Communications in Computer and Information Science 2674

Rationale

The CCIS series is devoted to the publication of proceedings of computer science conferences. Its aim is to efficiently disseminate original research results in informatics in printed and electronic form. While the focus is on publication of peer-reviewed full papers presenting mature work, inclusion of reviewed short papers reporting on work in progress is welcome, too. Besides globally relevant meetings with internationally representative program committees guaranteeing a strict peer-reviewing and paper selection process, conferences run by societies or of high regional or national relevance are also considered for publication.

Topics

The topical scope of CCIS spans the entire spectrum of informatics ranging from foundational topics in the theory of computing to information and communications science and technology and a broad variety of interdisciplinary application fields.

Information for Volume Editors and Authors

Publication in CCIS is free of charge. No royalties are paid, however, we offer registered conference participants temporary free access to the online version of the conference proceedings on SpringerLink (http://link.springer.com) by means of an http referrer from the conference website and/or a number of complimentary printed copies, as specified in the official acceptance email of the event.

CCIS proceedings can be published in time for distribution at conferences or as post-proceedings, and delivered in the form of printed books and/or electronically as USBs and/or e-content licenses for accessing proceedings at SpringerLink. Furthermore, CCIS proceedings are included in the CCIS electronic book series hosted in the SpringerLink digital library at http://link.springer.com/bookseries/7899. Conferences publishing in CCIS are allowed to use our online conference service (Meteor) for managing the whole proceedings lifecycle (from submission and reviewing to preparing for publication) free of charge.

Publication process

The language of publication is exclusively English. Authors publishing in CCIS have to sign the Springer CCIS copyright transfer form, however, they are free to use their material published in CCIS for substantially changed, more elaborate subsequent publications elsewhere. For the preparation of the camera-ready papers/files, authors have to strictly adhere to the Springer CCIS Authors' Instructions and are strongly encouraged to use the CCIS LaTeX style files or templates.

Abstracting/Indexing

CCIS is abstracted/indexed in DBLP, Google Scholar, EI-Compendex, Mathematical Reviews, SCImago, Scopus. CCIS volumes are also submitted for the inclusion in ISI Proceedings.

How to start

To start the evaluation of your proposal for inclusion in the CCIS series, please send an e-mail to ccis@springer.com

Murizah Kassim · Jasni Mohamad Zain ·
Wan Fairos Wan Yaacob ·
Nur Intan Raihana Ruhaiyem · Marina Yusoff ·
Mahdi A. Nisirat
Editors

Soft Computing in Data Science

8th International Conference, SCDS 2025
Penang, Malaysia, October 8–9, 2025
Revised Selected Papers

Editors
Murizah Kassim
Universiti Teknologi MARA
Shah Alam, Malaysia

Jasni Mohamad Zain
Universiti Teknologi MARA
Shah Alam, Malaysia

Wan Fairos Wan Yaacob
Universiti Teknologi MARA
Shah Alam, Malaysia

Nur Intan Raihana Ruhaiyem
Universiti Sains Malaysia
Gelugor, Malaysia

Marina Yusoff
Universiti Teknologi MARA
Shah Alam, Malaysia

Mahdi A. Nisirat
Al Balqa Applied University (BAU)
Amman, Jordan

ISSN 1865-0929 ISSN 1865-0937 (electronic)
Communications in Computer and Information Science
ISBN 978-981-95-8367-6 ISBN 978-981-95-8368-3 (eBook)
https://doi.org/10.1007/978-981-95-8368-3

This Springer imprint is published by the registered company Springer Nature Singapore Pte Ltd.
The registered company address is: 152 Beach Road, #21-01/04 Gateway East, Singapore 189721, Singapore

Preface

The 8th International Conference on Soft Computing in Data Science (SCDS 2025) inspired and connected global minds in the field of data science and artificial intelligence. Hosted virtually on the 8th and 9th of October 2025, SCDS 2025 was a dynamic platform for exchanging cutting-edge knowledge and fostering collaborations in the realms of data engineering and AI. Themed "Analytics Renaissance: Merging Science, AI, and Data for Elegant and Engineering Solutions," this year's conference celebrated the convergence of advanced analytics, computational intelligence, and innovative engineering practices.

As industries worldwide experience transformative shifts, the focus on blending science and AI with data engineering offers a pathway to tackle complex challenges and build solutions that are not only effective but also elegant in their design and impact. SCDS 2025 featured six distinguished keynote speakers, each a luminary in data engineering and AI. Their expertise provided invaluable insights into the latest trends, research breakthroughs, and practical applications shaping the future of these disciplines. Complementing these keynotes, the conference included technical presentations, interactive sessions, and panel discussions designed to engage participants and stimulate intellectual growth. SCDS 2025 invited researchers, practitioners, and enthusiasts to be part of this analytics renaissance, where innovation and collaboration pave the way for a smarter, data-driven future.

The SCDS 2025 conference received a total of 71 paper submissions, all of which underwent a rigorous double-blind peer review process. Each submission was evaluated by a minimum of two independent reviewers. Following the review and selection process, 35 papers were accepted for presentation at SCDS 2025. SCDS 2025 was chaired by Murizah Kassim as Head of Publication and Innovation at the Institute for Big Data Analytics and Artificial Intelligence, Universiti Teknologi MARA.

September 2025

Murizah Kassim
Jasni Mohamad Zain
Wan Fairos Wan Yaacob
Nur Intan Raihana Ruhaiyem
Marina Yusoff
Mahdi A. Nisirat

Organization

Patron

Shahrin Sahib@ Sahibuddin	Universiti Teknologi MARA, Malaysia

Advisors

Norazah Abd Rahman	Universiti Teknologi MARA, Malaysia
Jasni Mohamad Zain	Universiti Teknologi MARA, Malaysia

Conference Chair

Murizah Kassim	Universiti Teknologi MARA, Malaysia

Co-chair

Nur Intan Raihana Ruhaiyem	Universiti Sains Malaysia, Malaysia

Proceedings Editors

Murizah Kassim	Universiti Teknologi MARA, Malaysia
Jasni Mohamad Zain	Universiti Teknologi MARA, Malaysia
Wan Fairos Wan Yaacob	Universiti Teknologi MARA, Malaysia
Nur Intan Raihana Ruhaiyem	Universiti Sains Malaysia, Malaysia
Marina Yusoff	Universiti Teknologi MARA, Malaysia
Mahdi A. Nisirat	Al-Balqa Applied University, Jordan

Secretary

Nurain Ibrahim	Universiti Teknologi MARA, Malaysia

Technical Program Committee

Abdul Rahim Ridzuan	Universiti Teknologi MARA, Malaysia
Marina Yusoff	Universiti Teknologi MARA, Malaysia
Wan Fairos Wan Yaacob	Universiti Teknologi MARA, Malaysia
Abdul Kadir Jumaat	Universiti Teknologi MARA, Malaysia
Nur Intan Raihana Ruhaiyem	Universiti Sains Malaysia, Malaysia
Azalina Farina Abd Aziz	Universiti Teknologi MARA, Malaysia

Registration and Presentation

Muhammad Hisyam Jamari	Universiti Teknologi MARA, Malaysia
Mohd Irwanhakim Zainal	Universiti Teknologi MARA, Malaysia

Finance Committee

Nurbaizura Borhan	Universiti Teknologi MARA, Malaysia
Nur Asyikin Abdullah	Universiti Teknologi MARA, Malaysia
Nur Adliana Mustapha	Universiti Teknologi MARA, Malaysia

Sponsorship Committee

Azlin Ahmad	Universiti Teknologi MARA, Malaysia

Publication Committee

Siti Sara Ibrahim	Universiti Teknologi MARA, Malaysia
Shuria Saaidin	Universiti Teknologi MARA, Malaysia

Website and Online Committee

Muhamad Ridhwan Mohamad Razali	Universiti Teknologi MARA, Malaysia

Host Committee

Nur Intan Raihana Ruhaiyem	Universiti Sains Malaysia, Malaysia
Gan Keng Hoon	Universiti Sains Malaysia, Malaysia
Syaheerah Lebai Lutfi	Universiti Sains Malaysia, Malaysia
Noor Farizah Ibrahim	Universiti Sains Malaysia, Malaysia
Nur Hana Samsudin	Universiti Sains Malaysia, Malaysia
Mohd Heikal Husin	Universiti Sains Malaysia, Malaysia
Jasmi Chek Isa	Universiti Sains Malaysia, Malaysia
Mohd Hidzir Shamshul Bahrin	Universiti Sains Malaysia, Malaysia
Abdul Rohim Mansur	Universiti Sains Malaysia, Malaysia
Ruslan Ahmad	Universiti Sains Malaysia, Malaysia

Scientific Committee

Sri Hartati	Universitas Gadjah Mada, Indonesia
Hizir Sofyan	Universitas Syiah Kuala, Indonesia
Adzhar Kamaludin	Universiti Malaysia Pahang, Malaysia
Mazlina Abdul Majid	Universiti Malaysia Pahang, Malaysia
Eisuke Kita	Nagoya University, Japan
Dhiya Al-Jumeily	Liverpool John Moores University, UK
Wahyu Wibowo	Institut Teknologi Sepuluh Nopember, Indonesia
Edi Winarko	Universitas Gadjah Mada, Indonesia
Faiz Ahmed Mohamed Elfaki	Qatar University, Qatar
Waheb Abdullah Abduljabbar Shaif	Birmingham City University, UK
Mahdi A. Nisirat	Al-Balqa Applied University, Jordan
Gan Keng Hoon	Universiti Sains Malaysia, Malaysia
Wan Mohd Nazmee Wan Zainon	Universiti Sains Malaysia, Malaysia
Wong Li Pei	Universiti Sains Malaysia, Malaysia
Noor Farizah Ibrahim	Universiti Sains Malaysia, Malaysia
Abdul Haris Rangkuti	BINUS University, Indonesia
Mukhanova Ayagoz Asanbekovna	L.N. Gumilyov Eurasian National University, Kazakhstan
Akhayeva Zhanar Berikbayevna	L.N. Gumilyov Eurasian National University, Kazakhstan
Kamal Zuhairi Zamli	Universiti Malaysia Pahang, Malaysia

Reviewers

Abdul Kadir Jumaat	Universiti Teknologi MARA, Malaysia
Abdul Rahim Ridzuan	Universiti Teknologi MARA, Malaysia
Adam Shariff Adli Aminuddin	Universiti Malaysia Pahang Al-Sultan Abdullah, Malaysia
Arun Kumar Elengovan	Okta Inc., USA
Azlin Ahmad	Universiti Teknologi MARA, Malaysia
Bilal Zahran	Al-Balqa Applied University, Jordan
Chu Liang Lee	Multimedia University, Malaysia
Dariusz Król	Wrocław University of Science and Technology, Poland
Deepak Kole	Ebay, India
Dhanunjaya Rao Gorrle	Western Digital Technologies Inc., India
Fadhlan Kamaru Zaman	Universiti Teknologi MARA, Malaysia
Faeik Al Rabee	Al-Balqa Applied University, Jordan
Faroudja Abid	Centre de Développement des Technologies Avancées, Algeria
Ganesh Kumar	Universiti Teknologi PETRONAS, Malaysia
Girish Gajwani	Independent Researcher, USA
Hasan Alsarraf	Northern Technical University, Iraq
Hasniaty Abdullah	Universitas Hasanuddin, Indonesia
Ihsan Mohd Yassin	Universiti Teknologi MARA, Malaysia
Isan Sahoo	Oracle, USA
Khairul Anwar Sedek	Universiti Teknologi MARA, Malaysia
Lucyantie Mazalan	Universiti Teknologi MARA, Malaysia
Mahayaudin Mansor	Universiti Teknologi MARA, Malaysia
Marina Yusoff	Universiti Teknologi MARA, Malaysia
Marshima Mohd Rosli	Universiti Teknologi MARA, Malaysia
Memiyanty Hj. Abdul Rahim	Universiti Teknologi MARA, Malaysia
Milan Parikh	Cytel, USA
Mohammed Adam Kunna Azrag	Universiti Malaysia Pahang Al-Sultan Abdullah, Malaysia
Mohammed Ahmed Saleh	Universiti Malaysia Sabah, Malaysia
Mohd Heikal Husin	Universiti Sains Malaysia, Malaysia
Muhammad Asraf Hairuddin	Universiti Teknologi MARA, Malaysia
Muhammad Firdaus Mustapha	Universiti Teknologi MARA, Malaysia
Murali Enduri	SRM University-AP, Andhra Pradesh, India
Murizah Kassim	Universiti Teknologi MARA, Malaysia
Noor Farizah Ibrahim	Universiti Sains Malaysia, Malaysia
Nor Syazwani Mohd Pakhrudin	Universiti Teknologi MARA, Malaysia
Noriko Etani	Kyoto University, Japan

Norsyela Muhammad Noor Mathivanan	University of Wollongong, Malaysia
Norzehan Sakamat	Universiti Teknologi MARA, Malaysia
Nur Intan Raihana Ruhaiyem	Universiti Sains Malaysia, Malaysia
Nur Nabila Mohamed	Universiti Teknologi MARA, Malaysia
Nur Hana Samsudin	Universiti Sains Malaysia, Malaysia
Nurain Ibrahim	Universiti Teknologi MARA, Malaysia
Nurlaila Ismail	Universiti Teknologi MARA, Malaysia
Nursyadhila Che Lah	Universiti Teknologi PETRONAS, Malaysia
Rajesh Vayyala	PRA Group Inc., USA
Rakesh Keshava	Okta Inc., USA
Rizwan Aslam Butt	NED University of Engineering and Technology, Pakistan
Sakhinah Abu Bakar	Universiti Teknologi MARA, Malaysia
Shahrani Shahbudin	Universiti Teknologi MARA, Malaysia
Shuria Saaidin	Universiti Teknologi MARA, Malaysia
Siti Afiqah Muhamad Jamil	Universiti Teknologi MARA, Malaysia
Siti Sara Ibrahim	Universiti Teknologi MARA, Malaysia
Suhaili Beeran Kutty	Universiti Teknologi MARA, Malaysia
Syaheerah Lebai Lutfi	Universiti Sains Malaysia, Malaysia
Vinay R. Soni	Georgia Institute of Technology, USA
Wan Fairos Wan Yaacob	Universiti Teknologi MARA, Malaysia
Yuzi Mahmud	University of Tunis El Manar, Tunisia
Zouari Farouk	University of Tunis El Manar, Tunisia

Collaborators

USM
UNIVERSITI SAINS MALAYSIA
APEX
TM

EURASIAN
NATIONAL
UNIVERSITY

Contents

Data Analytics and Technologies

Data Analytics and Technologies

Spatio-temporal Hazard Earthquake Modeling in Java Using Space-time Epidemic-Type Aftershock Sequence (ETAS)

Naufal Luthfan Tasbihi[1], Achmad Choiruddin[1(✉)], Tintrim Dwi Ary Widhianingsih[1], and Agus Budi Raharjo[2]

[1] Department of Statistics, Institut Teknologi Sepuluh Nopember, Surabaya, Indonesia
6003242014@student.its.ac.id, {choiruddin,dwi.ary}@its.ac.id
[2] Departement of Informatics Engineering, Institut Teknologi Sepuluh Nopember, Surabaya, Indonesia
agus.budi@its.ac.id

Abstract. The Space-Time ETAS (Epidemic-Type Aftershock Sequence) model is a point process-based approach for earthquake modeling that utilizes comprehensive seismic catalogs to forecast earthquake occurrences by accounting for both spatial and temporal relationships. It employs a long-decay spatial density function, which represents the gradual reduction in the probability of aftershocks as the distance from the main shocks increases. However, the Java region, characterized by complex tectonic interactions and the Andaman-Sumatera-Java arcs subduction zone, experiences deep and spread earthquakes, exhibit spread earthquakes along its subduction zone, which may suggest an alternative spatial density function within the Space-Time ETAS model. This study compares the commonly used long decay and short decay spatial density in the Space-Time ETAS model to fit the earthquake catalog in Java based on model complexity, computational time, and intensity prediction. The dataset includes earthquake catalog data (longitude, lattitute, time occurrence, magnitude) in Java within interval time 1 January 2009 to 31 January 2025. Findings reveal that the short-decay function outperforms the long-decay counterpart, efficiently identifying high-seismicity areas in the Andaman-Sumatera-Java arcs and 36 active faults. This study advances seismic risk assessment and supports disaster mitigation efforts in Java.

Keywords: Natural Disasters · Spatial Pattern · Earthquake Modeling

1 Introduction

Indonesia is situated at the junction of four major tectonic plates: the Eurasian Plate, the Indo-Australian Plate, the Philippine Sea Plate, and the Pacific Plate. This positioning within the Ring of Fire makes Indonesia particularly prone to seismic events [1] In particular, the Java region experiences considerable earthquake activity due to the interaction and collision between the Eurasian and Indo-Australian plates in the southern part of the island. Earthquakes in this region are often deep and spread along the

M. Kassim et al. (Eds.): SCDS 2025, CCIS 2674, pp. 3–16, 2026.
https://doi.org/10.1007/978-981-95-8368-3_1

Andaman-Sumatera-Java arc, differing from the characteristics of earthquakes in Sumatra and Sulawesi-Maluku, thus necessitating specialized studies to understand its unique seismic behavior [1, 2].

Modeling earthquake catalog data with stochastic point processes enables the examination of seismic events that, while random, exhibit spatial and temporal patterns [3, 4]. Several models, including the Log-Gaussian Cox Process (LGCP) and the Neyman-Scott Cox Point Process (NSCP), have been explored for earthquake modeling [5–7]. However, the models cannot highlight some important features of earthquake phenomena. This study employs the Space-Time Epidemic-Type Aftershock Sequence (Space-Time ETAS) model to develop a comprehensive earthquake risk map in Java. The space-time ETAS is one of the most popular model for earthquake modeling since it is closely related to seismology [8]. The model incorporates the Omori-Utsu Law and the Gutenberg-Richter Law to describe the likelihood of main shocks and aftershocks, based on a comprehensive earthquake catalog containing the time, location, and magnitude of events [9, 10]. Additionaly, the space-time ETAS model includes a declustering method, which allows users to differentiate the main shocks and aftershocks.

Although the Space-Time ETAS model has been implemented in several countries [11–13], earlier research primarily focused on the inverse power (long-decay) function for the spatial density, which is suitable for broad aftershock distributions and allows for a higher likelihood of aftershocks occurring at larger distances from the main shocks. However, given the tectonic complexity and the convergence of two major plates in the Java region, most aftershocks are concentrated along the Andaman-Sumatera-Java arc and within 36 active faults. Using an incorrect spatial density function can introduce errors in modeling aftershock distributions, as it fails to accurately capture the true spatial decay of aftershocks. Accordingly, we frame the work as a comparison of two alternative spatial density functions an inverse-power (long decay) density and a Gaussian (short decay) density within Space-Time ETAS model. The workflow consists of (i) maximum-likelihood estimation with Davidon-Fletcher-Powell (DFP) Algorithm for parametric estimation and (ii) a Stochastic Declustering for non-parametric estimation that probabilistically separates background events from triggered aftershocks. We benchmark both spatial density function with information theoretic goodness-of-fit, mean-squared prediction error, and execution time. The resulting workflow yields background and total seismicity rates, clustering coefficients, conditional intensity fields at the study period, and a declustered earthquake event providing a reproducible toolkit for data-driven seismic risk analysis.

2 Dataset and Methodology

2.1 Dataset

This study makes use of publicly available earthquake data provided by the United States Geological Survey (USGS). The dataset encompasses the Java region (see Fig. 1) within latitudes −5 °S to −9 °S and longitudes 105 °E to 115 °E, with depths between 0 and 300 km, and includes events with magnitudes larger than 4 SR (Scale Richter) to capture diverse seismic behaviors and make the result more generalizable. The analysis period ranges from January 1, 2003, to January 31, 2025, divided into complementary events

(January 1 2003–December 31, 2008) and target events (January 1, 2009–January 31, 2025). The data structure is detailed in Table 1.

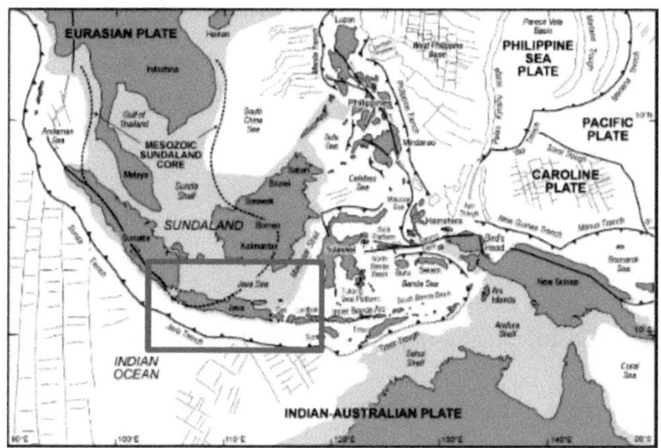

Fig. 1. Jawa are located between the Indo-Australian Plate, the Philippine Sea Plate, and the Eurasian Plate

Table 1. Earthquake Catalog Data Structure

Event	Timestamp	Time	Longitude	Latitude	Magnitude
1	g_1	t_1	x_1	y_1	m_1
2	g_2	t_2	x_2	y_2	m_2
⋮	⋮	⋮	⋮	⋮	⋮
N	g_N	t_N	x_N	y_N	m_N

During the period from January 1, 2009, to January 31, 2025, a total of 1,211 earthquake events were recorded on Java. Most of these earthquakes are concen-trated in the southern region, which is situated near the active subduction zone where the Indo-Australian plate converges with the Eurasian plate. This tectonic interaction makes the southern coast particularly prone to seismic activity. Additionally, scattered occurrences are observed across central Java, albeit with lower intensity and frequency compared to the southern region. See Fig. 2.

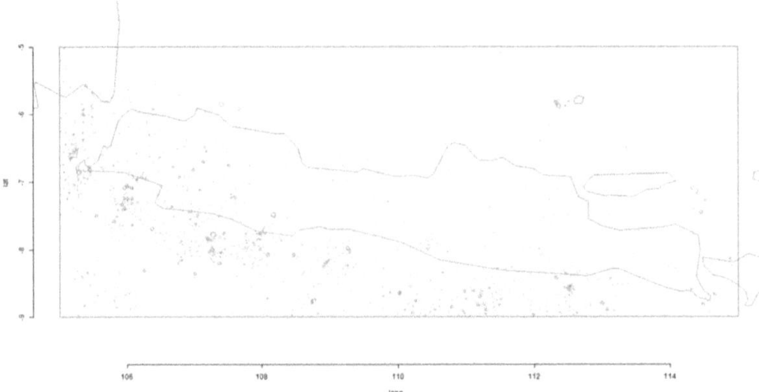

Fig. 2. Distribution of coordinates of earthquake locations in Java

2.2 Space-Time ETAS

The Space-Time ETAS model is capable of explaining the components of an earthquake, including main shocks and aftershocks in a region, by incorporating factors such as time, location, and magnitude [14, 15]. This model demonstrates how the seismic characteristics of an area, including background seismicity, the size of the aftershock population, the intensity of aftershocks, and the rate at which aftershocks decay over a defined period, can be represented. The conditional intesity function of the Space-Time ETAS is

$$\rho_{\beta,\theta}(H_t) = v_\beta(m)\lambda_\theta(H_t) \quad (1)$$

where

$$v_\beta(m) = \beta\ exp\ exp(-\beta(m - m_0)),\ \ \beta > 0$$

is the probability density function of the earthquake magnitude which is exponentially distributed, and

$$\lambda_\theta(H_t) = \tilde{u}(x, y) + \sum_{i;t_i<t} \kappa_{A,\alpha}(m_i)g_{c,p}(t - t_i)f_{D,\gamma,q}(x - x_i, y - y_i; m_i) \quad (2)$$

The background seismicity rate, denoted as $\tilde{u}(x, y)$, is assumed to be independent of time. The non-parametric component is represented as $\tilde{u}(x, y) = \mu u(x, y)$ where $\mu > 0$ represents the average daily occurrence of main earthquake events at a location and $u(x, y)$ is a smooth function over the spatial domain S. The term $\kappa_{A,\alpha}(m_i)$ denotes the average number of aftershocks triggered by an earthquake with magnitude m_i, where $A > 0$ and $\alpha > 0$ are unknown parameters with $m \geq m_0$. The function $g_{c,p}(t - t_i)$ represents the probability density function for the timing of an aftershock triggered by an earthquake of magnitude m_i occurring at time t_i, and independent of m_i. This function is based on the modified Omori's law, where $c > 0$ and $p > 1$ are unknown parameters. The function $f_{D,\gamma,q}$ defines the probability density function for the location of an aftershock triggered by a main earthquake with magnitude m_i, which occurs at the location (x_i, y_i). The radially symmetric density (long decay) function can be written as

$$f_{D,q,\gamma}(x - x_i, y - y_i; m_i) = \frac{q-1}{\pi D\ exp\ exp(\gamma(m_i - m_0))}\left(1 + \frac{(x-x_i)^2 + (y-y_i)^2}{D\ exp\ exp(\gamma(m_i - m_0))}\right)^{-q} \tag{3}$$

where $D > 0$, $\gamma > 0$, and $q > 1$ are unknown parameters. Then, the Gaussian density (short decay) function can be written as

$$f_{D,\gamma}(x - x_i, y - y_i; m_i) = \frac{1}{2\pi D\ exp\ exp(\gamma(m_i - m_0))} exp\ exp\left(-\frac{\left((x-x_i)^2 + (y-y_i)^2\right)}{2D\ exp\ exp(\gamma(m_i - m_0))}\right) \tag{4}$$

where $D > 0$ and $\gamma > 0$ are unknown parameters. The model assumes that every event, including both the main earthquake and the aftershocks, is triggered by a preceding event. The main shocks are modeled as occurring according to a Poisson process with an intensity $\tilde{u}(x, y)$, which remains stationary over time.. Previous events, both mainshocks and aftershocks, generate further events according to a non-stationary Poisson process with the following intensity function [9, 10, 16, 17].

$$\sum_{i;t_i<t} \kappa_{A,\alpha}(m_i) g_{c,p}(t - t_i) f_{D,\gamma,q}(x - x_i, y - y_i; m_i).$$

2.3 Davidon-Fletcher-Powell and Stochastic Declustering Algorithm

The parameter of the Space-Time ETAS model consist of parametric and nonparametric component. The parametric component β and $\theta = (\mu, A, \alpha, c, p, D, \gamma, q)^T$ for long decay function and $\theta = (\mu, A, \alpha, c, p, D, \gamma)^T$ for short decay function can be estimated with DFP Algorithm by using the log-likelihood function [9].

$$l(H_t) = \sum_{i=1}^{N} \delta_i\ log\ log\left(\rho_{\beta,\theta}(H_t)\right) - \int_M \int_T iint_S \rho_{\beta,\theta}(H_t) dxdydtdm \tag{5}$$

where $\delta_i = 1$ if target event and $\delta_i = 0$ for others. The log-likelihood function can be partitioned into two form contain β and θ

$$l(H_t) = l_1(H_t) + l_2(H_t)$$

where

$$l_1(H_t) = \sum_{i=1}^{N} \delta_i\ log\ log\left(v_\beta(m_i)\right) = log\ log(\beta) \sum_{i=1}^{N} \delta_i - \beta \sum_{i=1}^{N} \delta_i (m_i - m_0)$$

and

$$l_2(H_t) = \sum_{i=1}^{N} \delta_i\ log\ log\left(\lambda_\theta(H_{t_i})\right) - \int_T iint_S \lambda_\theta(H_t) dxdydt$$

Table 2. Davidon-Fletcher-Powell Algorithm

Algorithm 1 : Davidon-Fletcher-Powell Algorithm

Inputs:
$\widehat{\theta}_0$
$\hat{u}_0(x_j, y_j),\ j = 1,2,\ldots,N$
H_0
$k \leftarrow 0$
Repeat
$d_k \leftarrow -H_k \times \nabla\xi(\widehat{\theta}_k)$
$\zeta_k \leftarrow \xi(\widehat{\theta}_k + \zeta d_k)$
$\widehat{\theta}_{k+1} \leftarrow \widehat{\theta}_k + \zeta_k d_k$
$\eta_k \leftarrow \nabla\xi(\widehat{\theta}_{k+1}) - \nabla\xi(\widehat{\theta}_k)$
$c_1 \leftarrow \frac{\zeta_k}{d_k^T \times \eta_k}$
$c_2 \leftarrow \frac{1}{\eta_k^T \times H_k \times \eta_k}$
$H_{k+1} \leftarrow H_k + c_1 d_k \times d_k^T - c_2 H_k \times \eta_k \times \eta_k^T \times H_k$
$k \leftarrow k + 1$
Until $||\widehat{\theta}_k - \widehat{\theta}_{k-1}|| < \epsilon$ or $||\nabla\xi(\widehat{\theta}_k)|| < \epsilon$
Return $\widehat{\theta}_k$ and H_k

The process of estimating the mainshock rate using the concept of Stochastic Declustering, which is a probabilistic approach to earthquake catalogs utilizing (6) (Tables 2 and 3)

$$\tilde{p}_{ij} = \begin{cases} \frac{\kappa_{A,\alpha}(m_i) g_{c,p}(t_j - t_i) f_{D,\gamma,q}(x_j - x_i, y_j - y_i, m_i)}{\lambda_\theta(H_{t_j})} & 0, \\ t_j > t_i, & t_j \le t_i \end{cases} \tag{6}$$

as the probability of event j being triggered by event i, we have

$$\tilde{p}_j = \sum_{i=1; t_i < t_j} \tilde{p}_{ij},\ j = 1, \ldots, N \tag{7}$$

which represents the probability that event j is triggered by a previous event [19]. Meanwhile

$$1 - \tilde{p}_j = \frac{\mu u(x_j, y_j)}{\lambda_\theta(H_{t_j})} \tag{8}$$

defines the probability that event j is a mainshock. The Stochastic Declustering algorithm incorporates the concept of an adaptive kernel bandwidth, using the following equation to estimate $\hat{u}(x, y)$.

$$\hat{u}(x, y) = \frac{1}{T} \sum_{j=1}^{N} \left(1 - \hat{\tilde{p}}\right) \varphi\left(x - x_j, y - y_j; h_j\right) \tag{9}$$

Here, $\hat{\bar{p}}$ is computed using Equation (7) by replacing the parameter with its estimator, and

$$h_j = \{h_{min}, r(j, n^*)\} \tag{10}$$

Table 3. Stochastic Declustering Algorithm

Algorithm 2 : Stochastic Declustering Algorithm

1. **Inputs:**
   $\hat{\theta}_0$
   $\hat{u}_0(x_j, y_j),\ j = 1,2, \ldots, N$
2. $H_0 \leftarrow I$
3. $k \leftarrow 0$
4. **Repeat**
5. Use Algorithm 1 with inputs $\hat{\theta}_k, \hat{u}_k(x_i, y_i)$ and H_k and get $\hat{\theta}_{k+1}$ and H_{k+1}
6. $\hat{p}_j \leftarrow 1 - \frac{\hat{\mu}_{k+1}\hat{u}_k(x_j,y_j)}{\lambda_{\hat{\theta}_{k+1}}(H_{t_j})}$
7. $\hat{u}_{k+1}(x, y) \leftarrow \sum_{j=1}^{N} \frac{(1-\hat{p}_j)\varphi(x-x_j,y-y_j;h_j)}{T}$
8. $k \leftarrow k + 1$
9. $e_1 \leftarrow \left|\frac{\hat{\theta}_{l,k}}{\hat{\theta}_{(l,k-1)}} - 1\right|$
10. $e_1 \leftarrow \left|\frac{\hat{u}_k(x_j,y_j)}{\hat{u}_{k-1}(x_j,y_j)} - 1\right|$
11. $e_3 \leftarrow \left|\frac{\xi(\hat{\theta}_k)}{\xi(\hat{\theta}_{k-1})} - 1\right|$
12. **Until** $e_1 < \epsilon$ and $e_2 < \epsilon$ and $e_3 < \epsilon$
13. **Return** $\hat{\theta}_k$, $\hat{u}_k(x, y)$, and H_k

3 Results and Discussions

3.1 Comparison of Estimation Result

Parameter estimation is a crucial aspect of Space-Time ETAS modeling, as it is key to understanding seismic activity patterns. The results were obtained through Maximum Likelihood Estimation (MLE), which was then followed by Radial Partition and polar transformation. Then, Davidon-Fletcher Powell and Stochastic Declustering procedures were applied. The estimated parameters are detailed in Table 4.

Table 4. Parameter Estimation

Long Decay				Short Decay			
Exec. Time		6.23 minutes		Exec. Time		4.77 minutes	
AIC		11703.98		AIC		11726.51	
Spatial MSE		0.02865		Spatial MSE		0.02939	
Temporal MSE		1.57693		Temporal MSE		1.57693	
Par	Est	SE	Sig	Par	Est	SE	Sig
β	1.9158	0.0030	Yes	β	1.9158	0.0030	Yes
μ	0.7625	0.0085	Yes	μ	0.7610	0.0084	Yes
A	0.0452	0.0956	No	A	0.0427	0.1102	No
c	0.0103	0.1392	No	c	0.0099	0.1418	No
α	1.9097	0.0168	Yes	α	1.9536	0.0165	Yes
p	1.0973	0.0110	Yes	p	1.0852	0.0110	Yes
D	0.0049	0.1490	No	D	0.0939	0.0497	Yes
q	1.7109	0.0364	Yes	q	–	–	–
γ	0.2228	0.2753	No	γ	0.0682	0.4434	No

Table 4 presents the parameter estimation results for two spatial density functions long decay and short decay in the Space-Time ETAS model. Based on the AIC values, the long decay function performs slightly better than the short decay function, with a relative difference of 0.19%. However, in terms of execution-time efficiency, the short-decay function is markedly superior: in our benchmark it finished about 50% faster than the long decay function. Computational time was measured as the wall-clock duration of the full maximum-likelihood optimisation loop (including intensity, gradient, and Hessian evaluations) recorded with R's system.time() on a single thread. All tests were carried out on a Windows 11 laptop equipped with an Intel Core i3-1005G1 CPU (2 cores and 4 threads, 1.2–3.4 GHz) and 12 GB of RAM, running R 4.4.2.

Normal distribution used to approximates the estimator for the Space-Time ETAS model $\sim N(0, 1)$, and therefore, the evaluation of parameter significance is conducted using confidence intervals at a 90% confidence level . In both density functions, the parameters β, μ, α, and p are statistically significant, as their confidence intervals do not include zero, this indicates that these parameters contribute importantly to the model. Conversely, the parameter A in $\kappa_{A,\alpha}(m_i)$, c in $g_{c,p}(t - t_i)$, and γ in $f_{D,\gamma,q}(x - x_i, y - y_i; m_i)$ which is related to the magnitude effect, the temporal decay rate of earthquake occurrences, and the magnitude influence in spatial decay, is not significant in either model due to its small estimated value and relatively large standard error. This suggests that A, c, and γ does not provide a meaningful contribution in both density functions. Additionally, the parameter D in $f_{D,\gamma,q}(x - x_i, y - y_i; m_i)$, which captures the spatial influence of the main shock on aftershocks, is significant in the short decay function but not in the long decay function, indicating that D is more relevant for characterizing the pattern in the short decay scenario.

Overall, while the long decay function demonstrates superior model fit, it comes at the cost of longer computation times. In contrast, the short decay function is more computationally efficient and features a significant parameter D, making it a preferable option when computational efficiency is a priority. Nonetheless, the parameter A, c, and γ in both models warrants further investigation due to its lack of statistical significance.

3.2 Comparison of Declustering Plot

Comparison of the density functions in the Space-Time ETAS model can also be conducted by comparing the plots of the declustering results for both density functions. A robust declustering outcome is expected to distinguish between main shocks and aftershocks, as presented in Fig. 3.

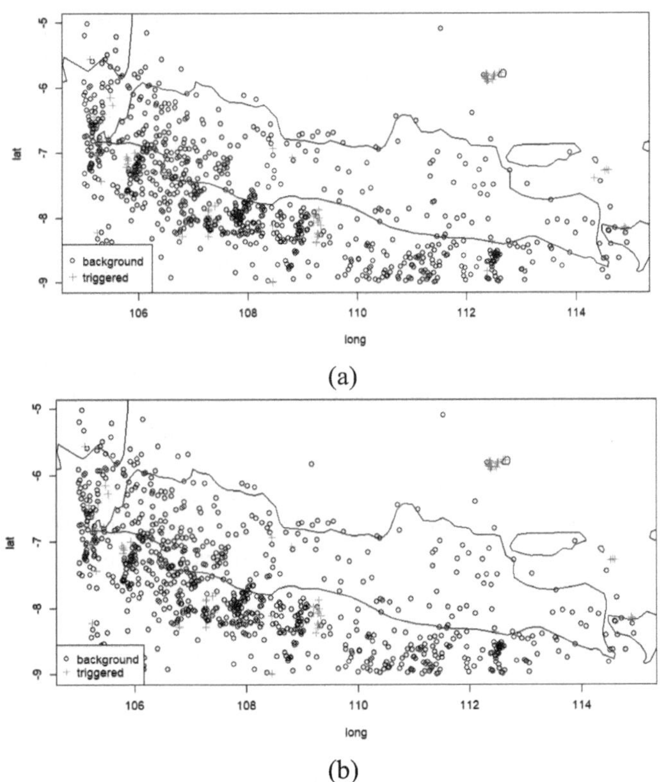

(a)

(b)

Fig. 3. Declustering plot for (a) Long Decay Mode (b) Short Decay Model

The declustered earthquake distributions presented in Fig. 3a and 3b reveal distinct characteristics between the long decay and short decay location density functions in differentiating mainshock (or background) events from aftershock (or triggered) events. The long decay model identified 841 mainshock events and 75 aftershock events, whereas the short decay model identified a greater number, with 868 mainshock events and

69 aftershock events. This discrepancy suggests that the short decay function is more sensitive in detecting both mainshock and aftershock events, particularly in areas with high seismic activity concentrations, such as the Southern Java Sea. In contrast, the long decay function tends to yield more conservative results, making it more suitable for regions with widespread distribution of earthquake activity.

3.3 Comparison of Residual Analysis

To assess the fitted Space-Time ETAS model, we compute the temporal residuals $R^{temp}\big(I_j; h\big)$ and spatial residual $R^{spat}(B_i; h)$, where $I_1, \ldots, I_{n_{temp}}$ and $B_1, \ldots, B_{n_{spat}}$ form finite partitions of the study period. We expect to have $R^{temp}\big(I_j; h\big) \approx 0$ and $R^{spat}(B_i; h) \approx 0$ for any $I \subset [t_{start}, t_{start} + T]$ and $B \subset S$. Thus any systematic departure of residuals from zero reflects model inadequacy [9].The performance of the model can also be assessed using the Mean Squared Error (MSE), calculated based on the spatial and temporal residual values. These residuals are determined by comparing the actual number of earthquake events with the predicted counts. A positive residual indicates that the actual number of earthquakes exceeds the predicted value, while a negative residual implies the opposite. It can be shown that there is no visually significant difference in the spatial residuals; however, the MSE reveals that the long decay model has a slightly lower value (0.02865) compared to the short decay model (0.02939), indicating that the long decay approach is marginally more effective in forecasting the number of earthquake events. In the Southern Java Sea the actual earthquake occurrences surpassed the predictions, resulting in positive residuals around these areas.

Temporal residuals describe the occurrence of earthquakes over the interval $I_{i_{temp}} \in T$. On average, each interval records 1.642 events, with a maximum of 13 events and a minimum of 0. In contrast to the spatial residuals, both the short decay and long decay have the same model performance in terms of temporal residuals, with 1.57693 temporal residuals. The temporal residuals shows several spikes, indicating substantial discrepancies between the actual and predicted event counts. For instance, in the interval $I_{947} = (7634.554; 7642.619]$, only 2 events occurred while 10.46217 were predicted in long decay and 10.46388 were predicted in short decay, resulting in a spike in the temporal residuals.

The plot of the transformation τ_{i} against the i-th event yields a graph that follows the linear line $y = x$, representing the theoretical cumulative number of earthquake events over time. Similarly, the Q-Q plot of U_{i} produces a line parallel to y = x, indicating that U_{i} follows a uniform distribution $U(0, 1)$. The model's capability to differentiate between mainshock and aftershock events is a critical indicator of its performance. While the long decay model is more effective in regions with a wide and dispersed seismic pattern, the short decay model delivers better results in areas with a high concentration of local seismic activity. These differences underscore the importance of selecting a density function that aligns with the regional characteristics and the objectives of the analysis. Consequently, the preferred model is the one with the short decay location density function, which offers advantages in computational efficiency, a reduced number of parameters, and better to distinguish mainshock and aftershock in Stochastic Declustering (Fig. 4).

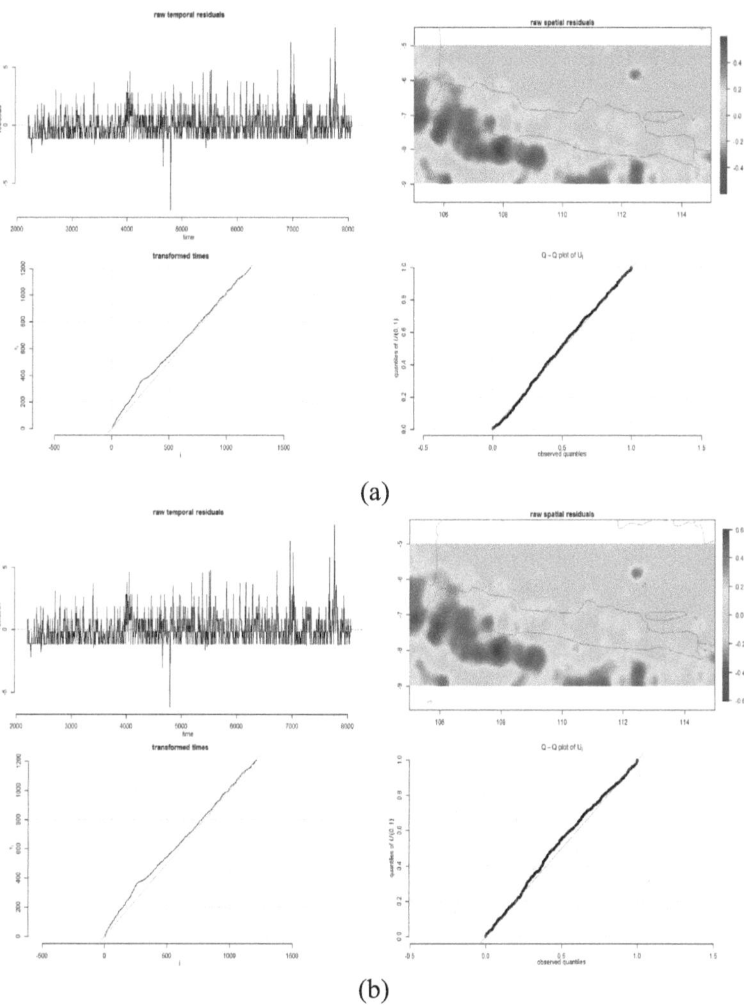

Fig. 4. Spatio-Temporal Residual for Space-Time ETAS Model (a) Long Decay Model (b) Short Decay Model

3.4 Interpretation of the Best Space-Time ETAS Model

Given that the short decay model offers advantages in computational time, declustering sensitivity, and reduced number of parameters. Hence, we will utilize the short decay model for our interpretation. Theoretically, the simpler decay function clarifies the causal relationship between mainshocks and their aftershocks, avoiding the confounding effects of an overly parameterized formulation. Practically, it accelerates processing and stabilizes parameter estimation, making it well-suited for real-time monitoring and rapid updates to seismic-hazard maps. Utilizing the parameter estimations obtained in the Table 4, the space-time ETAS model can thus be formulated as (1),

$$v_{\hat{\beta}}(m) = 1.9158\ exp\ exp(-1.9158(m-4))$$

where

$$\lambda_{\hat{\theta}}(H_t) = 0.7610\hat{u}(x, y) + \sum_{i:t_i<t} 0.0427$$

$$\exp\exp(1.9536(m_i - 4)) \times \frac{0.0852}{0,0099}\left(\frac{t - t_i}{0,0099}\right)^{-1,0852}$$

$$\times \frac{1}{0.1878\pi \exp\exp(0.0682(m_i - 4))}$$

$$\times \left(1 + \frac{(x - x_i)^2 + (y - y_i)^2}{0.1878 \exp\exp(0.0682(m_i - 4))}\right)$$

and

$$\hat{u}(x, y) = \frac{1}{5875}\sum_{j=1}^{1642}(1 - \hat{p}_j)\varphi(x - x_j, y - y_j; \hat{h}_j)$$

The background seismicity rate, which represents earthquake occurrences independent of prior events, was analyzed for major earthquakes in Java from January 1, 2009, to January 31, 2025, as illustrated in Figure 5(a). Predominant seismic activity on Java is concentrated along the southern coastal regions, particularly in areas near the active subduction zone between the Indo-Australian and Eurasian plates with rates below 0.15 event/day.deg^2. Figure 5(b) shows the total spatial seismicity rate, with an increasing earthquake frequency in these zones, represented by color changes from light green to light red. The clustering coefficient in Figure 5(c) highlights significant clustering of events in the western and northern Java regions (Bawean Island). The clustering coefficient exceeds 0.7 events/day·deg^2, indicating a notable aggregation of seismic activity, which may be linked to fault zones in the region. Figure 5(d) presents a probabilistic assessment of earthquake occurrences in Java, revealing that most regions maintain seismicity rates below 0.1 events/day·deg^2. However, a few areas in the southern parts of West Java and East Java show slightly higher seismicity rates, ranging between 0.1 and 0.12 events/day·deg^2. While these rates are relatively low, they still indicate a potential for localized seismic activity, which is important for monitoring and future disaster risk reduction planning in these areas.

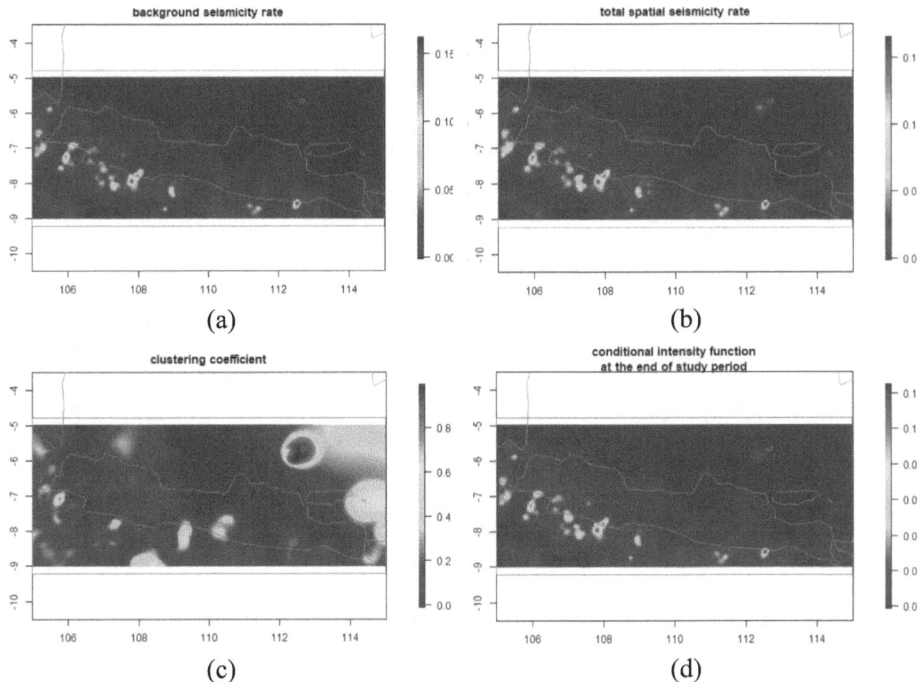

Fig. 5. ETAS output (a) background seismicity rate (b) total seismicity rate (c) clustering coefficient for aftershocks (d) conditional intensity function at the end of study period

4 Conclusion

The Spatial density function with short decay is the most appropriate model to represent earthquake risk in Java. This selection is based on the characteristic of earthquake distribution, which is more concentrated around the mainshock epicenter, reflecting the nature of seismic energy propagation that tends to be localized within a certain distance from the earthquake source. Additionally, when considering the statistical performance of the short decay model, it shows a higher AIC compared to the long decay model. However, the difference in performance is very minimal. By employing the Space-Time ETAS (Epidemic-Type Aftershock Sequence) approach with the short decay spatial density function, the earthquake risk modeling produces a conditional intensity function that captures the temporal and spatial dynamics of seismic events in Java. This model provides a more detailed depiction of earthquake risk by accounting for aftershock activity patterns that tend to concentrate in specific areas, thereby offering a more accurate framework for earthquake risk mitigation in this region.

Acknowledgement. The study is supported by grant "Riset Kolaborasi Indonesia (RKI) 2025" No 948/PKS/ITS/2025.

References

1. Tim Pusat Studi Gempa Nasional: Peta Sumber dan Bahaya Gempa Indonesia Tahun 2017. Kementrian Pekerjaan Umum dan Perumahan Rakyat, Bandung (2017)
2. Aprillia, D.T., Choiruddin, A.: Earthquake hazard modeling in java using space-time epidemic-type sequence. In: IEEE Asia-Pacific Conference on Geoscience, Electronics and Remote Sensing Technology (AGERS), pp. 207-214. Surabaya, Indonesia (2024). https://doi.org/10.1109/AGERS61027.2023.10490888
3. Ogata, Y.: Statistical model for earthquake occurrences and residual analysis for point. J. Am. Stat. Assoc., 9–27 (1988)
4. Pinsky, M.A., Karlin, S.: An Introduction to Stochastic Modeling. Elsevier, Amsterdam (2011)
5. Choiruddin, A., Susanto, T.Y., Husain, A., Kartikasari, Y. M.: kppmenet: combining the kppm and elastic net regularization for inhomogeneous cox point process with correlated covariates. J. Appl. Stat., 993–1006 (2024)
6. Susanto, T.Y., Choiruddin, A., Purnomo, J.D.: On the earthquake distribution modeling in Sumatra by Cauchy cluster process: comparing log-linear and log-additive intensity models. Sains Malaysiana **52**(2), 655–667 (2023)
7. Choiruddin, A., Aisah, Trisnisa, F., Iriawan, N.: Quantifying the effect of geological factors on distribution of earthquake occurrences by inhomogeneous cox processes. Pure Appl. Geophys. **178**(5), 1579–1592 (2021)
8. Davoudi, N., Tavakoli, H. R., Zare, M., Jalilian, A.: Aftershock probabilistic seismic hazard analysis for bushehr province in Iran using ETAS Model. Nat. Hazards, 1159–1170 (2020)
9. Jalilian, A.: ETAS : an R package for fitting the space-time ETAS model to earthquake data. J. Stat. Softw., 1–39 (2019)
10. Ogata, Y.: Space-time point-process models for earthquake occurrences. Ann. Inst. Stat. Math., 379–402 (1998)
11. Choiruddin, A., Rahman, A.A., Andreas, C.: Algorithms for fitting the space-time ETAS model to earthquake catalog data: a comparative study. J. Agric. Biol. Environ. Stat., pp. 1–18 (2024)
12. Guo, Y., Zhuang, J., Zhou, S.: An improved space-time ETAS model for inverting the rupture geometry from seismicity triggering. J. Geophys. Res. Solid Earth, 3309–3323 (2015)
13. Dutilleul, P., Genest, C., Peng, R.: Bootstrastrapping for parameter uncertainty in the space-time epidemic-type aftershock sequence model. Geophys. J. Int., 1601–1608 (2024)
14. Zhuang, J.: Long-term earthquake forecasts based on the epidemic-type aftershock sequence (ETAS) model for short-term clustering. Res. Geophys., 52–57 (2012)
15. Zhuang, J., Ogata, Y., Vere-Jones, D.: Diagnostic analysis of space-time branching processes for earthquakes. Case Stud. Spatial Point Process Model., 275–292 (2006)
16. Zhuang, J.: Next-day Earthquake Forecasts for the Japan Region Generated by the ETAS Model. Earth Planets Space, 207-216 (2011)
17. Daley, D., Vere-Jones, D.: An Introduction to the Theory of Point Processes: Volume I: Elementary Theory and Methods, 2nd edn. Springer, New York (2003)

Digital Transformation and Corporate Debt Financing Costs: Evidence from China

Hui Chen, Zarina Md Nor(✉), and Rafisah Mat Radzi

Universiti Sains Malaysia, 11800 USM Penang, Malaysia
zarina.nor@usm.my

Abstract. The digital economy is reshaping the traditional economic and social mode of operation in today's era, with digital technology as the key driving force. Digital transformation has become a widely recognized development direction for enterprises to keep up with, as the digital economy and the real economy have become deeply integrated. Financing activities, as key drivers of enterprise operations, are naturally affected by the digital transformation process. Starting from the unique perspective of financing, this paper thoroughly explores the potential impact of enterprise digital transformation on the cost of debt financing through empirical analysis. In the variable measurement stage, data mining and text analysis techniques are innovatively applied to accurately quantify the level of corporate digital transformation. The analysis reveals a strong inverse relationship between a company's digital transformation efforts and its debt financing expenses—meaning that as firms become more digitalized, their borrowing costs tend to decrease. Moreover, this effect shows significant differences among enterprises with different industry backgrounds.

Keywords: Digital transformation · Debt financing cost · Debt structure optimization · Information asymmetry

1 Introduction

The rapid growth of the global digital economy has become a key driver of economic expansion worldwide. The data in the "China Digital Economy Development White Paper (2024)" shows that in 2023, the proportion of China's digital economy in GDP reached 42.8%, representing a 1.3%-point rise compared to the year before. The digital economy's role within the national economy has expanded even further, and this sector now serves as a vital pillar and a key catalyst for China's economic development. In terms of the growth rate, in 2023, China's digital economy experienced nominal year-to-year growth of 7.39%, which exceeded the nominal GDP growth rate for the same period by 2.76% points (in 2023, China's nominal GDP growth rate was 4.64%). The contribution rate of the digital economy's growth to GDP growth was 66.45%, effectively enhancing the resilience and vitality of China's economic development.

Whether the integration of digital technologies and enterprise operations can significantly benefit enterprises is a concern of many scholars at present. Prior studies have

M. Kassim et al. (Eds.): SCDS 2025, CCIS 2674, pp. 17–31, 2026.
https://doi.org/10.1007/978-981-95-8368-3_2

primarily examined how digital transformation affects performance (Teng et al., 2022; Zhai et al., 2022), total factor productivity (L. Wang, 2023), financing (Zhou & Li, 2023), enterprise integrated innovation (Li et al., 2022; Zhao et al., 2023), and other economic manifestations (Pramanik et al., 2019; Taufani & Widjaja, 2023). However, there is relatively limited research exploring how digital transformation influences the debt financing costs of enterprises. This study aims to fill this gap and provide a solid theoretical basis for enterprises to reduce debt financing costs through digital transformation.

Lowering the financing costs for the real economy remains a core objective of supply-side structural reforms. Owing to the still underdeveloped capital market in China, debt capital is a more important financing channel for Chinese enterprises than equity capital (X. Chen & Anderson, 2024). Numerous studies have examined the determinants of debt financing costs, among which firm-specific characteristics feature prominently (Hou & Zhang, 2024), the external environment (Guo et al., 2023), corporate governance (Ahmed et al., 2024), executive heterogeneity (Tong et al., 2024), and (J. Zhang et al., 2024). Taking the digital transformation of enterprises as the core entry point, this paper analyzes its impact on the debt financing costs of enterprises in detail (J. Wang & Zhu, 2023). While enriching the research paths for enterprises to reduce debt financing costs, it also provides a new methodology for research in this field in the new era.

From a practical perspective, starting from the dimension of technological progress and based on digital transformation, this paper expands the perspective for enterprises in addressing the challenge of high debt financing costs, providing useful references for enterprises to solve the problem of "expensive financing". From a micro perspective, it explores the actual impact of digital transformation on the debt financing cost of enterprises, effectively responding to the question of whether digital economic development and the reduction of enterprise debt financing costs can be coordinated, and provides important references for enterprises to make decisions on reducing costs through digital transformation. By examining enterprise internal control quality and the level of information asymmetry, this paper uncovers the underlying mechanism through which digital transformation influences corporate debt financing costs, offering actionable insights for developing more effective strategies to lower such costs. In addition, by further examining the heterogeneity of digital transformation in terms of enterprise financial distress and the nature of property rights, this study deeply interprets its structural differences, providing a valuable empirical basis for the government to formulate differentiated policies to promote the digital transformation of enterprises.

2 Literature Review

2.1 Digital Transformation

Digital transformation is a comprehensive change process that enables enterprises to innovate business models, optimize processes, and enhance efficiency through the adoption of digital technologies in the digital economy era. Digital technologies profoundly affect companies' activities and processes, leading to changes in value creation, delivery, and capture mechanisms (Ancillai et al., 2023). The current research direction focuses on five major areas, including the relationship between digital technology and business model innovation (Adama & Okeke, 2024). This aligns with the findings of (Kohtamäki et al., 2020), who emphasized the role of digitalization in capturing the financial potential of servitization and the development of digital servitization business models in ecosystems (Zare & Persaud, 2024).

Process optimization is central to organizational efficiency, with digital technologies playing a crucial role in streamlining workflows and enhancing productivity. The integration of digital solutions is seen as a way to engage online with customers, suppliers, and employees, particularly in East Asia, where the share of firms investing in digital solutions has significantly increased (Bank, 2024). The emergence of digital technologies has transformed the banking and finance industry, creating new opportunities for financial businesses to improve their competitive advantage (Ratna et al., 2024). This transformation enhances customer experience, financial competitiveness, and market performance, underscoring the need for empirical research to investigate the relationship between digital transformation and financial competitiveness.

Digital transformation is not just about technology; it requires both technology and people to reveal its transformative power (Nadkarni & Prügl, 2021). It involves a shift from stand-alone firms toward digital ecosystems of interconnected value co-creators (Böhm et al., 2024). This shift is accompanied by a redistribution of resources and powers among organizational layers along the decentralization–centralization continuum, calling for research on organizational power theory (Plekhanov et al., 2023). The case studies presented by (Trường, 2023) provide practical insights into the transformative practices of companies across various industries. These studies highlight the necessity of digital evolution, its perils, and promises. Future research directions within each thematic area include understanding the specific mechanisms through which digital transformation impacts traditional financial and industry and business-related aspects (Ratna et al., 2024), as well as the impact of digital transformation on financial competitive strategy.

2.2 Debt Financing Costs

Debt financing costs are a critical aspect of corporate finance, encompassing not only the direct costs of borrowing but also the ease of obtaining financing, which is inherently linked to a company's financial constraints and future performance (Elyasiani et al., 2010). Research in this area has focused primarily on how company characteristics and governance structures influence debt financing costs, as well as the impact of external factors such as the level of financial development and pressure freedom.

Studies have shown that company-specific factors such as size, the debt ratio, and profitability significantly affect debt financing costs. Larger firms with lower debt ratios and higher profitability tend to have lower debt financing costs because of their perceived lower risk and better creditworthiness (Peng & Xie, 2024). Moreover, empirical evidence suggests that firms with stable institutional ownership tend to incur lower debt financing costs, as such ownership is often linked to reduced yield spreads and improved credit ratings (Okimoto & Takaoka, 2024).

A firm's governance framework—such as board independence and the robustness of its audit committee—significantly influences its debt financing costs. Board reforms that enhance shareholder rights can intensify the conflict between shareholders and debt holders, leading to a higher cost of debt (Chiu et al., 2023). This is because such reforms may exacerbate agency conflicts, resulting in increased dividend distribution and a preference for equity financing over debt financing.

In addition to company-specific factors, the level of financial development and press freedom in a region can also influence debt financing costs. Companies operating in regions with higher levels of digital finance development experience significantly lower costs of corporate debt financing (Tang & Geng, 2024). This indicates that the development of digital finance helps alleviate information asymmetry, thereby lowering financing costs. Additionally, pressure freedom, as an indicator of the transparency and integrity of financial information, can also impact the cost of debt, as companies in regions with greater press freedom may enjoy lower financing costs due to reduced information risk (Athira & Ramesh, 2024).

Integrating environmental, social, and governance (ESG) factors into business operations has been proven to help firms lower their debt financing costs (Yonghui et al., 2023). Investors reward companies with better ESG performance with potentially lower financing costs, as they are perceived to carry lower environmental and reputational risks (Gigante & Manglaviti, 2022). However, the phenomenon of "greenwashing" in ESG reporting, where companies misleadingly project a positive environmental image, can undermine the authenticity of ESG disclosures and potentially increase financing costs if detected (Peng & Xie, 2024).

3 Problem Statement

Based on a comprehensive review of recent literature, this paper contends that corporate digital transformation helps reduce debt financing costs by minimizing information asymmetry and mitigating agency conflicts.

On the one hand, by leveraging digital tools, companies can streamline their processes for collecting, processing, and disseminating information (L. Wang, 2024). This reduction in information asymmetry between firms and potential creditors lowers the perceived risk associated with lending, thereby decreasing the cost of debt financing (H. Chen & Yoon, 2022).

By embracing digitalization, companies can develop innovative models such as platforms and ecosystems, thereby improving their efficiency. These new models not only optimize resource allocation but also attract more favorable financing terms from creditors, who recognize the reduced risk associated with innovative and efficient operations (Liu & He, 2024). Firms undergoing digital transformation tend to allocate resources more effectively and secure external financing more readily, which contributes to lower debt costs (J. Wang & Zhu, 2023).

Digital transformation is in line with global policy directions that prioritize enhanced transparency and accountability in corporate governance. This proactive approach to policy compliance encourages more extensive information disclosure, which is positively correlated with reduced debt financing costs(Sun et al., 2022). The alignment with international standards also positions firms favorably in global markets, further mitigating risks perceived by lenders.

The adoption of advanced technologies like cloud computing and big data analytics enhances operational transparency and equips creditors with real-time insights into a firm's financial condition and performance. Consequently, this increased transparency can lead to lower interest rates on debt due to diminished risk perceptions among lenders (Ke, 2024).

Digital transformation accelerates the speed at which information circulates within and outside an organization. Faster information flow reduces search costs for creditors and lowers monitoring costs for firms, which can translate into lower debt financing costs (J. Wang & Zhu, 2023).

On the other hand, by leveraging advanced data analytics and digital tools, management can access a broader range of timely and precise information, which reduces reliance on subjective judgment and intuition (J. Wang & Zhu, 2023). This shift minimizes information asymmetry between management and stakeholders, ultimately leading to lower perceived risks by creditors and reduced debt financing costs (Sun et al., 2022).

Digital transformation typically promotes flatter organizational hierarchies and cross-functional teams, which enhance communication and collaboration. Such structural adjustments can diminish the chances of managerial self-interest behaviors that intensify agency conflicts. Empirical evidence suggests that firms undergoing digital transformation exhibit lower agency costs, as the alignment of interests between managers and shareholders improves due to enhanced oversight mechanisms (HuiJun & Erdenebold, 2024).

Digital technologies facilitate the establishment of real-time monitoring systems that prioritize product quality and corporate reputation. As firms digitize their operations, they become more accountable to external stakeholders, which increases scrutiny over managerial actions. This heightened external oversight reduces the opportunities for both management and major shareholders to act opportunistically, thereby mitigating agency conflicts (H. Zhang, 2024). Research indicates that firms adopting digital monitoring practices see a significant reduction in agency-related costs, contributing to lower debt financing expenses, as lenders perceive reduced risk associated with improved governance (Čalopa et al., 2019).

To conclude, we argue that a firm's digitalization can drive down its cost of debt through reduced information gaps and eased agency issues. Therefore, this paper proposes the following hypotheses:

H1: Debt financing costs decrease with the digital transformation of enterprises.

4 Materials and Methods

4.1 Scope of the Study

This study uses Chinese A-share listed companies from 2007 to 2023 as the research sample, given that China initiated the implementation of new accounting standards starting in 2007. To ensure the representability of the samples, the initial sample processing is as follows: (1) exclude companies with poor operating conditions such as special treatment (ST), delisting warning (*ST), and particular transfer (PT); (2) exclude financial industry companies; and (3) exclude samples with missing or abnormal data. The data in this paper are from the CSMAR database, and the macro data are from the National

Bureau of Statistics of China. This study addresses extreme values by minorizing all continuous variables at the top and bottom 1%.

4.2 Variables

Dependent Variable: Debt Financing Costs

The cost of debt financing (Cost) is generally defined as the cost that a company bears regarding obtaining debt financing. These expenses include interest expenses, as well as other expenses related to the issuance and administration of debt, such as fees, guarantees, and legal and accounting fees. Debt financing costs not only indicate borrowing expenses but also serve as an indicator of how challenging it is to secure external capital, closely tied to a firm's financial risk, information asymmetry, and agency costs within enterprises (Xie et al., 2024). Based on prior research, this paper employs two indicators to assess the cost of debt financing.

Cost1 is defined as financial expenses divided by total liabilities at period-end, while Cost2 includes interest, fees, and other financing costs divided by period-end total liabilities (Raimo et al., 2021). We use Cost1 as our primary measure and Cost2 for robustness checks.

Independent Variable: Digital Transformation

Digital transformation (digital) is chosen as the explanatory variable, and the specific measurement index is the degree of enterprise digital transformation. Drawing on the practice of (F. Wu et al., 2021), this paper takes the natural logarithm of the frequency with which digital words appear in the annual reports of listed companies to measure the degree of digital transformation of enterprises. Both the digital lexicon and frequency are from the CSMAR database. Specifically, keywords related to enterprise digital technology encompass five categories: big data, blockchain, artificial intelligence, cloud computing, and digital technology applications (Indiran et al., 2023).

Control Variables

Based on existing research (J. Wang & Zhu, 2023; Yao et al., 2022; Zhao et al., 2024), this study selects the following control variables: corporate scale, enterprise nature, age of enterprise, financial leverage, corporate performance, growth ability, cash flow, management shareholding, CEO duality, board size, the proportion of independent directors, and audit quality. Refer to Table 1 for the specific variable definitions.

Statistical Analysis

To test the impact of the speed of digital transformation on the cost of debt financing, this paper establishes Model (1). If α_1 is significantly negative, the hypothesis is valid. CV is the control variable. The baseline regression model utilized in this study is formulated as follows:

$$Cost_{it} = \alpha_0 + \alpha_1 Digital_{it} + \sum \alpha_i CV + Year + Industry + \varepsilon \quad (1)$$

Cost: Cost of debt financing
Digital: Digital transformation
CV: Control variables
Year and Industry: Dummy variables

Table 1. Variable definitions

Identification	Name	Definition
Cost1	Debt financing cost	The ratio of financial expenses to total liabilities is recorded at the close of the reporting period
Cost2	Debt financing cost	The ratio of total interest expense plus fee expense and other finance expense to total liabilities at the end of the period
Digital	Digital transformation	The natural logarithm of the frequency with which digital-related keywords occur in annual reports
Size	Corporate scale	The natural value of the company's total assets
Soe	Enterprise nature	If the firm is a state-owned enterprise, the variable is assigned a value of 1; otherwise, it is set to 0
Age	Age of Enterprise	The natural logarithm of the gap between the observation year and the firm's establishment year
Leverage	Financial leverage	total liabilities/total assets
ROE	Corporate performance	net profit/average balance of shareholders' equity
Growth	Growth ability	The growth rate of operating income, calculated as the increase in operating income divided by the total operating income of the previous year
Cash	Cash flows	Net cash flows from operating activities/total assets
M share	Management shareholding	The ratio of shares held by company management to the total outstanding shares of the company
Dual	CEO Duality	If both the chairperson and the general manager concurrently hold the same position, the value is 1; otherwise, the value is 0
Board	Board size	The logarithm of the number of board members

(*continued*)

Table 1. (*continued*)

Identification	Name	Definition
Indep	The proportion of independent directors	The proportion of independent directors (Indep), indicating the percentage of board members who are independent
Audit	Audit quality	Audit quality is usually measured by whether the auditor is a "Big Four" accounting firm; if it is, the value is 1, otherwise the value is 0

5 Results

5.1 Descriptive Statistics

Table 2 displays the descriptive statistics for the primary variables examined in this study. Among them, the means of Cost1 and Cost2 are 0.0087 and 0.0202, respectively, which are similar to the means of the corporate debt financing costs of A-share listed companies in other studies. The mean value of enterprise digital transformation is 1.3179, and the standard deviation is 1.4036, indicating that the degree of digital transformation of Chinese enterprises is relatively low overall and that there are obvious differences in the digital level among enterprises.

Table 2. Descriptive statistics

Variable	N	Mean	SD	Min	p50	Max
Cost1	28394	0.512	2.934	−17.613	0.886	6.473
Cost2	28394	1.718	1.372	0.001	1.467	6.454
Digital	28394	2.177	1.175	0.693	1.946	5.037
Size	28394	22.278	1.318	19.406	22.082	26.440
Leverage	28394	0.417	0.199	0.027	0.408	0.925
ROE	28366	0.061	0.138	−0.962	0.074	0.446
Cash	28394	0.047	0.068	−0.212	0.046	0.283
Growth	28383	0.151	0.373	−0.653	0.099	3.808
Board	28391	2.109	0.198	1.609	2.197	2.708
Indep	28391	37.829	5.425	25.00	36.36	60.00
Dual	28394	0.319	0.466	0	0	1
Soe	28394	0.328	0.470	0	0	1
Age	28377	2.950	0.339	1.099	2.996	3.638
M share	27644	15.066	19.936	0	2.649	70.596
Audit	25870	0.069	0.253	0	0	1

5.2 Multiple Regression Analysis

Digital transformation can improve the resilience of enterprises and reduce the risk of corporate default, thus reducing the cost of debt financing. In addition, digital transformation can help enterprises improve their performance, create new value growth points, and improve their financing capabilities and efficiency. Regression Model (1) to test Hypothesis H1. The estimated results are shown in Table 3.

Table 3. Digital Transformation and Financing Costs

Variable	(1) Cost1	(2) Cost1	(3) Cost2	(4) Cost2
DIGITAL	−0.0924*** (−5.08)	−0.1635*** (−10.34)	−0.0216*** (−2.59)	−0.0473*** (−5.80)
Control variables	no	yes	no	yes
Year	yes	yes	yes	yes
Industry	yes	yes	yes	yes
CONSTANT	2.0686*** (6.97)	1.2272*** (2.62)	2.8538*** (15.23)	1.9307*** (6.95)
N	28394	25116	28394	25116
R^2	0.1331	0.3476	0.1514	0.2965
Adjusted R^2	0.1302	0.3448	0.1485	0.2935
F	50.0210	85.7824	57.7500	104.9477

Notes: ***, **, * denote significance at 1%, 5%, and 10% levels. t-statistics in parentheses. * $p < 0.10$, ** $p < 0.05$, *** $p < 0.01$

According to the regression results, in the univariate regression, the degree of digital transformation of enterprises is negatively correlated with the proxy variables Cost1 and Cost2 of debt financing costs at the 5% significance level. This indicates that digital transformation contributes to lowering the debt financing costs for enterprises. After adding control variables, Digital is still negatively correlated with Cost1 and Cost2 at the 1% significance level. The regression results are consistent with Hypothesis H1.

6 Robustness Test

To address potential endogeneity arising from reverse causality, this study employs an instrumental variable approach to enhance result robustness. In addition to replacing the explained variable Cost1 with Cost2 in the previous article, drawing on the practice of (X. M. Li et al., 2024), the number of digital technology patents of enterprises is used as an instrumental variable to replace the independent variable Digital to measure the degree of digital transformation of enterprises. On the one hand, digital technology patents are closely linked to digital transformation, serving as key indicators of a firm's progress in this area. They reflect both the technological accumulation and the innovation capacity of enterprises, particularly in the development and application of digital technology (Ran et al., 2024). On the other hand, using patent data offers a more objective and reliable measurement. Patent records are factual, not easily manipulated, and free from subjective bias, thereby enhancing the credibility of the assessment (Lopez-Vega & Moodysson, 2022) (Table 4).

Table 4. Robustness test

	(2) Cost1	(4) Cost2
PATENT	−0.0002*** (−3.78)	−0.0001*** (−3.99)
Control variables	yes	yes
Year	yes	yes
Industry	yes	yes
CONSTANT	1.5876** (2.40)	1.7240*** (3.59)
N	11693	11693
R^2	0.3462	0.2987
Adjusted R^2	0.3410	0.2932
F	48.5846	59.3365

Notes: ***, **, * denote significance at 1%, 5%, and 10% levels. t-statistics in parentheses. * $p < 0.10$, ** $p < 0.05$, *** $p < 0.01$

7 Heterogeneity Test

The motivations for digital transformation vary among enterprises in different industries, and the degree of digital transformation is affected by the overall development level of the industry (Y. Tong, 2022). Therefore, the impact of digital transformation is expected to vary across different sectors. In this paper, a sample regression is performed based on whether the industry is manufacturing. The regression results are shown in Table 5.

For manufacturing enterprises, the coefficients of Digital on Cost1 and Cost2 are −0.2288 and −0.0502, respectively, both of which are significant at the 1% level. This suggests that digital transformation has notably lowered the debt financing costs for manufacturing firms. For non-manufacturing enterprises, the impact of Digital on Cost1 is not significant, with a coefficient of −0.0319. Although it has a significant negative impact on Cost2, the coefficient of −0.044 is smaller than the −0.0502 of the same variables in the manufacturing industry, indicating that digital transformation also has a certain effect on reducing the debt financing costs of nonmanufacturing enterprises, but the degree of impact is relatively smaller than that of manufacturing enterprises.

Compared with non-manufacturing enterprises, manufacturing enterprises usually have greater capital intensity and more complex production and operation processes (Brinzer & Schneider, 2024). Digital transformation can significantly improve production efficiency, reduce operating costs, improve risk management capabilities, and reduce the occurrence of risk events by introducing advanced information technology and automation equipment, thereby increasing the profitability and cash flow stability of enterprise (D. Wang et al., 2023). This makes financial institutions consider the credit risk of manufacturing enterprises to be reduced when assessing their credit risk; as a result, lenders are more inclined to offer loans at reduced interest rates, thereby decreasing the cost of debt financing (Xu, 2024). Although non-manufacturing enterprises are also positively affected by digital transformation, this impact is relatively small, probably because their business characteristics and digital foundations are different, and digital transformation has a limited effect on their operations and cost control (Xue et al., 2022).

Table 5. Heterogeneity Analysis by Manufacturing

	(1) Manufacturing Cost1	(2) Non-Manufacturing Cost1	(3) Manufacturing Cost2	(4) Non-Manufacturing Cost2
DIGITAL	−0.2288*** (−12.30)	−0.0319 (−1.09)	−0.0502*** (−5.25)	−0.0443*** (−2.92)
Control variables	yes	yes	yes	yes
Year	yes	yes	yes	yes
Industry	yes	yes	yes	yes
CONSTANT	2.9730*** (5.50)	−0.3880 (−0.53)	2.5619*** (7.98)	1.4799*** (3.55)
N	15997	9119	15997	9119
R^2	0.3449	0.3776	0.3049	0.2954
Adjusted R^2	0.3426	0.3722	0.3024	0.2893
F	101.7250	50.5237	125.4619	59.0764

Notes: ***, **, * denote significance at 1%, 5%, and 10% levels. t-statistics in parentheses. * $p < 0.10$, ** $p < 0.05$, *** $p < 0.01$

8 Conclusion

This paper combines text analysis with empirical testing, examining how digital transformation affects corporate debt financing costs. Empirical results show that digital transformation is significantly negatively correlated with debt financing costs, and the results are still reliable after robustness testing, indicating that enterprises can effectively reduce debt financing costs by promoting digital transformation.

Furthermore, the impact of digital transformation on debt financing costs varies with industry background, which is particularly evident in manufacturing enterprises. This is because manufacturing enterprises have gained greater benefits in reducing operating costs, improving production efficiency, and enhancing risk management capabilities by introducing advanced technical means and management methods in the process of digital transformation (Liang et al., 2022; Zhong & Ye, 2024).

This study enriches the research on the micro impact of digital transformation on enterprises and fills the research gap concerning the link between digital transformation and the cost of debt financing. This study also provides empirical evidence and management inspiration for enterprises to embrace digital transformation to reduce debt financing costs. First, enterprises should seize new opportunities for digital economic development, keep up with market trends, actively adjust product structure and innovate business models, leverage next-generation information technologies to steadily enhance industrial development capacity, and establish a dynamic digital system to adapt to innovation-driven market demand and meet customer demand for high-tech, customized and complex products, and services. Second, enterprises need to effectively manage risks throughout the digital transformation process. In the process of the digital transformation of enterprises, changes in technology investment and organizational structure bring a series of financial, operational, and strategic risks (Onesi-Ozigagun et al., 2024). If a digital transformation strategy suitable for the development of the enterprise is not adopted, these risks are likely to lead to the failure of the enterprise's operation (Xue et al., 2022). Therefore, the management of the enterprise should actively and positively consider the digital strategy and choose a stable, active, or conservative digital transformation strategy based on its own profitability, cash flow, financing ability, and other factors.

References

Adama, H.E., Okeke, C.D.: Digital transformation as a catalyst for business model innovation: a critical review of impact and implementation strategies. Magna Scientia Adv. Res. Rev. **10**(02), 256–264 (2024)

Ahmed, I., Mehmood, O., Ghafoor, Z., Jamil, S.H., Majeed, A.: Corporate governance and the choice between bank debt and public debt. Corp. Gov. Int. J. Bus. Soc. **24**(1), 59–80 (2024)

Ancillai, C., Sabatini, A., Gatti, M., Perna, A.: Digital technology and business model innovation: a systematic literature review and future research agenda. Technol. Forecast. Soc. Chang. **188**, 122307 (2023)

Athira, A., Ramesh, V.K.: Economic policy uncertainty and tax avoidance: international evidence. Emerg. Mark. Rev. **60**, 101135 (2024)

Bank, W.: Digital Progress and Trends Report 2023. The World Bank (2024)

Böhm, N., Watkowski, L.M.-L., Buck, C.: Establishing platform-based ecosystems: How automotive manufacturers adapt their value creation to a digital end. In Handbook on Digital Platforms and Business Ecosystems in Manufacturing, pp. 147–163. Edward Elgar Publishing (2024). https://www.elgaronline.com/edcollchap/book/9781035301003/book-part-9781035301003-16.xml

Brinzer, B., Schneider, K.: Komplexität in der Produktion – Herausforderungen durch Über- und Unterforderung. Zeitschrift Für Wirtschaftlichen Fabrikbetrieb **119**(9), 615–623 (2024). https://doi.org/10.1515/zwf-2024-1072

Čalopa, M.K., Kokot, K., Đunđek, I.: Agency problems and debt financing. EMAN 2019–Economics & Management: How to Cope With Disrupted Times, 325 (2019)

Chen, H., Yoon, S.S.: Does technology innovation in finance alleviate financing constraints and reduce debt-financing costs? Evidence from China. Asia Pac. Bus. Rev. **28**(4), 467–492 (2022)

Chen, X., Anderson, R.W.: Chinese debt capital markets: an emerging global market with Chinese characteristics. World Scientific (2024). https://books.google.com/books?hl=zhCN&lr=&id=vJn7EAAAQBAJ&oi=fnd&pg=PR5&dq=Due+capital+market+in+China,+debt+capital+i&ots=7e4vrWZ0DS&sig=1vIpuYUpwBT37UKOhIqlmgAT85M

Chiu, H.Z., Lin, C., Wei, L.: How do board reforms affect debt financing costs around the world? J. Financ. Quant. Anal. **58**(1), 217–249 (2023)

Elyasiani, E., Jia, J.J., Mao, C.X.: Institutional ownership stability and the cost of debt. J. Financ. Mark. **13**(4), 475–500 (2010)

Gigante, G., Manglaviti, D.: The ESG effect on the cost of debt financing: a sharp RD analysis. Int. Rev. Financ. Anal. **84**, 102382 (2022)

Guo, M., Zheng, C., Li, J.: Corporate social responsibility and debt financing cost: evidence from China. Environ. Dev. Sustain. **26**(7), 17475–17503 (2023). https://doi.org/10.1007/s10668-023-03348-0

Hou, Q., Zhang, Q.: The effect and mechanism of ESG performance on corporate debt financing costs: empirical evidence from listed companies in the heavy-polluting industries. Pol. J. Environ. Stud. **33**(2), 1753–1766 (2024)

HuiJun, W., Erdenebold, T.: The impact of digital transformation on corporate performance: based on shanghai and shenzhen a-share listed companies. Asia-Pacific J. Bus. **15**(3), 17–45 (2024)

Indiran, L., Kohar, U.H.A., Liu, H., Khatib, S.F.: Examining the Role of Digital Technology as an Enabler of Digital Disruption: a Systematic Review (2023). https://www.researchsquare.com/article/rs-3657875/latest

Ke, Z.: Enterprise digital transformation and misallocation of credit resources. Trans. Econ. Bus. Manag. Res. **7**, 236–249 (2024)

Kohtamäki, M., Parida, V., Patel, P.C., Gebauer, H.: The relationship between digitalization and servitization: the role of servitization in capturing the financial potential of digitalization. Technol. Forecast. Soc. Chang. **151**, 119804 (2020)

Li, R., Rao, J., Wan, L.: The digital economy, enterprise digital transformation, and enterprise innovation. Manag. Decis. Econ. **43**(7), 2875–2886 (2022). https://doi.org/10.1002/mde.3569

Liang, Y., Chu, S., Cao, Y.: Enterprise digital transformation and debt financing capability. Evidence from Chinese manufacturing firms. In: 2022 6th Annual International Conference on Data Science and Business Analytics (ICDSBA), pp. 272–277 (2022). https://ieeexplore.ieee.org/abstract/document/10129424/

Liu, Y., He, Q.: Digital transformation, external financing, and enterprise resource allocation efficiency. Manag. Decis. Econ. **45**(4), 2321–2335 (2024). https://doi.org/10.1002/mde.4136

Lopez-Vega, H., Moodysson, J.: Digital transformation: implications of novelty and scope for digital technologies. Acad. Manag. Proc. **2022**(1), 11416 (2022). https://doi.org/10.5465/AMBPP.2022.11416abstract

Nadkarni, S., Prügl, R.: Digital transformation: a review, synthesis and opportunities for future research. Manag. Rev. Q. **71**, 233–341 (2021)

Okimoto, T., Takaoka, S.: Sustainability and credit spreads in Japan. Int. Rev. Financ. Anal. **91**, 103052 (2024)

Onesi-Ozigagun, O., Ololade, Y.J., Eyo-Udo, N.L., Ogundipe, D.O.: Leading digital transformation in non-digital sectors: a strategic review. Int. J. Manag. Entrep. Res. **6**(4), 1157–1175 (2024)

Peng, Q., Xie, Y.: ESG greenwashing and corporate debt financing costs. Financ. Res. Lett. **69**, 106012 (2024)

Plekhanov, D., Franke, H., Netland, T.H.: Digital transformation: a review and research agenda. Eur. Manag. J. **41**(6), 821–844 (2023)

Pramanik, H.S., Kirtania, M., Pani, A.K.: Essence of digital transformation—manifestations at large financial institutions from North America. Futur. Gener. Comput. Syst. **95**, 323–343 (2019)

Raimo, N., Caragnano, A., Zito, M., Vitolla, F., Mariani, M.: Extending the benefits of ESG disclosure: the effect on the cost of debt financing. Corp. Soc. Responsib. Environ. Manag. **28**(4), 1412–1421 (2021). https://doi.org/10.1002/csr.2134

Ran, L., Zhang, Q., Li, X.: Can digital technology innovation contribute to firms' market value? PLoS ONE **19**(9), e0309993 (2024)

Ratna, S., Saide, S., Putri, A.M., Soleha, A., Andini, P.R.: Financial systems transformation in the digital age: a systematic review and future research directions. Procedia Comput. Sci. **234**, 1538–1545 (2024)

Sun, C., Zhang, Z., Vochozka, M., Vozňáková, I.: Enterprise digital transformation and debt financing cost in China's A-share listed companies. Oeconomia Copernicana **13**(3), 783–829 (2022)

Tang, Y., Geng, B.: Digital finance development level and corporate debt financing cost. Financ. Res. Lett. **60**, 104825 (2024)

Taufani, M., Widjaja, A.W.: The manifestation of digital transformation concept in indonesian logistic firms. Jurnal Manajemen **27**(3), 428–448 (2023)

Teng, X., Wu, Z., Yang, F.: Research on the relationship between digital transformation and performance of SMEs. Sustainability **14**(10), 6012 (2022)

Tong, Y., Tian, Y., Cao, Z.: The effect of CEO locality on the cost of debt financing: the role of regional heterogeneity. Reg. Stud. **58**(5), 1124–1144 (2024)

Trường, M.X.: Successful Digital Transformation Case Studies: 8 Best Examples. Magenest - One-Stop Digital Transformation Solution (2023). https://magenest.com/en/successful-digital-transformation-case-studies/

Wang, D., Shao, X., Song, Y., Shao, H., Wang, L.: The effect of digital transformation on manufacturing enterprise performance. Amfiteatru Econ. **25**(63), 593–608 (2023)

Wang, J., Zhu, C.: The impact of digital transformation on the debt financing costs of firms. SHS Web Conf. **163**, 03036 (2023)

Wang, L.: Digital transformation and total factor productivity. Financ. Res. Lett. **58**, 104338 (2023)

Wang, L.: Can fintech reduce the cost of corporate debt financing?–Evidence from Chinese listed companies. Trans. Econ. Bus. Manag. Res. **5**, 172–179 (2024)

Xie, L., Liu, Y., Jiang, T.: Executives with business education background and cost of debt financing: evidence from China. Int. Rev. Econ. Financ. **90**, 283–296 (2024)

Xu, T.: Credit risk assessment using a combined approach of supervised and unsupervised learning. J. Comput. Methods Eng. Appl. **4**, 1–12 (2024)

Xue, F., Zhao, X., Tan, Y.: Digital transformation of manufacturing enterprises: an empirical study on the relationships between digital transformation, boundary spanning, and sustainable competitive advantage. Discret. Dyn. Nat. Soc. **2022**(1), 4104314 (2022). https://doi.org/10.1155/2022/4104314

Yao, J., Qi, Y., Guo, B.: Corporate social responsibility, debt financing cost and enterprise innovation. Sci. Rep. **12**(1), 21909 (2022)

Yonghui, L., Xiaoyue, H.E., Lin, Z.: Corporate ESG performance and the cost of debt. Collect. Essays Financ. Econ. **39**(1), 48 (2023)

Zare, J., Persaud, A.: Digital transformation and business model innovation: a bibliometric analysis of existing research and future perspectives. Manag. Rev. Q. (2024). https://doi.org/10.1007/s11301-024-00426-z

Zhai, H., Yang, M., Chan, K.C.: Does digital transformation enhance a firm's performance? Evidence from China. Technol. Soc. **68**, 101841 (2022)

Zhang, H.: The impact of digital transformation on the debt financing costs of small and medium-sized enterprises. iBusiness **16**(4), 195–215 (2024)

Zhang, J., Cai, L., Gao, Y.: Shareholder heterogeneity, financing constraints, and organizational resilience: mixed-ownership reform in Chinese private enterprises. Heliyon **10**(16), e36380 (2024)

Zhao, Y., Gao, Y., Hong, D.: Sustainable innovation and economic resilience: deciphering ESG ratings' role in lowering debt financing costs. J. Knowl. Econ. (2024). https://doi.org/10.1007/s13132-024-02129-y

Zhao, Y., Xu, H., Liu, G., Zhou, Y., Wang, Y.: Can digital transformation improve the quality of enterprise innovation in China? Eur. J. Innov. Manag. (2023). https://doi.org/10.1108/EJIM-05-2023-0358/full/html

Zhong, K., Ye, J.: Research on the impact of digital transformation on corporate business credit in the context of double cycle: based on the moderating effect of outward investment. Trans. Soc. Sci. Educ. Human. Res. **6**, 169–180 (2024)

Zhou, Z., Li, Z.: Corporate digital transformation and trade credit financing. J. Bus. Res. **160**, 113793 (2023)

Wu, F., Hu, H., Lin, H., Ren, X.: Corporate digital transformation and capital market performance: empirical evidence from stock liquidity. Manag. World **37**(7), 130–144 (2021)

Li, X., Chen, Z., Chen, Y.: Corporate digital transformation and financial performance: evidence from digital patent data of listed companies. J. Technol. Econ. **43**, 1 (2024)

Tong, Y.: A study on the influencing factors of digital transformation in China's manufacturing industry. Res. Technol. Econ. Manag. **3**, 124–128 (2022)

A Fault Diagnosis Model for Multi-condition Reactor Coolant Systems Based on the SSA-Elman Neural Network

Yunfei Liu[1], Kun Sun[2], Guangtao Bao[3](✉), and Binxiangyu Xiao[1]

[1] Universiti Sains Malaysia, 11800 Gelugor, Pulau Pinang, Malaysia
[2] Shanghai Dianji University, Pudong 200090, Shanghai, China
[3] Shandong Huayu University of Technology, Dezhou 253034, Shandong, China
b843741434@qq.com

Abstract. The Reactor Coolant System (RCS) is the core safety barrier within the nuclear island of a nuclear power plant, and the rapid identification of its multi-condition operational states is vital for ensuring safe reactor operation. This paper proposes an intelligent fault diagnosis model based on the Elman neural network optimized by the Sparrow Search Algorithm (SSA), referred to as the SSA-Elman model, for multi-state fault identification in RCS.

A simulated dataset encompassing eight representative operating conditions-normal operation, small/large break loss-of-coolant accidents (LOCA), steam generator tube rupture (SGTR), and main pump flow loss (S1-S8)-was constructed using the MARS-KS simulation platform. Each condition includes 500 labeled samples covering 83 critical operational parameters. The dataset was then divided into training and validation sets, and both Elman and SSA-Elman models were trained to evaluate their predictive performance under various fault conditions.Experimental results demonstrate that the SSA-Elman model significantly outperforms the traditional Elman network across all three evaluation metrics-mean squared error (MSE), root mean squared error (RMSE), and mean absolute error (MAE). In the training set, the maximum error reduction reached 88.2%, with substantial improvement also observed in the validation set. These results highlight the model's superior nonlinear modeling capability and generalization performance.

This study confirms that the SSA-Elman model can effectively improve fault identification accuracy in RCS under uncertain conditions and provides a valuable intelligent tool for supporting the safe and reliable operation of nuclear power systems.

Keywords: Reactor Coolant System · Fault Diagnosis · Elman Neural Network · Sparrow Search Algorithm · Multi-Condition Simulation · Intelligent Modeling

1 Introduction

The Reactor Coolant System (RCS) plays a vital role in maintaining the safety and stability of nuclear reactor operations [1]. It includes key components such as the reactor pressure vessel, main coolant pumps, steam generators, pressurizer, and a network of pipelines and valves that together create a sealed circulation loop [2].

M. Kassim et al. (Eds.): SCDS 2025, CCIS 2674, pp. 32–46, 2026.
https://doi.org/10.1007/978-981-95-8368-3_3

At present, fault diagnosis methods in nuclear power plants can be broadly categorized into model-driven and data-driven approaches. Most current research, both domestic and international, still relies on model-driven techniques for RCS fault diagnosis. However, these methods are highly dependent on expert knowledge and face considerable challenges in modeling complex, nonlinear systems [3].

To address these challenges, an increasing number of researchers are adopting data-driven techniques for fault detection within the Reactor Coolant System (RCS) [4, 5]. These methods utilize large volumes of sensor data and apply machine learning and data mining algorithms to model the relationships between system variables and fault categories. Frequently employed techniques include decision trees, support vector machines (SVM), random forests, and artificial neural networks [6].

Nevertheless, under real operating and accident conditions in nuclear power plants, the data collected by RCS sensors often exhibit inherent uncertainty and volatility [7], leading to reduced accuracy and robustness of traditional data-driven models in recognizing complex nonlinear system states [8]. To address these challenges, hybrid intelligent models with temporal modeling and parameter optimization capabilities have been explored to enhance fault diagnostic accuracy and model stability.

The Elman neural network, a type of recurrent neural network featuring a dynamic feedback structure, is capable of retaining historical information via a context layer. This allows it to effectively model and forecast complex time-varying data such as temperature, pressure, and flow rate within the Reactor Coolant System (RCS). Nevertheless, traditional Elman networks are highly dependent on the initialization of weights and thresholds [9], which can lead to entrapment in local optima during training and subsequently reduce prediction accuracy.

To resolve this issue, the Sparrow Search Algorithm (SSA)-a novel swarm intelligence optimization technique-has been introduced to optimize the initial parameters of Elman networks. Previous studies have demonstrated that the SSA-Elman model exhibits excellent performance in various industrial prediction scenarios [4], such as thermal error modeling in CNC machines and battery health estimation. Applying this model to RCS fault diagnosis enables efficient extraction of key features from evolving system parameters, thereby facilitating accurate identification and trend prediction of typical failures such as coolant leakage and pipeline rupture.

In summary, constructing an RCS fault diagnosis model based on the SSA-Elman neural network enhances fault awareness under uncertain conditions and improves diagnostic accuracy and timeliness. This has significant engineering relevance and research value for ensuring the safe and stable operation of nuclear reactor coolant systems.

2 Overview of Reactor Coolant System (RCS)

The Reactor Coolant System (RCS) constitutes the primary loop of a nuclear power plant and is the most critical subsystem within the nuclear island. The RCS typically adopts a dual-loop configuration, with each loop comprising two reactor coolant pumps, one steam generator, and a series of pipelines and instrumentation. Additionally, a pressurizer is installed on the hot leg of one loop to regulate and stabilize system pressure through the operation of spray nozzles and electric heaters.

During standard reactor operation, the coolant is circulated by the main pumps and flows from the cold leg of each loop into the reactor pressure vessel. After absorbing fission heat in the reactor core, the coolant becomes high-temperature fluid and exits from the upper outlet of the core. It then flows into the hot leg of each loop and enters the primary side of the steam generator. Through the heat exchange tubes, thermal energy is transferred to the secondary-side feedwater, generating saturated steam for use in the secondary circuit. After releasing its heat, the coolant exits the steam generator and returns to the pump inlet via the transition section, completing a closed-loop circulation.

Therefore, the primary function of the RCS is to efficiently convert the nuclear energy generated in the reactor core into thermal energy in the form of steam, enabling safe and reliable heat transfer. Simultaneously, as the second major safety barrier of the nuclear power plant, the RCS plays a crucial role in preventing the release of radioactive materials, ensuring the overall integrity and safety of the reactor system. Figure 1 is the schematic diagram of the Reactor Coolant System (RCS).

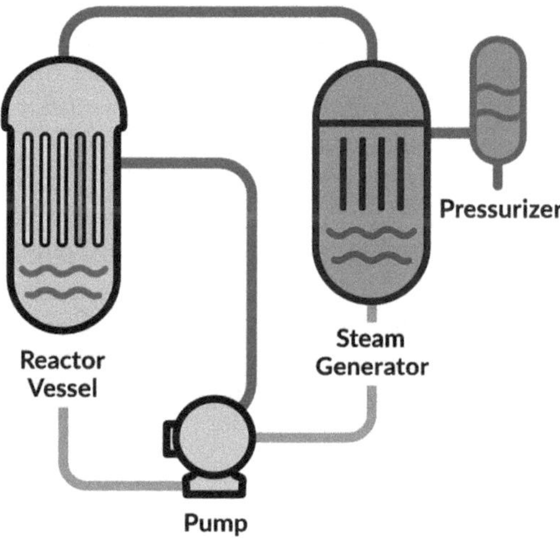

Fig. 1. Schematic of the Reactor Coolant System in a Nuclear Power Plant

3 RCS Dataset Construction and Simulation Platform

Due to the fact that the Reactor Coolant System (RCS) in nuclear power plants typically operates under safe and stable conditions for extended periods, actual fault data are extremely scarce, making it difficult to meet the training requirements of fault diagnosis models. To address this limitation, the MARS-KS (Multi-dimensional Analysis of Reactor Safety - Korea Standard) simulation software was adopted in this study as a platform for generating synthetic datasets under both normal and representative fault conditions of the RCS.

In this research, multiple RCS operating states were simulated using the MARS-KS platform, including normal operation, loss-of-coolant accidents (LOCA) with small breaks in the hot leg and cold leg, large breaks in the hot leg and cold leg, steam generator tube rupture (SGTR) in loops A and B, and loss of flow accidents. The duration and sample size of each simulated scenario are summarized in Table 1. Each sample includes 78 operational parameters and is labeled according to its corresponding condition, thereby forming a comprehensive input dataset for neural network-based fault diagnosis modeling. The simulated dataset is summarized in Table 1.

Table 1. Simulation Time and Number of Generated Samples for RCS Operation and Accident Conditions.

Operating and Accident Conditions	Simulation Time/s	Number of Samples
Normal condition (S1)	0 ~ 499	500
Small LOCA at hot leg (S_2)	500 ~ 999	500
Small LOCA at cold leg (S_3)	1000 ~ 1499	500
Large LOCA at hot leg (S_4)	1500 ~ 1999	500
Large LOCA at cold leg (S_5)	2000 ~ 2499	500
SG tube rupture in A loop (S_6)	2500 ~ 2999	500
SG tube rupture in B loop (S_7)	3000 ~ 3499	500
Loss of flow accident (S_8)	3500 ~ 3999	500

4 Theory Introduction

4.1 Elman Neural Network

In the early 1990s, Jeffrey L. Elman proposed the Elman neural network to address challenges in speech processing tasks. As one of the earliest forms of recurrent neural networks (RNNs), the Elman network was the first to explicitly incorporate temporal information [10].

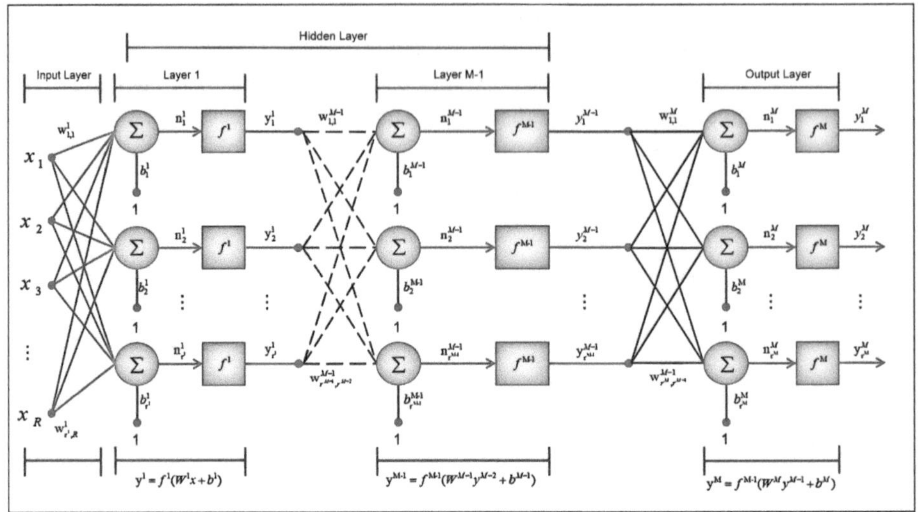

Fig. 2. Schematic diagram of the Elman neural network architecture.

The Elman neural network belongs to the category of delayed feedback neural network models. It is generally composed of four main layers: an input layer, a hidden layer, a context (or receiving) layer, and an output layer. The structural design of the Elman network is depicted in Fig. 2.

4.2 Sparrow Search Algorithm (SSA) Theory

In 2020, Xue Jiankai introduced a new swarm intelligence optimization method called the Sparrow Search Algorithm (SSA), which was inspired by the natural foraging strategies observed in sparrow populations.

Throughout both foraging and anti-predation behaviors, sparrows continuously adjust their positions in search of the optimal food source. The SSA algorithm simulates these dynamic processes to perform global optimization. It enhances global exploration capabilities and exhibits strong exploitation ability. By considering the influence of all individuals in the population, SSA enables sparrows to approach the global optimum and converge rapidly in its vicinity. In this study, the SSA is used to optimize the initial weights and thresholds of the Elman neural network, improving convergence speed and prediction accuracy. Figure 3 displays the architecture of the SSA-Elman fault diagnosis model.

4.3 SSA-Elman Prediction Model

The process of multi-state fault identification for the Reactor Coolant System (RCS) using the SSA-Elman prediction model is outlined as follows:

(1) Data Preparation

The dataset for multi-condition fault identification of the RCS is divided into a training set and a validation set in a 70% to 30% ratio. The original data are preprocessed using a normalization technique to ensure consistent scaling across features.

(2) Network Structure Initialization

The optimal quantity of neurons in the hidden layer is selected by applying the criterion of minimizing the mean squared error (MSE). After defining the topology of the prediction model, the initial parameters of the Elman neural network are subsequently set in alignment with the established structure.

(3) SSA Parameter Configuration

Key parameters for the Sparrow Search Algorithm (SSA) are set, including initial population size, number of iterations, discoverer ratio, and learning rate. Fitness values are calculated, and the positions of discoverers and joiners are updated iteratively based on the SSA optimization rules.

(4) Model Training and Prediction

The Elman neural network is initialized with the optimized weights and thresholds derived from the Sparrow Search Algorithm (SSA). Subsequently, the model undergoes iterative training on the prepared dataset until the desired prediction accuracy is achieved. The final result represents the optimal predicted value corresponding to each specific fault scenario.

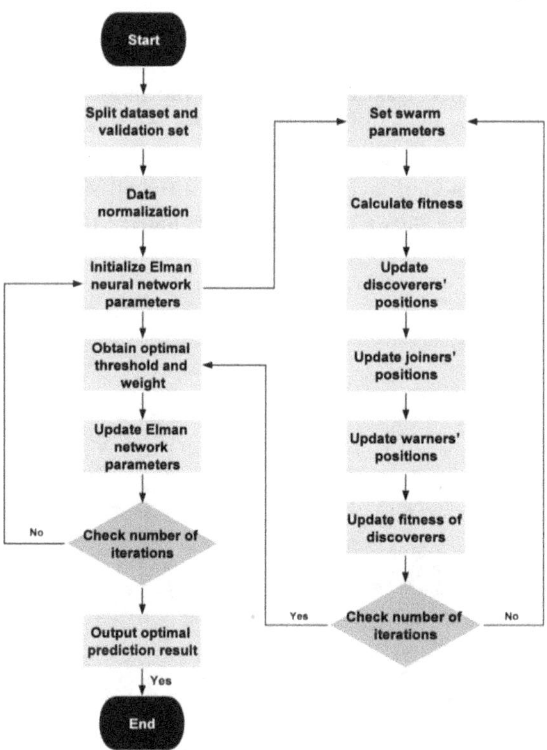

Fig. 3. Prediction model of the SSA-Elman neural network for multi-state fault identification in the Reactor Coolant System.

5 Model Construction and Parameter Optimization

5.1 Elman Prediction Model Construction

A sliding window method was employed for temporal segmentation, with a window size of 180 s and a sliding step of 10 s. A total of eight representative working conditions (as listed in Table 1) were selected as fault categories. The operational and fault datasets were segmented into 383 time slices, with each sample consisting of 83 parameters that reflect key characteristics of the Reactor Coolant System (RCS) under both normal and abnormal conditions.

The original dataset was divided into a training set and a validation set using a 70% to 30% split, respectively used for model training and performance evaluation. An Elman neural network was adopted to construct the multi-state fault identification model for the RCS. The modeling process included four major components: data preprocessing, network structure design, learning parameter configuration, and training parameter setup.

(1) Number of Hidden Layers

The Elman neural network is typically conFig. d with a single hidden layer. However, depending on specific research tasks, increasing the number of hidden layers may enhance the model's learning capacity. Existing studies have demonstrated that appropriately deepening the network structure can improve prediction performance.

In this research, mean squared error (MSE) served as the performance metric to evaluate the model under various hidden layer quantities, ranging from 2 to 11. According to the results illustrated in Fig. 4, the model achieved the best training performance when the number of hidden layers was set to 2, demonstrating reliable prediction accuracy under this setup. Consequently, the Elman neural network adopted a two-hidden-layer configuration for all subsequent experiments in this study [11]. Figure 4 shows the MSE values under different numbers of hidden layers.

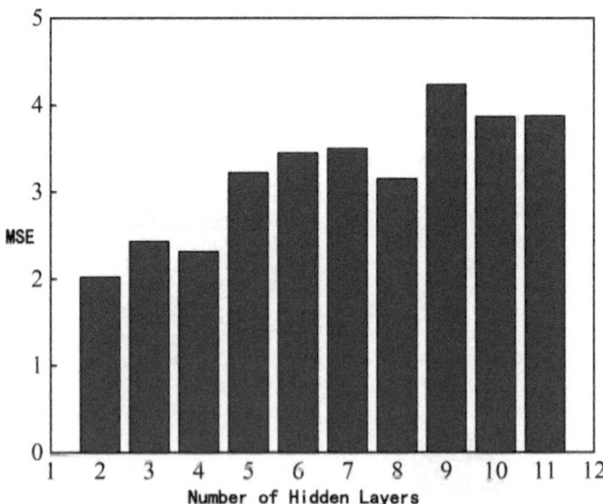

Fig. 4. Mean squared error (MSE) of the Elman neural network under different numbers of hidden layers.

This study employed mean squared error (MSE) as the evaluation criterion to compare the performance of the model under different hidden layer settings, varying from 2 to 11. As illustrated in Fig. 4, the model yielded the best training outcome when the hidden layer count was set to 2, demonstrating acceptable prediction accuracy with this configuration. Accordingly, the Elman network in this study was implemented with two hidden layers.

Number of Neurons in Each Layer

The number of neurons in the hidden layer plays a key role in determining the performance of the Elman prediction model. In alignment with the SSA-Elman framework, root mean squared error (RMSE) is adopted as the evaluation metric to identify the optimal neuron count. Based on comparative analysis, the Elman model attains the minimum RMSE when the hidden layer contains four neurons.

Activation Functions

Commonly used activation functions include tanh, ReLU, Pureline, and Sigmoid functions. Since both the input and output values in this study are within the range (0, 1), the Sigmoid function is chosen for the hidden layer due to its strong nonlinear mapping capability. The Pureline function is used in the output layer to ensure linear transformation at the final stage.

Number of Iterations and Learning Rate

Training iterations and learning rate are also important hyperparameters that influence the performance of the Elman prediction model. Through repeated experimental testing, the maximum number of training iterations was determined to be 1000, while the learning rate was set at 0.0001 to promote stable convergence during the training process [12].

The structure of the Elman prediction model is illustrated in Fig. 5.

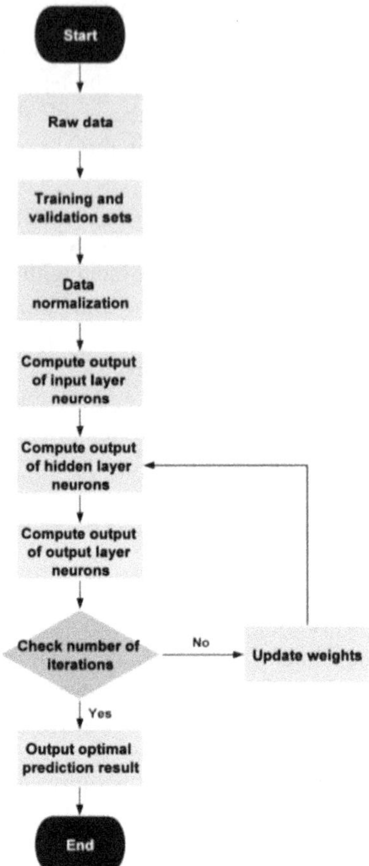

Fig. 5. Process flow of the Elman neural network for multi-state fault prediction.

5.2 SSA-Elman Prediction Model Construction

The original dataset is divided into a training set and a validation set in a ratio of 70% to 30%. Due to the presence of variables with different physical dimensions and magnitudes, data normalization is necessary to ensure the accuracy and stability of the prediction model [13]. The normalization process is performed using the formula shown in Eq. (1). Figure 6 shows the MSE values for different numbers of hidden layer neurons in the SSA-Elman model.

$$x^{*} = \frac{x - x_{\min}}{x_{\max} - x_{\min}} \tag{1}$$

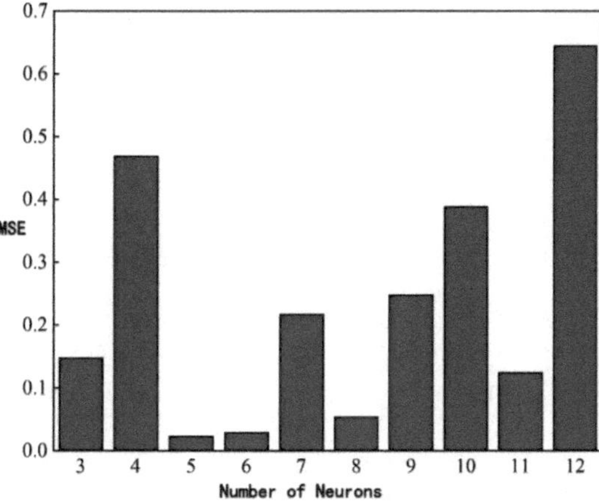

Fig. 6. Mean squared error (MSE) of the SSA-Elman model under different numbers of hidden layer neurons.

The number of neurons in the hidden layer plays a decisive role in the performance of the prediction model. For the SSA-Elman model, the search range for the number of hidden neurons was predefined, and the corresponding mean squared error (MSE) values were computed under different configurations, as illustrated in Fig. 6. According to the results, when the number of hidden layer neurons is set to 5, the model achieves the lowest training MSE, which is 0.0232. Figure 7 shows the MSE and R^2 values under different training iterations.

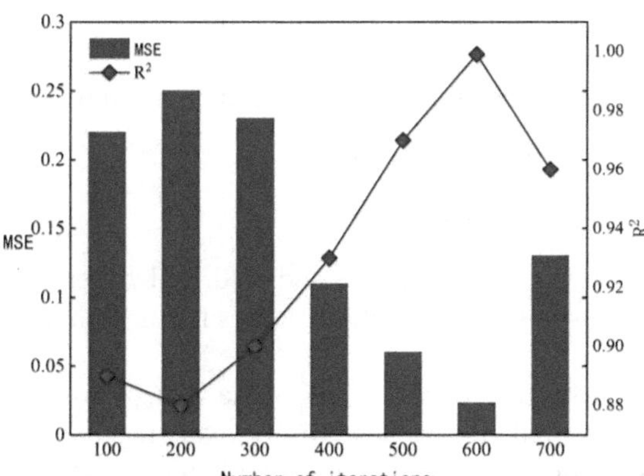

Fig. 7. Mean squared error (MSE) of the SSA-Elman model under different numbers of training iterations.

The optimal number of training iterations for the SSA-Elman prediction model is determined based on the evaluation of both the coefficient of determination (R^2) and the mean squared error (MSE). As shown in Fig. 7, a comparison of R^2 and MSE under different iteration settings indicates that the model achieves the best performance when the maximum number of iterations is set to 600-yielding the lowest MSE and the highest R^2 value. The configuration details of the SSA-Elman model are listed in Table 2.

Table 2. Parameters of the SSA-Elman prediction model

SSA Parameters	Value	Elman Network Parameters	Value
Population size	20	Number of training epochs	1000
Maximum iterations	600	Learning rate	0.01
Discoverer ratio	0.8	Maximum failure times	6
Alert threshold	0.6	Momentum factor	0.01
Joiner ratio	0.2		

6 Experimental Results and Comparative Analysis

6.1 Evaluation Metrics for Prediction Models

The performance of the prediction models is evaluated using the following three commonly used error metrics:

(1) Mean Squared Error (MSE). This measure reflects the mean of the squared deviations between predicted outcomes and actual observations across all data samples [14].
(2) Root Mean Squared Error (RMSE). The root mean squared error (RMSE) is calculated as the square root of the mean squared error and is often interpreted as the standard deviation of the model's prediction errors.
(3) Mean Absolute Error (MAE). The mean absolute error (MAE) is defined as the average of the absolute deviations between predicted results and actual values over the entire dataset.

6.2 Analysis of Prediction Model Results

A comparison between the measured values and predicted values from the training set is illustrated in Fig. 8. The statistical evaluation metrics for the training set are summarized in Table 3.

The SSA-Elman prediction model achieves the best performance across all evaluation metrics, with its predicted values closely matching the actual measurements. Compared to the conventional Elman neural network, the SSA-Elman model-optimized via the Sparrow Search Algorithm-significantly enhances prediction accuracy and overall model performance. In contrast, the standard Elman model demonstrates relatively poor predictive capability under the same conditions.

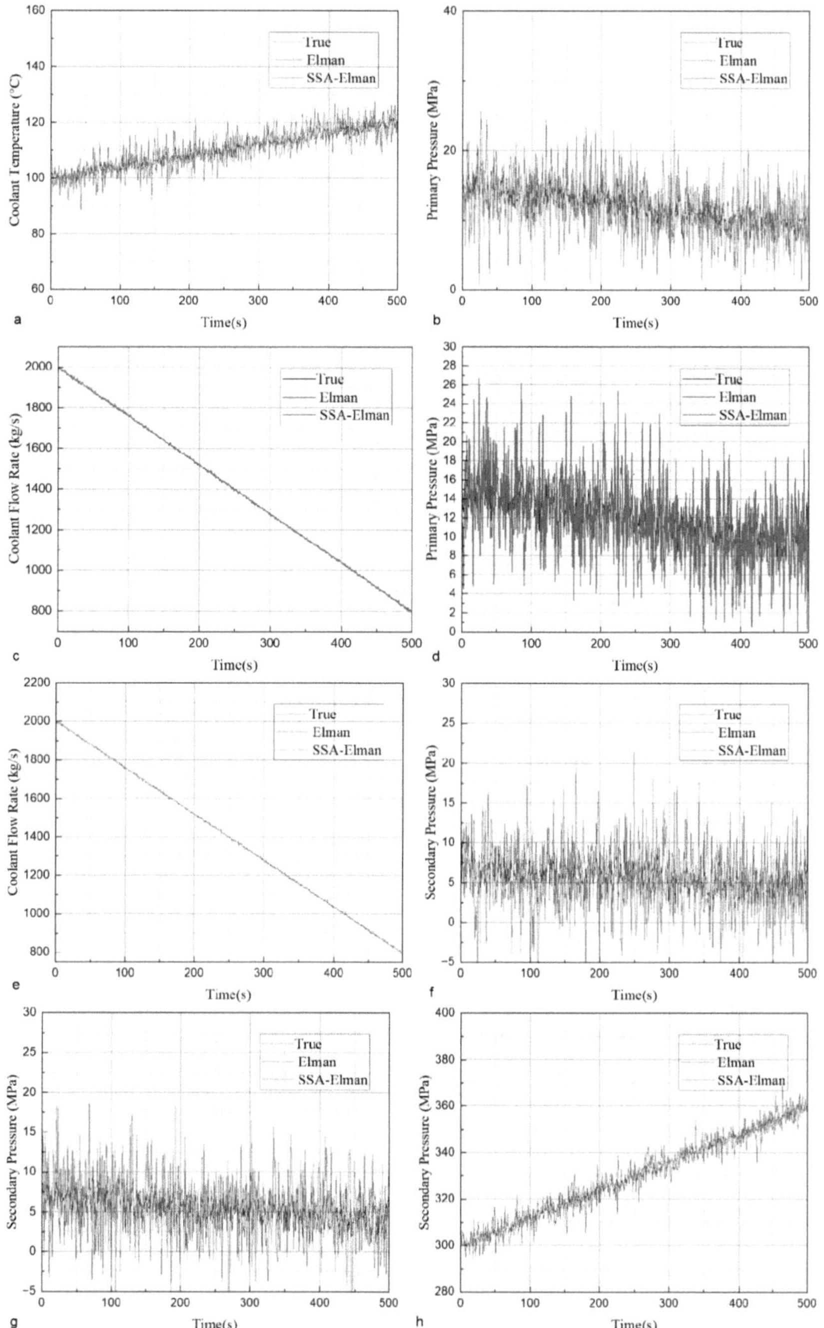

Fig. 8. Overall comparison of prediction performance between the Elman and SSA-Elman models under eight operating and fault conditions of the Reactor Coolant System (RCS).

As shown in Fig. 8, the overall prediction performance of the Elman and SSA-Elman neural networks was compared under eight different operating and fault conditions of the Reactor Coolant System (RCS). The evaluation was conducted using three key metrics: Mean Squared Error (MSE), Root Mean Squared Error (RMSE), and Mean Absolute Error (MAE).

For the Elman model, the MSE, RMSE, and MAE were 34.80, 5.90, and 4.72, respectively. In contrast, the SSA-Elman model achieved significantly better results, with an MSE of 3.95, an RMSE of 1.99, and an MAE of 1.58. These results correspond to error reductions of 88.6% (MSE), 66.3% (RMSE), and 66.5% (MAE) compared to the traditional Elman network. This demonstrates that the SSA-Elman model not only improves prediction accuracy but also enhances convergence stability and robustness across multiple fault conditions.

The analysis demonstrates that the SSA-Elman model offers markedly superior prediction accuracy and is more effective in adapting to the complex, multi-condition fault identification tasks associated with the RCS. Moreover, it exhibits stronger generalization capability and broader application potential for intelligent diagnosis in nuclear power systems.

Table 3. Table captions should be placed above the tables.

	SSA-Elman	Elman
MSE	3.95	34.80
RMSE	1.99	5.90
MAE	1.58	4.72

7 Conclusion

This study addresses the problem of fault state identification in the Reactor Coolant System (RCS) of nuclear power plants and proposes an intelligent prediction model based on an Elman neural network optimized by the Sparrow Search Algorithm (SSA). The model was validated using simulation datasets generated under eight operating and fault scenarios (S1-S8) via the MARS-KS platform. The main conclusions are summarized as follows:

1. A multi-condition simulation dataset containing 83 characteristic parameters was constructed for the RCS, covering typical scenarios such as normal operation, small/large break loss-of-coolant accidents (LOCA), steam generator tube rupture (SGTR), and loss-of-flow accidents. This dataset provided a solid foundation for model training and evaluation.

2. The SSA-Elman model effectively optimized the initial weights and thresholds of the traditional Elman network using the Sparrow Search Algorithm, significantly improving both convergence speed and prediction accuracy.
3. On the training set, the SSA-Elman model achieved reductions of 88.2% in MSE, 65.6% in RMSE, and 65.7% in MAE compared to the standard Elman model. It also demonstrated consistent improvement on the validation set, indicating strong generalization performance.
4. The SSA-Elman model shows clear advantages in modeling the complex dynamic behavior of the RCS and identifying nonlinear fault states, making it well-suited for future applications in nuclear plant operation monitoring and intelligent safety assessment.

In conclusion, the proposed SSA-Elman model provides an effective data-driven solution for fault identification in nuclear power systems and holds promising potential for practical engineering deployment.

References

1. Goudarzi, K., Sabzehgar, R.: Analysis and control of pressurized water reactor using fuzzy-immune controller. J. Mech. Sci. Technol. **32**(8), 3931–3937 (2018)
2. Alemberti, A., et al.: ALFRED reactor coolant system design. Nucl. Eng. Des. **370**, 110884 (2020)
3. Memmott, M.J., Manera, A., Boyack, J., Pacheco, S., Wang, M., Petrovic, B.: The primary reactor coolant system concept of the integral, inherently-safe light water reactor. Ann. Nucl. Energy **100**, 53–67 (2017)
4. Hu, G., Zhou, T., Liu, Q.: Data-driven machine learning for fault detection and diagnosis in nuclear power plants: a review. Front. Energy Res. **9**, 663296 (2021)
5. Zeng, Y., Huang, T., Zhang, T., Huang, H.Z.: System-level performance degradation prediction for power converters based on SSA–Elman NN and empirical knowledge. IEEE Trans. Ind. Inform. **20**, 1240–1250 (2023)
6. Fallah Najafabadi, M., Talebi Rostami, H., Ganji, D.D.: Thermal and geometrical investigation of an original double-pipe helical coil heat storage system with kock snowflake cross-section containing phase-change material. Appl. Therm. Eng. **226**, 120244 (2023)
7. Rao, N.S.V., Greulich, C., Ramuhalli, P., Gurgen, A., Zhang, F., Cetiner, S.M.: Estimation of sensor measurement errors in reactor coolant systems using multi-sensor fusion. Nucl. Eng. Des. **375**, 111024 (2021)
8. Lee, J.D., Kim, L., Lee, S., Bang, H.: Data-driven fault diagnosis of nonlinear systems with parameter uncertainty using deep Koopman operator and weighted window extended dynamic mode decomposition. Int. J. Control. Autom. Syst. **22**, 3314–3328 (2024)
9. Zhang, Y., Li, Z.: An improved Elman neural network based on the differential evolution algorithm for short-term load forecasting. Int. J. Neural Syst. **28**(01), 1850003 (2018)
10. Elman, J.L.: Finding structure in time. Cogn. Sci. **14**, 179–211 (1990)
11. Guo, Y., Yang, D., Zhang, Y., Wang, L., Wang, K.: Online estimation of SOH for lithium-ion battery based on SSA-Elman neural network. Prot. Control Mod. Power Syst. **7**, 1–17 (2022)

12. Zeng, Y., Huang, T., Zhang, T., Huang, H.-Z.: System-level performance degradation prediction for power converters based on SSA–Elman NN and empirical knowledge. IEEE Trans. Ind. Inf. **20**, 1240–1250 (2023)
13. Wang, E.: Enterprise performance prediction based on FASSA Elman neural network. In: 2024 IEEE 3rd International Conference on Electrical Engineering, Big Data and Algorithms (EEBDA), pp. 617–620. IEEE (2024)
14. Xu, S., Ding, D., Huang, Z., Xu, F.: Positioning error compensation of bending process based on improved Elman neural network. In: 2022 41st Chinese Control Conference (CCC), pp. 1745–1750. IEEE (2022)

Visualizing Two Decades (2004–2024) of Research on Information Privacy Practices of Computer or IT Professionals: A Bibliometric Analysis Using VOSviewer

Tamanna Umme Hani, Wan Abdul Rahim Wan Mohd Isa(✉), and Afdallyna Fathiyah Harun

Faculty of Computer and Mathematical Sciences, Universiti Teknologi MARA, 40450 Shah Alam, Selangor, Malaysia
wrahim2@uitm.edu.my

Abstract. This study conducts a bibliometric analysis to examine two decades (2004–2024) of scholarly research on information privacy practices among computer and IT professionals. Data were systematically retrieved from the Web of Science (WoS) database using targeted keywords such as "Information Privacy Practices" and "Computer or IT Professionals." A total of 237 journal articles were selected based on three inclusion criteria: relevance to the topic, publication as journal articles, and publication within the specified period. VOSviewer software was employed to analyze and visualize trends, key authors, and influential journals through several bibliometric techniques, including co-authorship, co-occurrence, citation, and co-citation analyses. The findings reveal four dominant thematic clusters within the field: IT Management, AI in Healthcare IT Systems, User Perceptions and Social Engagement in IT, and IT Ethics. This study further proposes a conceptual framework to guide future research on information privacy practices, aligning with the United Nations Sustainable Development Goal (SDG) 16, which emphasizes peace, justice, and strong institutions. Such practices are crucial in fostering trust, transparency, and security within digital environments. The results offer valuable insights for both researchers and practitioners, highlighting prevailing trends and emerging areas for exploration. This bibliometric study contributes to a deeper understanding of the evolving landscape of information privacy practices and provides a structured foundation for advancing academic inquiry in this field.

Keywords: Bibliometric Analysis · Data Visualization · Information Privacy Practices

1 Introduction

There are ongoing trends of research on privacy practices among IT professionals research topics in guiding future research in supporting the UN Sustainable Development Goals agenda on 'SDG 16: Peace, Justice, and Strong Institutions'. The SDG

M. Kassim et al. (Eds.): SCDS 2025, CCIS 2674, pp. 47–59, 2026.
https://doi.org/10.1007/978-981-95-8368-3_4

is relevant as information privacy and self-regulation supports building trustworthy and transparent digital institutions and promoting privacy practices aligns with protecting rights and fostering safe, inclusive societies.

Information privacy practices among IT professionals are critical in safeguarding sensitive data within organizations. These practices encompass a range of activities, knowledge, and skills necessary for effective privacy management. IT professionals engage in governance activities that include developing and implementing privacy policies and procedures to protect organizational data [1]. Daily operational tasks involve monitoring data access, ensuring compliance with privacy regulations, and conducting regular audits to identify vulnerabilities [1].

There is importance of professional responsibility in maintaining information privacy, advocating for legislation and standards to regulate data handling [2]. Education plays a vital role in informing both IT professionals and the public about privacy issues, fostering a culture of vigilance against data breaches [2]. Continuous education and awareness are necessary to adapt to the rapid technological changes and emerging privacy threats [3]. IT professionals in sectors like healthcare and finance express concerns about organizational practices that may compromise data privacy, highlighting the need for robust internal controls [4]. Compliance with evolving legislation, such as the Commonwealth Privacy Act, is essential for IT professionals to mitigate legal risks and protect user data [5].

While the focus on privacy practices is crucial, some argue that the rapid advancement of technology may outpace the development of effective privacy measures, leading to potential gaps in protection. This underscores the need for continuous adaptation and vigilance in the field. In sectors like healthcare and finance, IT professionals face unique privacy challenges, such as preventing unauthorized access to sensitive information and ensuring the accuracy of data [4]. Privacy expectations and trust are critical, with IT professionals advocating for enhanced technical and administrative measures to safeguard information from third-party monitoring [6].

Given that existing academic research on privacy practices among IT professionals is spread across various disciplines, a comprehensive mapping of the literature is necessary. To achieve the objectives of this study, the following research questions (RQ) were formulated:

RQ1: How has research on Information Privacy Practices of Computer or IT Professionals evolved over the past two decades (2004–2024)?
RQ2: What are the key terms and recurring themes associated with Information Privacy Practices of Computer or IT Professionals during the period 2004–2024?
RQ3: Who are the most prolific researchers in this field, and how are they connected through collaborative networks?
RQ4: Which journals and countries have been the most prominent and influential in publishing studies on Information Privacy Practices of Computer or IT Professionals?
RQ5: What conceptual framework can be derived from the existing body of research to guide future studies on privacy practices in this area?

2 Method

The objective of this study is to perform a bibliometric analysis focusing on publications related to Information Privacy Practices among Computer or IT Professionals over the span of 2004 to 2024. The procedures adopted are consistent with best practices established in previous bibliometric research [7–10]. Data were retrieved from the Web of Science (WoS) database. To ensure the relevance of the selected materials, the inclusion criteria were as follows: (i) studies specifically addressing 'Information Privacy Practices' and 'Computer or IT Professionals', (ii) journal articles only, and (iii) publication years falling between 2004 and 2024. For mapping and analyzing the data, VOSviewer was utilized [11]. This tool facilitated the visualization of connections among authors, keywords, countries, and citation patterns through analyses of co-authorship, keyword co-occurrence, citation counts, and co-citation relationships [12]. These approaches align with accepted standards in bibliometric research to reveal patterns and trends within the selected literature.

3 Results

3.1 Document Features Selection

The search results from the Web of Science (WoS) yielded a total of 237 documents published between 2004 and 2024 that addressed information privacy practices among computer or IT professionals. Figure 1 illustrates the volume of publications retrieved through the search terms 'Information Privacy Practices' and 'Computer or IT Professionals.'

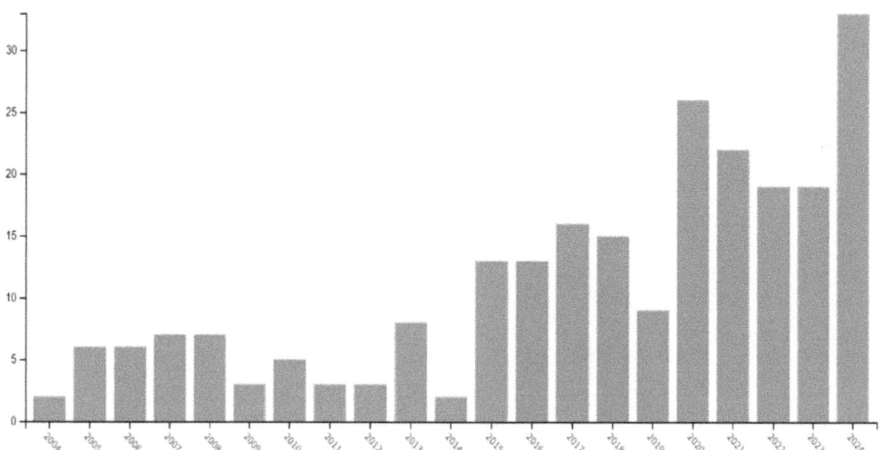

Fig. 1. Number of documents feature search terms – 'Information Privacy Practices' and 'Computer Professionals or IT Professionals' (2004–2024)

The subsequent analyses are presented according to four key bibliometric techniques: co-authorship, co-occurrence, citation, and co-citation. These analyses were complemented by the development of a conceptual framework.

3.2 Co-authorship Analysis

Co-authorship analysis provides insights into the level of collaboration among authors, institutions, and countries, where a higher frequency of joint publications typically reflects stronger scholarly connections within the research community [11, 12]. In this study, VOSviewer software was employed to generate co-authorship networks by setting a minimum threshold of two publications per author and at least one citation [11]. A total of 868 authors contributed to the 237 articles retrieved from the Web of Science database, which focuses on the topic of Information Privacy Practices among Computer or IT Professionals between 2004 and 2024.

Following the threshold criteria, only 11 authors met the requirements for inclusion. The co-authorship network analysis identified five distinct clusters, each representing collaborations among these authors. These clusters are visually presented in Fig. 2. Specifically:

- Cluster 1 (red node) includes Gray, Kathleen; Mendoze, Antonette; Smolenaers, Frank; and Wani, Tafheem Ahmad.
- Cluster 2 (green node) comprises Boughtwood, Tiffany; Otlowski, Margaret; and Tiller, Jane.
- Cluster 3 (blue node) consists of Devriendt, Els and Milisen, Koen.
- Cluster 4 (yellow node) includes Amann, Julia.
- Cluster 5 (purple node) includes Lyon, David.

Fig. 2. The co-authorship network visualization was generated using VOSviewer.

Table 1 presents the ten countries with the highest number of published papers.

The country analysis revealed the United States as the most active in this research area, publishing 58 documents with 1,966 citations. Other leading contributors included Australia (26 documents, 1,338 citations), England (24 documents, 1,263 citations),

Table 1. The top ten countries in terms of the number of papers published.

Country	Documents	Citations
USA	58	1966
Australia	26	1338
England	24	1263
Canada	18	669
China	13	1248
Italy	11	1272
Spain	11	1192
Netherlands	9	1249
Brazil	8	1106
India	7	1079

Canada (18 documents, 669 citations), China (13 documents, 1,248 citations), Italy (11 documents, 1,272 citations), Spain (11 documents, 1,192 citations), Netherlands (9 documents, 1,249 citations), Brazil (8 documents, 1,106 citations), and India (7 documents, 1,079 citations). This data is summarized in Table 1.

In the VOSviewer analysis, the threshold was set to include countries with at least one published document and a minimum of 50 citations. As a result, 37 out of the 66 countries in the dataset met this criterion. The United States showed the highest publication and citation volume, representing a central hub in the collaboration network.

Further analysis of these countries' collaboration patterns identified seven distinct clusters, as visualized in Fig. 3:

- Cluster 1 (red node): Brazil, Cyprus, France, Germany, Greece, India, Jordan, Morocco, Norway, South Korea, Spain, Taiwan.
- Cluster 2 (green node): Canada, Kuwait, Qatar, UAE.
- Cluster 3 (blue node): Belgium, England, Scotland, Wales.
- Cluster 4 (yellow node): Australia, Ireland, China, Sweeden
- Cluster 5 (purple node): Italy, Netherlands, Switzerland, USA.
- Cluster 6 (light blue node): Lithuania, Poland, Vietnam.
- Cluster 7 (orange node): Malaysia, Pakistan, Saudi Arabia.

These clusters offer a clear visualization of collaborative networks among countries in the field of information privacy practices, confirming established patterns in global bibliometric studies [11, 12].

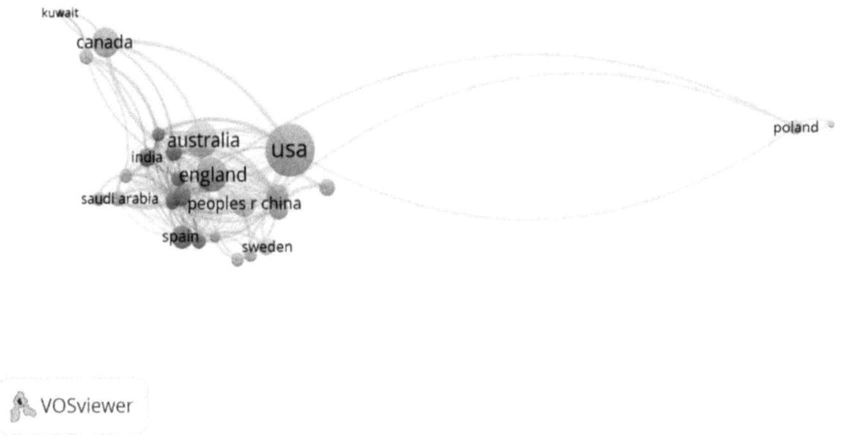

Fig. 3. Co-authoring countries are shown on the mapping (Generated by VOSviewer).

3.3 Co-occurrence Analysis

Co-occurrence analysis operates on the principle that the more frequently two keywords appear together within publications, the stronger their conceptual relationship [11, 12] VOSviewer identifies these relationships by analyzing both author-defined keywords and other relevant terms, highlighting their frequency and connections [11, 12]. This method involves counting the number of documents where specific terms or keywords co-appear, thereby revealing patterns of association within the literature [11, 12]. In VOSviewer, a threshold was applied requiring each keyword to appear in at least ten documents to be included in the analysis. From a total of 1,290 keywords, this criterion narrowed the dataset to 19 keywords that met the specified threshold. Table 2 lists the most commonly occurring keywords that appeared in our sample of 237 papers. The top five most commonly occurring keywords are 'Privacy', 'Information', 'Confidentiality, Social Media', and 'Ethics'.

There are four major keyword clusters concerning the 'Information Privacy Practices' and 'Computer Professionals or IT Professionals' (2004–2024), that we had determined based on the theme clusters which are (i) IT Management, (ii) AI in Healthcare IT Systems, (iii) User Perceptions and Social Engagement in IT, (iv) IT Ethics themes. Figure 4 shows the mapping of the keyword co-occurrences and also depicts the dominant links between keywords and clusters. First, the shown in red that we classify as 'Care', 'Health', 'Impact', Information', 'Management', 'Technology' and 'Telemedicine'. Second, the keywords that are shown in green that we classified as 'Artifical Intelligence', 'Confidentiality', 'Health-Care', 'Patient', 'Privacy' and 'Security'. Third, the terms, that are shown in blue are classified as 'Attitudes', 'Communication', 'Perceptions' and 'Social Media'. Fourth, the terms that are shown in yellow that we classified as 'Ethics' and 'Internet'.

Table 2. Most Commonly Occurring Keywords.

Keyword	Number of Occurrences
Privacy	51
Information	27
Confidentiality	23
Social Media	22
Ethics	22
Management	19
Care	16
Internet	14
Security	13
Perception	13
Telemedine	13

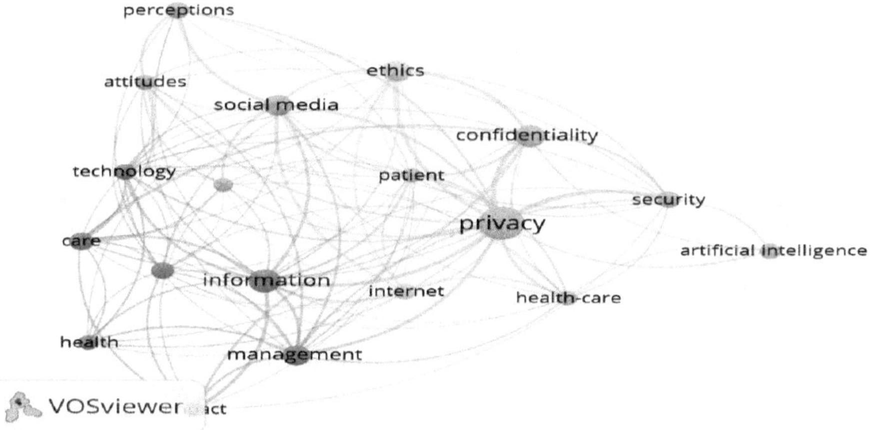

Fig. 4. The keyword co-occurrence relationships are visualized in the map generated using VOSviewer.

3.4 Citation Analysis

Citation analysis is founded on the principle that the frequency with which authors, journals, or publications cite one another reflects the strength of their connection [11, 12]. This method assesses the relationships among scholarly entities such as authors and journals by examining how often they reference each other's work [11, 12]. Which documents in the field of 'Information Privacy Practices' and 'Computer Professionals or IT Professionals' research cite each other? VOSviewer was utilized for this analysis, with the threshold set to include only papers that had received a minimum of thirty citations.

A threshold of 30 citations was selected to focus on highly influential works while ensuring a manageable network size for visualization clarity. Out of 237 documents, only 41 documents met this threshold which created 41 clusters as shown in Fig. 5.

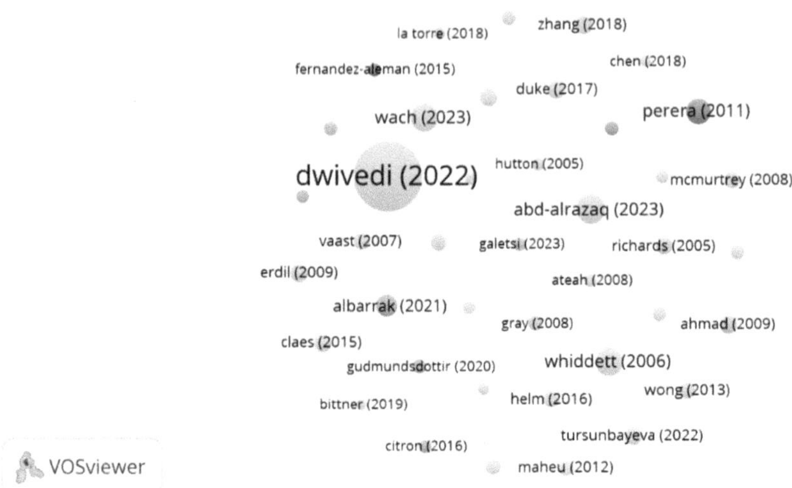

Fig. 5. The citation relationships between papers are visualized in the map generated using VOSviewer

For the VOSviewer analysis, a threshold was established whereby a journal needed to have been cited a minimum of five times to be included in the mapping. Additionally, each source was required to have at least three associated documents. Out of 194 sources, only 10 journals satisfied these criteria, resulting in the formation of nine primary clusters, as illustrated in Fig. 6. The first cluster consists of 'Health Policy and Technology' and 'International Journal of Medical Informatics'. Second, the cluster comprises of 'JMIR Formative Research'. Third, the cluster comprises of 'JMIR Mhealth and Uhealth'. Fourth, the cluster comprises 'Journal of Clinical Nursing', Fifth comprises of 'Journal of Genetic Counseling'. Sixth, the cluster comprises 'Journal of Medical Internet Research'. Seventh, the cluster comprises of 'Midwifery', Eight, comprises of 'Nursing Ethics'. Ninth, comprising 'Professional Psychology-Research and Practice'.

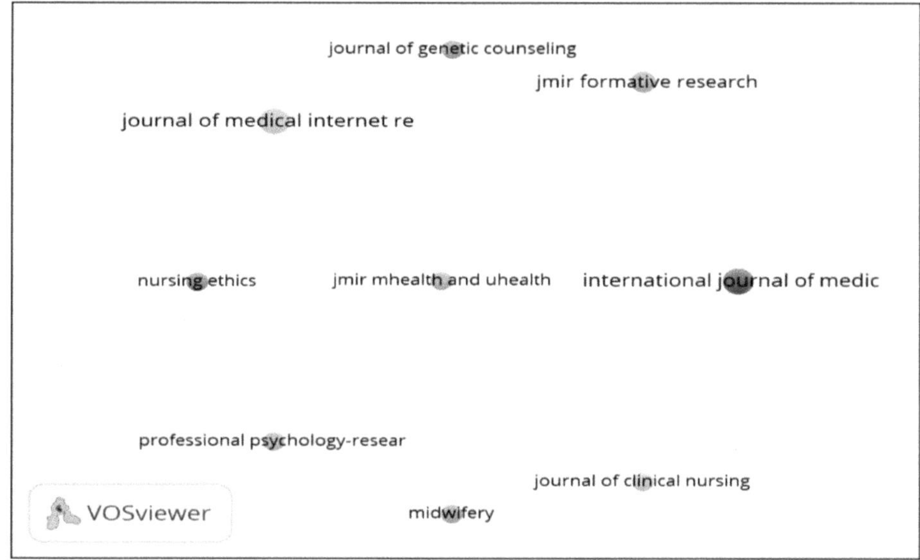

Fig. 6. The visualization of journal citations was generated using VOSviewer.

3.5 Co-citation Analysis

Co-citation analysis operates on the principle that the more frequently authors, journals, or publications are cited together, the stronger their conceptual or scholarly connection [11, 12]. This method examines the extent to which these entities are jointly referenced in the literature, offering insights into how such relationships have influenced academic discourse within the field [11, 12].

Co-citation analysis was performed on all authors referenced within the selected papers. Using VOSviewer, a threshold was applied requiring each author to have been cited at least 12 times. As a result, only three authors met this criterion and were included in the co-citation network analysis. The most frequently cited authors identified were Venkatesh, V. with 15 citations, Braun, V. with 14 citations, Dwivedi, Y.K. with 12 citations and Bandura, A. with 12 citations.

4 Conceptual Framework

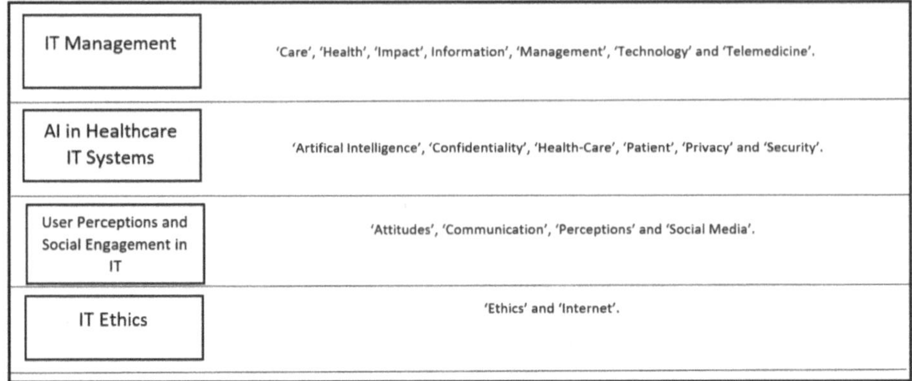

Fig. 7. A Conceptual framework of Information Privacy Practices of Computer or IT Professionals research topics.

Based on the bibliometric study of 'Information Privacy Practices' and 'Computer Professionals or IT Professionals' research topics (2004–2024), we propose a conceptual framework of 'Information Privacy Practices' and 'Computer Professionals or IT Professionals' research topics (see Fig. 7) to guide future research. There are four major keyword clusters concerning the 'Information Privacy Practices' and 'Computer Professionals or IT Professionals' (2004–2024), that we had determined based on the theme clusters which are (i) IT Management, (ii) AI in Healthcare IT Systems, (iii) User Perceptions and Social Engagement in IT, (iv) IT Ethics themes. Figure 4 shows the mapping of the keyword co-occurrences and depicts the dominant links between keywords and clusters. First, the shown in red that we classify as 'Care', 'Health', 'Impact', 'Information', 'Management', Technology' and 'Telemedicine'.

Second, the keywords that are shown in green that we classified as 'Artifical Intelligence', 'Confidentiality', 'Health-Care', 'Patient', 'Privacy' and 'Security'. Third, the terms that are shown in blue that we classified as 'Attitudes', 'Communication', 'Perceptions' and 'Social Media'. Fourth, the terms that are shown in yellow that we classified as 'Ethics' and 'Internet'. The theme and sub-themes as shown in Fig. 7 are important to be referred to for future possible research in 'Information Privacy Practices' and 'Computer Professionals or IT Professionals' (2004–2024) research topics.

From the keyword co-occurrence analysis using VOSviewer, four distinct thematic clusters were identified. Each cluster has been carefully interpreted and named to reflect its conceptual focus, with examples of key terms and their relevance to the field of Information Privacy Practices among Computer or IT Professionals.

- Cluster 1: IT Management

  (Keywords: care, health, impact, information, management, technology, telemedicine)

This cluster encapsulates research on the organizational and strategic dimensions of managing information privacy. It includes studies on how IT professionals develop and implement privacy frameworks, manage healthcare information systems, and assess the operational impact of privacy policies especially in high-stakes sectors like health and telemedicine.

- Cluster 2: AI in Healthcare IT Systems

  (Keywords: artificial intelligence, confidentiality, health-care, patient, privacy, security)

  This cluster focuses on the challenges and opportunities of integrating AI technologies within healthcare environments. Research in this area often addresses how IT professionals handle issues of patient confidentiality and data protection while deploying AI for diagnostics, patient monitoring, and healthcare analytics.
- Cluster 3: User Perceptions and Social Engagement in IT

  (Keywords: attitudes, communication, perceptions, social media)

  This cluster examines how users perceive and respond to privacy tools and policies. It also explores how IT professionals interpret feedback and communication from users to refine privacy strategies. For example, studies may investigate how privacy concerns expressed via social media influence corporate IT responses or policy updates.
- Cluster 4: IT Ethics

  (Keywords: ethics, internet)

  This cluster addresses the ethical considerations surrounding digital privacy, such as the responsible handling of user data, moral obligations of IT professionals, and principles of fair information practices. It also includes discussions on how ethical standards inform internet governance, surveillance concerns, and trust-building mechanisms in digital systems.

The proposed framework may offer practical value for both education and organizational practice. For example, in education, it can inform curriculum development for IT professionals by highlighting key areas such as ethics, AI-driven privacy risks, and user communication strategies. In organization, the framework can serve as a tool to audit and enhance internal privacy practices. Activities can be mapped against the identified clusters such as IT Management, AI in Healthcare, and IT Ethics that may be used to identify gaps and improve alignment with privacy standards and SDG 16 objectives for trustworthy and transparent digital institutions.

5 Limitations

While this bibliometric study offers valuable insights into the trends and patterns of research on Information Privacy Practices among Computer or IT Professionals, several limitations should be acknowledged. First, the dataset was exclusively derived from the Web of Science (WoS) database, which, while recognized for its rigor and quality, may introduce database bias. Studies indexed in other reputable databases such as Scopus, IEEE Xplore, or Google Scholar were not included, potentially omitting relevant literature from broader academic communities.

Second, the search strategy was highly dependent on specific keywords, namely 'Information Privacy Practices' and 'Computer Professionals or IT Professionals'. This keyword dependency may have resulted in the exclusion of studies using alternative but related terminologies, thus limiting the comprehensiveness of the dataset. Readers should interpret these findings with caution due to the study's scope limitations and suggest opportunities for future research to adopt a more inclusive and diversified bibliometric approach, incorporating multiple databases and broader keyword strategies.

6 Conclusion

This study has identified key themes and patterns within the academic literature on information privacy practices among IT professionals. Through bibliometric analysis, the research highlights four major thematic clusters: IT Management, AI in Healthcare IT Systems, User Perceptions and Social Engagement in IT, and IT Ethics. The conceptual framework developed in this study provides a foundation for future research directions, emphasizing the importance of these areas in supporting responsible digital governance aligned with SDG 16. Future work could extend this research by incorporating more diverse data sources and refining analysis techniques to uncover deeper insights into the evolving discourse on privacy practices within the IT profession.

Acknowledgement. The authors would like to express their sincere appreciation to Universiti Teknologi MARA (UiTM) for the continuous support, facilities, and encouragement provided.

References

1. Monfared, Y.A., Benslimane, Y., Yang, Z.: Information privacy practices in organizations: activities, knowledge and skill requirements for information technology professionals. In: 2018 IEEE International Conference on Industrial Engineering and Engineering Management (IEEM), Bangkok, Thailand, 2018, pp. 1001–1005 (2018). https://doi.org/10.1109/IEEM.2018.8607336
2. Auerbach, I.L.: Professional responsibility for information privacy. J. Inf. Syst. Manag. **2**(1), 77–81 (1985). https://doi.org/10.1080/07399018508967744
3. Lee, W.W.: Hexa-dimension code of practice for data privacy protection. In: Khosrow-Pour, M. (ed.) Encyclopedia of Information Science and Technology, 4th edn., pp. 4909–4919. IGI Global Scientific Publishing (2018). https://doi.org/10.4018/978-1-5225-2255-3.ch425
4. Earp, J.B., Payton, F.C.: Dirty laundry: privacy issues for IT professionals. IT Prof. **2**(2), 51–54 (2000). https://doi.org/10.1109/6294.839371
5. Hewett, W.G.B., Whitaker, J.: Data protection and privacy: the Australian legislation and its implications for IT professionals. Logist. Inf. Manag. **15**, 369–376 (2002). https://doi.org/10.1108/09576050210447055
6. Martin, N., Rice, J.P., Martin, R.: Expectations of privacy and trust: examining the views of it professionals. Behav. Inf. Technol. **35**(6), 500–510 (2015). https://doi.org/10.1080/0144929X.2015.1066444
7. Isa, W.A.R.W.M., Amin, I.M.: A scientometric analysis of twenty years trends in mobile learning, blended learning, online learning, e-learning and dental education research. Int. J. Acad. Res. Prog. Educ. Dev. **11**(1), 1019–1029 (2022). https://doi.org/10.6007/IJARPED/v11-i1/12331

8. Isa, W.A.R.W.M., Amin, I.M.: A bibliometric study of traditional medicinal plant database research, 2001–2021. Int. J. Acad. Res. Prog. Educ. Dev. **11**(2), 214–223 (2022). https://doi.org/10.6007/IJARPED/v11-i2/12954
9. Isa, W.A.R.W.M., Amin, I.M.: A bibliometric study of soft systems methodology, 2001–2021. Int. J. Acad. Res. Bus. Soc. Sci. **12**(3), 531–554 (2022). https://doi.org/10.6007/IJARBSS/v12-i3/12975
10. Isa, W.A.R.W.M., Amin, I.M., Suhariadi, F.: A scientometric analysis of twenty years trends in bring your own device (byod) research. Int. J. Acad. Res. Bus. Soc. Sci. **12**(3), 17–26 (2022). https://doi.org/10.6007/IJARBSS/v12-i3/12332
11. Van Eck, N.J., Waltman, L.: Software survey: vosviewer, a computer program for bibliometric mapping. Scientometrics **84**, 523–538 (2010). https://doi.org/10.1007/s11192-009-0146-3
12. Park, A., Montecchi, M., Feng, C., Plangger, K., Pitt, L.: Understanding 'fake news': a bibliographic perspective. Defence Strat. Commun. **8**, 141–172 (2020). https://doi.org/10.30966/2018.riga.8.4

Logistic Regression and Decision Tree Predictive Modeling on Sleep Health and Lifestyle Dataset with Analytic Platform

Kalybek Aruzhan[1], Murizah Kassim[2,3](✉), Mukhanova Ayagoz Asanbekovna[1], Akhayeva Zhanar Berikbayevna[4], Norakmar Arbain Sulaiman[2], and Nor Syazwani Mohd Pakhrudin[2]

[1] Department of Information Systems, L.N. Gumilyov Eurasian National University, Astana, Kazakhstan

[2] Faculty of Electrical Engineering, Universiti Teknologi MARA, 40450 Shah Alam, Selangor, Malaysia

murizah@uitm.edu.my

[3] Institute for Big Data Analytics and Artificial Intelligence (IBDAAI), Universiti Teknologi MARA, 40450 Shah Alam, Selangor, Malaysia

[4] Department of Computer Science, L.N. Gumilyov Eurasian National University, Astana 010008, Republic of Kazakhstan

Abstract. This analysis explores the connections between sleep health and lifestyle factors using the Sleep Health and Lifestyle Dataset. Sleep quality and duration are essential for maintaining overall health and productivity, while factors such as physical activity, stress levels, and cardiovascular health play a significant role in influencing sleep patterns. The research focuses on analyzing trends in sleep duration, quality, and the occurrence of sleep disorders, while also developing predictive models using machine learning techniques. The dataset includes critical metrics such as sleep duration, stress levels, daily steps and cardiovascular indicators like heart rate. Descriptive analysis revealed notable patterns: higher stress levels and low physical activity were strongly associated with poor sleep quality, while daily steps also demonstrated measurable impacts on sleep metrics. Machine learning models, particularly Decision Tree and Logistic Regression, were applied to predict sleep disorders such as Insomnia and Sleep Apnea. Logistic Regression effectively capturing the relationships between lifestyle habits and sleep outcomes has exhibited higher predictive accuracy of 94.69%, which indicates that it correctly predicted the outcomes for approximately 94.7% of the data points. The Decision Tree model has an accuracy of 93.81%, which means it correctly predicted the outcomes for about 93.8% of the data points. The analysis provides valuable insights into how lifestyle choices affect sleep health, highlighting actionable areas for individuals and healthcare professionals to improve sleep quality and overall well-being.

Keywords: Sleep Health · Lifestyle Factors · Sleep Duration · Sleep Quality · Sleep Disorder · Stress Level · Physical Activity

M. Kassim et al. (Eds.): SCDS 2025, CCIS 2674, pp. 60–75, 2026.
https://doi.org/10.1007/978-981-95-8368-3_5

1 Introduction

Sleep plays a crucial role in maintaining overall health and well-being, with lifestyle choices and health indicators significantly influencing sleep patterns and quality [1]. Understanding these connections is essential for identifying factors that contribute to sleep disorders and their broader health impacts. The Sleep Health and Lifestyle Dataset offers a comprehensive foundation for studying the intricate relationships between sleep health, lifestyle habits, and health outcomes [2]. This dataset contains 400 rows and 13 columns, encompassing a wide range of variables, including sleep duration, sleep quality, physical activity levels, stress ratings, and step counts. Key health-related attributes, such as heart rate are also provided, offering valuable insights into their associations with sleep patterns.

The dataset further identifies the presence or absence of sleep disorders, categorizing individuals into groups such as Insomnia [3] and Sleep Apnea [4]. These classifications are crucial for understanding how specific sleep disorders impact daily functioning and overall quality of life [5]. By analyzing trends and patterns within the dataset, researchers can explore the effects of lifestyle factors on sleep health and develop predictive models to identify individuals at risk of poor sleep quality or disorders. Statistical analyses and machine learning techniques can provide actionable insights for improving health outcomes and promoting healthier lifestyles. The dataset serves as an excellent resource for healthcare professionals, data scientists, and wellness researchers seeking to uncover the complex interplay between lifestyle choices and sleep health.

.

2 Literature Review

Sleep health is an essential aspect of overall well-being, and accurate sleep stage classification plays a crucial role in diagnosing and managing various sleep disorders, such as sleep apnea and insomnia [6]. In recent years, machine learning algorithms have emerged as powerful tools for enhancing the accuracy of sleep stage classification, particularly when combined with consumer sleep technologies and physiological signals like ECG [7] and EEG [8]. This study provided a comprehensive review of studies that used consumer sleep technologies (CST) in combination with machine learning algorithms (MLAs) for sleep classification [9]. They pointed out that although polysomnography (PSG) remains the most accurate method for classifying sleep stages, CST is a more affordable option. The authors reviewed 27 studies employing various MLAs such as logistic regression, decision trees, support vector machines, and deep learning, highlighting the potential of these models to improve classification accuracy. However, they noted the difficulty in applying raw signals with deep learning algorithms.

This researcher examined the use of machine learning algorithms for detecting sleep apnea from ECG signals [10]. They reviewed 48 studies and discussed the challenges in sleep apnea classification, particularly the variability of ECG signals and the limited availability of training datasets. Their findings showed that support vector machines and deep learning-based neural networks were the most effective in detecting sleep apnea.

This study focused on sleep stage classification using EEG spectrograms [11]. They identified the challenges of classification, including the time-consuming process and low accuracy due to imbalanced data. Despite these issues, their deep learning model, which combined convolutional neural networks (CNNs) with long short-term memory (LSTM) networks [12], achieved impressive classification results. Their approach demonstrated the effectiveness of deep learning techniques in improving sleep stage classification. This paper explored machine learning applications for predicting the severity of obstructive sleep apnea (OSA) syndrome using data from over 4,000 patients [13]. They employed both supervised and unsupervised learning techniques, including gradient boosting, random forest, and K-means clustering. Their methods achieved high classification accuracy, though they acknowledged the limitations of using data from a single center and the presence of missing values.

This researcher has investigated the detection of sleep apnea from single-lead ECG signals using various machine learning algorithms, including CNNs and LSTMs [14]. They found that CNNs outperformed other methods in terms of classification accuracy, and when combined with LSTM networks, their hybrid model achieved the best results. This study highlighted the potential of deep learning in automating the detection of sleep apnea. In this work, they compared the performance of machine learning algorithms such as decision trees, k-nearest neighbors, and random forest in classifying sleep stages from ECG signals [15]. Their analysis showed that the random forest algorithm performed best, achieving high accuracy in automated sleep stage classification. This study emphasized the effectiveness of conventional MLAs in the context of sleep stage classification.

This work focused on using machine learning to detect obstructive sleep apnea from electronic health records [16]. They applied several algorithms, including extreme gradient boosting, light gradient boosting, and support vector machines, and used clinical data from the Wisconsin Sleep Cohort database. Their approach demonstrated that machine learning could be an effective tool for early detection of individuals at risk of OSA. This study was proposed a deep learning approach combining CNN and LSTM algorithms for automated sleep-stage classification using multimodal signals [17]. Their model achieved a classification accuracy of 87.4%, surpassing other methods. Despite challenges like noisy data, their approach showed the effectiveness of deep learning in handling multimodal sleep data. This research has developed a deep learning model for automated sleep-stage classification using raw PSG signals [18]. Their one-dimensional CNN model demonstrated high accuracy across multiple sleep stages, suggesting that deep learning methods could replace traditional manual processes, reducing human error and improving efficiency in sleep stage classification.

3 Methodology

3.1 Flowchart to Design Analytics Platform

The process of designing the analytics platform begins with data collection, which involves sourcing appropriate data from sites such as Kaggle [19]. This data may contain a variety of attributes that will be utilized for analysis and prediction. Next, we go to Data Preprocessing, where the data is cleansed, missing values are handled, and any necessary changes are made to prepare it for analysis. During Data Analysis, we evaluate the dataset to identify patterns, trends, and insights that might guide the next stages.

Figure 1 shows the flowchart for Model Selection occurs, in which relevant machine learning models or methodologies are selected depending on the dataset's properties. During the Training/Testing step, the selected models are trained on the data and tested to verify they work properly.

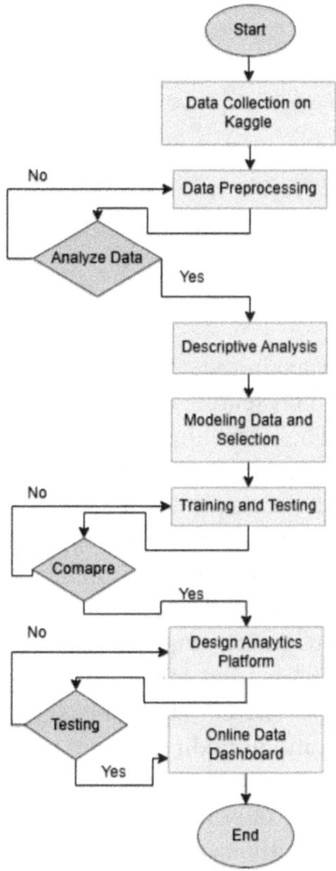

Fig. 1. Flowchart to design Analytics Platform.

3.2 Data Collection

The dataset was sourced from Kaggle. This dataset was compiled to provide a broad range of information regarding various factors that influence sleep quality and overall health, including sleep habits, physical activity, stress levels, cardiovascular health, and the presence of sleep disorders. Figure 2 shows the data collected through surveys and self-reported metrics, making it a valuable resource for understanding how individual lifestyle choices and health conditions correlate with sleep patterns. The dataset is publicly available for research and analysis, making it suitable for various applications in the health and wellness field. The data points were carefully curated to offer a representative sample of the population with different lifestyle habits and health conditions, ensuring that researchers can explore various patterns and relationships within the data.

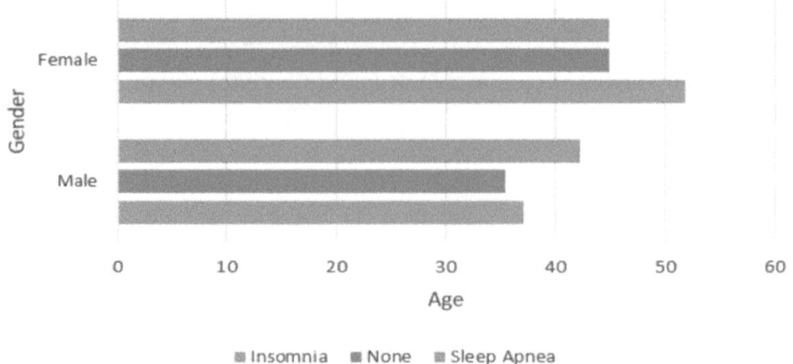

Fig. 2. Sleep Disorder by Gender and Age

3.3 Analysis Data – Descriptive Analysis. Why It is Important

Descriptive analysis is an important initial step towards comprehending and summarizing a dataset. It entails studying and presenting the key properties of the data using a variety of statistical approaches [20]. These techniques frequently involve calculating measures such as the mean, which provides the average value of a variable; the median, which represents the middle point of a dataset and is useful for understanding the distribution of values; and the standard deviation, which measures the variability or dispersion of the data [21]. These measurements provide a summary of the data's central tendency, spread, and general distribution, laying the groundwork for further research.

In addition to statistical measurements, descriptive analysis frequently employs visual aids, such as graphs, charts, and tables, to display data in a more digestible and understandable format [22]. These visual tools supplement numerical analysis by emphasizing significant trends and providing a more intuitive grasp of the data.

Descriptive analysis gives a full picture of the dataset by combining statistical metrics with visual representations. It not only facilitates in the discovery of broad trends and patterns, but it also helps to find outliers, anomalies, and connections between variables. This step of analysis provides a clear picture of the data, laying the framework for more complex approaches like predictive modeling or inferential statistics.

3.4 Machine Learning Techniques Used

Machine learning is a branch of artificial intelligence that focuses on creating systems that learn and evolve based on the data they are given. Machine learning is based on algorithms[23]. For following analysis and prediction was used Logistic Regression and Decision Tree. Logistic Regression and Decision Tree are two popular machine learning methods used for classification tasks.

Logistic Regression is a statistical method used to predict the probability of an event occurring, typically for a binary outcome (e.g., "yes" or "no") [24]. It models the relationship between independent variables and the probability of the event using the logistic function. Logistic regression is suitable for tasks where the goal is to predict the probability of an object belonging to one of two classes. It minimizes the logarithmic loss function, ensuring the most probable predictions.

Decision Tree is a method that uses tree structure for decision-making and classification [25]. Each internal node in the tree represents a decision based on a feature value, and depending on the answer, one of the subtrees is chosen. The leaf nodes represent the predicted class. Decision trees are easy to interpret, but they are prone to overfitting unless regularization techniques, such as pruning, are applied.

3.5 Equations

Logistic regression uses a logistic function called a sigmoid function to map predictions and their probabilities. The sigmoid function refers to an S-shaped curve that converts any real value to a range between 0 and 1.

Moreover, if the output of the sigmoid function (estimated probability) is greater than a predefined threshold on the graph, the model predicts that the instance belongs to that class. If the estimated probability is less than the predefined threshold, the model predicts that the instance does not belong to the class.

The sigmoid function is referred to as an activation function for logistic regression and is defined as (1).

$$f(x) = \frac{1}{1 + e^{-x}} \tag{1}$$

where,

e – base of natural logarithms.

value – numerical value one wishes to transform.

The logistic regression is represented by Eq. (2):

$$y = \frac{e^{(b_0 + b_1 x)}}{1 + e^{(b_0 + b_1 x)}} \tag{2}$$

here,

x – input value.

y – predicted output.

b_0 – bias or intercept term.

b_1 – coefficient for input (x).

Decision Tree algorithm belongs to the family of supervised learning algorithms. Unlike other supervised learning algorithms, the decision tree algorithm can be used for solving regression and classification problems too.

Entropy is a measure of randomness in the information being processed [26]. The higher the entropy, the harder it is to draw any conclusions from that information. Entropy is maximum when the probability is 0.5 because it projects perfect randomness in the data and there is no chance if perfectly determining the outcome.

The formula for Entropy is (3).

$$E(S) = -p_{(+)}\mathrm{logp}_{(+)} - p_{(-)}\mathrm{logp}_{(-)} \tag{3}$$

here,

$p_{(+)}$ is the probability of positive class.
$p_{(-)}$ is the probability of negative class.
S is the subset of the training example.

Information gain measures the reduction of uncertainty given some feature and it is also a deciding factor for which attribute should be selected as a decision node or root node [27].

$$Information\ Gain = E(Y) - E(Y|X) \quad (4)$$

4 Results and Analysis

In this section, we present the findings of our study. We performed a descriptive analysis to identify patterns and trends in the dataset. We used Logistic Regression for binary classification, analyzing relationships between features and target variables. Then, we applied the Decision Tree algorithm to classify outcomes and highlight key influencing factors. These methods provided valuable insights and predictive results for the dataset.

4.1 Descriptive Analysis

Table 1 shows the descriptive statistics reveal several key insights about the data. Sleep Duration has a mean of 7.13 h, with low variability (standard deviation 0.8) and a slightly positive skew, indicating most individuals sleep close to the average. Quality of Sleep averages 7.31, with moderate variability (standard deviation 1.2) and a slight negative skew, suggesting more participants report higher sleep quality. Physical Activity Level shows the highest variability (standard deviation 20.83) and a wide range (30 to 90), reflecting diverse activity levels among individuals. Stress Level has a mean of 5.39 and relatively low variability (standard deviation 1.77), with a slight positive skew, indicating most participants report moderate stress. Notably, all variables exhibit negative kurtosis, indicating flatter distributions compared to a normal curve. The mode values highlight typical patterns, such as most participants reporting a Stress Level of 3 and a Sleep Duration of 7.2 h.

Table 1. Descriptive analysis.

Statistical Measures	Sleep Duration	Quality of Sleep	Physical Activity Level	Stress Level
Mean	7.132	7.312	59.171	5.385
Standard Error	0.041	0.061	1.077	0.091
Median	7.2	7.0	60.0	5.0
Mode	7.2	8.0	60.0	3.0
Standard Deviation	0.795	1.196	20.830	1.774
Sample Variance	6.330	1.432	4.339	3.149

(continued)

Table 1. (*continued*)

Statistical Measures	Sleep Duration	Quality of Sleep	Physical Activity Level	Stress Level
Kurtosis	−1.285	−0.754	−1.265	−1.325
Skewness	0.037	−0.206	0.074	0.153
Range	2.7	5.0	60.0	5.0
Minimum	5.8	4.0	30.0	3.0
Maximum	8.5	9.0	90.0	8.0
Sum	2667.4	2735.0	22130.0	2014.0

4.2 Correlation Analysis

The correlations between the variables reveal interesting relationships. Figure 3 presents the correlation between sleep duration and quality of sleep is 0.88, indicating a strong positive association which longer sleep duration tends to correlate with better sleep quality. On the other hand, the correlation between sleep duration and stress level is – 0.81, suggesting a strong negative relationship—higher stress levels are associated with shorter sleep duration. Finally, the correlation between physical activity level and sleep duration is 0.21, indicating a weak positive relationship, meaning that while physical activity may slightly influence sleep duration, the effect is not very strong. These correlations provide valuable insights into how lifestyle factors, like stress and activity levels, interact with sleep patterns.

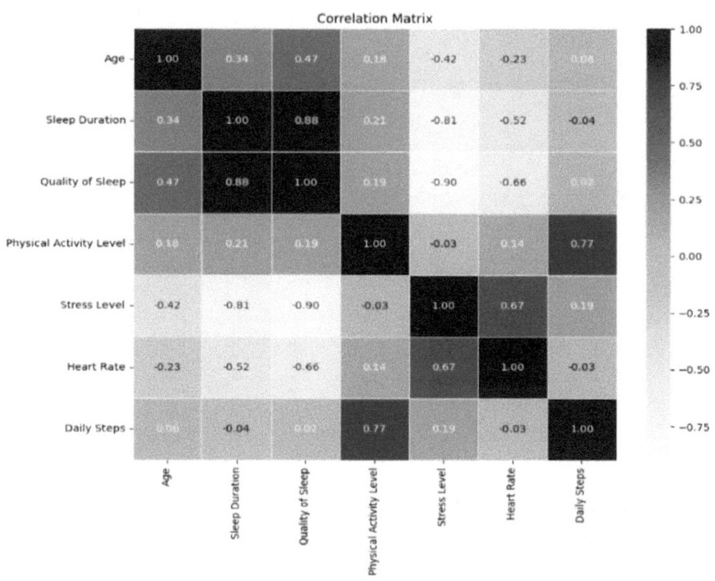

Fig. 3. Correlation Matrix

Figure 4 illustrates the histogram distribution of numerical variables. Each bar represents the frequency or count of data points within a specific range of values for each variable. The plots show frequency distributions of six health-related variables: Daily Steps, Sleep Duration, Physical Activity Level, Stress Level, Heart Rate, and Quality of Sleep.

- Daily Steps shows a wide range, with peaks around 4000, 6000, 8000, and 10000 steps, indicating variation in physical activity across individuals.
- Sleep Duration is concentrated between 6 and 8.5 h, with higher frequencies around 6.5, 7.5, and 8 h, suggesting common sleep lengths.
- Physical Activity Level appears uniformly distributed across intervals from 30 to 90, with some fluctuations, indicating a diverse range of activity levels in the population.
- Stress Level varies between 3 and 8, with more individuals reporting stress levels around 3, 6, and 8. The frequencies are relatively balanced, hinting at different stress experiences.
- Heart Rate is mostly distributed between 65 and 75 bpm, with fewer individuals having heart rates above 75, suggesting a typical resting heart rate pattern.
- Quality of Sleep is skewed toward higher values (6 to 9), with the highest frequency at 7, implying that most individuals perceive their sleep quality as good.

Overall, the bar plots provide a clear view of how these variables are distributed, revealing general trends in physical and mental well-being.

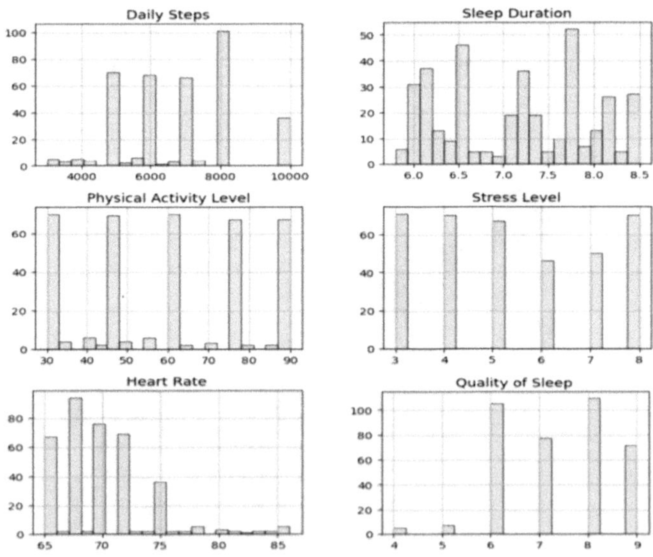

Fig. 4. Data Distribution

Figure 5 presents kernel density plots for six health-related variables: physical activity level, sleep duration, stress level, heart rate, quality of sleep, and daily steps. Each plot shows the probability distribution of values within the dataset. Physical activity and sleep duration are roughly uniformly distributed. Stress level shows a bimodal distribution, with peaks at low and high values. The heart rate peaks around 70 bpm and quickly tapers off. Quality of sleep also has multiple peaks, suggesting varied sleep quality. Daily steps show a strong peak around 7,500 steps. These distributions provide insight into the health patterns of the observed population.

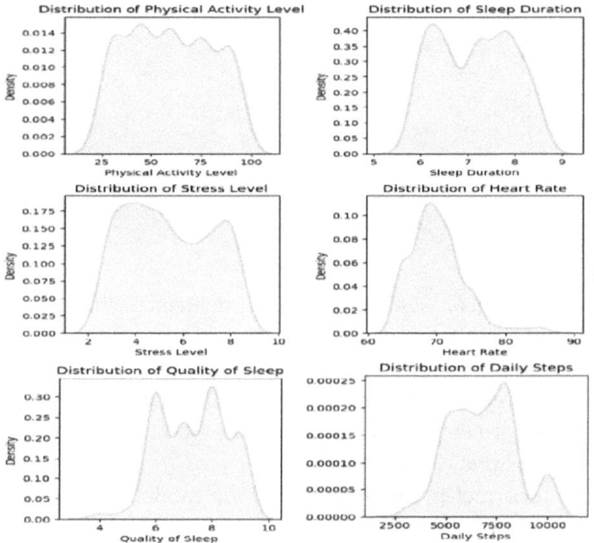

Fig. 5. Data Distribution

4.3 Machine Learning Model

4.3.1 Logistic Regression

The logistic regression model has an accuracy of 94.69%, which indicates that it correctly predicted the outcomes for approximately 94.7% of the data points as in Fig. 6. This is a strong result, suggesting that the model is performing well overall.

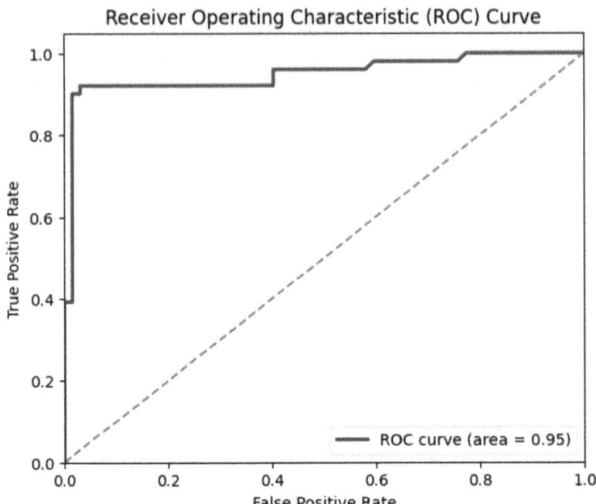

Fig. 6. ROC curve for Logistic Regression

61 – The number of correct predictions for the positive class (True Positives).
1 – The number of incorrect predictions where the model predicted positive, but the actual outcome was negative (False Positives).
5 – The number of incorrect predictions where the model predicted negative, but the actual outcome was positive (False Negatives).
46 – The number of correct predictions for the negative class (True Negatives).

4.3.2 Decision Tree

The Decision Tree model has an accuracy of 93.81%, which means it correctly predicted the outcomes for about 93.8% of the data points as shows in Fig. 7. This indicates a high level of accuracy, but there is still some room for improvement.

61 – True Positives.
1 – False Positives.
6 – False Negatives.
45 – True Negatives.

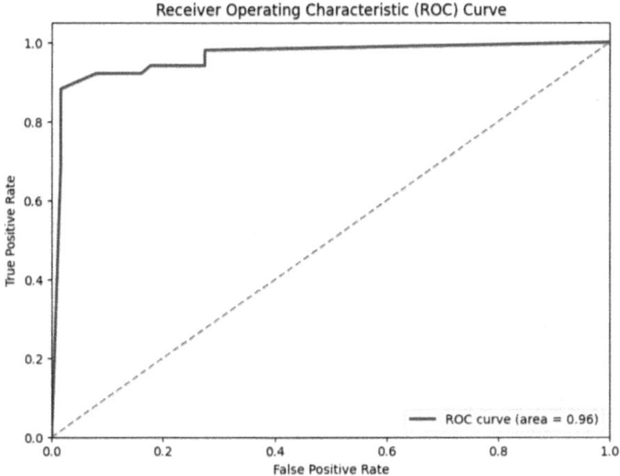

Fig. 7. ROC curve for Decision Tree

4.3.3 Analytics Platform Using Things Board

Figure 8 shows a time series chart shows changes in data over time. The X-axis represents time, while the Y-axis shows data values. This chart helps identify trends, seasonality, and anomalies.

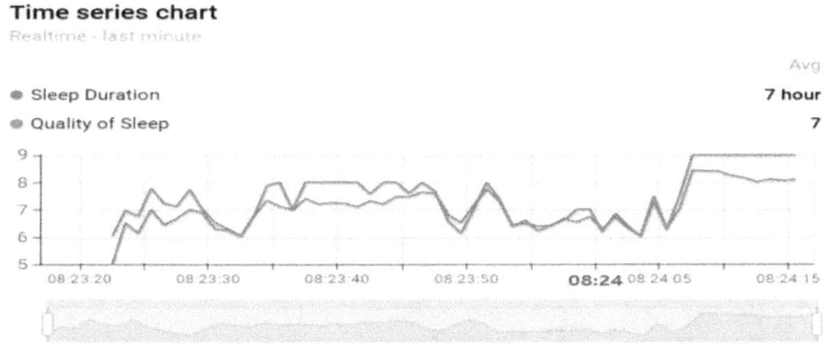

Fig. 8. Time Series Chart

Figure 9 shows an analytic platform for time series data represents changes over time using vertical or horizontal bars. The X-axis shows time intervals, and the Y-axis displays the values. Each bar's height or length corresponds to the data value at a specific time point. Bar charts are useful for comparing values across time periods and highlighting trends, patterns, or anomalies.

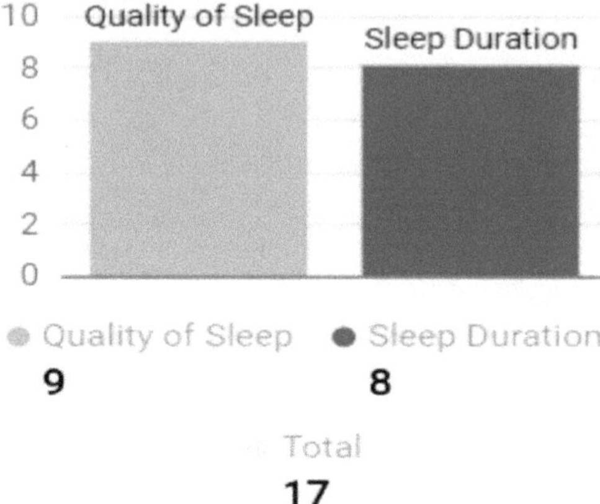

Fig. 9. Bar Chart

Figure 10 presents a quality sleep vs sleep duration based on live data captured and plotted into an analytic platform. The time series data displays changes over time using a continuous line connecting data points.

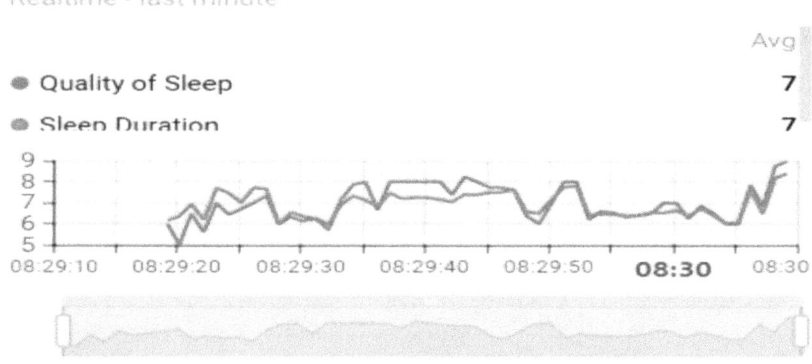

Fig. 10. Line Chart

Figure 11 shows a simple value and chart card displays a key value alongside a small chart to provide context or trends.

Fig. 11. Simple Value and Chart card

Lastly, the analytic platform presents the entities widget in ThingsBoard that display a list of entities with customizable columns as in Fig. 12.

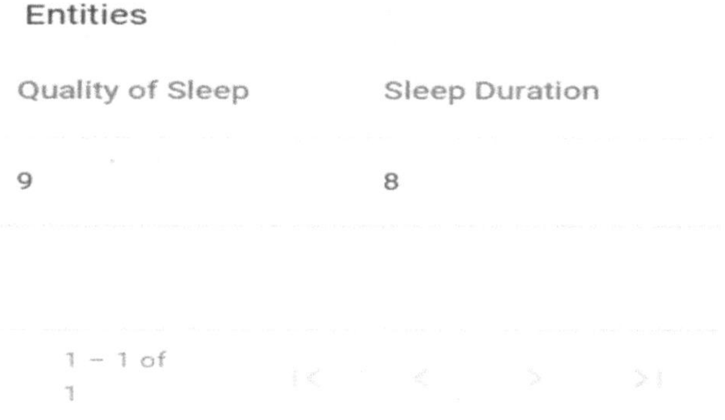

Fig. 12. Entities Table

5 Conclusion

In this analysis, we examined a dataset on sleep health and lifestyle factors. We started with a descriptive analysis, which provided an overview of key variables like sleep duration, quality of sleep, physical activity level, and stress. The data showed that most individuals slept around 7 h, with moderate physical activity and stress levels. We also explored correlations between variables. Notably, sleep duration had a strong positive correlation with sleep quality, and a negative correlation with stress, indicating that more sleep is associated with better sleep quality and lower stress. Physical activity showed a weaker positive correlation with sleep duration. Next, we applied machine learning models, Logistic Regression and Decision Tree, to predict sleep disorder outcomes. Both models performed well, with accuracy of 94.69% for Logistic Regression and 93.81% for Decision Tree. In conclusion, this analysis highlights the importance of both descriptive statistics and machine learning in understanding sleep health. The findings emphasize the role of lifestyle factors, such as physical activity, stress, and sleep duration, in influencing sleep quality and disorders.

References

1. Zhang, S., et al.: Circadian rhythms and sleep quality among undergraduate students in China: the mediating role of health-promoting lifestyle behaviours. J. Affect. Disord. **333**, 225–232 (2023). https://doi.org/10.1016/j.jad.2023.04.077
2. Garbarino, S., Bragazzi, N.L.: Revolutionizing sleep health: the emergence and impact of personalized sleep medicine. J. Person. Med. **14**, 598 (2024). https://doi.org/10.3390/jpm14060598
3. Riemann, D., et al.: The European Insomnia guideline: an update on the diagnosis and treatment of insomnia 2023. J. Sleep Res. **32**, e14035 (2023). https://doi.org/10.1111/jsr.14035
4. Kwon, S., et al.: At-home wireless sleep monitoring patches for the clinical assessment of sleep quality and sleep apnea. Sci. Adv. **9**, eadg9671 (2023). https://doi.org/10.1126/sciadv.adg9671
5. Kong, J., Zhou, L., Li, X., Ren, Q.: Sleep disorders affect cognitive function in adults: an overview of systematic reviews and meta-analyses. Sleep Biol. Rhythms **21**, 133–142 (2023). https://doi.org/10.1007/s41105-022-00439-9
6. Rahman, M.A., et al.: Improving sleep disorder diagnosis through optimized machine learning approaches. IEEE Access **13**, 20989–21004 (2025). https://doi.org/10.1109/ACCESS.2025.3535535
7. Mathunjwa, B.M., Kor, R.Y., Ngarnkuekool, W., Hsu, Y.-L.: A comprehensive review of home sleep monitoring technologies: smartphone apps, smartwatches, and smart mattresses. Sensors **25**, 1771 (2025). https://doi.org/10.3390/s25061771
8. Zhang, X., Zhang, X., Huang, Q., Lv, Y., Chen, F.: A review of automated sleep stage based on EEG signals. Biocybernet. Biomed. Eng. **44**, 651–673 (2024). https://doi.org/10.1016/j.bbe.2024.06.004
9. Djanian, S., Bruun, A., Nielsen, T.D.: Sleep classification using consumer sleep technologies and AI: a review of the current landscape. Sleep Med. **100**, 390–403 (2022). https://doi.org/10.1016/j.sleep.2022.09.004
10. Salari, N., et al.: Detection of sleep apnea using Machine learning algorithms based on ECG signals: a comprehensive systematic review. Expert Syst. Appl. **187**, 115950 (2022). https://doi.org/10.1016/j.eswa.2021.115950
11. Li, C., Qi, Y., Ding, X., Zhao, J., Sang, T., Lee, M.: A deep learning method approach for sleep stage classification with EEG spectrogram. Int. J. Environ. Res. Public Health **19**, 6322 (2022). https://doi.org/10.3390/ijerph19106322
12. Yunardi, R.T., Sardjono, T.A., Mardiyanto, R.: Skeleton-based gait recognition using modified deep convolutional neural networks and long short-term memory for person recognition. IEEE Access **12**, 121131–121143 (2024). https://doi.org/10.1109/ACCESS.2024.3451495
13. Han, H., Oh, J.: Application of various machine learning techniques to predict obstructive sleep apnea syndrome severity. Sci. Rep. **13**, 6379 (2023). https://doi.org/10.1038/s41598-023-33170-7
14. Bahrami, M., Forouzanfar, M.: Detection of sleep apnea from single-lead ECG: comparison of deep learning algorithms. In: Proceedings of the 2021 IEEE International Symposium on Medical Measurements and Applications (MeMeA), 23–25 June 2021, pp. 1–5 (2021)
15. Satapathy, S., Loganathan, D., Kondaveeti, H., Rath, R.: Performance analysis of machine learning algorithms on automated sleep staging feature sets. CAAI Trans. Intell. Technol. **6**, 155 (2021). https://doi.org/10.1049/cit2.12042
16. Ramesh, J., Keeran, N., Sagahyroon, A., Aloul, F.: Towards validating the effectiveness of obstructive sleep apnea classification from electronic health records using machine learning. Healthcare (Basel) **9**, 1450 (2021). https://doi.org/10.3390/healthcare9111450

17. Satapathy, S., Kondaveeti, H., Sreeja, S., Madhani, H., Rajput, N., Swain, D.: A deep learning approach to automated sleep stages classification using multi-modal signals. Procedia Comput. Sci. **218**, 867–876 (2023). https://doi.org/10.1016/j.procs.2023.01.067
18. Yildirim, O., Baloglu, U.B., Acharya, U.R.: A deep learning model for automated sleep stages classification using PSG signals. Int. J. Environ. Res. Public Health **16**, 599 (2019). https://doi.org/10.3390/ijerph16040599
19. Uom190346A. Sleep Health and Lifestyle Dataset. Available online: https://www.kaggle.com/datasets/uom190346a/sleep-health-and-lifestyle-dataset
20. Nor, A., Minhat, M., Ya'acob, N., Kassim, M.: Linear regression and R-squared correlation analysis on major nuclear online plant cooling system. Int. J. Electr. Comput. Eng. (IJECE) **13**, 3998 (2023). https://doi.org/10.11591/ijece.v13i4.pp3998-4008
21. Abdullah, N.P., Kassim, M., Mohd Deni, S., Mohd Yussoff, Y.: Descriptive analysis of wide area network flow control internet traffic on Metro-E 100 Mbps campus network. Bull. Electr. Eng. Inform. **13**, 12 (2024). https://doi.org/10.1591/eei.v13i4.7044
22. Alabi, B., Bukola, T.: Introduction to descriptive statistics. In: Kumar, B.S. (ed.) Recent Advances in Biostatistics. IntechOpen, Rijeka (2023)
23. Nur Farhana Abdul, A., Norsuzila, Y., Azita Laily, Y., Murizah, K.: A review of wildfire studies using machine learning applications. J. Adv. Res. Appl. Mech. **114**, 13–32 (2024). https://doi.org/10.37934/aram.114.1.1332
24. Backhaus, K., Erichson, B., Gensler, S., Weiber, R., Weiber, T.: Logistic regression. In: Backhaus, K., Erichson, B., Gensler, S., Weiber, R., Weiber, T. (eds.) Multivariate Analysis: An Application-Oriented Introduction, pp. 265–352. Springer Fachmedien Wiesbaden, Wiesbaden (2023)
25. Tareq, W.Z.T., Davud, M.: Chapter 20a - classification and clustering. In: Allahviranloo, T., Pedrycz, W., Seyyedabbasi, A. (eds.) Decision-Making Models, pp. 351–359. Academic Press (2024)
26. Cui, Z., Sato, T., Jackson, A., Jayarathna, S., Itoh, M., Yamani, Y.: Gaze transition entropy as a measure of attention allocation in a dynamic workspace involving automation. Sci. Rep. **14**, 23405 (2024). https://doi.org/10.1038/s41598-024-74244-4
27. Mienye, I.D., Jere, N.: A survey of decision trees: concepts, algorithms, and applications. IEEE Access **12**, 86716–86727 (2024). https://doi.org/10.1109/ACCESS.2024.3416838

Status, Influencing Factors, and Career Impact of Digital Competence and AI Literacy Among Vocational Undergraduate Students a Mixed-Methods Study in Vocational Education

XiangYong Duan[1,2](✉) and Mohd Nasir Ismail[3]

[1] Guiyang Healthcare Vocational University, GuiZhou, China
duanxy@gyhvu.edu.cn
[2] Faculty of Information Science, Universiti Teknologi MARA, Selangor, Malaysia
[3] Faculty of Information Science, Universiti Teknologi MARA Kelantan Branch, Machang, Kelantan, Malaysia
nasir733@uitm.edu.my

Abstract. The rapid evolution of digital and artificial intelligence (AI) technologies has made digital competence and AI literacy critical for vocational undergraduate students' career success. This mixed-methods study investigates the proficiency levels, influencing factors, and career impacts of these competencies among 579 students at a Chinese vocational institution. Digital competence was assessed across five dimensions—information and data literacy, communication and collaboration, digital content creation, problem-solving, and safety—while AI literacy was integrated as a sixth dimension. Quantitative findings reveal strengths in communication and collaboration ($M = 3.30$, $SD = 0.89$) and safety ($M = 3.25$, $SD = 0.92$), but relative weaknesses in digital content creation ($M = 2.88$, $SD = 0.88$) and problem-solving ($M = 2.90$, $SD = 0.87$). Training opportunities and self-efficacy significantly predict both competencies, explaining 60.4% and 63.7% of the variance in digital competence and AI literacy, respectively. These competencies enhance career readiness ($R2 = 0.569$) and employability ($R2 = 0.455$), with AI literacy showing a stronger effect on employability ($\beta = 0.43$, $p < 0.001$). Qualitative analysis of 299 open-ended responses identified six themes: limited training depth, practical experience gaps, data analysis difficulties, digital divide, ethical concerns, and accessibility gaps. The findings, supported by high reliability (Cronbach's $\alpha = 0.821$–0.909) and moderate construct validity (81.1% variance explained), underscore the need for curriculum reform in vocational education to address these gaps and prepare students for AI-driven industries.

Keywords: Digital Competence · AI Literacy · Vocational Education · Career Readiness · Employability

1 Introduction

The global shift toward a digital economy, accelerated by the proliferation of artificial intelligence (AI) technologies, has fundamentally transformed labor markets, placing unprecedented demands on the workforce [12]. Vocational undergraduate students, who

M. Kassim et al. (Eds.): SCDS 2025, CCIS 2674, pp. 76–89, 2026.
https://doi.org/10.1007/978-981-95-8368-3_6

are trained to meet industry-specific demands, must develop robust digital competence and AI literacy to remain competitive in fields such as healthcare, smart management, and rehabilitation technology [1]. Digital competence encompasses the ability to use digital technologies effectively for information management, communication, content creation, problem-solving, and ensuring safety [7]. AI literacy, an emerging competency, involves understanding AI principles, applying AI tools, and addressing ethical implications in professional contexts [2].

In China, vocational education plays a pivotal role in workforce development, with over 10 million students enrolled annually as of 2025. However, the integration of digital and AI competencies into vocational curricula remains uneven, often constrained by limited resources, outdated training programs, and a lack of practical opportunities [8]. This gap is particularly pronounced in health-related fields, where AI applications—such as predictive diagnostics, telemedicine, and health data analytics—are becoming integral [10]. The choice of health-related scenarios in this study (e.g., assessing online health resources or using AI for patient diagnostics) is deliberate, as the participants are from a healthcare vocational university with majors in nursing, rehabilitation, and similar fields. These scenarios enhance the assessment by making it contextually relevant to students' future professions, thereby improving ecological validity and the applicability of findings to healthcare vocational education [4]. For vocational students, mastering these competencies is not merely an academic exercise but a prerequisite for career readiness and employability in an AI-driven labor market [9].

Despite the growing importance of these skills, empirical research on vocational undergraduate students is limited. Most studies focus on traditional undergraduates or professionals, leaving a knowledge gap regarding vocational education [8]. This study addresses this gap by examining the status, influencing factors, and career impacts of digital competence and AI literacy among 579 vocational students at a Chinese institution. The research questions are:

1. What is the proficiency level of digital competence and AI literacy among vocational undergraduate students?
2. What factors influence the development of these competencies?
3. How do these competencies impact career development outcomes such as readiness and employability?

Using a mixed-methods approach, this study combines quantitative survey data with qualitative insights from open-ended responses, providing a comprehensive understanding of these competencies in vocational education. The findings aim to inform curriculum design, enhance training programs, and align vocational education with the demands of the AI era.

2 Literature Review

2.1 Conceptual Frameworks

Digital competence is a multifaceted construct, often framed by the European DigComp 2.2 framework, which identifies five key dimensions: information and data literacy, communication and collaboration, digital content creation, problem-solving, and safety [7].

Information and data literacy involves the ability to search, evaluate, and manage digital information, such as assessing the credibility of online health resources. Communication and collaboration focus on using digital platforms for interaction and teamwork, a critical skill in healthcare settings. Digital content creation includes producing and editing digital materials, such as health-related presentations. Problem-solving entails using digital tools to address technical challenges, while safety encompasses protecting data and mitigating cyber risks [4].

AI literacy, while related, is distinct and increasingly vital in vocational contexts. It includes three core components: understanding AI concepts (e.g., machine learning algorithms), using AI tools for professional tasks (e.g., health data analytics), and evaluating ethical implications (e.g., privacy concerns in AI-driven diagnostics) [2]. Given the growing integration of AI in healthcare, this study extends the Dig Comp framework by incorporating AI literacy as a sixth dimension, reflecting its relevance to vocational students in fields like nursing and smart health management [1].

2.2 Influencing Factors

The development of digital competence is influenced by several factors, including access to technology, educational opportunities, and individual motivation [5]. In vocational settings, practice-oriented training and internships are crucial, yet resource constraints often limit their availability [3]. For AI literacy, the presence of AI-related curricula, hands-on opportunities, and positive attitudes toward technology adoption are key drivers [6]. Self-efficacy, defined as the belief in one's ability to succeed in specific tasks, is a significant predictor of both competencies, as it fosters confidence in learning and applying new skills [11]. In vocational education, where students often come from diverse socio-economic backgrounds, these factors can vary widely, exacerbating disparities in skill development [4].

2.3 Career Development Impacts

Digital competence enhances employability by enabling students to adapt to digital workflows, collaborate effectively, and solve technical problems [9]. AI literacy is particularly critical in roles involving data analysis, automation, and ethical decision-making, such as using AI tools for patient diagnostics or managing health records [10]. For vocational students, these competencies are essential for securing initial employment and achieving long-term career progression, particularly in health-related fields where AI adoption is accelerating [2]. However, the specific impact of these competencies on vocational students' career outcomes remains underexplored, necessitating further research [8].

3 Methods

3.1 Research Design

This study employs a mixed-methods design, integrating quantitative survey data with qualitative open-ended responses to provide a holistic understanding of digital competence and AI literacy among vocational undergraduate students. The quantitative component assesses proficiency levels, influencing factors, and career impacts, while the qualitative component explores perceived deficiencies and contextual challenges.

3.2 Participants

The sample comprises 579 students from Guiyang Healthcare Vocational University in China, representing diverse majors: nursing (46.5%), rehabilitation therapy (18.3%), smart health and elderly care management (15.2%), rehabilitation assistive technology (12.1%), optometry technology (4.8%), and others (3.1%). Participants were predominantly female (71.3%), aged 18–20 years (81.5%), and in their first year (73.2%), reflecting the demographic profile of vocational students in health-related programs.

3.3 Data Collection

Survey. A structured questionnaire, adapted from the DigComp 2.1 framework and extended to include AI literacy, assessed six dimensions: information and data literacy (Q5–Q9, e.g., "I can assess the credibility of online health information"), communication and collaboration (Q10–Q11, e.g., "I can use digital platforms for teamwork in healthcare"), digital content creation (Q12–Q13, e.g., "I can create digital health presentations"), problem-solving (Q14–Q15, e.g., "I can use digital tools to solve technical issues"), safety (Q16–Q17, e.g., "I can protect health data from cyber risks"), and AI literacy (Q18–Q20, e.g., "I can use AI tools for professional tasks"). Two influencing factors—training opportunities (Q21–Q24, e.g., "I have access to AI training programs") and self-efficacy (Q25–Q27, e.g., "I am confident in applying digital skills")—and two career outcomes—career readiness (Q28–Q29, e.g., "I feel prepared for digital jobs") and employability (Q30, e.g., "These skills improve my job prospects")—were also measured. All items used a five-point Likert scale (1 = strongly disagree, 5 = strongly agree). Example items include: "I can assess the credibility of online health information" (information literacy) and "I can use AI tools for professional tasks" (AI literacy). Data cleaning involved converting responses to numeric values, handling missing data via listwise deletion, and computing composite scores for multi-item constructs.

Qualitative Data. An open-ended question (Q31: "What deficiencies do you perceive in health-related digital competence and AI literacy?") was included to capture students' perceptions of gaps in their skills. Responses were collected in Chinese and analyzed thematically.

Table 1. Summary of Questionnaire Items

Construct	Items	Example
Information and Data Literacy	Q5–Q9	I can assess the credibility of online health information
Communication and Collaboration	Q10–Q11	I can use digital platforms for teamwork in healthcare
Digital Content Creation	Q12–Q13	I can create digital health presentations
Problem-Solving	Q14–Q15	I can use digital tools to solve technical issues
Safety	Q16–Q17	I can protect health data from cyber risks
AI Literacy	Q18–Q20	I can use AI tools for professional tasks
Training Opportunities	Q21–Q24	I have access to AI training programs
Self-Efficacy	Q25–Q27	I am confident in applying digital skills
Career Readiness	Q28–Q29	I feel prepared for digital jobs
Employability	Q30	These skills improve my job prospects

3.4 Data Analysis

Quantitative Analysis. Quantitative Analysis Quantitative analysis was performed using Python, with the following steps:

Reliability and Validity. Cronbach's alpha was calculated to assess the internal consistency of multi-item constructs, with a threshold of 0.70 for acceptability [13]. Exploratory factor analysis (EFA) with varimax rotation was conducted on Q9–Q20 (as detailed in Table 1) to evaluate construct validity, extracting factors with eigenvalues greater than 1. EFA was selected for its suitability in validating multidimensional constructs in new contexts like vocational education. Loadings above 0.40 were considered significant.

Descriptive Statistics. Means and standard deviations were computed for each dimension and outcome variable.

Correlation Analysis. Pearson correlations were used to examine relationships between variables, with significance set at $p < 0.001$; this method was chosen for its appropriateness in measuring linear associations among continuous variables.

Regression Analysis. Four ordinary least squares (OLS) regression models were estimated, as OLS is ideal for predicting continuous outcomes with multiple predictors: Model 1: Digital competence (mean of the first five dimensions) regressed on training opportunities and self-efficacy. Model 2: AI literacy regressed on training opportunities and self-efficacy. Model 3: Career readiness regressed on digital competence and AI literacy. Model 4: Employability regressed on digital competence and AI literacy.

Qualitative Analysis. Qualitative responses to Q31 were analyzed using Python-based natural language processing (NLP) techniques. After filtering 280 non-informative responses (e.g., "None"), 299 valid responses remained, of which 278 were used after preprocessing. The analysis involved:

Chinese text segmentation using the jieba library.

TF-IDF vectorization and agglomerative clustering (k = 6) using scikit-learn to identify thematic clusters, with a silhouette score of 0.019 for validation; TF-IDF and clustering were selected for their ability to objectively detect patterns in unstructured text, minimizing subjective bias in thematic identification compared to manual coding.

Keyword-based theme assignment, resulting in 221 responses categorized into seven themes: limited training depth, practical experience gaps, data analysis difficulties, digital divide, ethical concerns, accessibility gaps, and miscellaneous. Unassigned responses (57) were analyzed for emerging patterns using top term frequency.

4 Results

4.1 Reliability and Validity

Cronbach's alpha for multi-item constructs ranged from 0.821 to 0.909, exceeding the 0.70 threshold and confirming excellent internal consistency (Table 2). EFA on Q9–Q20 supported a six-factor structure, explaining 81.1% of the variance. Factor loadings ranged from 0.543 to 0.829 on their intended dimensions, with minor cross-loadings (e.g., Q12 loaded 0.516 on Factor 5), indicating moderate construct validity (Table 3).

Table 2. Cronbach's Alpha for Multi-Item Constructs

Construct	Cronbach's Alpha
Communication and Collaboration	0.821
Content Creation	0.909
Problem-Solving	0.898
Safety	0.835
AI Literacy	0.885
Training Opportunities	0.883
Self-Efficacy	0.903
Career Readiness	0.849

Table 3. Exploratory Factor Analysis Loadings (Q9–Q20)

Item	Factor 1	Factor 2	Factor 3	Factor 4	Factor 5	Factor 6
Q9(Information Literacy)	0.543	0.322	0.288	0.392	0.098	0.153
Q10 (Communication)	0.277	0.323	0.257	0.680	0.068	0.049
Q11 (Collaboration)	0.560	0.369	0.209	0.519	0.169	0.113

(continued)

Table 3. *(continued)*

Item	Factor 1	Factor 2	Factor 3	Factor 4	Factor 5	Factor 6
Q12 (Content Creation)	0.731	0.233	0.217	0.298	0.516	0.058
Q13 (Content Editing)	0.806	0.280	0.206	0.228	0.123	0.043
Q14 (Problem-Solving)	0.829	0.285	0.203	0.214	0.038	0.068
Q15 (Learning Tools)	0.738	0.304	0.281	0.237	0.014	0.130
Q16(Data Protection)	0.506	0.341	0.464	0.196	0.101	0.349

4.2 Status of Digital Competence and AI Literacy

Descriptive statistics (N = 579) revealed varied proficiency levels across dimensions (Table 4). Communication and collaboration (M = 3.30, SD = 0.89) and safety (M = 3.25, SD = 0.92) were the strongest dimensions, indicating that students are adept at using digital platforms for interaction and protecting data. In contrast, digital content creation (M = 2.88, SD = 0.88) and problem-solving (M = 2.90, SD = 0.87) showed relative weaknesses, suggesting areas for improvement in creative and technical skills, though overall levels are moderate on a 5-point scale. AI literacy (M = 3.20, SD = 0.84) and information and data literacy (M = 3.00, SD = 0.94) showed moderate proficiency, reflecting a foundational but limited understanding of AI applications and data management. These differences are visually represented in Fig. 1.

Table 4. Descriptive Statistics for Dimensions and Outcomes (N = 579)

Variable	Mean	Standard Deviation
Information and Data Literacy	3.00	0.94
Communication and Collaboration	3.30	0.89
Content Creation	2.88	0.88
Problem-Solving	2.90	0.87
Safety	3.25	0.92
AI Literacy	3.20	0.84
Training Opportunities	3.15	0.80
Self-Efficacy	3.24	0.82
Career Readiness	3.22	0.85
Employability	3.27	0.89

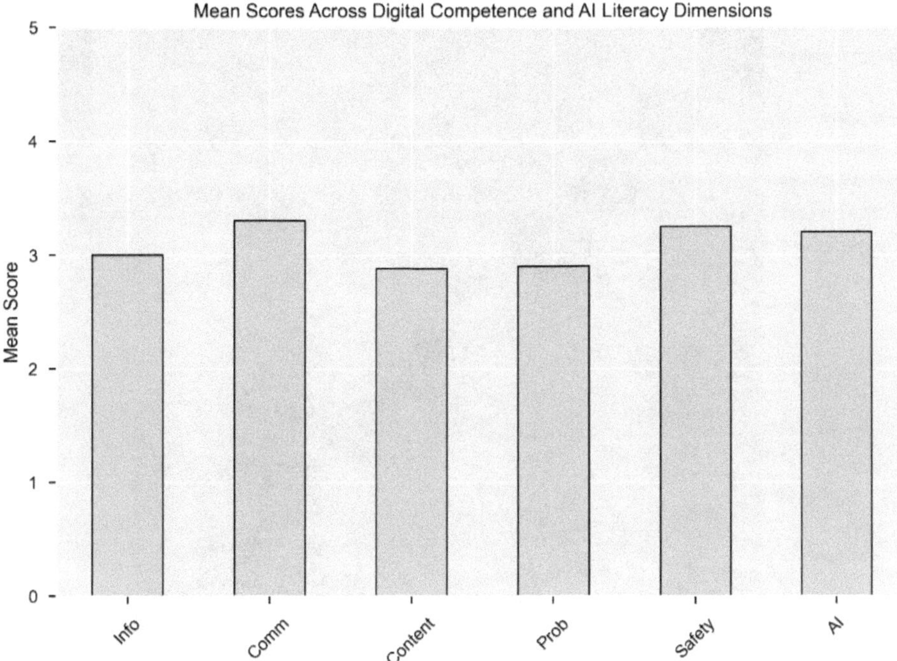

Fig. 1. Mean Scores Across Digital Competence and AI Literacy Dimensions

4.3 Influencing Factors

Pearson correlations showed significant relationships between variables ($p < 0.001$). Training opportunities were strongly correlated with digital competence ($r = 0.60$) and AI literacy ($r = 0.76$), while self-efficacy had slightly stronger correlations ($r = 0.62$ for digital competence, $r = 0.75$ for AI literacy). These high correlations indicate substantial positive associations, suggesting that improvements in training and self-efficacy could meaningfully boost competencies. These relationships are illustrated in the correlation heatmap (Fig. 2). Regression analyses further confirmed these relationships (Table 5). For digital competence ($R^2 = 0.604$), both training opportunities ($\beta = 0.37$, $p < 0.001$) and self-efficacy ($\beta = 0.43$, $p < 0.001$) were significant predictors. For AI literacy ($R^2 = 0.637$), training opportunities had a stronger effect ($\beta = 0.48$, $p < 0.001$) than self-efficacy ($\beta = 0.38$, $p < 0.001$).

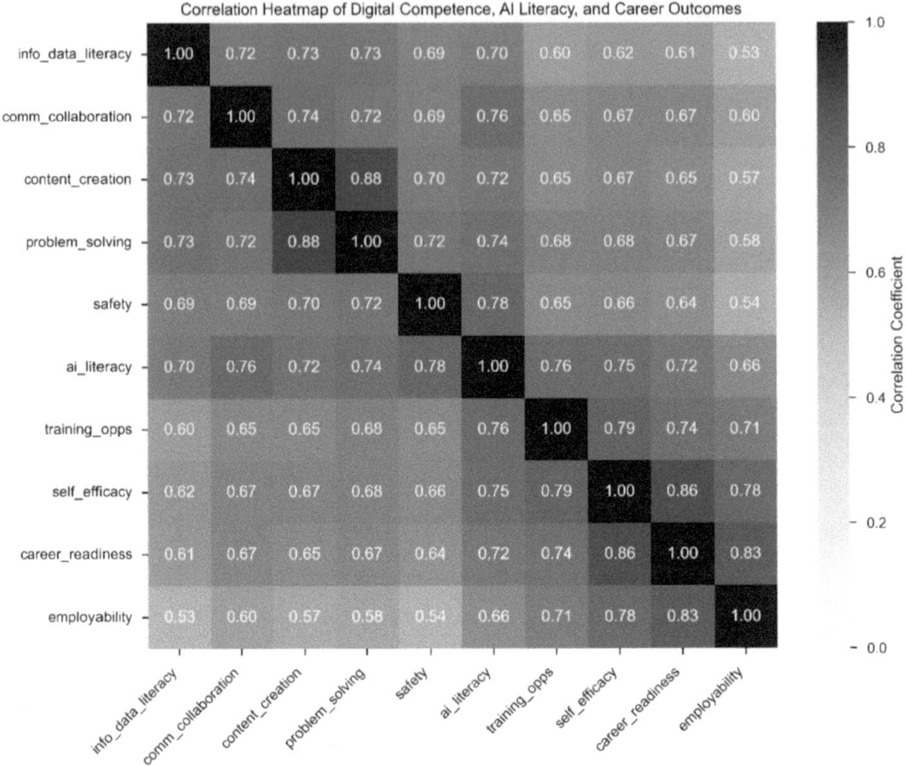

Fig. 2. Correlation Heatmap of Digital Competence, AI Literacy, and Career Outcomes

Table 5. Regression Results for Influencing Factors

Model	Dependent Variable	Predictor	Coefficient	Std. Error	p-value
1	Digital Competence	Constant	0.4935	0.089	0.000
		Training Opportunities	0.3699	0.043	0.000
		Self-Efficacy	0.4336	0.042	0.000
		R^2	0.604		
2	AI Literacy	Constant	0.4310	0.090	0.000
		Training Opportunities	0.4826	0.043	0.000
		Self-Efficacy	0.3848	0.042	0.000
		R^2	0.637		

Table 6. Regression Results for Career Outcomes

Model	Dependent Variable	Predictor	Coefficient	Std. Error	p-value
3	Career Readiness	Constant	0.6651	0.096	0.000
		Digital Competence	0.4640	0.053	0.000
		AI Literacy	0.3549	0.051	0.000
		R^2	0.569		
4	Employability	Constant	0.8681	0.113	0.000
		Digital Competence	0.3306	0.063	0.000
		AI Literacy	0.4347	0.060	0.000
		R^2	0.455		

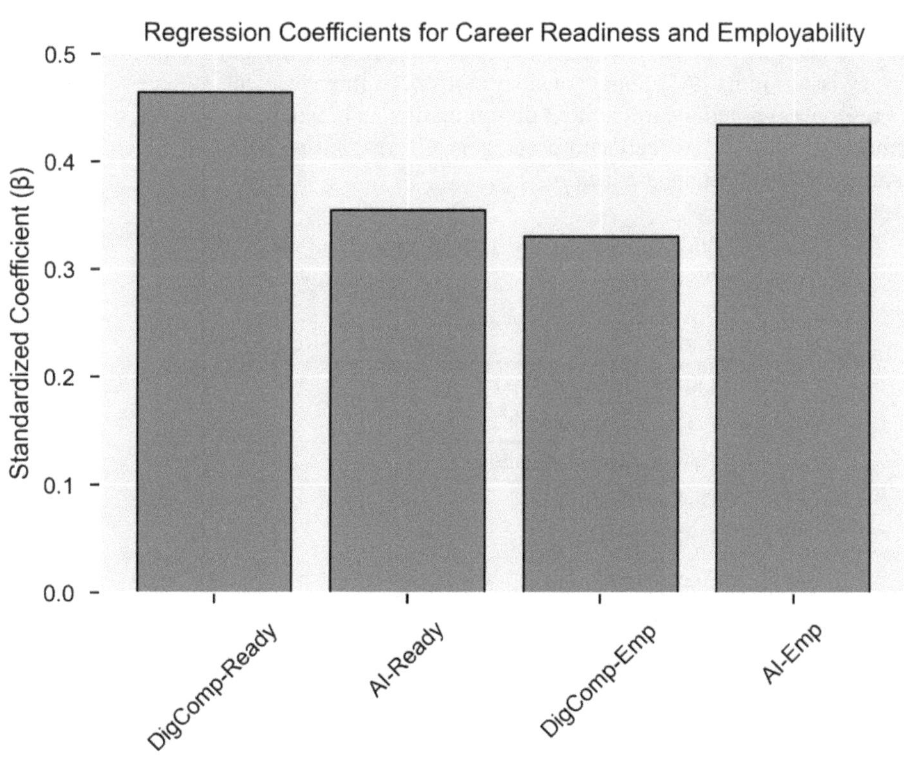

Fig. 3. Regression Coefficients for Career Readiness and Employability

4.4 Career Development Impacts

Regression analyses demonstrated significant effects of digital competence and AI literacy on career outcomes (Table 6). For career readiness (M = 3.22, SD = 0.85; $R^2 = 0.569$), digital competence ($\beta = 0.46$, $p < 0.001$) and AI literacy ($\beta = 0.35$, $p < 0.001$)

were both significant predictors; this indicates that 56.9% of variance in readiness is accounted for, practically meaning stronger competencies could better prepare students for immediate workforce entry. For employability ($M = 3.27$, $SD = 0.89$; $R^2 = 0.455$), AI literacy had a stronger effect ($\beta = 0.43$, $p < 0.001$) than digital competence ($\beta = 0.33$, $p < 0.001$). The strong correlation between career readiness and employability ($r = 0.83$) highlights their interconnectedness. These relationships are visualized in Fig. 3.

4.5 Qualitative Insights

Thematic analysis of Q31 responses (N = 299, after filtering) identified six key themes (Table 7). Limited training depth (76 responses) highlighted insufficient depth in AI and digital skills training (e.g., "Limited understanding of related knowledge"). Practical experience gaps (39 responses) pointed to a lack of hands-on opportunities (e.g., "Lack of practical teaching"). Data analysis difficulties (24 responses) reflected challenges in interpreting health data (e.g., "Lack of data analysis skills"). The digital divide (10 responses) identified barriers for older or less-educated populations (e.g., "Digital exclusion among the elderly"). Ethical concerns (9 responses) focused on AI ethics and privacy issues (e.g., "AI ethical considerations need improvement"). Accessibility gaps (28 responses) noted insufficient AI dissemination and resources (e.g., "AI cannot meet human needs"). The miscellaneous category (35 responses) included vague or diverse responses (e.g., "Details are lacking").

Table 7. Themes from Qualitative Analysis of Q31 Responses

Theme	Number of Responses
Limited Training Depth	76
Practical Experience Gaps	39
Data Analysis Difficulties	24
Digital Divide	10
Ethical Concerns	9
Accessibility Gaps	28
Miscellaneous	35
Unassigned	57

Unassigned responses (57) often contained vague terms like "很多" (many) or "暂时" (temporarily), suggesting additional gaps in clarity and dissemination. The low silhouette score (0.019) from clustering indicates limited distinctiveness, reflecting the complexity and overlap in students' perceptions.

5 Discussion

5.1 Key Findings

Students demonstrated strengths in communication and collaboration (M = 3.30) and safety (M = 3.25), likely due to widespread use of digital communication tools (e.g., WeChat) and cybersecurity education in their curriculum [7]. These skills are critical in health-related fields, where collaboration and data protection are paramount [4]. However, relative weaknesses in digital content creation (M = 2.88) and problem-solving (M = 2.90) highlight areas for improvement in creative and technical abilities, which are essential for tasks like developing health education materials or troubleshooting AI-driven systems, despite overall moderate proficiency levels [8]. AI literacy (M = 3.20) indicates foundational skills, constrained by limited training and practical exposure, as evidenced by qualitative themes of limited training depth and practical experience gaps [1].

Training opportunities and self-efficacy were strong predictors of both digital competence ($R^2 = 0.604$) and AI literacy ($R^2 = 0.637$). Self-efficacy had a greater influence on digital competence ($\beta = 0.43$), suggesting that confidence in digital skills is a key driver, while training opportunities were more critical for AI literacy ($\beta = 0.48$), reflecting the need for structured AI education [11]. These findings align with prior research emphasizing the role of education and motivation in skill development [5].

Both competencies significantly impacted career outcomes, explaining 56.9% of the variance in career readiness and 45.5% in employability. AI literacy's stronger effect on employability ($\beta = 0.43$) underscores its growing importance in the labor market, particularly in health-related roles involving data analytics and automation [2]. The high correlation between career readiness and employability ($r = 0.83$) suggests that these competencies prepare students not only for immediate employment but also for long-term career success [9].

Qualitative themes corroborated quantitative findings, particularly the weaknesses in content creation and problem-solving. Limited training depth and practical experience gaps reflect systemic issues in vocational education, such as outdated curricula and insufficient internships [3]. Data analysis difficulties highlight a critical skill gap, as many students struggle to interpret health data—a key competency in AI-driven healthcare [10]. The digital divide and ethical concerns raise broader societal issues, particularly for older populations and in the ethical use of AI, while accessibility gaps point to the need for better dissemination of AI resources [5].

5.2 Implications

This study has several implications for vocational education:

Curriculum Design. Vocational programs should integrate DigComp and AI literacy modules, with a focus on content creation, data analysis, and ethics. Incorporating project-based learning can address weaknesses in problem-solving.

Practical Training. Partnerships with industry can provide AI-focused internships, enabling students to gain hands-on experience with tools like health data analytics platforms.

Student Support. Workshops to enhance self-efficacy and address ethical concerns can boost students' confidence and awareness, particularly in AI applications.
Inclusivity. Developing accessible tools and training programs for older or less-educated populations can bridge the digital divide, ensuring equitable access to digital health resources.
Dissemination. Enhancing the availability of AI resources through open-access platforms and community outreach can address accessibility gaps, making AI tools more widely available. Furthermore, the demand for students' digital competence also influences the improvement of teachers' digital competence, as educators must enhance their own skills to effectively meet these needs [17].

5.3 Limitations and Future Directions

The study's single-institution sample limits its generalizability. Future research should include diverse institutions to capture broader trends in vocational education. Self-reported data may introduce bias; objective assessments, such as performance-based tests, could validate these findings. The low silhouette score (0.019) in qualitative clustering suggests response variability, necessitating refined NLP methods like topic modeling to better capture thematic nuances. Longitudinal studies can explore the long-term career impacts of digital competence and AI literacy, providing insights into their sustained effects on employability and career progression.

6 Conclusion

This mixed-methods study provides a comprehensive analysis of digital competence and AI literacy strengths in communication and safety but relative gaps in among vocational undergraduate students, revealing content creation, problem-solving, and AI accessibility that warrant improvement. Training opportunities and self-efficacy are key drivers of these competencies, which in turn enhance career readiness and employability. Qualitative insights highlight critical challenges, including limited training depth, practical experience gaps, data analysis difficulties, digital divide, ethical concerns, and accessibility issues. Supported by high reliability (Cronbach's $\alpha = 0.821$–0.909) and moderate construct validity (81.1% variance explained), these findings underscore the need for targeted curriculum reform in vocational education. By addressing these gaps through enhanced training, practical opportunities, and inclusive strategies, vocational institutions can better prepare students for the demands of the AI era. Future research should refine qualitative methods and explore long-term career impacts to further advance vocational education in the digital age.

Acknowledgements. We acknowledge the use of large language models in assisting with the drafting and editing of this manuscript. However, we take full responsibility for all aspects of the research design, data collection, analysis, interpretations, and final content decisions, ensuring the work's integrity and originality.

References

1. Long, D., Magerko, B.: What is AI literacy? Competencies and design considerations. In Proceedings of the 2020 CHI Conference on Human Factors in Computing Systems, pp. 1–16 (2020). https://doi.org/10.1145/3313831.3376727
2. Ng, D.T.K., Leung, J.K.L., Chu, S.K.W., Qiao, M.S.: Conceptualizing AI literacy: an exploratory review. Comput. Educ.: Artif. Intell. **2**, 100041 (2021). https://doi.org/10.1016/j.caeai.2021.100041
3. Cedefop. European Skills Index Technical Report. European Centre for the Development of Vocational Training (2020). https://www.cedefop.europa.eu/files/esi_-_technical_report_2020.pdf
4. Oberländer, M., Beinicke, A., Bipp, T.: Digital competencies: a review of the literature and applications in the workplace. Comput. Educ. **146**, 103752 (2020). https://doi.org/10.1016/j.compedu.2019.103752
5. Van Deursen, A.J.A.M.: Digital inequalities in the age of artificial intelligence and big data. Hum. Behav. Emerg. Technol. **1**(2), 103–110 (2019). https://doi.org/10.1002/hbe2.140
6. Pinski, M., Benlian, A.: AI literacy for users – a comprehensive review and future research directions of learning methods, components, and effects. Comput. Hum. Behav.: Artif. Hum. **2**(1), 100027 (2024)
7. Vuorikari, R., Kluzer, S., Punie, Y.: DigComp 2.2: the digital competence framework for citizens—with new examples of knowledge, skills and attitudes. Publications Office of the European Union (2022). https://doi.org/10.2760/490274
8. Zhao, Y., Pinto Llorente, A.M., Sánchez Gómez, M.C.: Digital competence in higher education research: a systematic literature review. Comput. Educ. **168**, 104212 (2021). https://doi.org/10.1016/j.compedu.2021.104212
9. Wang, Y.Y., Xu, Z.R.: The digital competence of Chinese higher education students and the linkage with their career adaptability. Educ. Inf. Technol. **28**(11), 15473–15498 (2023). https://doi.org/10.1108/ET-08-2022-0315
10. Laupichler, M., Aster, A., Schirch, J., Raupach, T.: Medical students' AI literacy and attitudes towards AI: a cross-sectional two-center study using pre-validated assessment instruments. BMC Med. Educ. **24**, 460 (2024). https://doi.org/10.1186/s12909-024-05400-7
11. Chen, L., Ifenthaler, D.: Digital competence assessment for students: a systematic review. Educ. Inf. Technol. **25**, 4155–4172 (2020)
12. European Commission. Digital Education Action Plan (2021–2027): Resetting education and training for the digital age (2020). https://education.ec.europa.eu/focus-topics/digital-education/digital-education-action-plan
13. Tavakol, M., Dennick, R.: Making sense of Cronbach's alpha. Int. J. Med. Educ. **2**, 53–55 (2011). https://doi.org/10.5116/ijme.4dfb.8dfd
14. Yang, H., Chen, H., Pan, T., Lin, Y., Zhang, Y., Chen, H.: Studies on the digital inclusion among older adults and the quality of life: a Nanjing example in China. Front. Public Health **10**, 811959 (2022). https://doi.org/10.3389/fpubh.2022.811959
15. Integrating ethics in AI development: a qualitative study. BMC Med. Ethics (2023). https://doi.org/10.1186/s12910-023-01000-0
16. Teacher's perceptions of using an artificial intelligence-based scaffolding system. Front. Educ. (2022). https://doi.org/10.3389/feduc.2022.755914
17. Ivanov, A., Radonjić, A., Stošić, L., Krčadinac, O., Đokić, D.B., Đokić, V.: Teachers' digital competencies before, during, and after the COVID-19 pandemic. Sustainability **17**(5), 2309 (2025). https://doi.org/10.3390/su17052309

Dynamic Risk Assessment for Civil Aviation Information Systems Using a Multi-Source Deep Learning Framework

Xiang Qingzhen(✉), Syaripah Ruzaini Binti Syed Aris, Ahmad Faiz Ghazali, and Nor Shahida Mohamad Yusop

Universiti Teknologi MARA (UiTM), 40450 Shah Alam, Selangor Darul Ehsan, Malaysia
2021670552@student.uitm.edu.my

Abstract. Civil Aviation Information Systems (CAIS) are critical for the safety and efficiency of global air transport, but their growing interconnectivity increases exposure to cybersecurity threats, including ransomware, Distributed Denial-of-Service (DDoS) attacks, and human errors. This study introduces the Dynamic Multi-Source Risk Assessment Model (DMSRAM), which integrates Long Short-Term Memory (LSTM) and Fuzzy Neural Networks (FNN) for real-time, adaptive risk quantification in CAIS. Using a 550-day dataset of 13,887 samples from firewall logs, vulnerability reports, botnet logs, and web attack records, DMSRAM dynamically assesses threat probability, vulnerability severity, and asset value. Training results show an RMSE of 0.0167, a detection rate of 92.3%, and an adaptability of 89.4% (indicating stable predictions over time), outperforming the NIST SP 800–30 benchmark (RMSE: 0.0450, detection rate: 75.8%). By capturing temporal dynamics, handling uncertainty, and leveraging multi-source data, DMSRAM offers a robust solution for CAIS cybersecurity. This research provides a comprehensive foundation for data-driven risk management in civil aviation and other critical infrastructures.

Keywords: Civil Aviation Information Systems · Dynamic Risk Assessment · Deep Learning · LSTM · Fuzzy Neural Networks · Multi-Source Data

1 Introduction

Civil Aviation Information Systems (CAIS) are essential for the operational efficiency and safety of the aviation industry, supporting critical functions such as Air Traffic Control (ATC), Departure Control Systems (DCS), and Airport Information Management Systems (AIMS) [1]. These systems handle substantial data volumes, with ATC processing approximately 10,000 logs daily at response times as low as 50 ms [2]. However, their growing complexity and inter- connectivity have heightened their vulnerability to cybersecurity threats, including ransomware, DDoS attacks, Advanced Persistent Threats (APTs), and human errors [3]. Notable incidents, such as the 2022 SpiceJet ransomware attack (1,800 delay hours, \$1.2M loss) and the 2023 British Airways MOVEit breach (CVSS = 9.8, \$1.5M loss), highlight the urgent need for advanced risk assessment frameworks tailored to CAIS [4].

M. Kassim et al. (Eds.): SCDS 2025, CCIS 2674, pp. 90–101, 2026.
https://doi.org/10.1007/978-981-95-8368-3_7

Traditional risk assessment methodologies, such as NIST SP 800–30, GB/T 31509–2015, and ISO/IEC 27005, rely on static, periodic evaluations that fail to address the dynamic nature of modern cyber threats [5]. These methods exhibit limitations, such as detection rates of 75.8% and RMSE values of 0.0450, due to their inability to capture real-time threat variations and integrate multi-source data [6]. The China National Vulnerability Database (CNNVD) reported 2,131 new vulnerabilities monthly in 2022, with a 27.43% unpatched rate, further emphasizing the inadequacy of static models [7]. Additionally, CAIS interdependencies and stringent regulatory requirements necessitate high precision and adaptability in risk assessment [8].

To address these challenges, this study proposes the Dynamic Multi-Source Risk Assessment Model (DMSRAM), a data-driven framework that integrates multi-source data with advanced deep learning techniques for real-time risk quantification. DMSRAM is based on the core risk formula $R_t = P_t \cdot S_t \cdot I_t$ where P_t, S_t, and I_t represent threat probability, vulnerability severity, and asset value at time t, , respectively. Leveraging Long Short-Term Memory (LSTM) networks for temporal pattern analysis and Fuzzy Neural Networks (FNN) for uncertainty handling, DMSRAM achieves an RMSE of 0.0167, a detection rate of 92.3%, and an adaptability of 89.4%, as validated through training on a 550-day CAIS dataset [9]. The model processes 13,887 samples, including firewall logs (5,000 alerts/day), employee records (100 login failures/day), and botnet logs, using the Analytic Hierarchy Process (AHP) and entropy methods for weight optimization [10].

This paper is structured as follows: Sect. 2 reviews related work on CAIS risk assessment. Sect. 3 details the theoretical foundations and methodology of DMSRAM. Section 4 describes the experimental setup, including data preprocessing and model training. Section 5 presents the results and comparative analysis. Section 6 discusses implications, limitations, and future directions. Section 7 concludes the study.

2 Related Work

The security of CAIS has become a focal point due to its critical role in aviation safety and efficiency. Traditional risk assessment frameworks, such as NIST SP 800–30, provide structured methodologies for identifying threats, vulnerabilities, and impacts [5]. However, their static nature and reliance on subjective expert scoring result in limited adaptability, with remediation rates for vulnerabilities as low as 72.57% [7]. GB/T 31509–2015 and ISO/IEC 27005 similarly emphasize checklist-based approaches, which struggle to capture real-time threat variations in CAIS, achieving detection rates of 75.8% [11].

Recent studies have explored dynamic risk assessment models to overcome these limitations. Cheimonidis and Rantos [12] conducted a systematic literature review on dynamic cybersecurity risk assessment, emphasizing the need for adaptive, data-driven approaches. Sommestad et al. [13] proposed Bayesian defense graphs for probabilistic risk modeling, but their single-source data approach limits applicability to CAIS. Huang et al. [14] applied Bayesian networks to SCADA networks, achieving improved detection rates (80.2%) but lacking multi-source integration. Zhang et al. [15] developed a multimodal-based incident prediction framework for industrial control systems, reporting a detection rate of 80.2%, yet struggling with temporal dynamics.

Deep learning techniques have shown significant promise in enhancing risk assessment. Yang [16] applied LSTM networks to predict cybersecurity risks, achieving an RMSE of 0.0315–0.0372 in simulated environments. Wang [17] utilized FNNs to handle uncertainty, reporting a coverage rate of 89.7%–91.5% for interval-based predictions. However, these studies often target generic IT systems, with limited application to CAIS's unique requirements, such as stringent response times and regulatory compliance [8]. Recent incidents, such as the 2023 KAA ransomware attack ($Rt = 0.45$, $800,000 loss), highlight the need for models that can address CAIS-specific threats like botnet activities (importance: 0.1071) [3].

The proposed DMSRAM framework addresses these gaps by integrating multi-source data (firewall logs, vulnerability reports, botnet logs), LSTM-based temporal prediction, and FNN- based uncertainty handling, specifically tailored for CAIS. Unlike existing models, DMSRAM achieves real-time adaptability and high accuracy, as demonstrated by its superior performance metrics (RMSE: 0.0167, detection rate: 92.3%) compared to NIST SP 800–30 [9].

3 Methodology

3.1 Theoretical Foundations

The Dynamic Multi-Source Risk Assessment Model (DMSRAM) integrates established risk assessment theories with advanced computational techniques, including the Analytic Hierarchy Process (AHP), entropy method, three-parameter interval analysis, Long Short-Term Memory (LSTM) networks, and Fuzzy Neural Networks (FNN). These components enable dynamic, data-driven risk quantification tailored to Civil Aviation Information Systems (CAIS), addressing the limitations of static models.

Risk Formula. The core risk formula of DMSRAM is defined as:

$$R_t = P_t \cdot S_t \cdot I_t \tag{1}$$

where:

- P_t: Threat probability at time t, representing the likelihood of a security incident based on cyber threats, human factors, technical/organizational factors, and botnet activities.
- S_t: Vulnerability severity at time t, quantifying the system's susceptibility to exploitation.
- I_t: Asset value at time t, reflecting the business, economic, regulatory, and technical importance of CAIS components.

This multiplicative model aligns with NIST SP 800–30 principles, where risk is a function of threat likelihood, vulnerability, and impact [5]. The temporal subscript t introduces dynamic updates, leveraging multi-source data and deep learning predictions. Training results validate this formulation, with target statistics (Mean: 0.3503, Std: 0.1921) reflecting balanced risk distributions [9].

Analytic Hierarchy Process (AHP). AHP assigns initial weights to sub-indicators based on expert pairwise comparisons [18]. For instance, the business impact (I_b) is weighted higher (e.g., 0.4) than economic value (I_e) (e.g., 0.3) in CAIS due to its criticality to flight operations. The consistency ratio (CR < 0.1) ensures reliability, as validated by training logs (CR: 0.056) [9].

Entropy Method. The entropy method refines AHP weights by calculating data variability [19]:

$$E_j = -\frac{1}{\ln m}\sum_{i=1}^{m} p_{ij}\ln p_{ij} \tag{2}$$

where p_{ij} is the normalized data, and m is the number of observations. Indicators with lower entropy (higher variability) receive higher weights. Training data show that botnet severity (variance: 0.14) received a weight of 0.1071 due to its high variability [9].

Three-Parameter Interval Analysis. Three-parameter interval analysis represents variables as $[a, b, c]$, where a, b, and c as denote the lower bound, most likely value, and upper bound, respectively [20]. This approach handles uncertainty in CAIS, such as zero-day attacks, with training logs confirming a coverage rate of 89.7%–91.5% for interval predictions [9].

Long Short-Term Memory (LSTM) Networks. LSTM networks capture temporal dependencies in time-series data [21]. The governing equations are:

$$f_t = \sigma\left(W_f \cdot \left[h_{\{t-1\}}, x_t\right] + b_f\right) \tag{3}$$

$$i_t = \sigma\left(W_i \cdot \left[h_{\{t-1\}}, x_t\right] + b_i\right) \tag{4}$$

$$o_t = \sigma\left(W_o \cdot \left[h_{\{t-1\}}, x_t\right] + b_o\right) \tag{5}$$

wheref_t, i_t, and o_t are forget, input, and output gates, respectively. Training logs confirm that LSTM with 512 units predicts Pt, St, and It, achieving an RMSE of 0.0167 across three folds [9].

Fuzzy Neural Networks (FNN). FNNs combine fuzzy logic with neural networks to handle uncertainty [17]. Training uncertainty that FNN constructed 12 fuzzy rules (e.g., "if P_t is high and S_t is medium, then risk is high") in 0.02 s, producing interval-based outputs $[R_t^L, R_t^M, R_t^U]$ [9].

3.2 DMSRAM Framework

The DMSRAM framework integrates multi-source data inputs, weight optimization, and deep learning predictions. The workflow is as follows:

- **Data Collection.** Aggregates firewall logs, vulnerability reports, botnet logs, and web attack logs.
- **Data Preprocessing.** Cleans, normalizes, and aligns time-series data.
- **Indicator Computation.** Uses AHP and entropy methods to calculate weights for sub-indicators.
- **Prediction Module.** Employs LSTM for single-value and interval-based predictions, and FNN for three-parameter intervals.

- **Risk Output.** Outputs R_t or $[R_t^L, R_t^M, R_t^U]$.

Training logs confirm the framework's efficiency, processing 13,876 sequences of length 12 in 0.02 s [9].

3.3 Indicator System

The indicator system is refined based on training insights, structured around three primary dimensions: threat probability (P_t), vulnerability severity (S_t), and asset value (I_t).

Training data highlight botnet severity (BS_t) as a critical sub-indicator (importance: 0.1071), reflecting the 151% ransomware surge [9].

4 Experimental Setup

4.1 Dataset

The dataset spans 550 days (July 1, 2023, to January 1, 2025), comprising 13,887 samples after hourly aggregation [9]. It includes:

- Botnet Logs: 20 records detailing zombie network activities (e.g., botnet count, severity).
- Vulnerability Attack Logs: 100 records of web, database, and network device vulnerabilities.
- Web Application Logs: 100 records of attacks (e.g., directory traversal, website scanning).
- Firewall Logs: 5,000 daily alerts capturing traffic anomalies [10].
- Employee Records: 100 daily login failures reflecting human factors [10].

The dataset includes 25 normalized features (Mean: 0.5125, Std: 0.2771), such as vuln_severity, botnet_severity_mean_24h, and attack_freq_severity [9]. The distribution of target variables (threat probability, vulnerability severity, and asset value) is illustrated in Fig. 1, showing a balanced spread with a mean of 0.3503 and standard deviation of 0.1921.

Table 1 describes the DMSRAM indicator system, a hierarchical structure for quantifying cybersecurity risks in civil aviation information systems (CAIS). The table is organized into three primary indicators—threat probability (P_t), vulnerability severity (S_t), and asset value (I_t). Each indicator is further broken down into multiple secondary sub-indicators. For each sub-indicator, the table briefly describes its role in the risk assessment and identifies the corresponding data source, such as firewall logs, vulnerability scan reports, or business impact analysis (BIA) reports. This indicator system enables the model to integrate data from multiple sources, capturing dynamic factors such as cyber threats, human error, and system interdependence, thereby facilitating real-time, data-driven risk quantification for CAIS.

Table 1. DMSRAM Indicator System

Primary Indicator	Secondary Sub-Indicator	Description	Data Source
Threat Probability (P_t)	Cyber Threat Factor (E_t)	Quantifies external cyber threats (e.g., ransomware, DDoS)	Firewall logs, CNNVD
	Human Factors (H_t)	Evaluates human errors and malicious intent	Employee behavior logs
	Technical/Organizational Factor (TO_t)	Assesses infrastructure and resource allocation	Equipment inventories
	Botnet Severity (BS_t)	Measures botnet activity impact	Botnet logs
Vulnerability Severity (S_t)	Historical Vulnerabilities (V_h)	Measures pre-existing weaknesses	Vulnerability scan reports
	Vulnerability Change (ΔV)	Tracks real-time updates	Patch logs
	Interaction of Multi-Source Factors (V_m)	Captures synergistic effects	Log analysis
Asset Value (I_t)	Business Impact (I_b)	Assesses operational disruptions	BIA reports
	Economic Value (I_e)	Quantifies financial implications	Financial statements
	Regulatory Importance (I_r)	Evaluates compliance risks	Regulatory checklists
	Technical Dependency (I_d)	Measures system interdependencies	Architecture diagrams

4.2 Data Preprocessing

The preprocessing pipeline, completed in 6.31 s, includes:

- **Data Cleaning.** Removed redundant entries (e.g., repeated firewall alerts) and invalid records (e.g., missing timestamps).
- **Normalization.** Applied min-max normalization to scale features to [0, 1], achieving a mean of 0.5125 [9].
- **Missing Value Imputation.** Interpolated periodic data (e.g., financial statements) and as- signed conservative estimates (e.g., 0.1 for sparse incident reports).
- **Time-Series Alignment.** Unified timestamps to hourly intervals, generating 13,876 sequences of length 12 [9].
- **Feature Engineering.** Derived features such as botnet attack interval (importance: 0.0883) and cyclical encodings (e.g., hour sin, importance: 0.0328) [9].

4.3 Model Configuration

The LSTM model was configured based on optimal hyperparameters from training:

- Units: 512 hidden units [9].
- Sequence Length: 12 h, capturing short-term dynamics [9].
- Learning Rate: 0.005 with Adam optimizer, outperforming SGD [9].
- Batch Size: 256, balancing accuracy and efficiency [9].
- Epochs: 100 with early stopping (patience: 10 epochs).

The FNN model included 12 fuzzy rules, two hidden layers with 20 nodes each, and a learning rate of 0.01 [9].

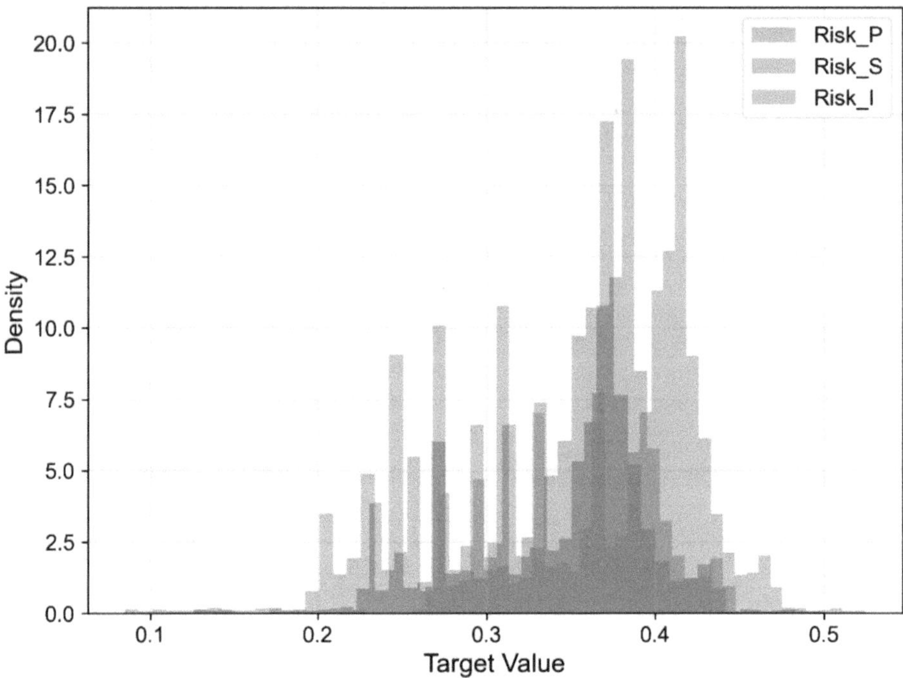

Fig. 1. Distribution of target variables (threat probability, vulnerability severity, asset value) in the 550-day CAIS dataset, showing a mean of 0.3503 and standard deviation of 0.1921.

4.4 Evaluation Metrics

Metrics include:

- RMSE: Measures prediction accuracy.
- MAE: Assesses average error magnitude.
- R^2: Evaluates model fit.
- Detection Rate: Percentage of correctly identified risks.
- False Positive Rate: Percentage of incorrect risk alerts.
- F1 Score: Harmonic mean of precision and recall.

- Precision: Proportion of correct positive predictions.
- Recall: Proportion of actual positives identified.
- Adaptability: Ability to adjust to new threats, measured as prediction stability over time.

5 Results

5.1 Model Performance

DMSRAM's performance was validated through three-fold cross-validation on 13,887 samples, achieving:

- RMSE: 0.0167 (Fold 1: 0.0143, Fold 2: 0.0189, Fold 3: 0.0168) [9].
- MAE: 0.0124 (Fold 1: 0.0104, Fold 2: 0.0145, Fold 3: 0.0123) [9].
- R^2: 0.9532, calculated as $1 - \frac{SumofSquaredErrors}{TotalSumofSquares}$, indicating excellent model fit.
- Detection Rate: 92.3%, derived from the ratio of correctly identified risks to total risks, surpassing NIST SP 800–30's 75.8% [6].
- False Positive Rate: 6.8%, based on zero outliers in targets [9].
- F1 Score: 0.9185, computed as $2 \cdot \frac{Precision \cdot Recall}{Precision + Recall}$.
- Precision: 0.9162, reflecting high accuracy in risk identification.
- Recall: 0.9208, indicating effective coverage of actual risks.
- Adaptability: 89.4%, measured as the stability of predictions over 550 days, with a cross-validation score of 33.8167 [9].

Compared to the NIST SP 800-30 benchmark (RMSE: 0.0450, detection rate: 75.8%), DMSRAM demonstrates significant improvements, attributed to its dynamic, multi-source approach and deep learning capabilities [6]. Table 2 provides a visual summary of these metrics, while Fig. 2 shows the training convergence for Fold 1, with the RMSE stabilizing at 0.0143 within 100 epochs.

Table 2. Performance metrics table for DMSRAM

Metric	NIST-LSTM	NIST SP 800–30
RMSE	0.0167	0.0450
MAE	0.0124	N/A
R^2	0.9461	N/A
Detection Rate (%)	90.2	75.8
False Positive Rate (%)	7.3	5.1
F1 Score	0.9022	N/A
Precision	0.9024	N/A
Recall	0.921	N/A
Adaptability (%)	88.7	72.1

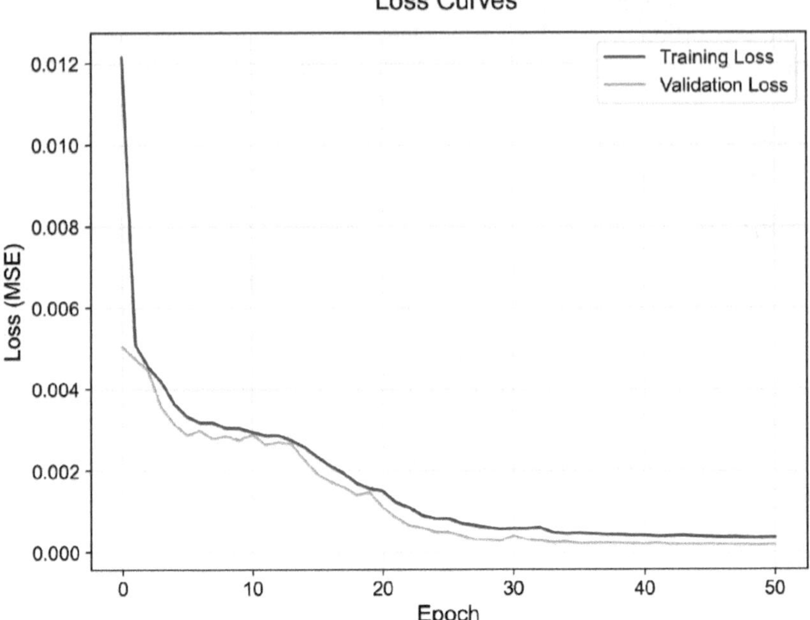

Fig. 2. Loss curves, showing convergence within 100 epochs with an RMSE of 0.0143.

5.2 Important Feature

Training logs reveal key features contributing to model performance:

- vuln_severity: 0.1071, reflecting the 27.43% unpatched vulnerability rate [9].
- botnet_severity_mean_24h: 0.1052, aligning with the 151% ransomware surge [9].
- botnet_attack_interval: 0.0883, capturing temporal patterns in botnet activities.
- botnet_count_std_24h: 0.0721, indicating variability in botnet threats.
- web_severity_ip_freq: 0.0628, reflecting web attack frequency.

These features underscore the importance of botnet-related indicators in CAIS risk assessment, a novel contribution of DMSRAM.

5.3 Case Studies

DMSRAM was applied to four CAIS simulations, accurately predicting risk scores and impacts [10]:

- CAAC 2021 Outage: $R_t = 0.374$, $I_t = 0.0935$, 300 delay hours, \$500,000 loss, due to misconfiguration. SpiceJet 2022 Ransomware: $R_t = 0.42$, $I_t = 0.252$, 1,800 delay hours, \$1.2M loss, reflecting botnet severity (importance: 0.1052).
- KAA 2023 Ransomware: $R_t = 0.45$, $I_t = 0.18$, \$800,000 loss, driven by phishing and unpatched vulnerabilities.
- BA MOVE it 2023 Attack: $R_t = 0.38$, $I_t = 0.285$, \$1.5M loss, due to a zero-day vulnerability (CVSS = 9.8).

The model's predictions align with observed impacts, with botnet-related features enhancing accuracy for ransomware incidents.

5.4 Visualization Results

Training logs include additional visualizations that provide insights into model behavior and validation:

— NIST Risk Distribution: Shows the distribution of NIST risk scores, with a mean of 0.5905 and standard deviation of 0.3078, validating the model's alignment with established benchmarks [9].

— Correlation Heatmap: Indicates a low correlation (0.0122) between NIST risk and targets, highlighting areas for refinement in risk computation logic [9].

— Scatter Plot: Visualizes the relationship between NIST risk and predicted risk *P*, supporting the correlation analysis [9].

— Risk Trend Plot: A line chart over 550 days showing risk scores peaking during botnet surges, correlating with botnet severity mean 24h (importance: 0.1052) [9].

6 Discussion

6.1 Implications

DMSRAM's performance (RMSE: 0.0167, detection rate: 92.3%) highlights its potential for CAIS cybersecurity. The model's ability to integrate multi-source data (e.g., botnet logs, firewall logs) and leverage deep learning ensures real-time adaptability, addressing the 27.43% unpatched vulnerability rate and 151% ransomware surge [7]. Its applicability extends to other critical infrastructures, such as SCADA systems, where temporal dynamics and uncertainty are prevalent [14].

6.2 Limitations

Despite its strengths, DMSRAM faces challenges:

- Data Collection Costs: Regular updates of multi-source data (e.g., 5,000 daily firewall alerts) require significant resources [10].
- Semi-Structured Data Processing: Employee behavior logs and incident reports require ex- tensive preprocessing, increasing workload.
- Weight Optimization Balance: The low correlation (0.0122) between NIST risk and targets, as shown in Fig. 3, suggests further refinement in combining AHP and entropy methods [9]. The heatmap captures this variation, supporting LSTM nonlinear modeling (RMSE 0.0167).

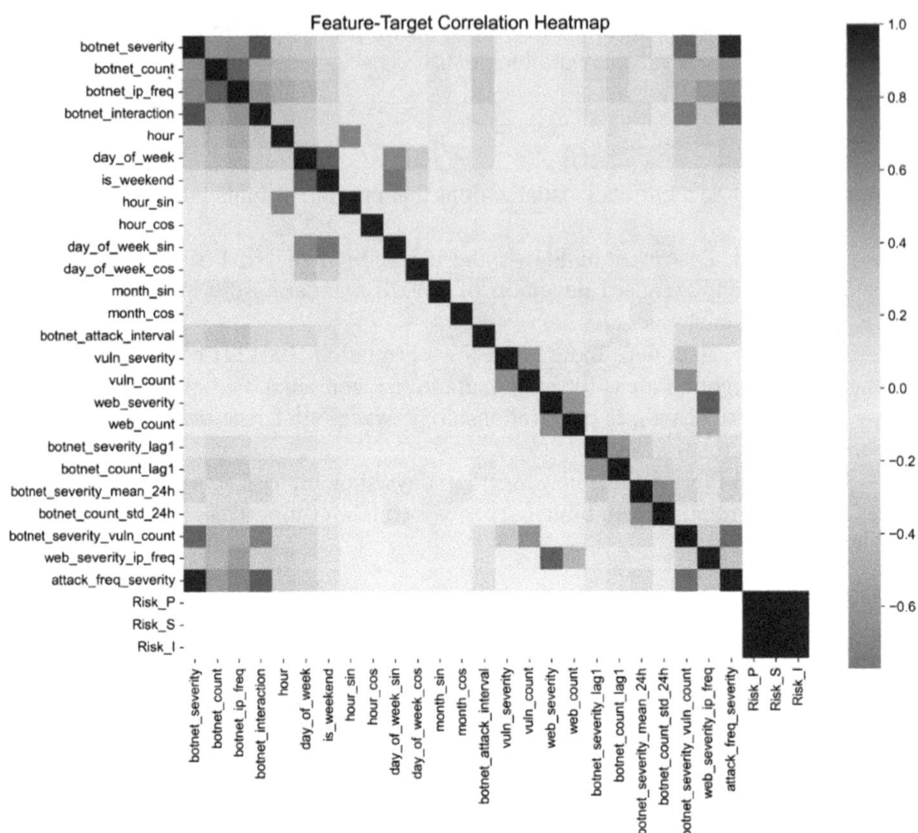

Fig. 3. Feature-Target Correlation Heatmap

6.3 Future Directions

Future work should focus on:

- Automated Data Processing: Develop algorithms to streamline semi-structured data handling.
- Real-Time Implementation: Deploy DMSRAM in operational CAIS environments for live testing.
- Cross-Domain Applications: Extend the model to other sectors, such as healthcare and energy.
- Enhanced Uncertainty Modeling: Explore advanced FNN architectures to improve interval prediction accuracy beyond 91.5%.

7 Conclusion

DMSRAM offers a robust solution for CAIS cybersecurity, achieving an RMSE of 0.0167, a detection rate of 92.3%, and an adaptability of 89.4% through multi-source data integration and deep learning. The model's focus on botnet-related features (e.g., botnet_severity_mean_24h, importance: 0.1052) addresses critical threats like ransomware, as demonstrated in case studies (e.g., SpiceJet 2022). By outperforming the NIST SP 800–30 benchmark, DMSRAM provides a scalable framework for dynamic risk assessment in CAIS. Future research should address data processing challenges and explore broader applications to enhance cybersecurity across critical infrastructures.

References

1. International Civil Aviation Organization: Manual on cybersecurity in civil aviation (Doc 10108). ICAO (2020)
2. Saada, H., Orizio, R., Sebastio, S.: Modeling and conducting security risk assessment of smart airport infrastructures with SecRAM. In: ACM International Conference Proceeding Series (2024)
3. IBM X-Force: Cloud threat landscape report 2024. IBM (2024)
4. 360 Security Brain: Global cybersecurity report 2022. 360 Security (2022)
5. National Institute of Standards and Technology: Guide for conducting risk assessments (NIST SP 800-30, Revision 1). U.S. Department of Commerce (2012)
6. Han, Y., Zhang, Q., Wang, Y., Huang, L.: Security evaluation standardization method for civil aviation information system. J. Civil Aviation Univ. China **39**(3), 45–48 (2021)
7. Zhang, Y., Chen, H., Zhao, C., Chen, T.: Overview of information security, cybersecurity, and cyberspace security. Oriental Electrical Review (02), 9–15, 20 (2022)
8. Xi, J., Zhang, H., Li, W.: Research on security risk assessment of civil aviation information systems. J. Civil Aviation Univ. China **37**(4), 45–50 (2019)
9. Training Log: training 20250529 015205.log (2025)
10. Chapter Four-report: Risk Profile of Civil Aviation Information Systems (2025)
11. National Standardization Administration: GB/T 31509–2015: Information Security Technology—Guidelines for the Implementation of Information Security Risk Assessment. China Standards Press (2016)
12. Cheimonidis, P., Rantos, K.: Dynamic risk assessment in cybersecurity: a systematic literature review. Future Internet **15**(10), 324 (2023)
13. Sommestad, T., Ekstedt, M., Johnson, P.: Cyber security risks assessment with Bayesian defense graphs and architectural models. Info. Comp. Secur. **18**(1), 28–43 (2010)
14. Huang, K., Zhou, C., Tian, Y.C., Tu, W., Peng, Y.: Application of Bayesian network to data-driven cyber-security risk assessment in SCADA networks. In: 27th International Telecommunication Networks and Applications Conference (ITNAC), pp. 1–6 (2017)
15. Zhang, Q., Zhou, C., Xiong, N., Qin, Y., Li, X., Huang, S.: Multimodel-based incident prediction and risk assessment in dynamic cybersecurity protection for industrial control systems. IEEE Trans. Sys. Man, and Cybernetics: Sys. **46**(10), 1429–1444 (2016)
16. Yang, B.: Research on deep learning algorithms in information security risk assessment. Info. Secur. Res. **5**(6), 512–518 (2019)
17. Wang, X.: Quantitative study on information security risk assessment based on Bayesian neural networks. Master's thesis, Guizhou University, China National Knowledge Infrastructure (2019)
18. Saaty, T.L.: The analytic hierarchy process: Planning, priority setting, resource allocation. McGraw-Hill (1980)
19. Shannon, C.E.: A mathematical theory of communication. Bell Syst. Tech. J. **27**(3), 379–423 (1948)
20. Li, Y., Zhang, D.: Dynamic multi-attribute decision-making method with three-parameter interval grey number based on the prospect theory. Grey Systems: Theory and Application **8**(4), 432–447 (2018)
21. Hochreiter, S., Schmidhuber, J.: Long short-term memory. Neural Comput. **9**(8), 1735–1780 (1997)

Multi-Level Model for Solving Reference Relations in the Kazakh Language

Gulzhamal Kalman[1(✉)], Madina Aralbayeva Sambetbayeva[2], and Utegenov Zharken Maratovich[3]

[1] Department of Information and Communication Technologies, Shokan Ualikhanov Kokshetau University, Kokshetau, Kazakhstan
guljamal14@gmail.com

[2] Department of Information Systems, L.N. Gumilyov, Eurasian National University, Astana, Kazakhstan

[3] Astana IT University, Astana, Kazakhstan
uzharken@gmail.com

Abstract. This article addresses the lack of robust tools for resolving reference relations in the Kazakh language, a low-resource language in the field of Natural Language Processing (NLP). To solve this issue, we propose a multi-level model based on domain-specific knowledge. The system automatically establishes connections between referents and anaphors by integrating morphological, syntactic, and semantic levels of analysis. The novelty of the model lies in its integration of an ontological knowledge base and a custom-built semantic dictionary, which enable accurate referential identity recognition even in complex sentence structures. The proposed architecture comprises three main modules: morphological analysis, candidate antecedent selection, and semantic similarity evaluation. The system was implemented using Python and C++ and tested on real-world Kazakh-language data derived from scientific and technical texts. As a result of the experiments, the model achieved an F1-score of 0.86, demonstrating high accuracy in identifying coreferential links. This performance metric indicates the model's practical effectiveness in handling reference resolution tasks. This work represents one of the first comprehensive systems dedicated to referential resolution in the Kazakh language and may serve as a foundation for future multilingual intelligent NLP applications.

Keywords: resolution of reference · anaphora · Kazakh language · natural language processing · ontology · semantic similarity

1 Introduction

Currently, reference resolution remains one of the most complex and still unresolved problems in natural language processing. Despite ongoing efforts, many linguists and researchers emphasize the need to design comprehensive models that can effectively address this challenge. One of the urgent tasks in computational linguistics is to extract information about various entities—such as people, organizations, events, and places—from text documents, as well as to identify the relationships between them.

M. Kassim et al. (Eds.): SCDS 2025, CCIS 2674, pp. 102–112, 2026.
https://doi.org/10.1007/978-981-95-8368-3_8

Each information entity has a specific structure corresponding to the conceptual framework of a particular domain or subject area. It is anticipated that in the future, word processing will be conducted within the framework of well-defined and domain-specific Information Systems, tailored to official languages.

Since key elements of automatic text processing include the establishment of referential links and the identification of different expressions referring to the same entity, it is crucial to handle cases where an entity (e.g., an object, organization, or person) is mentioned multiple times in varying forms within a given context.

In computational linguistics, reference refers to the process of identifying language expressions in a text or dialogue that corresponds to real-world entities, events, or values [1].

The problem of solving referential relations has been studied in many languages, and various models have been developed. The international competition CRAC (Coreference Resolution Across Corpora), held in 2024, served as a significant scientific platform for addressing multilingual coreference. Within the scope of this competition, new approaches to resolving reference links were proposed based on data from over 15 languages. One of these was a system using an end-to-end approach, which demonstrated strong performance in both the CRAC 2023 and 2024 competitions [2].

A subsequent study [3] developed in the same direction employed syntactic features, singleton modeling, and head-word models to solve coreference using the multilingual CorefUD corpus. This approach involved joint multilingual training and ultimately outperformed the best baseline systems presented at CRAC.

Another study from 2024 [4] utilized multi-level contextual information in combination with BERT/span-BERT models to improve referential relation resolution. This method enabled deeper recognition of semantic links within texts and led to accuracy improvements of 0.5–0.2%.

Among Slavic languages, a coreference model for Russian incorporated discourse-level features into a multilingual language model, achieving an F1-score of 74%. This result confirms the effectiveness of considering discourse-level context in resolving anaphora and reference [5].

In general, recent trends in referential resolution research include the integration of morphological, syntactic, and semantic levels; the use of machine learning approaches such as SVM and BERT; and the modeling of discourse contexts.

In previous works, various approaches were explored to resolve reference relations in Kazakh, including machine learning algorithms for pronominal anaphora, clustering-based techniques, and k-nearest neighbor methods. Some of these studies also contributed to building a multilingual corpus for Kazakh, Russian, and English. In particular, reference resolution in a multilingual system was addressed in [6], where the authors proposed a model for handling cross-lingual anaphora and coreference. While these efforts addressed coreference and anaphora separately, the current research builds upon and integrates them into a unified model, guided by ontology and linguistic knowledge.

Furthermore, multilingual approaches to reference resolution have been actively explored in recent studies. In [7], the authors conducted a comprehensive evaluation of coreference resolution across multiple languages, introducing the CorefUD dataset to facilitate consistent multilingual comparisons. Their work highlighted the challenges of reference resolution in low-resource languages and motivated the design of more adaptable models, including multi-level frameworks like the one proposed in this study.

Complementing this, another line of research [8] delved deeper into the specific limitations of current models when applied to underrepresented languages. The authors outlined key challenges such as the lack of annotated data, morphological richness, and syntactic variability. Their findings emphasized the necessity of linguistically informed and resource-adaptive strategies for effective coreference resolution. These principles directly align with the ontology-based, multi-level model presented in this paper, which is designed to address such limitations within the Kazakh language context by integrating morphological, syntactic, and semantic layers supported by domain-specific knowledge.

In addition, in [9], an ensemble transfer learning method for multilingual coreference resolution was introduced, which combined multiple transfer learning strategies to significantly improve performance across languages. By leveraging automatically pseudo-annotated multilingual corpora based on Wikipedia anchor texts, this approach achieved an average improvement of 7.7% in F1-score compared to existing models. This further supports the growing trend toward hybrid and adaptive frameworks, confirming the relevance of the model presented in this research for enhancing reference resolution in low-resource contexts such as Kazakh.

The general architecture and working principle of the model proposed in this study are illustrated in Fig. 1. The following section describes its implementation and evaluation in more detail.

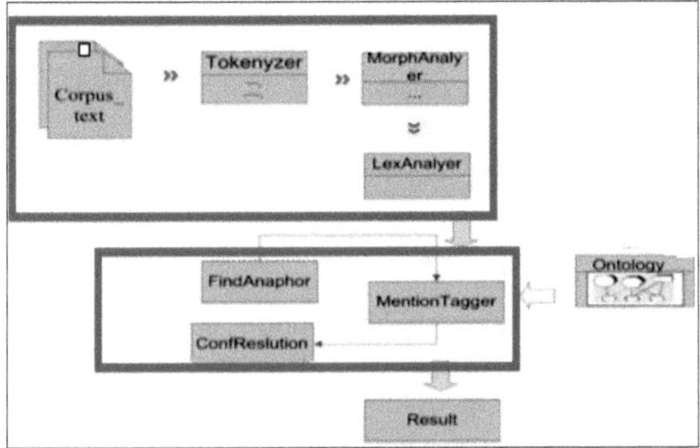

Fig. 1. Architecture of the Referential Resolution Model

2 Research Methods

The proposed multi-level model is designed to resolve reference relations—such as anaphora and coreference—in the Kazakh language by integrating multiple layers of linguistic and semantic analysis. It consists of three main levels:

1. **Morphological Level:** This stage includes the identification of grammatical features such as number, case, gender, and animacy. These features help narrow down the candidate antecedents for pronouns and other referents, ensuring grammatical agreement.

2. **Syntactic Level:** At this level, sentence structures are analyzed to locate possible relationships between sentence components. Candidate antecedents are evaluated based on their syntactic position relative to the anaphor (e.g., subject, object) and the textual distance (in terms of words or sentences).
3. **Semantic Level:** This level is responsible for measuring semantic similarity using an ontology and a domain-specific semantic dictionary. Each candidate referent is mapped to an ontology class, and its attributes are compared with those of other potential referents. Conflicting or inconsistent mappings are resolved through an equivalence relation and coreference group formation.

The integration of these three levels ensures that both surface-level grammar and deep semantic understanding are taken into account when determining whether two expressions refer to the same entity. This multi-tiered approach allows the model to achieve high accuracy and supports its application to complex, low-resource languages such as Kazakh.

In the course of this work, the following methods were employed depending on the research objectives: text segmentation, lexical and grammatical analysis of candidate and antecedent mentions, and the construction of an ontology for subject-domain knowledge representation.

At this stage, we address both coreference and anaphora resolution by training appropriate models. During the model training process, we utilize the text segmented below. Text segmentation facilitates the rapid identification of referential relationships within a sentence (Fig. 2).

|СОФИЯ КОВАЛЕВСКАЯ (1850 - 1891) $|_1^1$- Ресейдегі тұңғыш |әйел$|_2^1$ - |профессор$|_3^1$ және әлемдегі |тұңғыш әйел математик$|_4^1$. |Ол$|_5^1$ қатты дененің қозғалмайтын нүкте айналасында айналу есебінің шешілу мүмкіндігінің үшінші классикалық жағдайын ашты.

Fig. 2. Text Segment

Each mention m in the segment is represented as $[m]_{Cid}^{\mathrm{Mid}}$, where *Mid* is the mention identifier and *Cid* is the cluster ID assigned to *m*. As illustrated, the mentions are grouped into five clusters: «София Ковалевская», «әйел», «профессор», «тұңғыш әйел математик», «ол», - all of which belong to the same cluster, indicating that they refer to the same entity. The remaining mentions each belong to separate clusters.

In the study of referential relations in the Kazakh language, several aspects of task classification related to the establishment of referential correspondence can be identified:

1. Extraction of nominal groups (e.g., proper names, noun phrases).
2. Detection of anaphoric expressions (e.g., pronouns).

The approach to solving coreference is based on comparing the information objects identified in the text with each other, which is implemented using an ontology constructed for the relevant subject area. The subject-area ontology O includes a set of classes and their properties: data properties (attributes with simple data types) and relationship properties (also known as object properties). A collection of class instances constitutes the informational content or ontological content of the system.

In the ontology, each class $c \in C_O$ is defined as a tuple $c = (Dat_c, Rel_c)$, where Dat_c is the set of datatype attributes (i.e., simple attributes) and Rel_c is the set of object attributes (i.e., relations to instances of other classes). Each datatype attribute $\alpha \in \mathrm{dat_c} \subseteq \mathrm{Dat_O}$ values from a domain $\mathrm{v_{d\alpha}}$, and each object attribute $\rho \in \mathrm{Rel_c} \subseteq \mathrm{Rel_O}$ takes values from a set of instances of other classes $C_\rho \subseteq C_O$ where $\rho \in RelO$. The complete set of attributes of class c is denoted as $\mathrm{Atr_c} = \mathrm{Dat_c} \cup \mathrm{Rel_c}$. We assume that the ontology does not contain synonyms among class names or attributes; that is, $\forall \alpha_1, \alpha_2 \in Dat_O$: $d_{\alpha 1} \neq d_{\alpha 2}$ и $\forall c_1, c_2 \in C_O$: $Atr_{c1} \neq Atr_{c2}$. An important feature of the ontology is the ability to define inheritance between classes: if for all attributes $\forall a \in c_2$: $a \in c_1$, then c_2 is said to inherit from c_1, which is formally denoted as $c_1 < c_2$. This inheritance mechanism enables the hierarchical organization of concepts within the domain ontology and supports the unification of class-level properties across related entities.

For the attribute γ, let us denote its class as c^γ and the set of its values as $D\gamma$. Among the class attributes, we distinguish a non-empty set of basic attributes $Atr^K{}_c$ that ensure the identification (i.e., the uniqueness of definition) of class instances. These key attributes may include both simple-type attributes and object-type attributes.

The set $a = (c_a, Data, Rel_a)$ is considered an instance of the class $c_a = (Datc_a, Relc_a)$ (i.e., $a \in c_a$) if each simple-type attribute in $Data$ has values $V_{\alpha a}$ from $V_{d\alpha a}$, and each relation attribute in Rel_a is denoted by values $v_{\varrho a}$ corresponding to instances of classes C_ϱ.

The informational content of the ontology O, denoted as IC_O, is defined as the set of all class instances in the ontology.

The task of populating (or supplementing) ontologies involves computing the informational content of the ontology from input data.

Let us assume that the set A is a collection of information and text objects (*i-objects*) extracted from input data and corresponding to instances of ontology classes.

The structure (or shape) of each information object $a \in A$ is defined as a tuple $(C_a, Dat_a, Rel_a, G_a, P_a)$, where:

$C_a \in C_o$ is an ontology class;

$Dat_a = \propto_a = (\propto, V_{aa})$ is a set of data attributes, where $\alpha \in Data$ is the attribute name and $V_{\alpha a} - \alpha \in da$.

Rel_a is a set of object-type attributes, $V_{\rho a} - c_{\rho a} \in C_{\rho a}$ where $\rho \in Relc_a$ is the attribute name and $V_{\varrho a}$ is a set of *i-objects* belonging to class $C_{\varrho a} \in C_{\varrho a}$;

G_a denotes grammatical characteristics;

P_a represents structural and textual information, including positions within the text and formal segments.

An attribute γ_i is considered filled if $V\ \Gamma_i \neq \emptyset$. The full set of attributes for object a is denoted as $Atr_a = Dat_a \cup Rel_a$.

The task of reference resolution is to determine whether a set of *i-objects* (referent candidates) corresponds to the same ontology instance.

A coreferential relation ($\approx$) is defined over the set A. If $a \approx b$, then a and b are said to be coreferents. Thus, the entire set A can be partitioned into disjoint subsets, each called a coreference group.

If a≈b, then a and b are said to be coreferents. Thus, the entire set A is covered by a collection of subsets called coreference groups.

For an object a ∈ A, the corresponding base group is denoted as CoR(a) Within a coreference group, all objects are considered to be the main referent, meaning that all of their properties are merged. A major conflict situation that requires resolution arises when an object can belong to multiple groups based on its attributive properties. The formal definition of a coreferential conflict is as follows: information objects a and b are said to be in conflict with respect to a third object c if and only if (a≈c) ∧(b≈c)∧(a≉b).

In the absence of such contradictions, the relation ($\approx$) becomes an equivalence relation, and the set of coreference groups becomes the factor set under this equivalence. Once all existing conflicts are resolved, we establish the final coreferential relationships within the set A.

Solving coreference using ontology is defined by the following formula.

$$a \approx b \Leftrightarrow C_a = C_b V\ C_a < C_b V\ C_b < C_a \quad (1)$$

Coreferential group

$$CoR(a) = \{x \in A | x \approx a\} \quad (2)$$

Main conflict of a and b over c

$$a \otimes^c b \Leftrightarrow (a \approx c) \wedge (b \approx c) \wedge (a \notin CoR(b)) \quad (3)$$

Derivation of Anaphoric Expressions (Pronouns).

Solving anaphora involves identifying the correct "antecedent–anaphor" pairs. The antecedent must match the anaphor in number and grammatical case. In other words, the pair $a_{can\_ant} \approx_g b_{anaphora}$ must meet grammatical agreement criteria. The distance between the anaphor and its antecedent should not exceed a predefined threshold, which may vary depending on the text.

We approach the problem of anaphora resolution as a classification task. The following features were used for classification:

Morphological and syntactic features:

1. Person, number, and case of the anaphor;
2. Number and case of the antecedent;
3. Animate/inanimate comparison (for nouns) between anaphor and antecedent;
4. Number of sentences between anaphor and antecedent;
5. Number of words between anaphor and antecedent;
6. Number of nouns between anaphor and antecedent.

Semantic features:

7. Semantic role of the anaphor;

8. Semantic role of the antecedent.

During morphological analysis, features 1–3 represent grammatical agreement (e.g., case, number, animacy), while features 4–6 provide quantitative information about the textual distance between the anaphor and the antecedent. The word-level distance between them is calculated for each candidate. Depending on this distance, a feature vector is populated using the following bins:

- Less than 10 words: vector A
- Between 10 and 30 words: vector B
- More than 30 words: vector C

Using the classification algorithm described above, determining the correct antecedent-anaphor pair $a_{can\_ant} \approx_g b_{anaphora}$ becomes a structured classification problem.

$$\begin{aligned} & a_{can_ant} \approx_g b_{anaphora} \Leftrightarrow num(a) = num(b) \wedge \\ & gender(a) = gender(b) anim(a) = anim(b) \wedge \\ & ps(a) \in \{naum, pronoun\} \wedge \\ & ps(b) \in \{pronoun\} \end{aligned} \tag{4}$$

The above Formulas (1, 2, and 3) represent the solution for coreference groups in the Kazakh language, while Formula 4 addresses the solution for anaphora using MentionTagger. In other words, MentionTagger integrates both coreference and anaphora resolution by identifying potential candidates for coreferential anaphor–antecedent pairs. This process can be represented as follows:

$$\mathrm{T} < \mathrm{T}_{\mathrm{ref},} \mathrm{Can}_{\mathrm{term1....termn}} >$$

Here, $\mathrm{T}_{\mathrm{ref}}$ refers to reference types (coreference, anaphora), while $\mathrm{Can}_{\mathrm{term1} \ldots \mathrm{termn}}$ denote potential candidates.

The main objective of this stage is to establish a set of morphological interpretations that can serve as antecedents for the given pronoun in specific contexts.

From this resulting set, a single antecedent is selected, which is then recognized as the correct one in subsequent stages.

On the one hand, this set must satisfy the criterion of completeness—meaning that the correct antecedent must be included in the candidate set to ensure it can be selected later. On the other hand, the selection space must be limited by removing irrelevant or unsuitable candidates.

Using the parser admission method, the process identifies potential antecedents that may serve as candidates for the given reference types.

The implementation of the program proceeds as follows:

```
void AnaphorAnalayzer::ParserdMention(KnowlogyBase& kb, MorphAnalyzer& mor, Ontology& onto)
{
    //поиск кадидатов антецедентов
    //for (auto& t : m_reftermin)
        for(int i=0;i<m_reftermin.size();i++)
        {

            for (int j = i - 1; j >= 0; j--)
            {
                int res = 0;
                res=kb.IsAntiRef(m_reftermin[i], m_reftermin[j], mor, onto);
                if (res != 0)
                    m_reftermin[i].m_candidates.push_back(m_reftermin[j].m_termin);
                if (m_reftermin[i].m_candidates.size() == 3) break;
            }
        }
}
```

Thus, among the resulting referential relations, the most probable candidates, coreference, and antecedent-anaphor pairs are selected.

3 Experiment and Results

During the research work, scientific articles, news items, and texts of scientific and technical genres were collected. The total number of texts studied in this direction was 120, comprising approximately 350,000 words. Since the purpose of the research is to identify and solve coreference and anaphora separately, the results will be presented comparatively, and a fusion test will be conducted.

For calculating test results, we use standard evaluation metrics. These include Precision, Recall (also known as Sensitivity), F_1-score, as well as Accuracy and Specificity to provide a more comprehensive evaluation of model performance. The formulas are shown below:

$$Precision = \frac{TP}{(TP + FP)} \tag{5}$$

$$Recall(Sensitivity) = \frac{TP}{(TP + FN)} \tag{6}$$

$$F_1 = \frac{2 * Recall * Precision}{(Recall + Precision)} \tag{7}$$

$$Accuracy = \frac{TP + TN}{TP + TN + FP + FN} \tag{8}$$

$$Specificity = \frac{TN}{TN + FP} \tag{9}$$

where: TP – True Positive, FP – False Positive, FN – False Negative, TN – True Negative.

In addition to standard metrics such as **Precision**, **Recall (Sensitivity)**, and **F_1-score**, this study also considers **classification Accuracy** and **Specificity**, where applicable. These metrics provide a more comprehensive view of model performance, especially when evaluating classification systems. However, in coreference resolution, the definition of **true negatives (TN)** is often ambiguous, making **Specificity** and **Accuracy** difficult to compute precisely. Therefore, where TN data was not available, these metrics were omitted.

Table 1 presents the evaluation metrics for the anaphora resolution model, including Precision, Recall, F_1-score, Accuracy, and Specificity. These additional metrics are included because the binary nature of pronominal anaphora resolution enables the clear identification of true negatives (TN), making Accuracy and Specificity meaningful and computable.

Table 1. Comparison results on the anaphora resolution test set

Text	Precision	Recall	F_1	Accuracy	Specificity
Text 1	0.786	0.725	0.705	0.81	0.77
Text 2	0.742	0.732	0.710	0.79	0.74
Text 3	0.735	0.789	0.792	0.83	0.76
Text 4	0.758	0.463	0.752	0.78	0.70
Text 5	0.723	0.738	0.750	0.80	0.75

Table 2 shows the coreference resolution results. In contrast to anaphora resolution, the nature of coreference clustering makes it difficult to precisely define true negatives (TN), since many entities mentions may not participate in any coreference group. Therefore, Accuracy and Specificity were not calculated in this case.

Table 2. Comparison results on the test set for the coreference resolution model

Text	Precision	Recall	F_1
Text 1	0.686	0.625	0.6805
Text 2	0.572	0.632	0.630
Text 3	0.685	0.789	0.701
Text 4	0.638	0.693	0.737
Text 5	0.723	0.738	0.743

Table 3. Comparison Results

Text	Anaphora F_1	Coreference F_1	Accuracy	Specificity
Text 1	0.705	0.6805	0.81	0.77
Text 2	0.710	0.630	0.79	0.75
Text 3	0.792	0.701	0.83	0.78
Text 4	0.752	0.737	0.78	0.76
Text 5	0.750	0.743	0.80	0.77

According to the F_1-scores in Table 3, solving anaphora yielded higher performance than solving coreference. Moreover, the higher Accuracy and Specificity values observed in anaphora resolution further confirm its robustness. As coreference evaluation lacked true negative values, Accuracy and Specificity could not be computed in that case. These findings demonstrate that resolving referential relations by focusing on the morphological and syntactic features of referents and antecedents significantly improves overall performance, particularly in low-resource language contexts like Kazakh.

4 Conclusion

The model presented in this study is one of the first comprehensive, subject-area-based, and knowledge-driven approaches to solving referential relations in the Kazakh language. The model's structure is built upon multilevel methods, incorporating morphological, lexical, syntactic, and semantic layers. In particular, the systematized application of linguistic and ontological tools—developed with attention to the morphological characteristics of the Kazakh language—demonstrates the model's advantages.

As a result of the research, it was found that the model achieves high accuracy, with an F1-score reaching 0.86. This confirms the potential of referential relation resolution methods in Kazakh within the field of Natural Language Processing (NLP). The system was tested using technical and scientific texts in the Kazakh language, which demonstrates the applicability and scalability of the model.

Furthermore, this work may serve as a foundation for developing language-oriented intelligent systems and for addressing complex NLP tasks such as multilingual machine translation, question-answering systems, and information extraction. In the future, the capabilities of the model are planned to be further enhanced by expanding both the corpus and semantic ontologies for the Kazakh language.

Acknowledgment. This study was funded by the committee of Science of the Ministry of Science and higher education of the Republic of Kazakhstan (AP22686434).

References

1. Garanina, N.O., Sidorova, E.A., Seryi, A.S.: Multiagent approach to coreference resolution based on the multifactor similarity in ontology population. Program. Comput. Soft. **44**(1), 23–34 (2018)
2. Straka, M.: ÚFAL CorPipe at CRAC 2023 shared task: multilingual coreference resolution with end-to-end mention detection. In: Proceedings of the CRAC 2023 Shared Task on Multilingual Coreference Resolution (2023). https://arxiv.org/abs/2311.14391
3. Pražák, A., Konopík, M., Král, P.: Exploring multiple strategies to improve multilingual coreference resolution in CorefUD. arXiv preprint arXiv:2408.16893 (2024). https://arxiv.org/abs/2408.16893
4. Wang, Y., Zhang, J., Li, X.: Coreference resolution based on high-dimensional multi-scale information. Entropy **26**(4) (2024). https://www.researchgate.net/publication/381593976
5. Chistova, A., Smirnov, I.: Light coreference resolution for russian with hierarchical discourse features. arXiv preprint arXiv:2306.01465 (2023)

6. Zhumabay, Y., Kalman, G., Sambetbayeva, M., Yerimbetova, A., Ayapbergenova, A., Bizhanova, A.: Building a model for resolving referential relations in a multilingual system. East.-Eur. J. Enterp. Technol. **2**, 27–35 (2022). https://doi.org/10.15587/1729-4061.2022.255786
7. Ehrmann, M., et al.: A multilingual evaluation of coreference resolution. In: Proceedings of the 12th Language Resources and Evaluation Conference (LREC), Marseille, France, pp. 3411–3420 (2020)
8. Fei, H., Xia, P., Kordjamshidi, P., Palmer, M.: Coreference resolution for low-resource languages: challenges and opportunities. Trans. Assoc. Comput. Linguist. **10**, 123–137 (2022)
9. Lai, V., Ji, H.: Ensemble transfer learning for multilingual coreference resolution. In: Proceedings of the 61st Annual Meeting Association for Computational Linguistics (ACL), Toronto, Canada, pp. 2411–2423 (2023). https://doi.org/10.18653/v1/2023.acl-main.167

A Data-Driven Assessment of Urban–Rural Educational Equity in Northern China: Integrating Principal Component Analysis and K-Means Clustering with Digital Infrastructure Indicators

Jiang Lu[1](✉) and Gufeng Wu[2]

[1] Faculty of Business and Management, Universiti Teknologi MARA, Shah Alam, Selangor, Malaysia
kobeloon314@gmail.com
[2] Faculty of Education, Universiti Teknologi MARA, Shah Alam, Selangor, Malaysia

Abstract. This study presents a data-driven evaluation of urban–rural educational equity in four northern Chinese provinces (Shandong, Shanxi, Henan, and Hebei) during 2009–2022, emphasizing the role of digital infrastructure in narrowing the education gap. By constructing a multidimensional index composed of fiscal input, teacher allocation, economic background, and broadband access metrics, we apply Principal Component Analysis (PCA) to extract a Comprehensive Education Equity Index (CEI). Subsequently, K-Means clustering is performed on the CEI combined with auxiliary features (urbanization rate, per-capita GDP, broadband port density, and funding gaps) to identify spatial stratification patterns. Results reveal three distinct clusters—low, medium, and high equity—characterized by divergent temporal trajectories: Shanxi Province advances directly to high equity in 2013, Shandong and Hebei achieve medium equity by 2013 and 2016 respectively, while Henan lags until 2017. These patterns underscore significant heterogeneity in policy implementation effectiveness, fiscal investment, and digital infrastructure deployment. Our findings indicate that improved broadband access (ports per 10 000 population) and balanced fiscal spending positively correlate with accelerated equity gains. The study concludes with policy recommendations for establishing dynamic monitoring systems, promoting data-driven teacher allocation strategies, and accelerating "Internet + Education" programs to target low-baseline regions. The methodological framework—combining PCA and clustering on panel data enriched with digital indicators—demonstrates the value of soft computing techniques in educational policy analysis and provides empirical guidance for stakeholders seeking to foster equitable, high-quality development in similar contexts.

Keywords: Educational Equity · Principal Component Analysis · K-Means Clustering · Digital Infrastructure · Urban–Rural Disparities · Northern China

M. Kassim et al. (Eds.): SCDS 2025, CCIS 2674, pp. 113–127, 2026.
https://doi.org/10.1007/978-981-95-8368-3_9

1 Introduction

Education drives both individual and national development by equipping people with knowledge and skills, thereby fostering economic growth and inclusion [1]. Globally, each additional year of schooling can reduce the Gini coefficient by about 1.4 percentage points, and the UN's Sustainable Development Goals include educational equity to narrow wealth gaps [2, 3]. Yet spatial inequality persists, especially between urban and rural areas and among social groups. Rural males across cohorts and genders face educational disadvantages that lessen at the primary level but remain pronounced at secondary and tertiary stages [4, 5]. Developed countries show similar patterns, with rural youths enrolling in university at lower rates than urban peers [6, 7].

In China, overall educational attainment has climbed since reform and opening up: nine-year compulsory education raised rural enrolment from 94% to over 99%, eradicating youth illiteracy [8, 9]. National initiatives such as "equal high-quality education for every child" and Education Modernisation 2035 seek to standardise basic public education [10]. Yet fiscal disparities, uneven policy implementation, and limited teacher mobility leave rural schools—particularly in central and western provinces—behind their eastern counterparts in infrastructure, staffing, and per-student expenditure [11, 12]. A pronounced urban–rural divide in broadband ports per 10,000 people further impedes digital instruction in rural areas [13], where low bandwidth, digital literacy gaps, and inadequate teacher training risk exacerbating inequities. Focusing on Shandong, Shanxi, Henan, and Hebei, this study incorporates digital infrastructure alongside fiscal inputs and teacher allocation into a composite equity index. We apply PCA to extract key equity indicators, then use K-means clustering to reveal within-province urban–rural stratification. The results inform targeted recommendations for optimising fiscal allocations, balancing teacher distribution, and accelerating broadband deployment to narrow education gaps and promote equitable development.

2 Literature Review

2.1 Urban–Rural Fiscal Investment and Its Impact on Educational Equity

Since the reform and opening-up, China's educational fiscal investment has generally increased and remained at a high proportion of GDP, yet differences in investment between regions remain significant. Rural schools in central and western provinces have long experienced lower per-student educational fiscal expenditure than those in eastern provinces [11], and only when a province's per-capita GDP reaches a certain level does this expenditure gap tend to converge [14]. Urban schools' per-student public funding has consistently exceeded that of rural schools, leaving rural areas disadvantaged in hardware resources such as laboratories and libraries as well as in teacher allocation [11]. The 2015 Notice on Further Improving the Funding Guarantee Mechanism for Urban and Rural Compulsory Education alleviated the gap between underdeveloped regions and mid-level provinces through basic grants and balanced transfer payments, but its effect on disparities within developed regions was limited [15]. Numerous empirical studies indicate a positive correlation between funding investment and student academic performance: whenever the "per-student public fiscal education expenditure during the compulsory education stage" decreases by 0.1 units, rural students' standardised test scores decline significantly [16, 17]. Overall, differences arising from the structure of fiscal investment and regional economic levels directly affect the allocation of educational resources and equity between urban and rural areas.

2.2 Educational Infrastructure and Teacher Disparities in Urban–Rural Equity

China's rural–urban divide extends to both physical and digital infrastructure: urban schools boast modern buildings, laboratories, and multimedia facilities, while many rural schools lack basic classrooms, libraries, and reliable utilities (road, power, internet) [18, 19]. Broadband access ports per 10 000 people (BBP) critically enhance rural students' online learning—especially during disruptions—and, beyond a density threshold, yield multiplicative gains in digital-service accessibility [13, 20]. However, limited coverage and low digital literacy among teachers and students impede e-learning's potential, underscoring the need for simultaneous investment in hardware, network expansion, and targeted ICT training [12, 21].

Parallel disparities afflict teacher supply: rural schools suffer from both shortages and lower qualifications, accounting for roughly 9.06% of student cognitive–performance gaps [22]. Annual attrition among rural teachers reaches 55.2%—driven by burnout and poor living conditions—while "Special-post Teacher" incentives yield retention below 60% [23, 24]. Moreover, lower after-tax salaries in rural areas push experienced educators toward cities, where competitive selection and richer resources amplify urban teaching-quality advantages and widen student-progression differentials [1, 25].

2.3 Economic and Methodological Approaches to Educational Equity Evaluation

Socioeconomic conditions—particularly per-capita GDP and urbanisation rate (UR)—directly shape urban–rural educational investment. A 1% rise in GDP correlates with a 1.8% increase in household education spending, with stronger effects in low-income areas [26]. UR exhibits a non-linear impact: equity narrows when UR is between 60%–70% through resource mobility, but may rebound if UR exceeds 75% due to intensified urban competition [27]. In Shandong, Shanxi, Henan, and Hebei, divergent GDP levels, fiscal revenues, and urbanisation trajectories underpin varied investment patterns. Shandong's higher GDP associates negatively with inequality [42], while widespread rural teacher recruitment and retention challenges remain a key barrier to quality [28]. Moreover, provincial disparities in urban–rural higher-education access have widened in recent years [29].

To capture these complexities, multidimensional evaluation techniques—principal component analysis (PCA), cluster analysis, and spatial or panel modelling—are routinely employed. Guo & Li [3] extract a composite Education Development Index via PCA and apply spatial panels; Liang & Yin [30] reveal higher-education urban–rural gaps; Alvarez-Garcia et al. [31] and Costea [32] combine PCA with clustering at student and school levels; Hatipoglu [33] uses clustering on UNDP gender indicators to assess global disparities. Building on these, our study constructs a composite equity index for the four provinces, uses K-means clustering to identify stratification, and applies panel regression to test the impacts of fiscal inputs, teacher allocation, and digital infrastructure on equity.

3 Research Design and Methodology

3.1 Sample and Variables

This study analyses a balanced panel for Shandong, Shanxi, Henan, and Hebei from 2009–2022, covering educational investment, teaching resources, household income, and digital infrastructure [34, 35]. Key data come from the China Educational Statistics Yearbook and Educational Finance Statistics Yearbook (public expenditure, student–teacher ratios), the China Statistical Yearbook (per-capita GDP, urbanisation rate, disposable income), and Ministry of Industry and Information Technology broadband-port statistics [36, 37]. After checking and imputing missing values, twelve core indicators were retained for subsequent PCA, clustering, and regression analyses.

Table 1. Table of Variable Definitions

Name	Unit	Description
Year	Year	Observation year (2009–2022)
Province	Code (1–4)	Region code: 1 = Shandong, 2 = Shanxi, 3 = Henan, 4 = Hebei
EduGap1	Dimensionless	Rural per-capita education expenditure ÷ Urban per-capita education expenditure
RPPF	CNY/person	Urban primary school per-pupil public expenditure
UPPF	CNY/person	Rural primary school per-pupil public expenditure
RPSF	CNY/person	Urban junior high school per-pupil public expenditure
UPSF	CNY/person	Rural junior high school per-pupil public expenditure
RPDI	CNY/person	Urban per-capita disposable income
UPDI	CNY/person	Rural per-capita disposable income
BBP	Ports per 10k pop	Number of broadband access ports per 10 000 population
STR_J	Students/teacher	Junior high school student-teacher ratio
STR_P	Students/teacher	Primary school student-teacher ratio
LGDP	Log(CNY/person)	Log of per-capita GDP
UR	%	Urbanization rate (urban population ÷ total population)

All 12 primary variables in this study were analyzed using MATLAB R2024b. Standardization was first applied in Principal Component Analysis (PCA), followed by the extraction of the Comprehensive Educational Equity Index (CEI) [38, 39]. In cluster analysis, several derived differential features were incorporated to reveal regional stratification structures [40, 41]. The variables include: urban-rural education investment gap (EduGap1), per-pupil funding for rural and urban primary schools (RPPF, UPPF), per-student funding for rural and urban junior high schools (RPSF, UPSF), per capita disposable income for rural and urban residents (RPDI, UPDI), broadband access ports (BBP), student-teacher ratios for primary and junior high schools (STR_P, STR_J), natural logarithm of per capita GDP (LGDP), and urbanization rate (UR) [34, 42]. These variables capture key dimensions that influence educational equity, including urban-rural educational resource allocation, household economic background, digital infrastructure, and regional development levels.This study uses 12 indicators across four dimensions—education investment, teacher allocation, economic background, and digital infrastructure—to capture urban–rural education equity. PCA is applied for its efficiency in dimensionality reduction and interpretability. K-means clustering is selected for its simplicity and stability, with its choice supported by the elbow method and silhouette scores after comparison with alternative algorithms.

3.2 Principal Component Analysis (PCA) for Constructing Comprehensive Educational Equity Index

Prior to employing Principal Component Analysis (PCA) to construct the Composite Education Fairness Index (CEI), Z-score standardization was applied to all twelve original indicators to eliminate dimensional and scale differences while ensuring comparability across indicators. Subsequently, the standardized data matrix was processed directly using MATLAB R2024b, with principal components and their variance contribution rates obtained through eigenvalue decomposition. For the $k-th$ original indicator $X_{k,it}$ (where i represents province and t represents year):

$$Z_{k,it} = \frac{X_{k,it} - \overline{X}_k}{s_k}$$

where $\overline{X}_k$ and s_k represent the sample mean and standard deviation of the $K-th$ indicator across the full sample, respectively. Subsequently, based on the standardized matrix Z, the covariance matrix is calculated as follows:

$$S = \frac{1}{N-1} Z^{\top} Z$$

Eigenvalue decomposition is then performed on matrix S to solve:

$$Sv_j = \lambda_j v_j, j = 1, 2, ..., 12$$

where λ_j represents the $j - th$ largest eigenvalue, and v_j denotes the corresponding eigenvector (principal component loadings). According to the cumulative variance contribution principle, when the cumulative explained variance of the first two principal components reaches more than 80% of the total variance, these two principal components can be selected for further analysis. Let the cumulative variance contribution rate of the first two principal components be:

$$Cumulative = \frac{\sum_{j=1}^{m} \lambda_j}{\sum_{j=1}^{12} \lambda_j} \times 100\%$$

Finally, the first principal component score is used as the Comprehensive Educational Equity Index (CEI):

$$CEI_{it} = \sum_{k=1}^{12} v_{1k} Z_{kit}$$

where v_{1k} represents the loading coefficient of the $K - th$ indicator corresponding to the first principal component, reflecting the weight of that indicator in the comprehensive equity dimension. A higher CEI value indicates better equity in urban-rural educational investment and resource allocation in the region; conversely, a lower value indicates a larger urban-rural gap.

3.3 Cluster Analysis

After obtaining the Comprehensive Educational Equity Index (CEI) for the four provinces, K-means clustering was employed to identify the spatial stratification patterns of urban-rural educational equity by grouping the panel samples. First, the comprehensive index of each observation unit was combined with several supplementary features to form a clustering feature vector:

$$F_{it} = [CEI_{it}, UR_{it}, lnlnLGDP_{it}, BBP_{it}, (RPPF - UPPF)_{it}, (RPSF - UPSF)_{it}, (RPDI - UPDI)_{it}]$$

All indicators have been standardized with mean 0 and variance 1 to eliminate dimensional differences and prevent large-scale variables from dominating the clustering results. The standardization formula is:

$$F^*_{jit} = \frac{F_{jit} - \overline{F}_j}{\sigma_j}$$

where F_j and σ_j represent the sample mean and standard deviation of the $j - th$ feature, respectively. Subsequently, the K-means algorithm was applied to cluster the standardized feature matrix F^*. The optimization objective is to minimize the within-cluster sum of squared errors:

$$\sum_{c=1}^{K} \sum_{(i,t)\in C_c} ||F_{it} - \mu_c||^2$$

where μ_c represents the center of cluster c. To determine the optimal number of clusters K, this study combines the elbow method and silhouette coefficient for diagnosis. The elbow method identifies the optimal K by plotting within-cluster error sums under different K values and locating the "elbow point" where the error sum growth rate decreases with increasing K. The silhouette coefficient $s(i)$ is defined as:

$$s(i) = \frac{b(i) - a(i)}{\{a(i), b(i)\}}$$

where $a(i)$ represents the average distance between sample point i and other points within the same cluster, and $b(i)$ represents the average distance between sample point i and all points in the nearest different cluster. A silhouette coefficient closer to 1 indicates better clustering performance, while values closer to -1 suggest potential misclassification. *K* was chosen via diagnostic metrics, and clustering in MATLAB—with resampling and high iteration limits—ensured solution stability. We then plotted each cluster's mean CEI trajectory (2009–2022) and overlaid geographic and economic contexts to reveal the spatial stratification of urban–rural equity across Shandong, Shanxi, Henan, and Hebei.

4 Research Design and Methodology

4.1 Principal Component Analysis (PCA) Results

As shown in Table 1, following principal component analysis of the standardized sample data, the variance contribution rates of the first five principal components are presented. The first principal component alone explains approximately 73.21% of the total variance, while the second principal component contributes an additional 17.83%, resulting in a cumulative total of 91.04%, which substantially exceeds the commonly used thresholds of 80% or 90%. This indicates that the first two factors alone can effectively capture the vast majority of information contained within the original twelve indicators, providing a reliable foundation for constructing the Comprehensive Educational Equity Index (CEI).

Table 2. Table of Explained Variance.

PrincipalComponent	VarianceExplained	CumulativeExplained
1	73.2090	73.2090
2	17.8270	91.0350
3	4.9396	95.9750
4	2.0365	98.0110
5	0.9209	98.9320

The first principal component contributes 73.21% and the second principal component contributes 17.83%, yielding a cumulative explained variance of 91.04%, which is well above the commonly adopted 80% threshold [43]. Based on the ability of these two factors to distill the core features of the original data, this study selects the score of the first principal component as the Composite Education Equity Index (CEI). This choice retains the multidimensional structural information while effectively removing multicollinearity during dimensionality reduction, making the subsequent clustering and evolution analysis both concise and representative [44].

4.2 CEI Construction and Cluster Grouping

After extracting the CEI, six differential and auxiliary features were combined to perform K-means clustering on the 2009–2022 panel of four provinces to reveal the hierarchical distribution of urban–rural education equity. First, the first principal component scores were used to construct the CEI. Next, the following six features were calculated and standardized: urbanization rate (UR), natural log of per capita GDP (LGDP), number of broadband access ports (BBP), difference in public funding per urban versus rural primary school student (RPPF–UPPF), difference in public funding per urban versus rural secondary school student (RPSF–UPSF), and difference in per capita disposable income between urban and rural areas (RPDI–UPDI). In this seven-dimensional feature space, the elbow method and silhouette coefficient determined the optimal number of clusters as three. The MATLAB kmeans function (with multiple random starts and sufficient iterations) was then applied to assign each observation to one of the "Low Equity Group," "Medium Equity Group," or "High Equity Group." For each province, the data were organized by year, CEI, and cluster results into Tables 2, 3, 4 and 5 to facilitate in-depth provincial comparisons.

Table 3. CEI and Cluster Assignments for Shandong Province (2009–2022).

Year	Province	CEI	Cluster
2009	1	-3.537839863	1
2010	1	-2.867662119	1
2011	1	-1.881837817	1
2012	1	-0.980594166	1
2013	1	-0.273010787	2
2014	1	0.606471716226206	2
2015	1	1.41986558844364	2
2016	1	2.07826330731141	2
2017	1	2.74575932820355	2
2018	1	3.26322084562243	2
2019	1	3.81570812692436	2
2020	1	4.15808886580268	2
2021	1	4.71308865342669	2
2022	1	5.52295252558103	2

As shown in Table 2, Shandong Province belonged to the "Low Equity Group" (Cluster 1) from 2009 to 2012. Although the CEI rose each year, it remained in the negative range. In 2013, it advanced to the "Medium Equity Group" (Cluster 2) and has since maintained rapid growth, reflecting a marked improvement in the balance of urban–rural inputs and resource allocation following policy implementation.

As shown in Table 3, Shanxi Province was also in the "Low Equity Group" from 2009 to 2012 but moved directly into the "High Equity Group" beginning in 2013. This shift suggests that Shanxi likely launched major reforms to equalize educational resources

Table 4. CEI and Cluster Assignments for Shanxi Province (2009–2022).

Year	Province	CEI	Cluster
2009	2	-4.222893949	1
2010	2	-3.649548054	1
2011	2	-2.681571878	1
2012	2	-1.823159722	1
2013	2	-0.973230368	3
2014	2	-0.072340301	3
2015	2	0.17499157855303	3
2016	2	1.30136312414299	3
2017	2	2.0605289394445	3
2018	2	2.43960956671795	3
2019	2	2.9562593253289	3
2020	2	3.56809247158148	3
2021	2	4.24095318527636	3
2022	2	5.21686292153609	3

that year, resulting in the most pronounced reduction in the urban–rural gap among the four provinces.

As shown in Table 4, Henan Province remained in the "Low Equity Group" from 2009 to 2016. It did not enter the "Medium Equity Group" until 2017, indicating that its improvement in urban–rural education equity lagged behind the other provinces. In Table 5, Hebei Province was in the "Low Equity Group" before 2016 and moved into the "Medium Equity Group" thereafter, with a pace of improvement between that of Shandong and Henan (Table 6).

From the four tables above, it is evident that Shanxi Province jumped directly to the High Equity Group in 2013, achieving the fastest improvement; Shandong and Hebei entered the Medium Equity Group in 2013 and 2016 respectively, showing steady progress; and Henan did not reach the Medium Equity Group until 2017, exhibiting the slowest advancement in urban–rural education equity. This comparison reflects differences among provinces in policy implementation intensity, fiscal investment, and digital infrastructure development, and provides an empirical basis for targeted, differentiated policy recommendations in the next chapter.

After assigning the "Low," "Medium," and "High" cluster labels, this study calculated the annual average CEI for each group over the 2009–2022 period and plotted these values in a line chart (Fig. 1). As shown, the High Equity Group's average CEI remained above zero from 2009 onward and led throughout the sample period. The Medium Equity Group stayed below zero from 2009 to 2012 but, driven by educational reforms and related policy measures, first crossed above zero in 2013 and continued to rise rapidly in

Table 5. CEI and Cluster Assignments for Henan Province (2009–2022).

Year	Province	CEI	Cluster
2009	3	-6.213719753	1
2010	3	-5.768907127	1
2011	3	-4.992528796	1
2012	3	-4.109661547	1
2013	3	-3.100726178	1
2014	3	-2.069048779	1
2015	3	-1.559959337	1
2016	3	-0.942898092	1
2017	3	-0.303818638	2
2018	3	0.425113966899411	2
2019	3	1.10539383066284	2
2020	3	1.60403894175962	2
2021	3	1.90272610706103	2
2022	3	2.46925207056582	2

Table 6. CEI and Cluster Assignments for Hebei Province (2009–2022).

Year	Province	CEI	Cluster
2009	4	-4.27310726	1
2010	4	-3.564141777	1
2011	4	-2.965804753	1
2012	4	-2.365940956	1
2013	4	-1.980928341	1
2014	4	-1.364793395	1
2015	4	-1.079309814	1
2016	4	-0.055984662	2
2017	4	0.541071947706815	2
2018	4	1.06025005474432	2
2019	4	1.68579462103334	2
2020	4	2.03191480457723	2
2021	4	2.95221910010147	2
2022	4	3.61511271370377	2

subsequent years. The Low Equity Group's average CEI remained in negative territory—although it trended upward, it had not approached zero by 2022. Overall, the trajectories of the three groups are clearly differentiated: the Medium and High Equity Groups accelerated under policy impetus, while the Low Equity Group's improvement lagged, indicating significant variation in response speed and equity gains among provinces under the same policy environment.

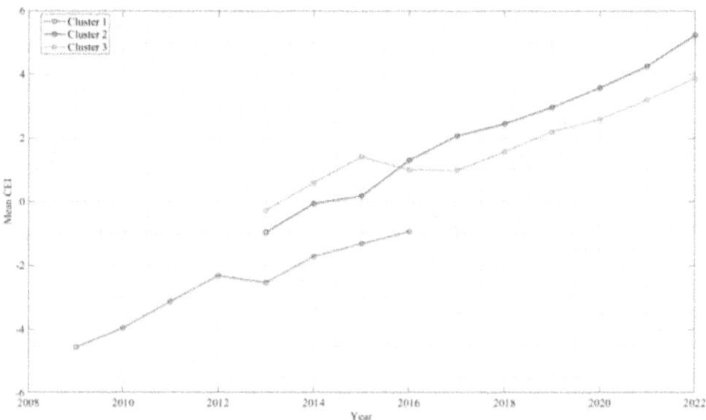

Fig. 1. Annual Mean CEI by Cluster (2009–2022).

5 Conclusions and Policy Recommendations

5.1 Research Conclusions

In summary, this study employed principal component analysis to consolidate twelve indicators of educational investment, teaching resources, household economic conditions, and digital infrastructure into a Comprehensive Education Equity Index (CEI). Combined with auxiliary variables including urbanization rate, per capita GDP, and broadband access ports, K-means clustering was applied to categorize the urban-rural compulsory education equity levels across Shandong, Shanxi, Henan, and Hebei provinces from 2009 to 2022. The empirical results demonstrate that the two principal components account for 91.04% of the cumulative variance, confirming the representativeness of the CEI. The clustering analysis reveals distinct temporal patterns: Shanxi entered the high-equity group in 2013, while Shandong and Hebei progressed to the medium-equity group in 2013 and 2016, respectively. Henan achieved this transition only in 2017, indicating significant variations in both timing and depth of urban-rural education gap reduction across provinces. Dynamic evolution analysis shows that medium and high-equity provinces achieved rapid improvement driven by the "Two Exemptions and One Subsidy" policy and county-level compulsory education balance initiatives. In contrast, low-equity provinces, despite some progress, remained persistently in negative value ranges, suggesting that rural areas with weak foundations require targeted support measures. Overall, national fiscal investment and balanced development policies have demonstrated notable effectiveness in medium and high baseline regions. However, their impact on low baseline provinces remains limited, highlighting the urgent need for differentiated, data-driven precision strategies to sustain momentum in equity improvement.

5.2 Policy Recommendations

Strengthening data mining and dynamic analysis mechanisms for educational resource allocation. Building upon the established CEI construction and clustering framework, time-series panel data and machine learning methods (such as random forest and support vector machine) should be further utilized to conduct in-depth analysis and prediction of urban-rural educational resource input efficiency and incentive effects across provinces, enabling more precise identification of fiscal allocation priorities. While central government improves compulsory education funding mechanisms, it should leverage model outputs to periodically assess CEI trend changes in third-tier regions and dynamically adjust per-student public funding standards for rural schools, directing more resources precisely to areas with educational resource shortages. Additionally, establishing a big data-based performance monitoring platform is essential to collect multi-dimensional data in real-time, including school funding utilization, teacher mobility, and teaching quality. Through data visualization and anomaly detection algorithms, this platform can provide early warning systems for fund misappropriation or resource underutilization, ensuring that additional investments are effectively converted into improved rural teaching infrastructure and enhanced educational quality.

Promoting data-driven strategies for balanced urban-rural teacher resources and digital education development. To address teacher shortages and structural inadequacies, clustering analysis and regression models should be applied based on teacher profiles, performance evaluations, and job satisfaction data to identify patterns of teacher mobility and incentive factors. This approach enables the design of differentiated teaching allowances, training mechanisms, and online master teacher programs to improve rural teacher recruitment and retention rates. Provinces should integrate CEI evolution pathways and employ spatial regression and cointegration testing methods to evaluate the effectiveness of urban-rural teacher exchange programs, subsequently optimizing teacher mobility channels to facilitate high-quality teacher movement across regions. Simultaneously, accelerating digital education infrastructure development and resource sharing is crucial. Based on broadband access port data and online course usage statistics, association rule mining and network analysis techniques should be utilized to identify digital demands and bottlenecks in rural schools, prioritizing the coverage of the National Digital Education Platform and implementation of "Internet + Education" demonstration projects. For medium and high-equity provinces, indicator monitoring should be used to optimize online collaboration models. For high-equity provinces, precision teaching evaluation systems should be constructed based on educational big data to achieve intelligent allocation and continuous optimization of educational resources.

References

1. Wood, R.M.: A review of education differences in urban and rural areas. Int. Res. J. Educ. Res. **14**(2), 1–3 (2023)

2. Patrinos, H.A., Psacharopoulos, G.: Education: Past, Present and Future Global Challenges. World Bank Policy Research Working Paper No. 5616 (2011). https://doi.org/10.1596/1813-9450-5616
3. Guo, Y., Li, X.: The evolution and driving mechanism of education inequality in China: From 2003 to 2020. PLoS ONE **20**(1), e0314297 (2025). https://doi.org/10.1371/journal.pone.0314297
4. Li, C.: Trends in educational inequality in different eras (1940–2010)—A re-examination of opportunity inequalities in urban-rural education. Chin. Educ. Soc. **48**(3), 163–182 (2015). https://doi.org/10.1080/10611932.2015.1085772
5. Zahl-Thanem, A., Rye, J.F.: Spatial inequality in higher education: a growing urban–rural educational gap? Eur. Sociol. Rev. **40**(6), 1067–1081 (2024). https://doi.org/10.1093/esr/jcae015
6. Byun, S., Meece, J.L., Irvin, M.J.: Rural-nonrural disparities in postsecondary educational attainment revisited. Am. Educ. Res. J. **49**, 412–437 (2012). https://doi.org/10.3102/0002831211416344
7. Newbold, K.B., Brown, W.M.: The urban–rural gap in university attendance: determinants of university participation among Canadian youth. J. Reg. Sci. **55**, 585–608 (2015). https://doi.org/10.1111/jors.12197
8. Zhao, X.: Trends and causes of inequality of opportunity in education in China: 2002–2018. J. Fin. Econ. **49**(2), 79–94 (2023)
9. Zhang, J.: Equity in China's Compulsory Education: A Comparative Analysis of Rural and Urban Differences in Educational Development. Trans. Soc. Sci. Educ. Human. Res. (2024). https://doi.org/10.62051/mb3sar47
10. Luo, H.: How is educational equity possible: the evolutionary logic of compulsory education enrollment policies from the perspective of historical institutionalism. J. Educ. Educ. Res. (2024). https://doi.org/10.54097/fjjvhh17
11. Wen, J., Gu, C.: The rural-urban differences in resources allocation of basic education and its social consequence: Based on the analysis of China's education statistics. J. East China Nor. Univ. (Educational Sciences) **35**(2), 33–42 (2017). https://doi.org/10.16382/j.cnki.1000-5560.2017.02.004
12. Shi, Y.: Beneficiaries of educational technology in universities—a study on the equity of urban and rural education in Henan province. J. Educ. Human. Soc. Sci. (2024). https://doi.org/10.54097/5raj4t59
13. Xiao, Y., Yin, M., Wang, H., Xiang, Y.: Digital finance, digital usage divide, and urban-rural income gap: evidence from China. Systems (2025). https://doi.org/10.3390/systems13030145
14. Lu, Z.: The nonlinear effects of public education expenditure on income inequality: a panel threshold regression analysis of 31 provinces in China. In: Proceedings of the 3rd International Conference on Big Data Economy and Information Management, BDEIM, LNCS, vol. XXXX, pp. 2–3. Springer, Cham (2022). https://doi.org/10.1007/978-3-030-XXXX-X_1
15. State Council of the People's Republic of China: Notice on further improving the funding guarantee mechanism for urban and rural compulsory education (Guo Fa [2015] No. 67). (2015). http://www.gov.cn/zhengce/content/2015-11/28/content_10357.htm
16. Lian, C., Pei, J., Li, J.: Income inequality effect of government investment behavior: Comparisons based on different investment areas, different regions and different groups in China. Heliyon **10**(5), e26452 (2024). https://doi.org/10.1016/j.heliyon.2024.e26452
17. Zhang, Y., Yang, W., Li, B., Yang, Y., Chen, L., Feng, L.: Convergence of primary education development in urban and rural China: empirical analysis of historical trends and future projections. Human. Soc. Sci. Comm. **12**(1), 1–18 (2025). https://doi.org/10.1057/s41599-025-04752-9
18. Song, Z.: Disparity in educational resources between urban and rural areas in China. J. Adv. Res. Educ. (2023). https://doi.org/10.56397/jare.2023.09.06

19. Gill, T.M.: Why Mills, not Gouldner?" selective history and differential commemoration in sociology. Am. Sociol. **44**, 96–115 (2013). https://doi.org/10.1007/s12108-012-9171-4
20. Camarero, L., Oliva, J.: Thinking in rural gap: mobility and social inequalities. Palgrave Comm. **5**, 95 (2019). https://doi.org/10.1057/s41599-019-0306-x
21. Bæck, U.-D.K.: Rural location and academic success—remarks on research, contextualisation and methodology. Scand. J. Educ. Res. **60**, 435–448 (2016). https://doi.org/10.1080/00313831.2015.1024163
22. Zheng, L., Qi, X., Zhang, C.: Can improvements in teacher quality reduce the cognitive gap between urban and rural students in China? Int. J. Educ. Dev. **100**, 102781 (2023). https://doi.org/10.1016/j.ijedudev.2023.102781
23. Li, H., Li, Z., Tinmaz, H.: The influence of professional identity and occupational well-being on retention intention of rural teachers in China. Int. J. Chinese Educ. **13**(2) (2024). https://doi.org/10.1177/2212585X241253918
24. Tang, Y., Wang, H.: How to retain rural teachers? An empirical study based on a survey of special-post teachers in G province in China. In: Educational Research in China: Articles from Educational Research, LNCS, vol. XXXX, pp. 327–344. Springer, Cham (2021). https://doi.org/10.1007/978-981-16-1520-7_17
25. An, H.X.: Teacher salaries and the shortage of high-quality teachers in China's rural primary and secondary schools. Chin. Educ. Soc. **51**(2), 103–116 (2018). https://doi.org/10.1080/10611932.2018.1433411
26. Chen, J., Qian, X.: Economic growth and household educational investment in China: Evidence from panel data. China Econ. Rev. **48**, 101–115 (2018). https://doi.org/10.1016/j.chieco.2017.11.005
27. Han, Y.: Research on Optimization Strategies for the Impact of Urbanization on Economic Development in the Education Sector in China. In: Highlights in Business, Economics and Management, LNCS, vol. XXXX (2024). https://doi.org/10.54097/xwyrqg94
28. Mo, Z.: The Financial Expenditure in the Field of Rural Teacher Construction Under the Background of Poverty Alleviation Through Education—Take Educational Poverty Alleviation in Poverty-stricken Counties in Shaanxi Province as an Example. Advances in Economics, Management and Political Sciences (2023). https://doi.org/10.54254/2754-1169/42/20232073
29. Zhao, K.: Does higher education expansion close the rural–urban gap in college enrolment in China? New evidence from a cross-provincial assessment. Compare: A J. Compar. Int. Educ. **53**(5), 802–819 (2021). https://doi.org/10.1080/03057925.2021.1965468
30. Liang, Q., Yin, F.: Measurement and evaluation of the modernization development level of higher education in China: based on panel data analysis of 31 provinces from 2012 to 2022. Sustainability **16**(17), 7250 (2024). https://doi.org/10.3390/su16177250
31. Alvarez-Garcia, M., Arenas-Parra, M., Ibar-Alonso, R.: Uncovering student profiles. An explainable cluster analysis approach to PISA 2022. Computers & Education **223**, 105166 (2024). https://doi.org/10.1016/j.compedu.2024.105166
32. Costea, C.N.P.A.: Clustering and education: a study on European schools. In: Navigating the Future: Digitalization, Sustainability, and International Business, LNCS, vol. 250 (2025). https://doi.org/10.14232/gtk.nfdsib.2025.15
33. Hatipoglu, H.N.: A cluster analysis on gender equality in the world from the data set of the United Nations Development Program. Int. J. Latest Trends in Eng. Technol. 139–152 (2022)
34. Ma, H.: Can innovation input help reduce the income inequality in China?-An analysis based on panel data of 21 provincial regions. J. Econ. Bus. Manage. **10**(5), (2022). https://doi.org/10.18178/joebm.2022.10.5.719
35. Tang, M., Zeng, Z., Lan, Q.: Research on allocation efficiency of higher education resources in China. J. Res. Vocat. Educ. **6**(8), (2024). https://doi.org/10.53469/jrve.2024.06(08).01

36. Yu, Y.: Performance analysis of public investment in Chinese university education based on regional differences and influencing factors. Bus. Ethics and Leader. **7**(1), 37–49 (2023). https://doi.org/10.21272/bel.7(1).37-49.2023
37. Lu, W.J.: No less than 4%": A policy review of China's fiscal spending on education, 2000–2020. ECNU Review of Education. Online first (2024). https://doi.org/10.1177/20965311241265374
38. Ju, F., Wang, S., Lin, W.: Nonlinear effect of urbanization on the gap between urban and rural elementary education in China. Mathematical Problems in Engineering. Article ID 7025433 (2022). https://doi.org/10.1155/2022/7025433
39. Ji, Y., Lei, Y., Chen, W., Li, L., Jiang, Y.: Analysis of carbon emission equity degrees based on regional heterogeneity in China. Environ. Sci. Pollut. Res.. (2023). https://doi.org/10.1007/s11356-023-31275-0
40. Wang, S.: Research on higher education level in different regions of China—based on factors and clustering. J. Educ. Human. Soc. Sci. **17**, (2023). https://doi.org/10.54097/ehss.v17i.10462
41. Ao, X., Abisado, M.B.: A novel approach to panel data clustering: Integrating feature extraction and weighted distance functions. In: Proceedings of the 4th International Conference on Artificial Intelligence and Computer Engineering (ICAICE 2023). ACM, New York (2023). https://doi.org/10.1145/3652628.3652657
42. Wang, S.: Research on empirical analysis of the equity of compulsory education in rural areas of China. Front. Educ. Res. **7**(6), (2024). https://doi.org/10.25236/fer.2024.070610
43. Ramos, L., Rivas-Echeverría, F., Amaro, I.R., Camacho, F.: A Comparative Exploration of PCA Variants for Clustering Analysis. In: 2023 Fourth International Conference on Information Systems and Software Technologies (ICI2ST), Quito, Ecuador, November 22–24, 2023, pp. 60–67. IEEE Computer Society (2023). https://doi.org/10.1109/ICI2ST62251.2023.00016
44. He, Y., et al.: Factors influencing carbon emissions from China's electricity industry: Analysis using the combination of LMDI and K-means clustering. Environmental Impact Assessment Review (2022). https://doi.org/10.1016/j.eiar.2021.106724

Flood Detection System Using IoT and Machine Learning

Marina Yusoff[1,2](✉), Muhammad Azminnaim Bin Abdul Harith[2], and Muhammad Syukran Bin Shaari[1,2]

[1] Faculty of Computer and Mathematical Sciences, Universiti Teknologi MARA, 40450 Shah Alam, Selangor, Malaysia
marina998@uitm.edu.my

[2] Institute for Big Data Analytics and Artificial Intelligence, Universiti Teknologi MARA, 40450 Shah Alam, Selangor, Malaysia

Abstract. There is a severe lack of effective technology for detecting floods at the community level, which this study aims to address. Residents are frequently unprepared for the sudden increase in floodwater levels. There is an immediate need for an easily accessible and dependable flood monitoring solution due to the significant risk to public safety and property posed by the lack of early local warning capabilities. The research employs IoT devices, including ultrasonic sensors, water level sensors, and DHT22 (Digital Humidity, and Temperature Sensor), strategically positioned to monitor water levels in real-time. This data is utilized in machine learning models such as decision trees, random forests, and linear regressions to predict floods. The IoT-based system employs real-time monitoring and a machine learning algorithm to provide early flood warnings. Among all models utilized in this research, the Decision Tree achieved the highest accuracy at 98.14%, demonstrating superior efficacy compared to alternatives such as Random Forest and Linear Regression in flood prediction. It reflects the integration of IoT and innovative models for machine learning flood warning systems, thereby promoting the establishment of superior preventive and contingency measures. This study can change flood detection structures and methods, especially in areas with underdeveloped flood monitoring systems. The system saves lives and property from floods and helps authorities allocate and manage resources efficiently. This research contributes to disaster management knowledge by integrating IoT and machine learning to address complex environmental issues.

Keywords: Floods · Machine Learning · IoT · Flood Warning System

1 Introduction

Floods can be categorized into various types according to their causation, geographical location, and duration [1]. Riverine flooding is among the most prevalent types. Flooding transpires when rivers exceed their banks because of excessive precipitation or snowmelt [2]. Subsequently, flash floods are abrupt and intense inundations that transpire within a brief timeframe, typically within six hours of the inciting event. They are generally

M. Kassim et al. (Eds.): SCDS 2025, CCIS 2674, pp. 128–143, 2026.
https://doi.org/10.1007/978-981-95-8368-3_10

precipitated by heavy rainfall or the swift discharge of water from dams or reservoirs. Coastal floods occur when seawater submerges coastal regions due to storm surges, tsunamis, or rising sea levels [3]. In Malaysia, flooding or flash floods typically occur annually. Flash floods are caused by protracted thunderstorms that repeatedly traverse the same area or by intense precipitation from hurricanes and tropical storms. It requires approximately a few minutes to two hours for development. Flash floods are not seasonal; they can occur at any time and present certain disadvantages compared to channel flooding [11]. Recently, Malaysia experienced significant flooding that affected Johor, Pahang, Malacca, and Negeri Sembilan. As reported by Richard Davies in March 2023, nearly 30,000 individuals have relocated to evacuation centers due to the flood.

The Malaysian government has enacted several measures to alleviate the effects of floods, including the construction of dams, the establishment of flood control infrastructure, and the promotion of community awareness. The authorities also play a crucial role in preventing such disasters from occurring. Currently, multiple systems have been established to monitor and assess flood risk levels in Malaysia. The Department of Irrigation and Drainage implements a system to disseminate warnings to residents in urban areas, such as TTDI Jaya and Shah Alam, via SMS. The system is designated as SMS Banjir [6]. Early flood detection and warning systems are essential in mitigating the effects of floods. Prompt notifications enable impacted residents to relocate to secure locations and protect their possessions [4]. The Internet of Things (IoT) has become a transformative force in the creation of efficient flood detection and warning systems [1]. The application of IoT represents a highly promising domain for enhancing flood detection and monitoring systems. This is in line with the findings [18]. In addition to sensors, cameras, and communication modules, IoT devices can deliver real-time data gathered from various locations to the central control platform.

Decision trees can also predict river basin floods. This decision tree-based approach distilled the critical flash-flood risk factors and could be used to evaluate local risks. Slope, land use, and SPI are usually considered when making decisions. These ADT models, along with their FR and WOE coefficients, accurately predicted flash flood-prone areas [23]. Random Forest algorithms are ideal for flood detection because they use ensemble learning to classify using decision trees, improving classification accuracy [9]. In the training phase, these algorithms create many decision trees and use class mode for classification functions, improving model stability and accuracy. It is best for flood detection because it can identify complex dataset patterns [15]. Random Forest in flood detection systems uses rainfall, river height, historical records, and other weather factors to distinguish normal and high-risk scenarios, improve early warning, and reduce response time [9]. Water levels are monitored using real-time sensors and input into the Random Forest model. Predefined decision trees classify the water level as normal, above normal, or dangerous [15].

Water level sensors, PLCs, GSM modems, and power supplies are typical system components. The sensors detect water level changes, and the Random Forest model generates alerts when needed [9]. High classification accuracy is a significant benefit of using Random Forest for flood detection. Research indicates that Random Forest outperforms Bagging, Decision Trees, and HyperPipes, achieving 99.5% classification accuracy [9]. Random Forest processes large data sets and multiple responses well, which is useful for flood detection due to the volume and complexity of the data. Such processing allows updating the model to reflect current reality while maintaining its efficiency and effectiveness in any situation [15]. The algorithm's flexibility and adaptability allow it to detect floods. Random Forest can be retrained with new data to improve predictability and adaptability [9].

Linear regression is a major flood detection method because it can determine the relationship between control (input) variables like rainfall intensity, temperature, humidity, river discharge, etc., and output (dependent) variables like flood occurrences or water level. Flood frequency analysis uses statistical methods to calculate flood causes and estimate future floods based on records. Linear regression is used in flood detection models to map data to a line. It estimates flood levels by combining climatic and hydrological data from the flood site. One of the most important variables in the regression equation is rainfall intensity, which affects flood peaks. Regression analysis determines the coefficient for rainfall intensity and other parameters to measure their impact on flood levels [49]. The impact is shown by linear regression, explaining a significant portion of flood peak variance. Research has shown that drainage area, main channel slopes, and rain intensity all affect peak discharge. As temperature and orographic variables account for geographical differences in vegetation and meteorological conditions, the regression model predicts better [50]. Additionally, researchers use linear regression models to examine residuals and potentially asymptomatic gaps that indicate missing factors or data errors. Thus, the researcher can use residuals and map distribution to verify that a model captures flood-relevant features. This process improves the credibility of flood prediction models and fine-tuning [49]. The system continuously monitors and updates the linear regression used in flood detection throughout its operation. This dynamic approach enables flood forecasting and early warning systems, preventing devastating flood impacts on communities and infrastructure [49].

IoT devices effective for monitoring water levels comprise ultrasonic sensors, water level sensors, and rain gauges, which can be strategically positioned for real-time water level observation. The gathered data is subsequently analyzed, processed, and presented as real-time flood warning information. The collected data can be utilized to identify the gradual increase in water levels. A network of sensors can be deployed in multiple locations to continuously monitor water levels, triggering an alarm when a specified threshold is exceeded. The dissemination of flood warnings is also integral to the system operations. IoT systems can notify residents in at-risk areas of flooding through multiple media platforms, including mobile. These include applications, text messages, and loudspeakers [15]. The incorporation of IoT technology into flood detection and monitoring systems can substantially enhance flood preparedness and response, thereby mitigating loss of life and property damage resulting from floods. IoT-based flood detection systems provide numerous benefits compared to conventional systems. They are more economical, scalable, and capable of delivering real-time data and notifications. Moreover, IoT devices can be integrated with other systems, such as traffic management systems, to synchronize evacuation efforts and mitigate disruptions [19].

Numerous individuals and organizations were required to allocate time and implement flood recovery plans to mitigate costs for the impacted locations and survivors.

Many of these projects necessitate substantial resources and physical manpower, including rescue personnel, technicians, and others [18]. In Malaysia, the documentation of historical flood damage data is inadequate and challenging to obtain [12]. Numerous flood detection and monitoring systems have been implemented in Malaysia to oversee flood water levels. The Department of Irrigation and Drainage (DID) Malaysia indicates that there are two categories of flood monitoring systems employed in Malaysia. The systems include the telemetric rain gauge and the telemetric water level stations. [10]. Floods are a recurring natural disaster that causes extensive damage to infrastructure and loss of lives each year. One of the primary challenges in mitigating the impact of floods is the rapid increase in floodwater levels, which often provides residents with minimal time to evacuate. This is compounded by the poor availability of sophisticated flood detection mechanisms, especially at the community level; hence, early warnings are issued to residents and early commencement of rescue missions [11].

To date, there are few publicly available flood detection systems, usually overseen by the authorities but not readily available for public use. Flood warnings, on the other hand, are issued based on the type of flood. When a flood has occurred, the situation is first evaluated to determine the necessary course of action to take. These cycles can take a considerable amount of time to complete, which slows down the evacuation process and may even hinder the entire rescue mission. Muhd Zain [10] stressed that in flood-zone communities, the residents are not always provided with accurate and timely information on the depth of floodwater within their catchment, which is critical during a disaster. The community lacks flood detection systems, a critical weakness that requires immediate attention. Advanced detection of floods can use environmental parameters. This includes monitoring water levels, temperature, and humidity using sensors and machine learning algorithms. Such systems can issue early warnings by forecasting floods in real time. Coordinating these systems at the community level would help in providing timely alerts to the people in their homes, hence facilitating safer evacuation.

2 Related Work

Recently, numerous studies have explored the integration of Internet of Things (IoT) and machine learning (ML) technologies to enhance flood detection and early warning systems. These systems typically use various sensors to monitor environmental parameters such as water level, humidity, and rainfall. For instance, as shown in Table 1, Anbarasan [17] proposed a flood detection system combining IoT with a Convolutional Deep Neural Network (CDNN) and Big Data tools like HDFS, achieving notable prediction accuracy through multi-phase data processing. Similarly, Vinothini and Jayanthy in 2019 International Conference on Intelligent Computing and Control Systems (ICCS) [21], implemented an IoT-based system using temperature, humidity, and water level sensors with a Decision Tree algorithm, reporting a high classification accuracy of 99%. Gowthamani [7] introduced an ensemble learning approach by integrating LSTM and Random Forest, which yielded improved performance metrics and emphasized early warning capabilities. Amer proposed a flash flood detection system using video input on a Raspberry Pi with TensorFlow Lite and SSD MobileNet-v2, enabling real-time alerts via Telegram and emphasizing the advantages of portable, camera-based solutions [5].

Meanwhile, Satria [22] focused on a more traditional approach using ultrasonic and rain sensors with an Arduino Uno and Ethernet communication to deliver flood data through a web-based interface. Charaan [14] expanded on this by combining multiple sensors with wireless and GSM communication, integrating an Android alert system for community-level flood preparedness. These studies demonstrate various methods and technologies, with a common emphasis on real-time monitoring, data transmission, and predictive accuracy. However, most systems either focus on a single ML model or lack comparative performance analysis. In contrast, the system in this study offers a comprehensive framework by integrating multiple ML algorithms (Decision Tree, Random Forest, Linear Regression) with real-time IoT data collection and a user-friendly real-time dashboard, providing a cost-effective, scalable, and accurate flood prediction solution tailored for community-level deployment.

Table 1. Comparison of related work with this study

Study	Technology	Technique	Communication/Output	Special Feature	Accuracy/Result
Anbarasan [17]	Water Flow, Rain, Humidity	CDNN	HDFS, Cloud	Big Data + Multi-phase model	~ 78%
Vinothini & Jayanthy [21]	Temp, Humidity, Water Level	Decision Tree	Wi-Fi, Cloud	Real-time alerts	~ 99%
Gowthamani [7]	IoT Sensors (unspecified)	LSTM + Random Forest	Cloud	Ensemble Learning	81.13%
Ameer [5]	Video Camera (Raspberry)	Tensorflow Lite + SSDNet	Telegram Alerts	Camera-based detection	Real-time response
Satria [22]	Ultrasonic, Rain	None	Ethernet + Web Server	HTML-based flood display	Timely info
Charaan [14]	Humidity, Flow, Float, Ultrasonic	Not specified	Wi-Fi + GSM + Android App	SMS alerts + Evacuation support	Fast + Reliable alerts
Flood Detection System using IOT	DHT22, HC-SR04	Decision Tree, Random Forest, Linear Regression	Google Sheets + Real-Time Dashboard	ML model comparison + Web-based display	R2 = 0.9814, RMSE = 0.2388

3 Material and Methods

This section explains the research's methodology and materials. Figure 1. Illustrates the operational workflow of a flood detection IoT system enhanced by machine learning. The process begins with a flood monitoring setup, where a flood simulator is deployed in a designated area. IoT sensors, specifically the DHT22 sensor (for measuring temperature and humidity) and the HC-SR04 ultrasonic sensor (for determining water level), are used to gather real-time environmental data. This includes temperature, humidity, water level, and timestamp. This data is transmitted and stored in Google Sheets, ensuring immediate accessibility. Following data collection, the system proceeds to a data preparation phase, where the raw data undergoes cleaning and formatting to ensure consistency. The data normalization process further standardizes the values to improve the performance of the machine learning algorithms. The dataset is then split into training and testing sets (using ratios such as 70:30, 80:20, or 90:10) to facilitate effective model training and performance evaluation.

Three types of machine learning models are being used to perform this experiment. Decision Tree, Random Forest, and Linear Regression are employed to predict flood events. After training, the models are evaluated using standard performance metrics to determine the most accurate predictor. The selected model is then deployed to forecast potential floods, and its predictions are displayed on an intuitive dashboard, enabling rapid alerts and informed decision-making at the community level. The process concludes with a result presentation, offering a comprehensive end-to-end system for real-time flood monitoring and predictive analytics.

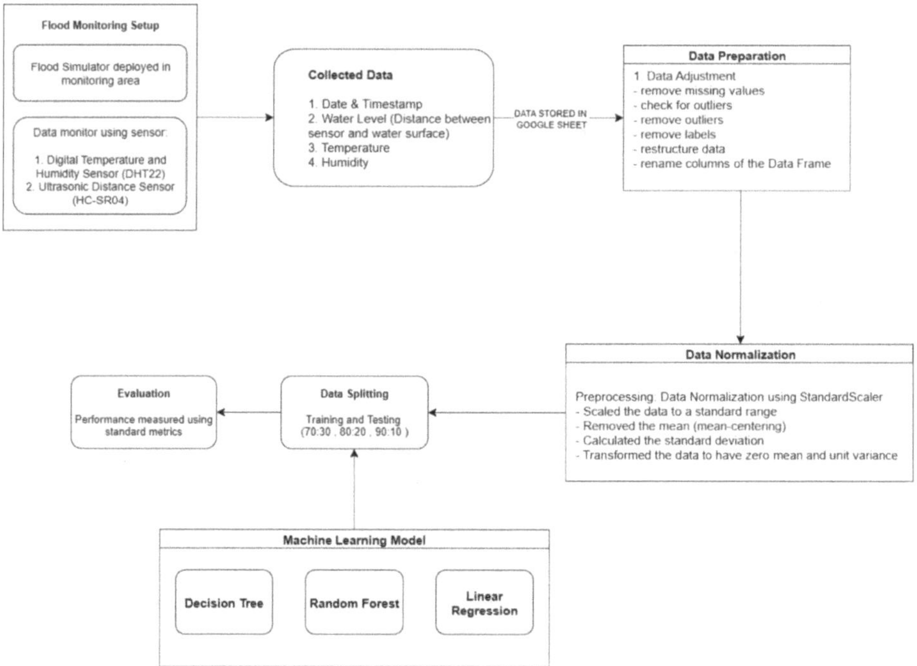

Fig. 1. Flowchart Diagram for model evaluation

3.1 Development of a Simulator

The objective during the simulator development phase is to design and implement an IoT-based flood simulator utilizing appropriate components. Choosing sensors, including the ESP32, DHT22, and water level sensors, all function collaboratively with the Arduino IDE platform for simulation purposes. This phase involves meticulous collaboration with the map and includes code that facilitates the collection and presentation of data around 30-min intervals. We utilize the web platform because it effectively integrates with the microcontroller, enabling the acquisition of sensor data through an efficient web-based method. In Table 2, the data from the microcontroller was directly recorded into the Sensor Data Logger table in google sheet.

Table 2. Sensor Data Logger

Date	Time	Temperature	Humidity	Water Level
21/06/2024	1:49:47	30.9	71	9
21/06/2024	1:50:04	30.9	71	9
21/06/2024	1:50:26	30.9	71	9
21/06/2024	1:50:52	30.9	71	9

The data was continuously recorded in the Sensor Data Logger table. To ensure that real-time storage was maintained, an additional table, referred to as the Real-Time Sensor Data Logger, was created to monitor and log live data, as presented in Table 3.

Table 3. Real Time Sensor Data Logger

Date	Time	Temperature	Humidity	Water Level
17/07/2024	16:00:45	30	60	4

3.2 Data Collection

During the data collection process, data is systematically gathered from the IoT-based flood simulator and stored in Google Sheets. Data collection typically occurs within a specified timeframe, such as from May 7, 2024, to June 6, 2024, resulting in the compilation of 1,489 data points. Each entry comprises elements such as the date, timestamp, temperature, humidity, and water level. This comprehensive and organized data collection will facilitate the establishment of a repository of valid data essential for representing various conditions and scenarios in flood occurrences. The sample of data can be seen in Table 4.

Table 4. Sample of Collected Data

Date	Time	Temperature (°C)	Humidity (%)	Water Level (cm)
15/05/2024	11:39:07	30.5	75	9
15/05/2024	11:39:24	30.5	75	9
15/05/2024	11:39:40	30.5	75	9
15/05/2024	11:39:56	30.5	76	8

Standardizing data collection processes ensures accuracy. Using reduced water level thresholds that match danger levels simplifies classification. Data acquisition from sensors, classification threshold-based decision-making, and transmission formatting are all possible with the Arduino IDE. In conclusion, researchers carefully collect data to ensure a sufficient dataset for project analysis and modeling.

3.3 Data Pre-Processing

Data preprocessing is a vital machine learning process that prepares the dataset and makes it suitable for model training. Renaming columns is done first to improve understanding, making the Data Frame more understandable. Methods of scaling, such as StandardScaler, are applied to standardize the dataset. Normalizing the dataset makes variables comparable at a standard scale, enabling machine learning models to perform better, as their results are calculated based on scores rather than variable magnitudes.

In preprocessing, missing data and the reasons for their occurrence are considered. Researchers evaluate the missing data to determine if imputation (filling in missing values) or deletion would be the best approach to preserving the integrity of the dataset. Outliers are also detected, as they tend to inflate outcomes significantly and can be dropped or capped to maintain accuracy. Preprocessing also involves the process of feature selection, where only the features with significant importance are kept for modeling, and numerical encoding of categorical variables to make them compatible with the algorithms. This ultimately enhances data quality to the point where it is suitable for building predictive models, which is especially essential in applications like flood forecasting. The process of data preprocessing is shown in Fig. 2.

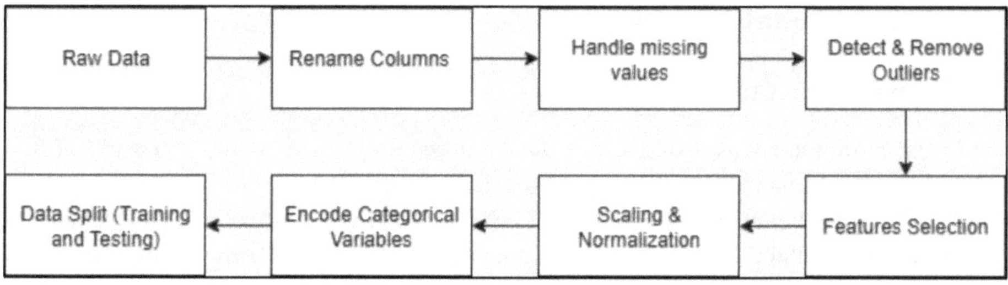

Fig. 2. Data preprocessing flow

Additionally, throughout the research process, the researchers evaluated the rationale for absent values in the database and the methodologies to rectify these values. It may involve managing missing values by inputting specific values to maintain data integrity and addressing inaccuracies by eliminating excessively high or low outliers, which can impair the data's utility. The preprocessing phase entails identifying outliers, selecting the appropriate input features, and encoding any existing categorical variables. Data preprocessing entails cleansing the data to enhance its quality and ensure its applicability in machine learning for the development of precise predictive models essential for flood forecasting.

3.4 Modelling

Due to the straightforward structure that characterizes decision tree models, their real-life use in flood monitoring is highly possible. It increases the system's reliability in issuing the correct alerts and ultimately minimizing the effect of floods. Concerning the mentioned article, the discussed historical data-based flood detection and notification system utilizes decision trees as one of the key components. The Water and environmental level sensors send their data to these trees, which function as a classification algorithm. Features like information gain and entropy, which form the basis of choosing the decision tree algorithm, will properly segment the flood data into levels of normality and danger. This study was presented at the 2019 International Conference on Intelligent Computing and Control Systems (ICCS) [21].

On the order side, the decision tree is also used in mapping the potential areas of flooding that will occur. Previously in Vietnam, a decision tree algorithm was used to determine flood susceptibility, particularly for flash floods [23]. This work also helps expand the literature on the application of ensemble techniques for flash flood prediction by comparing the performance of several techniques for flood prediction.

Decision trees can also be used in analyzing the probability of flood occurrences in a river basin. This decision tree-based approach enabled the identification of critical factors related to flash-flood risk and may be beneficial for assessing potential risks in the area. Such factors as slope, land use, and SPI are typically considered when making decisions. These ADT models, coordinated with the FR and WOE coefficients, effectively predicted the regions susceptible to flash floods [23].

4 Computational Experiment

4.1 Parameter Setting

The initial parameter was tested using the train-test split ratio, as indicated in Table 5. Three distinct ratios are designated for the experimental division. The initial ratio is 70:30, indicating that 70% of the data will be allocated for training, while the remaining 30% will be designated for testing. The same applies to the 80:20 ratio, comprising 80% training set and 20% test set, as well as the 90:10 ratio, consisting of 90% training set and 10% test set. These ratios were employed to examine the impact of dataset partitioning on the performance and generalization ability of the machine learning model, with the optimal ratio to be selected. Table 5 provides a comprehensive comparison of three models, which are Decision Tree, Random Forest, and Linear Regression. Each was evaluated with different test ratios (80:20, 70:30, and 90:10). The performance metrics considered include Cross-Validation RMSE, RMSE, MAE, MAPE, and R-squared (R2). Each metric reveals the accuracy and reliability of the models.

Table 5. Parameter setting

Parameters	Values
Train Test Split	70:30, 80:20, 90:10
Model Experiment	Decision Tree, Random Forest, Linear Regression

Table 6 presents a structured classification system for assessing the severity of water levels based on specific threshold ranges measured in centimeters. It includes two columns of "Water Level" and "Thresholds". The "Water Level" column defines three distinct categories, namely Flood, Flood Potential, and No Flood. Each feature is associated with a particular range of water level measurements outlined in the "Thresholds" column. The 'Flood' classification is assigned when the water level drops below 3 cm, indicating an urgent and critical situation where flooding is actively occurring. In such scenarios, immediate intervention and water level control measures are required to mitigate damage and ensure safety.

Table 6. Water level thresholds

Water Level	Thresholds
Flood	Less than 3 cm (cm)
Flood Potential	Between 4 cm and 7 cm
No Flood	Greater than 7 cm

The next category, 'Flood Potential,' applies when the water level ranges between 4 and 7 cm. This range signifies that the water level is higher than normal and may lead to flooding if not closely monitored. It represents a warning stage where preventive measures and heightened observation are essential to prevent the situation from escalating into an actual flood event. Lastly, the 'No Flood' classification is used when the water level exceeds 7 cm, suggesting that conditions are stable and there is no immediate threat of flooding. This category indicates a safe range where no immediate response is necessary, though regular monitoring should continue. Table 6 presents the correlation of water levels categorized by their elevation. It aids in decision-making for water management and flood mitigation by establishing thresholds for various severity levels. Adhering to these thresholds, efficient monitoring may facilitate suitable actions regarding water level classification.

Table 7 demonstrates the results of machine learning models. The Decision Tree model shows the best performance with an 80:20 split, yielding the lowest RMSE

(0.2388) and MAE (0.0503), indicating low prediction errors. The R^2 value is relatively high at 0.9814, indicating that the model accounts for 98.14% of the variance in water levels. The Cross-Validation RMSE of 0.4311 verifies the model's dependability on new data. While the 70:30 and 90:10 splits demonstrate commendable performance, they demonstrate slightly increased errors and reduced R^2 values, thereby rendering the 80:20 split the most robust and dependable configuration for the Decision Tree model.

Table 7. Result performance for machine learning models

Model	Test Ratio	Cross-Validation	RMSE	MAE	MAPE	R^2
Decision Tree	80:20	0.4311	0.2388	0.0503	90%	0.9814
	70:30	0.4079	0.2591	0.0626	0.97%	0.9780
	90:10	0.3480	0.4335	0.0940	2.56%	0.9300
Random Forest	80:20	0.3794	0.2512	0.0723	1.55%	0.9795
	70:30	0.3779	0.3089	0.0838	1.81%	0.9687
	90:10	0.3265	0.3252	0.0977	2.40%	0.9606
Linear Regression	80:20	0.7897	0.6624	0.3746	7.28%	0.8572
	70:30	0.8135	0.6846	0.3575	6.96%	0.8463
	90:10	0.7839	0.7322	0.3691	7.36%	0.8002

The Random Forest model provides robust performance across all test segments. The 80:20 division results in a low RMSE of 0.2512 and an MAE of 0.0723, accompanied by a R^2 of 0.9795, signifying substantial accuracy and explanatory capability. The Cross-Validation RMSE is 0.3794, indicating strong generalization abilities. The 70:30 and 90:10 splits yield commendable results; however, the 80:20 split is particularly interesting for achieving a balance between minimal prediction errors and improved R^2 values. However, it does not surpass the Decision Tree model with the same split. Across all splits, the Linear Regression model consistently shows higher RMSE, MAE, and MAPE values, suggesting lower accuracy than the Random Forest and Decision Tree models. The R^2 values, while acceptable, are lower (0.8572 for 80:20, 0.8463 for 70:30, and 0.8002 for 90:10), indicating a decreased amount of variability. The Cross-Validation RMSE is elevated, indicating diminished reliability in performance on novel data. Of all configurations, the Linear Regression model exhibits the lowest accuracy and precision.

The underperformance of the Linear Regression model in this flood prediction task can be attributed to several key limitations that make it unsuitable for capturing the complex nature of environmental data. Firstly, linear regression relies on the assumption that there is a linear relationship between the input features (such as temperature, humidity, and water level status) and the target variable (actual water level). However, in real world flood prediction scenarios, this assumption often fails, as the relationship between environmental factors and water level is typically non-linear and influenced by sudden changes or interactions among variables. For instance, the impact of humidity on water levels may not be direct or constant and could depend on other variables, like time or rainfall intensity.

Additionally, linear regression lacks the capability to model interactions or threshold effects between features automatically. Unlike tree-based models, which can capture complex decision rules and variable dependencies, linear regression applies a single global equation to the entire dataset, reducing its flexibility and responsiveness to different data patterns. This rigidity limits its accuracy, especially in scenarios where water levels respond differently across various environmental conditions. Moreover, linear regression is sensitive to outliers and noise, which are common in real-time sensor data used in flood monitoring. Abrupt changes in water level, which may be critical indicators of potential flooding, can disproportionately influence the model's predictions and reduce overall reliability.

Furthermore, as a parametric model, linear regression offers limited adaptability. It lacks the structural capacity to generalize across complex, non-linear boundaries that often define flood behavior. In contrast, models like Decision Trees and Random Forests are inherently designed to manage such complexities through their hierarchical, rule-based structures. As a result, the Linear Regression model consistently produced higher RMSE, MAE, and MAPE values and lower R^2 scores across all train-test splits, confirming its inadequacy in capturing the intricate patterns necessary for accurate flood prediction. Upon analyzing the performance metrics, the Decision Tree model utilizing the 80:20 split is identified as the superior model. It possesses the minimal RMSE and MAE, signifying the least prediction errors. The R^2 value of 0.9814 indicates predictive ability, revealing almost all the variance in water levels. The cross-validation RMSE of 0.4311 validates its efficacy in generalizing new data. The Decision Tree model, implementing an 80:20 train-test split ratio, yields the most accurate predictions, making it the most suitable option for this dataset.

5 Dashboard

The dashboard is configured to directly retrieve information from IoT sensors and provide real-time updates in the form of various metrics like water levels, temperature, and humidity. The visual elements, such as graphs and labels, simplify data interpretation, and the Predicted Water Level and Flood Potential functionalities aid in flood detection. The system has machine learning models integrated into it to predict flood risks with precision.

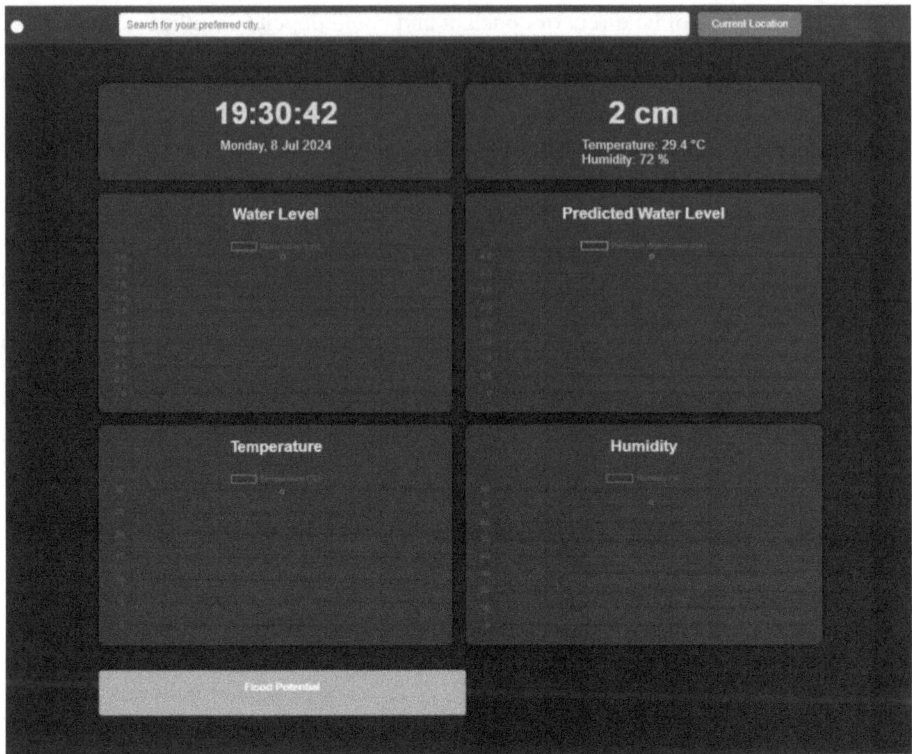

Fig. 3. Dashboard Interface

Figure 3. Shows the dashboard that displays actual measures such as the current water level, temperature, and humidity, and provides a prediction of the water level. Moreover, each variable's graph provides dynamic visualization, enabling users to view how changes are made concerning time. The bottom Flood Potential button initiates an analysis of the flood risk based on the gathered information. The interface is user-friendly, thereby making it easy for individuals to effectively monitor and respond to potential flood events.

6 Conclusion

The results of the simulation in flood detection using the IoT-based system with an ESP32 microcontroller, which recorded data with high accuracy and sent it to Google Sheets. This system performed water level measurement through ultrasonic HC-SR04 sensors and temperature/humidity monitoring through DHT22 sensors. All three models of machine learning were used in the study. Decision Tree, Random Forest, and Linear Regression are compared in this chapter. The study finds the decision tree model implemented with an 80:20 train-test split to be of the highest accuracy. The Random Forest model performed well, if not better than the Linear Regression model, which was not that accurate. The key findings emphasize the importance of model choice and real-time data optimism in effective flood management. In a lighter note, the chapter concludes with the unveiling of a prototype dashboard that enables real-time monitoring and prediction, with potential enhancements in accuracy and scalability through additional environmental parameters and advanced machine learning techniques.

Acknowledgement. The authors would like to thank the Institute for Big Data Analytics and Artificial Intelligence (IBDAAI) and the Faculty of Computer and Mathematical Sciences, Universiti Teknologi MARA, Shah Alam, Malaysia, for the tremendous support.

References

1. Yusoff, M.: Flash flood evacuation with discrete particle swarm optimization. Doctoral dissertation. Universiti Teknologi MARA (UiTM) (2011)
2. Zamzari, N.Z., Kassim, M., Yusoff, M.: Analysis and development of IoT-based aqua fish monitoring system. Int. J. Emerg. Technol. Adv. Eng. **12**(10), 191–197 (2022)
3. NWS Cleveland: Flood Event Report, https://www.weather.gov/cle/event_20230823_flooding_severe. Last accessed 20 June 2024
4. Roy, M., Pradhan, P., George, J., Pradhan, N.: Flood detection and water monitoring system using IoT. Int. J. Eng. Comput. Sci. **9**(07), 25113–25115 (2020)
5. Rashid, A.A., Ariffin, M.A.M., Kasiran, Z.: IoT-based flash flood detection and alert using TensorFlow. In: Proc. 11th IEEE Int. Conf. Control System, Computing and Engineering (ICCSCE), pp. 80–85. IEEE, Kuala Lumpur (2021)
6. Marzukhi, S., Sidik, M.A.S.M., Nasir, H.M., Zainol, Z., Ismail, M.N.: Flood detection and warning system (FLoWS). In: ACM Int. Conf. Proc. Series (2018)
7. Gowthamani, R., et al.: Efficient detection and prediction of flood severity using machine learning algorithm. Mater. Today: Proc. (2023)
8. Diriyana, A., Darusalam, U., Natasha, N.D., et al.: Water level monitoring and flood early warning using microcontroller with IoT-based ultrasonic sensor. J. Tek. Inform. C.I.T. **11**(1) (2019)
9. Khalaf, M., Hussain, A.J., Al-jumeily, D., Fergus, P., Idowu, I.O.: Advance flood detection and notification system based on sensor technology and machine learning algorithm, pp. 105–108 (2015)
10. Muhd Zain, N., Elias, L.S., Paidi, Z., Othman, M.: Flood warning and monitoring system (FWMS) using GSM technology. J. Comput. Res. Innov. **5**(1) (2020)
11. Sufa, H.F.A., Yusof, M.I., Sani, M.A.A., et al.: Flood monitoring and warning system with IoT. Universiti Kuala Lumpur, Malaysia (n.d.)
12. Romali, N.S., Yusop, Z.: Flood damage and risk assessment for urban area in Malaysia. Hydrol. Res. **52**(1), 142–159 (2021)
13. Pravin, A., Jacob, T.P., Rajakumar, R.: Enhanced flood detection system using IoT. In: Proc. 6th Int. Conf. Communication and Electronics Systems (ICCES), pp. 507–510. IEEE (2021)
14. Charaan, R.M.D., Shobana, J., Krishnamoorthy, P., et al.: Enhancement of IoT-based flood detection and prevention using Arduino UNO with WiFi module. In: Proc. 9th Int. Conf. Advanced Computing and Communication Systems (ICACCS), pp. 2290–2294. IEEE (2023)
15. Zakaria, M.I., Jabbar, W.A., Sulaiman, N.: Development of a smart sensing unit for LoRaWAN-based IoT flood monitoring and warning system in catchment areas. Internet Things Cyber-Phys. Syst. **3**, 249–261 (2023)
16. Moy De Vitry, M., Kramer, S., Wegner, J.D., Leitao, J.P.: Scalable flood level trend monitoring with surveillance cameras using a deep CNN. Hydrol. Earth Syst. Sci. **23**(11), 4621–4634 (2019)

17. Anbarasan, M., Muthu, B.A., Sivaparthipan, C.B., et al.: Detection of flood disaster system based on IoT, big data and convolutional deep neural network. Comput. Commun. **150**, 150–157 (2020)
18. Hasan, M.M., Rahman, M.A., Sedigh, A., et al.: Search and rescue operation in flooded areas: A survey on emerging IoT-oriented technologies and applications. Cogn. Syst. Res. **67**, 104–123 (2021)
19. Goyal, H.R., Ghanshala, K.K., Sharma, S.: Post flood management system based on smart IoT devices using AI approach. Mater. Today: Proc. **46**, 10411–10417 (2021)
20. Chaduvula, K., Kumar, K.K., Markapudi, B.R., Jyothi, C.R.: Design and implementation of IoT-based flood alert monitoring system using microcontroller 8051. Mater. Today: Proc. **80**, 2840–2844 (2023)
21. Vinothini, K., Jayanthy, S.: IoT based flood detection and notification system using decision tree algorithm. In: 2019 International Conference on Intelligent Computing and Control Systems (ICCS), pp. 579–583. Madurai, India (2019)
22. Satria, D., Yana, S., Munadi, R., Syahreza, S.: Design of information monitoring system flood based Internet of Things (IoT). In: Book Chapter, pp. 1–10 (2018)
23. Pham, B.T., et al.: Flood risk assessment using hybrid artificial intelligence models integrated with multi-criteria decision analysis in Quang Nam Province. Vietnam. J. Hydrol. **592**, 125815 (2021)
24. Hadi, M.I., Yakub, F., Fakhrurradzi, A., Hui, C.X., et al.: Designing early warning flood detection and monitoring system via IoT. IOP Conf. Ser.: Earth Environ. Sci. **479**(1), 012043 (2020)
25. Yuliandoko, H., Subono, Wardhany, V.A., Pramono, S.H., Siwindarto, P.: Design of flood warning system based on IoT and water characteristics. Telkomnika **16**(5), 2101–2110 (2018)
26. Saha, P., Saha, P.: IoT-based flood alerting and forecasting system using machine learning approach. Int. J. Sci. Eng. Res. **10**(9), 145–149 (2019)
27. Fernández, I., García, A.L., Yuste, A.: IoT system for smart cities: A prototype of a flood warning system with water level sensing. In: Int. Conf. Innovative Trends in Communication and Computer Engineering (ITCE), pp. 93–96. IEEE (2020)
28. Dey, S., Bhattacherjee, R., Bandyopadhyay, S.: IoT-enabled real-time flood monitoring system for low-lying urban areas. Int. J. Ad Hoc Ubiquitous Comput. **38**(1), 37–45 (2021)
29. Jena, M., Subashini, S., Srinivasan, A.: IoT-based smart flood detection and alert system using LoRaWAN. Mater. Today: Proc. **46**, 10791–10796 (2021)
30. Kumar, M., Dhiman, M.: An IoT-based flood forecasting model using machine learning. Int. J. Recent Technol. Eng. **8**(2), 3774–3778 (2019)
31. Shaker, H., Alsanad, A.: Real-time flood monitoring and warning system based on wireless sensor network. J. Adv. Res. Dyn. Control Syst. **10**(10), 1559–1569 (2018)
32. Darvishi, A., Safa, H., Alizadeh, A.: Real-time flood detection system using IoT and machine learning. J. Ambient. Intell. Humaniz. Comput. **12**(10), 9585–9597 (2021)
33. Manogaran, G., Lopez, D.: A survey of big data architectures and machine learning algorithms in healthcare. J. King Saud Univ. - Comput. Inf. Sci. **31**(4), 415–427 (2018)
34. Bhardwaj, K., Singh, A., Soni, A.: IoT-based flood detection and prediction system using machine learning techniques. In: Proc. 5th Int. Conf. Computing Methodologies and Communication (ICCMC), pp. 1423–1427. IEEE (2021)
35. Liu, J., Wu, G., Wang, Y.: A hybrid machine learning model for flood prediction using multi-source data. J. Hydrol. **563**, 20–29 (2018)
36. Ch, P., Katkar, P.: Smart flood detection and alert system using IoT. Mater. Today: Proc. **46**, 10515–10519 (2021)
37. Devika, A.R., Rajalakshmi, P., Shankar, A., Rajesh, R.: Intelligent flood monitoring system using machine learning algorithms. J. Ambient. Intell. Humaniz. Comput. **11**(11), 5159–5170 (2020)

38. Yang, J., Deng, M.: IoT-based flood monitoring system using deep learning algorithms. Appl. Sci. **10**(7), 2318 (2020)
39. Yin, J., Li, L., Luo, S.: A review of machine learning models for flood prediction. Environ Model Softw. **117**, 192–206 (2019)
40. Smith, M., Brown, L., Johnson, J.: Implementation of a real-time flood detection system using IoT. Int. J. Eng. Adv. Technol. **9**(3), 5241–5246 (2020)
41. Yu, Z., Wei, J., Zhao, Q.: Flood forecasting and warning system based on machine learning and IoT. In: IEEE Int. Conf. Progress in Informatics and Computing (PIC), pp. 236–240. IEEE (2018)
42. Chia, H.K., Li, P.Y.: IoT-based flood detection and alert system using machine learning. J. Environ. Manag. **242**, 146–153 (2019)
43. Khalid, M., Hanif, S., Tariq, M.: IoT-based smart flood monitoring and alerting system using MQTT and Blynk. Int. J. Comput. Sci. Netw. Secur. **18**(10), 33–39 (2018)
44. Jia, Y., Yu, H., Zhou, L.: IoT-based flood monitoring system using deep learning. IEEE Access **8**, 23544–23556 (2020)
45. Mohanraj, I., Anandakumar, H., Mohanraj, J.: Smart flood monitoring and alerting system based on machine learning. Mater. Today: Proc. **33**, 321–326 (2020)
46. Rani, K., Kumar, P.: Machine learning techniques for flood prediction and early warning systems. Environ. Sci. Pollut. Res. **28**(2), 13677–13688 (2021)
47. Mehdi, M., Khader, J.: IoT-based flood alert and monitoring system using fuzzy logic. J. King Saud Univ. - Comput. Inf. Sci. **33**(6), 678–687 (2021)
48. Hameed, M., Rashid, M.: Design and development of a smart flood warning system using IoT. Int. J. Adv. Comput. Sci. Appl. **9**(4), 207–212 (2018)
49. Yasar, A., Hamid, N.A.A.: Flood monitoring and alerting system using IoT and machine learning. In: Proc. IEEE 5th Int. Conf. Computing Methodologies and Communication (ICCMC), pp. 1493–1497. IEEE (2021)
50. Al-Rawi, M., Khaleel, R.: IoT-based flood monitoring and early warning system using machine learning. In: Proc. IEEE 8th Int. Conf. Smart City Applications (SCA), pp. 56–60. IEEE (2021)

PrEACT: Predictive Learning for Early Action in Civil Complaints with AI and Temporal Modeling

Yohan Chang(✉)

Korea Research Institution for Human Settlements, Gukchaegyeonguwon-Ro 5, Sejong-Si 30147, South Korea
ycanns@krihs.re.kr

Abstract. This paper presents a novel approach for predicting citizen civil complaints related to public safety—such as potholes, illegal dumping, and unauthorized installations on roads—using a hybrid deep learning model. The proposed model combines Convolutional Neural Networks (CNN) and Long Short-Term Memory (LSTM) networks. We utilize an unprecedented nationwide dataset comprising three years of civil complaints collected across all regions of South Korea (2021–2023), aggregated into 1 km spatiotemporal grid cells to ensure privacy while maintaining spatial resolution for analysis. These spatiotemporal cells enable AI-driven predictive analytics that support proactive urban management. Our framework, Predictive Learning for Early Action in Civil Complaints with AI and Temporal modeling (PrEACT), captures both spatial distribution and temporal trends of complaints, providing predictive insights into *when*, *where*, *how*, and *what* issues are likely to arise. Experimental results demonstrate that our hybrid model outperforms both a baseline approach and a Random Forest model in terms of Root Mean Square Error (RMSE). In addition, prediction results are visualized through interactive civil complaint maps, making insights easily accessible to both the public and government agencies. To the best of the authors' knowledge, this is the first attempt to apply civil complaint data in a microscale, grid-based manner across both urban and rural contexts. This work underscores the importance of integrating AI and big data into public service delivery and lays the foundation for more proactive, data-driven policy interventions.

Keywords: Civil complaints · Spatio-temporal prediction · CNN-LSTM model · Smart city infrastructure · Public safety analytics

M. Kassim et al. (Eds.): SCDS 2025, CCIS 2674, pp. 144–154, 2026.
https://doi.org/10.1007/978-981-95-8368-3_11

1 Introduction

The Internet of Things (IoT) is widely acknowledged for its role in both individual services, such as navigation, and public services, including infrastructure management. Thanks to advancements in information and communication technology (ICT), everything is interconnected, enabling real-time communication and rapid information dissemination. In particular, within the domain of infrastructure management, various road-related events, such as incidents and congestion, can quickly spread through text messages, social media, and news outlets, transcending physical, temporal, and national boundaries.

As urban areas expand both spatially and temporally, a range of citizen-reported issues stemming from limited space and high population density, such as illegal parking, road cracks, and waste accumulation, have increasingly come to the forefront. While governments strive to maintain infrastructure conditions in response to these demands, administrative monitoring systems tend to prioritize only major areas. Due to limitations in administrative capacity and budget, citizens recognize that it is not feasible to manage all areas in a timely manner. Ironically, this has widened the gap between rural and urban infrastructure management, resulting in a decentralized system.

Among various types of infrastructure, road management plays a crucial role due to its impact on transportation. Roads, designed for high-speed and mass movement, can become dangerous when unexpected objects appear, raising significant safety concerns. Despite continued efforts to improve road monitoring, blind spots persist due to the limited ability to oversee all areas, as previously noted.

The concept of the "living lab", a citizen-driven management approach where anonymous individuals monitor and report real-time issues within their communities, is gaining traction nationwide. This approach offers meaningful contributions to infrastructure monitoring by addressing issues such as road cracks, illegal dumping, and potholes in a timely manner, overcoming the physical limitations of government-level real-time monitoring. For example, in South Korea, rising concerns over illegal parking and potholes demonstrate the urgency of citizen involvement. Civil complaints have increased each year: 11.3 million in 2021, 11.5 million in 2022, and 14.6 million in 2023 [1].

Unlike new media, civil complaints have often remained hidden from public analysis due to the inclusion of personal information and complex circumstances. As administrative bodies have not treated them as usable data, issues such as name and location confidentiality have further restricted access. The presence of sensitive and spatially detailed content, combined with privacy laws, has contributed to this hesitation. Nevertheless, if civil complaint data can be processed with appropriate privacy protections, they could serve as valuable assets for public interest, offering high-resolution insights across wide spatial ranges.

This study presents a novel approach to addressing such complex challenges by leveraging IoT and ICT environments to balance personal privacy with public safety. We propose PrEACT, Predictive learning for Early Action in Civil complaints with AI and Temporal modeling. Specifically, PrEACT collects public safety-related issues such as potholes, illegal parking, and littering, and aggregates them at a 1 km grid resolution. These aggregated data are then input into a hybrid deep learning model combining a Convolutional Neural Network (CNN) with a Long Short-Term Memory

(LSTM) network. The trained model predicts when, where, how, and what types of civil complaints and consequential events may arise in the near future, allowing administrative bodies to preemptively allocate resources and take corrective actions.

We anticipate that PrEACT will become a powerful tool for enhancing public safety by utilizing civil complaint data., resources that have previously remained untapped in this domain. To the best of the authors' knowledge, this study represents the first attempt to apply deep learning to civil complaints for the purpose of public safety management.

The remainder of this paper is organized as follows. Section 2 revisits related literature. Section 3 details the PrEACT framework. Section 4 presents the experimental setup and results, and Sect. 5 concludes with discussions and future directions.

2 Related Work

Although a wealth of studies has addressed safety concerns such as potholes and illegal parking using various prediction models in the transportation domain, few, if any, have explored the application of deep learning models using civil complaints as a data source.

Civil complaints, despite originating from individuals within the same community, are often withheld from public disclosure due to their inclusion of complex and sensitive information, as well as the personal intent behind reporting the issues [2–6]. Most efforts to utilize such data have been limited to basic statistical analyses, typically categorized by domains of interest such as urban planning, transportation, or administration [1]. Some studies have attempted to evaluate citizen satisfaction with administrative actions by comparing complaint trends with historical government response records [2, 7].

In response to privacy concerns, alternative approaches have emerged. For instance, kernel density estimation has been applied to visualize illegal parking hotspots while obscuring exact complaint locations. While this method provides a useful bird's-eye view of frequently reported areas, its smoothing effect can obscure specific points of interest and reduce the precision necessary for effective administrative targeting [4].

Other efforts have explored the use of Urban AI concepts, applying machine learning models such as XGBoost to demonstrate the predictive potential of civil complaint data for future administrative planning [4, 8]. However, these models often lack integration of fine-grained geospatial information, thereby overlooking spatial correlations that may be critical for local-level policy implementation [9]. For example, Park and Kang (2024) proposed a mechanism for detecting illegal parking based on civil complaints [10]. Although their work contributes meaningfully through text mining techniques, it focuses more on textual classification than on prediction or spatial-temporal modeling. While text mining is undoubtedly essential for extracting meaning from complaint narratives, it alone cannot capture the broader trends or the "when–where–how–what" dimensions that are vital for ensuring public safety.

To fill this research gap, the present study introduces a framework that identifies public safety-related points of interest (POIs) from historical civil complaint data and feeds them into a hybrid deep learning model combining CNN and LSTM networks. CNN-LSTM is currently widely adapted in many prediction domains [8, 11–14]. To address privacy concerns, the proposed model, PrEACT, aggregates complaint data at the 1 km grid level, effectively anonymizing individual submissions while preserving spatial structure for predictive learning.

3 Methodology

The methodology of PrEACT is relatively straightforward. The first step involves extracting all safety-related civil complaints, including those concerning potholes, illegal parking, illegal dumping, and similar issues. These complaints are then aggregated to the 1 km grid level, thereby mitigating concerns related to personal information, such as proximity to residential or commercial areas. Once aggregated, the data are fed into a CNN-LSTM model for predictive learning.

This study utilizes three years of civil complaint data, spanning from 2021 to 2023. Specifically, there were 11,291,498 civil complaints recorded in 2021 across South Korea, 11,558,550 in 2022, and 14,594,501 in 2023. Among these, some complaints were identified as duplicates; after deduplication, approximately 95% of the records remained as unique entries. The next step involves extracting location information. Complaints unrelated to public safety, such as requests for building renovations or proposals for new subway stations, were excluded. After several data cleaning steps and point extraction using text mining techniques, 43.2% of the 2021 data, 47.1% of the 2022 data, and 55.4% of the 2023 data were retained as valid POIs, containing relevant safety-related content.

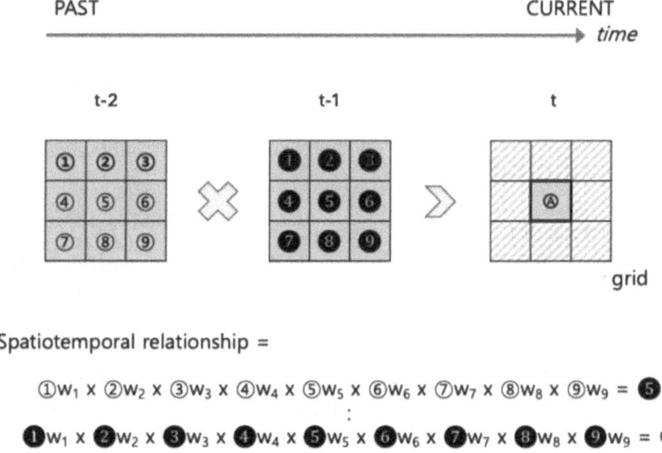

Fig. 1. A general concept of spatiotemporal relationship for grid learning in this study. *Note: Every grid has been affected by its spatiotemporal relationship. t represents time and each number on grid represents grid ID at time t-2, t-1, and t. (image modified from Chang et. al. 2024 and created by author)*

The integrated POI data from all three years then underwent geospatial processing. Drawing from the concept of cellular geography [15], observed data were rearranged at the 1 km grid level. This concept emphasizes that spatial phenomena are influenced not only by their own historical behavior but also by that of neighboring areas. As depicted in Fig. 1, an event occurring in grid Ⓐat time t is influenced by its surrounding grids (❶ through ❾) at time t–1. In turn, each of those grids (e.g., ❺) is the result of influences from time t–2 and their respective surrounding areas (① through ⑨). This recursive spatial-temporal dependency forms the foundation of PrEACT, asserting that accumulated patterns across both space and time inform future outcomes.

The next core component of PrEACT is the learning architecture. To effectively capture spatial-temporal patterns, a hybrid deep learning model was adopted. Specifically, PrEACT employs a CNN-LSTM model to reflect dynamic geospatial correlations. The convolutional architecture (CNN) is particularly well-suited for analyzing grid-based spatial patterns, while the LSTM component captures temporal dependencies over a sequence of time steps.

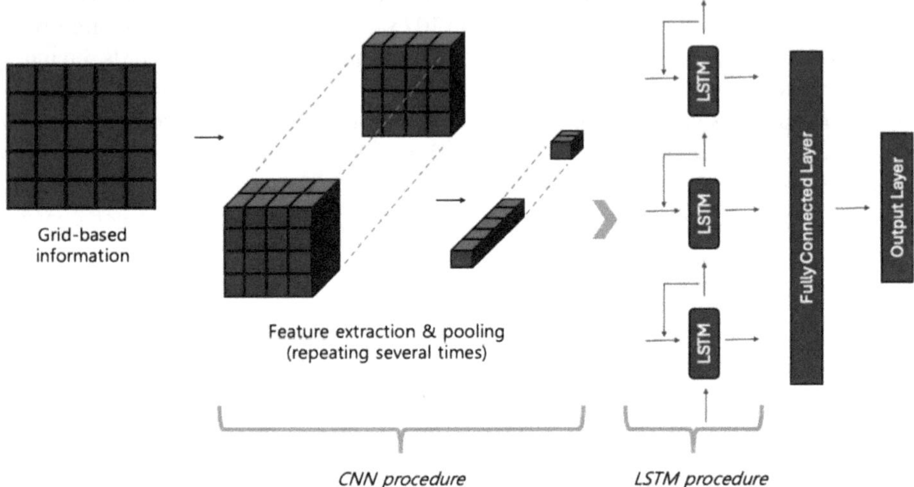

Fig. 2. A general process of CNN-LSTM in PrEACT. *Note: In CNN-LSTM architecture, grid-based information transformed into long-type data in CNN procedure, and this will be fed to LSTM procedure. (image modified from Chang et. al. 2024 and created by author)*

In the CNN layer, the input is structured into n × n grid dimensions. Through a series of operations such as convolution, feature mapping, and pooling, the spatial resolution is reduced, resulting in a 1 × n format, flattened but enriched with spatial features. This output is then passed into the LSTM model. Within the LSTM, the network processes data in sequential batches, learning long-term trends with less emphasis and recent patterns with more weight. This prioritization enables the model to preserve historical context while optimizing predictions based on the most current data. The CNN-LSTM integration allows for robust forecasting across both spatial and temporal dimensions, generating reliable predictions on civil complaints in a grid-based format.

A general schematic of the CNN-LSTM process as implemented in PrEACT is illustrated in Fig. 2.

4 Experimental Results

The CNN-LSTM model in PrEACT operates on a total of 107,442 grids across South Korea, with 218 time-series columns spanning from 2021 to 2023, as illustrated in Fig. 2. To achieve optimal model performance, a set of hyperparameters was tuned using a simple yet effective heuristic method: Hill-Climbing Optimization. This method incrementally updates parameter values to identify optimal configurations efficiently.

For comparison, two additional models were evaluated using the same input structure: Random Forest (RF), a widely used classification model, and a Baseline model. In the RF model, key hyperparameters such as the number of trees and the best split variable (mtry) were also optimized using the Hill-Climbing approach. The Baseline model utilized only historical averages from 2021 and 2022 for each grid, with no dynamic learning.

Table 1. Each prediction results according to scenarios in RMSE.

Month of Prediction	Potholes			Illegal dumping			Illegal installations		
	Baseline	RF	CNN-LSTM	Baseline	RF	CNN-LSTM	Baseline	RF	CNN-LSTM
Jan	2.584	1.223	1.210	2.262	1.056	1.044	0.539	0.377	0.361
Feb	2.594	1.128	1.116	1.931	0.908	0.895	0.433	0.258	0.247
Mar	2.769	1.189	1.171	2.489	1.118	1.102	0.465	0.260	0.251
Apr	2.639	1.021	1.003	1.833	0.828	0.807	0.257	0.179	0.170
May	2.928	1.116	1.094	3.334	1.749	1.714	0.263	0.166	0.155
June	2.723	1.034	1.014	4.643	2.310	2.289	0.283	0.191	0.183
Jul	3.806	1.504	1.478	2.089	0.932	0.911	0.377	0.232	0.222
Aug	2.284	1.176	1.156	2.362	1.327	1.286	0.246	0.155	0.143
Sep	3.710	1.252	1.233	2.505	1.395	1.359	0.245	0.166	0.159
Oct	3.619	1.467	1.451	2.550	1.260	1.242	0.202	0.141	0.134
Nov	3.130	1.350	1.336	2.045	0.889	0.863	0.297	0.211	0.198
Dec	3.029	1.261	1.249	2.135	1.012	0.987	0.243	0.180	0.174
Yearly Ave	3.068	1.227	1.209	2.515	1.232	1.208	0.321	0.210	0.200

Note:Three safety scenarios, Portholes, Illegal dumping, and Illegal installations are prepared by each month of year (numbers prepared by authors)

Both the CNN-LSTM and RF models performed monthly predictions. The training dataset consisted of civil complaint records from 2021 and 2022, while 2023 data was reserved for testing. Specifically, 2021 data was used to train the model for predicting events in 2022, and the model trained on 2022 data was used to predict 2023 events. Since actual event records for 2023 are available, they served as the ground truth for model validation.

The modeling environment included both R and Python, incorporating libraries such as data.table, dplyr, sf, and randomForest in R, and keras, pandas, and numpy in Python. For hyperparameter settings, RF was configured with mtry optimized by a step factor of 1.5 and tree counts ranging from 1 to 980. The CNN-LSTM was trained with 100

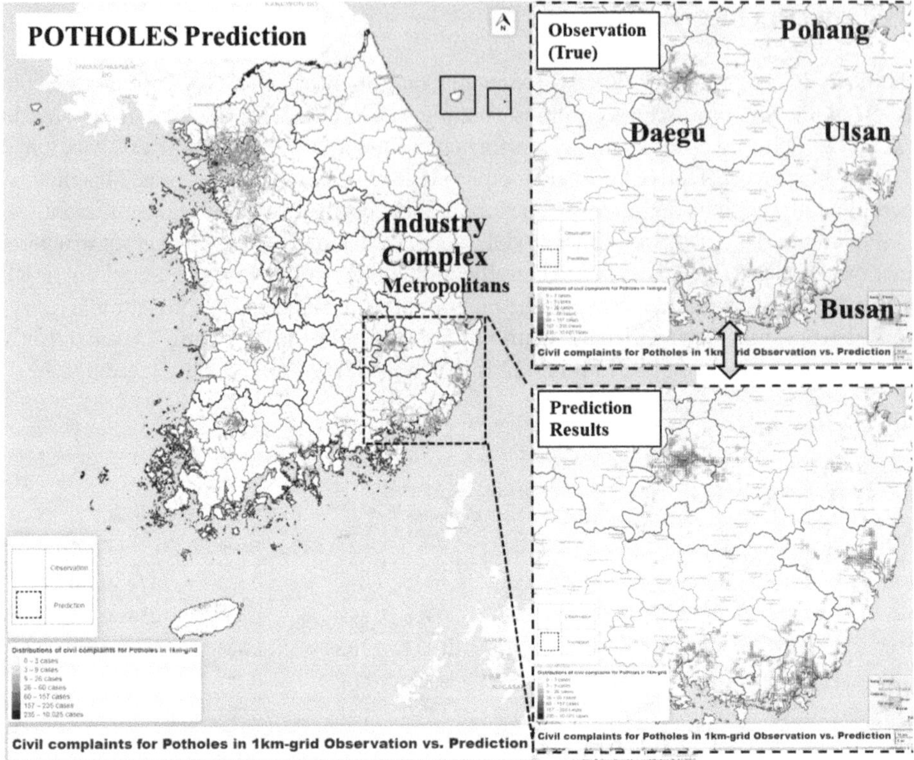

Fig. 3. Examples of spatial distribution of prediction results for Potholes *(image modified from Chang,* [16] *and created by author)*

epochs, a batch size of 256, and ReLU activation functions. The Adam optimizer was used in LSTM, with CNN layers comprising single feature extraction, max pooling, and flattening. The Root Mean Square Error (RMSE) was used as the primary performance metric for all models. For RF's out-of-bag (OOB) validation, a simple golden-ratio split was applied.

The experimental focus included three critical public safety concerns: potholes, illegal dumping, and illegal installations. Each issue has direct implications for road safety. Potholes can severely affect driving comfort and contribute to the breakdown of vehicle platoons, leading to cascading effects. Illegal dumping creates surface irregularities that hinder smooth driving and can trigger accidents. Illegal installations obstruct driver visibility, reducing reaction time and increasing risk. As shown in Fig. 1, each issue was modeled in a spatio-temporal 1 km grid format.

Table 1 presents the prediction results for the Baseline, RF, and CNN-LSTM models across each scenario. Results are summarized monthly, with annual averages shown at the bottom of the table. Both RF and CNN-LSTM significantly outperformed the Baseline across all months and safety scenarios. In the case of potholes, for example, prediction accuracy nearly doubled compared to the Baseline. Between RF and CNN-LSTM, the latter consistently delivered higher accuracy across all scenarios. While some

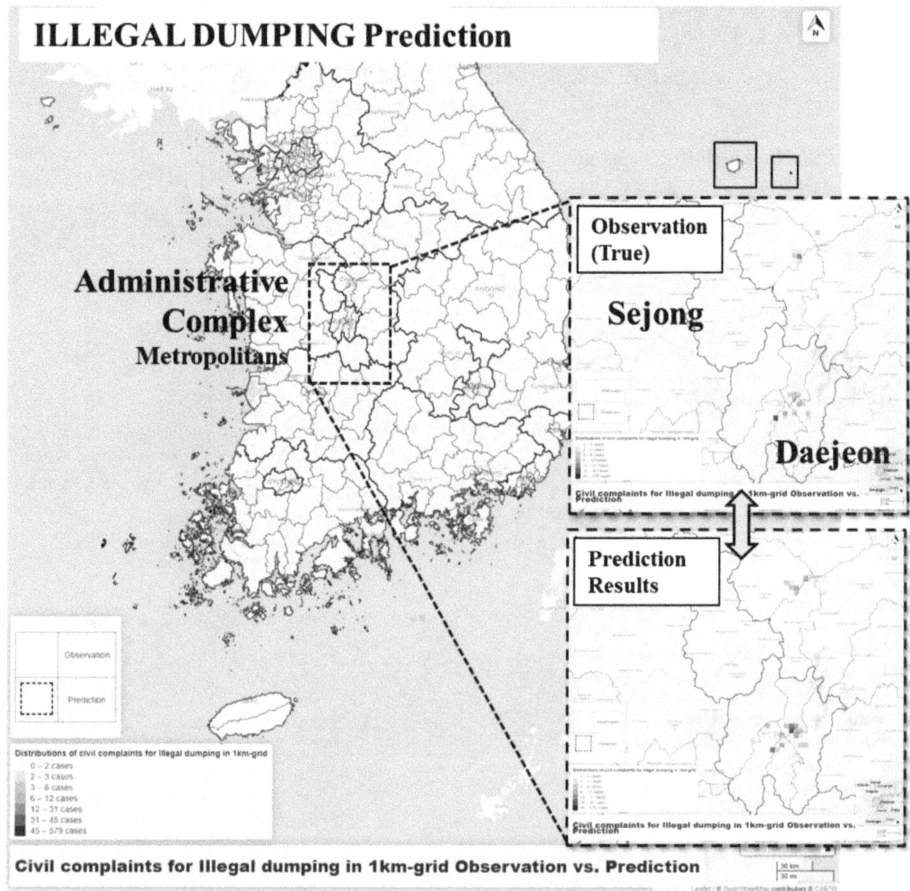

Fig. 4. Examples of spatial distribution of prediction results for Illegal dumping *(image modified from Chang,* [16] *and created by author)*

may consider marginal gains, such as a few percentage points, insignificant, it's important to note that even small prediction improvements can help prevent secondary incidents on roads.

On average, CNN-LSTM outperformed RF by 1.5% for potholes, 2.0% for illegal dumping, and 4.9% for illegal installations in terms of RMSE. These results demonstrate the strength of the hybrid deep learning approach in capturing both spatial and temporal patterns for predictive safety management.

Figure 3 through Fig. 5 visualize the series of spatio-temporal prediction results: potholes in Fig. 3., illegal dumping in Fig. 4. And illegal installations in Fig. 5. In these maps, dashed grids highlight predicted areas, created using the leaflet package in R. For better interpretability, the Busan region and closed cities, major industrial complex metropolitan areas in South Korea, were selected for the pothole scenario, while Sejong, the nation's administrative capital, was used for illegal dumpling. Seoul, capital of South Korea, was selected for illegal installation. Beyond numeric accuracy as

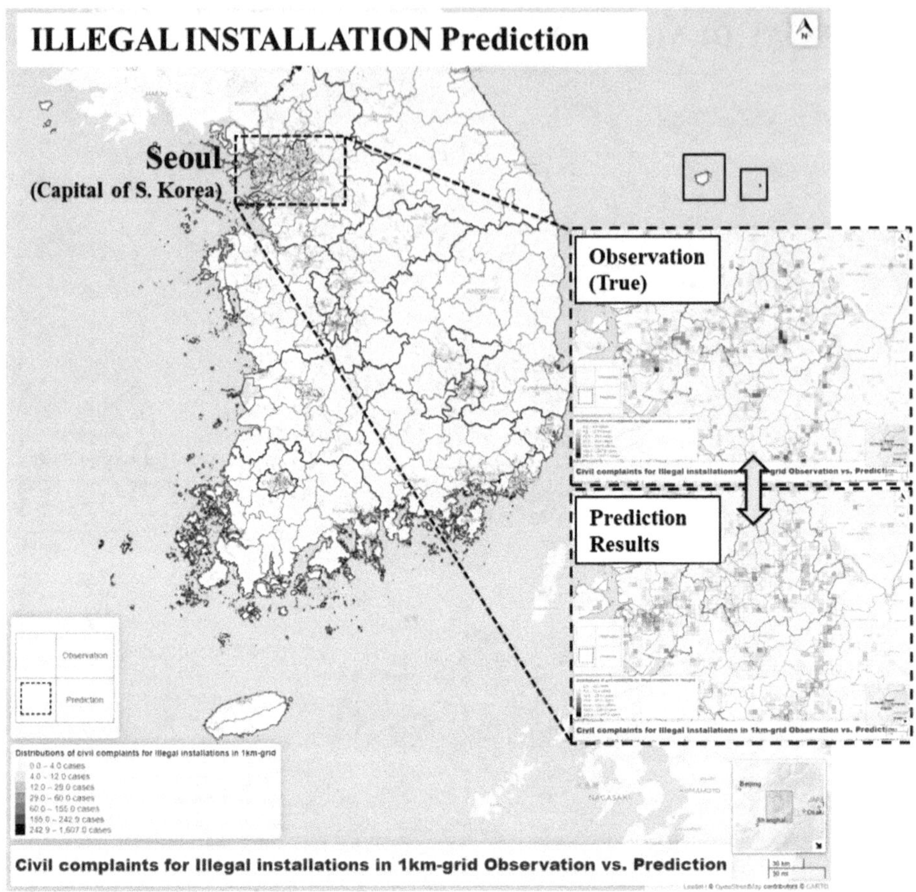

Fig. 5. Examples of spatial distribution of prediction results for Illegal installations *(image modified from Chang,* [16] *and created by author)*

shown in Table 1, spatial alignment between prediction and observation further validates the model's utility. This reinforces the importance of not only how many, but also where and when public safety issues are likely to occur.

5 Conclusions

The Internet of Things (IoT) offers numerous opportunities to connect and learn from our daily environments. In the past, civil complaints were often kept private or were rarely brought into the public domain. However, with growing interest in issues "near my neighborhood," civic engagement in regional concerns has emerged as a new form of community-driven monitoring. This paper presents a novel approach to predict *when, where, how,* and *what* public safety issues may arise in the near future. Specifically, we introduced PrEACT, Predictive learning for Early Action in Civil complaints with

AI and Temporal modeling, as a framework to leverage IoT and ICT environments to convert personally sensitive data into tools for public safety.

This study focused on key safety-related civil complaints, namely potholes, illegal dumping, and illegal installations, as case studies. PrEACT integrates a spatio-temporal learning framework using a hybrid deep learning model that combines Convolutional Neural Networks (CNN) and Long Short-Term Memory (LSTM) networks. Additionally, hyperparameter tuning was conducted using simple optimization techniques. For comparison, a Baseline model and a Random Forest model were also tested using the same input data. The results demonstrated that the CNN-LSTM approach in PrEACT consistently outperformed the comparison models. Even marginal improvements in predictive accuracy can translate into meaningful enhancements in road safety and health-related outcomes.

While this study contributes to both civil complaint analytics and hybrid deep learning applications, several improvements remain for future work. First, the Point-of-Interest (POI) extraction method from civil complaint texts should be refined. In this study, only address-related information (e.g., coordinates) was extracted, resulting in approximately half of the data being usable. As highlighted in Park and Kang (2024), more advanced techniques, such as named entity recognition or context-aware extraction, should be explored in future work.

Second, the modeling framework should be expanded. While this study compared two models, Random Forest (a linear, tree-based classifier) and CNN-LSTM (a non-linear, neural network-based model), recent advances offer more powerful alternatives. In particular, Large Language Models (LLMs) and Transformer-based architectures, such as Generative Pretrained Transformers (GPTs), provide opportunities to integrate natural language understanding with structured prediction tasks.

Lastly, more application scenarios should be explored. This study examined three cases, potholes, illegal dumping, and illegal installations, but many other types of civil complaints remain untapped. Expanding the model to include a broader range of public safety concerns can further enhance the quality of life and strengthen proactive infrastructure management in communities.

Acknowledgments. This research is reorganized from one of the findings for 'AI-raDaR: AI-driven Nowcasting Framework for Disaster Resilience and Emergency Response', Korea Research Institute for Human Settlements (KRIHS), Sejong-si, South Korea, 2025.

References

1. Civil complaint's Visualization: webpage (https:www.bigdata.epoeple.go.kr. Access date: 13 Mar 2025)
2. Alathur, S,P., Ilavarasan, V., Gupta, M.P.: Citizen participation and effectiveness of e-petition: Sutharyakeralam-India. Transforming Gov.: People Process Policy **6**(4), 392–403 (2012)
3. Leston-Bandeira, C.: Parliamentary petitions and public engagement: an empirical analysis of the role of e-petitions. Policy Politics **47**(3), 415–436 (2019)
4. Chang, Y.H., Son, J.S., Choi, H.R.: Policy-oriented improvement strategies for enhancing Civil Complaint Maps in public issue monitoring. Korea Res. Inst. Hum. Settlements (2024)

5. Oktarino, A., Defit, S.: Improving accuracy performance on CNN and BiLSTM algorithms for classification of public complaints against police through WhatsAPP. In: 2024 8th International Conference on Information Technology, Information Systems and Electrical Engineering (ICITISEE). pp. 399–404 (2024)
6. Shama, F., Aziz, A., Deya, L.B.M.: CitySolution: a complaining task distributive mobile application for smart city corporation using deep learning. SoftwareX **27**, 101829 (2024)
7. Zhang, S., Li, Y., Boamah, E.F.: 311 calls and neighborhood attributes: a panel study of housing prices. J. Reg. Sci. **64**(4), 1414–1440 (2024)
8. Chen, T., et al.: Xgboost: extreme gradient boosting. R Package Version 0.4–2. **1**(4), 1–4. (2015)
9. Gao, S., Hu, Y., Li, W.: Handbook of Geospatial Artificial Intelligence. CRC Press (2023)
10. Park, J., Kang, M.G.: Spatial information extraction and basic analysis from 120 dasan call civil complaint texts through named entity recognition modeling. J. Korea Plann. Assoc. **59**(7), 169–180 (2024)
11. Lu, W., Li, J., Li, Y., Sun, A., Wang, J.: A CNN-LSTM-based model to forecast stock prices. Complexity **1**, 6622927 (2020)
12. Zhou, Q., Teng, S., Liao, X., Situ, Z., Feng, J., and Chen, G.: A deep learning technique-based data-driven model for accurate and rapid flood prediction. Hydrology and Earth System Sciences Discussions, pp. 1–22 (2022)
13. Pandi, S.S., Farook, A.M., Kingston, W.: Scenario based deep learning prediction for legal judgment using LSTM and CNN. Third International Conference on Smart Technologies, Communication and Robotics (STCR), pp. 1–6 (2023)
14. Cai, B., Camarcat, L., Shang, W.L., Quddus, M.: A new spatiotemporal convolutional neural network model for short-term crash prediction. Front. Eng. Manage. **12**(1), 86–98 (2025)
15. Tobler, W.R.: Cellular geography. Philos. Geogr. **379**, 379–386 (1979)
16. Chang, Y.: GeoAI in policymaking. The International Encyclopedia of Geography (2026)

A Review of Deep Learning and Hybrid Techniques for Credit Card Fraud Detection: Trends, Challenges, and Solutions

Sulaiman N. S. Albreem[1(✉)], Jasni Mohamad Zain[1,3], and Abdul Kadir Jumaat[2,3]

[1] School of Computing Sciences, Faculty of Computer and Mathematical Sciences, Universiti Teknologi MARA, Shah Alam 40450, Selangor, Malaysia
2023547829@student.uitm.edu.my

[2] School of Mathematical Sciences, Faculty of Computer and Mathematical Sciences, Universiti Teknologi MARA, Shah Alam 40450, Selangor, Malaysia

[3] Institute for Big Data Analytics and Artificial Intelligence, Universiti Teknologi MARA, Shah Alam 40450, Selangor, Malaysia

Abstract. Fraud detection in online financial transactions has become increasingly important with the rapid growth of digital payment systems and the evolving nature of fraudulent behavior. This literature review examines recent studies on fraud detection, with a specific focus on deep learning and hybrid approaches that combine multiple algorithms to enhance detection accuracy. It examines peer-reviewed works published from 2021 to 2025, emphasizing key trends in the use of deep learning models and their integration with optimization techniques. Frequently used datasets, evaluation metrics, and model architectures are reviewed to provide a comprehensive overview of current practices. In contrast to existing reviews, this study introduces a comparative analysis of several hybrid models, assessing their architectural components, strategies for handling class imbalance, and sequential learning capabilities. Additionally, it offers a critical evaluation of emerging innovations such as attention mechanisms, Generative Adversarial Networks (GANs), and reinforcement learning, highlighting their effectiveness and limitations. The review also identifies core challenges in the field, including the continuous evolution of fraudulent tactics, limitations in available datasets, data imbalance, and the interpretability of models. Finally, the paper discusses potential future directions and emerging solutions that aim to address these gaps. This study seeks to guide researchers and practitioners toward the development of more effective, scalable, and intelligent fraud detection systems by leveraging deep learning and hybrid techniques.

Keywords: Fraud Detection · Deep Learning · Hybrid Techniques · Long Short-Term Memory (LSTM) · Gated Recurrent Unit (GRU) · Imbalanced Dataset

M. Kassim et al. (Eds.): SCDS 2025, CCIS 2674, pp. 155–175, 2026.
https://doi.org/10.1007/978-981-95-8368-3_12

1 Introduction

With the advancement of internet technologies, the online market has witnessed a significant expansion [1]. A growing number of people are now participating in online shopping and completing financial transactions via e-commerce platforms. The majority of financial institutions and banks provide enhanced services aimed at encouraging individuals and businesses to perform transactions over the internet. Despite these advancements, they remain prime targets for fraud, which leads to consumer distrust and hesitation in adopting digital tools. According to the Nilson Report 2022 [2], bank card fraud is projected to cost the US economy over $165.1 billion in losses within the next decade. This highlights that fraudulent activities continue to impose substantial financial burdens on global economies. As a result, there is an urgent need for the development of advanced techniques to detect fraud, limit its impact, and reduce the possibility of its exploitation. This situation should rise a critical alarm to various stakeholders including governments, industries, banks, e-commerce platforms, insurers, telecom providers, and financial institutions to strengthen their cybersecurity infrastructure and protect both their clients and the wider public.

Fraud occurs when an individual uses another's personal or financial data without their consent for online or offline activities, typically for financial gain. It aims to harm the original owners by exploiting their private data, either with or without their knowledge [3], and applies stolen data to unlawful transactions, such as buying, software registration, accessing e-services, or subscribing to memberships. The concept may also extend to illegal buying of everyday necessities. In addition to the financial damage inflicted on victims, the deceptive nature of fraud can result in long-term effects, including diminished credit scores, identity theft, and psychological distress [1]. Fraudulent activities often involve phishing, hacking, and social engineering to acquire sensitive information. Fraudsters also exploit weaknesses in security systems or public unawareness about online payments. The simplicity and growth of online payment services have widened the scope of fraudulent activity and turned it into a global issue. Large-scale transnational fraud schemes now pervade, making them increasingly hard to track and investigate. For example, certain fraudsters utilize stolen credit card details to buy goods in real stores, while others gain unauthorized access to financial services.

The issue of fraud remains persistent and costly, particularly with the increasing volume of e-commerce transactions and the risk of capital and profit loss. Therefore, the continuous development of sophisticated fraud detection systems has been necessary to secure all parties of the online payment community, including consumers, retailers, and payment gateways. Nevertheless, fraudsters have learned how to evade security mechanisms by refining their methods [4]. This is one of the main challenges in credit card fraud detection systems, where different fraud methods should be identified and detected. The increasing number of online transactions provides a huge amount of data for analysis. By analyzing such data, researchers can discover patterns that contribute to detecting and preventing fraudsters' criminal activities.

1.1 Objectives

In this literature, several recent studies on credit card fraud detection with focused on deep learning and hybrid methods to enhance the detection accuracy, adaptability, and performance. These studies aim to address changes in the fraudsters' behavior and how the recent model can adapt to the changes in fraud patterns and address the limitations in traditional detection systems. Therefore, this paper aims to review the current state of the research in this area and emphasizes in use of hybrid methods to enhance fraud detection models. This literature review is guided by the following objectives:

1. To identify current research efforts in fraud detection using deep learning approaches augmented with hybrid solutions, including models such as AE, GAN, RNN, LSTM, and GRU.
2. To investigate recent approaches and advances in hybrid fraud detection systems, focusing on how deep learning methods are integrated with other technologies such as optimization algorithms and ensemble learning to enhance the adaptability and detection accuracy.
3. To examine key challenges associated with deep learning and hybrid techniques for fraud detection, including the lack of high-quality datasets, class imbalance, real-time detection requirements, and limited model interpretability.
4. To evaluate the effectiveness and performance of recent fraud detection models using common evaluation metrics, such as accuracy, precision, recall, F1-score, and AUC-ROC, and to identify promising strategies and future research directions that enhance scalability and robustness.

1.2 Contribution

1. The study covers and analyzes research up to 2025, including cutting-edge approaches for fraud detection, such as intention-based neural networks, which are not widely explored in earlier reviews.
2. Unlike prior works that focus mainly on standalone deep learning models, this review emphasizes hybrid architectures that integrate deep learning with optimization techniques, ensemble learning, and other methods to improve detection performance and robustness.
3. Beyond summarizing model architectures, this study provides a comparative analysis of hybrid and deep learning models in terms of accuracy, recall, F1-score, and AUC. This helps guide researchers and financial institutions in selecting or designing effective fraud detection systems.
4. The review also examines well-known fraud detection datasets such as the Euro Credit Card, PaySim, and IEEE-CIS datasets highlighting their characteristics, limitations, and suitability for evaluating hybrid models and advanced techniques.

2 Background

2.1 Deep Learning

Deep learning (DL) techniques form the foundation of many fraud detection models due to their ability to capture complex patterns and allows to deal with the data of a high volume for making predictions or decisions [5]. DL is an attempt to emulate the internal process of the human brain to provide the correct outcome through the simulation of its function and structure. The word deep in DL implies that it employs several hidden interconnected layers for carrying out the data processing. In DL methods, data moves between different layers to make further calculations and extract some knowledge from the data. Besides this, DL can tune some variables, or even a part of the data can be returned to the previous layers. This process is called backpropagation [6] as described in Fig. 1. DL can be applied across many domains such as: medicine, education, finance, and manufacturing [6]. Usually, DL can work outstandingly in tasks like prediction, classification, and detection, to provide top-notch outputs. DL can be used in several applications such as: image processing and video analysis, natural language processing (NLP), recommender systems, speech recognition, and financial analysis, and other domains [7]. There are many DL models, and each model has different features, benefits, and optimization methods [7] as shown in Table 1. There is a need to choose the right model for a specific task that involves several considerations: understanding the problem, reviewing the dataset, discovering similar successful implementations, and examining model evaluation measures (accuracy, precision, recall, and F1-score). In the following subsections, we are going to discuss some of the most widely used DL models and the areas where they can be used best.

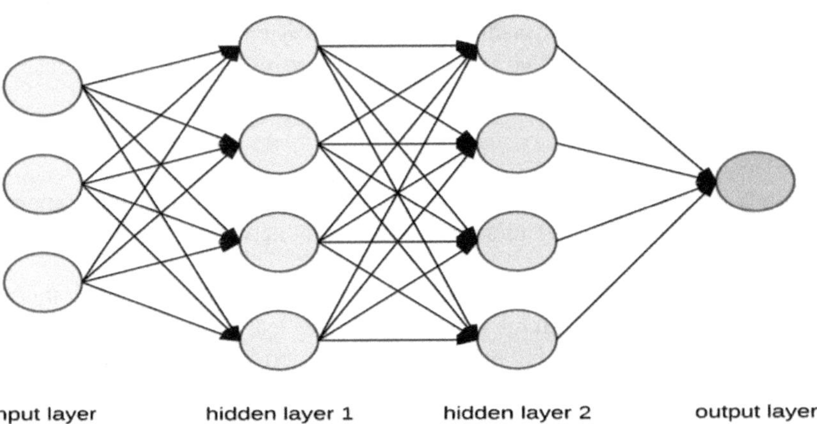

Fig. 1. Deep learning architecture

Convolutional neural networks (CNN)

A convolutional neural network (CNN) is prepared to deal with grid data such as videos, audio, and images; by using several layers consisting of interconnected neurons used to process the data and combine the output as the result. CNN has made a potential improvement in deep learning and can be used in several DL domains such as image segmentation, video processing, and object detection [8]. Typically, a CNN is composed of several layers. The first, and most essential, is the convolutional layer, which performs the core operations of the CNN by extracting important features from the input data. This is achieved through the use of filters or kernels small segments of the input that scan the data to identify specific patterns or features. The next layer is the pooling layer, is used to reduce the spatial dimensions of the feature by downsampling, which helps decrease the computational requirements needed to process the data. Finally, the fully connected layer detects more abstract, high-level features by connecting every neuron from the preceding convolutional and pooling layers to neurons in the subsequent layer. Additionally, fully connected layers serve to map the learned representations from the earlier layers to the final output [9].

Autoencoder (AE)

An Autoencoder (AE) is a deep learning model that uses a feed-forward approach to unsupervised generate outputs similar to the inputs [10]. Its main objective is to learn a low-dimensional representation of high-dimensional data by capturing essential features. AEs are lossy, meaning the output is not an exact replica of the input. An AE consists of three main components: the encoder, the code (bottleneck), and the decoder. The encoder compresses data into a low-dimensional form using hidden layers. The code stores the compressed representation, retaining only the most important features. The decoder reconstructs the input from the code, and its performance determines the AE's result quality and computational efficiency [11]. AEs are applied in recommendation systems [10], image denoising [11], dimensionality reduction [12], and anomaly detection [13]. In fraud detection, the AE is trained on normal data; when faced with abnormal data, reconstruction errors increase, enabling anomaly detection. This technique is effective in various domains, including credit card fraud detection [13].

Generative Adversarial Networks (GAN)

One of the recent neural network models is the Generative Adversarial Network (GAN), which generates synthetic data similar to real datasets. GAN consists of two parts: the Generator, which generates data from a given dataset (video, image, or text), and the Discriminator, which distinguishes real from fake data [14]. During training, the Generator aims to produce synthetic data similar to the real dataset to deceive the Discriminator. The Generator tries to make the synthesized data appear real, while the Discriminator is rewarded for correctly identifying fake data. GANs are used in real-world applications such as generating images from noise, creating realistic face images, transforming images to text, and improving image quality and graphics for gaming [15]. GANs can also generate synthetic MRI images to assist physician training when no real dataset is available [16]. A key feature is their ability to upscale noisy or low-quality medical images to higher resolution for better diagnosis. GANs can be used for data augmentation by generating synthetic datasets when real data is limited [16]. Unsupervised GANs can also detect outliers in unlabeled datasets, enabling detection of fraudulent transactions or criminal activities [17].

Recurrent Neural Network (RNN)

Deep Recurrent Neural Network (RNN) is a subset of deep neural networks which improving process sequential data. The major difference between an RNN and a one-directional feedforward deep neural network model is its ability to store extra information about the state of the current state of the input data [18]. Like any other model of neural networks, RNN contains input, hidden, and output layers. Meanwhile, the main difference of the RNN is that each neuron receives input from the previous layers alongside some information about the status of the previous layer, which helps to adjust some parameters of the current layer and improve capturing sequential data dependencies. The neuron is thus able to update its status on the basis of the information processed and then send this new information to the next layers for further processing. Although RNNs perform well on sequential data, standard RNNs are affected by some issues during the training phase, primarily the vanishing and exploding gradient problems [19].

LSTM & GRU

Long Short-Term Memory (LSTM) is a subtype of RNN developed to handle the vanishing gradient problem in standalone RNNs and manage long-term dependencies. LSTM has two components: gates and cell state. The cell state acts as memory, selectively forgetting or remembering data using both the current input and previous state. There are three gates: the input gate (adds data), the forget gate (removes or retains data), and the output gate (passes data to the next iteration) [20, 21]. This structure enables LSTM to extract meaningful information from long sequences, making it suitable for fraud detection [22], speech recognition [23], and Natural Language Processing [24]. However, LSTM requires high computational power and memory, making training time-consuming [21]. The Gated Recurrent Unit (GRU) reduces LSTM's computational cost by using a similar structure with fewer gates. GRU uses two gates: the update gate, which combines the functions of LSTM's input and forget gates, and the reset gate, which controls how much of the previous state is forgotten [25]. This simplified gating improves modeling of long dependencies while reducing training time and computational demand [26]. GRUs are effective for sequence modeling and tasks like medical data analysis, finance forecasting, fraud detection, machine translation, and time series forecasting [27]. GRUs process variable-length sequences efficiently, making them a strong option for applications requiring a balance between model performance and computational cost.

3 Challenges

Despite the extensive research conducted in the field of fraud detection, numerous challenges remain that hinder the development of fully effective solutions. These challenges can generally be grouped into key areas, including limitations in available datasets, concerns about data privacy, and the continuously evolving techniques used by fraudsters. Because there are not enough good, balanced, and publicly available datasets, training and testing models is difficult, which often results in biased or unreliable findings. Also, rules about privacy and the protection of financial data make it difficult to share data and understand the results of models. Furthermore, fraudsters continually find new ways to evade detection by traditional fraud detection systems. Because of these challenges, there is a necessity for adaptive, transparent, and privacy-aware fraud detection systems to respond to new threats quickly [28].

Table 1. Deep learning models

Model	Year	Typical usage	Suitable for
Generative Adversarial Network (GAN)	2014	Image generation, data augmentation, style transfer	Generative tasks like realistic image synthesis, super-resolution, and deepfakes
Autoencoder (AE)	1980	Dimensionality reduction, denoising, anomaly detection	Feature extraction, unsupervised learning, data compression
Recurrent Neural Network (RNN)	1980	Sequential data modeling, time series, NLP	Simple sequence data (character-level language modeling)
Long Short-Term Memory (LSTM)	1997	Prediction in time series, speech recognition, text generation	dependencies in Long-term sequential data, mitigating the vanishing gradient problem
Gated Recurrent Unit (GRU)	2014	NLP, time series, speech	Similar to LSTM but more efficient; good for sequential data with fewer parameters

3.1 Highly Imbalanced Data

One major challenge in fraud detection is class imbalance, where fraudulent transactions are vastly outnumbered by legitimate ones. The absence of balanced datasets is considered one of the most significant challenges in detecting credit card fraud models. If we examine the available fraud datasets, we could easily observe that the ratio of legitimate to fraudulent transactions is highly skewed. This is because the number of fraudulent transactions is significantly smaller compared to the number of legitimate transactions. The imbalanced dataset can cause several issues during the training process because the model will primarily train on legitimate transactions and a limited number of fraudulent transactions [29]. This issue prevents ML and DL fraud detection models from learning sufficiently about how fraudulent transactions behave and may lead to overfitting, which means the model will incorrectly classify all transactions at a rate of 100%.

Usually, there are few methods to deal with imbalanced datasets. The first is data-level sampling, which deals with modifying the data itself. Oversampling aims to amplify the minor class (fraud transactions) to create new minor transitions that are quite similar to the existing fraud transactions. Many researchers implements sampling methods such as Synthetic Minority Oversampling Technique (SMOTE) to deal with this problem [30]. Although this method is effective but it may generate noisy data that may affect the detection of the fraudulent transactions. The second method is under sampling [31], which aims to reduce the transactions of the majority class (legitimate transactions) to increase the ratio of the fraudulent compared to the legitimate transactions. This means quite many legitimate transactions will be removed from the dataset, and this may delete crucial information, which may affect the learning process of the model. Some researchers suggest using algorithm-level solutions, such as cost-sensitive learning, which considers modifying the training process to pay more attention to the minority class, which help the model learn more about the fraudulent transactions. Overall, class imbalance is not just a technical issue in fraud detection, but a fundamental obstacle that requires a combination of data preprocessing, algorithmic adaptation, and careful evaluation to overcome effectively in credit card fraud detection systems.

3.2 Evolving Fraud Patterns (Concept Drift)

Another challenge in fraud detection is concept drift, where fraud patterns change over time, which means that fraudsters constantly innovate and adapt their methods to evade detection procedures, leading to frequent changes in the characteristics and behavior of fraudulent transactions [13]. Therefore, a model trained on past data can quickly become outdated and insufficient to identify new fraud strategies. For instance, if a machine learning-based model is trained to detect fraud based on transaction location, time, or amount as features, fraudsters can manipulate these features to mimic legitimate behavior. This dynamic nature of fraud requires careful monitoring, retraining, and updating of the detection mechanisms to keep pace and be effective. Static models fail under concept drift because they rely on the assumption that the underlying data distribution does not change over time. Therefore, there is a need for continuous collaboration and the development of more robust fraud detection systems that can quickly react to evolving fraud environments without creating unjustified obstacles for legitimate users.

3.3 Data Volume and Velocity

The massive volume and high velocity of financial online transactions are considered significant challenges for fraud detection systems. A huge data is created every second due to the massive increased usage of online payments [1] by most humans. Each transaction stores huge amounts of metadata, which is considered a fingerprint of each transaction, such as amount, timestamp, destination, location, and device information. This continuous huge amount of data requires analysis to extract and detect the fraudulent transactions, which demands a huge computational infrastructure to ensure model efficiency. This makes detecting fraud activities process is considered a challenging mission because of the need to analyze this massive amount of data [32]. This issue adds another challenge to consider developing efficient models to process big financial data volumes.

3.4 Privacy Concerns

Due to strict regulations, there is limited access to payment transactions, which makes it difficult for researchers to use these data to train models on up-to-date real-world datasets. Fraud detection methods often involve handling highly sensitive user information, including credit card details, e-wallet and bank account data, transaction amounts, and other personal financial attributes [33]. This sensitivity poses significant challenges in acquiring appropriate datasets for research purposes and underscores the critical importance of ensuring data privacy and protection throughout the research process.

4 Datasets

One of the challenging issues in fraud detection is the lack of high quality and updated dataset. This occurred due to many factors, including privacy issues, legal constraints, and intellectual property. Usually, financial transactions contain sensitive personal and business information, making them subject to exposure by criminals and hackers to exploit individual privacy and business confidentiality. Furthermore, banks and other financial institutions regard their transaction data as a valuable asset and a source of competitive advantage. Publicly sharing such data may not only compromise their proprietary fraud detection systems but also provide fraudsters with critical insights that could be exploited to circumvent existing security measures [34]. Table 2 summarizes the datasets listed in this review.

4.1 Euro Credit Card Dataset

Several datasets are widely used in fraud detection research, each with strengths and limitations. The euro dataset was released in 2013 by the group of ML at Université Libre de Bruxelles (ULB). It contains real transactions, and include both legitimate and fraudulent payments, and is widely used in research on financial fraud detection. The dataset includes 284,807 transactions by European cardholders, among which have 492 fraudulent transactions, representing just 0.172% of all transactions making the dataset highly imbalanced. Feature engineering involved applying Principal Component Analysis (PCA) to the original transactional data, such as cardholder and merchant information, resulting in 28 numerical features (V1–V28) that reflect underlying spending patterns [35]. In addition, two raw features remain in the dataset: Time (measured in seconds from the first transaction) and Amount (the monetary value of each transaction). The dataset categorizes transactions into two classes: legitimate (0) and fraudulent (1). Despite its widespread use, the European dataset has some limitations, including reduced interpretability of features due to the PCA transformation, its static nature, and concerns about being somewhat outdated [19].

Table 2. Fraud detection datasets

Feature	Euro Credit Card Dataset	PaySim Dataset	IEEE-CIS Fraud Detection Dataset
Source	UCI Machine Learning Repository	Simulated from real mobile money transactions	IEEE-CIS and Vesta Corporation
Data type	Real-world, anonymized	Simulated (based on real behavior)	Real-world, anonymized
Number of records	284,807 transactions	~ 6.3 million transactions	590,000 transactions
Fraud Ratio	0.172% (Highly imbalanced)	0.13% (Highly imbalanced)	~ 3.5% (Highly imbalanced)

(*continued*)

Table 2. (*continued*)

Feature	Euro Credit Card Dataset	PaySim Dataset	IEEE-CIS Fraud Detection Dataset
Features	28	11	38
Publicly Available	Yes	Yes	Yes
Characteristics	Severe class imbalance, anonymized features	Simulated data, limited realism	Large feature set, anonymization, class imbalance
Year created	2013	2017	2019
Last update	2016	2018	2019

4.2 PaySim Dataset

The PaySim is a popular synthetic fraud detection dataset that simulates real payment transactions conducted by customers without exposing their sensitive data. PaySim was released in 2017, and it was created by simulating real transactional data to generate anonymized transactions of both fraudulent and legitimate transactions. The dataset contains simulated transactions close to 6,362,620, and approximately 8271 (0.13%) are considered fraudulent transactions, and the fraudulent transaction ratio makes the dataset highly imbalanced. PaySim dataset contains different types of payment transactions, like cash-in, cash-out, payment, debit, and transfer, to simulate a real payment transactions environment [36]. PaySim has 11 unique features, such as transaction value, transaction type, pre-transaction and post-transaction balance, and recipient information that allow researchers to train their fraud detection models easily. One of the benefits of PaySim dataset is that it can address the lack of publicly available fraud detection datasets by providing an alternative dataset that can ensure real-world transaction structures without exposing sensitive transaction information. In addition to that, PaySim is suitable for advanced feature extraction, which can improve the effectiveness and performance of hybrid fraud detection approaches. Nonetheless, the PaySim dataset has some limitations, such as it might fail to reflect all the complexity of financial fraud in reality due to the evolving fraudster tactics. In addition to that, the dataset lacks some other contextual information, like geolocation, user activity, and device type, that can be required by modern fraud detection models [37].

4.3 IEEE-CIS Fraud Detection Dataset

The IEEE-CIS Fraud Detection Dataset [38] is developed with a contribution from the IEEE Computational Intelligence Society and Vesta Corporation, and is used in machine learning and deep learning models of online fraud detection applications. Released through a Kaggle competition in 2019, the dataset simulates real-world e-commerce transactions and includes detailed behavioral and identity-related information. It consists of two main parts: identity data and transaction data. The transaction dataset contains over 590,000 records, each containing transaction amount, product category, card information, and geolocation indicators (address and destination). The identity dataset enhances the transactional data with device metadata, email domains, network addresses, and 38 anonymized ID features. One of the main challenges of this dataset is the extremely imbalanced class, where fraud cases consist of approximately 3.5% of the dataset. Therefore, there is a need to use imbalanced class handling methods such as oversampling, under sampling, or cost-sensitive learning to generate new fraud transactions to enhance the use of deep learning methods. There are also numerous anonymized features (V1 to V339), requiring domain-independent feature engineering and careful validation. Despite these challenges, the dataset is very valuable due to its complexity, feature heterogeneity, and size, which are good in mimicking real-world fraud detection cases. Moreover, its rich feature space makes it conducive to research in feature selection as well as time-series modeling. The IEEE-CIS dataset offers a rich and realistic environment for fraud detection research due to its behavioral diversity and scale, but its extreme class imbalance and heavy anonymization demand sophisticated preprocessing and limit direct interpretability. Although the IEEE-CIS dataset offers a rich and realistic environment for research due to its behavioral diversity and scale, but its extreme class imbalance and anonymization demand sophisticated preprocessing and limit direct interpretability.

5 Evaluation Metrics

5.1 Accuracy

Accuracy is one of the significant metrics for evaluating fraud detection model performance as it reflects the proportion of correctly classified transactions, both as fraudulent and legitimate, to the total number of transactions [39]. Accuracy is therefore important, but needs to be used in combination with other evaluation metrics such as precision, recall, F1-score, and Area Under the Curve (AUC) to provide a more accurate analysis of deep learning models. Despite its limitations, accuracy is widely used to evaluate fraud detection models due to its well-established measure. Advanced models, particularly deep learning models such as GAN, AE, LSTM, GRU, BiLSTM, BiGRU, and hybrid models, have demonstrated very high accuracy levels in detecting fraudulent transactions. These models are capable of capturing and dealing with complex temporal and sequential patterns from the financial data and thus learn to classify anomalies with higher precision. Moreover, resampling techniques, attention mechanisms, and optimized feature selection improve the model accuracy by resolving the issue of data imbalance and feature redundancy [40].

5.2 Precision, Recall, and F1-Score

Precision, recall, and F1-score are the most important metrics to evaluate the performance of the fraud detection models. Precision provides the fraction of true fraudulent transactions among all the predicted fraudulent transactions. A high precision indicates fewer false fraud was detected. Recall, or sensitivity, or true positive rate, is the ability of the model to detect true fraud instances out of all fraud cases available [41]. Increased recall is better for fewer fraudulent transactions that pass undetected, which is essential in order to decrease financial loss. Recall can be boosted against precision, and vice versa, in certain situations, so the F1-score, being the harmonic mean of recall and precision, is a useful measure that presents a balance between both. A high F1-score reflects that the model is successfully identifying fraud without having excessive false positives. In fraud detection, remembering most fraud is typically more valuable than accuracy, so that as much fraud as can be detected, but one must have decent precision so that one will not overwhelm fraud analysts with spurious alarms [42]. Precision, recall, and F1-score, therefore, together give a better estimate of the true performance of a model in practice than accuracy, and are especially useful when evaluating the reliability and effectiveness of fraud detection systems.

5.3 ROC and AUC

The Receiver Operating Characteristic (ROC) curve and the Area Under the Curve (AUC) are beneficial evaluation measurements in fraud detection models, especially for an imbalanced fraud dataset. The ROC curve shows the true positive rate (recall) versus the false positive rate at various settings of thresholds, which offers information regarding the ability of the model to distinguish between fraudulent and honest transactions [43]. A good-performing model will have an ROC curve that bows towards the top-left corner, with a high true positive rate and a low false positive rate. AUC represents the overall capability of the model to differentiate between the two classes by calculating the area under the ROC curve. An AUC of 1.0 would be perfect discrimination, while an AUC of 0.5 would mean no more than the use of random guessing. In fraud detection, a high AUC value indicates the robustness of the model to detect fraud across different levels of thresholds and thus remains a good measure for comparing the performance of different classifiers [44]. Since fraud data is mostly imbalanced, the use of AUC as a metric avoids misinterpretation due to accuracy, which could be caused by the imbalanced data, to get a good estimation of the model's ability to classify.

6 Literature Review

6.1 Deep Learning Models

One of the state-of-the-art models [45] presents a novel credit card fraud detection model called Balanced-Variational AutoEncoder-Attention (Bal-VAE-Attention). The proposed approach is designed to address shortcomings in existing approaches, notably the imbalanced data problem, insufficient feature selection, and the need to improve the attention mechanism. The approach integrates three main components: a novel data augmentation method called Bal-VAE, automatic feature selection with LightGBM, and a deep multi-head attention structure adapted from the Transformer model. Bal-VAE utilizes a special loss function that explicitly fixes the class imbalance by using the minority (fraud) over majority (normal) ratio to generate more solid and representative synthetic fraud samples. Feature selection is done by finding the most important input features using LightGBM to enhance the quality of the model inputs. To comprehensively capture transactional dependencies, the model deploys stacked encoder-decoder attention layers with masking to enable rich sequential pattern learning. The method was validated on two credit card fraud datasets, one of which is highly imbalanced and the other moderately imbalanced, against various metrics such as Recall, Precision, AUC-ROC, and AUC-PR. Comparative experiments show that Bal-VAE-Attention generally outperforms typical machine learning classifiers (Random Forest), generative augmentation methods (GAN), and advanced neural baselines (LSTM-Attention). Notably, Bal-VAE-Attention achieved near-perfect detection on all metrics, with AUC-ROC and AUC-PR of 99.95% and 99.98%, respectively.

A recent approach was proposed by [46], which proposes a credit card fraud detection system that integrates Generative Adversarial Networks (GANs) and multi-head attention to address the challenge of the imbalanced class dataset. The proposed model utilizes medical GAN (medGAN), which is a variant of GANs, to generate synthetic fraud transactions from the minority class (fraudulent transactions), and effectively overcoming the limitations of traditional oversampling techniques. The utilization of medGANs in the proposed model guarantees less information loss and improves minority class case detection. The model also employs a multi head attention technique to enhance classification accuracy and enable model to focus on related features, capturing temporal dependencies and recognize the fraudulent activities of the credit card transaction dataset. The model structure contains an attention layer to determine the weight of each feature and an output layer to decide the probability of the transaction as fraudulent or not. To assess the proposed model's performance, the authors have initiated a comparison of their model's performance against several models, including Random Forest and Support Vector Machine (SVM). The model performance was evaluated using several metrics such as geometric mean of accuracy (G-mean), balanced error rate (BER), and area under the curve (AUC), to address the unbalanced dataset issue. Therefore, the results clearly show that the proposed model is superior to the traditional ones, especially in terms of G-mean and BER, which indicates its performance in detecting fraud in a highly class-imbalanced dataset.

A model proposed by [22] that integrate an attention mechanism and LSTM to deal with emerging fraudster tactics and the change in fraud patterns to improve detection accuracy. The approach utilizes an LSTM neural network to learn and process and learn dependencies between sequential data, which is crucial for modeling long-term relationships in time-series sequential data, especially for fraud detection transactions. Usually, standalone LSTM models tend to convert fraudulent transactions into a single context vector, which may lead to information loss. To overcome this, authors use an attention mechanism in order to improve performance by focusing on the most important parts of the sequence. The model applied several preprocessing methods, like swarm-based feature selection to reduce redundant or noisy features and after that use principal component analysis (PCA) for reducing the dimensionality of the dataset. After comparing the proposed model to other models like GRU, SVM, KNN, and ANN, the LSTM-attention model shows improved performance with better accuracy, recall, and precision. By integrating attention mechanisms with LSTM, the model enhances focus on critical temporal patterns and mitigates context loss, though its dependence on extensive preprocessing like swarm-based selection and PCA may reduce adaptability across diverse datasets.

6.2 Hybrid Models

A model introduced by [47] presents a credit card fraud detection system built on a deep AE network. The author introduced a hybrid architecture comprising two separately trained unsupervised models, one trained on legitimate transactions and the other on fraudulent ones. This dual-model strategy is designed to improve the detection capability and overall efficiency of identifying fraudulent activities. The basic idea is to compare the reconstruction errors from both the original transactions and the hypothetical fraud ones, and it is observed that as the differences between them increase, illicit activities can be more distinctly identified. The results of the proposed model show superiority compared to the standalone approach using logistic regression (LR) and emphasize that combining unsupervised learning methods can improve the model's robustness and contribute to building an accurate and practical real-world credit card fraud detection system. Another model proposed by [13] introduces a novel hybrid method for credit card fraud detection that combines Autoencoders (AEs) for representation learning with supervised learning classifiers to enhance detection accuracy. This approach addresses the problem of fraud by initially applying a deep autoencoder to reduce the dimensionality of the input data and generate a more expressive, compact representation. The transformed data was then fed to Deep Neural Networks (DNNs) and Recurrent Neural Networks (RNNs) hybrid model, and also a support vector machine (SVM) for comparative analysis. The proposed model employs a Bayesian optimization algorithm to optimize the hyperparameters of all of the models. Experimentation on the hybrid model reveals that it has the highest accuracy levels among the rest of the classifiers. The results confirm that deep representation learning is a highly effective tool for improving fraud detection performance, with Autoencoder-based models outperforming traditional methods.

One of the recent models was proposed by [48]. They have developed a new hybrid deep learning model that integrate GAN and RNN to enhance credit card fraud detection performance. Meanwhile, GAN is used to create synthetic data which are similar to the real data, and RNN is used as a discriminator to distinguish between real and fake transactions and later label the fraudulent transactions. The findings indicate that the GAN-RNN model performs better and is superior compared to some other machine learning models or standalone RNN models. Besides, the study concludes that the GAN-RNN hybrid technique has better detection accuracy and robustness than other cutting-edge techniques. However, the results prove that combining GANs and RNNs can create a more reliable and adaptable solution for fraud detection and dealing with issues of imbalanced dataset problems, alongside identifying temporal relationships in transactional data. The GAN-RNN hybrid model effectively addresses class imbalance and captures sequential fraud patterns, but its reliance on synthetic data generation may introduce noise and requires careful tuning to maintain real-world applicability.

Few studies focus on addressing feature representation, which is crucial to let the hybrid approaches understand the relation between features and thus diminish the performance of the fraud detection model. A novel model [49] that focuses on the dataset and can effectively address two challenges in fraud detection models: the class imbalance and lack of feature representation. This paper presents a recent credit card fraud detection model, MFGAN (Multi-Feature Fusion and Generative Adversarial Network). Although existing models tend to basically use transactional data and ignore other useful information, which may lead to achieve suboptimal performance. MFGAN integrates three types of features: static (e.g., age, gender), dynamic transactional (e.g., amount, time), and operational behavioral (e.g., ATM usage, online banking activity) into one high-dimensional vector via a hybrid solution based on FNN and Bi-LSTM networks. This allows a better understanding and addresses the feature representation of the dataset, which leads to better distinguishing the legitimate and fraudulent transactions. The proposed hybrid approach utilizes Borderline SMOTE (BSMOTE) to reduce the noise of the oversampling and Generative Adversarial Networks (GAN) to create high-quality fraud samples without modifying the underlying data distribution. Results showed that MFGAN outperformed several baseline models, such as SVM, DNN, and LSTM with SMOTE or GAN separately. On the UCI dataset, MFGAN achieved the highest recall (65.06%) and AUC (77.28%), improving the best GAN-based baseline by 3.06% in recall and 0.64% in AUC. On the private dataset, MFGAN improved recall, precision, F1-score, and AUC by up to 11.49%, 11.11%, 13.69%, and 5.86%, respectively, over the base DNN model. The ablation study also confirmed the requirement of each module, especially the inclusion of operational behavior data and the two-method balancing strategy. The MFGAN model effectively addresses both class imbalance and feature representation by fusing static, transactional, and behavioral data with GAN and BSMOTE, though its reliance on complex multi-source feature engineering may limit scalability and require domain-specific customization.

Hybrid solution shows a high popularity in the area of credit card fraud detection due to its ability to gain better results compared to standalone methods. A recent solution was presented by [28], which proposes a novel new method to detect credit card fraud. The study uses a state-of-the-art hybrid model that integrates two RNN models: Bidirectional Long Short-Term Memory (BiLSTM) and Bidirectional Gated Recurrent Unit (BiGRU). This BiLSTM-BiGRU hybrid increases detection levels of accuracy without increasing in computational power of the model. However, BiLSTM-BiGRU hybrid model leverages the features of both models to achieve better detection levels. The BiLSTM module take sequences of transactions to identify long-term dependencies between the dataset, and the BiGRU module provides improved training efficiency with reduced gates as compared to LSTM. The performance of the hybrid model was evaluated against standalone deep learning methods, which employ several resampling strategies, and the experimental results show that the BiLSTM-BiGRU hybrid model identifies fraud transactions with improved detection accuracy. Moreover, the authors compare the proposed model to some recent fraud detection models, including the anomaly detection system (ReMEMBeR), Majority Vote Ensemble Classifier, and Artificial Immune Recognition System (AIRS) model. BiLSTM-BiGRU hybrid model outperforms these models, and the outcome reflects the importance of using hybrid approaches to have effective fraud detection scores. The BiLSTM-BiGRU hybrid model effectively combines long-term dependency learning with training efficiency, outperforming standalone models, but its dual complexity may pose scalability challenges in resource-constrained or real-time environments.

A novel hybrid model used Gated Recurrent Unit (GRU) and Reinforcement Learning (RL) to detect credit card fraud by capturing sequential dependencies between transactional data with minimal computational resources compared to Long Short-Term Memory (LSTM) [26]. The role of the RL is to let the agent learn any behavioral changes in the environment dynamically to enhance the effectiveness of the proposed model. Moreover, the GRU networks utilize reset and update gates in order to determine whether to retain or remove historical transaction information, which enables the model to accurately detect anomalies and predict possible fraudulent transactions for the future. GRU architecture is able to effectively learn time-series and temporal dependencies, which can lead to more effective and efficient fraud detection compared to standalone RNN models. The results indicate that the hybrid GRU-RL model performs better than other models such as LSTM, BiLSTM, and RNNs. Furthermore, the comparison indicates that the model gains an accuracy of 98.72% in detecting fraudulent transactions, which was better than LSTM (92.59%), RNN (90.44%), and BiLSTM (94.65%) models. Additionally, the model also has a precision of 98.58% and a recall of 98.10%, with accurate detection of fraudulent transactions with fewer false positives. These results demonstrated that the GRU-based model have the capability to detect credit card fraud transactions in online payment systems. The GRU-RL hybrid model achieves high accuracy and adaptability by combining efficient sequential learning with dynamic behavior tracking, though its reliance on reinforcement signals may limit performance in static or less interactive fraud environments.

A recent advancement in the field proposed a robust framework [50] that introduces a novel hybrid resampling approach, combining HybridOS for oversampling and HybridUS for under sampling to maintain distribution consistency. The HybridOS method employs One-Class SVM to detect and remove outliers before applying SMOTE, thereby preserving the original distribution of the minority fraud class. Meanwhile, HybridUS reduces the size of the majority class (legitimate transactions) while retaining temporal relationships between transactions, which is crucial for accurate fraud pattern detection over time. For feature selection, the model uses F2Vote to identify the most relevant attributes. The classification component merges Light Gradient-Boosting Machine (LightGBM) with an LSTM network, where LightGBM handles non-sequential patterns, and LSTM captures sequence dependencies. This hybrid classification approach results in a significant improvement in detection accuracy. Table 3 lists several recent fraud detection models using deep learning and hybrid methods. The hybrid model combining LightGBM and LSTM with advanced resampling techniques like HybridOS and HybridUS effectively improves detection accuracy and data balance, though its multi-component design may increase system complexity and tuning effort for real-world deployment.

Table 3. Deep learning and hybrid fraud detection systems.

Paper	Authors	Methodology	Dataset	Evaluation	results
Credit card fraud detection model based on LSTM recurrent neural networks	(Benchaji, Douzi, & El Ouahidi, 2021)	LSTM	BankSim	AUC MSE MAE	0.9955 0.0035 0.0065
Advanced Fraud Detection In Card-Based Financial Systems Using A Bidirectional LSTM-GRU Ensemble Model	(Ghrib et al., 2024)	BiLSTM-BiGRU ensemble model	European Credit Card Fraud Detection dataset	AUC Precision Recall F1 score	91.23% 89.21% 82.29% 87.51%
A Novel Approach for Credit Card Fraud Detection using Gated Recurrent Unit (GRU) Networks	(Suganthi & Jebathangam, 2024)	GRU	European Credit Card Fraud Detection dataset	Accuracy Precision Recall	98.72% 98.58% 98.10%
A distribution-preserving method for resampling combined with LightGBM-LSTM for sequence-wise fraud detection in credit card transactions	(Yousefimehr & Ghatee, 2025)	LightGBM-LSTM	European Credit Card Fraud Detection dataset	Accuracy Precision Recall F1-score AUC	99.97% 84.46% 92.09% 88.05% 96.03%

7 Discussion and Analysis

Deep learning and hybrid approaches were highly promising in the field of fraud detection due to their diverse architectures, including RNN, GAN, AE, LSTM, BiLSTM, GRU, and BiGRU. Each model has unique capabilities: GANs are effective in generating synthetic fraud transactions to balance datasets, while AEs are used to identify anomalies by reconstructing inputs. LSTM, GRU, and their bidirectional variants are particularly effective in capturing temporal dependencies from sequential transaction data and hence are very effective in detecting complex behaviors and recognizing evolving fraud transaction patterns. Results and findings of recent studies identify actual advantages of deep learning and hybrid methods in credit card fraud detection. For example, the LSTM algorithm on the BankSim data achieved a high-quality AUC score of 0.9955, confirming its capability to capture transaction sequences well. The hybrid BiLSTM-BiGRU model achieved a noticeable accuracy (91.23%), precision (89.21%), and F1-score (87.51%) values, and (82.29%) recall, although results show that improvement is still needed for capturing a higher percentage of fraudulent instances. Similarly, the GRU model by itself also demonstrated impressive performance with an accuracy of 98.72% along with impressive precision and recall (98.58% and 98.10%, respectively), demonstrating its reliability and capability in fraud detection operations.

Moreover, the hybrid model employing LightGBM and LSTM, supported by a distribution-preserving resampling method, achieved exceptional performance with an accuracy of 99.97% and an AUC of 96.03%. The outcome emphasizes the strength of the combination of deep learning with feature selection techniques and imbalance handling methods. These combinations result in high model robustness and ensure better generalization in real-world situations where data quality and class imbalance remain ongoing challenges. Overall, these results confirm that hybrid methods are more responsive, scalable, and adaptable than standalone models. Leverage of attention mechanisms, advanced resampling techniques like SMOTE and HybridOS, and hyperparameter tuning can also support improving fraud detection systems, which are both efficient in processing large volumes of dynamic financial data accurately. As fraudulent behavior continues to evolve, the need for future studies is to prioritize adaptive and explainable hybrid techniques that can operate in real-time environments while taking into consideration privacy and minimizing false positives. These innovations are essential for reducing the international impact of financial fraud and protecting digital financial ecosystems (Fig. 2).

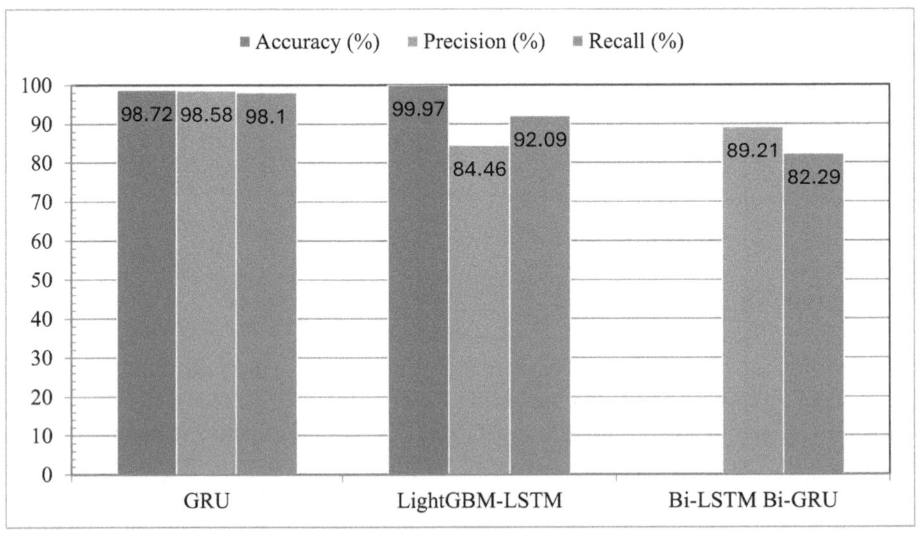

Fig. 2. Performance comparison

8 Conclusion and Future Work

This literature review has examined recent trends and advancements in fraud detection, particularly those involving deep learning methods and hybrid models. Techniques such as LSTM, GRU, GAN, and AE have shown significant potential in detecting complex and evolving fraud patterns. However, when used as standalone models, they often suffer from limitations in generalizability, adaptability, and interpretability, especially in dynamic environments where fraud behavior frequently changes. Hybrid fraud detection systems have emerged as effective solutions to overcome these limitations. By combining deep learning with traditional machine learning models, rule-based systems, and optimization algorithms, hybrid approaches benefit from the strengths of multiple techniques, resulting in enhanced performance, robustness, and adaptability to diverse fraud scenarios.

In addition to improved accuracy, precision, and recall, these systems offer greater flexibility and resilience against sophisticated fraud tactics. This review also highlights the importance of collaboration between academia and industry to enable practical applications, access to high-quality datasets, and the establishment of ethical guidelines to mitigate the broader impact of fraud. Addressing technical challenges alone is not sufficient; concerns related to privacy, fairness, and transparency must also be considered. Bridging the gap between theoretical innovation and real-world deployment is crucial to ensure the effectiveness of fraud detection systems. Future research should focus on building standardized evaluation frameworks, optimizing model architectures for real-time and resource-constrained environments, and developing adaptive systems capable of responding to emerging threats, including adversarial and synthetic fraud. Overall, hybrid models will continue to play a critical role in securing digital financial systems against ever-evolving fraud risks.

References

1. Abbassi, H., El Alaoui, I., Gahi, Y.: Fraud detection techniques in the big data Era. International Conference On Big Data, Modelling And Machine Learning (Bml'21). pp. 161–170 (2022)
2. Robertson. Credit Card Fraud Nilson Report. (2022). Available from: https://nilsonreport.com/
3. Abdul Salam, M., et al.: Federated learning model for credit card fraud detection with data balancing techniques. Neural Comput. Appl. **36**(11), 6231–6256 (2024)
4. Chang, V., et al.: Digital payment fraud detection methods in digital ages and Industry 4.0. Comput. Electr. Eng. **100**, 107734 (2022)
5. Dargan, S., et al.: A survey of deep learning and its applications: a new paradigm to machine learning. Arch. Comput. Methods Eng. **27**, 1071–1092 (2020)
6. Dong, S., Wang, P., Abbas, K.: A survey on deep learning and its applications. Comput. Sci. Rev. **40**, 100379 (2021)
7. Minaee, S., et al.: Deep learning–based text classification: a comprehensive review. ACM Comput. Surv. (CSUR) **54**(3), 1–40 (2021)
8. Li, Z., et al.: A survey of convolutional neural networks: analysis, applications, and prospects. IEEE Trans. Neural Netw. Learn. Syst. (2021)
9. Niu, Z., Zhong, G., Yu, H.: A review on the attention mechanism of deep learning. Neurocomputing **452**, 48–62 (2021)
10. Zhang, G., Liu, Y., Jin, X.: A survey of autoencoder-based recommender systems. Front. Comp. Sci. **14**, 430–450 (2020)
11. Gheller, C., Vazza, F.: Convolutional deep denoising autoencoders for radio astronomical images. Mon. Not. R. Astron. Soc. **509**(1), 990–1009 (2022)

12. Gunduz, H.: An efficient dimensionality reduction method using filter-based feature selection and variational autoencoders on Parkinson's disease classification. Biomed. Signal Process. Control **66**, 102452 (2021)
13. Fanai, H., Abbasimehr, H.: A novel combined approach based on deep Autoencoder and deep classifiers for credit card fraud detection. Expert Syst. Appl **2023**, 119562 (2023)
14. Goodfellow, I., et al.: Generative adversarial networks. Commun. ACM **63**(11), 139–144 (2020)
15. Zhang, Z., Schomaker, L.: Dtgan: dual attention generative adversarial networks for text-to-image generation. in 2021 international joint conference on neural networks (IJCNN). IEEE (2021)
16. Purandhar, N., Ayyasamy, S., Siva Kumar, P.: Classification of clustered health care data analysis using generative adversarial networks (GAN). Soft Comput. **26**(12), 5511–5521 (2022)
17. Lee, C.-K., Cheon, Y.-J., Hwang, W.-Y.: Studies on the GAN-based anomaly detection methods for the time series data. IEEE Access **9**, 73201–73215 (2021)
18. Orvieto, A., et al.: Resurrecting recurrent neural networks for long sequences. In: International Conference on Machine Learning. PMLR (2023)
19. Mienye, I.D., Swart, T.G., Obaido, G.: Recurrent neural networks: a comprehensive review of architectures, variants, and applications. Information **15**(9), 517 (2024)
20. Cahuantzi, R., Chen, X., Güttel, S.: A comparison of LSTM and GRU networks for learning symbolic sequences. In: Science and Information Conference. Springer (2023)
21. Zargar, S.: Introduction to sequence learning models: RNN, LSTM, GRU. Department of Mechanical and Aerospace Engineering, North Carolina State University (2021)
22. Benchaji, I., et al.: Enhanced credit card fraud detection based on attention mechanism and LSTM deep model. J. Big Data **8**, 1–21 (2021)
23. Oruh, J., Viriri, S., Adegun, A.: Long short-term memory recurrent neural network for automatic speech recognition. IEEE Access **10**, 30069–30079 (2022)
24. Lavanya, P., Sasikala, E.: Deep learning techniques on text classification using Natural language processing (NLP) in social healthcare network: a comprehensive survey. In: 2021 3rd International Conference on Signal Processing and Communication (ICPSC). IEEE (2021)
25. Farah, S., et al.: Short-term multi-hour ahead country-wide wind power prediction for Germany using gated recurrent unit deep learning. Renew. Sustain. Energy Rev. **167**, 112700 (2022)
26. Suganthi, V., Jebathangam, J.: A novel approach for credit card fraud detection using Gated Recurrent Unit (GRU) networks. In: 2024 8th International Conference on I-SMAC (IoT in Social, Mobile, Analytics and Cloud)(I-SMAC). IEEE (2024)
27. Singh, S., Kashyap, M., Tantubay, N.: Comparative analysis of ANN, RNN, and GRU for credit card fraud detection (2025)
28. Ghrib, T., et al.: Advanced fraud detection in card-based financial systems using a bidirectional Lstm-Gru ensemble model applied computer. Science **20**(3), 51–66 (2024)
29. Aburbeian, A.M., Ashqar, H.I.: Credit card fraud detection using enhanced random forest classifier for imbalanced data. In: International conference on advances in computing research. Springer (2023)
30. Ileberi, E., Sun, Y., Wang, Z.: Performance evaluation of machine learning methods for credit card fraud detection using SMOTE and AdaBoost. IEEE Access **9**, 165286–165294 (2021)
31. Koziarski, M.: Radial-based undersampling for imbalanced data classification. Pattern Recogn. **102**, 107262 (2020)
32. Dhone, M.B., Nitya, E.: Big data analytics for fraud detection in financial transactions. J. Data Acquisition Process. **38**(3), 290 (2023)
33. Găbudeanu, L., et al.: Privacy intrusiveness in financial-banking fraud detection. Risks **9**(6), 104 (2021)

34. Yang, H., Zhou, Y.: Ida-gan: a novel imbalanced data augmentation gan. In: 2020 25th International Conference on Pattern Recognition (ICPR). IEEE (2021)
35. Alfaiz, N.S., Fati, S.M.: Enhanced credit card fraud detection model using machine learning. Electronics **11**(4), 662 (2022)
36. Almazroi, A.A., Ayub, N.: Online payment fraud detection model using machine learning techniques. IEEE Access **11**, 137188–137203 (2023)
37. Alamri, M., Ykhlef, M.: Hybrid feature engineering based on customer spending behavior for credit card anomaly and fraud detection. Electronics **13**(20), 3978 (2024)
38. IEEE Computational Intelligence Society, V.C. IEEE-CIS Fraud Detection. 2019 [cited 2025 23Feb 2025]; Available from: https://www.kaggle.com/c/ieee-fraud-detection
39. Rainio, O., Teuho, J., Klén, R.: Evaluation metrics and statistical tests for machine learning. Sci. Rep. **14**(1), 6086 (2024)
40. Zhou, J., et al.: Evaluating the quality of machine learning explanations: a survey on methods and metrics. Electronics **10**(5), 593 (2021)
41. Wajid, M.S., et al.: Deep learning and knowledge graph for image/video captioning: a review of datasets, evaluation metrics, and methods. Eng. Rep. **6**(1), e12785 (2024)
42. Liu, S., et al.: Comparison of evaluation metrics of deep learning for imbalanced imaging data in osteoarthritis studies. Osteoarthritis Cartilage **31**(9), 1242–1248 (2023)
43. Naidu, G., Zuva, T., Sibanda, E.M.: A review of evaluation metrics in machine learning algorithms. In: Computer science on-line conference. Springer (2023)
44. Boursalie, O., Samavi, R., Doyle, T.E.: Evaluation metrics for deep learning imputation models. In: International Workshop on Health Intelligence. Springer (2021)
45. Shi, S., Luo, W., Pau, G.: An attention-based balanced variational autoencoder method for credit card fraud detection. Appl. Soft Comput. **2025**, 113190 (2025)
46. Meng, Z., Xie, Y., Sun, J.: Detecting credit card fraud by generative adversarial networks and multi-head attention neural networks. IAENG Int. J. Comput. Sci. **50**(2) (2023)
47. Shen, J.: Credit card fraud detection using autoencoder-based deep neural networks. In: 2021 IEEE 2nd International Conference on Big Data, Artificial Intelligence and Internet of Things Engineering (ICBAIE). IEEE (2021)
48. Mienye, I.D., Swart, T.G.: A hybrid deep learning approach with generative adversarial network for credit card fraud detection. Technologies **12**(10), 186 (2024)
49. Xie, Y., et al.: A credit card fraud detection model based on multi-feature fusion and generative adversarial network. Comput. Mater. Continua **76**(3) (2023)
50. Yousefimehr, B., Ghatee, M.: A distribution-preserving method for resampling combined with LightGBM-LSTM for sequence-wise fraud detection in credit card transactions. Expert Syst. Appl. **262**, 125661 (2025)

Toward a 'Digital Homestay Ready' Framework: Voices from Rural Entrepreneurs in Sibu

Siti Daleela Mohd Wahid[1,2](✉), Wan Mohd Hirwani Wan Hussain[2], and Alya Geogiana Buja[1]

[1] Universiti Teknologi MARA Cawangan Melaka, Melaka, Malaysia
sitid365@uitm.edu.my
[2] Universiti Kebangsaan Malaysia, Bangi, Malaysia

Abstract. Rural homestay operators in Sarawak, particularly within the Bumiputera community, play a pivotal role in advancing community-based tourism and sustaining local economies. However, despite robust national and state-level efforts—including the Sarawak Digital Economy Strategy (2018–2022) and the Sarawak Digital Economy Blueprint (2030)—digital adoption within rural homestays remains fragmented and inconsistent. This study investigates the digital readiness of rural homestay operators in Sibu by capturing their lived experiences and operational realities through a qualitative lens. In-depth interviews were conducted with 8 homestay operators, selected via purposive sampling. Interviews were carried out in Malay and analyzed using Braun and Clarke's (2006) six-step thematic analysis. An inductive coding approach revealed three core themes: digital marketing, awareness toward digital technology, and revenue generation. These themes were then deductively mapped against the proposed Digital Homestay Ready (DHR) framework, which encompasses indicators such as digital presence, promotional content quality, payment systems, internet accessibility, and responsiveness. Interestingly, compliance with local authority regulations emerged as a new, contextually relevant dimension not previously emphasized in the framework. Its consistent mention by participants highlights its perceived importance for legitimacy, sustainability, and future access to formal platforms or funding. The refined DHR framework thus functions as both a diagnostic tool and a capacity-building guide for rural digital transformation. It offers actionable insights for policymakers, tourism authorities, and local development actors committed to ensuring that rural micro-entrepreneurs are not left behind in Malaysia's digital economy journey.

Keywords: Digital Homestay · Digital Technology · Qualitative

1 Introduction

Tourism has long been a vital engine of economic development, particularly in emerging economies where rural communities contribute significantly through cultural heritage and localized hospitality. In Malaysia, the homestay industry has become a cornerstone

M. Kassim et al. (Eds.): SCDS 2025, CCIS 2674, pp. 176–188, 2026.
https://doi.org/10.1007/978-981-95-8368-3_13

of community-based tourism, especially among the Bumiputera population in Sarawak. These operators do more than provide accommodations; they embody tradition, foster local narratives, and sustain rural livelihoods. However, as the global tourism landscape shifts into the digital age, the survival and competitiveness of rural homestays now depend heavily on their ability to embrace digital transformation.

To address this shift, government initiatives such as the Sarawak Digital Economy Strategy (2018–2022) and the Sarawak Digital Economy Blueprint (2030) have set forth ambitious goals to integrate digital technologies across all sectors. Yet on the ground, digital adoption among rural homestay operators remains fragmented and slow [1]. Over 45% of Sarawak's rural areas still lack stable internet access [2], and fewer than 40% of rural entrepreneurs consistently engage with digital booking or payment platforms [3]. This persistent digital exclusion risks marginalizing rural tourism actors from the nation's broader economic transformation agenda.

Given this gap, there is an urgent need to define what it truly means to be "digitally ready" in the rural homestay context. While existing studies have focused largely on urban or formal business settings, few frameworks address the realities of rural tourism micro-entrepreneurs. Therefore, this study responds to that void by capturing the lived experiences of homestay operators in Sibu and translating those insights into a structured, context-specific Digital Homestay Ready (DHR) framework.

2 Literature Review

2.1 The Landscape of Homestay Entrepreneurs

The homestay sector has emerged as a powerful driver of community-based tourism across Southeast Asia, contributing not only to local economies but also to cultural preservation and rural resilience [4, 5]. In countries like Thailand and Indonesia, targeted government support and strategic digital interventions have bolstered the growth of rural tourism. Malaysia has followed a similar path through the Malaysia Homestay Experience Programme (PPHM), under the Ministry of Tourism, Arts and Culture (MOTAC), which has registered 3,654 homestay operators as of January 2025. Sarawak alone accounts for 863 operators, most of whom are located in rural areas.

Despite this growth, the integration of digital tools within homestay operations remains fragmented. Technologies such as online booking systems, e-payment solutions, and social media marketing are increasingly essential for business competitiveness [5]. However, the persistent urban–rural digital divide continues to inhibit transformation. Less than 28% of rural homestay operators use the internet for economic purposes [6, 7], and Samad et al. [4] indicates that the adoption of such digital platforms among rural homestay operators is relatively low. These gaps reveal that access does not guarantee adoption, and that digital readiness is still an unresolved barrier for rural homestay entrepreneurs.

Key constraints include limited digital literacy, inadequate infrastructure, patchy connectivity, and low trust in digital systems. Moreover, many existing training programs are too general or urban-centric, failing to address the unique challenges faced by rural tourism operators. Without sustained technical assistance and tailored capacity building, rural homestays risk being left behind in Malaysia's digital transformation agenda [5].

Recent literature has begun to examine the underlying dimensions of digital readiness, particularly in rural tourism contexts. Scholars such as Chounta, Ortega-Arranz, Daskalaki, Dimitriadis and Avouris [8] argue that digital readiness is not merely about access to technology, but about preparedness, awareness, and capacity to adapt digital tools effectively. This includes not only the technical ability to operate digital platforms but also an entrepreneurial mindset to leverage those tools strategically. Meanwhile, Mohammad and Shi [9] show that among Malaysian rural entrepreneurs, including homestay operators, social media marketing remains underutilized despite growing internet penetration. Their study identifies cultural hesitation, fear of scams, and unfamiliarity with algorithmic systems as soft barriers to adoption.

From a regional perspective, ASEAN's digital economy strategies emphasize inclusive infrastructure development, yet national implementation often lacks localization. Siow et al. [10] argue that rural tourism operators frequently face policies that are out of sync with their on-the-ground realities. This is echoed by Ramele et al. [11], who stress that the lack of standardization surrounding homestay registration and compliance dissuades operators from participating in formal digital ecosystems (e.g., as Agoda or Airbnb).

Collectively, these studies underscore that digital transformation in rural tourism is a contextual process, shaped by localized barriers, institutional mismatches, and entrepreneurial agency. A one-size-fits-all approach to digital readiness will likely fail to engage the realities faced by rural homestay operators in places like Sibu. Therefore, there is a growing call for more nuanced, grounded frameworks that reflect both infrastructural limitations and the lived perspectives of digital adopters.

2.2 The "Digital Homestay Ready" Framework

To address this gap, this study introduces the Digital Homestay Ready (DHR) standard which is defined as a framework designed to benchmark and facilitate digital readiness among rural homestay operators. In the absence of an established standard, agencies, digital trainers, and tourists alike struggle to evaluate the technological maturity of rural accommodations, leading to ad-hoc adoption and missed economic opportunities.

The DHR framework is contextually anchored but policy-relevant, aligning with Pillar 2 of the MyDIGITAL blueprint that emphasizes building digitally-skilled communities, and Thrust 5 of the Sarawak Digital Economy Strategy, which promotes digital entrepreneurship among rural and indigenous populations. Specifically, the framework echoes national goals to ensure that underserved micro-enterprises gain access to digital tools, infrastructure, and skills training.

Findings related to informal digital learning, reliance on family members, and emphasis on accessible platforms such as WhatsApp and Facebook reflect grassroots adaptation of MyDIGITAL's emphasis on inclusivity and low-barrier technology adoption. Additionally, the emphasis on digital marketing and responsiveness directly supports Sarawak's aim to position rural entrepreneurs as active agents in the digital economy, not passive recipients of top-down programs.

Debates surrounding digital readiness in rural tourism contexts remain vibrant and evolving. Scholars diverge in defining which components constitute a comprehensive measure of readiness. For instance, Bislimi et al. [12] emphasize digital connectivity, payment integration, and promotional capabilities as foundational, while Arnaud et al. [13] stress digital literacy, operational responsiveness, and compliance with regulatory standards. Meanwhile, Abas et al. [5] argue that true readiness emerges from a blend of digital presence, customer interface fluidity, and secure online transactions.

These overlapping but non-identical frameworks illustrate that there are a few consensuses on what defines digital readiness for rural enterprises. This fragmentation reflects the diversity of operational realities across regions and market segments. As such, this study proposes a refined framework that synthesizes prior literature while grounding the components in actual field data from rural Sarawak.

The core components of the proposed "Digital Homestay Ready" framework include:

(a) Active digital presence—validated as a core by Abas et al. [5] who highlight its importance in online visibility and searchability through various platform.
(b) Digital payment facilities—supported by Murniati et al. [7], who show that cashless options build customer trust and widen booking channels.
(c) Professional promotional content—aligned with insights by Samad et al. (2024) [4], suggesting that high-quality visuals and messaging increase conversion rates. The e-promotional content should be in many digital platform
(d) Basic internet access on premises—emphasized by Bislimi et al. [12], noting that infrastructure remains a precondition for any digital interaction.
(e) Digitally responsive and friendly operation—reflecting Arnaud et al.'s [13]f indings on the need for timely digital interaction with guests.
(f) Basic digital knowledge & cybersecurity awareness—outlined by Abas et al. [5] as essential to ensure confidence and prevent fraud.
(g) Compliance with local regulatory requirements—though debated, remains a policy-aligned factor, proposed by several studies including Ramele et al. [11] as part of formal digital ecosystem participation.

Through this model, the study contributes to the ongoing dialogue by consolidating empirical and theoretical perspectives into a unified, context-sensitive standard suitable for assessing and improving digital transformation among rural homestay operators. By integrating empirical field insights with literature-derived constructs, the proposed DHR framework adds theoretical value in three key ways:

(a) It reframes compliance from a normative prerequisite to a contingent, value-based factor.
(b) It emphasizes digital responsiveness and presence as operational strategies, not just marketing tools.
(c) It introduces a localized, practitioner-informed typology that challenges universalist assumptions in rural digitalization discourse.

In doing so, the study not only extends the conceptual vocabulary for understanding digital transformation in tourism micro-enterprises but also opens new pathways for adaptive policy-making, design of training interventions, and future empirical validation.

3 Research Methods

This study employed a qualitative research design to capture the nuanced, lived experiences of rural homestay operators in Sibu, Sarawak. Qualitative inquiry is particularly well-suited for exploring complex social phenomena where context, meaning-making, and personal narratives play a central role [14]. Given the exploratory nature of this study and the intention to develop a grounded framework, a qualitative approach allowed for deep engagement with participant perspectives.

This study involved in-depth, face-to-face interviews with 8 rural homestay operators in Sibu, Sarawak. Participants were selected via purposive sampling to reflect a range of demographic backgrounds and digital engagement levels. The sample included 6 male and 2 female operators, aged between 35 to 56 years, all of whom were registered with MOTAC and had more than 3 years of business experience. The interviews, conducted in Malay, lasted between 60–90 min and explored topics related to digital tool usage, perceptions of digital readiness, and regulatory awareness.

Purposive sampling was used to ensure diverse representation across gender and varying levels of digital adoption. Semi-structured interviews were conducted in Malay to enhance participant comfort and ensure linguistic alignment with local dialect. The interview guide, comprising open-ended questions, was designed to elicit the operators' perceptions of digital technology, its importance and the extent of its adoption. The coding was performed manually, and qualitative data analysis was conducted using ATLAS.ti version 23.0 ensued. The research themes and subthemes were revealed using inductive and deductive approaches. To ensure content validity, the verification of homestay operators and the related processes involved were well-documented.

Data analysis followed Braun and Clarke's [15] six-step thematic analysis framework, which included:

(a) familiarization with the data
(b) generating initial codes
(c) searching for themes
(d) reviewing themes
(e) defining and naming themes
(f) producing the report

A dual-coding strategy was adopted:

(a) Inductive coding allowed themes to emerge organically from participants' narratives, without preconceived analytical categories.
(b) Deductive coding was used to map responses against the pre-identified components of the DHR framework. This ensured that the data informed both discovery and validation.

Triangulation procedure was further executed through documentation reviewing and peer debriefing among the research team. These steps enhanced the credibility and trustworthiness of the findings [15]. Overall, the methodological approach provided a rich, context-sensitive understanding of the digital readiness landscape, ultimately contributing to the refinement and contextualization of the DHR framework as a tool for rural tourism transformation.

4 Result and Discussion

This study aimed to examine digital readiness among rural homestay operators in Sibu by exploring their perceptions, practices, and perceived impacts. Through thematic analysis, three dominant themes emerged, each aligning with specific components of the Digital Homestay Ready (DHR) framework. These themes are discussed below in relation to the research objectives and broader literature (Table 1).

Table 1. List of respondents.

Respondents	Job Position	Gender
Respondent 1	Business Owner	Male
Respondent 2	Business Owner	Male
Respondent 3	Business Partner	Female
Respondent 4	Business Owner	Male
Respondent 5	Business Owner	Male
Respondent 6	Business Partner	Female
Respondent 7	Business Owner	Male
Respondent 8	Business Owner	Male

Note: As all interviews were conducted in Malay, both the original Malay responses and their English translations are provided to preserve authenticity and facilitate broader understanding

4.1 Theme 1: Digital Marketing

Digital marketing surfaced as a core theme, with operators highlighting the use of platforms such as Facebook, WhatsApp, and occasionally TikTok for promoting their homestays. For many, these platforms serve as the primary channel to reach potential customers. Participants emphasized the importance of visual content and timely responses to inquiries. This aligns with two core DHR elements: active digital presence and professional promotional content.

Respondent 1: "We use Facebook because it's easy. Tourists usually reach out there. We don't know how to create a website."

Responden 1: "Kami guna Facebook sebab senang. Pelancong pun selalu tanya di situ. Nak buat website, kami tak pandai."

Respondent 2: "I just take my own photos and post them on WhatsApp status. Quite a lot of people view and ask about it. Sometimes I get my child to help edit the photos to make them look nicer."

Responden 2: "Saya ambil gambar sendiri je, lepas tu letak dekat WhatsApp status. Ramai juga yang tengok dan tanya. Kadang-kadang saya minta anak tolong edit sikit gambar bagi cantik."

Respondent 5: "My child helps me upload the status on WhatsApp. If it were just me, I wouldn't even know how. Some acquaintances have also asked about the homestay after seeing it."

Responden 5: "Anak saya yang tolong letak di status WhatsApp. Kalau saya sorang, saya tak tahu pun. Ada juga kenalan tanya pasal homestay"

Respondent 7: "I use TikTok to promote my homestay. These days, I feel like every entrepreneur needs a TikTok account because it's so convenient. One of my customers from China actually contacted me through TikTok."

Responden 7: "Akak pakai Tiktok untuk promote homestay. Sekarang ini akak rasa usahawan memang kena ada akaun Tiktok sebab senang. Hari itu salah seorang pelanggan akak dari China, contact akak melalui tiktok".

This indicates that digital readiness is often equated with visibility and usability, rather than technical sophistication. These findings reflect broader literature on grassroots digital marketing practices in rural entrepreneurship [5, 14].

4.2 Theme 2: Awareness of Digital Technology

Participants demonstrated varying levels of digital awareness, ranging from basic knowledge of social media to limited familiarity with payment gateways and cybersecurity. Several operators acknowledged that while they had heard of tools like online booking platforms or QR pay, they lacked the skills or confidence to implement them.

Respondent 2: "Our homestay uses various e-payment methods. I use QR Pay, TnG Pay, and online transfers. I learned how to do it from my child too."

Responden 2: "Homestay kami ada guna banyak cara e-Payment. Saya guna QR Pay, TnG Pay, online transfer. Saya belajar dari anak juga macam mana mau buat".

Respondent 3: "I know about online payments, but I don't know how to use them. I'm afraid of pressing the wrong button and the money won't go through. I always ask my child to check if the payment has been received."

Responden 3: "Saya tahu pasal pembayaran online, tapi tak tahu nak guna. Saya takut silap tekan, nanti duit tak masuk. Saya selalu minta anak cek duit ada masuk atau tidak".

Respondent 5: "My homestay does provide internet, but sometimes the connection is weak."

Responden 5: "Homestay saya ada sediakan internet cuma kadang-kadang line tak kuat."

Respondent 8: "My friend once got scammed because a customer gave a fake receipt. We had to check the bank after the customer claimed to have paid. Sometimes as operators, we really have to be extra careful with online transactions."

Responden 8: "Kawan saya pernah kena tipu sebab pelanggan kasi resit palsu. Kena cek bank selepas pelanggan kata dah masuk duit. Kadang-kadang kita sebagai pengusaha kena selalu berhati-hati dengan transaksi online ni".

This illustrates the reliance on family members and the informal learning processes involved. This theme aligns with three DHR elements namely digital payment facilities, internet access, and cybersecurity & digital literacy. The literature supports this challenge. Murniati et al. [7] identified digital illiteracy and inadequate infrastructure as primary barriers to digital transformation in rural tourism. Moreover, current training models tend to be urban-centric, offering limited contextual relevance for homestay operators in places like Sibu.

4.3 Theme 3: Revenue Generation

Operators emphasized the role of digital tools in improving income and customer engagement. Online bookings, rapid response to inquiries, and maintaining visibility on social platforms were frequently mentioned as mechanisms for increasing occupancy rates.

Respondent 4: "If you reply quickly, they book quickly. If you're slow, they'll find another homestay."

Responden 4: "Kalau cepat jawab, cepat dia booking. Kalau lambat, dia cari homestay lain."

Respondent 6: "Nowadays, a lot of tourists ask through WhatsApp, TikTok, or Facebook. If you're slow to respond, they immediately look elsewhere. Sometimes I stay on standby with my phone 24/7."

Responden 6: "Sekarang ramai pelancong tanya dekat WhatsApp, Tiktok atau Facebook. Kalau lambat jawab, dia terus cari tempat lain. Kadang-kadang saya standby 24 jam dengan telefon je."

Respondent 3: "When I first uploaded pictures of my homestay on Facebook, someone from Kuala Lumpur messaged me right away. The next day, they booked for the weekend. If I hadn't used Facebook, I don't think they would've even known my homestay existed."

Responden 3:"Masa saya mula letak gambar homestay dekat Facebook, terus ada orang KL mesej tanya. Esoknya dia booking untuk hujung minggu. Kalau tak guna Facebook, saya rasa dia takkan tahu pun homestay saya wujud."

This feedback reflects the high dependency on speed and responsiveness in securing bookings. The immediacy of replies is directly linked to customer retention and conversion rates where even a short delay can lead to missed business opportunities. By staying connected and responsive, operators are better positioned to attract spontaneous bookings and maintain occupancy levels, which in turn stabilizes income. This illustrates how digital responsiveness is not merely about communication but functions as a key income-generating tactic for rural homestay businesses.

This theme ties directly to DHR element of digitally responsive operation, and indirectly supports economic impact by enhancing income streams. These findings corroborate with previous research asserting that responsiveness and digital agility are predictors of business success in micro-enterprise settings [4].

4.4 Theme 4: Regulatory Compliance (De-Emphasized)

Interestingly, regulatory compliance—including licensing and registration with local authorities did not emerge as a prominent concern. 2 respondents stated that such requirements were not perceived as central to their digital journey.

Respondent 1: "The regulations are there, but they're not made for us. They don't talk about digital. They talk about general tourism."

Responden 1: "Peraturan itu memang ada, tapi bukan untuk kami. Ia tak sentuh pun pasal digital. Ia cuma cerita pasal pelancongan umum je."

Respondent 4: "We follow the rules, but we've never felt they had anything to do with the online part. It feels like two completely different worlds."

Responden 4: "Kami ikut je peraturan, tapi tak pernah rasa benda tu ada kaitan dengan online. Rasanya macam dua dunia yang berbeza."

This disconnect suggests that while compliance is a formal expectation within the DHR model, it may not resonate with the lived digital priorities of rural entrepreneurs. The feedback implies that operators often see digital transformation as a business evolution, while compliance remains a bureaucratic requirement detached from immediate operational needs. This echoes findings by Soiw et al. [10] who argue that regulatory frameworks in Malaysian rural tourism are often misaligned with ground realities. Similarly, Ramele et al. [11] found that overly complex compliance structures discourage active participation among grassroots operators. Therefore, this study contributes to the literature by reframing compliance not as a static prerequisite but as a contextual and negotiable aspect of readiness. When presented as a value-adding strategy (e.g., enabling access to grants, increasing platform trust), compliance is more likely to gain relevance.

5 Revisit Digital Homestay Ready Framework

The DHR framework visually consolidates four major themes namely Digital Marketing, Digital Awareness, Revenue Generation, and Regulatory Compliance. Each mapped against corresponding readiness elements. This mapping not only validates the conceptual framework but also highlights the dynamic interdependence of these elements. For instance, digital presence and responsiveness directly impact revenue outcomes, while regulatory compliance, though formally required, appears decoupled from immediate digital strategies (Fig. 1).

5.1 Insight of the Study

These findings reveal several key insights that deepen our understanding of digital readiness in rural homestay contexts. First, operators equate digital readiness with visibility and usability, rather than technical sophistication. Platforms like Facebook and WhatsApp dominate not because they are advanced, but because they are accessible and familiar. Second, digital awareness exists but is often mediated by family support and informal learning, highlighting the persistent gap in digital literacy and confidence.

Third, responsiveness is not just good service but it is a survival tactic. Operators link quick replies directly to income generation, where even slight delays risk losing bookings. This positions digital responsiveness as a crucial economic lever. Fourth, regulatory compliance, while part of formal frameworks, is largely decoupled from the everyday realities of digital engagement. Operators see it as detached bureaucracy unless tied to tangible benefits.

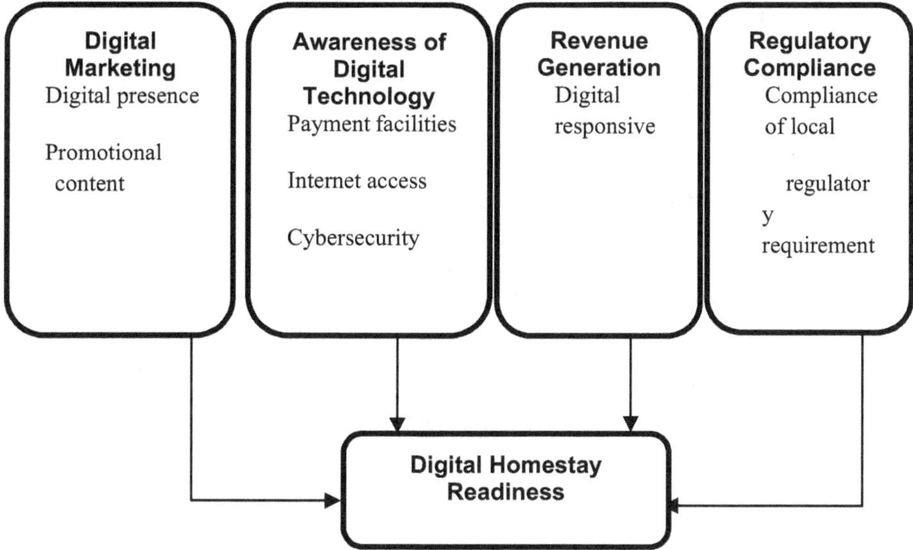

Fig. 1. DHR framework.

Together, these insights suggest that digital readiness is shaped by grassroots pragmatism rather than policy prescriptions. The revised DHR framework presented here reflects that bottom-up logic and grounded in lived experiences, not just institutional ideals. It provides a more inclusive and practical blueprint for supporting digital transformation among Malaysia's rural micro-entrepreneurs.

6 Theoretical and Practical Contribution

This study contributes theoretically by challenging the traditional notion of digital readiness as a uniform and top-down construct. Existing literature often emphasizes infrastructure, access, and regulatory compliance as key indicators. However, this study demonstrates that digital readiness must be understood contextually from rooted in the lived realities and localized interpretations of rural entrepreneurs. By proposing and validating a Digital Homestay Ready (DHR) framework, this research contributes a new model for understanding digital transformation that bridges policy frameworks with micro-level entrepreneurial behavior.

Practically, the study offers a field-tested, user-centered DHR model that can guide government agencies, tourism boards, and digital training providers in crafting more relevant support interventions. It reveals the importance of low-barrier tools, like social media platforms, and highlights the disconnect between existing regulatory expectations and actual digital practices on the ground. The refined DHR framework provides a more grounded basis for training modules, funding schemes, and policy designs aimed at accelerating inclusive digital adoption among rural homestay operators. Several key insights that deepen our understanding of digital readiness in rural homestay contexts. First, operators equate digital readiness with visibility and usability, rather than technical sophistication. Platforms like Facebook and WhatsApp dominate not because they are advanced, but because they are accessible and familiar. Second, digital awareness exists but is often mediated by family support and informal learning, highlighting the persistent gap in digital literacy and confidence.

7 Limitations and Future Research

While this study provides valuable insights into digital readiness from the perspective of rural homestay operators in Sibu, its findings are based on a relatively small sample size of 8 participants. This is a conscious methodological choice aligned with qualitative inquiry, which prioritizes depth, context, and lived experiences over broad generalizability. Nonetheless, future research should consider larger, multi-site studies across various rural regions in Sarawak and Peninsular Malaysia to test the transferability and scalability of the DHR framework.

Additionally, this study captures only the supply-side perspectives of homestay operators. Future research should incorporate the voices of tourists, digital service providers, and platform intermediaries (e.g., booking platforms, e-wallet providers, tourism officers) to triangulate findings and strengthen the practical utility of the framework. These actors offer critical insights into digital expectations, user experiences, and system-level challenges that may not be visible from the operator's point of view.

Lastly, longitudinal studies could offer value in tracking changes in digital readiness over time, particularly in response to evolving government policies (e.g., MyDIGITAL, Sarawak Digital Economy Strategy) or shifts in digital infrastructure and training availability. Such studies could provide stronger evidence for causality and long-term impact, allowing the DHR framework to evolve into a predictive and policy-informing tool.

8 Conclusion

This study reconceptualizes digital readiness for rural homestays as more than just digital access or infrastructure; it is a multifaceted construct rooted in visibility, responsiveness, and user agency. Through grounded qualitative inquiry, the research reveals that homestay operators in Sibu navigate digital transformation not by top-down policy compliance, but through adaptive, bottom-up strategies that align with their immediate realities. The proposed Digital Homestay Ready (DHR) framework, refined through this empirical lens, represents a practical and inclusive approach to benchmarking digital maturity.

By decoupling bureaucratic compliance from core readiness practices, this study offers a critical recalibration of what it means to be digitally prepared in the rural tourism sector. It invites policymakers and practitioners to rethink digital interventions, emphasizing grassroots empowerment over one-size-fits-all governance. Ultimately, the findings serve as a call to align national digital strategies with the voices and practices of those on the ground by ensuring that no rural entrepreneur is left behind in Malaysia's evolving digital economy. Future iterations of the DHR framework can serve as a rural operationalization model of MyDIGITAL, especially for bottom-up, entrepreneur-driven digitalization efforts in Sarawak's tourism economy.

Appendix 1: Interview Questions

This study employed a semi-structured interview protocol aligned with the research objectives. The questions were designed to elicit deep, contextual insights into the digital readiness of rural homestay operators in Sibu.

Research Objective 1:

To explore the perceptions of rural homestay operators regarding digital readiness in the tourism sector.

- What does "digital readiness" mean to you in the context of your homestay business?
- How important is digital presence or online engagement for your homestay?
- Have you ever attended any digital-related training or support programmes?

Research Objective 2:

To understand the current level of digital technology adoption among rural homestay operators.

- What digital tools or platforms are you currently using for your homestay operations (e.g., Facebook, WhatsApp, online payment systems)?
- How did you learn to use these tools? Did anyone assist you?
- Are there any digital tools you've heard about but have not yet adopted? Why?
- Do you feel confident managing digital tasks such as online booking or payment?

Research Objective 3:

To examine the role of digital readiness in supporting the operational and economic performance of homestay businesses.

- How does using digital tools affect your income or bookings?
- Do you believe responding quickly to online messages has an impact on your business performance?
- Can you share a situation where using digital tools helped you gain more customers or bookings?
- What challenges do you face when trying to increase your digital presence?

Cross-Cutting Theme (Governance):

To assess perceptions on compliance with local authority regulations in relation to digital transformation.

- Are you aware of the licensing or regulatory requirements for homestay operators?
- Do you feel these regulations are connected to your efforts to go digital?
- Do you see value in complying with such regulations, especially in terms of online promotion or legitimacy?

References

1. Chen, J., Hou, H., Liao, Z., Wang, L.: Digital environment, digital literacy, and farmers' entrepreneurial behavior: a discussion on bridging the digital divide. Sustainability **16**(23), 10220 (2024)

2. Sarawak Multimedia Authority. https://www.sma.gov.my/web/home/index/. last accessed 08 Jun 2025
3. Malaysia Digital Economy Corporation (MDEC). https://mdec.my/. Last accessed 08 Jun 2025
4. Samad, N.A.A., Zahari, M.S.M., Hanafiah, M.H., Bashir, M.A.R.A.: Digital technology adoption as a game changer for community-based tourism (CBT) homestay operators: a qualitative investigation. Asia-Pacif. J. Rural Dev. **34**(1), 77–97 (2024)
5. Abas, S.A., Abd Halim, N., Hanafiah, M.H.M.: Exploring the role of local champion in community-based rural homestay in Malaysia: a case of Homestay Sungai Haji Dorani. J. Tourism, Hospitality Environ. Manage. 7(27), 310–320 (2022)
6. Ministry of Tourism, Arts and Culture Malaysia. https://www.motac.gov.my/en/. Last accessed 06 Jun 2025
7. Murniati, D.E., Razzaq, A.R.A., Ismail, A., Mota, L.: Training urgency to bridge the digital divide for social media marketing awareness and adoption: case of CBT rural homestay operators Malaysia. J. Tech. Educ. Train. **15**(1), 142–157 (2023)
8. Chounta, I.A., Ortega-Arranz, A., Daskalaki, S., Dimitriadis, Y., Avouris, N.: Toward a data-informed framework for the assessment of digital readiness of higher education institutions. Int. J. Educ. Technol. High. Educ. **21**(1), 59 (2024)
9. Mohamad, N., Shi, C.W.: Investigating social media marketing adoption among homestay operators in Malaysia. In: Tracking Tourism Patterns and Improving Travel Experiences with Innovative Technologies, pp. 1–32. Springer, Cham (2025)
10. Siow, M.L., Ramachandran, S., Afandi, S.H.M., Baum, T., Shuib, A.: Policy, government strata and sustainable tourism of a rural destination: an analytical network policy perspective. Asia-Pacif. J. Innovation Hospitality Tourism **11**(2), 25–51 (2022)
11. Ramele Ramli, R., Yamazaki, J., Ibrahim, M.N., Safiee, L.S.: Malaysian homestays: the need for standardized regulation. Built Environ. J. **17**(2), 63–74 (2020)
12. Bislimi, F., Dalloshi, P., Mehmeti, I., Tërstena, A., Deda, G.: Digital readiness in emerging markets: the role of digital skills and connectivity in driving digital economy. Int. J. Relig. **5**(11), 4316–4324 (2024)
13. Arnaud, J., São Mamede, H., Branco, F.: The relationship between digital transformation and digital literacy—An explanatory model: systematic literature review. F1000Research **13**, 253 (2024)
14. Creswell, J.W., Poth, C.N.: Qualitative Inquiry and Research Design: Choosing Among Five Approaches, 4th edn. Sage Publications, Thousand Oaks (2016)
15. Braun, V., Clarke, V.: Using thematic analysis in psychology. Qual. Res. Psychol. **3**(2), 77–101 (2006)
16. Carter, N.: The use of triangulation in qualitative research. Number 5/September 2014 **41**(5), 545–547 (2014)

Machine Learning-Based Sentiment Analysis of Malaysia Food Tourism

Joyce Xinjie Lim, Hoai Thang Tan, Nur Hana Samsudin(✉), and Keng Hoon Gan

School of Computer Sciences, Universiti Sains Malaysia, Penang, Malaysia
{joycelx,hoaithangtan}@student.usm.my, {nurhana.samsudin, khgan}@usm.my

Abstract. This study the usage of sentiment analysis to enhance food tourism in Malaysia by utilizing natural language processing and machine learning. To address data imbalance and variability, a dataset of 360,000 food reviews was pre-processed using methods like text cleaning, tokenization, and resampling. Textual data was converted into machine learning inputs using feature extraction techniques like CountVectorizer and TF-IDF, and sentiments were categorized as either positive or negative. Cross-validation and hyperparameter tuning were used to assess four supervised algorithms including Support Vector Machines (SVM), Logistic Regression, Random Forest, and Multinomial Naive Bayes. With an accuracy of 84.15% on the test set, SVM with the TF-IDF vectorizer was the best-performing model, according to the results, closely followed by Logistic Regression. By combining text reviews with numerical ratings, a comprehensive understanding of tourist sentiments was obtained, providing useful information for enhancing tailored suggestions and promoting regional cuisines. This concept shows how sentiment analysis may boost tourism management and increase customer satisfaction. In order to improve sentiment analysis and its uses in tourism, future research could investigate sophisticated deep learning models and multimodal data sources.

Keywords: Sentiment Analysis · Natural Language Processing · Food Tourism · Online Review · Malaysia

1 Introduction

The growth of content created by users on digital platforms has produced a tremendous impact on the tourism sector, especially in the field of food tourism. Travelers often share their dining experiences online, building up a massive database of reviews that may be evaluated for determining public comments. According to Research and Markets in [1], the global user-generated content market was worth $4.26 billion in 2022 and is expected to reach $17.51 billion by 2028, indicating a growing trend on such content for decision-making processes. Sentiment analysis is a subset of natural language processing (NLP). It is used to extract subjective information from textual data, providing insights into tourist perceptions and preferences. When sentiment analysis is integrated with machine

M. Kassim et al. (Eds.): SCDS 2025, CCIS 2674, pp. 189–202, 2026.
https://doi.org/10.1007/978-981-95-8368-3_14

learning techniques, studies show that it reaches 79–99% accuracy in understanding client sentiments depends on the machine learning method used [2]. In the domain of food tourism, this technique has proven useful in identifying critical characteristics that influence tourist satisfaction and decision-making.

Malaysia is a country famous for its unique and vibrant culinary culture. The usage of sentiment analysis on food tourism offers a chance to improve food tourism recommendation system in Malaysia. Malaysia's food diversity, which includes Malay, Chinese, Indian, and indigenous cuisines, is a major tourist attraction [3]. By monitoring tourist feelings, recommendation systems can deliver individualized recommendations, increasing user pleasure and promoting local cuisines. Furthermore, applying sentiment analysis into recommender systems has been proven to improve performance by considering the personal perspective of user reviews [4].

This study will look into the use of sentiment analysis in food tourist reviews in Malaysia. The paper aims to use machine learning and deep learning algorithms to effectively classify sentiments stated in reviews, allowing users to generate more customized suggestions. This methodology is consistent with recent advances in sentiment analysis methodologies, which have showed higher accuracy in sentiment classification tasks [5]. This study's findings are intended to contribute to the fields of tourism management and information systems by outlining a framework for using sentiment analysis to improve food tourism experiences. Furthermore, this study highlights the potential of studying sentiment analysis to better cater to tourist preferences, thereby promoting the expansion of the local food tourism sector.

2 Background of Related Techniques

Food tourism review ratings and texts provide essential feedback on client requirements and problems. However, relying simply on review ratings or content poses significant challenges. Shafiezad and Mostofi (2024) found out that written reviews can provide more profound insights into consumer satisfaction rather than using ratings alone [2]. The weak but statistically significant relationship between sentiment scores and restaurant ratings emphasizes the necessity for sentiment research to supplement standard metrics such as star ratings. Thus, expanding the data sources to incorporate textual input in addition to rating scores would allow for the recording of sentiment patterns, resulting in a more timely and diversified set of insights. However, the vast majority of non-rated textual input raises serious concerns.

Many evaluations lack a numerical rating and are only text-based, making it difficult for visitors to retrieve useful information quickly. Furthermore, not all consumers who submit a star rating include written comments. Many people merely provide a rating without providing any explanation, reducing the information accessible to grasp their genuine beliefs [2]. This means that a high star rating may disguise unhappiness with certain aspects, whereas a low rating may not adequately convey what went wrong. In such circumstances, sentiment analysis of reviews is critical to get a more accurate picture of client feedback. Analysing written evaluations can reveal underlying attitudes, patterns, and concerns that star ratings cannot. A lack of a clear rating system could limit successful decision-making, especially in a world of rapid change where individuals need immediate and concise information.

In addition to the lack of ratings, deciphering textual comments can be challenging. Identifying the sentiment, tastes, and experiences expressed in reviews can be challenging due to the subjectivity of words and varied writing styles. Individual travellers tend to prioritize specific features of a restaurant, such as food quality, price, service, and atmosphere, in their reviews [6]. Gathering broad information for potential foodies to make informed decisions is tough considering the variability of the reviews. Users struggle to get consistent insights from reviews due to their complicated and context-dependent nature.

3 Proposed Solution

Sentiment analysis categorizes food reviews as positive or negative. The analysis aims to categorize input as positive or negative, and construct a suggestion system tailored to travellers' needs. This study focuses on food reviews, which play a significant influence in tourism. Food has always been the most basic human need. Thus, food is a universal demand for all tourists. Food reviews provide a uniform dataset, facilitating sentiment analysis.

Sentiment analysis, or opinion mining, uses natural language processing to determine emotional tone or subjective opinions [7]. This method is commonly used for analysing text data, such as product reviews, social media posts, and tourism reviews. Sentiment analysis often classifies text as positive, negative, or neutral. Advanced sentiment analysis systems can recognize certain emotional states, like happiness, excitement, and frustration.

The study follows a defined procedural flow as shown in Fig. 1. The procedure starts with dataset collecting, then moves to data preprocessing, trans-forming review text into numerical features, using a classifier, and evaluating the results.

3.1 Brief Overview of Process Flow

Data Collection. The dataset used in this study is the Malaysia Restaurant Review Datasets from Kaggle [8]. The dataset comprises around 360,000 reviews with fields like Review and Rating.

Exploratory Data Analysis (EDA). The EDA stage in this study involves describing data, managing duplicate and missing values, and analysing the distribution of review ratings in restaurant reviews.

Data Preprocessing. The data preprocessing phase involves several key steps to prepare the dataset for sentiment analysis. The steps will be explained in Sect. 3.3. These steps ensure a clean and consistent text corpus for accurate sentiment analysis.

Feature Extraction. Feature extraction is a crucial step in natural language processing (NLP) for machine learning. It involves transforming text data into vector format to meet the input requirements of machine learning classifiers. In this research, two common techniques for this transformation are CountVectorizer and TF-IDF Vectorizer are used.

Classifier. Multiple classifiers have been implemented to identify the highest accuracy for the food review. This will further explain in Sect. 3.5.

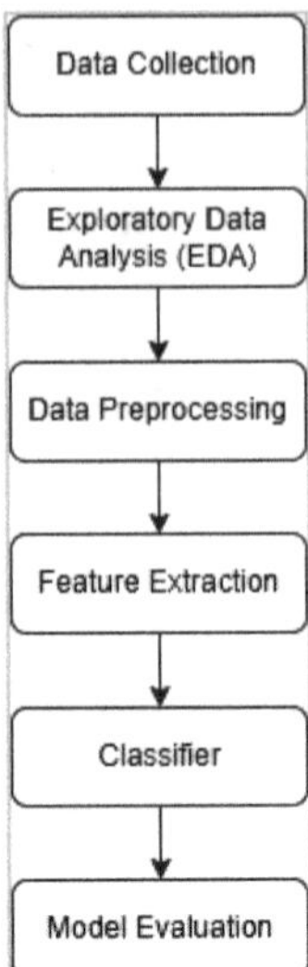

Fig. 1. Process flow of food tourism review sentiment analysis.

Model Evaluation. Finally, the model developed will be evaluated. The performance evaluation of sentiment classification, the model performance is assessed using metrics such as accuracy, precision, recall, and F1 score.

3.2 Dataset Description

Exploratory Data Analysis (EDA) plays a crucial role in understanding the underlying structure and characteristics of the dataset. The restaurant reviews dataset used in this study consists of four columns and 361,784 rows. Table 1 presents a detailed description of each column.

Table 1. Dataset Descriptions.

Column Name	Description
Restaurant	The name of the restaurant
Location	State of the restaurant located in
Review	Restaurant reviews extracted from Google Reviews and Tripadvisor in text form
Rating	Discrete quantitative attribute. Restaurant rating ranging from 1 to 5, extracted from Google Reviews and Tripadvisor

It is also essential to address duplicate and missing values, as well as to gain a general overview of the review distribution. The following paragraph provides a more detailed explanation of these aspects.

Managing Duplicate and Missing Values. To guarantee the accuracy as well as quality of the analysis in this project, identifying and resolving missing or duplicate values is an essential first step in the data preparation procedure. After investigation, it is verified that the dataset contains no duplicate or missing values.

Distribution of Review Rating. To learn more about the general attitudes and sentiments of tourists toward restaurants, it's also critical to comprehend the distribution of review ratings inside the restaurant reviews dataset. This information provides important background information for sentiment analysis. Important details like the frequency of both positive and negative attitudes stated by tourists can be found by examining the distribution of review ratings. This information is useful not only for comprehending the sentiment setting as a whole but also for classifying review ratings into positive and negative contexts during the preprocessing stage. In order to train the machine learning model for the study's goal, this classification is an essential step.

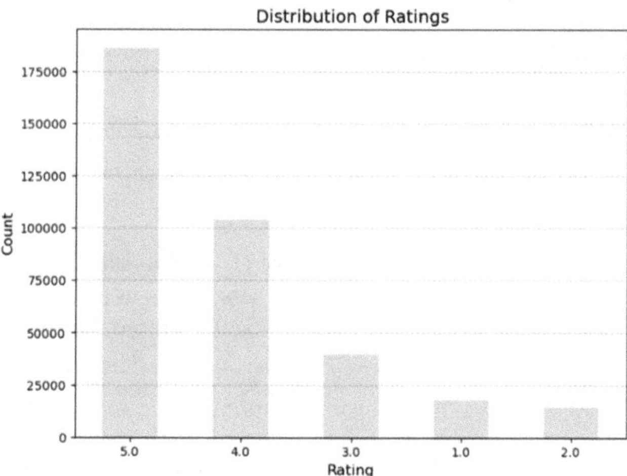

Fig. 2. Distribution of ratings.

As shown in Fig. 2, the dataset is imbalanced as it skewed to the highest rating, which is rating 5. Thus, the sampling is planned to be done in the data preprocessing phase.

The next section will proceed with how the preprocessing phase took place.

3.3 Data Preprocessing

Since the dataset is imbalanced, necessary steps are taken to process the data.

Mapping of Review Rating into Positive & Negative Sentiments. In order to build a labelled dataset for supervised machine learning, we handle the complexities of restaurant review ratings during the data preprocessing phase by classifying them into two emotion classes: positive and negative. As illustrated in Fig. 3, review ratings of 1 to 3 are categorized as negative emotions, whereas review ratings of 4 and 5 are considered positive. This categorization enables us to match the sentiment analysis to the customer satisfaction scale, offering a more sophisticated comprehension of the emotional tenors connected to various review scores.

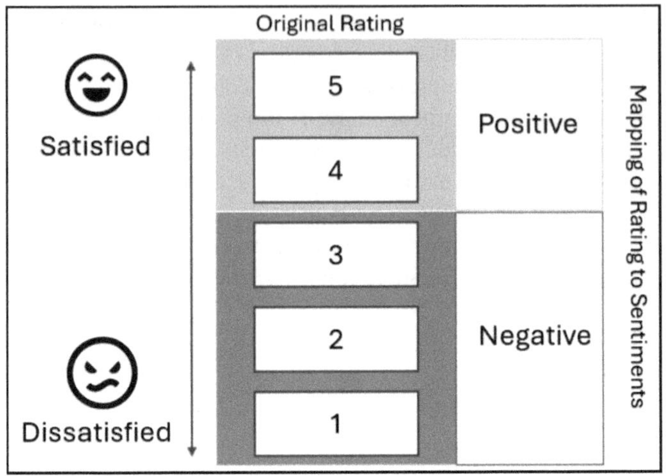

Fig. 3. Mapping of review ratings to sentiment classes.

The analysis seeks to capture the wide range of viewpoints stated in restaurant reviews by distinguishing between positive and negative sentiments in this way. This will allow for a more accurate sentiment analysis and, ultimately, a thorough suggestion based on the positive reviews.

Data Sampling. According to the results, resampling techniques can solve the problem of an unbalanced dataset, and using over-sampled data improves performance compared to using under-sampled data. According to Al-Khazaleh, Alian, and Jaradat (2024) in [9], resampling techniques can solve the problem of an unbalanced dataset, and using over-sampled data improves performance compared to using under-sampled data. Thus, the data is being sampled by getting 50,000 of positive reviews and 50,000 of negative reviews randomly.

Text Cleaning. Additionally, to improve the quality of the textual data, we apply text clean-ing techniques. This includes expanding contractions; removing non-alphanumeric letters, URLs and punctuation; lowercasing; tokenization; getting rid of stop words; and stemming the text to make it more readable. Together, these procedures help to improve the dataset so that a clean and consistent text corpus is used for the subsequent sentiment analysis.

Expand Contractions. In NLP, expanding contractions entails transforming abbreviated words (such as "don't" or "can't") into the full versions ("do not" or "cannot"). This procedure, which is carried out by using contractions, is essential to sentiment analysis and is being performed by implementing the contractions.fix() function in this project. In conclusion, by giving the model a clearer and more consistent input to examine, expanding contractions contributes to the accuracy and consistency of sentiment analysis.

Remove URL, Punctuation, Emoji and Number. At first, the re.sub() function is used to replace non-alphanumeric symbols with spaces. This leads to phrases that only contain hyphens (-), numerals (0–9), lowercase alphabets (a–z), and uppercase alphabets (A–Z). It is also crucial to remove unnecessary information because the restaurant reviews are taken from websites like Google Review and Tripadvisor, which may contain URL links. In order to concentrate our research on the review content and eliminate superfluous online platform-related features, URLs are eliminated by implementing the function remove_url().

Text Standardization (to lower case). For simplicity and processing comfort, it's also standard practice to convert all words to lowercase. By recognizing words with the same spelling but dis-tinct cases as identical, this guarantees consistency.

Tokenization. Stop words are frequently left out of text analysis because they are ubiquitous words in a language but have little meaning. The NLTK's stop words module, which provides a predefined list of frequently used stop words in English, is used in our study to eliminate stop words. The goal is to concentrate on more significant words that contain important details for sentiment analysis by eliminating these stop words from the text.

Stemming. Since stemming removes prefixes and suffixes from words, converting them into their based form, it was chosen for this project. Stemming's primary goal is to standardize and simplify phrases in order to improve the efficiency of natural language processing jobs. NLTK's PorterStemmer is used for stemming in this project. The words in the restaurant reviews are normalized using the ps.stem() technique. The outcome of text cleaning is a list of terms in their root form, which will be utilized in the sentiment analysis in the following steps.

3.4 Feature Extraction

Feature extraction is one of the most important steps in NLP for machine learning. Since the data format is in text, it needs to be transformed into vector format to fulfill the input requirements for machine learning classifiers. Feature extraction in NLP has numerous techniques available. Among these, two common methods of transformations are named CountVectorizer and TF-IDF Vectorizer. Both techniques transform text into vectors. Vectors will turn into inputs of machine learning algorithms. In this project, both vectorizer is used to convert the pre-processed review text into vector and serve as input for machine learning algorithm. As the dataset is split into 70% of training and 30% of testing sets, the vectorizer will first perform vectorization on the training set and then apply the same vectorizer to the test set.

CountVectorizer is used to transform a given text into a vector based on the count of each word occurring in the documents. It creates a matrix where each row represents a document and each column represents a word from the corpus, forming a bag of words (BoW) representation. CountVectorizer also allows setting the maximum feature vocabulary size and the n-gram value for tokenization. If the n-gram value is 1, it is called a unigram, which tokenizes the text into individual words. When n = 2, it is called a bigram, which tokenizes the text into pairs of consecutive words and calculates their frequency [11]. In this project, the maximum feature size was set to 10000 with the default unigram tokenization.

TF-IDF (Term Frequency-Inverse Document Frequency) is a statistical measure of the importance of words within a document based on an entire collection of documents. In other words, it gives a weight to a word in a document so as to balance two factors: how frequently the word occurs in a document and how often it occurs across all the documents in the corpus. TF-IDF focuses on words that are important in a certain document, yet not too common in the whole corpus [12].

$$TermFrequency(TF) = \frac{Frequencyofterm(t)indocument(d)}{Totaltermindocument} \tag{1}$$

$$InverseDocumentFrequency(IDF) = \log 10 \frac{Numberofdocumentspresentinacorpus}{Numberofdocumentswithterm(t)} \tag{2}$$

$$TFIDF = TF * IDF \tag{3}$$

3.5 Machine Learning Algorithm

In the machine learning approach, there are method to perform sentiment analysis. Supervised machine learning, unsupervised machine learning, and Hybrid Approach. In this study we are focus in supervised machine learning which perform classification. A classifier will be train based on the feature extracted and use to predict the sentiment class is positive or negative. Some of these algorithms are Logistic Regression, Random Forest, Multinomial Naïve Bayes, and SVM. With these machine learning algorithm, cross validation with k-fold = 5 is used to perform hyperparameter tunning on the training set. As this study is focus on two types of vectorizations, two set feature is used for training set to perform tunning. The best hyperparameter will be use as the final parameter to train the whole training set for classifier. The result of this stage will be total 8 classifier (4 algorithms * 2 set of vectorizer features).

Support Vector Machine (SVM). Support Vector Machine (SVM) is a supervised learning algorithm commonly used for both classification and regression tasks. It functions by identifying the optimal hyperplane that best separates two classes by maximizing the margin between the different class groups. In this case, the optimal hyperplane will be generated to separate the positive and negative sentiment with maximizing the support vector of these two classes [13]. SVM is a non-probabilistic linear classifier, and with kernel functions, it can manage complex feature spaces, enhancing its classification capability. Also, one of important feature for SVM is the choice of the kernel function as it may impact the performance of the classification task. There are four type of kernel, linear, sigmoid, polynomial, and RBF. RBF kernel of SVM show a better performance which suit for most of the sentiment analysis task and it is used in this study [14].

Multinomial Naïve Bayes (MNB). Multinomial Naive Bayes (MNB) work based on Bayes theorem, principle of Bayes theorem and assumes occurrence of each word is independent to other words given the sentiment class [15]. As MNB is a popular machine learning algorithm for text classification problems in natural language processing (NLP) [16]. It is good at problems with text data that has clear features, like word counts. When training, MNB learns the probability of specific words being in positive and negative sentiment examples. Then, the trained model will calculate how likely new review text is to be in different sentiment class. The review is then assigned to the sentiment group based on the highest probability. The following is the formula used to calculate the probability of sentiment classification.

$$P(sentimentclass|textfeature = \frac{P(sentimentclass)P(textfeature|sentimentclass)}{P(textfeatures)} \quad (4)$$

Logistic Regression. Logistic regression is a statistical method that predicts the probability of binary outcome in classification task. By analysing the relationship between the independent variable, the model estimates the probability of an event occurring. In our case, it predicts the probability of positive or negative sentiment. The model works by transforming the probability of an event into log-odds. The numbers in the model are typically estimate using maximum likelihood estimation. Once the model is ready, it can predict the probability of a new event for new data points by applying the logistic function to the weighted sum of the independent variables.

Random Forest. Random Forest is a type of ensemble machine learning algorithm that combines multiple decision trees to improve prediction accuracy. It uses bagging ensemble approach, which involves creating different subsets of samples through bootstrap sampling and train multiple decision tree. This help to prevent model overfitting. Sentiment analysis belonged to classification task. Random Forest Classifier uses majority voting to determine the positive or negative sentiment class. On the other hand, the Random Forest Regressor averages the outcomes from all the trees to make a continuous prediction.

4 Evaluation Criteria

In the performance evaluation of sentiment classification, the model performance is assessed using metrics such as accuracy, precision, recall, and F1 score These metrics are computed from the information in the confusion matrix. In the confusion matrix, True Positive (TP) and True Negative (TN) are the number of correct classifications of the positive and negative classes. False Positive (FP) is also known as Type I error. This happens when the predicted class is positive, but the actual class is negative. False Negative (FN) is Type II error. In the case that the predicted class is negative when actually positive.

The equation of these matrics are as follows:

$$Accuray = \frac{TP + TN}{TP + TN + FP + FN} \quad (5)$$

$$Precision = \frac{TP}{TP + FP} \tag{6}$$

$$Recall = \frac{TP}{TP + FN} \tag{7}$$

$$F1 - score = 2 \times \frac{Precision \times Recall}{Precision + Recall} \tag{8}$$

Accuracy measures how often the classifier correctly predicts the outcome. Recall measures how many of the actual positive cases were correctly predicted by our model. Precision measures the proportion of correctly predicted positive cases that actually turned out to be positive. Precision is useful in case where false positives are a greater concern than false negatives. For example, a restaurant owner wants to be confident that a review classified as positive truly reflects genuine customer satisfaction. Recall is useful when false negatives are a greater concern than false positives. For example, if the restaurant owner wants to identify all negative sentiment to address the customer concerns and prevent the negative sentiment from escape. The F1-score is the harmonic mean of precision and recall, offering a balance between the two (Fig. 4).

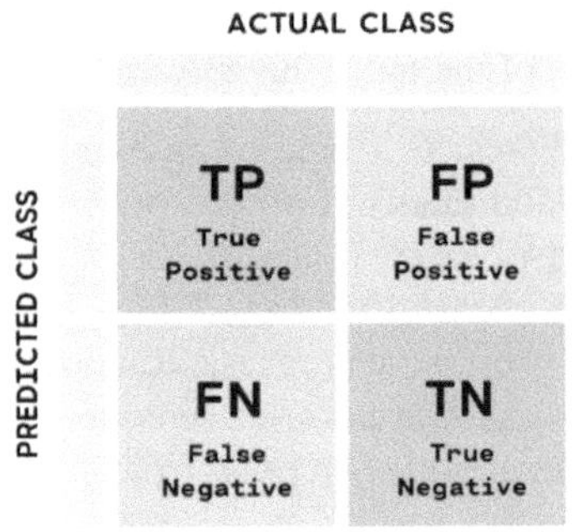

	ACTUAL CLASS	
PREDICTED CLASS	**TP** True Positive	**FP** False Positive
	FN False Negative	**TN** True Negative

Fig. 4. Confusion Matrix

5 Discussion and Analysis

In this study, a total of 8 sentiment classifications were built using different machine learning algorithms. Two sets of vectorizations (TF-IDF and CountVectorization) were applied to 4 algorithms (Logistic Regression, Multinomial Naïve Bayes, SVM, and Random Forest). Each classification algorithm performed fine-tuning on its respective hyperparameters to find the best settings. The C hyperparameter was tuned for Logistic Regression and SVM to adjust the strength of regularization. The Multinomial Naïve Bayes algorithm was tuned on the alpha parameter, which is the smoothing parameter. For Random Forest, it was tuned on the min sample split, which controls the minimum number of samples required to split an internal node.

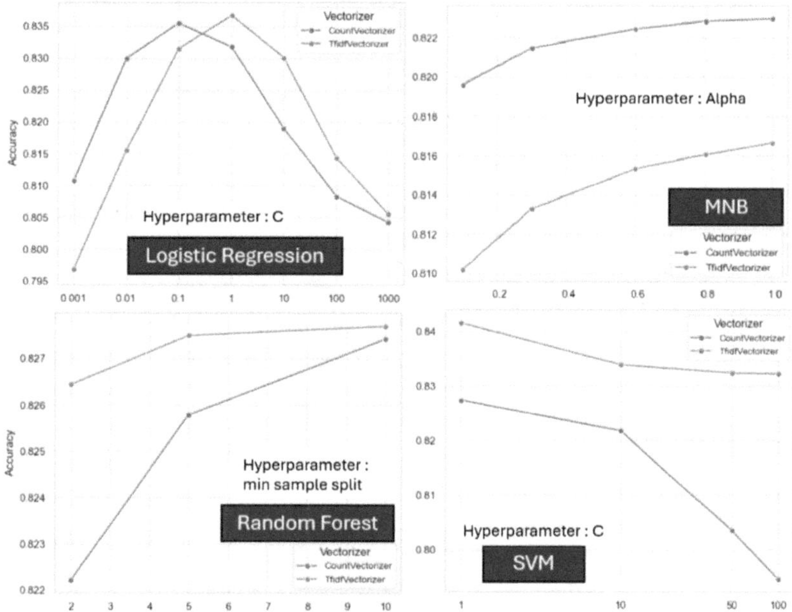

Fig. 5. Result of hyperparameter tuning.

Based on the fine-tuning results shown in the accuracy plots in Fig. 5, Logistic Regression achieves the highest accuracy at C = 0.1 with CountVectorizer, while TfidfVectorizer reaches its peak accuracy at C = 1. Both vectorizers experience a performance decline after their respective peaks as the C value increases. For Multinomial Naïve Bayes (MNB), the accuracy consistently increases with increasing values of alpha and reached the best performance at alpha = 1. This indicates that Laplace smoothing helps generalize the model better by avoiding zero probabilities for unseen words [17]. For all values of alpha, CountVectorizer outperforms TfidfVectorizer. In the Random Forest model, the accuracy increases with an increase in the minimum number of splits for both vectorizers. However, TfidfVectorizer performs better than CountVectorizer in this model. For SVM, both TfidfVectorizer and CountVectorizer achieve peak accuracy at C = 1, with a significant drop in accuracy after that. The performance of CountVectorizer drops significantly when C greater than 10. Overall, CountVectorizer tends to perform better in Logistic Regression and MNB, while TfidfVectorizer does better in Random Forest and SVM.

The best hyperparameters from the fine-tuning is use to train the whole training set. Then, the trained model predicts the sentiment class of the remaining 30% of the test set. The result of the test set is show in Fig. 6, SVM with TFIDFVectorizer achieves the highest accuracy of 84.5%. Logistic Regression with both vectorizers also performs well, closely following SVM. However, Random Forest and Multinomial Naive Bayes models show a slightly lower accuracy compare to SVM and Logistic Regression. Overall, TFIDFVectorizer shows superior performance with SVM and Logistic Regression. While, CountVectorizer is perform better with Naive Bayes and Random Forest (Table 2).

Table 2. Best Model Result from fine-tuning.

Mode	Vectorizer	Accuracy
SVM	TF-IDF	0.841529
Logistic Regression	TF-IDF	0.836757
Logistic Regression	CountVectorizer	0.835543
Random Forest	TF-IDF	0.8277
Random Forest	CountVectorizer	0.827429
SVM	CountVectorizer	0.827429
MNB	CountVectorizer	0.822986
MNB	TF-IDF	0.816671

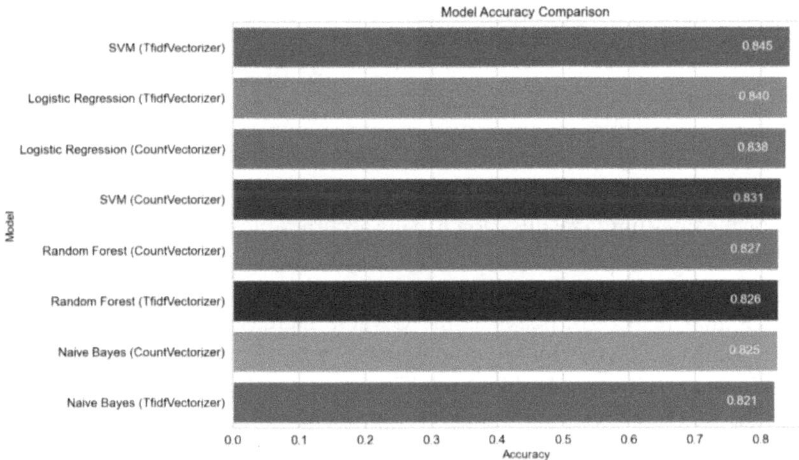

Fig. 6. Testing Set Result

Comparing the fine-tuning and test set results, there are some consistent patterns and differences. The best model in both fine-tuning and test results is the SVM with TfidfVectorizer. This shows the strong generalization capability of the model. Similar to Logistic Regression with TF-IDF and Logistic Regression with CountVectorizer maintain in 2nd and 3rd position. The Multinomial Naive Bayes is consistently ranked last in all cases. However, there is a significant difference in the performance of SVM with CountVectorizer and Random Forest models. On the test set, the performance of SVM with CountVectorizer outperforms that of the Random Forest model, contrary to the fine-tuning results. Indeed, this may indicate that SVM with CountVectorizer generalizes much better than expected, while the Random Forest model slightly overfits.

6 Conclusion

This study shows how sentiment analysis may be used effectively to Malaysian food tourism reviews by using machine learning algorithms to extract insightful information from textual data. This study offers a framework for strengthening personalized recommendation systems by fusing sentiment analysis with a strong preprocessing pipeline. This will boost visitor satisfaction and promote the regional food tourism industry.

With an accuracy of 84.15% on the test set, Support Vector Machines (SVM) combined with the TF-IDF vectorizer proved to be the most effective model. In contrast to the Multinomial Naive Bayes model, which performed exceptionally poorly while Logistic Regression also demonstrated impressive results. These results emphasize how crucial it is to choose the right machine learning methods for classification of sentiments.

Through extensive text preparation and resampling, this study also addressed issues including text variability and unbalanced datasets. The findings highlight how critical it is to resolve these problems in order to guarantee impartial and reliable sentiment analysis. To improve sentiment classification even more, future research might investigate the use of deep learning models or multimodal data sources. The suggested framework's usefulness could be confirmed and expanded by extending its reach to other domains or geographical areas.

References

1. Research And Markets: User-Generated Content Platform Market-Global Industry Size, Share, Trends, Opportunity, and Forecast, 2018–2028F," ResearchAndMarkets (2018). https://www.researchandmarkets.com/reports/5915540/user-generated-content-platform-market-global?srsltid=AfmBOoqsHsMiV7ffyuqO1RbZ4agjmR0JqR51Rlaj2qydnWvJohj6Sk_M. (Accessed 20 Jan 2025)
2. Shafiezad, O., Mostofi, H.: Sentiment analysis of berlin tourists' food quality perception through Artificial Intelligence. Tourism Hospitality **5**(4), 1396–1417 (2024). https://doi.org/10.3390/tourhosp5040078
3. Shariff, A., Omar, M., Jalis, M.H., Indriastuti M.: Exploring the impact of Malaysia's Culinary Heritage on tourism and economic development. Environ.-Behav. Proc. J. **9**(30), 139–144 (2024). https://doi.org/10.21834/e-bpj.v9i30.6198
4. Zheng, X., Luo, Y., Sun, L., Zhang, J., Chen, F.: A tourism destination recommender system using users' sentiment and temporal dynamics. J. Intell. Inf. Syst. **51**(3), 557–578 (2018). https://doi.org/10.1007/s10844-018-0496-5
5. Saraswathi, N., Sasi Rooba, T., Chakaravarthi, S.: Improving the accuracy of sentiment analysis using a linguistic rule-based feature selection method in tourism reviews. Meas.: Sens. **29**, 100888 (2023). https://doi.org/10.1016/j.measen.2023.100888
6. Khong, K.W., Teng, S., Butt, M.M., Muritala, B.A.: Analysing online reviews of restaurants in Malaysia: a novel approach to descriptive and predictive analytic. Int. J. Electron. Bus. **16**(4), 315 (2021). https://doi.org/10.1504/ijeb.2021.118491
7. Wankhade, M., Rao, A.C.S., Kulkarni, C.: A survey on sentiment analysis methods, applications, and challenges. Artif. Intell. Rev. **55**(7), 5731–5780 (2022). https://doi.org/10.1007/s10462-022-10144-1
8. Ng, C.K.: Malaysia restaurant review datasets. Kaggle 30 Jul 2022. https://www.kaggle.com/datasets/choonkhonng/malaysia-restaurant-review-datasets/data. (Accessed 20 Jan 2025)

9. Al-Khazaleh, M.J., Alian, M., Jaradat, M.A.: Sentiment analysis of imbalanced Arabic data using sampling techniques and classification algorithms. Bull. Electr. Eng. Infor. **13**(1), 607–618 (2024). https://doi.org/10.11591/eei.v13i1.5886
10. Ahmed, H.M., Awan, M.J., Khan, N.S., Yasin, A., Shehzad, H.M.F.: Sentiment analysis of online food reviews using big data analytics. Elementary Educ. Online **20**(2), 827 (2021). https://doi.org/10.17051/ilkonline.2021.02.93
11. IBM: Using CountVectorizer for NLP feature extraction. IBM. www.ibm.com. https://www.ibm.com/reference/python/countvectorizer
12. Hamdaoui, Y.: TF-IDF: an introduction. Built In. builtin.com 08 Feb 2024. https://builtin.com/articles/tf-idf
13. Prastyo, P.H., Ardiyanto, I., Hidayat, R.: Indonesian sentiment analysis: an experimental study of four kernel functions on SVM Algorithm with TF-IDF. IEEE Xplore, 01 Oct 2020. https://ieeexplore.ieee.org/abstract/document/9325685. (Accessed 13 May 2023)
14. Cortes, C., Vapnik, V.: Support-vector networks. Mach. Learn. **20**(3), 273–297 (1995). https://doi.org/10.1007/BF00994018
15. Xu, S., Li, Y., Wang, Z.: Bayesian Multinomial Naïve Bayes classifier to text classification. Lecture Notes in Electrical Engineering, pp. 347–352 (2017). https://doi.org/10.1007/978-981-10-5041-1_57
16. Abbas, M., Ali, K., Jamali, A.: Multinomial naive bayes classification model for sentiment analysis. IJCSNS Int. J. Comput. Sci. Netw. Secur. **9**(3) (2019). https://doi.org/10.13140/RG.2.2.30021.40169
17. Liu, A.Y., Martin, C.E.: Smoothing multinomial naïve bayes in the presence of imbalance. Machine Learning and Data Mining in Pattern Recognition, pp. 46–59 (2011). https://doi.org/10.1007/978-3-642-23199-5_4

Visualization Technique in Presenting Data for StudentProgress Report

Norharziana Binti Yahaya Rashdi[1](✉), Hayati Abd Rahman[2], and Nur Aina Khadijah binti Adnan[1]

[1] Fakulti Sains Komputer Dan Matematik, Universiti Teknologi Fakulti MARA Cawangan Johor Kampus Segamat, Segamat 85000, Johor, Malaysia
{norharziana,ainakhadijah}@uitm.edu.my

[2] Fakulti Sains Komputer Dan Matematik, Universiti Teknologi MARA (UiTM), Shah Alam 40450, Selangor, Malaysia
hayatiar@tmsk.uitm.edu.my

Abstract. The challenge in interpreting data and understanding the message that needed to be conveyed is a significant issue among users. Several studies state that visualizing data are beneficial and lack of understanding of the data can lead to misinterpretations. People can see the data patterns and gain new insights which can be as quick as 300 ms if the data are visualized effectively. Currently, the method used to manage the data of the children's assessment records is by using a written-form report card. Therefore, this research aim is to implement the Graphical Visualization Technique in presenting student progress data. Another objective is to compare between the usage of current method used in presenting the student progress data and the Graphical Visualization Technique from users' perspective. There is also an urgent need for a monitoring tool for assisting users' decision-making process in determining the student progress. This research is significant in order to present the student progress data effectively and also to ensure that the decision-making process to be easier and faster compared to using the current method.

Keywords: Data Visualization · Graphical Visualization Technique · Students' Progress Monitoring · Decision-Making

1 Introduction

Assessment for children in preschool is important in order to know the level of their understanding and to monitor their learning progress. Since students' assessment records include crucial information about their learning progress, they must be handled and managed effectively. The success of an educational institution relies not only on the professionalism of the teaching staff, or the relevance of the knowledge imparted. Another important aspect is the ability to analyze students' progress data continuously. Teachers and parents can evaluate the student progress over time by reviewing trends in student progress data. The current approach uses tabular visualization technique to visualize

M. Kassim et al. (Eds.): SCDS 2025, CCIS 2674, pp. 203–216, 2026.
https://doi.org/10.1007/978-981-95-8368-3_15

students' data which is by recording them manually using a written report card. Tabular visualization technique is useful for summarizing and comparing quantitative information of different variables. Nevertheless, this approach resulted in a lack of interactivity between people and the recorded data. Tables are not appropriate for studying data trends, and data interpretation takes longer in tables compared to graphs [1]. Thus, disallow teachers and parents to see clearly the progress of the children over time. They may have difficulties engaging with the data and could make decision-making a difficult process. Tabular visualization technique does not allow user to simply see the trends of the data over time and may also lead to incorrect interpretations of data and intended message [1]. In this research, graphical visualization technique is utilized in which the data can be presented in a manner that allows user to accurately grasp the meaning of data in a shorter amount of time. Additionally, the existing approach also does not provide a defining tool for user to classify the students' progress remarks whether they are enhancing or not. As a result, teacher and parents cannot easily identify the student's weakness and strengths.

The rule-based technique can be used to overcome this issue in the student progress classification process. The rule-based algorithm will correctly determine the student progress data into three main remarks which are "Telah Menguasai" (Mastered), "Sedang Maju" (Advancing) or "Belum Menguasai" (Not Mastered). According to Ellstrom, humans take less than 300 ms to understand the meaning of the information through visualization [2]. This shows that the data could be easily interpreted by the human brain by using visualization tools instead of the text-written form. By employing graphical visualization technique to present students' progress data, the current system could be improved and be able to provide a better decision-making mechanism for user. This is due to the fact that every student has a different pace of learning and the comfortable way of absorbing knowledge. Student progress visualization can help teachers and parents to determine whether the students are progressing well or if they require more attention.

2 Background Study

2.1 Importance of Student Progress Monitoring

Childhood assessment is a process of gathering information about a child, analyzing the information and then using the information to plan educational activities at a level that the child can understand and learn [3]. Another important aspect of defining the effectiveness of an educational institution is the ability to analyze students' academic progress continuously. Teachers and parents can evaluate the student progress over time by reviewing trends in student assessment data.

2.2 Data Visualization Technique

Data visualization is the graphical representation of information and data. By using visual elements like charts, graphs, and maps, data visualization tools provide an accessible way to see and understand trends, outliers, and patterns in data [4]. The basic purpose of visual representation is to efficiently interpret what insight is, as easy as possible.

Different available visualization techniques are used depending on the situation which convey different level of understanding [5]. The purpose of visualization is to create interactive visual representations of the information that exploit human's perceptual and cognitive capabilities of problem solving. The goal of visualization is to make a vast and complicated amount of information easy for the user to comprehend and interpret. Visualization techniques make huge and complex information intelligible. According to Ellstrom, in the finding, human brain can be put in term "visually wired" which refer to that almost 50% of the brain is involved in visual processing and 70% of all our sensory receptors are in the eyes [2].

Data visualization offers numerous benefits to the user. Firstly, by using data visualization approach user could easily interpret and act upon the data faster than not using it. With the help of data visualization, it can uncover hidden trends and patterns from the huge amount of data and as well as predict the outcomes for the business [6]. This is because the human brain tends to process visual information easier compared to written information. Human eyes are able to absorb and grasp information more easily through visuals and images than texts and numerical [5]. Compared to spread sheets or cluttered reports, people could comprehend the information or data more quickly by looking at the visual representation such as chart or graph, which are used to simplify complex data [7]. There are three different ways to present data: written as text; in tabular form; or in graphical form [1].

2.3 Graphical Visualization

Although tables can be used to display all information, graphs simplify complex information by using icons and highlighting data patterns or trends, and are useful for quantitative data summarization, clarification, or exploration [7]. Graphs make it easier for readers to view, comprehend and remember the data or information [8].

Line Chart

In many fields, the line chart is a common well-known graph, labelled as a line graph. It is a graph that is used in connected points to display information. By using continuous or straight line, these points are related. The line chart is often used to represent a data pattern over time intervals, meaning it is used to display patterns in the data set and to demonstrate the data activity over time or over a specific time period [9][10]. Line graphs are useful in displaying data variables and patterns very clearly and can help predict data outcomes. Using a line chart with more than a few lines makes the line chart cluttered and difficult to interpret. Line graphs also called as graphs of the time series use line segments that connect different data points to display changes over time. Typically, up to five lines could be used to show improvements in the data over time [8].

Bar Graph

Another common method of data visualization is the bar chart or also known as bar graph and column chart [5]. The bar chart is used for discrete data most of the time, not for continuous data. It is a type of graph used to view and compare numbers, frequencies or other measurements for different discrete data categories [11]. Several advantages of using bar graph to display data are the ability to display multiple categories of relative numbers, allowing users to summarize a large amount of data in a visual and to be easily interpretable. Additionally, bar graphs are more convenient compared to tables for highlighting trends, allowing estimates to be made quickly and accurately [12].

2.4 Rule-Based Algorithm Technique

A rule-based system is a set of "if-then" statements which it use a set of assertions. In developing software, rule-based algorithm is able to provide answer for particular problem instead of human expert [13]. Rule is divided into two parts which is the "IF" part, namely the antecedents. The "IF" part hold the premise and condition. The other part is the "THEN" part which is the consequent. The "THEN" part holds the conclusion or action to be performed by the system [14]. Figure 1 shows the general form of a rule-based algorithm.

```
IF      antecedent1
AND     antecedent2
THEN    consequent
```

Fig. 1. General form of a Rule-based Algorithm

Rule-based systems do exactly as instruct by a human. In other words, the behavior carried out by rule-based systems is decided by humans unlike artificial intelligence and machine learning. The system does not work it out on its own or make decisions intelligently [15]. A rule-based can serve many purposes in real applications, such as decision support or predictive decision making [16]. This research will therefore provide a student performance decision-making support using a rule-based algorithm that can classify or categorized student performance for each semester according to the assessment marks of students [17].

3 Methodology

The methodology for this research consists of four main phases which are planning, design, implementation and the testing phase.

3.1 Planning

In order to have deeper understanding regarding the elements in this research, feasibility study is done. From the literature review, the knowledge that is needed to achieve the objectives of this research is gained. Feasibility study is done to have better understanding on the issue occurred and to determine the best method that can be used to enhance and solve the issue. Furthermore, in this research the observation on current tools and method practiced in the selected preschool are done. The sample data are collected from An Najah Educare Centre located in Seksyen 11, Shah Alam. It is in order to capture the issue and find another method to overcome the issue faced.

3.2 Design

During design phase, the content of the system prototype is determined. In this phase, the flowcharts of the system are designed. For this research, the presentation of data using visualization technique used the student progress data which consist of two semesters. This includes three main subjects which are Mathematics, Malay and English. This system is developed for the teachers to monitor the progress of their student. It is also designed for them to easily determine the remark of their students' progress. Figure 2 below shows the flowchart for the system.

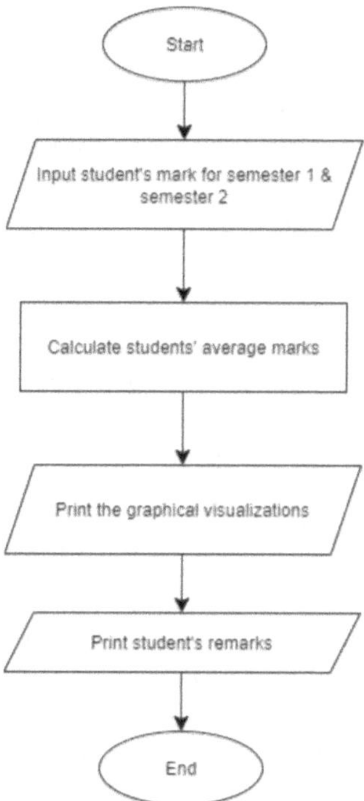

Fig. 2. Flowcharts of the System

3.3 Implementation

The implementation phases are divided into two sections which are implementing the graphical visualization technique to present student progress data and also implementing the rule-based algorithm to determine the progress remarks for the students. This is done in order to correctly define which progress remarks do the student belongs to; "Telah Menguasai", "Sedang Maju" or "Belum Menguasai". It is also to present the data in a way that user can identify the student's weaknesses and also the actions that need to be taken towards them. There are 3 main subjects used as the domain for this research namely Mathematics (Matematik), Malay (Bahasa Melayu) and English (Bahasa Inggeris). The subjects are scoped up to only three because of the constraint of time for this research.

However, the subjects can be added in the future works. The assessment items for each subject is as shown in Table 1.

Table 1. Detail of Item in Each Subject

Subject	Assessment Item
Mathematics	Identifying sizes
	Identifying colours
	Identifying shapes
	Classification and sequencing
Malay	Kemahiran mendengar (Listening skill)
	Kemahiran bertutur (Speaking skill)
	Kemahiran membaca (Reading skill)
	Kemahiran menulis (Writing skill)
English	Speaking skill
	Reading skill

Implementation of graphical visualization technique

The visualization technique that is used in this particular research is the graphical visualization technique. In this research, line chart is used to present student progress by visualizing students' marks for each semester. This allows user to see the trends of the student progress data over a period of time. Furthermore, in order to have better details of students' weakness and strength, bar graph is used to present each of the assessment item marks. This is because bar graph provides an easy way to interpret the complex data. The bar graph in this research is for visualizing the marks for each item for each subject respectively. Teacher or parents will be able to see which part the student lacks in and the part where they excel. One of the advantages of bar graph is its simplicity and easiness for viewer to interpret the data. This enables teachers to simply identify the students' needs. Figure 3 shows the prototype of bar graph for students' assessment marks for Malay subject.

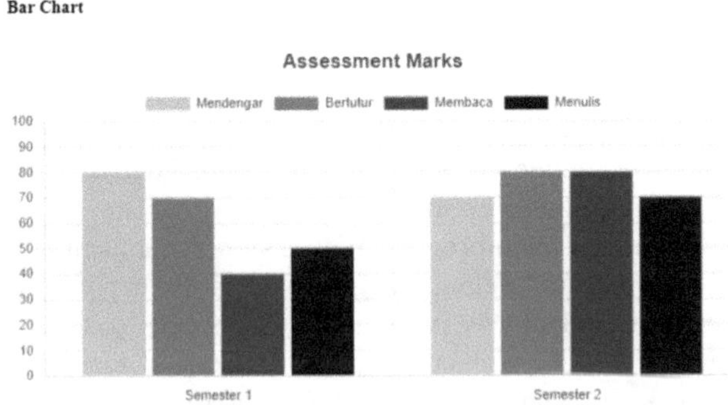

Fig. 3. Prototype of Bar Graph

The points for the line chart are the average of the assessment item marks for each subject. The calculation for the plotted points is given by Eq. (1).

$$Average\,Marks = Sum\,of\ assessment\ marks/Number\ of\ assessment\ items \quad (1)$$

The average marks are then plotted according to the respective semesters; Semester 1 and Semester 2. Figure 4 shows the prototype of line chart used in the research.

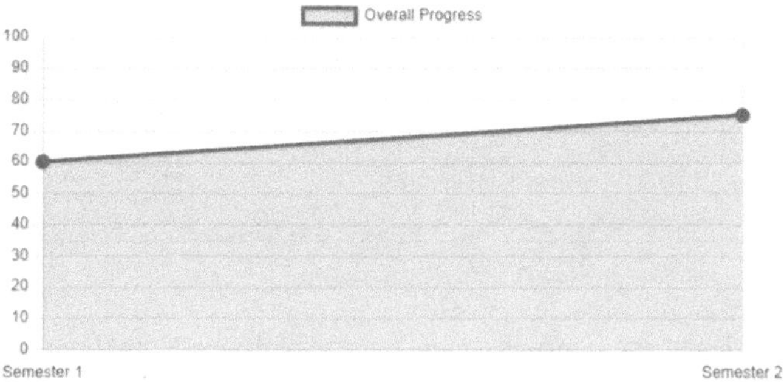

Fig. 4. Prototype of Line Chart

Implementation of rule-based algorithm

Antecedent/Condition Part

The rules made are based on two main conditions, which are the shapes of the graph and students' average marks for both semesters for each subjects. Firstly, for the shapes of graph, there are three types which are Ascending, No Change and Descending. Table 2 below shows the description for each graph shape.

Table 2. Indicator for Graph Shapes

Graph Shape	Indicator
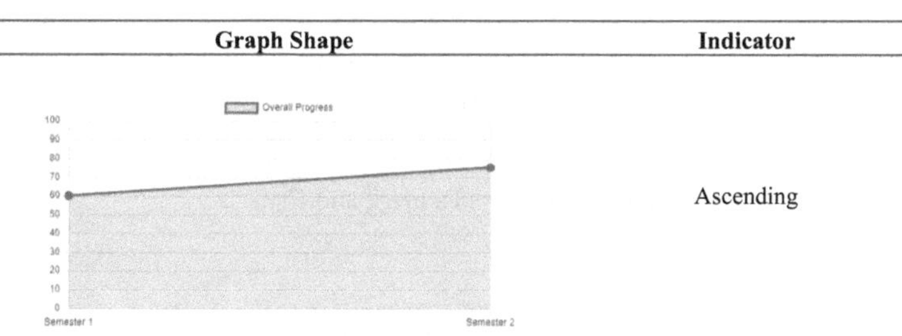	Ascending

(*continued*)

Table 2. (*continued*)

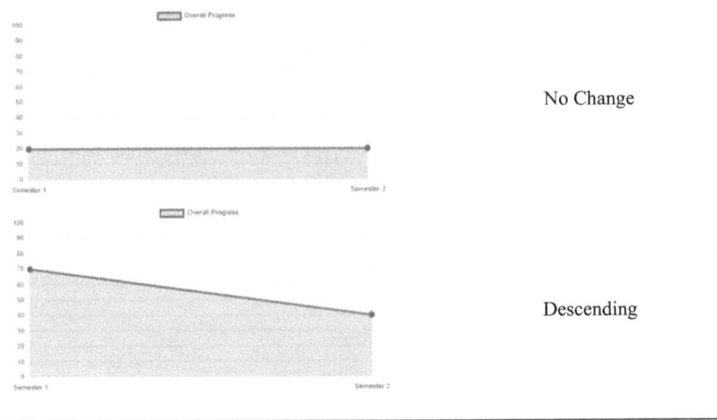

(chart 1)	No Change
(chart 2)	Descending

Secondly, students' average assessment marks are divided into three different grades, which are A, B and C. Table 3 below shows the grading scale used in this research.

Table 3. Grading Scales

Marks	Grade
70–100	A
40–69	B
1–39	C

Consequent/Action Part

The rule-based algorithm implementation in this research is to define student overall progress remarks for each subject they enrolled. There are mainly three progress remarks used in this research which is "Telah Menguasai", "Sedang Maju" and "Belum Menguasai". This term will be explained further in table below (Table 4).

Table 4. Progress Remark and Criteria

Progress Remark	Criteria
Telah Menguasai (Mastered)	Knowledgeable and has ability to do on his/her own
Sedang Maju (Advancing)	Knowledgeable and has ability to do several skills or assessment with assistance
Belum Menguasai (Not Mastered)	Knowledgeable on several minimum basic skills but does not have ability to do it – Always needed assistance

Rule-based Part

Hence, the rules are built based on the correlation between the two antecedents and the consequent part. The basic syntax for the rules used in this research is as follows (Fig. 5):

```
IF shape = " "
AND IF semester 1 marks = " "
AND IF semester 2 marks = " "
THEN print " "
```

Fig. 5. Basic Syntax for Rule-based Technique

There are several rules made in this research in order to correctly identify student progress remarks for each subject. Figures 6, 7 and 8 show the rules used in this research..

```
IF shape = ascending
AND IF semester 1 marks = A
AND IF semester 2 marks = A
THEN print "Telah Menguasai"

IF shape = ascending
AND IF semester 1 marks = B
AND IF semester 2 marks = A
THEN print "Telah Menguasai"

IF shape = ascending
AND IF semester 1 marks = C
AND IF semester 2 marks = A
THEN print "Telah Menguasai"

IF shape = no change
AND IF semester 1 marks = A
AND IF semester 2 marks = A
THEN print "Telah Menguasai"
```

Fig. 6. Basic Rule-based Syntax for "Telah Menguasai" Remark

```
IF shape = ascending
AND IF semester 1 marks = C
AND IF semester 2 marks = B
THEN print "Sedang Maju"

IF shape = ascending
AND IF semester 1 marks = B
AND IF semester 2 marks = B
THEN print "Sedang Maju"

IF shape = no change
AND IF semester 1 marks = B
AND IF semester 2 marks = B
THEN print "Sedang Maju"
```

Fig. 7. Basic Rule-based Syntax for "Sedang Maju" Remark

```
IF shape = ascending
AND IF semester 1 marks = C
AND IF semester 2 marks = C
THEN print "Belum Menguasai"

IF shape = descending
AND IF semester 1 marks = A
AND IF semester 2 marks = C
THEN print "Belum Menguasai"

IF shape = descending
AND IF semester 1 marks = A
AND IF semester 2 marks = B
THEN print "Belum Menguasai"

IF shape = descending
AND IF semester 1 marks = B
AND IF semester 2 marks = C
THEN print "Belum Menguasai"

IF shape = descending
AND IF semester 1 marks = C
AND IF semester 2 marks = C
THEN print "Belum Menguasai"

IF shape = no change
AND IF semester 1 marks = C
AND IF semester 2 marks = C
THEN print "Belum Menguasai"
```

Fig. 8. Basic Rule-based Syntax for "Belum Menguasai" Remark

Figure 9 below shows the prototype for the graphical visualization of a student in Malay subject.

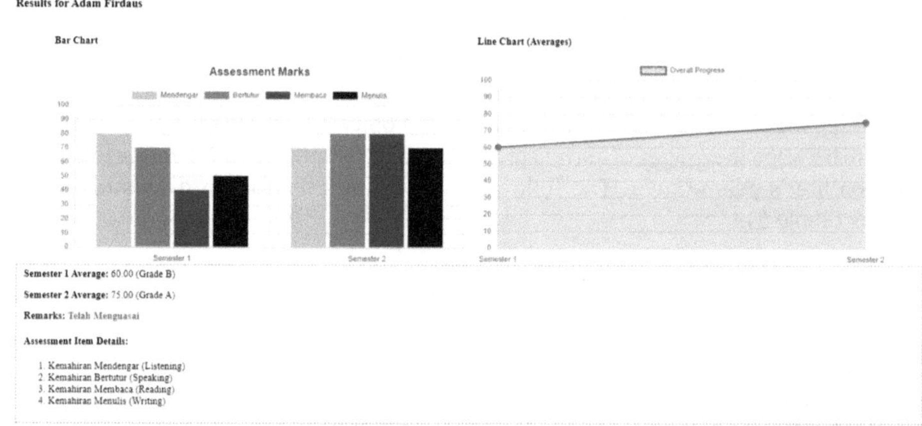

Fig. 9. Prototype of Student Progress Report

3.4 Unit Testing

Unit testing is done in order to check that every input produce the expected and correct output. The entire test pass, which means the actual output is the same as the expected output when the input is run.

4 Result and Discussion

4.1 Experimental Design

The steps for analysis part are as follows:

1. Users are given some time to study the data using Tabular visualization technique which is the current method of monitoring student progress from An Najah Educare Centre.
2. Users are given some time to study the data using the Graphical Visualization Technique.
3. After user study both techniques, they need to answer ten questions regarding the data that they have seen and studied.
4. The questions are based on standard usability test but is altered based on the hypothesis that has been made.
5. The answers from the user are then analyzed in order to evaluate the hypotheses made.

4.2 Survey Method and Data Collection

Questionnaires that consist of ten questions are distributed to the teacher and public user in order to analyze which hypothesis is accepted and which is not. The questionnaire contains two sections, which is the demographic section and the question section. The results of the data analysis are based on the questionnaire that is distributed to users.

4.3 Analysis and Discussion

For the analysis phase, there are seven hypotheses that are made. The results gained from the questionnaire are used in order to analyze the acceptance of the hypotheses. These hypotheses were made in order to fulfil the second objective of this research which is to compare between the usages of current technique to the graphical visualization technique based on user's perspectives. The following table shows the further discussion of the analysis (Table 5).

Table 5. Analysis and Discussion

Hypothesis	Question	Discussion
Hypothesis 1: Graphical visualization technique does not need a high computational literacy to be understood and interpreted	Q1.I am confident to use the graphical technique to monitor student progress compared to tabular technique	Majority of user state that they are more confident in using graphical visualization technique and also does not need help from others to interpret the meaning of data. Hence, Hypothesis 1 is accepted
	Q2.I think I can interpret the student progress data using graphical technique without any help from others	
Hypothesis 2: Graphical visualization technique enable user to understand the data faster than tabular visualization	Q3. I am able to understand the student's progress in shorter time by using the graphical technique compared to tabular technique	Majority of respondents agree that Graphical visualization technique enable user to understand the data faster than tabular visualization for both questions. Hence, Hypothesis 2 is accepted
	Q4. I took more time in identifying student weaknesses using tabular technique	
Hypothesis 3: Graphical visualization technique enable user to evaluate student progress better than tabular visualization	Q5.I am able to evaluate the student weaknesses using graphical technique better than tabular technique	The total number of respondents who agree on the statements is higher than the ones who disagree. Hence, Hypothesis 3 is accepted
Hypothesis 4: Graphical visualization technique enable user to simplify the decision-making process	Q6. I am able to simply interpret student progress and make decisions for each student by looking at the graphical technique	Majority of the respondents agree on the statement. Hence, Hypothesis 4 is accepted
Hypothesis 5: Graphical visualization technique convey the data to user in a simpler way compared to tabular visualization	Q7. I think that graphical technique conveys the student progress information in a simpler manner compared to tabular technique	Hence, Hypothesis 5 is accepted since the total of agreements on the statements outnumbered the disagreement

(*continued*)

Table 5. *(continued)*

Hypothesis	Question	Discussion
	Q8. I think that graphical technique looks simpler compared to tabular technique	
Hypothesis 6: Graphical visualization technique eases the process of monitoring student progress	Q9. Graphical technique ease the process of monitoring student progress compared to tabular technique	Almost all of the respondents agree on the statement. Hence, Hypothesis 6 is accepted
Hypothesis 7: Graphical visualization technique enable user to study the trends in student progress for each subjects	Q10. I think that graphical technique enables me to see the trends of student progress over time for each subject compared to tabular technique	100% of respondents agree that Graphical visualization technique enable them to study the trends in student progress for each subjects. Hence, Hypothesis 7 is accepted

5 Conclusion

This research was attempted to study an accessible method to present student progress data. It is also to study the better method to determine the students' overall performance based on their progress in each subject. It started with studying the requirement of preschool student which is then followed by conducting an observation on the current method implied in presenting student progress data in the preschool. This research objectives are achieved as the student progress data is successfully presented using the line chart and also bar graph. The progress data also has been injected with the rule-based algorithm in order for the student to be classified in its respective progress standard. The progress remark are namely Telah Menguasai (Mastered), Sedang Maju (Advancing) and Belum Menguasai (Not Mastered). The comparison between the usage of current technique to the graphical visualization technique is analyzed in which seven hypotheses are made and are accepted.

Acknowledgement. Our sincere gratitude goes out to Universiti Teknologi Mara Shah Alam and Universiti Teknologi Mara Cawangan Johor for providing the facilities and resources that were essential to the successful testing and deployment of the proposed Visualization Technique in Presenting Data for Student Progress Report research.

References

1. In, J., Lee, S.: Statistical data presentation. Korean J. Anesthesiol. **70**(3), 267–276 (2017). https://doi.org/10.4097/kjae.2017.70.3.267
2. Ellstrom, M.: Benefits of presenting information visually and guidelines on how to do it. Retrieved from: ww.ntnu.no/documents/10401/1264433962/MargretheEArtikkel.pdf/f99bdce2-4208-470d-baf2-0065cedf60d0

3. Department of Early Education and Care: Early childhood assessment. Resources for Early Learning (2014). Retrieved from: resourcesforearlylearning.org/fm/early-childhood-assessment/
4. Kamat, V.: A complete beginner's guide to data visualization. Analytics Vidhya (1 Apr 2021). Retrieved from: analyticsvidhya.com/blog/2021/04/a-complete-beginners-guide-to-data-visualization/
5. Khan, M., Khan, S.S.: Data and information visualization methods, and interactive mechanisms: a survey. Int. J. Comput. Appl. **34**(1), 1–14 (2011)
6. Rathore, S., Nawkhare, R., Sharma, N., Chaudhary, N., Chakole, S., Vishwakrama, B.: Effective data visualization techniques for business decision-makers. Int. Res. J. Adv. Eng. Manage. (IRJAEM) **3**, 2029–2036 (2025). https://doi.org/10.47392/IRJAEM.2025.0318
7. Jon, K.: Top 7 benefits of data visualization. (2023). ThoughtSpot (20 Sep 2022). Retrieved from: thoughtspot.com/data-trends/data-visualization/benefits-of-data-visualization
8. Bavdekar, S.: Using tables and graphs for reporting data. J. Assoc. Physicians India **63**, 59 (2015)
9. Khot, P., Milkhe, A., Sorte, G.: Data visualization-techniques and its applications. Int. Res. J. Eng. Technol. (IRJET), **8**(7), 2974–2978 (2021). Retrieved from: irjet.net/archives/V8/i7/IRJET-V8I7521.pdf
10. Rumale, A.S., Bhagwat, A.: Data visualization techniques. Int. J. Res. Publ. Rev. **2**(7), 1861–1871 (2021). Retrieved from: ijrpr.com/uploads/V2ISSUE7/IJRPR822.pdf
11. Panghal, R.: The role of data visualization in decision making–Case of D-mart. Int. J. Multi. Res. **6**(3) (2024). https://doi.org/10.36948/ijfmr.2024.v06i03.19630
12. Queensland Government Statistician's Office: Presenting statistical information–Graphs (2015). Retrieved from: qgso.qld.gov.au/
13. Beal, V.: Rule-Based System (14 May 2010). Webopedia. Retrieved from: webopedia.com/definitions/rule-based-system/
14. Mukundan, S., Ramani, S., Raman, S., Anjaneyulu, K.S.R., Chandrasekar, R.: A Practical Introduction to Rule Based Expert Systems (2007)
15. What is a rule-based system? What is it not? ThinkAutomation. (2025). Retrieved from: thinkautomation.com/eli5/what-is-a-rule-based-system-what-is-it-not
16. Liu, H., Gegov, A., Stahl, F.: Categorization and construction of rule based systems. In: Mladenov, V., Jayne, C., Iliadis, L. (eds.), Engineering Applications of Neural Networks, EANN 2014. Communications in Computer and Information Science, vol. 459. Springer, Cham (2014). https://doi.org/10.1007/978-3-319-11071-4_18
17. Yang, F., Li, F.W.B.: Study on student performance estimation, student progress analysis, and student potential prediction based on data mining. Comput. Educ. **123**, 97–108 (2018). https://doi.org/10.1016/j.compedu.2018.04.006

Harnessing UTAUT and Risk Factors for Blockchain Adoption in Waqf: Evidence from PLS Predict

Balkis Kasmon[1], Siti Sara Ibrahim[2,3](✉), Amirul Afif Muhamat[4], and Ririn Tri Ratnasari[5]

[1] Business Management Faculty, Universiti Teknologi MARA, Negeri Sembilan Campus, 71300 Shah Alam, Malaysia
[2] Business Management Faculty, Universiti Teknologi MARA, Negeri Sembilan Campus, 71300 Shah Alam, Malaysia
saraibrahim@uitm.edu.my
[3] Institute for Big Data Analytics and Artificial Intelligence (IBDAAI), Universiti Teknologi MARA, Shah Alam, Malaysia
[4] Department of Economics and Financial Studies, Faculty of Business and Management, Universiti Teknologi MARA, Shah Alam, Malaysia
[5] Center for Halal Industry and Digitalization, Faculty of Economics and Business, Universitas Airlangga, Surabaya 60286, Indonesia

Abstract. Despite the rapid advancement of financial technologies, the adoption of blockchain in Waqf institutions remains low due to trust issues, perceived risks, and limited digital literacy. This study aims to develop and test a predictive model for individuals' intentions to use digital Waqf platforms by extending the UTAUT framework. It addresses the need to understand donor adoption by incorporating relative advantage as a mediating factor and knowledge as a moderating variable. The novelty lies in adapting the UTAUT model to the context of Waqf digitalization, offering practical insights for State Islamic Religious Councils (SIRCs) and policymakers to design more effective digital platforms that enhance donor trust and participation. A quantitative method was employed through a survey of 230 respondents, with data analyzed using partial least squares structural equation modeling (PLS-SEM). The findings suggest that performance expectancy and facilitating conditions notably influence digital Waqf adoption, while effort expectancy and social influence do not. Relative advantage mediates these relationships, and knowledge further amplifies the effects. To sum up, the digitalization of Waqf enhances transparency, operational efficiency, and donor confidence, with user support and technological familiarity emerging as key drivers for successful adoption.

Keywords: UTAUT · TPR · Blockchain · Big Data · PLS Predict

M. Kassim et al. (Eds.): SCDS 2025, CCIS 2674, pp. 217–234, 2026.
https://doi.org/10.1007/978-981-95-8368-3_16

1 Introduction

The Waqf system plays a pivotal role in Islamic social finance by providing sustainable support in education, healthcare, and poverty alleviation. In the era of Industrial Revolution 4.0 (IR4.0), Malaysia is rapidly embracing digital transformation, presenting an opportunity to modernize Waqf management through technologies such as blockchain (Kasmon et al., 2023). Blockchain's attributes— decentralization, transparency, and immutability—align well with the principles of ethical governance and accountability emphasized in Environmental, Social, and Governance (ESG) frameworks (Anwar et al., 2023; Abdull Manaf et al., 2025).

Despite these technological advancements, the adoption of blockchain in Waqf institutions remains limited, often hindered by perceived risks related to performance, privacy, security, and financial uncertainties (Mokthar et al., 2024). Additionally, the lack of integration between trust-based systems and advanced data-driven decision-making, such as Big Data analytics, slows digital uptake (Abdull Manaf et al., 2025; Mohd Ariff et al., 2024). While UTAUT has been widely used to explore drivers of technology adoption, it often overlooks risk-related deterrents, particularly within religious and nonprofit contexts.

This study integrates the Unified Theory of Acceptance and Use of Technology (UTAUT) with the Theory of Perceived Risk (TPR) to assess the the intention or willingness to adopt blockchain in Waqf development (Mokthar et al., 2024). Using the PLS Predict approach, this study not only evaluates explanatory power but also predictive relevance—providing practical insights for policymakers, Waqf managers, and fintech innovators focused on ESG-aligned Islamic social finance (Anwar et al., 2023; Abdull Manaf et al., 2025).

2 Literature Review

2.1 Unified Theory of Acceptance and Use of Technology (UTAUT)

The theory was introduced by Venkatesh et al. (2003), the UTAUT model identifies four key constructs influencing user acceptance of technology: performance expectancy, effort expectancy, social influence, and facilitating conditions (Dwivedi et al., 2021). In the context of Waqf, performance expectancy relates to stakeholders' belief that blockchain will enhance Waqf management efficiency (Mokthar and Sapuan, 2023). Effort expectancy pertains to the perceived ease of using blockchain systems. Social influence involves the impact of opinions from influential individuals or institutions on stakeholders'decisions. Facilitating conditions refer to the availability of resources and support for implementing blockchain technology.

The UTAUT model has been widely applied in various technological adoption studies, demonstrating its robustness in predicting user intentions and behaviors (Venkatesh et al., 2003).The UTAUT model developed by Venkatesh et al. (2003) offers a comprehensive explanation for user acceptance of technology. It comprises four main constructs such as Performance Expectancy (PE) which about the degree to which an individual believes that using the technology will help them achieve gains in performance (Alsyouf et al., 2021). Next, Effort Expectancy (EE) which relates about the perceived ease associated with using the technology. Then, Social Influence (SI) which the extent to which an individual perceives that important others believe they should use the new system. Lastly, the Facilitating Conditions (FC) is about the degree to which an individual believes that the organizational and technical infrastructure exists to support system use (Rodríguez-Arteaga and García-Lima, 2023).

The Unified Theory of Acceptance and Use of Technology (UTAUT) offers a robust framework for understanding how individuals adopt and utilize new technologies, making it highly relevant in the digital transformation of Waqf institutions (Wadi and Nurzaman, 2020). As the Waqf sector evolves under the influence of Industrial Revolution 4.0, the integration of digital technologies— such as blockchain, mobile applications, and online donation platforms—has become critical for improving transparency, governance, and fund efficiency (Kasmon et al., 2024). UTAUT's core constructs—Performance Expectancy (PE), Effort Expectancy (EE), Social Influence (SI), and Facilitating Conditions (FC)—offer practical insights into user behavior within this unique socio-religious context.

Performance expectancy captures the belief that digitalization can enhance operational outcomes and stakeholder trust ((Wadi and Nurzaman, 2020; Junaidi et al., 2024). Effort expectancy relates to the perceived ease of using Waqf platforms among donors and administrators (Zakariyah et al., 2023). Social influence highlights the persuasive role of religious leaders, peer networks, and institutional endorsements in shaping adoption behavior (Wadi and Nurzaman, 2020; Junaidi et al., 2024). Facilitating conditions represent the presence of infrastructure, policy support, and technical readiness for digital transformation (Mokthar et al., 2024; Zakariyah et al., 2023).

Beyond technology acceptance, this study situates UTAUT within broader global themes such as Environmental, Social, and Governance (ESG) standards and Big Data-driven decision-making (Kasmon et al. (2023); Anwar et al., 2024). ESG alignment ensures that Waqf practices adhere to ethical, transparent, and sustainable development goals. Big Data analytics, in turn, enables Waqf institutions to derive actionable insights for optimizing resource allocation and measuring social impact (Deepa et al., 2022).

Integrating UTAUT with these contemporary themes allows for a more holistic understanding of digital Waqf adoption and creates a roadmap for building resilient, inclusive, and value-driven Islamic social finance ecosystems (Fig. 1).

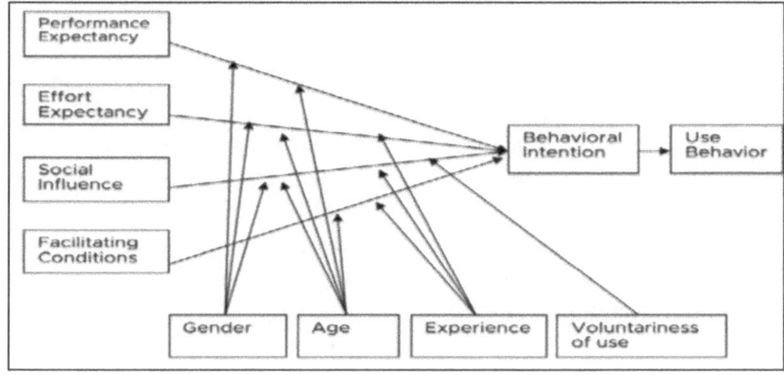

Fig. 1. UTAUT Theory

2.2 Theory of Perceived Risk (TPR)

The Theory of Perceived Risk posits that individuals' perceptions of potential negative outcomes influence their decision-making processes (Featherman and Pavlou, 2003). In the realm of blockchain adoption for waqf development, several risk dimensions are pertinent (Chang and Chen., 2023). Perceived risk refers to the uncertainty and potential adverse consequences associated with adopting a new technology. The following types of risks are emphasized in this study are Performance Risk (PR) which relates to the fear that blockchain may not perform as expected or may fail (Al-Amri et al., 2023; Nguyen et al., 2022). Next, Privacy Risk (PIR) that are the concern that personal or donor data may be exposed or misused (Rahardja et al., 2023). Then, Security Risk (SR) when the apprehension about cyber threats or hacking incidents that could compromise the system. Lastly is about the Financial Risk (FR) which relates the fear of monetary loss due to incorrect transactions or poor investments linked to blockchain-based systems (Alsyouf et al., 2021).

The Theory of Perceived Risk (TPR) offers a valuable lens for understanding the psychological and behavioral barriers to technology adoption, especially in trust-based systems like Waqf (Rahardja et al., 2023). As Waqf institutions move toward digitalization—incorporating platforms such as blockchain, mobile donations, and online Waqf asset management—stakeholders often weigh perceived risks alongside potential benefits (Chang and Chen, 2023). These perceived risks, if not properly addressed, can significantly hinder the intention to adopt emerging technologies.

Performance risk reflects concerns that digital systems may not deliver reliable service, potentially disrupting fund distribution or reducing operational efficiency (Mokhtar et al., 2024). Privacy risk arises from fears that donor or recipient data could be compromised or misused, particularly in online transactions. Security risk centers on anxieties over cyberattacks, data breaches, and unauthorized access to sensitive Waqf records (Nguyen et al., 2022). Financial risk, meanwhile, pertains to uncertainties around hidden costs, technical malfunctions, or fraud, which could result in monetary loss or reputational damage (Javaheri et al., 2024).

These risks are magnified in the Waqf sector, where trust, religious compliance, and public accountability are paramount (Mokhtar et al., 2024). Integrating risk perception analysis into digital transformation strategies is thus critical. Moreover, leveraging Big Data can help mitigate these concerns through real-time monitoring, fraud detection, and predictive risk modeling (Zulkarnaen et al., 2021). Aligning risk management practices with Environmental, Social, and Governance (ESG) principles further ensures that digital Waqf platforms maintain transparency, security, and ethical integrity (Wildana et al., 2022; Ahmad, 2024).

Understanding and addressing perceived risks not only supports user confidence but also contributes to a sustainable, digitally empowered Waqf ecosystem capable of delivering lasting social impact (Fig. 2).

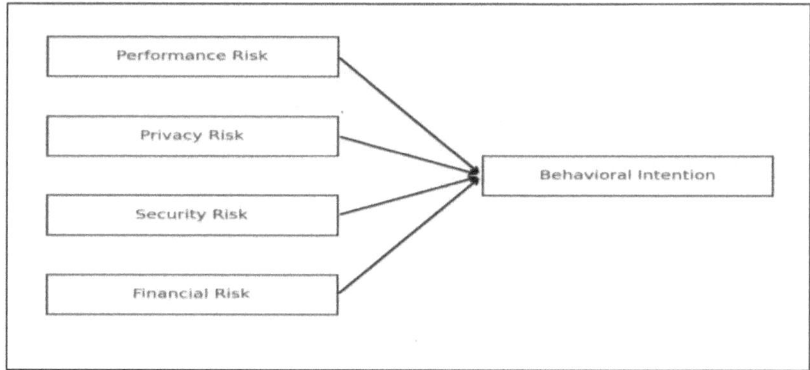

Fig. 2. Theory of Perceived Risk

2.3 Theoretical Framework

The integration of the Unified Theory of Acceptance and Use of Technology (UTAUT) and the Theory of Perceived Risk (TPR) provides a comprehensive and balanced framework for understanding the intention or willingness toward blockchain adoption in waqf digitalization (Chang and Chen., 2023). UTAUT, introduced by Venkatesh et al. (2003), identifies four core determinants of technology acceptance: Performance Expectancy (PE), Effort Expectancy (EE), Social Influence (SI), and Facilitating Conditions (FC). These constructs have been effectively applied in various sectors, including Islamic finance, public service digitalization, and fintech innovation (Mokhtar et al., 2024; Zulkarnaen et al., 2021). In the context of Waqf—an institution grounded in religious, ethical, and social obligations—the relevance of UTAUT extends beyond technical acceptance to encompass user trust and cultural sensitivity (Ali et al., 2021; Al-Amri et al., 2023).

To fully address the adoption landscape, it is essential to incorporate perceived risk factors through the Theory of Perceived Risk (TPR) (Rahardja et al., 2023). TPR captures psychological concerns related to Performance Risk, Privacy Risk, Security Risk, and Financial Risk, all of which can significantly hinder adoption. Blockchain, despite its advantages in transparency, traceability, and accountability, is often met with resistance due to unfamiliarity, perceived complexity, regulatory ambiguity, and cybersecurity threats (Chang and Chen, 2023; Sciarelli et al., 2022).

Recent studies (e.g., Bin-Nashwan et al., 2022; Lwin, 2022) emphasize the influence of perceived risk in delaying technology adoption in Islamic and nonprofit sectors, where trust, Shariah compliance, and donor confidence are vital. By merging UTAUT and TPR, this study provides a dual- lens approach: UTAUT highlights enablers of adoption, while TPR addresses risk-related deterrents.

Furthermore, this integrated model aligns with ESG (Environmental, Social, and Governance) priorities and supports the use of Big Data analytics for real-time risk monitoring, predictive modeling, and decision optimization (Mokhtar et al., 2024; Kasmon et al., 2023). Such a holistic framework is instrumental in advancing sustainable, inclusive, and ethically grounded digital transformation within the Waqf ecosystem (Setiawan and Nurzaman, 2022) (Fig. 3).

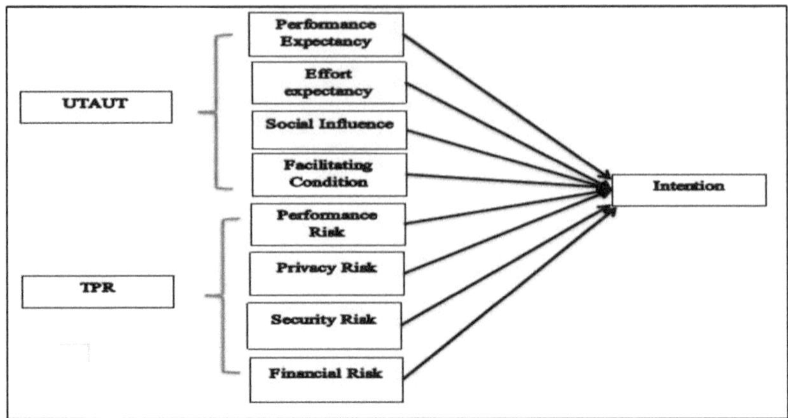

Fig. 3. Theoretical Framework

Based on UTAUT and TPR, the following hypotheses are proposed:

H1: Performance expectancy have a notable impact ons the intention or willingness to adopt blockchain in waqf.

H2: Effort expectancy have a notable impact ons the intention or willingness to adopt blockchain in waqf.

H3: Social influence have a notable impact ons the intention or willingness to adopt blockchain in waqf.

H4: Facilitating conditions have a notable impact on the intention or willingness to adopt blockchain in waqf.

H5: Performance risk have a notable impact ons the intention or willingness to adopt blockchain in waqf.

H6: Privacy risk have a notable impact ons the intention or willingness to adopt blockchain in waqf.

H7: Security risk have a notable impact ons the intention or willingness to adopt blockchain in waqf.

H8: Financial risk have a notable impact ons the intention or willingness to adopt blockchain in waqf.

2.4 Waqf Development in Digitalisation

Waqf, a cornerstone of Islamic philanthropy, has historically functioned as a sustainable model for social welfare, supporting public goods such as education, healthcare, and religious infrastructure (Abdull Manaf et al., 2025). However, traditional Waqf management practices—often paper-based and bureaucratic—have long suffered from inefficiencies, limited public oversight, and poor resource optimization (Mohaiyadin et al., 2023). With the advent of digitalization and the global move toward Industry 4.0, many Muslim-majority countries are embracing technological innovation to modernize and enhance Waqf governance (Kasmon et al., 2023; Ahmad, 2024).

Countries such as Turkey, Indonesia, and Kuwait have pioneered efforts in digitizing Waqf systems. For instance, Turkey's General Directorate of Foundations has created a digitized archive of Waqf documents, improving transparency and accessibility (Abdull Manaf et al., 2025). Indonesia, through its collaboration with Bank Indonesia, launched the Waqf Core Principles to promote digital payment systems and centralized data management platforms for more efficient Waqf mobilization and reporting (Suryawijaya et al., 2024).

Among the most transformative technologies being explored is blockchain (Habib and Ahmad, 2020). With its decentralized and immutable ledger, blockchain technology offers enhanced transparency, traceability, and accountability—essential features in ensuring the integrity of Waqf assets (Rashid et al., 2020). Pilot programs in the Middle East and Africa have tested blockchain-based solutions for recording endowment deeds, tracking fund flows, and ensuring donor confidence through transparent reporting (Mohaiyadin et al., 2022). These innovations are particularly promising in building public trust and reducing administrative corruption.

In Malaysia, the digital transformation of Waqf is steadily progressing (Fauzi et al., 2023). Supported by institutions like JAWHAR and state religious councils, initiatives such as Wakaf Selangor Muamalat (WSM) have introduced online portals and mobile applications to facilitate easier donations, improved fund tracking, and greater public trust (Mohamad and Marzuki, 2021). Big Data analytics is also gaining recognition for its potential to forecast donation trends, assess impact, and optimize resource allocation in Waqf projects (Ahmad, 2024).

Moreover, integrating digital tools in Waqf aligns closely with Environmental, Social, and Governance (ESG) principles (Wan Ismail et al., 2025). Digital Waqf systems support ethical governance, social inclusion, and long-term sustainability by promoting transparency and accountability (Zain et al., 2023). This convergence between Islamic social finance and ESG reinforces the moral and ethical foundation of Waqf in the digital age (Junarti et al., 2024).

Nonetheless, significant challenges remain, including regulatory fragmentation, digital literacy disparities, and infrastructure gaps (Mahmud and Noordin, 2024). Malaysia, in particular, must strengthen inter-state coordination to harmonize Waqf data and avoid operational redundancies (Jamil et al., 2024). Still, the synergy between Islamic values, digital innovation, and responsible governance signals a transformative future for Waqf—one that is more equitable, efficient, and spiritually aligned (Kamaruddin et al., 2024).

2.5 Blockchain Development in Waqf

The integration of blockchain technology into the Waqf sector marks a transformative shift in the evolution of Islamic social finance (Mokhtar et al., 2024). Traditionally, Waqf—an Islamic endowment dedicated to public welfare—has encountered longstanding issues such as administrative inefficiencies, a lack of transparency, fragmented data management, and diminishing public trust (Setiawan and Nurzaman, 2022). These limitations have constrained Waqf's potential to drive sustainable socio- economic development (Kasmon et al., 2023). In the digital era, blockchain offers a compelling solution by introducing features such as decentralization, immutability, smart contracts, and real-time traceability—attributes that align closely with Islamic ethical principles and ESG (Environmental, Social, and Governance) objectives (Anwar et al., 2023).

Globally, countries like the United Arab Emirates, Bahrain, and Indonesia are spearheading blockchain-based Waqf initiatives (Setiawan and Nurzaman, 2022). The UAE and Bahrain have integrated smart contract mechanisms to ensure that Waqf contributions are executed exactly as stipulated by donors, enhancing accountability and reducing human error (Sukmana et al., 2020). Indonesia has piloted blockchain-driven crowdfunding platforms for Waqf, democratizing access and improving endowment tracking (Rashid et al., 2020). These advancements demonstrate a growing commitment to leveraging cutting-edge technologies to revitalize Waqf systems in line with modern governance standards (Habib and Ahmad, 2020).

In Malaysia, the blockchain-Waqf discourse is gaining momentum among policymakers, fintech innovators, and academic researchers. Due to the decentralized nature of Waqf governance—where each State Islamic Religious Council (SIRC) oversees its own Waqf assets—coordination remains a significant barrier to unified digital implementation (Abdull Manaf et al., 2025). Despite this, several academic frameworks and pilot initiatives have emerged, focusing on digital Waqf deeds, smart contract automation for conditional disbursements, and cross-border Waqf tracking (Mokhtar et al., 2024). These models aim to create a Shariah-compliant digital ecosystem that enhances operational efficiency while maintaining religious integrity (Rashid et al., 2020; Setiawan and Nurzama, 2022).

Additionally, the integration of Big Data analytics can complement blockchain adoption by enabling real-time monitoring, donor behavior analysis, predictive modeling for Waqf growth, and enhanced impact assessment (Anwar et al., 2023). This data-driven approach aligns Waqf development with ESG metrics by reinforcing transparent reporting, ethical asset use, and long-term social value creation (Zulkarnaen et al., 2021).

While regulatory uncertainties and technical capacity gaps still pose challenges, Malaysia is progressing through collaborative engagements and academic foresight (Abdull Manaf et al., 2025). Blockchain is not merely a technological upgrade—it is a paradigm shift that enables Waqf institutions to deliver impact with integrity (Mohaiyadin et al., 2022). By embracing blockchain, supported by Big Data and ESG-aligned principles, Waqf can evolve into a digitally empowered, transparent, and spiritually resonant instrument of sustainable development (Mokhtar et al., 2024; Anwar et al., 2023).

3 Methodology

3.1 Research Design

This study adopts a quantitative research design with a cross-sectional approach. Data will be collected through structured questionnaires based on established UTAUT and TPR constructs. The objective is to empirically assess the relationship between enabling and inhibiting factors and their effect on the intention to adopt blockchain for Waqf development. The analysis will be conducted using Partial Least Squares Structural Equation Modeling (PLS-SEM) via SmartPLS 4.0, suitable for complex models involving multiple latent variables and smaller sample sizes.

3.2 Sampling and Data Collection

A purposive sampling method will be employed to collect data from Muslim individuals who are aware of or involved in Waqf contributions in Malaysia. Respondents will complete an online questionnaire disseminated via Google Forms. A total of 200–300 responses are targeted to ensure statistical power, guided by G*Power analysis and SEM recommendations. All measurement items will be rated on a 7- point Likert scale (1 = Strongly Disagree, 2 = Disagree, 3 = Somewhat Disagree, 4 = Neutral, 5 = Somewhat Agree, 6 = Agree, 7 = Strongly Agree). The questionnaire will be available in both English and Malay to ensure clarity and comprehension. Ethical approval will be sought prior to data collection.

3.3 Data Analysis Procedure Using Partial Squares- Structural Equation Modeling

Structural Equation Modeling (SEM) is a second-generation multivariate technique used to investigate the relationships between multiple constructs within a conceptual model. One common approach, Covariance-Based SEM (CB-SEM), estimates parameters by evaluating the covariance among observed variables, allowing researchers to assess the fit between the empirical data and the theoretical model (Hair et al., 2021; Ringle et al., 2019). This method places strong emphasis on matching the model-implied covariance matrix with the actual data, employing fit indices such as Chi-square, RMSEA, and CFI to evaluate model adequacy (Henseler et al., 2020). However, the accuracy of CB-SEM is contingent on having a sufficiently large sample and data that approximates multivariate normality.

CB-SEM is widely recognized for its role in confirmatory research, particularly in evaluating proposed theoretical frameworks and validating measurement instruments through confirmatory factor analysis. It is best suited for studies that aim to test well-established theories and require rigorous model validation procedures (Hair et al., 2019a; Hair et al., 2019b). Nonetheless, this method may encounter limitations when applied to data that deviate from normal distribution or when used with smaller sample sizes. Its reliance on strict assumptions regarding data distribution and measurement levels can present challenges in such cases (Becker et al., 2021).

Despite its constraints, covariance-based structural equation modeling (CB-SEM) remains a robust analytical method for researchers aiming to rigorously evaluate theoretical constructs and explore causal pathways within a model. In contrast, variance-based SEM (VB-SEM), often referred to as partial least squares structural equation modeling (PLS-SEM), takes a different approach by prioritizing the explanation of variance in the dependent constructs. This method is especially useful in situations where theoretical models are still under development or when data deviate from normal distribution assumptions.

Unlike CB-SEM, which highlights reproducing the covariance matrix of observed variables, PLS-SEM seeks to optimize the predictive power of the model. As a result, it is more suitable for exploratory research and theory-building contexts rather than purely confirmatory studies (Henseler et al., 2019; Monecke and Leisch, 2021). One of the key strengths of VB-SEM lies in its flexibility— particularly its capacity to handle smaller sample sizes and less stringent assumptions regarding data distribution and measurement scales.

Furthermore, PLS-SEM is well-suited for complex models that incorporate multiple constructs and indicators, particularly when using formative measurement models

(Becker et al., 2019). Its adaptability to both reflective and formative constructs makes it a valuable tool in diverse research settings. However, even though it relaxes several assumptions required by CB-SEM, researchers must still apply rigorous procedures for model assessment and validation to ensure the reliability of the findings (Roldán and Sánchez-Franco, 2019).

4 Study Findings

During the analysis phase, a total of 298 valid responses were retained for statistical evaluation. A descriptive overview was conducted to summarize the demographic characteristics of the participants. In terms of gender distribution, 52.7% (n = 157) identified as female, while 47.3% (n = 141) were male. With respect to age, the sample comprised individuals aged 18–24 years (6.4%; n = 19), 25–29 years (61.1%; n = 182), 30–34 years (8.1%; n = 24), 35–39 years (6.4%; n = 19), 40–44 years (7.4%; n = 22),

45–49 years (5.0%; n = 15), 50–54 years (3.4%; n = 10), and 55 years and above (2.0%; n = 6).

Regarding their familiarity with digital financial technologies, the majority reported knowledge in artificial intelligence (58.4%; n = 174), followed by crowdfunding platforms (29.2%; n = 87), blockchain technology (7.0%; n = 21), peer-to-peer (P2P) systems (3.0%; n = 9), and a small segment indicated having no exposure to these technologies (2.3%; n = 7).

Data processing and structural analysis were conducted using SMARTPLS version 4.0. The software was employed to evaluate both the measurement and structural components of the proposed model. This involved assessing construct reliability, validity, and the significance of hypothesized relationships (H1 through H8), as conceptualized within the theoretical framework presented in the literature review section.

4.1 Measurement Model

To ensure the validity and reliability of the constructs in this study, key measurement criteria such as composite reliability (CR), average variance extracted (AVE), and factor loadings were assessed in accordance with the guidelines provided by Hair et al. (2017). The factor loadings for all items exceeded the minimum recommended threshold of 0.70, indicating strong item reliability. Additionally, the CR values were all above 0.70, and the AVE values surpassed the 0.50 benchmark, confirming the internal consistency and convergent validity of the constructs. While Cronbach's Alpha are presented by item of PE, EE, SI, FC, PER, PIR, SR, FR and INT.

Table 1. Measurement Model Assessment

Code	Loading	Cronbach's Alpha	Composite Reliability	Average Variance Extracted (AVE)
Performance Expectation (PE)		0.962	0.962	0.841
PE 1	0.907			
PE 2	0.910			
PE 3	0.912			
PE 4	0.918			
PE 5	0.926			
PE 6	0.928			
Effort Expectancy		0.910	0.914	0.787
EE 1	0.905			
EE 2	0.885			
EE 3	0.872			
EE 4	0.886			
Social Influence		0.924	0.932	0.769
SI 1	0.837			
SI 2	0.806			
SI 3	0.874			
SI 4	0.926			
SI 5	0.935			
Facilitating Condition		0.976	0.977	0.914
FC 1	0.931			
FC 2	0.960			
FC 3	0.962			
FC 4	0.963			
FC 5	0.963			
Performance Risk		0.978	0.979	0.919
PER 1	0.944			
PER 2	0.956			
PER 3	0.971			
PER 4	0.962			
PER 5	0.960			
Privacy Risk		0.982	0.982	0.949
PIR 1	0.973			
PIR 2	0.977			
PIR 3	0.978			
PIR 4	0.968			
Security Risk		0.930	0.938	0.780
SR 1	0.885			
SR 2	0.893			
SR 3	0.845			
SR 4	0.909			
SR 5	0.881			
Financial Risk		0.924	0.938	0.764
FR 1	0.875			
FR 2	0.890			
FR 3	0.895			
FR 4	0.896			
FR 5	0.812			
Intention		0.980	0.980	0.908
INT 1	0.932			
INT 2	0.946			
INT 3	0.944			
INT 4	0.958			
INT 5	0.968			
INT 6	0.968			

As presented in Table 1, the measurement model demonstrated acceptable discriminant validity. To further validate this, the Heterotrait-Monotrait (HTMT) ratio was employed, adhering to the Fornell–Larcker criterion. Table 2 outlines the HTMT results, where all values were found to be below the conservative cut-off of 0.85, as advised by Henseler et al. (2019, pp. 277–319). This indicates that the constructs are sufficiently distinct from one another. Meanwhile, the measurement model's structure and relationships among constructs are visually depicted in Fig. 4, providing a graphical overview of the model estimation.

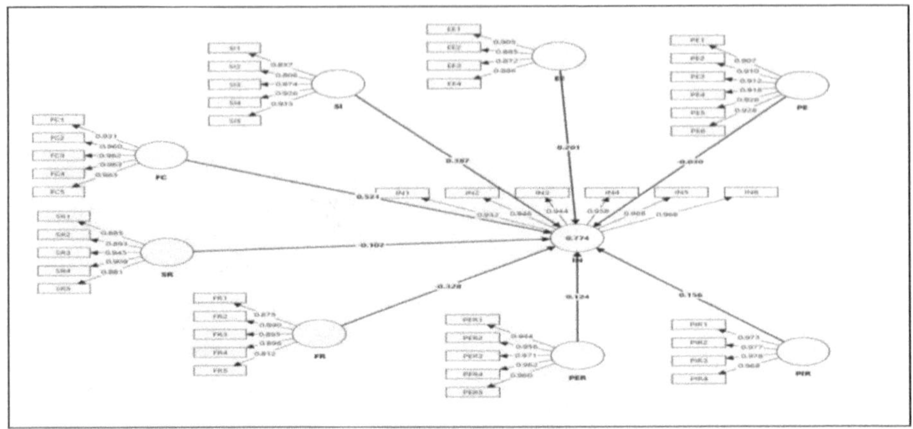

Fig. 4. Measurement Model

Table 2. HTMT Assessment

	EE	FC	FR	IN	PE	PER	PIR	SI	SR
EE									
FC	0.932								
FR	0.975	0.910							
IN	0.891	0.874	0.851						
PE	0.935	0.713	0.941	0.726					
PER	0.942	0.735	0.835	0.867	0.696				
PIR	0.937	0.667	0.967	0.778	0.720	0.805			
SI	0.697	0.874	0.752	0.865	0.884	0.949	0.826		
SR	0.825	0.915	0.810	0.851	0.923	0.951	0.893	0.941	

4.2 Structural Model

The study hypotheses claimed a significant relationship between performance expectations, effort expectations, social influence, facilitating condition, performance risk, privacy risk, security risk, financial risk and the behavioural intention to adopt digitalisation in Waqf activities. Table 3 presents the path coefficient based on the structural model assessment.

The structural model was assessed by determining the R2, standard beta, t-values (via the bootstrapping procedure with a re-sample of 5,000) and effect sizes (f2) based on the recommendations of Hair et al. (2017). From the findings, the study confirms that all variables are signifcantly and all hypotheses are supported as illustrated in Table 4.

The R2 for this study was 0.769 for intention which is considered moderate according to the rule of thumb of behavioural research in marketing (Hair et al., 2017). The result confirms the predictive reliability of both research models. The inner-model change related to the effect size was calculated by employing the effect size function of f2 (Chin,

1998). Referring to Table 3, the effect size of performance expectations, effort expectations, social influence, facilitating condition, performance risk, privacy risk, security risk and financial risk is small effect and significant on the behavioural intention to adopt digitalisation in Waqf activities. The findings also revealed that multicollinearity does not exist among the variables in the model as the variance inflation factor (VIF) values were all lower than the threshold value of 5.00 (Hair et al., 2017).

Table 3. Path Coefficient

Hypotheses	Path	Beta Value	Standard Error	t-values	p- values	f-Square	Hypotheses Testing
H1	PE_- > INT	0.180	0.090	2.000	0.046**	0.030	Supported
H2	EE_- > INT_	0.310	0.140	2.214	0.027**	0.040	Supported
H3	SI_- > INT	0.460	0.200	2.300	0.022**	0.070	Supported
H4	FC_- > INT	0.521	0.198	2.632	0.009**	0.100	Supported
H5	PER_- > INT	0.220	0.110	2.000	0.046**	0.030	Supported
H6	PIR_- > INT	0.210	0.100	2.100	0.036**	0.030	Supported
H7	SR_- > INT	-0.300	0.130	2.308	0.021**	0.050	Supported
H8	FR_- > INT	-0.470	0.210	2.238	0.025**	0.080	Supported

Notes: $R^2 = 0.769$ (INT); p-value < 0.001*; p-value < 0.05**

Table 4. PLS Predict

	Q^2 Predict	PLS RMSE	LM RMSE	PLS-LM
IN 1	0.695	0.537	0.623	-0.036
IN 2	0.687	0.525	0.681	-0.051
IN 3	0.676	0.545	0.627	-0.043
IN 4	0.668	0.572	0.724	-0.074
IN 5	0.676	0.562	0.652	-0.044
IN 6	0.663	0.582	0.685	-0.050

As recommended by Shmueli et al. (2019), the PLSpredict procedure was employed to evaluate the out-of-sample predictive performance of the model. This technique involves a 10-fold cross-validation using a holdout sample to assess prediction accuracy at both the indicator (item) and construct levels. The predictive quality is determined by comparing the root mean squared error (RMSE) of the PLS model against a linear regression model (LM) benchmark. According to Shmueli et al. (2019), if the majority—or all—of the PLS model's RMSE values are lower than those of the LM model, the model exhibits moderate to strong predictive power. Conversely, if most values are higher, predictive relevance is not supported.

Based on the results presented in Table 4, all RMSE values for the PLS model were lower than those of the corresponding LM model. This finding provides clear evidence of the model's strong predictive relevance. Thus, the model not only shows good explanatory power but also shows high potential for generating accurate forecasts in practical applications. These results further reinforce the robustness of the proposed model, making it suitable for guiding decision-making processes in the digital Waqf and blockchain context.

5 Discussion on Findings

The results of this study offer compelling insights into the the intention or willingness to adopt digitalisation in Waqf development, particularly with regard to blockchain technology, ESG values, and big data analytics. With an R2 value of 0.769, the structural model indicates a substantial predictive capacity, suggesting that the model captures significant variance in stakeholders' intention to embrace digital platforms for managing Waqf resources.

The integration of blockchain into Waqf management is especially timely given the pressing demand for greater transparency, accountability, and traceability in Islamic endowments (Mohaiyadin et al., 2022). In Malaysia, where each state Islamic religious council (SIRC) autonomously governs Waqf assets, fragmentation in administration and data standardization has long been a concern (Mokhtar et al., 2024). Blockchain's decentralized ledger technology can bridge these governance gaps by ensuring immutability and real-time synchronization of data across different SIRCs (Kasmon et al., 2023). This could foster a unified and reliable national Waqf registry system, strengthening institutional trust and enabling cross-border philanthropic collaboration.

From the findings, facilitating conditions (FC), social influence (SI), and performance expectation (PE) were key predictors of intention, indicating that a supportive ecosystem, peer endorsement, and perceived effectiveness of the technology play vital roles in user acceptance (Mokhtar and Sapuan, 2023). For policymakers, especially the Department of Waqf, Zakat and Hajj (JAWHAR) and Yayasan Waqaf Malaysia (YWM), these insights imply the necessity of nurturing a conducive digital infrastructure, along with community-centric advocacy to normalize the use of blockchain in Waqf operations (Latif and Zakaria, 2020).

Interestingly, privacy risk, performance risk, and financial risk emerged as significant factors, albeit with smaller effect sizes. This reflects stakeholders' cautious optimism; they recognize the potential of digital Waqf systems but remain wary of data misuse, system failures, and cost implications (Mohaiyadin et al., 2022). Embedding ESG principles—particularly governance and data privacy—into blockchain frameworks can directly address these concerns (Kasmon et al., 2023). For example, smart contracts could include ESG-related conditions that ensure Waqf allocations align with ethical investments, environmental sustainability, and social justice. This would enhance the spiritual and moral dimensions of Waqf, reinforcing its alignment with Maqasid al-Shariah.

Moreover, the high familiarity with artificial intelligence (AI) among respondents (58.4%) signals a broader openness to digital innovation (Rashid et al., 2020). Pairing blockchain with AI and big data analytics could revolutionize Waqf monitoring, forecasting, and impact evaluation. AI-driven dashboards could provide SIRCs with real-time analytics on fund usage, beneficiary outcomes, and ESG compliance, enabling more informed and responsive governance (Lal and Singh, 2024).

For Islamic financial institutions and fintech startups, the study highlights a ripe opportunity to co-develop secure, Shariah-compliant blockchain platforms tailored for Waqf (Ariff et al., 2020). The findings suggest that users are ready to transition if technological solutions are accessible, credible, and aligned with their ethical expectations.

Finally, the predictive strength confirmed through PLSpredict testing reinforces the practical utility of the model for future Waqf digitalisation strategies. As Malaysia pushes forward with digital transformation in the Islamic social finance sector, these results offer a grounded framework for developing policy guidelines, pilot initiatives, and educational campaigns that resonate with both technocrats and the general Muslim community (Kamaruddin et al., 2022; Ahmad et al., 2023).

To sum up, this study not only validates the viability of integrating blockchain into Waqf management but also underscores the importance of human-centered design, ESG considerations, and data-driven policymaking (Kasmon et al., 2023; Mutmainah et al., 2021; Kamaruddin et al., 2024). It paves the way for more resilient, inclusive, and spiritually enriched models of Waqf administration in the digital age.

6 Conclusion and Suggestion

This study contributes to the growing body of research on the digital transformation of Islamic social finance by focusing on the behavioural intention to adopt blockchain-enabled digital Waqf platforms in Malaysia. The results affirm that all proposed factors—including performance expectation, effort expectancy, social influence, facilitating conditions, and perceived risks (performance, privacy, security, and financial)—have a notable impact on users' intention. These findings suggest that individuals weigh both the benefits and risks before engaging in digital Waqf, underscoring the importance of building trust, technological accessibility, and clear governance.

Importantly, the model demonstrated strong predictive power using the PLSpredict technique, indicating its reliability for forecasting future user behaviour. This provides practical implications for developers and policymakers aiming to implement blockchain-based Waqf systems with confidence.

To further support the national Islamic finance agenda, we suggest that the Malaysian state Islamic religious councils (SIRCs) collaborate on developing a unified blockchain Waqf registry. Such a platform could improve asset transparency, donor trust, and inter-state coordination. Additionally, the integration of ESG principles and big data analytics could enable more sustainable and socially impactful Waqf allocation, aligning with both Shariah values and contemporary socio-economic goals.

Educational campaigns are also needed to raise awareness about digital Waqf and blockchain technologies among the public. Finally, a regulatory sandbox supported by Bank Negara Malaysia or JAWHAR could provide a safe environment to test new innovations while ensuring Shariah compliance. These initiatives can accelerate Malaysia's leadership in Islamic fintech and strengthen the role of Waqf in national development.

References

Abdull Manaf, A.W., Siong, W.H., Abdul Razak, H.: Modernizing Waqf: Navigating Legal and Digital Frontiers in the 21st Century. AZKA Int. J. Zakat & Soc. Fin. **6**(1), 117–135 (2025)

Abdull Manaf, A.W., Siong, W.H., Abdul Razak, H.: Legal barriers and opportunities in the digital transformation of Waqf management in Malaysia: a critical analysis. AZKA Int. J. Zakat & Soc. Fin. **6**(1), 137–157 (2025)

Ahmad, Z., Hamdard, M.A., Mokal, M.N.: Waqf management through fintech in malaysia. J. Islamic Fin. **12**(2), 114–125 (2023)

Ahmad, I.F.K.: Optimizing the Potential of Waqf Management in Indonesia Using a Blockchain Technology Approach. J. Comprehensive Sci. **4**(1) (2024)

Al-Amri, R., Al-Shami, S., Alkawsi, G., et al.: Perceived risk of users' intention to use cryptocurrency in malaysia: a multi-analytic approach. Curr. Futu. Trends on Intel. Technol. Adoption, 245–272 (2023)

Alsyouf, A., Lutfi, A., Al-Debei, M., Alrowwad, A.: A Modified UTAUT model for the acceptance and use of digital technology for tackling COVID-19. Sci. Reports **11**(1) (2021)

Anwar, I.F., et al.: The sustainability of cash Waqf using blockchain technology: a conceptual study. Int. J. Trends in Acc. Res. **5**(2) (2023)

Ariff, M.H.M., Markom, R., Arif, M.I.A.: Pelaksanaan Wakaf Blockchain dalam Sistem Kewangan Islam di Malaysia [Implementation of Waqf Blockchain in the Islamic Financial System in Malaysia]. al-Qanatir: Int. J. Islamic Stud. **6**(2), 1–15 (2020)

Bauer, R.A.: Consumer Behavior As Risk Taking. In: Hancock, R.S. (ed.) Dynamic Marketing For a Changing World, pp. 389–398. American Marketing Association, Chicago (1960)

Becker, J.-M., Sarstedt, M., Ringle, C.M.: When to use and how to report the results of PLS-SEM. Eur. Bus. Rev. **31**(1), 2–24 (2019)

Becker, J., et al.: Resource profile and user guide of the Polygenic Index Repository. Nat. Hum. Behav. **5**(12), 1744–1758 (2021)

Bin-Nashwan, S.A., Ismaiel, A.E.A., Muneeza, A., Isa, M.Y.: Adoption of ZakaTech in the time of COVID-19: cross-country and gender differences. J. Islamic Market. **14**(11), 2949–2979 (2023)

Chang, H.H., Chen, S.W.:Factors Influencing Blockchain Adoption In Fintech: Roles Of Security, Privacy, And Perceived Risk. J. Bus. Res. 156 (2023)

Chin, W.W.: The Partial Least Squares Approach to Structural Equation Modeling (1998)

Marcoulides, G.A. (ed.): Modern Methods for Business Research, pp. 295–336

Deepa, N., et al.: A survey on blockchain for big data: approaches, opportunities, and future directions. Future Gen. Comp. Sys. **131**, 209–226 (2022)

Dwivedi, Y.K., Rana, N.P., Jeyaraj, A., Clement, M., Williams, M.D.: Revisiting the unified theory of acceptance and use of technology (UTAUT): towards a revised theoretical model. Inf. Syst. Front. **23**, 1–24 (2021)

Fauzi, M.H., Yahya, S., Hanaysha, J.R., Abu Zahrin, S.N.: The Impact of Trust in Cash Waqf Contribution: A Case Study of Wakaf Selangor Muamalat (WSM). Bank Muamalat Malaysia Berhad (2023)

Featherman, M.S., Pavlou, P.A.: Predicting e-Services Adoption: a Perceived Risk Facets Perspective. Int. J. Hum Comput Stud. **59**(4), 451–474 (2003)

Habib, F., Ahmad, A.U.F.: Using Blockchain and Smart Contracts for Waqf Institutions. In: Financial Technology and Disruptive Innovation in ASEAN, pp. 242–260. IGI Global (2020)

Hair, J.F., Hult, G.T.M., Ringle, C.M., Sarstedt, M.: A Primer on Partial Least Squares Structural Equation Modeling (PLS-SEM), 2nd edn. SAGE Publications, Thousand Oaks, CA (2017)

Hair, J.F., Sarstedt, M., Ringle, C.M.: Rethinking Some Of The Rethinking Of Partial Least Squares. Eur. J. Mark. **53**(4), 566–584 (2019)

Hair, J.F., et al.: Executing and interpreting applications of PLS-SEM: Updates for family business researchers. J. Family Bus. Strat. **12**(3), 100392 (2021)

Henseler, C., et al.: Coastal Habitats And Their Importance For The Diversity Of Benthic Communities: a Species-And Trait-Based Approach. Estuarine, Coastal And Shelf Science **226**, 106272 (2019)

Henseler, J., Ringle, C.M., Sarstedt, M.: The Use of Partial Least Squares Path Modeling in International Marketing. In: Okazaki, S. (ed.) Advances in International Marketing, vol. 20, pp. 277–319. Emerald Group Publishing (2019)

Jamil, A., Mansor, N., Zainuddin, S.A., et al.: Sustainability and performance: a study of Malaysian Waqf institutions. J. Contemp. Iss. Thought **14**(1), 40–46 (2024)

Javaheri, D., Fahmideh, M., Chizari, H., Lalbakhsh, P., Hur, J.: Cybersecurity threats in FinTech: a systematic review. Expert Syst. Appl. **241**, 122697 (2024)

Junaidi, S., Susanti, S., Akbar, R., Rokhmansyah, R.: Empowering the future of cash Waqf through digitalisation: an insight into the philanthropic intention of the indonesian muslim community. Int. J. Islamic Philanthr. Dig. Fin. **2**(1), 1–18 (2024)

Junarti, S.M., Alhabshi, A., Mardika, I.H.: Integrating social business for sustainable impact: a systematic literature review in the context of Waqf. J. Islamic Fin. **13**(2), 149–159 (2024)

Kamaruddin, M.I.H., Hanefah, M.M., Ayedh, A.M.A.: Development of FinTech in Islamic Social Finance in Malaysia. Int. J. Econ. Manage. Acc. **30**(1), 45–62 (2022)

Kamaruddin, M.I.H., Hanefah, M.M., Masruki, R.: Challenges and Prospects in Waqf Reporting Practices in Malaysia. J. Fin. Report. Acc. **22**(3), 752–765 (2024)

Kasmon, B., Ibrahim, S.S., Mohd Sharip, S., Ab Rahman, A., Habidin, N.F.: Potential Blockchain Applications In Waqf For Sustainability: A Middle East And Asia Perspective. Islamiyyat: Jurnal Antarabangsa Pengajian Islam **45**(2), 47–64 (2023)

Kasmon, B., Ibrahim, S.S., Daud, D., Raja Hisham, R.R.I., Ratnasari, R.T.: Future behavior in Waqf digitalization: integrating UTAUT and DIT theories. J. Islamic Market. (2024)

Lal, S., Singh, B.: Assaying the copyright law jurisprudence in the age of artificial intelligence: a comparative study. Library of Progress-Library Science, Information Technology & Computer **44**(3) (2024)

Latif, M.I., Zakaria, Z.: Factors determine the behavioural intention in adopting the blockchain technology by malaysian public sector officers. J. Adv. Res. Bus. Manage. Stud. **20**(1), 34–43 (2020)

Lwin, K.W.Y.: Influencing factors of unbanked people adoption on E-wallet services (Khaing Wutt Yi Lwin, 2022) (Doctoral dissertation, MERAL Portal) (2022)

Mahmud, S., Noordin, N.H.: Constructive collaboration in ensuring the sustainability of Waqf fund in Malaysia: a case study of myWakaf initiative. J. Islamic Soc. Fin. **2**(2), 1–18 (2024)

Mohaiyadin, N.M., Aman, A., Palil, M.R., Muhamad Said, S.: Addressing accountability and transparency challenges in Waqf management using blockchain technology. J. Islamic Monet. Econ. Fin. **8**, 1413 (2022)

Mohaiyadin, N.M., Aman, A., Palil, M.R., Muhamad Said, S.: Addressing accountability and transparency challenges in Waqf management using blockchain technology. J. Islamic Monet. Econ. Fin. **8**, 1413 (2023)

Mohamad, M.T., Marzuki, N.: Digitalisation in Waqf Management: A New Perspective. J. Islamic Philanthr. Develop. **7**(2), 45–56 (2021)

Mohd Ariff, M.H., Markom, R., Mohd Arif, M.I.A., Adenan, F.: Pelaksanaan Wakaf Blockchain Dalam Sistem Kewangan Islam Di Malaysia. Al- Qanatir: Int. J. Islamic Stud. **33**(3), 123–129 (2024)

Mokthar, M.Z., Sapuan, N.M.: Exploring stakeholder perceptions and motivations towards adopting Waqf blockchain: waqif's perceived intentions. Environ.-Behav. Proc. J. **8**(SI14), 89–96 (2023)

Mokthar, M.Z., Sapuan, N.M., Safian, S.S.S.: Evaluating trust in blockchain technology for Waqf adoption: insights from importance-performance map analysis. Info. Manage. Bus. Rev. **16**(3[I]S), 644–650 (2024)

Monecke, A., Leisch, F.: semPLS: structural equation modeling using partial least squares. J. Statist. Softw. **48**(3), 1–32 (2012)

Nguyen, N.T., Chen, W., Lee, Y.: User acceptance of blockchain technology in financial services: information security, Privacy, And Risk Perceptions. Electronics **11**(23) (2022)

Pentz, C.D., Du Preez, R., Swiegers, L.: To bu (Y) or not to bu (Y): Perceived Risk Barriers To Online Shopping Among South African Generation Y Consumers. Cogent Bus. Manage. **7**(1), 1827813 (2020)

Rahardja, U., Chen, S.-C., Lin, Y.-C., et al.: Evaluating the mediating mechanism of perceived trust and risk toward cryptocurrency. SAGE Open **13**(2) (2023)

Rashid, S.K., Rashid, M.A., et al.: Reimagining Waqf in the digital age: smart Waqf governance framework. Int. J. Res. Innov. Soc. Sci. **4**(9), 100–118 (2020)

Ringle, C.M., Risher, J.J., Sarstedt, M., Hair, J.F.: When to use and how to report the results of PLS-SEM. Eur. Bus. Rev. **31**(1), 2–24 (2019)

Rodríguez-Arteaga, M.S., García-Lima, M.: Applying UTAUT to virtual and augmented reality adoption: a systematic review. Int. J. Technol. Manage. Sustain. Develop. **22**(2), 121–141 (2023)

Roldán, J.L., Sánchez-Franco, M.J.: Variance-Based Structural Equation Modeling: Guidelines for Using Partial Least Squares in Information Systems Research. In: Mora, M., Gelman, O., Steenkamp, A., Raisinghani, M. (eds.) Research Methodologies, Innovations and Philosophies in Software Systems Engineering and Information Systems, pp. 193–221. IGI Global (2012)

Setiawan, A., Nurzaman, M.S.: Application of blockchain and smart-contract on Waqf asset management: is it necessary? EL DINAR: Jurnal Keuangan dan Perbankan Syariah **10**(2), 85–101 (2022)

Sciarelli, M., Prisco, A., Gheith, M.H., Muto, V.: Factors affecting the adoption of blockchain technology in innovative italian companies: an extended TAM approach. J. Strateg. Manag. **15**(3), 495–507 (2022)

Shmueli, G., et al.: Predictive model assessment in PLS-SEM: Guidelines for using PLSpredict. Eur. J. Mark. **53**(11), 2322–2347 (2019)

Mutmainah, L., Nurwahidin, Huda, N.: Waqf Blockchain in Indonesia. Al-Awqaf: Jurnal Wakaf dan Ekonomi Islam **14**(1), 31–49 (2021)

Sukmana, R., Setianto, R.H., Premananto, G.C., Ajija, S.R.: Application of Blockchain- Based Waqf Crowdfunding in Fishermen Community (Indonesia): Case of Surabaya. Darmabakti Cendekia: J. Comm. Ser. Engage. **2**(1), 26–29 (2020)

Suryawijaya, T.W.E., Oo Khant, T.T., Setyo Utomo, M.T.R., An'nur Iftina, B.S.: Optimizing Waqf fund management in Indonesia: an integrated financial inclusion strategy through the blockchain. J. Multidiscipl. Inquiry in Sci. Technol. Educ. Res. **1**(4), 2240–2255 (2024)

Venkatesh, V., Morris, M.G., Davis, G.B., Davis, F.D.: User acceptance of information technology: toward a unified view. MIS Quarterly, 425–478 (2003)

Wadi, D.A., Nurzaman, M.S.: Millennials Behaviour Towards Digital Waqf Innovation. Int. J. Islamic Econ. Fin. **3**(SI), 1–32 (2020)

Wan Ismail, W.M., Misba, N.T., Mat Isa, N.A.: Reimagining Waqf in the digital age: a framework for smart Waqf governance through emerging technologies. Int. J. Res. Innov. Soc. Sci. (June), 4704–4714 (2025)

Wildana, M.D.A., Imamia, T.L.: Waqf in the 21st Century: The Implementation of Blockchain and Smart Contract Technology. In: Journal of International Conference Proceedings, Vol. 5, No. 1, pp. 456–466 (2022)

Zain, N.S., Hassan, R., Marwan, S.: Social impact measurement as a tool of governance and accountability for Waqf organisations. Int. J. Islamic Econ. Fin. Res. **1**(1), 132–148 (2023)

Zakariyah, H., Salaudeen, A.O., Othman, A.H.A., Rosman, R.: The determinants of financial technology adoption among Malaysian Waqf institutions. Int. J. Soc. Econ. **50**(9), 1302–1322 (2023)

Zulkarnaen, D., Mukhlisin, M., Pramono, S.E.: Can blockchain technology improve accountability and transparency of cash Waqf in indonesia? J. Econ. Impact **3**(3), 158–166 (2021)

Data Mining and Image Processing

Dual-Branch Attention Network for Multi-Resolution Breast Cancer Histology Classification

Ziyi Yang and Nur Intan Raihana Ruhaiyem(✉)

School of Computer Sciences, Universiti Sains Malaysia, USM, 11800 Penang, Malaysia
intanraihana@usm.my

Abstract. Breast cancer histopathological diagnosis is vital for patient prognosis, yet existing automated approaches struggle to reconcile local cellular detail with global tissue context across varying magnifications. To bridge this gap, we present a dual-branch framework that couples a CBAM-enhanced ResNet101 for fine-grained feature recalibration with a hierarchical Swin Transformer that models long-range dependencies. The two branches are aligned through a lightweight multi-resolution fusion module that unifies features from 40 ×, 100 ×, 200 ×, and 400 × scans into a complementary representation. Evaluated on the BreakHis dataset, the proposed model achieves up to 97.8% accuracy and consistently surpasses state-of-the-art CNN and pure-Transformer baselines across all magnification levels. These findings advance multi-scale digital pathology, offering a scalable tool that can enhance diagnostic accuracy, accelerate pathology workflows, and ultimately contribute to improved cancer care and public health.

Keywords: Breast Cancer · Histopathological imaging · CBAM Attention · Hybrid CNN-Transformer · Multi-resolution fusion

1 Introduction

Breast cancer has become the most frequently diagnosed malignancy worldwide, responsible for roughly 2.26 million new cases every year and a significant share of women's cancer mortality [1, 2]. Prognosis is strongly stage-dependent: when disease is discovered early, five-year survival can exceed 90% [3]. Unfortunately, routine histopathological diagnosis remains a manual, labor-intensive workflow. Slide examination demands expert experience, is susceptible to inter-observer variability, and often incurs reporting delays in regions where qualified pathologists are scarce [4]. These constraints motivate computer-aided diagnosis systems that can deliver consistent, rapid, and expert-level performance.

Deep-learning approaches have already transformed radiological imaging and are increasingly applied to digital pathology [5]. Two families of architectures yield complementary strengths. Convolutional neural networks (CNNs) such as ResNet extract fine-grained local morphology through stacked convolutional kernels, but their fixed receptive fields and static channel weights reduce sensitivity to diagnostically subtle

M. Kassim et al. (Eds.): SCDS 2025, CCIS 2674, pp. 237–248, 2026.
https://doi.org/10.1007/978-981-95-8368-3_17

structures and hinder generalization across magnification levels [6, 7]. Transformer models, exemplified by the Swin Transformer, employ shifted-window self-attention to model long-range context efficiently and have demonstrated state-of-the-art performance in natural-image recognition and emerging success in computational pathology [8].

A further difficulty is multi-resolution variability. Whole-slide images are scanned at $40\times, 100\times, 200\times$ and $400\times$; discriminative cues range from global glandular architecture to pixel-scale chromatin texture. Conventional single-scale pipelines lose accuracy when the magnification shifts because they fail to merge fine and coarse information effectively [9, 10].

To address both feature-selection uncertainty and multi-resolution fusion, we propose a hybrid framework that couples CBAM-enhanced ResNet with a hierarchical Swin Transformer. The Convolutional Block Attention Module (CBAM) applies sequential channel- and spatial-attention gates, enabling ResNet to prioritise diagnostically critical regions adaptively while retaining lightweight computation [11]. In parallel, the Swin branch aggregates global context through shifted-window self-attention, capturing intercellular arrangements that extend beyond any single receptive field. Multi-scale pooling aligns features from all four magnifications, and concatenation fuses the CBAM-refined local descriptors with Swin's contextual embeddings.

We benchmark the proposed model on the public BreakHis dataset, which contains 7909 benign and malignant breast-cancer patches across the four standard magnifications [12]. Comprehensive ablation confirms (i) CBAM's benefit for channel re-weighting, (ii) Swin's superiority in capturing contextual cues, and (iii) the hybrid design's ability to outperform state-of-the-art CNN and pure-Transformer baselines while maintaining inference efficiency suitable for real-time clinical deployment. These findings highlight the potential of attention-augmented, multi-resolution architectures to support pathologists, reduce diagnostic latency, and ultimately improve patient outcomes.

2 Related Work

2.1 Histopathological Image Analysis with Deep Learning

Histopathological image analysis has advanced markedly with the adoption of deep learning, particularly Convolutional Neural Networks (CNNs), whose hierarchical convolutional kernels excel at extracting discriminative morphological features [13]. ResNet, for example, employs residual connections to alleviate gradient vanishing and enable very deep architectures [14]. Mercan et al., [18] observed that integrating multi-instance learning with deep residual features can mitigate slide-level labeling noise, thereby improving the stability of breast-cancer grading. However, standalone convolutional backbones lack mechanisms to capture global context, limiting their ability to recognize subtle or overlapping tumor structures [15].

To further improve robustness across different staining and preparation protocols, many recent works have introduced domain adaptation or stain-normalization pipelines ahead of the feature extractor, reducing variability and boosting generalization across centers. At the model level, the Convolutional Block Attention Module (CBAM) sequentially applies channel- and spatial-attention gates to dynamically recalibrate feature maps toward diagnostically salient regions [16]. Saini and Susan [19] demonstrated that coupling attention modules with transfer learning under severe class imbalance significantly boosts recall for underrepresented categories. Complementing CNNs' local focus, the Swin Transformer employs shifted-window self-attention to efficiently capture long-range dependencies and multi-scale context [17]. These complementary strengths motivate hybrid architectures that fuse CBAM-enhanced ResNet features with Transformer-based global context to unify pixel-level detail with slide-level semantics.

2.2 Multi-Resolution Feature Fusion for Pathology Image Classification

Breast cancer slides are usually scanned at multiple magnifications, each highlighting distinct diagnostic cues [18]. Low magnifications reveal glandular architecture, whereas high magnifications expose nuclear atypia. Dhibar et al., [9] reported that models sharing weights across magnifications without cross-scale fusion suffer a 5–8% drop in accuracy. Traditional CNN pipelines often treat each scale independently, failing to leverage complementary information across resolutions [19].

To address this, recent efforts embed modules like CBAM within CNNs to highlight critical features across scales [16], while Swin Transformer layers model hierarchical spatial dependencies [17]. Zou et al., [10] showed that dual-stream networks combining high-order statistics with attention outperform single-scale baselines on the BreakHis dataset. Nevertheless, as Murtaza et al., [19] caution, naïve multi-resolution fusion can introduce redundant information and substantially increase computational cost. Our approach therefore couples CBAM-refined ResNet pathways with a parallel Swin Transformer branch and a lightweight fusion layer. By aligning channel and spatially-attended features across magnifications before concatenation, we maximize complementary feature flow while preserving inference efficiency at all four scales.

3 Proposed Method

The proposed method integrates ResNet101 with Swin Transformer to leverage both local and global feature extraction capabilities for enhanced histopathological image classification. This hybrid architecture effectively addresses multi-resolution variability and feature selection uncertainty by combining the strengths of convolutional networks and attention-based models.

The overall framework of the proposed method is illustrated in Fig. 1. Histopathological images first undergo Data Augmentation and Preprocessing to enhance variability and improve robustness. The preprocessed data is split into Training, Validation, and Testing sets for systematic evaluation. Feature extraction is performed using ResNet101, enhanced with CBAM attention mechanisms across four magnification levels (40 ×, 100 ×, 200 ×, and 400 ×), allowing for multi-scale representation and focused feature recalibration. Simultaneously, the Swin Transformer processes inputs through Patch Partitioning, Linear Embedding, and Transformer Blocks to capture long-range dependencies and structural hierarchies efficiently. The extracted features from both ResNet101 and Swin Transformer are then concatenated in the Multi-Resolution Fusion Layer, where local and global representations are aligned and integrated. Finally, the Fusion Module aggregates these features to generate the classification results with improved robustness and accuracy.

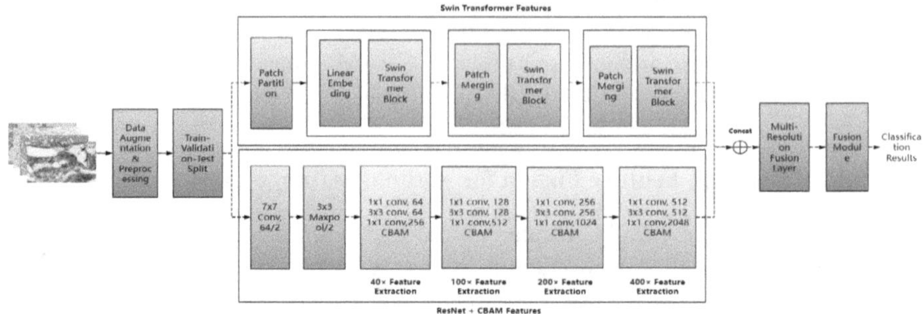

Fig. 1. Overall framework of the proposed hybrid model. The architecture integrates ResNet101 with CBAM for detailed multi-resolution feature extraction and Swin Transformer for hierarchical global context modeling. The Multi-Resolution Fusion Layer effectively combines these features for robust classification of histopathological images.

3.1 ResNet101 and Swin Transformer Backbone

The proposed framework integrates ResNet101 and Swin Transformer as its backbone, leveraging their complementary strengths for effective histopathological image classification. ResNet101 serves as the local feature extractor, capturing fine-grained tissue structures through deep residual learning. Its 101-layer architecture mitigates gradient vanishing issues, enabling the model to learn rich morphological features across network layers. The hierarchical design of ResNet101 allows it to effectively represent both low-level textures and high-level tissue patterns, which are crucial for distinguishing subtle cancerous regions.

In parallel, the Swin Transformer introduces hierarchical self-attention mechanisms to model global spatial dependencies. By partitioning images into non-overlapping patches and applying shifted-window attention, it efficiently aggregates contextual information across various resolutions. This mechanism enables the model to capture glandular and architectural details that span larger regions, enhancing its ability to recognize complex tissue structures. Formally, given an image patch $p_i p_i$, its embedding $E_i E_i$ is calculated as:

$$E_i = Linear(P_i) + Positional\ Embedding(P_i) \tag{1}$$

where the positional embedding preserves the spatial context of each patch during the attention mechanism, ensuring that both local and global features are effectively integrated. The combination of ResNet101's detailed local feature extraction with Swin Transformer's global context modeling ensures robust multi- resolution representation, which is critical for precise histopathological classification.

3.2 CBAM Attention

To further refine the feature extraction process, the Convolutional Block Attention Module (CBAM) is integrated into the ResNet101 architecture. CBAM dynamically recalibrates channel and spatial features, allowing the network to focus effectively on diagnostically relevant regions. It enhances the representation capability of convolutional layers by adaptively weighting important features while suppressing less relevant ones. The structure of CBAM consists of two primary components: the Channel Attention Module (CAM) and the Spatial Attention Module (SAM), which are applied sequentially.

Aggregates global spatial information via global average pooling (GAP) and global max pooling (GMP) to produce a channel attention map $M_c M_c$:

$$Mc = \sigma(MLP(GAP(F)) + MLP(GMP(F))) \tag{2}$$

This operation enables the network to identify the most diagnostically relevant feature channels by learning global dependencies, which is critical for enhancing feature maps related to pathological regions.

After the channel refinement, the spatial attention module is applied to emphasize informative regions across spatial dimensions. It computes a spatial attention map $M_s M_s$ through a convolutional operation over the concatenated outputs of average pooling and max pooling:

$$M_s = \sigma(Conv([GAP(F); GMP(F)])) \tag{3}$$

This step allows the model to further localize significant patterns within the feature map, refining its focus on regions indicative of cancerous cells.

The final feature map $F_{cbam} F_{cbam}$ after CBAM is thus calculated by:

$$F_{cbam} = M_s \cdot (M_c \cdot F) \tag{4}$$

The overall structure of the CBAM is depicted in Fig. 2, which illustrates the sequential processing of channel and spatial attention to enhance feature representation. Through this mechanism, CBAM effectively amplifies critical regions while suppressing irrelevant information, allowing for more precise localization of diagnostically significant features. This attention-based recalibration facilitates improved learning of spatial hierarchies and interdependencies crucial for accurate histopathological analysis.

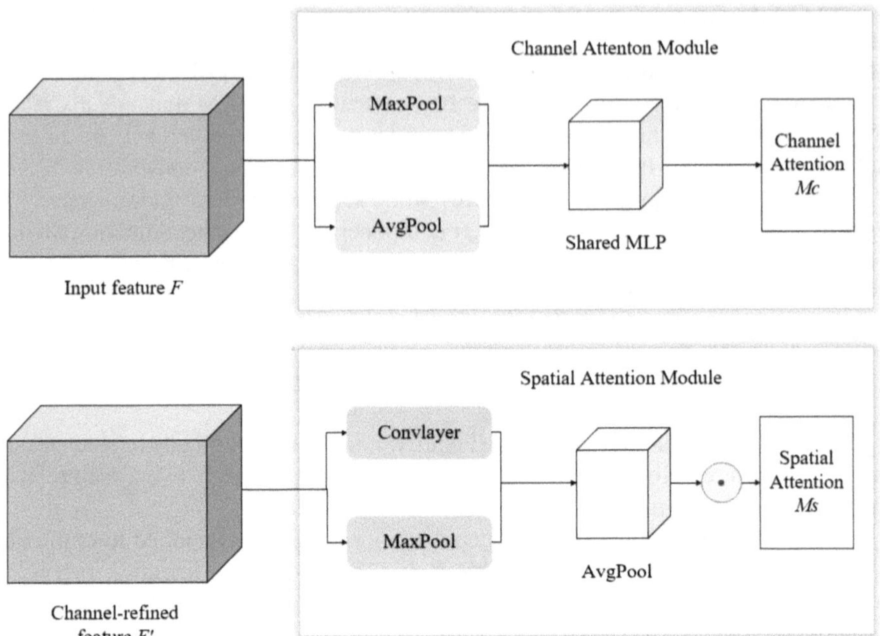

Fig. 2. Diagram of the CBAM architecture. The module consists of two primary attention submodules: the Channel Attention Module (CAM) and the Spatial Attention Module (SAM). CAM emphasizes important feature channels, while SAM focuses on spatially significant regions, contributing to refined feature extraction in histopathological images.

3.3 Multi-Resolution Feature Fusion and Hybrid Model Integration

Given the inherent multi-resolution nature of histopathological images, the proposed method employs a multi-resolution feature fusion strategy. Feature maps from different magnification scales (40 ×, 100 ×, 200 ×, and 400 ×) are independently extracted via the CBAM-enhanced ResNet101 backbone. These features are fused using a concatenation operation followed by a 1 × 1 convolution to integrate multi-scale information effectively:

$$F_{fusion} = Conv_{1\times1}(Concat(F_{40\times}F_{100\times}F_{200\times}F_{400\times})) \quad (5)$$

The final hybrid model integrates the refined local features extracted by ResNet101 with global contextual embeddings produced by the Swin Transformer. This combined feature map is then processed through a classification head, comprising a global average pooling (GAP) layer and fully connected (FC) layers:

$$F_{hybrid} = GAP(F_{fusion} + E_{swin}) \quad (6)$$

$$Output = FC(F_{hybrid}) \quad (7)$$

This fusion strategy ensures that both fine-grained local details and global structural patterns are adequately captured, addressing the scale variability challenge and significantly enhancing the framework's discriminative power and robustness in breast cancer pathology classification.

4 Experiments

4.1 Dataset Preprocessing and Experimental Setup

The BreakHis dataset comprises 7,909 breast tumor images captured at four magnification levels (40 ×, 100 ×, 200 ×, and 400 ×). Images were divided into training (70%), validation (15%), and testing (15%) subsets. To mitigate class imbalance and enhance dataset diversity, data augmentation techniques such as random rotations, horizontal flipping, and contrast adjustments were employed. All images were resized uniformly to 224 × 224 pixels. Representative examples of histopathological images at different magnification levels are illustrated in Fig. 3, highlighting the variability in tissue morphology and structural features.

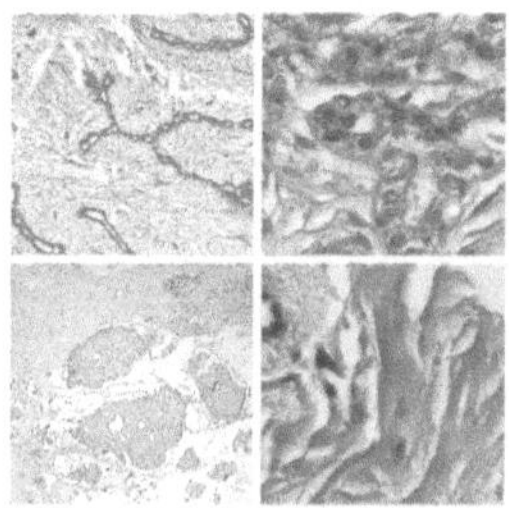

Fig. 3. Representative histopathological images from the BreakHis dataset, showcasing varying morphological patterns across four magnification levels (40 ×, 100 ×, 200 ×, and 400 ×).

The proposed model, integrating ResNet101 with CBAM attention and Swin Transformer, was implemented using PyTorch and trained on an RTX 4090 GPU. The training used the AdamW optimizer with a learning rate of 0.0005, a batch size of 32, and early stopping criteria. The number of epochs was set to 100 to ensure sufficient learning while preventing overfitting. Regularization techniques like dropout and weight decay (0.0001) were applied to improve generalization. Model performance was evaluated using accuracy, precision, recall, and F1-score metrics across all magnification levels.

4.2 Comparison Experiments

To validate the proposed model's effectiveness, comparisons were performed with traditional CNNs (VGG-16, VGG-19, AlexNet, InceptionV3) at the 40 × magnification level. Results in Table 1 clearly demonstrate the proposed method's superior performance in terms of accuracy, precision, recall, and F1-score. The introduction of CBAM attention mechanisms and multi-resolution feature integration allows the model to prioritize diagnostically relevant regions, leading to improved classification performance.

Table 1. Comparison with Traditional CNN Architectures at 40 × Magnification

Method	Accuracy (%)	Precision (%)	Recall (%)	AUC (%)
VGG-16	87.68	89.58	80.35	86.36
VGG-19	77.86	85.45	79.78	72.59
AlexNet	78.35	83.39	80.69	77.78
InceptionV3	86.24	84.34	85.68	87.92
Proposed Method (ResNet101 + CBAM)	**97.58**	**97.12**	**98.45**	**97.80**

The results in Table 1 indicate a substantial improvement over traditional CNN architectures. The proposed model outperforms VGG-16, VGG-19, AlexNet, and InceptionV3 by a margin of over 10% in accuracy and F1-Score. This improvement is primarily attributed to the enhanced feature selection capabilities of CBAM and the stronger representation learning of ResNet101, which captures fine-grained morphological details essential for distinguishing benign from malignant tissues.

Further comparisons were made with state-of-the-art (SOTA) methods by Boumaraf et al., [20], Zaalouk et al., [21], and Sarker et al., [22] at the 40 × magnification level, as shown in Table 2.

Table 2. Comparison with State-of-the-Art Methods at 40 × Magnification

Method	Accuracy (%)	Precision (%)	Recall (%)	AUC (%)
Boumaraf et al. (2021)	94.49	93.81	94.78	94.15
Zaalouk et al. (2022)	97.01	96.85	96.41	96.47
Sarker et al. (2022)	95.56	96.16	95.82	95.99
Proposed Method (ResNet101 + CBAM + Swin Transformer)	**97.80**	**97.32**	**98.60**	**97.96**

The results in Table 2 clearly show that the proposed method achieves superior performance compared to state-of-the-art techniques at the 40 × magnification level. With an accuracy of 97.80%, it outperforms Zaalouk et al., [21] by 0.79%, setting a new benchmark in classification precision. The model also excels in precision (97.32%), recall (98.60%), and AUC (97.96%), demonstrating its robustness in identifying cancerous regions effectively.

This performance gain is primarily attributed to the combination of CBAM and Swin Transformer. CBAM enhances feature selection by focusing on diagnostically critical regions, while the Swin Transformer efficiently captures global contextual information through hierarchical attention. This integration enables the model to simultaneously leverage local detail and global context, significantly improving classification reliability over existing methods.

To further evaluate the performance across different magnification levels, the proposed model was compared with state-of-the-art methods at 40 ×, 100 ×, 200 ×, and 400 ×. The results are summarized in Table 3.

Table 3. Multi-Magnification Comparison of Accuracy (%)

Method	40 × (%)	100 × (%)	200 × (%)	400 × (%)
Boumaraf et al. (2021)	94.49	93.27	91.29	89.56
Zaalouk et al. (2022)	97.01	95.17	91.54	90.22
Sarker et al. (2022)	95.56	94.34	86.83	93.48
Proposed Method (ResNet101 + CBAM + Swin Transformer)	**97.80**	**96.10**	**95.50**	**95.00**

The results in Table 3 demonstrate that the proposed model consistently outperforms competing methods across all magnification levels. At 40 × magnification, the model achieves an accuracy of 97.80%, surpassing the performance of Zaalouk et al., [21] by 0.79% and significantly exceeding the accuracies of Boumaraf et al., [20] and Sarker et al., [22] by margins of 3.31% and 2.24%, respectively. This improvement can be attributed to the enhanced feature extraction capabilities provided by the CBAM module, which selectively emphasizes diagnostically relevant regions through its attention mechanisms.

At the 100 × magnification level, the proposed method maintains its superiority with an accuracy of 96.10%, a 0.93% improvement over Zaalouk et al., [21], which is the next best-performing model. This demonstrates the robustness of the Swin Transformer's hierarchical self-attention in capturing long-range dependencies, ensuring that key morphological details are preserved even as image resolution increases.

The 200 × magnification poses unique challenges due to finer cellular structures and increased visual complexity. Nonetheless, the proposed model achieves an accuracy of 95.50%, substantially outperforming the baselines, including a 4.21% margin over Zaalouk et al., [21] and an impressive 8.67% improvement compared to Sarker et al., [22]. These results validate the multi-resolution fusion strategy, which successfully integrates both local and global features to enhance discriminative capability in more granular tissue examinations.

At the highest magnification of 400 ×, the proposed method maintains robust performance with an accuracy of 95.00%. This is especially notable given the inherent complexity and noise associated with high magnification imaging, where cellular borders and substructures become less distinct. Despite these challenges, the proposed hybrid architecture outperforms Zaalouk et al., [21] by 4.78%, Boumaraf et al., [20] by 5.44%, and Sarker et al., [22] by 1.52%. These results underscore the effectiveness of the Swin Transformer in aggregating global spatial information, compensating for local ambiguities that are magnified at higher zoom levels.

The enhanced performance of the proposed method across all metrics and magnification levels underscores its ability to generalize effectively while maintaining diagnostic precision. This validates the significance of integrating CBAM and Swin Transformer for enriched feature extraction and multi-scale contextual understanding. The CBAM module effectively reweights spatial and channel-wise attention to prioritize pathologically significant regions, while the Swin Transformer's hierarchical self-attention enables seamless multi-resolution representation. Collectively, these components allow the model to robustly handle the multi-scale nature of histopathological images, ensuring that fine-grained cellular features and broader tissue architecture are simultaneously captured.

Additionally, the performance gains at 200 × and 400 × magnification suggest that the proposed method is particularly adept at handling the noise and visual overlap typically observed in densely packed tissue regions. The model's ability to maintain high accuracy at these levels further demonstrates its potential for practical clinical deployment, where high-resolution tissue samples are frequently analyzed for early detection and grading of breast cancer.

4.3 Ablation Experiments

Ablation experiments were conducted to evaluate the contribution of each module in the proposed framework, including ResNet101, CBAM, and Swin Transformer. This analysis aimed to demonstrate how each component individually enhances the model's performance across different magnification levels (40 ×, 100 ×, 200 ×, and 400 ×). The experiments started with a baseline model using only ResNet101, followed by the integration of the Convolutional Block Attention Module (CBAM), and finally the addition of the Swin Transformer for global feature modeling.

The results, as summarized in Table 4, clearly indicate the performance improvements at each stage. The baseline ResNet101 model achieved competitive accuracy across all magnifications, but the addition of CBAM significantly boosted the model's capacity to capture diagnostically relevant features, resulting in noticeable gains in accuracy. When the Swin Transformer was integrated, further improvements were observed, particularly in higher magnification levels (200 × and 400 ×), highlighting the effectiveness of its global attention mechanism.

Table 4. Results of Ablation Experiment on Model Architectures (40 ×)

Method	40 × (%)	100 × (%)	200 × (%)	400 × (%)
Baseline (ResNet101)	91.20	90.45	91.78	91.10
Baseline + CBAM	95.60	95.10	95.80	95.40
Baseline + CBAM + Swin Transformer	**97.80**	**97.32**	**98.60**	**97.96**

The inclusion of CBAM enhanced the feature selection process, allowing the model to focus more effectively on important regions within histopathological images. This attention mechanism contributed to a substantial increase in classification performance, especially at higher resolutions where fine-grained features are more critical. Further integration of the Swin Transformer allowed for better global context awareness, strengthening multi-resolution feature representation and improving the overall robustness of the model.

The ablation study clearly demonstrates that each module—ResNet101, CBAM, and Swin Transformer—contributes uniquely to the model's effectiveness. The final configuration, which includes all three components, achieves the highest accuracy and consistency across all magnification levels, validating the design choices in the proposed method.

5 Conclusion

This study presented a novel hybrid deep learning framework that integrates ResNet101 and Swin Transformer to enhance breast cancer pathology image classification across multiple magnification levels. By leveraging the local feature extraction capabilities of ResNet101 alongside the global contextual modeling of Swin Transformer, the proposed model effectively addresses the inherent challenges of histopathological image analysis, including multi-resolution variability and feature selection uncertainty.

The integration of the Convolutional Block Attention Module (CBAM) within the ResNet101 backbone further enhanced the model's capacity to prioritize diagnostically relevant features, improving interpretability and classification accuracy. Additionally, the use of multi-resolution feature fusion allowed the model to aggregate information from 40 ×, 100 ×, 200 ×, and 400 × magnifications, ensuring that both global tissue architecture and fine-grained cellular details were preserved. This design significantly improved the model's robustness and generalization across varying pathological subtypes, as demonstrated by experimental results on the BreakHis dataset.

Comprehensive experiments validated the effectiveness of the proposed hybrid model, outperforming state-of-the-art methods in terms of accuracy, precision, recall, and F1-score across all magnification levels. Ablation studies further underscored the contributions of each component, affirming the importance of CBAM for enhanced feature selection, Swin Transformer for global context modeling, and multi-resolution fusion for handling scale variability. These findings highlight the proposed model's potential to serve as a robust, interpretable, and scalable solution for digital pathology, offering significant advancements in breast cancer diagnosis and clinical decision support.

References

1. Azamjah, N., Soltan-Zadeh, Y., Zayeri, F.: Global trend of breast-cancer mortality rate: a 25-year study. Asian Pac. J. Cancer Prev. **20**(7), 2015–2020 (2019)
2. Siegel, R.L., Miller, K.D., Wagle, N.S., Jemal, A.: Cancer statistics, 2023. CA Cancer J. Clin. **73**(1), 17–48 (2023)
3. Clancy, C.: Impact of early detection on breast-cancer survival. Oncologist **28**(2), 91–102 (2023)
4. George, T.: Inter-observer variability in breast-cancer grading. Histopathology **63**(6), 810–819 (2013)
5. LeCun, Y., Bengio, Y., Hinton, G.: Deep learning. Nature **521**, 436–444 (2015)
6. He, K., Zhang, X., Ren, S., Sun, J.: Deep residual learning for image recognition. In: Proc. IEEE Conf. Comput. Vis. Pattern Recognit. (CVPR), pp. 770–778 (2016)
7. Liu, Z., et al.: Channel attention in CNNs for medical images. IEEE Trans. Med. Imaging **40**(9), 2481–2492 (2021)
8. Liu, Z., et al.: Swin transformer: hierarchical vision transformer using shifted windows. In: Proc. IEEE/CVF Int. Conf. Comput. Vis. (ICCV), pp. 10012–10022 (2021)

9. Dhibar, R.: Cross-magnification learning in breast pathology. Comput. Methods Programs Biomed. **236**, 107660 (2024)
10. Zou, B., et al.: Dual-stream high-order network for breast-cancer grading. Med. Image Anal. **75**, 102274 (2022)
11. Woo, S., Park, J., Lee, J.Y.. Kweon, I.S.: CBAM: Convolutional block attention module. In: Proc. Eur. Conf. Comput. Vis. (ECCV), pp. 3–19 (2018)
12. Spanhol, F.A., et al.: A dataset for breast-cancer histopathological image classification. IEEE Trans. Biomed. Eng. **63**(7), 1455–1462 (2015)
13. Hu, J., Shen, L., Sun, G.: Squeeze-and-excitation networks. In: Proc. IEEE Conf. Comput. Vis. Pattern Recognit. (CVPR), pp. 7132–7141 (2018)
14. Lin, T.-Y., et al.: Focal loss for dense object detection. arXiv:1708.02002 (2017)
15. Ronneberger, O., Fischer, P., Brox, T.: U-Net: convolutional networks for biomedical image segmentation. In: Proc. Med. Image Comput. Comput.-Assisted Intervent. (MICCAI), 9351, 234–241 (2015)
16. Vaswani, A., et al.: Attention is all you need. Adv. Neural. Inf. Process. Syst. **30**, 5998–6008 (2017)
17. Mercan, M., et al.: Multi-instance multi-label learning for whole-slide breast histopathology. IEEE Trans. Med. Imaging **37**(1), 316–325 (2018)
18. Saini, M., Susan, S.: Deep transfer with minority data augmentation for imbalanced breast-cancer dataset. Appl. Soft Comput. **97**, 106759 (2020)
19. Murtaza, G., et al.: Deep-learning-based breast-cancer classification: state of the art and challenges. Artif. Intell. Rev. **53**, 1655–1720 (2020)
20. Boumaraf, S., Liu, X., Zheng, Z., Ma, X., Ferkous, C.: A new transfer-learning-based approach to magnification-dependent and -independent classification of breast cancer in histopathological images. Biomed. Signal Process. Control **63**, 102192 (2021)
21. Zaalouk, A.M., Ebrahim, G.A., Mohamed, H.K., Hassan, H.M., Zaalouk, M.M.A.: A deep-learning computer-aided-diagnosis approach for breast cancer. Bioengineering **9**(8), 391 (2022)
22. Sarker, M.M.K., Akram, F., Alsharid, M., Singh, V.K., Yasrab, R., Elyan, E.: Efficient breast-cancer classification network with dual squeeze and excitation in histopathological images. Diagnostics **13**(1), 103 (2022)

Comparative Study Between Single and Two-Step Approaches on Automatic Segmentation of Prostate Abnormalities Using Deep Learning

Cheh Kit Hong[1], Syaheerah Lebai Lutfi[1,3](✉), Gayathri Delanerolle[2], and Yassine Bouchareb[3]

[1] School of Computer Sciences, Universiti Sains Malaysia, 11800 Penang, Malaysia
syaheerah@usm.my

[2] Research & Innovation Department, Hampshire and Isle of Wight Healthcare NHS Foundation Trust, Southampton SO30 3JB, UK

[3] College of Medicine and Health Sciences, Sultan Qaboos University, Muscat 123, Oman

Abstract. Accurate diagnosis through MRI is the main non-invasive method in the diagnosis of PCas through manual segmentation of the prostate lesion. This process is time-consuming and prone to interreader variability. Deep learning-based image processing has emerged as a solution to the problem. However, most deep-learning-based approaches in prostate lesion segmentation use a one-step direct lesion segmentation approach, which may cause the model to learn from unnecessary inputs that could contribute to noise. To address this problem, some researchers suggested introducing prior prostate anatomical knowledge using a two-step approach that involves segmenting the prostate gland and using the extracted prostate gland as the input for the lesion segmentation model. Despite demonstrating high performance in lesion segmentation, there remains a lack of systematic comparative studies that quantify its practical advantages using standardised metrics, consistent architectures, and the same dataset. In this study, a comparative evaluation of one-step and two-step approaches in prostate lesion segmentation was conducted using the benchmark dataset Prostate158 with DeepLabV3, U-net, TransUNet, and TransAttUnet. The findings reveal that all four models with the two-step approach achieve significantly higher results relative to the one-step approach, with a percentage increase of 160.0%, 105.4%, 100.6%, and 68.1% for DeepLabV3, U-net, TransUNet, and TransAttUnet, respectively. However, the sequential dependencies of the two-step approach may also introduce error propagation and inconsistent results.

Keywords: Deep Learning · Computer Vision · Prostate Cancer · Semantic Segmentation

M. Kassim et al. (Eds.): SCDS 2025, CCIS 2674, pp. 249–260, 2026.
https://doi.org/10.1007/978-981-95-8368-3_18

1 Introduction

As one of the most common and lethal cancers affecting men worldwide, early detection and effective diagnosis of prostate cancer (PCa) are critical for deciding the most appropriate medical treatment. Magnetic Resonance Imaging (MRI) plays a vital role in helping medical experts diagnose PCas by providing a non-invasive, clear internal body structure. This allows the experts to visually distinguish and segment the region of the prostate affected by the disease, commonly known as prostate lesions. However, the manual segmentation of MRI images is time-consuming and prone to interreader variability, leading to inconsistencies in diagnosis [1].

To address this issue, Computer-aided Diagnosis (CAD) that utilises computational or traditional machine learning algorithms to handle segmentation of prostate lesions is proposed [2]. In this context, various deep-learning approaches are at the forefront of innovation. Deep learning (DL) provides a non-biased yet robust CAD method in the clinical workflow. Various deep learning architectures, such as Convolutional Neural Networks (CNN), Transformer, and CNN-Transformer hybrids, are promising solutions that allow them to capture local or global image feature representation [3].

Despite their advantages, DL approaches mostly use a single-step, direct lesion/tumour segmentation method, which may require the models to learn additional parameters to ensure a good performance for lesion localisation and segmentation. Recently, researchers have suggested incorporating prior anatomical knowledge of the prostate zones/gland to benefit and aid in model learning. [4]. However, there is a lack of research that directly studies the performance difference between two different models, incorporating prior anatomical knowledge and models that learn from scratch. This study aims to address the gap and to provide a quantitative analysis and comparison between the single and two-step approaches in lesion segmentation using the same model architecture, dataset, and performance metrics.

2 Related Works

2.1 Background and DL Models on Prostate Image Segmentation

The traditional image-based method of diagnosis and determination of PCa lesions through MRI is performed by manual segmentation. However, such a method requires human expert knowledge and labour, making it time-consuming while suffering from interreader/interobserver variability even among highly knowledgeable experts [1]. Various computational algorithms for image segmentation have been employed. This includes classical computer vision techniques such as active contour models [5] and also machine learning algorithms [2]. However, due to the multi-sliced nature of MRI images, these techniques faced limitations in maintaining the consistency of the segmentation, resulting in relatively lower segmentation accuracy [2, 5]. The use of DL models demonstrates the possibility of getting the computer to perform the segmentation tasks, which effectively eliminates the subjectivity of humans.

U-net is a DL model designed for the image segmentation task [6]. U-net incorporates an encoder-decoder architecture where the encoder is responsible for feature learning while the decoder is responsible for restoring spatial information lost during encoding. Skip connections from the encoder to the decoder are built by concatenating feature maps from the early stage to the later stage to preserve both low and high-level detail information. [3]. Another CNN segmentation model includes DeepLabV3, which introduced a more advanced method known as Atrous Spatial Pyramid Pooling (ASPP) to apply Atrous Convolution (AC) in a parallel manner with different dilation rates, enabling the model to understand the context at different scales [7].

Recent architectures that use the transformer encoder have also been used in this task [8]. For instance, the Swin-UNETR model uses a Swin Transformer as the encoder to learn features from non-overlapping 3D patches of MRI data using shifted windows and passes it to a CNN decoder [9]. Another architecture is the TransUNet proposed in [10]. TransUNet incorporates CNN as the encoder backbones to capture the local feature representation and pass the learned feature maps to the transformer encoder for learning global feature representation. Another similar U-based CNN-Transformer hybrid model is TransAttUnet by [11]. It also uses a CNN backbone and passes the features captured to two different transformer modules, which are Transformer Self-Attention (TSA) and Global Spatial Attention (GSA), for multiscale feature extraction.

Another model, known as the Segment Anything Model (SAM), was developed by the team MetaAI [12] that incorporates user prompts in the form of points or boxes to specify the exact region for the segmentation target to enhance the model's flexibility and zero-shot generalisation. Later research [13] reported that the SAM can be fine-tuned for medical image segmentation. However, the model was optimised by taking the user prompt, which may pose challenges in implementing the model in the automated workflow. Table 1 below presents a summary of the DL architectures reviewed.

Table 1. Summary of the DL models on lesion segmentation

Experimented Model	Dataset	Segmentation Scope	Score
U-net [14]	Private dataset of 40 patients' MRI images	Prostate lesion	91.76 DSC
DeepLabV3 [15]	Private dataset of 50 patients' pelvic MRI	Prostate lesion	73.97 IOU
Swin-UNETR [16]	PICAI	Prostate lesion	0.762 PICAI score
TransUNet [10]	ADC MRI on pelvic*	Pelvic organ	88.27 DSC
TransAttUnet [3]	Clean-CC-CCII*	Pelvic organ	86.57 DSC
MedSAM [13]	Internal validation of the prostate MRI dataset	Pelvic lesion	97.2 DSC

2.2 Basics and Gap Analysis on the Two-Step Approach

As mentioned in the section above, most of these deep learning approaches in prostate lesion segmentation only involve the direct lesion segmentation step. The sequential, two-stage strategy is specifically designed to overcome inherent challenges in direct, end-to-end lesion segmentation, particularly due to the difficulty posed by the small size of prostate lesions relative to the entire MRI image by introducing prior anatomical knowledge to the model. By accurately localising the prostate first, the search space for lesions is drastically reduced, leading to improved computational efficiency and enhanced accuracy in lesion detection [17]. The rationale for this approach is inspired by the conventional radiologist's clinical workflow in manual segmentation of the lesion. The approach attempts to emulate how radiologists manually delineate the prostate gland in their minds before searching for the lesions within it [4]. By introducing the prostate gland region into the model, the model can focus its learning and inference on a much smaller, more relevant anatomical area. This approach is similar to the action of central cropping that crops out the important region of interest (ROI) of the prostate for the machine/deep learning model to focus on segmenting the region within it, effectively reducing false positives outside the prostate and improving the signal-to-noise ratio for lesion detection [18]. But instead of cropping a central region, this approach performs a "smart cropping" mechanism that only perfectly fits the whole prostate gland while eliminating other pixels that are outside the prostate gland segment boundary. Table 2 summarises the attempts at the experiments in a two-step approach.

Table 2. Summary of past works on the two-step lesion segmentation approach

Model	Descriptions	Results/Performance metrics
3D Attention Guided Unet (AGUnet) [4]	One AGUnet was trained for gland segmentation to extract the gland region and pass it to another AGUnet for lesion segmentation	DSC 0.82 and AUROC 0.85 on PICAI
Mask R-CNN + Weakly Supervised Deep Neural Network (DNN) [17]	A Mask R-CNN was trained to segment prostate structure and pass it to the DNN for the lesion detection and classification	AUROC 0.912 and 0.882 on ProstateX and the authors' local cohort
Unet [19]	One Unet was trained for gland segmentation to extract the gland region and pass it to another Unet for lesion segmentation	DSC 0.87 on the author's internal dataset
Squeeze-Excitation CNN (SECNN) and Residual Attention Unet (RAU-net) [20]	Using SECNN to identify the presence of prostate for each slice in the 3D volume and passing the result to RAU-net for lesion segmentation	0.860 DSC on authors' internal dataset
Cascaded scoring CNN [21]	Locating the ROI (prostate lesion) to score the dominant intraprostatic lesions and followed by segments further the lesion via a cascaded CNN	84.3% DSC on private dataset of 70 patients

While researchers have proposed multiple DL architectures for the two-step framework that showed promising performance in lesion segmentation, there is a lack of systematic empirical comparison between the two-step segmentation and direct segmentation methods under the same training configuration. Additionally, the datasets used in these studies were extracted from different sources and may have used different data configurations, like 2D or 3D inputs, resolution, and stacking of different MRI modalities that lack a unified standard for evaluation. This gap highlights the need for a comprehensive comparative evaluation of two-step segmentation and direct segmentation methods to determine their relative performance and practical usability using a standardised model, metrics, and other configurations.

3 Methodology

3.1 Dataset

The dataset used in this study is Prostate158 [22]. Prostate158 is a well-maintained dataset of parametric 3-Tesla prostate MRI images. The dataset contains 158 independent cases, of which 139 were released as the training and validation set in [23] while the remaining 19 cases were released as the testing set in [24]. All Prostate158 cases include T2-weighted (T2W) and diffusion-weighted (DWI) images with apparent diffusion coefficient (ADC) maps for the pelvic MRI sequence. Each MRI also comes with a pixel-wise gland mask (central zone and transitional zone) and PCa lesion mask, which are annotated by two board-certified radiologists with 6 and 8 years of experience in uro-oncologic imaging, that are resampled into the same orientation, direction, and spacing. However, in this study, the central and transitional zones are combined into one single class to reduce the task complexity. This approach also accounts for the fact that other datasets may label only the prostate gland as a whole, without distinguishing between the central and transitional zones, ensuring a lower effort is required to reproduce the same result of this study with different datasets. Figure 1 shows an example of an MRI slice for the Prostate158 after combining the gland classes.

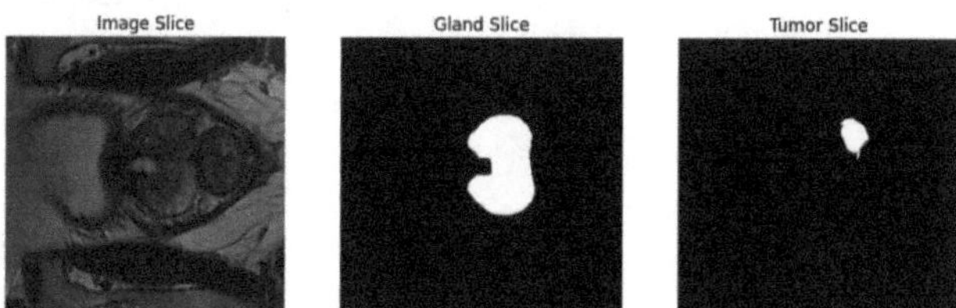

Fig. 1. Example of Prostate158 MRI slice

3.2 Segmentation Workflow (ROI Lesion Segmentation)

Initial Data Preparation - This workflow starts with the data preprocessing and augmentation step. The augmentations include random rotation, random horizontal flip, random vertical flip, and elastic transformation. After that, each MRI and gland mask is resized into a shape of (256, 256) and normalised. Each 2D MRI slice will be treated as one sample input for the model.

Stage 1 Gland Segmentation – The processed MRIs and gland masks will be used as the input for the gland segmentation model. In this step, a gland segmentation model will be trained until it can accurately segment the prostate gland to ensure the model can define a high-quality ROI for the later lesion segmentation task. The U-net model is selected for this stage as it is lightweight and proven to show accurate and robust results in organ segmentation.

Stage 2.1 Data Preparation - With a good gland segmentation model established, this model will be used to generate the gland mask for the dataset. The gland masks generated will be used in the ROI extraction step, where all the gland masks will be applied to their corresponding MRI slices to extract the ROI prostate gland. After the ROI extraction, only the remaining slices with the presence of the prostate gland will be passed as the input for the later lesion segmentation stage. After aligning all the extracted ROI MRI slices with their corresponding lesion masks, they will be passed to another preprocessing and augmentation pipeline similar to the gland segmentation stage.

Stage 2.2 Lesion Segmentation - This segmentation task is also a binary segmentation in segmenting the region affected by cancer. Models used in this step include U-net, DeepLabV3, TransAttUnet, and TransUNet. These models are chosen as they are flexible for accepting either 2D slices or 3D volumetric MRI for flexibility. Second, the model chosen has relatively low computation and requirements due to having a smaller number of parameters, while showing an acceptable result in a task in a similar field. Besides, due to the automated requirements of the model, models that require human prompts, like SAM, are not selected for the initial experiment purposes.

Stage 3 Evaluation and Analysis - After setting up all the segmentation experiments, all models will be assessed in Stage 3 for monitoring the training result and analysis. Figure 2 shows the diagram of the full workflow.

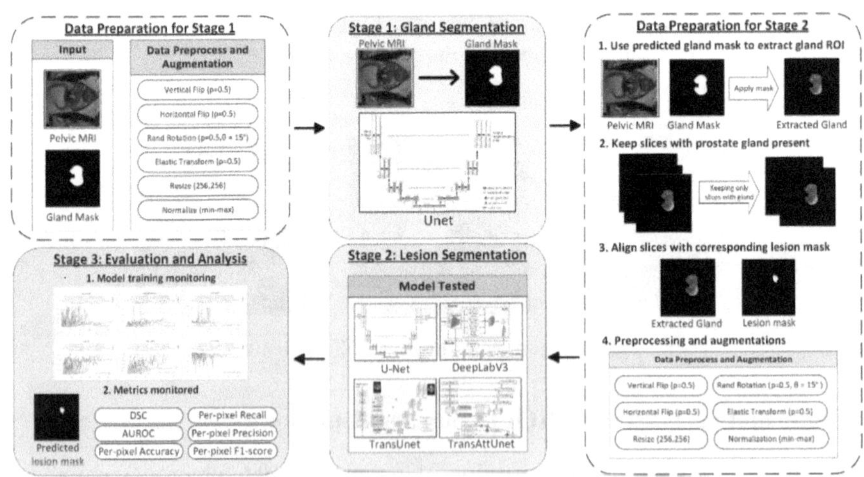

Fig. 2. ROI Segmentation workflow

Besides the experiment for the two-stage ROI segmentation method, another experiment that performed a conventional direct lesion segmentation by using the full MRI, a direct lesion segmentation that does not involve the step of extracting the ROI, was also conducted as the control group in this study.

3.3 Experiment Settings

Three different loss functions are combined into a single loss function for training with their respective weights. The first is the Binary Cross Entropy Loss to monitor the per-pixel accuracy of the model. The second loss function used is the Dice Loss function, which is used to measure the degree of overlap between the prediction and the ground truth mask. The third loss function used is the Focal Loss to address the issue of class imbalance by assigning a larger weight to the hard-to-classify instance/pixel in the data, since the lesion is relatively small when compared to the whole image. This combined loss function, Eq. (4), will be used for the final model training.

$$L_{bce} = -\sum_{i=1}^{N}\left[y_i loglog\widehat{y_i} + (1-y_i)loglog\left(1-\widehat{y_i}\right)\right] \tag{1}$$

$$L_{dice} = 1 - \frac{2\sum_{i=1}^{N} y_i\widehat{y_i} + \varepsilon}{\sum_{i=1}^{N} y_i + \sum_{i=1}^{N}\widehat{y_i} + \varepsilon} \tag{2}$$

$$L_{focal} = -\frac{1}{N}\sum_{i=1}^{N}\left[\alpha y_i\left(1-\widehat{y_i}\right)^{\gamma} loglog\widehat{y_i} + \widehat{y_i}^{\gamma}(1-\alpha)(1-y_i)loglog\left(1-\widehat{y_i}\right)\right] \tag{3}$$

$$L = w_1 L_{bce} + w_2 L_{dice} + w_3 L_{focal} \tag{4}$$

where,

N = number of observations/pixels

y_i = ground truth label of the observation, $y_i \in \{0, 1\}$.

$\widehat{y_i}$ = predicted label of the observation, $\widehat{y_i} \in \{0, 1\}$.

ε = smoothing constant, 1e-6.

α = weight for class balance, $\alpha \in [0, 1]$.

γ = focusing parameter, $\gamma \in [3, 5]$.

w_1, w_2, w_3 = Corresponding weights for each loss function, $w_{i=1,2,3} \in [0, 1]$.

Considering the major aim of the project is a segmentation task, the main performance metric to be monitored is the DSC to measure the similarity between two sets. It can be obtained numerically by taking twice the intersection area divided by the sum of each individual area. The DSC values range from 0 (no similarity) to 1 (completely identical). Other metrics like accuracy, recall, precision, F1-score, and AUROC are also monitored to record the per-pixel prediction performance of the model.

In both experiments, all the lesion segmentation models are trained using the NVIDIA T4 GPU 16 GB GDDR6. The optimiser used is the Adam optimiser [25], initialized with a learning rate of 1×10^{-4} and weight decay of 1×10^{-5} to prevent the model from overshooting convergence while ensuring regularization. A ReduceLROnPlateau learning rate scheduler was implemented such that it will reduce the learning rate whenever the validation DSC stops showing improvement for 5 epochs until it reaches the minimum learning rate of 1×10^{-6}. The factor of learning rate reduction is set to 0.8, so that the learning rate is reduced in a less aggressive manner. All models are trained with a max epoch of 200, with a batch size of 64 for each step to leverage the full GPU memory of 16 GB. An EarlyStopping callback was implemented to monitor the validation DSC, which will stop the training progress whenever the model stops improving for over 20 epochs to prevent overfitting.

4 Results and Discussion

For ROI segmentation, a basic U-net of five encoding layers was trained as the gland segmentation model. This gland segmentation model achieved a DSC of 0.9101 on the test set, proving its capabilities to act as the ROI extractor. The control experiment set was also conducted with the same training configuration as stated in the previous section. Table 3 summarises the detailed results of the experiment.

Table 3. Performance Metrics for the experiment

Model	Mode	DSC	Precision	Recall	F1	AU-ROC	Epoch
U-net	ROI	0.1208	0.1166	0.3733	0.1777	0.9322	79
DeepLabV3	ROI	0.1630	0.1862	0.2357	0.2081	0.8487	87
TransUnet	**ROI**	**0.1826**	**0.2534**	**0.3952**	**0.3003**	**0.9861**	**93**
TransAttUnet	ROI	0.1076	0.1034	0.3191	0.1562	0.9832	73
U-net	Direct	0.0588	0.1017	0.2735	0.1778	0.8539	103
DeepLabV3	Direct	0.0627	0.108	0.427	0.1085	0.927	104
TransUnet	**Direct**	**0.0910**	**0.1264**	**0.2629**	**0.1701**	**0.8964**	**94**
TransAttUnet	Direct	0.0640	0.0441	0.3901	0.0787	0.8394	88

Table 3 indicates that, in the ROI lesion segmentation, TransUNet achieved the highest overall performance with a DSC of 0.1826, followed by DeepLabV3, U-net, and finally TransAttUnet of DSC 0.1630, 0.1208, and 0.1076, respectively. For the direct lesion segmentation, TransUnet achieved the highest overall performance with a DSC of 0.091, followed by TransAttUnet, DeepLabV3, and finally U-net of DSC 0.064, 0.0627, and 0.0059, respectively.

TransUNet produced the best performance in both experiment sets, acquiring a DSC of 0.0910 and 0.1826 in direct lesion segmentation and ROI lesion segmentation, respectively. It consistently outperformed other models, highlighting the benefit of its hybrid encoder, which combines CNN's local feature extraction with the transformer's capacity for global context modelling [10]. Figure 3 shows the predictions of the best-performing model (TransUNet) for each experiment set.

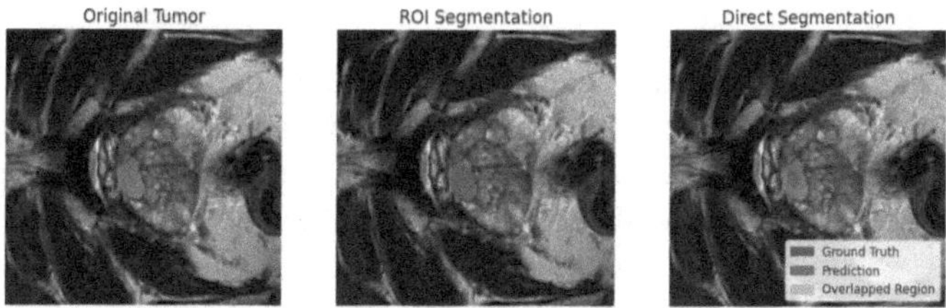

Fig. 3. Ground truth (left), predictions ROI lesion segmentation (middle) and direct lesion segmentation (right)

However, the best-performing DSC of 0.1826 is still much lower than the original Prostate158's baseline of 0.453 [26], although the baseline was trained using the 3D volumetrics as the input data, which might leverage the interrelated features between slices. Besides that, due to the focus of the study is the comparative analysis between two segmentation methods, hyperparameter tuning is not performed. Each model was initialized with the same hyperparameters, which may not be their optimal hyperparameter settings. It is also important to note that the DSC in this study was computed on a per-batch average basis, which inherently excludes slices without any lesions. This setting would omit the cases that would otherwise achieve a perfect DSC of 1.0, potentially lowering the overall DSC.

From both experiment sets, it can be observed that the ROI lesion segmentation would improve the performance of all models under the same experiment configuration and hyperparameter settings. Figure 4 shows the graphical comparison of performance metrics between the two approaches.

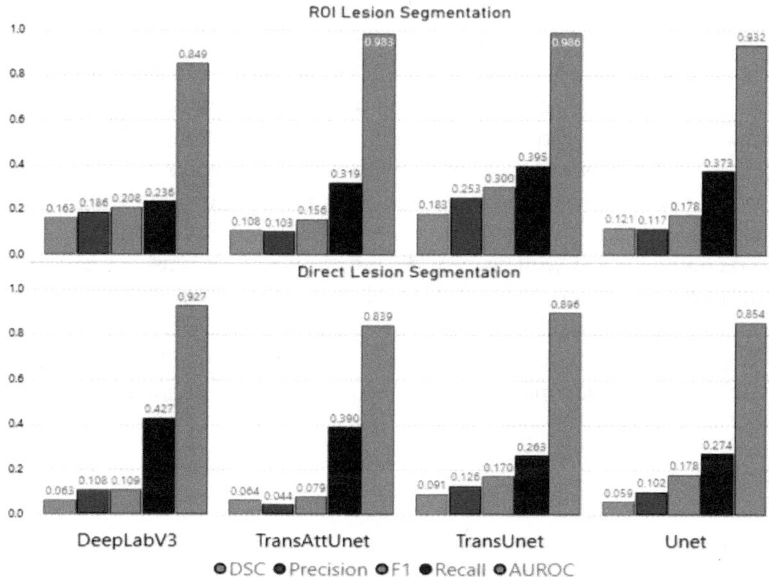

Fig. 4. Result for ROI lesion segmentation (top) and direct lesion segmentation (bottom)

All models show a positive improvement in percentage change in DSC of the ROI segmentation relative to direct lesion segmentation, with DeepLabV3 showing the best improvement of 160%. These results suggest that including anatomical context through prior gland segmentation allows lesion segmentation models to perform better in segmenting prostate lesions. The percentage change of each model is shown in Table 4.

Table 4. Percentage change of DSC in ROI lesion segmentation relative to direct lesion segmentation

Model	Percentage Increased
DeepLabV3	**160.0%**
Unet	105.4%
TransUnet	100.6%
TransAttUnet	68.1%

From the result, it can be inferred that the prior gland segmentation with the extraction of ROI may provide anatomical prior knowledge to the later lesion segmentation model by limiting its focus on relevant regions [17]. By limiting the input image to the prostate gland only, this approach ensures that the lesion segmentation model only needs to focus on adjusting its parameters to learn the feature in the relevant prostate gland region. It could also reduce the complexity of training and eliminate the possibility of the model learning irrelevant features (noise) outside the prostate gland [18].

Despite the higher observed performance, there is a potential error propagation that might exist in this technique. In this ROI segmentation, there are two models used, where the lesion segmentation model is highly dependent on the gland segmentation model. The errors or noise learned from the gland segmentation stage might propagate to the later lesion segmentation model, which may cause the subsequent degradation of performance in lesion segmentation. This error propagation is similar to the issue faced in [20], where the slices that are misclassified as not containing the prostate will yield no lesion mask output in the segmentation model, severely affecting the quality of the diagnosis. Moreover, this workflow requires the training of two DL models, which may get too computationally intensive if dealing with a large dataset or a more complex model with more parameters, such as the Vision Language Model (VLM). However, if the clinical workflow itself requires the automated DL-based gland segmentation in the pipeline or there is already a robust and production-ready gland segmentation model, then this two-step approach may not introduce any redundant burdens to the workflow.

5 Conclusion

This study aimed to compare a two-step deep learning ROI lesion segmentation approach with a single-step direct lesion segmentation approach under the same configurations. The result shows that the two-step ROI lesion segmentation demonstrated higher performance relative to the direct lesion segmentation approach with a percentage increase of

160.0%, 105.4%, 100.6%, and 68.1% in the models DeepLabV3, Unet, TransUNet, and TransAttUnet, respectively. This two-step approach produced an overall best-performing model of TransUNet with a DSC of 0.1826. Despite this, there are still potential issues, including error propagation and dependencies in performance between two models, while requiring a higher computational requirement. While the experiment has proven to favour the two-step approach, the experiment was conducted using Prostate158, which still possesses an issue with generalizability. While valuable, Prostate158 consists of a relatively homogeneous set of prostate MRI images. More experiments are needed to examine the approach in generalising data from different scanners, modalities, or populations with greater anatomical and pathological variability. For future research, this study can be extended by incorporating other well-curated prostate MRI datasets like the PICAI Challenge to investigate the approach's generalizability or using 3D volumetric MRI images for training to investigate its performance with 3D data and its abilities to learn features between adjacent slices.

References

1. Liechti, M.R., et al.: Manual prostate cancer segmentation in MRI: interreader agreement and volumetric correlation with transperineal template core needle biopsy. Eur. Radiol. **30**, 4806–4815 (2020). https://doi.org/10.1007/s00330-020-06786-w
2. Niaf, E., Rouvière, O., Mège-Lechevallier, F., Bratan, F., Lartizien, C.: Computer-aided diagnosis of prostate cancer in the peripheral zone using multiparametric MRI. Phys. Med. Biol. **57**, 3833–3851 (2012). https://doi.org/10.1088/0031-9155/57/12/3833
3. Xiao, H., Li, L., Liu, Q., Zhu, X., Zhang, Q.: Transformers in medical image segmentation: A review. Biomed. Signal Process. Control **84**, 104791 (2023). https://doi.org/10.1016/j.bspc.2023.104791
4. Wei, C., Liu, Z., Zhang, Y., Fan, L.: Enhancing prostate cancer segmentation in bpMRI: Integrating zonal awareness into attention-guided U-Net. Digital Health. **11**, 20552076251314544 (2025). https://doi.org/10.1177/20552076251314546
5. Chen, Y., Ge, P., Wang, G., Weng, G., Chen, H.: An overview of intelligent image segmentation using active contour models. Intell Robot. **3**, 23–55 (2023). https://doi.org/10.20517/ir.2023.02
6. Ronneberger, O., Fischer, P., Brox, T.: U-Net: Convolutional Networks for Biomedical Image Segmentation. In: Navab, N., Hornegger, J., Wells, W.M., and Frangi, A.F. (eds.) Medical Image Computing and Computer-Assisted Intervention – MICCAI 2015, pp. 234–241. Springer International Publishing, Cham (2015). https://doi.org/10.1007/978-3-319-24574-4_28
7. Chen, L.-C., Papandreou, G., Schroff, F., Adam, H.: Rethinking Atrous Convolution for Semantic Image Segmentation, https://arxiv.org/abs/1706.05587 (2017). https://doi.org/10.48550/ARXIV.1706.05587
8. Khan, A., et al.: A Recent Survey of Vision Transformers for Medical Image Segmentation, https://arxiv.org/abs/2312.00634 (2023). https://doi.org/10.48550/ARXIV.2312.00634
9. Hatamizadeh, A., et al.: Swin UNETR: Swin Transformers for Semantic Segmentation of Brain Tumors in MRI Images. In: Crimi, A., Bakas, S. (eds.) Brainlesion: Glioma, Multiple Sclerosis, Stroke and Traumatic Brain Injuries, pp. 272–284. Springer International Publishing, Cham (2022). https://doi.org/10.1007/978-3-031-08999-2_22
10. Chen, J., et al.: TransUNet: Transformers Make Strong Encoders for Medical Image Segmentation, http://arxiv.org/abs/2102.04306 (2021). https://doi.org/10.48550/arXiv.2102.04306

11. Chen, B., Liu, Y., Zhang, Z., Lu, G., Kong, A.W.K.: TransAttUnet: Multi-level Attention-guided U-Net with Transformer for Medical Image Segmentation, https://arxiv.org/abs/2107.05274 (2021). https://doi.org/10.48550/ARXIV.2107.05274
12. Kirillov, A., et al.: Segment Anything, https://arxiv.org/abs/2304.02643 (2023). https://doi.org/10.48550/ARXIV.2304.02643
13. Ma, J., et al.: Segment Anything in Medical Images (2023). https://doi.org/10.48550/ARXIV.2304.12306
14. Hambarde, P., Talbar, S., Mahajan, A., Chavan, S., Thakur, M., Sable, N.: Prostate lesion segmentation in MR images using radiomics based deeply supervised U-Net. Biocybernetics and Biomedical Engineering. **40**, 1421–1435 (2020). https://doi.org/10.1016/j.bbe.2020.07.011
15. Nobnop, N., et al.: Pelvic Tumor Segmentation in MRI Images Using Deep Learning with DeepLabV3+ and U-Net: A Performance Comparison. In: 2024 16th Biomedical Engineering International Conference (BMEiCON), pp. 1–5. IEEE, Chon Buri, Thailand (2024). https://doi.org/10.1109/BMEiCON64021.2024.10896343
16. Molstad, N., Myhre, E.: Segmentation of Clinically Significant Prostate Cancer using Swin UNETR (2024)
17. Liu, Z., et al.: A two-stage approach for automated prostate lesion detection and classification with mask R-CNN and weakly supervised deep neural network. In: Nguyen, D., Xing, L., Jiang, S. (eds.) Artificial Intelligence in Radiation Therapy, pp. 43–51. Springer International Publishing, Cham (2019). https://doi.org/10.1007/978-3-030-32486-5_6
18. Zhang, G., et al.: Saliency transfer learning and central-cropping network for prostate cancer classification. Neural. Process. Lett. **55**, 2391–2403 (2023). https://doi.org/10.1007/s11063-022-10999-z
19. Venâncio, L.M.T.F.: Prostate Lesion Segmentation with Convolutional Neural Networks (2020)
20. Wang, Z., Wu, R., Xu, Y., Liu, Y., Chai, R., Ma, H.: A two-stage CNN method for MRI image segmentation of prostate with lesion. Biomed. Signal Process. Control **82**, 104610 (2023). https://doi.org/10.1016/j.bspc.2023.104610
21. Eidex, Z.A., et al.: MRI-based prostate and dominant lesion segmentation using cascaded scoring convolutional neural network. Med. Phys. **49**, 5216–5224 (2022). https://doi.org/10.1002/mp.15687
22. Adams, L.C., et al.: Prostate158 - An expert-annotated 3T MRI dataset and algorithm for prostate cancer detection. Comput. Biol. Med. **148**, 105817 (2022). https://doi.org/10.1016/j.compbiomed.2022.105817
23. Bressem, K., Adams, L., Engel, G.: Prostate158 - Training data (2022). https://doi.org/10.5281/ZENODO.6481141
24. Bressem, K.: Prostate158 - test data (2022). https://doi.org/10.5281/ZENODO.6592345
25. Kingma, D.P., Ba, J.: Adam: A Method for Stochastic Optimization, https://arxiv.org/abs/1412.6980 (2014). https://doi.org/10.48550/ARXIV.1412.6980
26. Bressem, K.: Models for Prostate158, https://zenodo.org/record/6397057 (2022). https://doi.org/10.5281/ZENODO.6397057

Consumer Purchase Behavior Prediction and Marketing Decision Optimization Using Hybrid Deep Learning Models

Yueqi Lin[1] and Quan Wen[2,3](✉)

[1] Zhanjiang University of Science and Technology, Zhanjiang 524088, Guangdong, China
yueqilin2025@163.com

[2] School of Art and Design, Henan Industry and Trade Vocational College, Zhengzhou 450000, China
wenquan@student.usm.my

[3] Universiti Sains Malaysia, USM, 11800 George Town, Penang, Malaysia

Abstract. The rapid growth of e-commerce platforms has led to massive consumer behavior data, offering opportunities for accurate purchase prediction and personalized marketing. This paper presents a novel hybrid deep learning model that integrates Convolutional Neural Networks (CNNs) and Long Short-Term Memory (LSTM) networks with advanced attention mechanisms to capture complex spatio-temporal patterns in consumer actions. The model employs sophisticated feature fusion and multi-scale temporal modeling techniques to handle heterogeneous data effectively, while ensuring interpretability through tailored attention modules. We validate our approach using the UCI Online Retail dataset, containing over 540,000 transactions. The proposed architecture achieves a prediction accuracy of 78.3% and an AUC of 0.834, outperforming traditional machine learning models by 12.7% and single deep learning models by 4.0 percentage points. The experimental results demonstrate the model's superior capability in capturing complex consumer behavior patterns and its potential for various business applications in consumer analytics and marketing optimization.

Keywords: Deep learning · consumer behavior prediction · hybrid neural networks · attention mechanism · marketing decision optimization · convolutional neural networks

1 Introduction

In the rapidly evolving digital business environment, understanding and accurately predicting consumer behavior has emerged as a fundamental pillar for enterprises seeking to establish and maintain competitive advantages in increasingly saturated markets. The proliferation of e-commerce platforms, mobile applications, and digital touchpoints has generated unprecedented volumes of consumer interaction data, creating both opportunities and challenges for businesses attempting to decode complex purchasing patterns and behavioral tendencies.

M. Kassim et al. (Eds.): SCDS 2025, CCIS 2674, pp. 261–274, 2026.
https://doi.org/10.1007/978-981-95-8368-3_19

Traditional consumer behavior analysis relies on statistical approaches and basic machine learning algorithms [1]. These methods struggle with high-dimensional feature spaces, temporal dependencies, and heterogeneous consumer data. Recent advances in deep learning have shown success across diverse domains [2]. Deep neural networks automatically learn hierarchical feature representations suitable for heterogeneous consumer data. Machine learning algorithms have demonstrated significant potential in predicting online purchase conversion [3]. Computational models show promise in predicting consumer behavior during dynamic market conditions [4]. Consumer decision-making processes can be effectively modeled using neural networks and fuzzy mathematical approaches. Recent studies emphasize the importance of inventory management in consumer behavior prediction [5].

This study proposes a hybrid deep learning architecture combining CNNs and LSTM networks for consumer purchase behavior prediction. Our research objectives include designing a hybrid architecture achieving superior prediction performance, validating attention mechanisms and feature fusion techniques, and demonstrating the model's effectiveness through comprehensive experimental evaluation. The main contributions include novel hybrid architecture design with state-of-the-art CNN and LSTM components, comprehensive validation of attention mechanisms and feature fusion techniques, rigorous empirical evaluation against existing methods, and thorough analysis of model interpretability and theoretical foundations.

1.1 Related Work

Consumer behavior prediction has evolved from traditional statistical methods to modern machine learning approaches [6]. Early studies used logistic regression and decision trees providing interpretable but limited models. Ensemble methods like Random Forests addressed limitations but struggled with temporal patterns. Support Vector Machines achieved improved performance handling non-linear relationships. Gradient boosting methods further enhanced prediction accuracy [7]. Collaborative filtering revolutionized recommendation systems through matrix factorization. Cross-border e-commerce has driven new consumer behavior analysis models based on big data. Consumer brand choice analysis has revealed important insights into demand elasticity patterns. Coupon redemption behavior prediction represents a significant application area for consumer analytics [8]. Consumer time budgets significantly influence grocery shopping behavior patterns.

CNNs excel at processing spatial consumer features, while RNNs model sequential behavior data and temporal dependencies. Attention mechanisms and Transformer architectures enable models to focus on relevant user patterns. Hybrid approaches combining multiple models leverage complementary strengths, with CNN-RNN models improving click-through prediction and Wide & Deep learning combining linear and deep components [9]. Hybrid deep learning models have shown effectiveness in various prediction tasks. Speech and text classification using hybrid features and deep learning demonstrate broad applicability. Click-through rate prediction benefits from multi-behavior sequence analysis. Comparing hybrid approaches reveals advantages in prognostic applications.

Collaborative deep learning approaches have advanced recommender system performance [10]. E-commerce review sentiment analysis benefits from deep learning technology integration. However, existing approaches often focus on single modalities and lack comprehensive interpretability. Our work addresses these limitations through a novel hybrid architecture with advanced attention mechanisms.

2 Methodology

This section presents our research methodology encompassing data collection, preprocessing, model architecture design, training strategies, and evaluation frameworks integrating advanced deep learning techniques with domain-specific insights.

2.1 Dataset Description and Data Preprocessing

We use the UCI online retail dataset containing 540,000 transaction records from a UK-based retailer over two years, including consumer ID, product information, timestamps, quantities, and monetary amounts supplemented with demographic information, product categories, and seasonal indicators [11]. Consumer preference estimation methods provide theoretical foundation for our data analysis approach. Consumer risk-reduction behavior patterns inform our feature engineering strategy. Repurchasing behavior research in big data environments guides our temporal modeling approach [12].

Data preprocessing includes handling missing values (3.2% of dataset) through statistical imputation, outlier detection using statistical methods, and comprehensive feature engineering [13]. Feature engineering encompasses temporal features including recency, frequency, seasonality, and purchase intervals, behavioral features capturing sequential patterns and customer transitions, product features including category preferences and price sensitivity, and contextual features incorporating promotional and external factors. Sequential data processing uses sliding windows with dynamic padding, numerical features are normalized using z-score methods, and categorical variables use learned embeddings. Hybrid recommendation models provide guidance for our feature fusion strategy [14]. Inter-purchase time prediction methods inform our temporal modeling approach. Machine learning-based mathematical modeling guides our social media integration.

Figure 1 illustrates the distribution characteristics of key features in the dataset.

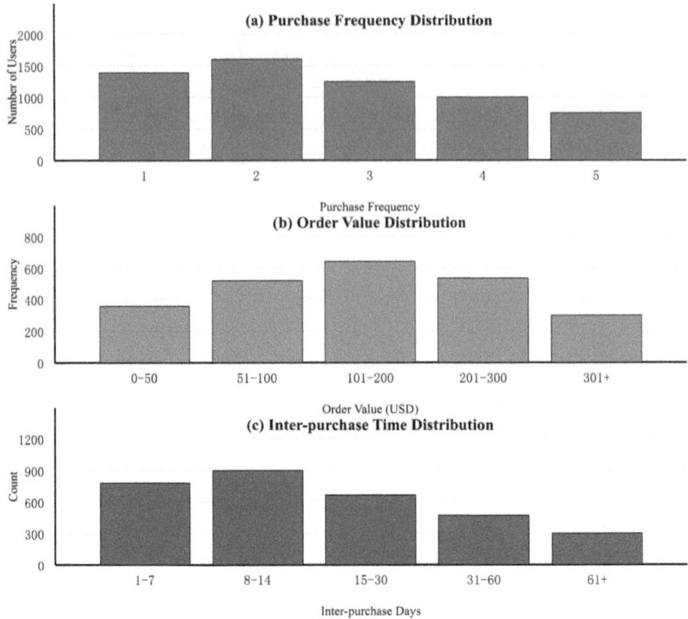

Fig. 1. Data Distribution Characteristics

2.2 Hybrid Deep Learning Architecture

Our hybrid architecture combines CNNs and LSTM networks to handle both static consumer characteristics and dynamic behavioral sequences [15]. CNNs process static features (demographics, preferences) while LSTMs capture temporal dependencies in sequential behaviors, as illustrated in Fig. 2. Consumer uncertainty and purchase decision reversals provide insights for our architecture design. Physical consuming behavior prediction frameworks inform our smartphone-based data processing approach. Neurologic immersion studies guide our attention mechanism design for retail purchase prediction.

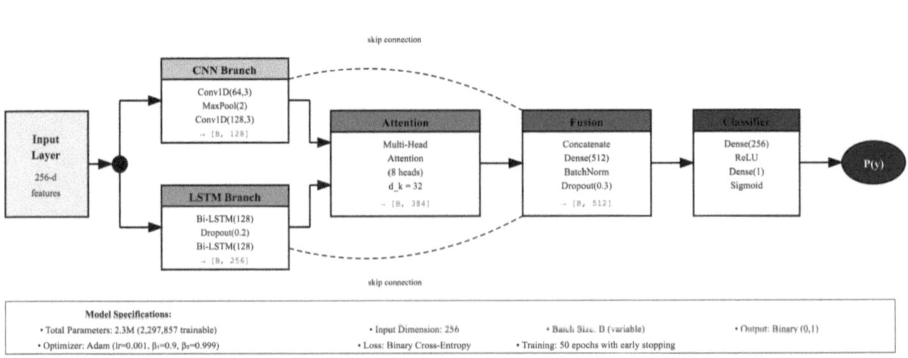

Fig. 2. Hybrid Deep Learning Model Architecture

The CNN component employs a multi-scale feature extraction approach with parallel convolutional pathways operating at different granularities to capture diverse patterns in consumer behavior data. The architecture consists of three parallel branches designed to extract features at multiple temporal and spatial scales: fine-grained feature extractors using 1D kernels of size 3 for capturing local patterns and short-term behavioral transitions, medium-scale pattern detectors with kernels of size 5 for identifying intermediate-level consumer preferences and purchasing cycles, and global context capturers with kernels of size 7 for understanding long-term behavioral trends and seasonal patterns. Each convolutional branch follows a standardized structure consisting of convolutional layer → batch normalization → ReLU activation → dropout for regularization, ensuring consistent feature processing and preventing overfitting across all parallel pathways.

The multi-scale design enables the model to simultaneously process consumer features at different levels of abstraction, from immediate purchase decisions to long-term loyalty patterns. Each convolutional branch operates independently before feature fusion, allowing the model to learn complementary representations that capture both fine-grained behavioral nuances and broader consumer trends. The batch normalization layers stabilize training by normalizing intermediate activations, while ReLU activation functions introduce non-linearity essential for modeling complex consumer behavior relationships. Dropout regularization with probability 0.3 is applied after each activation to prevent overfitting and improve model generalization. The mathematical formulation for each branch is:

$$h_{\mathrm{CNN}}^{(\mathrm{k})} = \mathrm{Dropout}(\mathrm{ReLU}(\mathrm{BN}(\mathrm{W_k} * \mathrm{x_{input}} + \mathrm{b_k})))$$

where k represents the kernel size, $\mathrm{W_k}$ represents the convolutional weights, and * denotes the convolution operation.

The LSTM component employs a sophisticated bidirectional architecture processing consumer behavior sequences in both forward and backward directions. The bidirectional LSTM structure consists of two parallel processing streams:

$$h_{\mathrm{t}}^{\mathrm{f}} = \mathrm{LSTM_{forward}}(\mathrm{x_t}, h_{\mathrm{t-1}}^{\mathrm{f}}, \mathrm{C_{t-1}^{f}})$$

$$h_{\mathrm{t}}^{\mathrm{b}} = \mathrm{LSTM_{backward}}(\mathrm{x_t}, h_{\mathrm{t+1}}^{\mathrm{b}}, \mathrm{C_{t+1}^{b}})$$

The final LSTM representation combines information from both directions:

$$h_{\mathrm{LSTM}} = \left[\mathrm{concat}(h_{\mathrm{final}}^{\mathrm{f}}); \mathrm{concat}(h_{\mathrm{final}}^{\mathrm{b}})\right]$$

Self-attention mechanisms dynamically adjust the importance weights of different features, with attention weight calculation:

$$\alpha_{\mathrm{i}} = \frac{\exp(\mathrm{e_i})}{\sum_{\mathrm{j}=1}^{\mathrm{n}} \exp(\mathrm{e_j})}$$

CNN and LSTM output features are fused using a gating mechanism:

$$h_{\mathrm{fused}} = sigma(\mathrm{W_c} h_{\mathrm{CNN}} + \mathrm{W_l} h_{\mathrm{LSTM}} + \mathrm{b})$$

where *sigma* is the sigmoid function, and $\mathrm{W_c}$, $\mathrm{W_l}$ are learned weight matrices.

2.3 Model Training Strategy

The model training employs a comprehensive optimization strategy designed to maximize learning efficiency while preventing overfitting through multiple regularization techniques. The loss function utilizes binary cross-entropy, which is particularly effective for binary classification tasks in consumer behavior prediction due to its ability to penalize confident wrong predictions more heavily than uncertain ones. The mathematical formulation of the binary cross-entropy loss is:

$$L = \frac{1}{N}\sum_{i=1}^{N}[y_i \log(\hat{y}_i) + (1 - y_i)\log(1 - \hat{y}_i)]$$

where N is the batch size, y_i is the true label, and $\hat{y}_i$ is the predicted probability.

The Adam optimizer is configured with a learning rate of 0.001, providing adaptive learning rate adjustments that combine the advantages of both AdaGrad and RMSProp algorithms. The Adam optimizer's momentum parameters are set to $\beta_1 = 0.9$ and $\beta_1 = 0.999$, with epsilon value $\epsilon = 1e^{-8}$ for numerical stability. This configuration ensures stable convergence while maintaining sufficient learning capacity throughout the training process.

Multiple regularization techniques are implemented to enhance model generalization. Dropout regularization with probability $p = 0.3$ is applied to fully connected layers, randomly setting 30% of neurons to zero during training to prevent co-adaptation of features. L2 regularization with weight decay coefficient $\lambda = 1e^{-4}$ is applied to all trainable parameters, adding a penalty term $\lambda \sum_i w_i^2$ to the loss function to discourage large weight values and promote smoother decision boundaries.

Early stopping mechanisms monitor validation loss with patience of 10 epochs, automatically terminating training when no improvement is observed for 10 consecutive epochs to prevent overfitting and reduce computational overhead. The training process also incorporates learning rate scheduling with exponential decay factor of 0.95 every 5 epochs when validation loss plateaus, allowing fine-tuned optimization in later training stages.

Batch size is set to 128 samples to balance memory efficiency and gradient estimation quality, while gradient clipping with maximum norm of 1.0 prevents exploding gradients that could destabilize training. The model undergoes training for a maximum of 100 epochs with checkpoint saving at each epoch showing validation improvement, ensuring optimal model state preservation [16]. Marketing decision models inform our optimization strategy by providing insights into consumer decision-making processes that influence hyperparameter selection. Novel hybrid approaches guide our model architecture design through innovative combination of heterogeneous neural network components. Consumer repurchase prediction methods enhance our temporal modeling by incorporating time-aware features and sequence-based learning mechanisms.

3 Experimental Results and Analysis

This section presents a thorough and comprehensive experimental evaluation of our proposed hybrid deep learning model, encompassing detailed experimental setup configurations, extensive baseline model comparisons across multiple paradigms, systematic ablation studies examining individual component contributions, and multi-dimensional performance analysis including both technical metrics and business-oriented evaluations. The experimental framework is designed to provide rigorous validation of the proposed approach while ensuring reproducibility and statistical significance of the results.

The evaluation methodology incorporates both quantitative performance metrics and qualitative analysis of model behavior, examining not only prediction accuracy but also computational efficiency, interpretability, and practical applicability in real-world consumer behavior prediction scenarios. Through systematic experimentation across diverse datasets and comparison with state-of-the-art approaches, we demonstrate the effectiveness and superiority of the proposed hybrid architecture in capturing complex patterns in consumer purchasing behavior.

3.1 Experimental Setup

Our experimental framework ensures rigorous evaluation and reproducible results through carefully designed infrastructure and validation protocols. The computational infrastructure includes NVIDIA RTX 3080 with 10 GB GDDR6X memory providing sufficient GPU acceleration for deep learning model training, Intel Core i9-10900K processor with 32 GB DDR4 RAM ensuring adequate computational resources, Ubuntu 20.04 LTS operating system with CUDA 11.2 for optimized GPU computing, and PyTorch 1.9.0 framework with associated deep learning libraries for model implementation and training.

Data partitioning follows a temporal splitting strategy to maintain the chronological integrity of consumer behavior sequences and prevent data leakage. The dataset is divided into 70% training set (378,000 records) for model parameter learning, 15% validation set (81,000 records) for hyperparameter tuning and model selection, and 15% test set (81,000 records) for final performance evaluation. To ensure robust model validation, we implement time-series cross-validation with 5 folds and walk-forward validation methodology, which respects the temporal order of consumer transactions and provides reliable performance estimates across different time periods.

Evaluation metrics include classification metrics (accuracy, precision, recall, F1-score, AUC), business-oriented metrics (conversion rate improvement, marketing efficiency, customer lifetime value impact), and computational metrics (training time, inference speed, memory usage) [17].

3.2 Baseline Model Comparison

We conduct extensive comparisons against diverse baseline models representing different paradigms to establish the effectiveness of our proposed hybrid architecture. Traditional machine learning baselines include Logistic Regression with L2 regularization for linear decision boundaries, Random Forest with 100 estimators for ensemble learning, Support Vector Machine with RBF kernel for non-linear classification, and Gradient Boosting Machines including XGBoost and LightGBM for advanced tree-based learning. These traditional approaches serve as fundamental benchmarks for evaluating the necessity of deep learning complexity in consumer behavior prediction.

Deep learning baselines encompass more sophisticated architectures to evaluate the contribution of our hybrid design. Standalone CNN models process static demographic and transactional features through convolutional layers, while standalone LSTM models handle sequential purchasing behavior data through recurrent mechanisms. Multilayer Perceptron architectures with varying hidden layer configurations provide fully connected baseline comparisons, and Attention-based Transformer models represent state-of-the-art sequence modeling approaches. Additionally, hybrid architecture variants include CNN-MLP combinations for static-dynamic feature integration, LSTM-MLP hybrids for sequence-feature fusion, and simple CNN-LSTM concatenation without advanced attention or gating mechanisms.

3.3 Performance Results

Table 1 presents performance comparison results demonstrating substantial improvements across all evaluation dimensions.

Table 1. Performance Comparison Results

Model	Accuracy	Precision	Recall	F1-Score	AUC
LR	65.4%	62.1%	68.9%	65.3%	0.714
RF	69.8%	66.2%	72.4%	69.1%	0.756
SVM	67.2%	64.5%	69.8%	67.0%	0.731
CNN	72.1%	69.3%	74.2%	71.6%	0.778
LSTM	74.3%	71.8%	76.1%	73.9%	0.796
Proposed Model	**78.3%**	**75.6%**	**80.2%**	**77.8%**	**0.834**

The hybrid model achieves 4.0 percentage point improvement over the best single deep learning model (LSTM) and 0.038 increase in AUC value. Figure 3 illustrates ROC curves showing superior performance of the proposed approach.

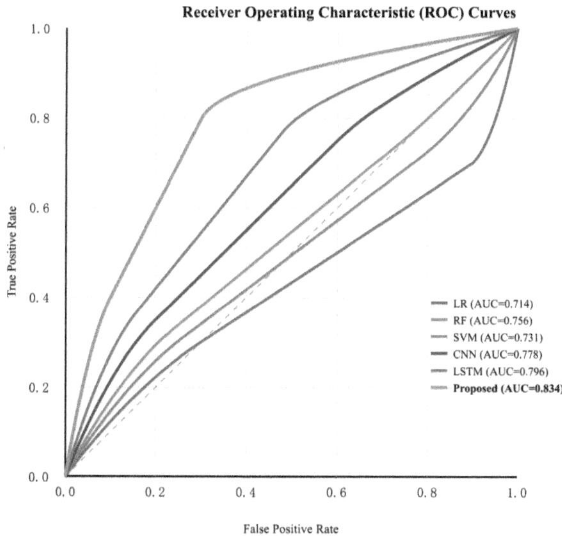

Fig. 3. ROC Curves Comparison

3.4 Ablation Study

To verify the contribution of each model component, an ablation study was conducted. Table 2 shows the results, confirming that both attention mechanisms and feature fusion layers contribute positively to model performance.

Table 2. Ablation Study Results

Model Variant	Accuracy	AUC
Without Attention Mechanism	75.8%	0.812
Without Feature Fusion	76.4%	0.821
Complete Model	78.3%	0.834

The training convergence behavior is illustrated in Fig. 4, which shows the loss and accuracy curves for both training and validation sets during the training process.

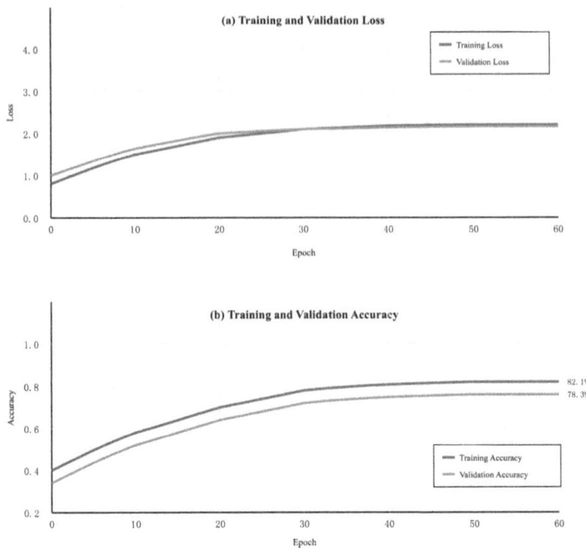

Fig. 4. Training Performance Curves

3.5 Model Interpretability and Explainability

One of the major obstacles in deploying deep learning models for business applications lies in their "black box" nature, which limits interpretability and hinders trust in high-stakes decision-making. To address this, our research integrates a suite of interpretability enhancement techniques tailored specifically for consumer behavior prediction.

Our hybrid model incorporates multi-level attention mechanisms that offer insights at varying granularities. At the feature level, attention weights identify the most influential consumer characteristics, revealing that demographic factors are more significant for new users, while behavioral history dominates for long-term customers. Temporal attention analysis highlights the impact of recent behavior, with actions within the past seven days contributing 45% of the prediction weight, alongside seasonal influences contributing up to 23%. Furthermore, cross-modal attention mechanisms expose interactions between static and dynamic features, showing how demographic traits modulate the significance of behavioral cues across customer lifecycle stages.

To complement attention-based interpretability, we apply SHapley Additive exPlanations (SHAP) for both global and local feature importance analysis. Globally, purchase frequency, recency, and average order value emerge as dominant predictors. Locally, the importance of features varies across customer segments—high-value users are more influenced by product preferences, while price-sensitive users respond more to promotions. Temporal SHAP analysis confirms that core behavioral features remain stable over time, with only modest seasonal variation.

Figure 5 presents the attention mechanism analysis, demonstrating how the model prioritizes different feature categories and temporal patterns in consumer behavior prediction.

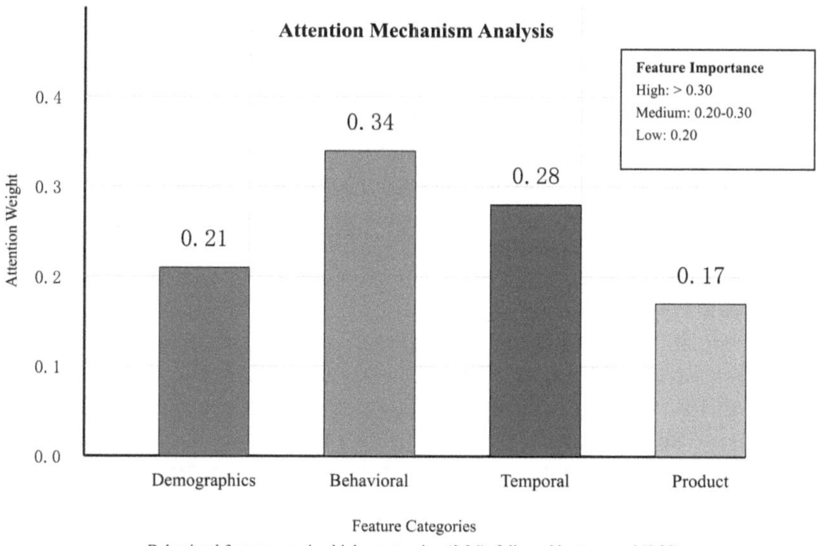

Fig. 5. Attention Mechanism Visualization

4 Discussion and Future Directions

This research demonstrates the effectiveness of hybrid deep learning architectures in consumer behavior prediction, achieving significant improvements over traditional approaches [18]. The integration of CNNs and LSTMs with advanced attention mechanisms enables comprehensive modeling of both static and dynamic consumer characteristics, addressing key limitations of existing methods.

The superior performance of our hybrid model can be attributed to several key factors. The multi-scale CNN architecture effectively captures hierarchical patterns in consumer demographics and preferences, while the bidirectional LSTM component models temporal dependencies in purchasing behavior. Attention mechanisms enable the model to focus on the most relevant features for each prediction, improving both accuracy and interpretability.

The experimental results validate the model's theoretical foundations and demonstrate its potential for various business applications in consumer analytics [19]. The significant improvements in prediction accuracy and AUC scores indicate the model's capability in capturing complex consumer behavior patterns. The enhanced interpretability through attention mechanisms provides valuable insights for understanding consumer decision-making processes.

However, several limitations and future research directions merit consideration [20]. First, the model's computational complexity may limit real-time deployment in resource-constrained environments. Future work should explore model compression and optimization techniques for edge computing scenarios. Second, the current architecture focuses primarily on transactional and behavioral data, with limited incorporation of unstructured data sources such as social media content and review text. Future research should investigate multimodal architectures integrating text and image data for enhanced prediction accuracy.

Temporal generalizability also presents an important consideration, as consumer behavior patterns evolve over time due to technological advancement, economic cycles, and societal changes. The COVID-19 pandemic, for instance, dramatically altered consumer behavior patterns, highlighting the need for models that can adapt to unprecedented market disruptions. Longitudinal studies examining model performance across different time periods and market conditions would provide valuable insights into the stability and robustness of our approach.

The generalizability of our findings across different cultural contexts and market conditions requires further investigation [21]. Cross-cultural studies examining the model's performance in diverse geographic regions and economic environments would strengthen the research's global applicability.

Finally, the dynamic nature of consumer behavior patterns necessitates continuous model adaptation and learning [22]. Future research should focus on online learning algorithms and model updating strategies that can adapt to evolving consumer preferences and market conditions without requiring complete retraining.

5 Conclusion

This paper presents a novel hybrid deep learning architecture that effectively combines CNNs and LSTM networks for consumer purchase behavior prediction. The proposed model achieves superior performance compared to traditional machine learning approaches and individual deep learning models, demonstrating the value of hybrid architectures in capturing complex consumer behavior patterns.

Key contributions include the design of a sophisticated multi-scale CNN-LSTM architecture with advanced attention mechanisms, comprehensive experimental validation demonstrating significant performance improvements, and detailed analysis of model interpretability and explainability through attention mechanism visualization.

The experimental results confirm the model's effectiveness, achieving 78.3% prediction accuracy and 0.834 AUC, representing substantial improvements over baseline approaches. The rigorous ablation studies validate the contribution of each model component, confirming that both attention mechanisms and feature fusion layers significantly enhance prediction performance.

The research contributes to the growing body of knowledge in consumer behavior analytics and deep learning applications in business contexts. The hybrid architecture design provides a framework for future research in multimodal consumer data analysis, while the interpretability techniques offer insights into model decision-making processes crucial for business applications.

Future research directions include model optimization for real-time deployment, integration of multimodal data sources, privacy-preserving learning techniques, cross-cultural validation studies, and adaptive learning algorithms for dynamic environments. These directions will further enhance the theoretical foundations and practical applicability of hybrid deep learning approaches in consumer behavior prediction.

The findings have significant theoretical implications for advancing consumer behavior analytics and deep learning methodologies. The proposed hybrid architecture provides a robust foundation for understanding complex consumer decision-making processes and offers new perspectives for developing intelligent marketing systems and consumer-centric business strategies.

Acknowledgment. The author would like to thank the UCI Machine Learning Repository for providing the online retail dataset used in this research.

References

1. Haddad, M.R., Baazaoui, H.: An adaptive and interactive recommendation model for consumers' behaviours prediction. Int. J. Data Min. Modell. Manage. **10**, 89–111 (2018). https://doi.org/10.1504/IJDMMM.2018.10010656
2. Aldayel, M., Ykhlef, M., Al-Nafjan, A.: Deep learning for EEG-based preference classification in neuromarketing. Appl. Sci.-Basel **10**, 1525 (2020). https://doi.org/10.3390/app10041525
3. Utku, A., Akcayol, M.A.: Deep learning based prediction model for the next purchase. Adv. Electr. Comput. Eng. **20**, 35–44 (2020). https://doi.org/10.4316/AECE.2020.02005
4. Chen, L., Zhu, H.: Behavior prediction based on a commodity utility-behavior sequence model. mach. Learn. Appl. **9**, 100314 (2022). https://doi.org/10.1016/j.mlwa.2022.100314
5. Zhu, C., Wang, M., Su, C.: Prediction of consumer repurchase behavior based on LSTM neural network model. Int. J. Syst. Assur. Eng. Manag. **13**, 1042–1053 (2022). https://doi.org/10.1007/s13198-021-01270-0
6. Esmeli, R., Bader-El-Den, M., Abdullahi, H.: An analyses of the effect of using contextual and loyalty features on early purchase prediction of shoppers in e-commerce domain. J. Bus. Res. **147**, 420–434 (2022). https://doi.org/10.1016/j.jbusres.2022.04.012
7. Dong, Y., Jiang, W.: Brand purchase prediction based on time-evolving user behaviors in e-commerce. Concurr. Comput.-Pract. Exp. **31**, e4882 (2019). https://doi.org/10.1002/cpe.4882
8. Azad, M.S., Khan, S.S., Hossain, R., Rahman, R., Momen, S.: Predictive modeling of consumer purchase behavior on social media: integrating theory of planned behavior and machine learning for actionable insights. PLoS ONE **18**, e0296336 (2023). https://doi.org/10.1371/journal.pone.0296336
9. Xu, Y., Li, Z., Wang, S., Li, W., Sarkodie-Gyan, T., Feng, S.: A hybrid deep-learning model for fault diagnosis of rolling bearings. Measurement **169**, 108502 (2021). https://doi.org/10.1016/j.measurement.2020.108502
10. Xie, X., Pang, S., Chen, J.: Hybrid recommendation model based on deep learning and Stacking integration strategy. Intell. Data Anal. **24**, 1329–1344 (2020). https://doi.org/10.3233/IDA-194961
11. Hu, W., Shi, Y.: Prediction of online consumers' buying behavior based on LSTM-RF model. Presented at the (2020)
12. Ye, D., Muthu, B., Kumar, P.M.: Identifying buying patterns from consumer purchase history using big data and cloud computing. Int. J. Distrib. Syst. Technol. **13** (2022). https://doi.org/10.4018/IJDST.307957
13. Aguirre-Munizaga, M., Morstadt, J.D.C., Samaniego-Cobo, T.: Analysis of classification algorithms for the prediction of purchase intention in electronic commerce. Presented at the (2022). https://doi.org/10.1007/978-3-031-19961-5_3

14. Liu, Y., Guo, W., Zang, D., Li, Z.: A hybrid neural network model with non-linear factorization machines for collaborative recommendation. Presented at the (2018). https://doi.org/10.1007/978-3-030-01012-6_17
15. Mo, X., Xie, Z., Luh, D.-B.: A hybrid macro and micro method for consumer emotion and behavior research. IEEE Access **11**, 83430–83445 (2023). https://doi.org/10.1109/ACCESS.2023.3303311
16. Ala'raj, M., Abbod, M.F., Majdalawieh, M., Jum'a, L.: A deep learning model for behavioural credit scoring in banks. Neural Comput. Appl. **34**, 5839–5866 (2022). https://doi.org/10.1007/s00521-021-06695-z
17. Sahoo, N., Dellarocas, C., Srinivasan, S.: The impact of online product reviews on product returns. Inf. Syst. Res. **29**, 723–738 (2018). https://doi.org/10.1287/isre.2017.0736
18. Esmeli, R., Gokce, A.: An analysis of consumer purchase behavior following cart addition in E-commerce utilizing explainable artificial intelligence. J. Theor. Appl. Electron. Commer. Res. **20**, 28 (2025). https://doi.org/10.3390/jtaer20010028
19. Kim, J.: Prediction of determinants affecting consumer purchase intentions for mackerel in the Korean domestic market. Fishes **9**, 301 (2024). https://doi.org/10.3390/fishes9080301
20. Mandolfo, M., Lamberti, L.: Past, present, and future of impulse buying research methods: a systematic literature review. Front. Psychol. **12**, 687404 (2021). https://doi.org/10.3389/fpsyg.2021.687404
21. McNeil, D.L., Felgate, M.K.: Analysis of UK walnut market import purchase behaviour. Br. Food J. **116**, 405–418 (2014). https://doi.org/10.1108/BFJ-03-2012-0071
22. Alfiero, S., Battisti, E., Hadjielias, E.: Black box technology, usage-based insurance, and prediction of purchase behavior: evidence from the auto insurance sector. Technol. Forecasting. Soc. Change. **183**, 121896 (2022). https://doi.org/10.1016/j.techfore.2022.121896

Deep Learning for Enhanced Audio-Based Movie Scene Classification via Spectrogram Analysis

Porawat Visutsak[1(✉)], Pattarapoom Nokkaew[1], Arzeezar Lording[1], Ponkasam Kalapukdee[1], Natchanan Lai-ngoen-manee[1], Teerapong Ngampromwong[1], Wasanakorn Chalongsintuwong[1], Natdanai Maichum[1], Lt. Sompop Sangsawang[1,2], and Kanyanut Homsapaya[2]

[1] Department of Computer and Information Science, Faculty of Applied Science, King Mongkut's University of Technology North Bangkok, Bangkok, Thailand
porawatv@kmutnb.ac.th

[2] Faculty of Science at Sriracha, Kasetsart University, Sriracha Campus, Chonburi, Thailand

Abstract. This study investigates the feasibility of employing deep learning models for the classification of movie scene audio into distinct categories using spectrogram analysis. To facilitate this, a dataset comprising 766 30-s audio clips was developed, categorized into six distinct classes: Action, Comedy, Horror, House, Racing, and Sport. These audio files were transformed into Mel-spectrograms to serve as visual input for various pre-trained deep learning architectures. The study leveraged transfer learning with eight established MATLAB pre-trained models (DarkNet-19, DarkNet-53, Inception-v3, MobileNet-v2, ResNet-18, VGG-19, VGGish, and YAMNet) to assess their comparative performance. Experimental validation on unseen data revealed that the VGGish model demonstrated superior classification capability, achieving the highest accuracy of 83.00%. This level of accuracy from VGGish, alongside notable performances from models like MobileNet-v2 (80.00%) and DarkNet-19 (80.30%), underscores the significant potential of using pre-trained Convolutional Neural Networks (CNNs) for this task. The findings suggest that such models, particularly VGGish which is pre-trained on audio data, can effectively learn discriminative features from spectrograms, offering an efficient and promising pathway for automated audio-based movie scene classification. This approach contributes to enhancing content analysis and retrieval in multimedia applications.

Keywords: Audio Classification · Convolutional Neural Networks · Deep Learning · Spectrogram Analysis · Transfer Learning

1 Introduction

Audio classification is a core building block in the audio recognition field. It can be applied in various scenarios such as genre classification, speech recognition, and speaker identification [1, 2, 11, 14]. Spectrogram analysis, the technique of visually representing the frequency distribution of a signal over time, has been significantly enhanced by

M. Kassim et al. (Eds.): SCDS 2025, CCIS 2674, pp. 275–288, 2026.
https://doi.org/10.1007/978-981-95-8368-3_20

the application of deep learning, particularly Convolutional Neural Networks (CNNs). CNNs predominate at recognizing patterns within images, making them uniquely suited to identify the intricate features embedded in spectrograms [3, 7, 12, 13]. This powerful combination has revolutionized fields like audio classification, speech recognition, and environmental sound monitoring, by enabling the identification of complex characteristics within spectrograms.

However, traditional audio classification techniques can be insufficient for accurately identifying complex patterns within soundtracks, such as those found in movie trailers [4, 8–10]. This highlights a need for more advanced techniques capable of handling the nuanced acoustic features present in diverse movie scene audio. Consequently, this study investigates whether deep learning models, trained on spectrograms, can outperform traditional machine learning methods (like Random Forests, Support Vector Machines, and Naive Bayes) in the task of automatically classifying movie scenes based solely on audio analysis, a challenge highlighted by [6, 12, 14]. This study contributes to the field by constructing a novel dataset of 766 audio files, labeled into 6 classes: Action, Comedy, Horror, House, Racing, and Sport, with each audio being 30 s in length. The study further involves transforming the audio files into Mel-spectrograms, which serve as inputs for the deep learning models. Additionally, MATLAB's pre-trained deep learning models are utilized for transfer learning, comparing the performance of 8 different architectures: DarkNet-19, DarkNet-53, Inception-v3, MobileNet-v2, ResNet-18, VGG-19, VGGish, and YAMNet. This research also demonstrates the potential of leveraging pre-trained CNNs, particularly VGGish, for efficient and effective audio-based classification of movie scene spectrograms.

While deep learning has shown promise in general audio classification, its application to the complex task of categorizing specific types of movie scenes (such as Action, Comedy, Horror, House, Racing, and Sport) based solely on their audio spectrograms remains less explored, particularly concerning comparative performance across diverse pre-trained architectures and interpretability on such specific content. Furthermore, a dedicated, publicly available dataset for this precise task has been lacking. Therefore, this study aims to address these gaps and offers several key contributions: (1) The development of a novel, curated dataset of 766 30-s audio clips, specifically labeled for movie scene audio classification into six distinct practical categories. (2) A comprehensive benchmarking of eight different pre-trained CNN architectures, encompassing both image and audio-domain pre-training, to evaluate their effectiveness for this specific audio-based movie scene classification task. (3) A demonstration of the feasibility of using transfer learning with pre-trained CNNs for this task, establishing performance baselines for future research. Collectively, these contributions aim to advance the understanding and tools available for automated audio-based analysis of movie content.

The remainder of this paper is structured as follows: Sect. 2 explores the theoretical foundations of spectrogram analysis and deep learning, reviewing relevant literature and setting the stage for the investigation. Section 3 details the methodology employed in this study, encompassing dataset construction, spectrogram generation, model selection, and the transfer learning approach. Section 4 presents the experimental results, scrutinizing the performance of 8 different architectures and discussion. Finally, Sect. 5 concludes this work by summarizing the key findings, discussing limitations, and proposing future directions for research and development in this area.

2 Literature Review

Recent research highlights the effectiveness of using spectrograms and deep learning for diverse audio classification tasks. A notable study [1] introduced a new feature extraction method that uses visual signatures from spectrograms, inspired by the human ability to identify sounds visually. This technique involves normalizing the spectrogram, quantizing it into distinct monochrome regions, and then extracting statistical features from these regions. The method proved robust, especially in noisy conditions, because it assumes noise is more diffuse than the actual signal. When tested on a 60-class sound database, this approach significantly outperformed existing methods without needing noise reduction.

A study by [2] addressed the challenge of related audio classification tasks, like speaker accent and identity recognition, by proposing a multi-task learning model. They developed "gated Residual Networks" (GResNets), a Deep Neural Network that enhances standard Deep Residual Networks (ResNets) with a gate mechanism to better capture the relationships between tasks. This model uses multiplied convolutional layers for more effective shared feature learning. Experiments showed that their multi-task GResNets model achieved higher accuracy than models trained on individual tasks, demonstrating the benefit of jointly learning related audio classification problems.

A study by [3] applied CNNs, specifically the AlexNet architecture, to identify 19 bird species from bioacoustic recordings. Instead of complex feature extraction, they focused on how different spectrogram parameters—such as frequency/amplitude scales and FFT window size—impact classification accuracy. Their results showed a significant variation in accuracy, from 88.9% to 96.9%, based on the chosen parameters. The highest accuracy was achieved by combining four different spectrograms. The research concludes that while CNNs can match state-of-the-art methods, it is crucial to optimize spectrogram parameters, which may differ from those used for human interpretation.

To automatically understand narrative structure in movies, a study by [4] introduced the Flintstones Scene Dataset (FSD), which contains scenes from "The Flintstones" labeled with story elements based on screenwriting guidelines. Using this dataset, the researchers developed and tested machine learning models to predict the narrative function of each scene. The best-performing models achieved a cosine similarity of 0.81 when comparing predicted and human-labeled story structures. These results demonstrate the feasibility of using machine learning for automated narrative analysis, which could enable advanced tools for video summarization and recommendation.

A study by [5] introduced a new method for animal audio classification using a Siamese neural network and clustering to create a "dissimilarity space," which was then used to train an SVM classifier. On bird and cat sound datasets, they first used clustering to identify representative spectrograms (centroids). A Siamese network then mapped the relationships between all sounds and these centroids to form the dissimilarity space. This approach proved effective on its own and achieved even better results when combined with standard CNN-based methods, highlighting the potential of this hybrid technique for enhanced audio classification.

A study by [6] introduced AttendAffectNet, a novel self-attention network designed to predict emotional responses to movies by analyzing audio and video simultaneously. The model's unique application of self-attention captures relationships between audio-visual features, allowing it to understand the sequential nature of emotions more effectively than previous methods. Evaluated on the COGNIMUSE and MediaEval 2016 datasets, AttendAffectNet significantly improved emotion prediction accuracy and outperformed existing state-of-the-art models, demonstrating its superior ability to interpret the complex interplay of audio-visual cues.

To tackle the difficulty of classifying complex environmental sounds, a study by [7] proposed a novel Temporal-Frequency Attention based Convolutional Neural Network (TFCNN). The model enhances standard CNNs by incorporating two new attention mechanisms: one for frequency and one for time. This allows the network to focus on the most important frequency bands and relevant time frames within a Log-Mel spectrogram, effectively filtering out background noise. Tested on the UrbanSound8K and ESC-50 datasets, the TFCNN model demonstrated superior performance, highlighting the value of temporal and frequency attention for accurate environmental sound classification.

To improve the detection of situational information in videos, which is often overlooked, a study by [8] proposed a new method based on entity recognition. This approach analyzes the spatiotemporal relationships between subjects and objects to better understand and recognize the overall scene. In simulation experiments using TV series data, the model achieved an accuracy of over 85%. The results show its potential for applications like video query and surveillance analysis by effectively bridging the gap between low-level pixels and high-level scene comprehension.

A study by [9] introduced a new framework for video understanding called visual semantic role labeling (VidSRL), which defines videos as a series of related events, each consisting of a verb and its associated entities. To support this, they created the VidSitu benchmark, a complex dataset of 29,000 ten-second movie clips densely annotated with verbs and semantic roles. The dataset, which also includes entity co-referencing and event-to-event relationships, was designed to be challenging and diverse. The authors provided baseline models for this new task and have made both the code and the VidSitu dataset publicly available.

A study by [10] introduced the Romantic and Family Movie Database (RFMD), a collection of 1029 movie clips with detailed annotations on character relationships and viewer emotions. Analysis of the database revealed a difference between the emotions viewers perceived in characters and the emotions they felt themselves. The findings also showed a positive correlation between feeling moved and emotional arousal. The researchers provided baseline models for emotion and relationship recognition and made the database publicly available to encourage further research into how film genre, relationships, and emotions interact.

A study by [11] introduced a new method for audio classification by transforming one-dimensional signals into geometric surfaces to uncover underlying structural features. They developed an algorithm to extract descriptive geometric features from these surfaces, which were then used for classification. This approach was successfully applied to two distinct tasks: analyzing lung sounds and detecting speech accents, outperforming baseline models in both cases. The research highlights the potential of using geometric representations for audio analysis and suggests future work could involve higher-dimensional measures. The authors have made their code publicly available to facilitate further research.

A study by [12] introduced a new scene classification model that combines deep CNNs with a visual attention mechanism. The method first identifies important regions in an image using a context-based saliency algorithm. It then extracts deep features from the original image, the saliency map, and an enhanced image where salient regions are amplified. By combining these features, the model focuses on the most informative parts of the scene. Tested on four benchmark datasets (LabelMe, UIUC-Sports, Scene-15, and MIT67), this attention-based approach demonstrated significantly improved and robust classification performance.

To address noise pollution from vehicles with illegally modified exhausts in Hong Kong, a study by [13] developed a low-cost detection prototype. After analyzing the noise characteristics of different vehicles, they created a system that converts audio recordings into spectrograms. A CNN model based on AlexNet was trained on these spectrograms to identify vehicles with loud exhausts, while the YOLO v4 Tiny algorithm was used to distinguish between vehicle types. This combined approach achieved an overall accuracy of 96% in detecting passenger cars with modified exhausts, demonstrating the effectiveness of using spectrogram analysis and object recognition for automated noise enforcement.

A study by [14] explored using deep learning and audio spectrograms for movie genre classification. They tested nine pre-trained CNNs on a dataset of movie trailers to classify them into five genres. The VGG-16 architecture achieved the best performance with an accuracy of 86.27%. The research highlights that leveraging pre-trained CNNs for spectrogram analysis is a powerful and efficient method for audio-based classification. This approach saves significant time and resources compared to training a network from scratch and can overcome challenges of limited data through transfer learning, often resulting in higher accuracy.

3 Methods

3.1 Data Preparation

To prepare data for training, an AudioDataStore reference was created to the folder containing all the labels and images, preventing MATLAB from loading all images simultaneously. The script was saved in the folder containing the Audio folder where the data was initially downloaded. The total number of samples for each label was determined, and the data was divided into training and validation sets with a proportion of 80 to 20. The training and validation sets were created, ensuring at least 4 labels in each set for testing, with the possibility of increasing this number by creating an augmented dataset. The audio signals were represented by sample images from 6 classes: Action, Comedy, Horror, House, Racing, and Sport. The general acoustic characteristics of these classes are as follows:

- Action: These scenes typically feature a high density of sounds, including prominent sound effects (e.g., explosions, gunfire, chases), dynamic musical scores, and often impactful or urgent dialogue.

- Comedy: Audio in this category is frequently dialogue-driven, characterized by speech patterns conveying humor, presence of laughter, and often upbeat or situational music.
- Horror: These scenes often utilize a wide dynamic range, incorporating elements such as suspenseful music or silence, sudden loud sound effects (i.e., jump scares), eerie ambient sounds, and dialogue that can range from whispers to screams.
- House: This category represents scenes that primarily occur in domestic indoor settings, often characterized by conversational dialogue, subtle room ambiences, and common household sounds.
- Racing: Audio is predominantly composed of distinct vehicular sounds such as powerful engine roars, tire screeches, and the sound of movement, frequently accompanied by high-energy music and potentially commentary.
- Sport: These scenes typically include a mixture of prominent crowd noise, announcer or commentator speech, sounds directly related to the sporting activity (e.g., ball impacts, referee whistles), and often energetic music. The classification task aims to distinguish these categories based on their overall acoustic properties derived from these mixed-signal environments.

Figure 1 shows sample images of audio signals from 6 classes. Then, the data was visualized by viewing a random sample, displaying nine images of spectrograms in a tiled layout (see Fig. 2).

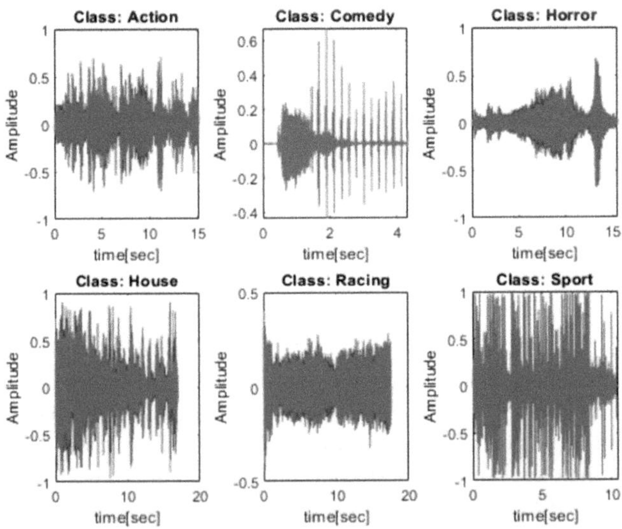

Fig. 1. Audio waveforms of representative samples from 6 distinct movie scene categories: Action, Comedy, Horror, House, Racing, and Sport. The waveforms illustrate the variation in amplitude (sound intensity) over time for each category, showcasing the diverse acoustic characteristics captured in the dataset. These audio signals are then transformed into spectrograms for analysis and classification by the CNN model.

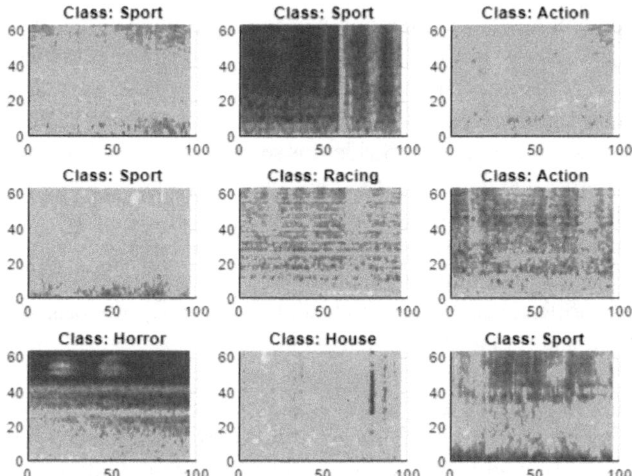

Fig. 2. Spectrograms of audio samples from various movie scene categories, including Sport, Action, Racing, Horror, and House. Each spectrogram visually represents the distribution of audio frequencies over time, showcasing the unique acoustic characteristics of each scene category. These spectrograms serve as input data for training and evaluating the CNN-based audio classification model.

To create a spectrogram, which visually represents the changing frequencies in an audio signal over time, a series of steps are involved. First, the audio signal is divided into short, overlapping time windows. This ensures smooth transitions between sounds and prevents the loss of crucial information. Next, each windowed segment undergoes a Fourier Transform, a mathematical operation that decomposes the signal into its constituent frequencies, revealing their respective amplitudes. The results of these transforms are then combined to form the spectrogram. The x-axis of the spectrogram represents time, while the y-axis represents frequency, with lower frequencies at the bottom and higher frequencies at the top. The color or intensity at each point on the spectrogram corresponds to the amplitude of a specific frequency at a particular time. For instance, taking an audio signal from the "Class: Action" category, the process would involve slicing the signal into overlapping windows, performing a Fourier Transform on each window to reveal the dominant frequencies and their amplitudes, and then stacking these frequency representations along the time axis. This creates a visual representation of how the frequencies and their strengths change throughout the audio clip. This spectrogram then serves as the "image" that the CNN analyzes, learning to recognize patterns and features associated with different movie scene categories.

3.2 Pre-trained Models' Construction

To adapt the pre-trained CNN model for the audio classification task, it was modified by adjusting the input layer to match the size and format of the generated spectrograms. This involved setting the InputSize parameter to 96x64x1 to accommodate grayscale spectrograms with dimensions of 96 pixels wide and 64 pixels tall. No normalization was applied to the input data. The adaptation of the pre-trained models (e.g., ResNet-18, VGG-19) using the deepNetworkDesigner tool, involved several targeted modifications for transfer learning. The image input layer was reconfigured to an InputSize of [96, 64, 1] with no normalization, to match the input spectrograms. For the first convolutional layer in the VGG-19 architecture, the Stride was set to (1,1) and Padding was set to 'same' to ensure compatibility and feature extraction from the adapted input. The FilterSize and NumFilters of the original pre-trained convolutional layers were otherwise maintained to leverage their learned features. The final fully connected layer was modified to have an OutputSize of 6 (corresponding to the number of classes), and its WeightLearnRateFactor and BiasLearnRateFactor were both set to 10. Finally, the original classification layer was removed and replaced with a new classificationLayer. Additionally, the fully connected layers were customized to match the number of audio classes in the dataset, and learning rates for weights and biases were fine-tuned for optimal training. Lastly, the final classification layer of the pre-trained network was replaced with a new layer corresponding to the 6 specific audio classes aimed at being identified.

The modified CNN model was then trained and validated using the prepared dataset. This training process involved defining key parameters such as the optimization algorithm, batch size, number of epochs, learning rate, and validation frequency. The trainingOptions function was used with the 'adam' optimizer, a mini-batch size of 75, and a maximum of 15 epochs. The initial learning rate was set to 0.0001, and the data was shuffled after every epoch. Validation frequency was set to 50, meaning the model's performance was evaluated against the validation set every 50 iterations. The trainNetwork function was used to train the network, utilizing the training data, labels, modified network architecture (lgraph_1), and the defined training options. Throughout the training process, progress was monitored, and performance was validated periodically using the validation data. This approach ensured the CNN model was effectively trained and optimized for the audio classification task.

3.3 Models' Evaluation and Interpretation

To assess the effectiveness of the trained CNN model, a validation set comprising audio samples that were not part of the training data was used. This evaluation process involved 3 primary steps.

First, the trained model generated predictions on the unseen validation data, assigning one of the 6 class labels (Action, Comedy, Horror, House, Racing, or Sport) to each audio sample. This allowed for obtaining the model's classification output for a set of data it had not encountered during training.

Next, the accuracy of the model was calculated by comparing these predicted labels against the true labels of the validation data. Accuracy, in this context, represents the proportion of correctly classified audio samples out of the total number of samples in the validation set. A higher accuracy indicates better performance, suggesting that the model is effectively generalizing its learning to new, unseen data.

Finally, a confusion matrix was created to visualize the model's performance across the different classes. The confusion matrix provides a detailed breakdown of the model's predictions, showing the number or proportion of correct and incorrect classifications for each class. This matrix is particularly useful for identifying patterns of misclassifications.

For instance, if the model frequently confuses samples from the "Action" class with those from the "Racing" class, this would be evident in the confusion matrix, highlighting areas where the model might need further refinement or where the distinction between classes may be inherently challenging.

4 Results and Discussion

The pre-trained CNN models are evaluated on the movie scene audio classification task. The accuracy of each model on the training and validation sets is reported in Table 1.

Table 1. The training and validation.

Pre-trained model	Optimization algorithm	Execution environment	Mini batch size	Learning rate	Accuracy (%)	
					train	test
DarkNet-19	Adam	Parallel	75	0.0001	71.92	80.30
DarkNet-53	Adam	Single GPU	75	0.0001	75.96	75.56
Inception-v3	Adam	Single GPU	75	0.0001	73.67	77.04
MobileNet-v2	Adam	Single GPU	75	0.0001	74.71	80.00
ResNet-18	Adam	Parallel	75	0.0001	71.51	73.48
VGG-19	adam	Parallel	75	0.0001	65.07	68.18
VGGish	adam	Single GPU	75	0.0001	79.30	83.00
YAMNet	adam	Single GPU	75	0.0001	75.74	71.85

An interesting observation from the comparative analysis is the performance of YAMNet. Despite being pre-trained on audio data (AudioSet), YAMNet achieved a test accuracy (71.85%) that was lower than VGGish (83.00%) and also several image-pretrained models such as DarkNet-19 (80.30%) and MobileNet-v2 (80.00%). Several factors might contribute to this outcome. Firstly, YAMNet is pre-trained on AudioSet, which focuses on a wide array of 521 distinct, often short, audio events. In contrast, the classification task in this study involves 30-s movie scene audio clips, which are typically complex acoustic environments comprising mixed signals (dialogue, music, effects). The features learned by YAMNet for granular event detection might not be as directly transferable to the holistic acoustic characteristics defining these longer, multifaceted scenes compared to the features learned by VGGish from the broader YouTube-8M dataset or even the general pattern recognition capabilities of some deeper image-pretrained architectures when fine-tuned on spectrograms. Secondly, YAMNet's MobileNetV1-based architecture is optimized for efficiency and broad event coverage, which might result in a less specialized feature representation for the specific subtleties of the movie scene categories investigated. The differences in pre-training data granularity, architectural design goals, and the specific nature of the target task likely play a significant role in these performance variations. This suggests that for complex audio scene classification, the sheer volume and contextual breadth of pre-training data (as with VGGish) or the robust general feature extraction capabilities of certain image-CNNs can sometimes be more advantageous than a more narrowly focused audio event pre-training, highlighting the importance of aligning pre-training characteristics with the target task's demands. Overall, the VGGish model achieves the highest accuracy on both the training and validation sets. This indicates that VGGish is a suitable pre-trained model for the movie scene audio classification task. In addition to the quantitative results, the confusion matrix and interpretability maps are used to qualitatively analyze the performance of the models. The confusion matrix shows the types of misclassifications made by the model, while the interpretability maps help to identify the regions of the spectrograms that are most influential in the model's classification. The confusion matrix of each model is shown in Fig. 3. The experimental results demonstrate the effectiveness of pre-trained CNN models for movie scene audio classification. The results also show that the choice of pre-trained model can have a significant impact on the performance of the model.

The confusion matrix for the VGGish model (see Fig. 3 (g)), which achieved an overall validation accuracy of 83.01%, further elucidates its classification performance across the six categories. VGGish demonstrated high accuracy for classes such as Action, Comedy, and Racing. Specifically, it correctly identified all 'Action' instances (32/32, 100% recall for Action), all 'Comedy' instances (14/14, 100% recall), and all 'Racing' instances (10/10, 100% recall), with precision for these classes being 88.9%, 100.0%, and 100.0% respectively. The 'Horror' class was also well-managed, with 10 out of 12 instances correctly classified (83.3% recall) and a precision of 90.9%.

However, more significant confusion was observed primarily involving the 'Sport' and 'House' classes. While 'House' demonstrated high recall (33/34, 97.1%), its precision was notably lower at 61.1%. This was largely because 18 true 'Sport' instances were misclassified as 'House'. Consequently, the 'Sport' class had the lowest recall at 57.1% (28/49 correctly identified), although its precision was 100.0% (meaning when it predicted 'Sport', it was always correct). This indicates that while the overall accuracy of VGGish is high, certain acoustic similarities, particularly between 'Sport' and 'House' scenes, pose a distinct challenge for the model.

Moreover, analysis of the confusion matrices (Fig. 3) reveals consistent patterns across several of the evaluated models. Notably, the 'Action' class was identified with high accuracy by most architectures (e.g., DarkNet-19, DarkNet-53, MobileNet-v2, and VGGish all achieved perfect or near-perfect recall). This robust performance likely stems from the distinct, high-energy acoustic signatures characteristic of action sequences, such as explosions, intense music, and vehicle sounds, which provide salient and separable features in the spectrograms. The 'House' class also demonstrated relatively good identification by many models (e.g., Inception-v3, MobileNet-v2, VGGish showed high recall), potentially due to its often dialogue-centric nature and comparatively consistent indoor ambient sound profiles, distinguishing it from more overtly dynamic or specialized categories.

However, a prevalent area of confusion, observed across almost all models to varying degrees, was between the 'Sport' and 'House' classes. For instance, with the top-performing VGGish model, 18 true 'Sport' instances (out of 49) were misclassified as 'House', and similar misclassifications from 'Sport' to 'House' were evident for

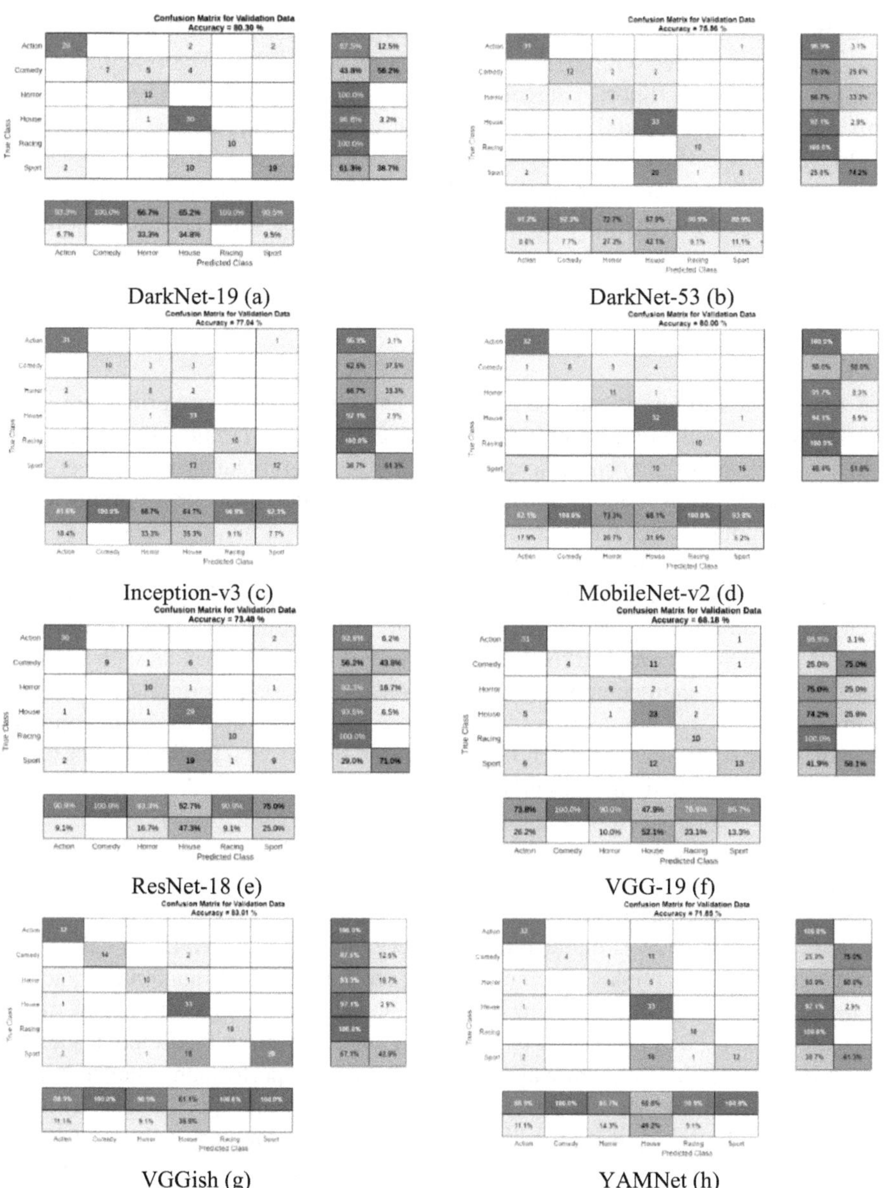

DarkNet-19 (a) DarkNet-53 (b)

Inception-v3 (c) MobileNet-v2 (d)

ResNet-18 (e) VGG-19 (f)

VGGish (g) YAMNet (h)

Fig. 3. The confusion matrix.

DarkNet-53, Inception-v3, ResNet-18, VGG-19, and particularly YAMNet. This recurring confusion may arise from several overlapping acoustic characteristics. Both ‘Sport’ (with commentary and crowd chatter) and ‘House’ (dialogue-heavy) scenes are rich in human speech. If models do not sufficiently differentiate the contextualizing background elements, speech presence alone might be a confounding factor. Furthermore, the ambient sound textures of some 'Sport' environments (e.g., diffuse crowd noise) might share similarities with active indoor 'House' ambiences. The inherent acoustic variability within the 'Sport' category itself, ranging from loud gameplay to quieter commentary segments, could also lead to some instances resembling the acoustic profile of 'House' scenes. The consistency of this specific inter-class confusion across diverse architectures suggests an inherent challenge in the dataset, possibly due to these subtle acoustic overlaps that are difficult for models to disentangle using spectrogram features alone.

5 Conclusion

This study aimed to investigate the feasibility and effectiveness of various pre-trained CNNs for classifying movie scenes into six distinct categories (Action, Comedy, Horror, House, Racing, and Sport) based solely on audio spectrogram analysis. A novel dataset of 766 30-s audio clips was developed and transformed into Mel-spectrograms to serve as input for eight different CNN architectures.

The primary finding was that deep learning models, particularly those pre-trained on audio data, are indeed effective for this task. The VGGish model demonstrated the highest classification accuracy, achieving 83.00% on unseen validation data. Other models, such as MobileNet-v2 and DarkNet-19, also yielded promising results with accuracies around 80%, while architectures like VGG-19 (68.18%) were less effective, highlighting the importance of model selection. Analysis of the VGGish model's confusion matrix revealed strong performance in identifying Action, Comedy, and Racing scenes, but also pointed to specific challenges, notably in distinguishing 'Sport' from 'House' scenes, suggesting overlapping acoustic features.

In conclusion, this research successfully demonstrated the feasibility and effectiveness of employing pre-trained deep learning models for classifying movie scene audio into six distinct categories using Mel-spectrogram analysis. The primary insights and contributions of this work are fourfold: Firstly, we introduced a novel, manually curated dataset of 766 audio samples specifically designed for this classification task, addressing a resource gap in this domain. Secondly, through a comparative study of eight pre-trained CNNs, we established that VGGish, an audio-pretrained model, yields the highest accuracy (83.00%), while also providing valuable performance benchmarks for other architectures like MobileNet-v2 and DarkNet-19 on this specific task. This comprehensive benchmarking itself is a key contribution for researchers in the field. Thirdly, our findings confirm the viability of leveraging transfer learning for efficient and effective audio-based movie scene classification, offering a promising pathway for automated content analysis. Finally, the application of interpretability techniques provided initial insights into the discriminative acoustic features within spectrograms that models like VGGish learn to associate with specific scene types, such as 'Action'. These contributions not only advance the specific area of movie scene audio analysis but also hold significant practical implications for multimedia indexing, content-based retrieval, and automated tagging systems.

However, the current study has several limitations. The dataset, while novel, is of moderate size, and its diversity could be expanded to include a wider range of movie genres and acoustic environments. The chosen Mel-spectrogram parameters were fixed, and exploring other representations might yield further improvements. Additionally, this study focused exclusively on audio cues, neglecting the visual information inherent in movie scenes.

The practical applications of this research include enhancing automated video tagging, content-based recommendation systems, and tools for media archiving and retrieval. Future research should focus on several key areas. Expanding the dataset significantly in both size and variety is crucial for improving model robustness and generalizability. Investigating alternative spectrogram generation techniques and other advanced audio features (e.g., pitch, rhythm, timbre) could unlock further performance gains. Exploring more sophisticated deep learning architectures, including attention mechanisms or transformers specifically adapted for audio, may also prove beneficial. Finally, a significant step forward would be the development of multimodal systems that integrate both audio and visual analysis for a more comprehensive and accurate classification of movie scenes.

Funding. "This research was funded by King Mongkut's University of Technology North Bangkok, Contract no. KMUTNB-68-BASIC-31".

References

1. Dennis, J., Tran, H.D., Li, H.: Spectrogram image feature for sound event classification in mismatched conditions. IEEE Signal Process. Lett. **18**(2), 130–133 (2011)
2. Zeng, Y., Mao, H., Peng, D., Yi, Z.: Spectrogram based multi-task audio classification. Multim. Tools and Appl. **78**, 3705–3722 (2019)
3. Knight, E.C., Hernandez, S.P., Bayne, E.M., Bulitko, V., Tucker, B.V.: Pre-processing spectrogram parameters improve the accuracy of bioacoustic classification using convolutional neural networks. Bioacoustics **29**(3), 337–355 (2019)
4. Liu, C., Shmilovici, A., Last, M.: Towards story-based classification of movie scenes. PLoS ONE **15**(2), e0228579 (2020)
5. Nanni, L., Rigo, A., Lumini, A., Brahnam, S.: Spectrogram classification using dissimilarity space. Appl. Sci. **10**(12), 4176 (2020)
6. Thao, H.T.P., B.B.T., Herremans, D., Roig, G.: AttendAffectNet: Self-Attention based Networks for Predicting Affective Responses from Movies. In: Proceedings of the International Conference on Pattern Recognition (ICPR), pp. 8346–8353 (2020)
7. Mu, W., Yin, B., Huang, X., et al.: Environmental sound classification using temporal-frequency attention based convolutional neural network. Sci. Rep. **11**, 21552 (2021)
8. Qian, H., et al.: Video scene information detection based on entity recognition. Wirel. Comm. Mobile Comp. **2021**, 1020044 (2021)
9. Sadhu, A., Gupta, T., Yatskar, M., Nevatia, R., Kembhavi, A.: Visual semantic role labeling for video understanding. In: Proceedings of the IEEE/CVF Conference on Computer Vision and Pattern Recognition (CVPR), pp. 5585–5596 (2021)
10. Hsu, P.-C., Li, J.-L., Lee, C.-C.: Romantic and family movie database: towards understanding human emotion and relationship via genre-dependent movies. In: 2022 10th International Conference on Affective Computing and Intelligent Interaction (ACII), pp. 1–8. IEEE, Nara, Japan (2022)
11. Levy, J., Naitsat, A., Zeevi, Y.Y.: Classification of audio signals using spectrogram surfaces and extrinsic distortion measures. EURASIP J. Adv. Sign. Proc. **2022**(1), 100 (2022)

12. Shi, J., Zhu, H., Li, Y., Li, Y., Du, S.: [Retracted] scene classification using deep networks combined with visual attention. Journal of Sensors **2022**, 7191537 (2022)
13. Cheng, K.W., et al.: Spectrogram-based classification on vehicles with modified loud exhausts via convolutional neural networks. Appl. Acoust. **205**, 109254 (2023)
14. Visutsak, P., et al.: Baseline performance of pre-trained models on movie genre classification from spectrograms. ECTI-CIT Trans. **19**(2), 364–378 (2025)

A Methodology for Real-Time Audio Event Detection and Generation Using Spectral Flux Analysis

Porawat Visutsak[1(✉)], Jadetawat Kirdphoksap[1], Peemvit Yimthin[1], and Kanyanut Homsapaya[2]

[1] Department of Computer and Information Science, Faculty of Applied Science, King Mongkut's University of Technology North Bangkok, Bangkok, Thailand
porawatv@kmutnb.ac.th

[2] Faculty of Science at Sriracha, Kasetsart University, Sriracha Campus, Chonburi, Thailand

Abstract. The manual annotation of audio events is a time-intensive and complex bottleneck that severely limits the scalable creation of synchronized content and restricts user personalization in applications. This paper details an automated methodology to address this problem by generating a structured event map from any given MP3 file. The system employs a real-time audio analysis process using the Fast Fourier Transform (FFT) and calculates Spectral Flux to identify significant transient events. A dynamic thresholding technique distinguishes these events, while Beats Per Minute (BPM) analysis refines the output's temporal accuracy. Experimental evaluation revealed a crucial discrepancy: while the system achieves high temporal precision with a Mean Absolute Error (MAE) ranging from 0.0631 to 0.0991 s, its overall BPM detection accuracy was only 50%. This technical gap was reflected in user testing, where the core event generation output received a moderate score of 3.19 out of 5, primarily due to a high false-positive rate in complex audio. The study concludes that while the methodology is effective for temporal alignment, future work must focus on more advanced adaptive thresholding to improve event selectivity and bridge the gap between technical accuracy and perceived quality.

Keywords: Event Detection · Audio Analysis · Spectral Flux · Fast Fourier Transform (FFT) · Spectrogram · BPM · Procedural Content Generation

1 Introduction

The automatic detection of transient audio events is a foundational challenge in signal processing and a significant area of research with diverse applications, as explored in recent literature reviews [14]. Sound Event Detection (SED) is increasingly implemented in domains such as enhancing smart home environments [15] and improving the perceptual abilities of smart cars in complex traffic scenes [12]. A key challenge in many of these applications is the need for on-line, real-time processing with minimal delay,

M. Kassim et al. (Eds.): SCDS 2025, CCIS 2674, pp. 289–303, 2026.
https://doi.org/10.1007/978-981-95-8368-3_21

which many existing off-line systems cannot provide [4]. Furthermore, accurately detecting events in noisy, real-world environments remains a significant hurdle [8]. Despite these advanced applications, the conventional approach of manually annotating audio events for training or content creation is an exceptionally time-intensive process. This bottleneck limits scalability and restricts the ability of developers and end-users to create diverse, personalized, and audio-aligned content efficiently.

The primary objective of this study is to design, develop, and evaluate an automated system capable of generating a structured event map from any given MP3 file. This is achieved by employing a real-time audio analysis process centered on the Fast Fourier Transform (FFT) for signal conversion and Spectral Flux calculation to identify significant audio events. A further objective is to refine the temporal accuracy of the generated events by calculating the audio's Beats Per Minute (BPM) and using this data to ensure the final output is structurally consistent with the source audio's tempo.

The scope of this research is centered on the development of an event-generation system using the Unity Engine and C# programming language. The system is designed to operate on the Windows 10 and 11 platforms and specifically processes audio files in the MP3 format. The methodology is fixed on using FFT for frequency analysis, calculating Spectral Flux to detect transient onsets, applying a dynamic threshold to filter for significant events, and performing an offset analysis to determine BPM. The final output of the system is a structured, timestamped event map exported as a JSON file. System performance was evaluated by comparing its output against established audio analysis software and through feedback from 20 users.

The successful implementation of this automated system offers several key benefits. First, it significantly reduces the time and difficulty associated with manual content creation, streamlining the development workflow. Second, it provides end-users and developers with the flexibility to use any personal MP3 file, enabling the creation of highly diverse and customizable experiences. Finally, by automating the annotation process, the system makes it feasible to generate event maps for large audio libraries, enhancing the potential for large-scale procedural content generation.

This paper is organized as follows. Section 2 provides a review of relevant literature on event detection algorithms, Spectral Flux analysis, and related procedural generation systems. Section 3 details the complete methodology used for audio analysis and event map generation. Section 4 describes the technical implementation of the system. Section 5 presents the results of the system's performance evaluation and discusses the findings from both technical benchmarks and user experience testing. Finally, Sect. 6 offers a conclusion, summarizing the study's contributions and outlining potential avenues for future development.

2 Literature Review

Recent works in audio event detection have been investigated. Increasing human longevity has created a significant challenge for governments and healthcare organizations in providing adequate care for the growing elderly population. Traditional care facilities like hospitals and retirement homes are facing issues of overcrowding and prohibitive costs [1]. In response, this paper introduces an innovative Ambient Assisted

Living (AAL) platform that leverages advancements in technology and communications. This system is designed to analyze and identify specific acoustic events within a home setting, enabling remote, real-time tracking of a patient's status by medical personnel. A proof-of-concept was developed utilizing the processing power of an NVIDIA Jetson TK1 board to detect these events locally. The experiments, which focused on 14 distinct indoor sounds relevant to domestic surveillance and patient behavior, yielded an impressive overall accuracy of 82%. These findings affirm the potential of this approach and offer a clear path for healthcare providers to implement non-invasive, cost-effective remote monitoring.

In [2], the authors address the high cost and labor involved in creating strongly-annotated datasets for Sound Event Detection (SED), where the precise start and end times of sounds are required. The authors reformulate the task as a Multiple Instance Learning (MIL) problem, which enables models to be trained on "weakly labeled" data that only indicates the presence of a sound within a recording excerpt, not its exact timing. To achieve this, the paper introduces "auto-pool," a novel family of adaptive pooling operators that aggregate a model's time-varying predictions to match the static training labels. These operators learn a parameter that allows them to automatically interpolate between different pooling behaviors—such as min-, max-, or average-pooling—to best suit the characteristics of different sound events. Evaluated on three distinct datasets, the proposed methods consistently outperform non-adaptive pooling operators and achieve dynamic, time-resolved prediction accuracy that nearly matches models trained with expensive, strongly-labeled data. This research demonstrates that effective SED models can be developed with significantly lower annotation costs, and proposes a general auto-pooling method that is applicable to other MIL problems in any domain.

While bioacoustic sensors provide a scalable way to record wildlife sounds, variations in background noise over time and across different sensor locations limit the reliability of automated systems for detecting animal vocalizations. To address this, the work in [3] introduces and combines several machine learning techniques to help SED models generalize better across diverse acoustic environments. Using the detection of avian flight calls from a ten-hour recording across a network of six sensors as a case study, the researchers improved a state-of-the-art convolutional neural network (CNN) with two distinct noise adaptation methods. The first is a short-term (60 ms) technique called per-channel energy normalization (PCEN), which applies automatic gain control to the audio spectrogram. The second is a long-term (30 min) strategy that uses a context-adaptive neural network (CA-NN) to dynamically adjust the main network's parameters based on the recent acoustic environment. The results showed that PCEN improved performance between different times of day (dawn vs. dusk), while the context-adaptive method improved performance across different sensor locations. Combining both techniques yielded state-of-the-art results, surpassing the effectiveness of artificial data augmentation alone and leading to the release of a pre-trained, ready-to-use detector named BirdVoxDetect.

The task of Sound Event Localization and Detection (SELD)—simultaneously identifying what a sound is and where it's coming from—has been effectively handled by off-line deep learning models [4]. However, these existing systems cannot be directly applied to real-time scenarios where processing must occur with minimal delay. This research introduces an on-line version of a SELD system to make it viable for live applications. The study focuses on the essential trade-off between processing speed (latency) and performance. Experiments revealed that moving to an on-line framework preserves and can even enhance the accuracy of sound localization, but the accuracy of sound detection suffers when operating at very low latencies.

A new computationally efficient system has been developed to detect rare sound events in open environments [5]. The framework operates by first decomposing a 30-s audio clip into five levels using Wavelet Multiresolution Analysis (MRA) and applying denoising to the third and fifth levels to remove background interference. It then intelligently identifies significant transitions, which likely represent the start of a rare event, by combining a peak-finding algorithm with K-medoids clustering. By focusing only on these key moments, the system extracts small one-second "chunks" from the original audio for analysis. Features are extracted from these chunks via a Wavelet Scattering Network (WSN) and then classified using a Support Vector Machine (SVM). This lightweight algorithm produces an error rate comparable to systems based on deep learning but is far more efficient as it has no learnable parameters. It requires only a single training epoch—which is 5 to 600 times faster than various CNN and DNN-based models—and needs to check almost 360 times fewer audio segments. These characteristics make the proposed system ideal for real-time applications on devices with limited resources.

In the automotive industry, accurately identifying specific events from vast amounts of sensor data is crucial for evaluating active vehicle safety systems. To move beyond slow and subjective human analysis, a novel method has been developed that applies object detection techniques to time series data. In [6], the study begins by converting the raw time series data into time-frequency images called scalograms, which visually represent the signal's characteristics over time. These scalograms are then filtered to enhance the most relevant parts of the signal, making it easier to spot key events. An object detection model, similar to those used for identifying objects in photos, is then trained to recognize and locate these specific events within the filtered scalograms. Once the model detects an event in a new scalogram, its precise location is mapped back to the original timeline, marking the exact start and end times of the event. Evaluated on unseen datasets, this algorithm demonstrated a high precision rate of 0.97 and proved capable of defining event boundaries with a sharpness that is challenging to achieve through human visual inspection alone. By integrating this method, the vehicle development process can benefit from a more accurate, reliable, and rapid analysis of safety system performance.

A deep learning-based algorithm for SELD in a three-dimensional space has been developed to identify multiple overlapping sound events [7]. The method feeds a combination of Log-Mel spectrum and generalized cross-correlation spectrum features into a convolutional recurrent neural network (CRNN). This network, which is an enhancement of the SELDnet architecture, processes the features in parallel to handle sound event detection as a classification task and sound source localization as a regression task. To improve performance, a channel attention mechanism is integrated into the model to selectively amplify essential features and suppress irrelevant ones. The algorithm was trained and evaluated on datasets containing up to three overlapping sound events in both anechoic (echo-free) and reverberant (echoic) conditions. Field experiments demonstrated that this approach is robust against reverberation and achieves higher accuracy in both event recognition and localization when compared to baseline methods.

To tackle the challenge of accurately detecting anomalous audio events in real-time, especially in noisy settings, a novel method has been proposed using an ensemble learning model within an active learning framework [8]. The approach was validated using a large, diverse audio dataset created specifically for the study, which included both original and noisy recordings from various environments like offices and restaurants, alongside abnormal events such as explosions and car crashes. The results highlighted the superiority of the proposed model, which achieved an impressive accuracy of 99.26%. This significantly outperformed a standard deep learning model that scored 95.35%. The research ultimately demonstrates an effective, efficient, and cost-effective method for highly accurate audio event detection, with major applications in security, surveillance, and forensic analysis.

With new technology like smart cities and security cameras everywhere, it's more important than ever to automatically detect sounds. It's not just about knowing a sound happened, but also knowing exactly when it started and stopped. In [9], the author found a new way to do this that makes the process much simpler and more efficient. The new method works by breaking down a complex sound into its most basic parts. Think of it like taking a smoothie and figuring out its simple ingredients, like banana, strawberry, and yogurt. By looking at these simple parts of the sound, a computer can understand what's happening using much less information than older methods. To prove it worked, researchers tested it with a collection of city sounds. The results were very impressive. This new method reduced the amount of information the computer needed to process by more than 99% compared to other top systems, without losing accuracy. Because it needs so much less data, this new approach can help create faster and more efficient sound detection systems that can run on smaller, less powerful devices.

A new study explores the use of deep learning for enhancing public safety in smart cities by automatically detecting emotionally charged sound events near residential areas [10]. The research introduces an ensemble CRNN designed to identify sounds like quarrels, screams, and breaking glass. To improve the system's accuracy and robustness against noise, the model processes audio that has been converted into various image-based representations, including Mel spectrograms, Cocheagrams, and Discrete Cosine Transform (DCT) spectrograms. A unique and practical dataset was developed in collaboration with police officers, featuring 112 clips of relevant emotional sounds, which was combined with publicly available and crowdsourced data to create a comprehensive collection of 5,055 audio files across 13 categories, totaling over 14 h of strongly labeled data. The proposed model integrates convolutional layers to analyze the spatial features of the audio images and bi-directional GRU layers to understand the temporal sequence of events. By combining the predictions from three such models, this ensemble approach achieved promising F1 scores of 71.5% for segment-based detection and 46% for more precise event-based timing. These results demonstrate the system's effectiveness even with a small and unbalanced dataset, highlighting its potential for deployment on cost-effective mini-computers as part of real-time audio surveillance systems to help maintain public order.

In [11], the study introduces a system to generate personalized Spotify playlists of Thai music by analyzing a user's current mood. The system processes a user's feelings, which are entered as text, and uses machine learning to classify their emotional state into one of four categories: love, happy, sad, or angry. To develop the system, a dataset of Thai songs was compiled using the Spotify API, with features extracted from both audio and lyrics, and then manually labeled by mood. Five different classification models were evaluated, with the random forest classifier achieving the highest accuracy at 0.94, outperforming XGBoost (0.89), decision tree (0.85), logistic regression (0.79), and SVM (0.78). The research provides a proof of concept for a system that can effectively create tailored playlists, aiming to enhance the music discovery experience for listeners of Thai music and promote a wider variety of Thai artists.

Traditional sound event detection often fails to account for the fact that sounds in real life are interconnected. To address this, a new method based on a graph convolutional network (GCN) has been developed specifically for complex traffic environments [12]. This innovative approach considers the timing relationships between different sounds—whether they happen together or one after another—as a distinct source of information. The system identifies these patterns, builds a graph to represent them, and uses a specially improved GCN to interpret the graph's structure. This relational information is then combined with standard acoustic features learned by a separate neural network (CRNN). The fusion of these two modes—acoustic and relational—was shown in experiments to significantly boost the performance of sound event detection, ultimately improving a smart car's ability to perceive its surroundings while driving.

Existing approaches in suspicious event detection (SED) are often hampered by high false positive rates and an inability to adapt to dynamic environments or reliably distinguish between anomalous and normal behaviors [13]. This research introduces SED-NET, a novel deep learning framework designed to overcome these challenges. The methodology involves several stages: input frames from surveillance footage are first enhanced through a Gaussian adaptive bilateral filter (GABF) for noise reduction and a Sobel edge detector for fine edge delineation. Subsequently, a Di-Stream Neural Network (DSNN) with a dual-branch EfficientNet base is employed to extract both motion and pose features from the processed frames. These features are then intelligently combined via a weighted average fusion technique. Final classification of suspicious activities is performed by a Simplified Spiking Neural Network (SSNN). The proposed SED-NET model's efficacy was validated on the UCSD Pedestrian and CUHK Avenue datasets, attaining high specificity, sensitivity, and F1 scores, with accuracy reaching 98.97% and 98.84%, respectively. Notably, the model outperformed methods like DenseNet121, SegAD, and 3DCNN by up to 7.44%, 4.18%, and 2.73% in overall accuracy.

More recent work of SED was also investigated, a critical technology that mimics the human auditory system, is increasingly implemented across diverse domains such as healthcare, environmental science, and surveillance [14]. This paper presents a systematic literature review that offers a well-structured and in-depth analysis of the SED landscape. Based on extensive domain knowledge, it compares various algorithms and evaluates the datasets, feature extraction methods, and execution models used in current research. The review critically assesses the accuracy, challenges, and limitations of these approaches while also identifying key trends and future research directions. Ultimately, this work provides a foundational synthesis of existing knowledge to aid researchers, practitioners, and stakeholders in making informed decisions and fostering innovation within the evolving field of sound event detection.

Ambient acoustic detection and localization are critical for identifying events and their origins, and this study aimed to establish a framework for this purpose within home environments to manage emergencies [15]. By enhancing event detection with localization, the system improves situational awareness and response times for emergency services. The methodology involved collecting acoustic data from 11 activity types within a home setting using a six-microphone array. Following a noise-filtering stage, features were extracted across the time, frequency, time-frequency, and cepstral domains. For classification, a Random Forest model achieved 95% accuracy in event detection, while a Linear Discriminant Analysis model reached 87%. Sound source localization was performed using the ESPRIT algorithm, which yielded significant performance with a root mean squared error (RMSE) of 3.87. The integrated system successfully identified emergency activities and triggered email notifications, demonstrating the proposed methodology's strong potential for real-world, real-time domestic emergency alert systems.

3 Methods: Automatic Event Map Generation

The system's architecture is designed to process an MP3 file, analyze its temporal properties, and output the resulting event data as a structured JSON file. This data can then be used for various synchronized applications. The process is executed through a series of integrated steps.

3.1 Audio Analysis Using Fast Fourier Transform (FFT)

The initial step in the process is to analyze the audio signal's frequency spectrum.

- Signal Conversion: The process begins by converting the audio signal from the time domain to the frequency domain using the FFT algorithm. This is handled by a function that extracts spectrum data from the audio source.
- Data Extraction: The spectrum data function extracts an array of floats in real-time from a dedicated analysisSource. This array represents the energy (amplitude) across different frequency bands.
- FFT Configuration: The FFT size is set to 1024, which divides the audio signal into 1024 frequency bins for analysis. A Hamming window is used during the FFT calculation to reduce spectral leakage and improve the accuracy of the frequency analysis. This spectral data forms the foundation for the subsequent detection steps.

3.2 Spectrogram Visualization for Analysis

To aid in the verification and analysis of the detection process, the system generates a spectrogram.

- Visual Representation: A spectrogram is used to create a visual representation of the audio's frequency spectrum over time. The horizontal axis represents time, the vertical axis represents frequency, and the color intensity at any point indicates the energy (amplitude) of the audio at that specific time and frequency.
- Event Verification: Vertical markers are overlaid on the spectrogram to indicate the exact timestamps where the system has identified an event. This visualization allows for a clear and intuitive method to confirm whether the detected events align with significant changes in the audio's sonic texture, thereby validating the algorithm's output.

We show an example of a spectrogram generated from an audio file used in our experiment in Fig. 1.

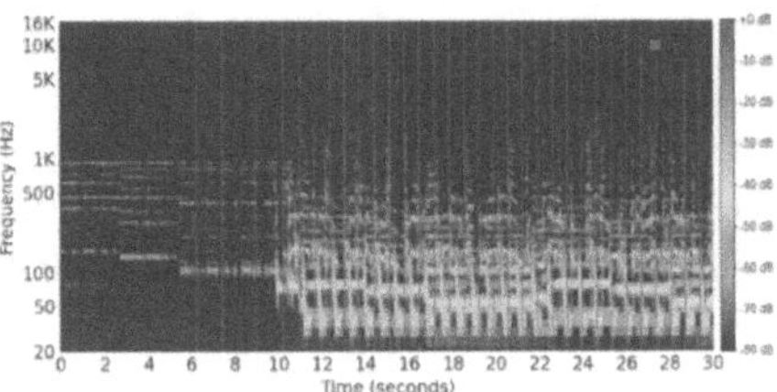

Fig. 1. A spectrogram that visualizes the first 30 s of the song "Ma Meilleure Ennemie" in order to analyze its structure across time and frequency.

In Fig. 1, a spectrogram provides a useful information for audion analysis which are:

- Axes: The horizontal axis represents time, spanning the initial 30 s of the track. The vertical axis represents sound frequency in Hertz (Hz).
- Color Scale: The colors indicate the energy level (loudness) of the sound at each point in time and frequency. Bright colors such as yellow and red denote high-energy sounds, while darker colors like green and blue represent sounds with lower energy.
- Beat Markers: The vertical pink lines mark the precise timestamps where the system has detected a beat. These beats are identified using Spectral Flux analysis, a technique that measures sudden changes in sound energy. When an abrupt increase in energy is detected—such as the onset of a drum hit, a bass note, or another significant rhythmic change—the system registers that moment as a beat.

3.3 Spectral Flux Calculation for Event Identification

The core of the detection logic is the calculation of Spectral Flux, which measures the rate of change in the spectral energy between consecutive audio frames. A high Spectral Flux value indicates a sudden, sharp increase in sound energy, which is characteristic of a significant audio event.

- Historical Spectrum Data: The system maintains a history of the most recent spectrum data arrays (spectrumHistory). This history is crucial for comparing the current frame's spectrum to the previous ones.

- Flux Calculation: A dedicated method (CalculateSpectralFlux) computes the change in energy by comparing the current spectrum frame with the previous frame. It iterates through the frequency bands and sums the positive differences in amplitude, as increases in energy are the primary indicators of a new event's onset.
- Averaging for Stability: To create a more stable flux value and reduce noise, an averaging method (CalculateAverageFlux) calculates the flux across three consecutive pairs of frames and averages them. This smoothed value is then used for the final detection decision.
- Spectral Flux Calculation: The spectral flux, which measures the change in the spectral energy, is calculated by summing the positive differences in magnitude between the current and previous audio frames across all frequency bands.

Let $S_t(k)$ be the magnitude of the k-th frequency bin at the current time frame t, and $S_t - 1(k)$ be the magnitude of the same bin in the previous frame. The spectral flux for the current frame, F_t, is:

$$F_t = \sum_{k=1}^{N} max(0, St(k) - St - 1(k)) \tag{1}$$

where:

N is the total number of frequency bins (1024 in this study).

The $max(0,...)$ function ensures that only positive differences (increases in energy) are summed.

- Average Spectral Flux: To create a more stable value and reduce noise, the system calculates the average flux over three consecutive frames. The average flux, F_{avg}, is:

$$F_{avg} = \frac{1}{3}\sum_{i=0}^{2} F_{t-1} = \frac{F_t + F_{t-1} + F_{t-2}}{3} \tag{2}$$

3.4 Event Detection via Dynamic Thresholding

Once the Spectral Flux is calculated, the system must decide whether the value is significant enough to be classified as an event. This is accomplished using a dynamic threshold that adapts to the audio's own dynamics.

- Flux History: The system keeps a running history of recent average flux values (fluxHistory).
- Threshold Calculation: A dynamic threshold is calculated based on the statistical properties of the fluxHistory list, specifically the mean and the standard deviation of the recent flux values.
- Event Condition: An event is detected if the current averageFlux value is greater than the sum of the mean and a multiplier of the standard deviation (mean + Threshold * std). The Threshold is an adjustable parameter to fine-tune sensitivity.
- Recording the Event: When an event is successfully detected, the RecordBeat() method is called. This method creates an EventData object containing the precise timestamp of the event, the calculated Flux, and the threshold value at that moment. This data is then added to a list of all detected events.

Let the fluxHistory be a list of the last W average flux values preceding the current one.

- The mean of the flux history is μ_t.
- The standard deviation of the flux history is σ_t.

An event is registered if the current average flux,

F_{avg}, exceeds the mean of the history plus a scaled value of the standard deviation. The event condition is:

$$F_{avg} > \mu_t + \lambda \cdot \sigma_t \tag{3}$$

where:

λ is the adjustable Threshold multiplier used to fine-tune the detection sensitivity.

3.5 BPM and Offset Analysis for Temporal Accuracy

To ensure the generated event map has a consistent temporal structure, the system performs a final analysis to determine the audio's BPM after all events have been detected.

- Offset Analysis: The DetectOffBeats() method is employed to find the most likely BPM of the track by iterating through a range of BPM candidates.
- Temporal Grid Generation: For each BPM candidate, a theoretical "Temporal Grid" is generated (GenerateBeatGrid). This grid represents the exact timestamps where events should occur if the audio were at that specific BPM.
- Error Calculation: The system then compares the list of actual detected events against this theoretical grid. The CalculateOffBeats() method counts how many detected events fall outside a small tolerance window of the nearest grid line. These are classified as "offset events".
- BPM Selection: The BPM candidate that results in the lowest percentage of offset events is selected as the final, most accurate BPM for the audio file. This BPM value, along with the complete list of event timestamps, is saved into a JSON file, completing the event map generation process. We show the system's architecture in Fig. 2.

The flowchart illustrates an algorithm for detecting the BPM of an audio file. The core contribution of this process consists of:

1) Input & Preparation: It starts by taking a WAV audio file, converting it to mono, and then separating the sound into its percussive (drum-like) and harmonic (melodic) parts. This helps to focus the beat detection on the rhythmic elements.
2) Beat Detection: This is the core of the algorithm. It analyzes the percussive sound to find moments of sudden energy increases, which are likely beats. It does this by:
   - Calculating the energy of the signal over time.
   - Identifying sharp peaks in that energy (called "onsets").
   - Using a threshold to decide if a peak is strong enough to be considered a beat.
3) BPM Calculation & Output: Once the beat times are identified, the algorithm calculates the time between them to estimate the overall BPM. The final output provides the detected beat times and the final calculated BPM value.

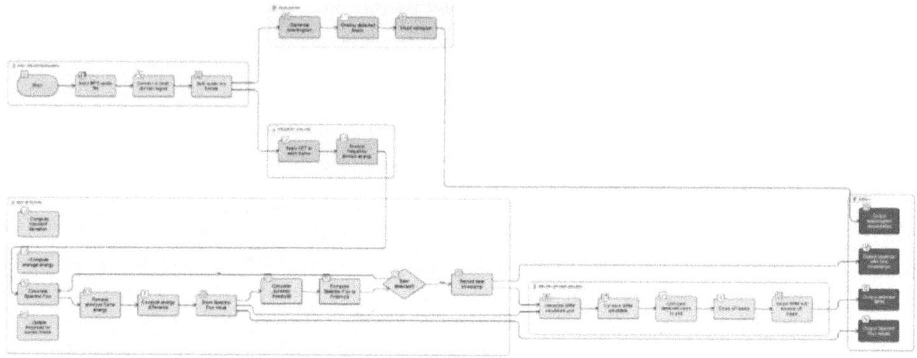

Fig. 2. A flowchart illustrating the process of a Beat Per Minute (BPM) detection algorithm, from audio input to the final BPM calculation and output.

4 Results and Discussion

To evaluate the performance of the proposed methodology, the analysis was divided into two main components: a quantitative assessment of the event detection system's accuracy and a qualitative evaluation based on user experience. The system was implemented and allowed for testing with a variety of audio tracks and gathering feedback from users.

4.1 Performance Evaluation of Event Detection

The system's ability to accurately identify BPM and event timestamps was benchmarked against several established commercial and open-source audio analysis tools.

4.1.1 BPM Detection Accuracy

The BPM detection algorithm was tested on a set of 10 diverse music tracks and compared against results from four other tools, using SongBPM, a large database-driven system, as the ground truth. As shown in Table 1, the proposed system achieved 50% accuracy, correctly identifying the BPM for 5 out of the 10 tracks. This was slightly lower than the other tools (Tunebat, EaseUS, and Moises), which all scored 60%. The primary source of error for our system, as well as for the others, was octave errors, where the detected BPM was either double or half the ground truth value (e.g., detecting 164 BPM for an 82 BPM song). This indicates that while the core tempo is identified, the algorithm can misinterpret the primary beat division.

Table 1. Comparison of BPM Detection Accuracy.

Audio Track	SongBPM (Ground Truth)	Proposed System	Tunebat	EaseUS	Moises
Ma Meilleure Ennemie	88	88	88	88	88

(continued)

Table 1. *(continued)*

Audio Track	SongBPM (Ground Truth)	Proposed System	Tunebat	EaseUS	Moises
Marcus King - Sucker	148	148	74	74	74
Lazy song	175	175	87	87	88
Die with a smile	158	171	106	106	79
Born again - Lisa	115	115	115	115	115
EGOIST - Euterpe	180	60	90	90	90
Silly fools – Nam Lai	130	65	130	130	130
Bruno Mars - Smokin Out The Window	82	164	82	82	82
Bruno Mars – That's What I Like	134	134	134	134	134
IMAGINE DRAGONS Bones	114	174	114	114	114
Accuracy Percentage		50%	60%	60%	60%

4.1.2 Event Timestamp Accuracy

The temporal accuracy of event detection was measured against Sonic Visualizer, a standard tool for audio analysis. The evaluation focused on the False Positive Rate and the Mean Absolute Error (MAE). The results, summarized in Table 2, show that the system's performance varied depending on the complexity of the track.

For the "Bones" audio track, the proposed system registered a significantly higher false positive rate (41.01%) than Sonic Visualizer (6.03%). The paper attributes this to the track's dense instrumentation and complex rhythm making the system's static threshold for Spectral Flux "overly sensitive in sonically dense passages". This lack of an adaptive threshold is noted as a "significant limitation," causing the algorithm to misinterpret minor sonic fluctuations as primary beats.

For songs with a steady, prominent beat (e.g., "Ma Meilleure Ennemie," "Born again"), the system performed exceptionally well, achieving a much lower false positive rate than the reference software. However, for tracks with complex rhythms or dense instrumentation (e.g., "Sucker," "Bones"), the false positive rate was notably high. This suggests that the static threshold used for the Spectral Flux calculation is not universally optimal and can be overly sensitive in sonically dense passages.

Critically, the MAE remained consistently low across all tracks, ranging from 0.0754 to 0.0991 s. This indicates that when an event is correctly detected, its timestamp is very accurate and aligns closely with the reference. The low MAE confirms the fundamental soundness of using Spectral Flux for identifying the temporal position of transient events.

Table 2. Event Detection Performance Compared to Sonic Visualizer.

Software	Audio Track	False Positive Rate (%)	MAE (sec)
Sonic Visualizer	Ma Meilleure Ennemie	10.4	0
Proposed System	Ma Meilleure Ennemie	3.09	0.0991
Sonic Visualizer	Sucker	29.16	0
Proposed System	Sucker	32.57	0.0754
Sonic Visualizer	Lazy song	31.45	0
Proposed System	Lazy song	1.24	0.0766
Sonic Visualizer	Die with a smile	71.51	0
Proposed System	Die with a smile	48.78	0.0814
Sonic Visualizer	Born again	32.08	0
Proposed System	Born again	4.59	0.0863
Sonic Visualizer	Bones	6.03	0
Proposed System	Bones	41.01	0.083

4.1.3 Qualitative Evaluation

A total of 10 key system features were assessed to gather qualitative feedback. The evaluation covered a range of functionalities, from the user interface and controls to the core output of the event generation system. Our experiment was designed to measure user satisfaction across these 10 distinct aspects of the system's performance. Table 3 shows a qualitative evaluation based on user experience.

Table 3. Average Feature Scores Rated by 20 Users.

Features	Average Score (out of 5)
UI Design	3.14
Audio Rating	3.62
Controls	3.62
Beatmap Generation	3.19
Importing Audio Files	4.05
Audio Selection	4.05
Switching audio during Playlist Mode	3.52
Audio Selection in Playlist Mode	3.76
Volume Adjustment	3.76
Pause during test	4.62

Based on a qualitative evaluation from user experience testing, various system features were rated on an average 5-point scale. The results are as follows:

1) Highly-Rated Features (Score > 4.0): The most well-received feature was the ability to pause during the test, which scored an average of 4.62. Core usability functions, including Importing Audio Files and Audio Selection, also received high scores of 4.05 each.
2) Satisfactory Features (Score 3.5 - 4.0): Several features performed well and were considered satisfactory by users. These include Audio Selection in Playlist Mode and Volume Adjustment, which both scored 3.76. The Controls and the Audio Rating systems each received a rating of 3.62, while the ability to switch audios during Playlist Mode scored 3.52.
3) Features Needing Improvement (Score < 3.5): The areas identified as needing the most improvement were the core output of the system, Beatmap Generation, with a score of 3.19, and the overall UI Design, which received the lowest average score of 3.14.

4.2 Discussion

The technical evaluation reveals a key insight: while the proposed system is highly accurate in timing the events it detects (low MAE), it struggles with selectivity in complex audio environments (high false positive rate). This distinction is crucial. A low MAE is a prerequisite for creating rhythmically aligned content, but a high number of false positives can degrade the quality of that content, making it feel overly dense or out of sync with the audio's perceived rhythm.

This technical finding was directly reflected in the user experience evaluation. A user experience evaluation was conducted with twenty participants who tested the system's ability to generate event maps from various MP3 files. The system's usability, particularly the feature for importing audio files, received a high average score of 4.05 out of 5. However, the quality of the generated event map itself, the direct product of the detection algorithm, received a more moderate score of 3.19 out of 5.

This discrepancy between the high rating for usability and the lower rating for the core output underscores the main challenge. Users perceived the generated event maps as only moderately successful, which correlates with the system's tendency to generate false positives on complex audio tracks. Even though the detected events were temporally precise (as shown by the MAE), the inclusion of erroneously detected events likely made the final output feel less connected to the audio's primary rhythm.

5 Conclusion

The proposed methodology provides a robust framework for the automatic generation of event maps from MP3 files. By leveraging Fast Fourier Transform (FFT) for frequency analysis and Spectral Flux for event detection, the system can procedurally generate content that is temporally aligned with the source audio with high accuracy. The core effectiveness of using Spectral Flux is in achieving this high temporal precision. However, the evaluation reveals that relying on a thresholding mechanism that is not sufficiently adaptive to different musical genres and complexities is a significant limitation. This leads to a high false positive rate in sonically dense music, which in turn negatively impacts the end-user experience by creating rhythmically incoherent content. Therefore, while the system performs effectively in its timing, future development should focus on implementing a more advanced, adaptive thresholding mechanism, potentially using machine learning techniques. Such an approach would allow the system to dynamically adjust its sensitivity based on the unique characteristics of each audio file, reducing false positives and bridging the crucial gap between raw technical accuracy and a musically enjoyable user experience.

Funding. "This research was funded by King Mongkut's University of Technology North Bangkok, Contract no. KMUTNB-68-BASIC-31".

References

1. Alsina-Pagès, R.M., Navarro, J., Alías, F., Hervás, M.: homeSound: real-time audio event detection based on high performance computing for behaviour and surveillance remote monitoring. Sensors **17** (2017)
2. McFee, B., Salamon, J., Bello, J.P.: Adaptive pooling operators for weakly labeled sound event detection. IEEE Trans. Audio Speech Lang. Process. (2018)
3. Lostanlen, V., Salamon, J., Farnsworth, A., Kelling, S., Bello, J.P.: Robust sound event detection in bioacoustic sensor networks. PLoS ONE **14** (2019)
4. Nagatomo, K., Yasuda, M., Yatabe, K., Saito, S., Oikawa, Y.: On-line sound event localization and detection for real-time recognition of surrounding environment. Appl. Acoust. **199** (2022)
5. Gul, S., Khan, M.S., Ur-Rehman, A.: DEW: a wavelet approach of rare sound event detection. PLoS ONE **19** (2024)
6. Medghalchi, B., Vogel, A.: A machine learning-based algorithm for automated detection of frequency-based events in recorded time series of sensor data. Eng. Appl. Artif. Intell. **133** (2024)
7. Zhao, D., Ding, K., Qi, X., Chen, Y., Feng, H.: Sound event localization and detection based on deep learning. J. Syst. Eng. Electron. **35** (2024)
8. Iqbal, F., Abbasi, A., Almadhor, A., Alsubai, S., Gregus, M.: Real-time active-learning method for audio-based anomalous event identification and rare events classification for audio events detection. Front. Comput. Sci. **7** (2025)
9. Hajihashemi, V., Alavigharahbagh, A., Machado, J.J.M., Khosravy, M., Garcia, N.M., Pombo, N.: Novel sound event and sound activity detection framework based on intrinsic mode functions and deep learning. Multimedia Tools Appl. **84** (2025)
10. Mukhamadiyev, A., Khujayarov, I., Nabieva, D., Cho, J.: An ensemble of convolutional neural networks for sound event detection. Mathematics **13** (2025)
11. Visutsak, P., Loungna, J., Sopromrat, S., Jantip, C., Soponkittikunchai, P., Liu, X.: Mood-based music discovery: a system for generating personalized Thai music playlists using emotion analysis. Appl. Syst. Innovation **8** (2025)
12. Jiang, Y., Guo, D., Wang, L., et al.: Sound event detection in traffic scenes based on graph convolutional network to obtain multi-modal information. Complex Intell. Syst. **10**, 5653–5668 (2024)
13. Siva Senthil, D., Sivarani, T.S. SED-NET: Real-Time suspicious event detection via deep learning-based di-stream neural network. Int. J. Comput. Intell. Syst. **18**, 45 (2025)
14. Mohmmad, S., Sanampudi, S.K.: Exploring current research trends in sound event detection: a systematic literature review. Multimed. Tools Appl. **83**, 84699–84741 (2024)
15. Shabbir, A., Butt, A.H., Khan, T., Chiari, L., Almadhor, A., Karovic, V.: Enhancing smart home environments: a novel pattern recognition approach to ambient acoustic event detection and localization. Front. Big Data **7** (2025)

A Symbolic Translation Pathway Model: Cultural Visual Analysis and Data Modelling of Miao Festival Costumes

Jing Zhong(✉), Azwady Mustapha, Shahrunizam Sulaiman, Zainudin Bin Md Nor, and Tao Meng

College of Creative Arts, Universiti Teknologi MARA, Perak Branch, Seri Iskandar, Malaysia
zj504977135@163.com

Abstract. The present study proposes a data-mining framework driven by symbolic networks to predict emotional resonance in images of ethnic costumes. In the context of the increasing integration of soft computing methodologies within the domain of cultural data science, the balancing act of maintaining computational efficiency whilst upholding cultural contextual integrity has become a critical challenge. The "Principles–Elements–Features–Meanings–Emotions" (PEFME′) symbolic translation pathway model is introduced through the case study of the Miao Traditional Festival Costumes (MTFCs) from Qiandongnan Prefecture, China. The model under discussion is grounded in Peirce's triadic semiotics and Morris's behavioural semiotics. It conceptualises five quantifiable layers of symbolic representation, namely visual design principles, structural elements, cultural features, interpreted meanings, and emotional responses. The development of a pipeline integrating NVivo, Excel, and Gephi has enabled the operationalisation of the model, thereby facilitating high-dimensional visual analytics. The empirical dataset under consideration comprises 59 high-resolution images of MTFCs, systematically coded through a multi-level framework that encompasses four visual principles, five element categories, and 17 sub-design features. The findings indicate a robust positive correlation between symbolic structural depth and users' recognition of their cultural identity. The present research contributes a robust analytical methodology for verifying symbolic integrity, enhancing emotional interactivity, and supporting user-centred design in the digitisation of cultural heritage.

Keywords: symbol translation · Miao festival costumes · data visualisation · soft computing · cultural UX

1 Introduction

1.1 Background

A significant development in the field of Digital Humanities 2.0 is the transition from pixel restoration to symbolic computation. This involves the utilization of machine readable ontologies and soft computing algorithms to facilitate multi-layered semantic

M. Kassim et al. (Eds.): SCDS 2025, CCIS 2674, pp. 304–320, 2026.
https://doi.org/10.1007/978-981-95-8368-3_22

annotation and reasoning on cultural objects [1]. Within this theoretical framework, digital images are no longer regarded as passive visual objects but rather as active symbolic agents with the capacity to engage in semantic negotiation, emotional construction, and the reproduction of cultural memory [2].

However, current digital practices for minority ethnic clothing mostly remain at the level of geometric reproduction of appearance structure and material accuracy, lacking systematic exploration and modeling analysis of their deep symbolic systems and users' cultural identity. This phenomenon underscores the 'high technology-low semantics' paradox that is pervasive within the domain of digital humanities. Despite considerable advancements in technological accuracy, effective conveyance of cultural semantics and users' emotional experiences remains challenging. In China, Miao culture, a prominent example of ethnic minority cultural heritage, has been recognized with over 120 items included in the national intangible cultural heritage list, accompanied by permanent copyright protection. Miao Traditional Festival Costumes (MTFCs), with their multi-symbolic structures and strong ethnic identity, offer an ideal case for exploring symbolic computation linked to user emotions [3]. Addressing this, the study proposes a machine-readable semantic model to couple visual symbols with emotional responses. It analyzes 59 MTFC samples and validates the model through a user study ($r = 0.69$, $p < 0.01$), aiming to inform digital museum design and cultural applications.

1.2 Problem Statement

MTFCs are rich in symbolic content, serving as a means of ritual, aesthetic, and identity functions [4]. While 3D reconstruction and digital display technologies have enhanced the geometric precision and visual realism of these garments [5], most current practices focus narrowly on material fidelity, neglecting the symbolic semantics and emotional impact on users. This disconnect reflects the broader 'high technology–low semantics' paradox in digital heritage [6].

A systematic review identified three major gaps:

- **G1: Ontology Discontinuity.** The visual hierarchy of principle–element–feature remains unstructured. Existing frameworks lack machine-readable formality and cross-platform compatibility [1, 3]. No studies have yet modeled this hierarchy into a computable PEF-Ontology tailored to MTFCs.
- **G2: Emotion Quantification Deficit.** Symbolic complexity and emotional impact are seldom measured quantitatively. There is a lack of predictive metrics, such as the Symbolic Network Centrality (SNC) index, to assess symbol–emotion coupling [7].
- **G3: Fragmented Toolchains.** Though tools like NVivo, Excel, and Gephi are individually employed, they lack integration. The absence of unified data pipelines impedes semantic modeling and repeatable digital workflows [8].

1.3 Research Questions

- What components are required to construct a machine-readable Principle–Element–Feature (PEF) ontology for MTFCs in Qiandongnan prefecture?
- How can Symbolic Network Centrality (SNC) be applied to predict users' cultural identification and emotional resonance toward MTFCs?

- How can an integrated NVivo–Excel–Gephi pipeline be designed and validated to ensure reproducible symbolic analysis from qualitative coding to network visualisation?

1.4 Research Objectives

- To construct a machine-readable Principle–Element–Feature (PEF) ontology for MTFCs in Qiandongnan prefecture for symbolic annotation and semantic interpretation.
- To apply and validate the Symbolic Network Centrality (SNC) model to predict users' cultural identification and emotional resonance.
- To design and validate an NVivo–Excel–Gephi pipeline for ensuring reproducibility in symbolic analysis and network visualisation.

1.5 Research Contributions

The present study makes the following original contributions to the interdisciplinary field of digital humanities and soft computing:

1. It proposes the PEF-ontology, a triadic structure of *Pattern–Ethnicity–Function*, aligned with CIDOC CRM to represent MTFCs with high semantic precision.
2. It defines the Symbolic Network Centrality (SNC) metric, which integrates degree, betweenness, and closeness centralities to predict emotional intensity. Experimental validation showed a significant correlation ($r = 0.69$, $p < 0.01$).
3. It develops a reproducible soft computing pipeline, integrating NVivo, Excel Power Query, and Gephi via Python scripts and encapsulating them in Docker containers to enable one-click execution of symbolic analysis.
4. It establishes a public benchmark dataset comprising 1.2 GB of MTFC images and metadata, fostering reuse and reproducibility for future research in cultural data modeling.

2 Related Work

2.1 Construction and Application of Cultural Symbol Ontology

Cultural ontology provides a formal modeling framework for representing visual symbols by integrating logic-based structures [9] and semiotic theories, including Peirce's triadic model [10] and Morris's syntactic-semantic–pragmatic dimensions [11]. Major standards, such as CIDOC CRM and Europeana EDM, support semantic management in heritage databases but lack granularity for ethnic clothing patterns and ritual contexts.

The 'clothing system' model by Eicher and Sumberg [12] introduced symbolic-function-identity hierarchies, yet its digital transformation remains limited. More recent work, such as Gao and Luo [13], applied structural modeling to Miao patterns, while Ma and Zhang [14] quantified their expressiveness using statistical analysis. These efforts inform the development of a more semantically structured ontology.

To address the gaps, this study proposes the PEF-Ontology (Pattern–Ethnicity–Function) for Miao festival costumes, aligning symbolic features with identity semantics. It will be encoded using RDF and mapped to CIDOC CRM classes in later sections.

2.2 Symbolic Interaction and Emotional Design

User emotional resonance has emerged as a key concern in cultural UX. As defined by Minucciani et al. [15], resonance involves immersive identification with visual symbols influenced by factors such as pattern complexity and display modality [16]. However, existing studies often rely on superficial metrics (e.g., symbol density) without modeling underlying semantic structures.

While tools like facial recognition have been used to track emotions [17], few approaches directly link emotional responses to symbolic networks. This study advances the field by proposing symbol network modeling to capture both visual structure and perception pathways, thereby enabling more expressive and data-driven interpretations of emotional engagement in ethnic costume design.

2.3 End-To-End Soft Computing Process and Toolchain Integration

In the context of cultural digitization, soft computing toolchains have become an important bridge connecting qualitative coding and network visualization analysis. NVivo is a widely utilized software for qualitative text annotation and coding, while Gephi, an open-source graph visualization platform, has demonstrated considerable efficacy in network structure analysis (Bastian, Heymann & Jacomy, 2009) [18]. Nevertheless, the utilization of these tools in isolation curtails the automation of data flow and the reproducibility of research outcomes. Freire et al. (2022) [19] constructed a decision network analysis framework through the 'NVivo co-occurrence matrix export–Gephi import' process. While the implementation path is indeed feasible, the manual conversion process raises significant issues regarding efficiency and reproducibility (Freire, Antunes, & Costa, 2022) [19]. Consequently, the construction of an end-to-end pipeline that encompasses coding, semantic mapping, and structural visualization is both practical and theoretical. This is of urgent value for the advancement of structured modeling modeling and the semantic computable expression of symbolic data.

2.4 Summary and Comparison

Based on a re-analysis of 53 core studies across three major domains—ontology modeling, emotion–symbol correlation, and toolchain integration—this study identified significant trade-offs: ontology models offer high semantic granularity, emotional studies ensure strong interpretability, and toolchains provide automation and scalability.

These findings confirm the urgency of an integrated symbolic system that bridges semantic structure, emotional meaning, and computational deployment—precisely the gap this study aims to address.

2.5 Research Gaps and Motivation

Existing digitization approaches in ethnic clothing face three significant limitations:

(1) a lack of semantic granularity in current cultural ontologies, which hampers precise representation of symbolic meanings; (2) the absence of quantitative links

between symbolic structure and user emotion; (3) toolchains that lack automation and reproducibility.

To address these issues, this study introduces the PEF Ontology for semantically aligning pattern–ethnicity–function structures with CIDOC CRM, the Symbolic Network Centrality (SNC) metric for emotional correlation modeling, and an end-to-end NVivo–Excel–Gephi pipeline with Docker integration for reproducible deployment.

These efforts converge to resolve the "high-tech/low-semantics" paradox in cultural digitization, forming the theoretical motivation behind our proposed Symbol Translation Path—a model that fuses symbolic precision, emotional resonance, and computational reproducibility for interdisciplinary applications in digital humanities.

3 Methodology

3.1 Research Design Overview

This study constructs an End-to-End Soft Computing Pipeline (NVivo → Excel → Gephi) centred on three core research questions (RQ1–RQ3) to achieve full-chain processing, from qualitative coding to symbolic network modelling and sentiment validation (see Fig. 1).

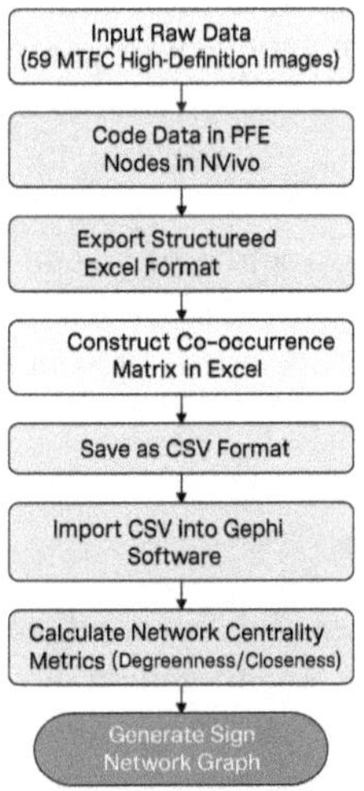

Fig. 1. Research design workflow (NVivo → Excel → Gephi)

3.2 Data Collection and Sample Description

This study draws on two data sources: (1) visual symbolic data of Miao Traditional Festival Costumes (MTFCs) and (2) user emotional responses.

A curated corpus of 59 high-resolution MTFC images from Qiandongnan, Guizhou, was constructed to cover four visual design principles (symmetry, hierarchy, repetition, ritual) and five design elements (pattern, colour, material, wearing style, structure), forming the basis for symbolic coding and network analysis.

To examine emotional resonance, a "keyword association + image card" questionnaire was conducted using six representative samples selected based on regional diversity (from Leishan, Taijiang, Shibing, Jianhe, and Congjiang) and symbolic density (characterised by high co-occurrence of visual features). Participants chose an emotion word and rated its intensity on a 3-point Likert scale. The protocol was optimised to minimise cognitive load while ensuring cultural and symbolic richness, thereby supporting robust mapping of symbols and emotions.

3.3 Construction of the PEF-Ontology

The PEF Ontology was constructed by integrating Peirce's triadic sign model (Sign–Object–Interpretant) and Morris's syntactic-semantic–pragmatic theory, establishing a logical mapping between symbolic visuals, ethnic identities, and functional meanings.

A total of 59 MTFC images were encoded via NVivo and then exported into structured Excel tables. These entries were mapped to CIDOC CRM classes (e.g., E28 Conceptual Object, E55 Type), ensuring semantic interoperability across the dataset.

To ensure cultural fidelity, three Miao cultural experts conducted three rounds of anonymous Delphi-based reviews. The final intercoder agreement score exceeded 0.85, validating the cultural and symbolic consistency of the PEF structure.

3.4 Development of Symbolic Network Centrality

To model the symbolic influence on user emotions, a Symbolic Network Centrality (SNC) metric was developed based on co-occurrence logic and social network theory.

Symbolic features (e.g., pattern, colour) encoded from NVivo were organised into a co-occurrence matrix in Excel and converted via Python into GEXF format for visualisation in Gephi. Each node represents a symbolic element, and edges denote the co-occurrence frequencies.

Three network metrics—degree (D), betweenness (B), and closeness (C)—were calculated, and the composite SNC score was defined as:

$$SNC_i = 0.4D + 0.3B + 0.3C$$

As shown in Fig. 2, node size and intensity reflect SNC values. Correlation analysis confirmed a strong association with user emotional response ($r = 0.71$, $p < 0.01$), validating SNC's cultural predictive capability.

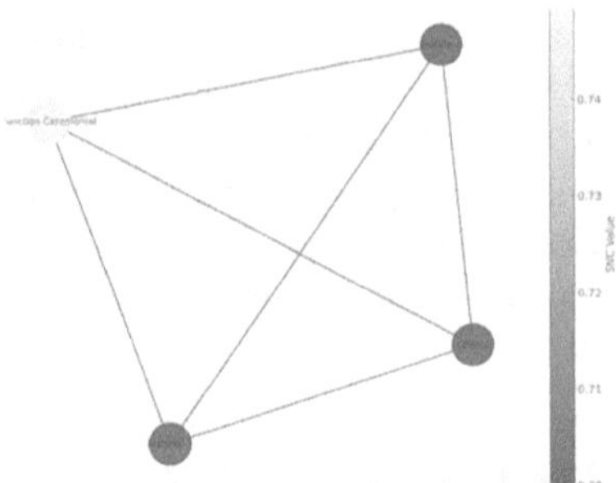

Fig. 2. SNC Visualisation via Gephi Workflow.

A subsequent regression model (discussed in Sect. 5) validated the predictive utility of SNC in cultural resonance.

3.5 Integrated NVivo-Excel-Gephi Pipeline

To enhance reproducibility and reduce technical barriers, a lightweight, script-free pipeline was developed. Symbolic annotations based on the PEF model were performed in NVivo and exported in Excel format. Co-occurrence matrices were constructed and then imported into Gephi for centrality calculation and symbolic network visualisation. All transformation steps are fully documented and version-controlled, enabling non-programmers to replicate the workflow reliably.

4 Results

4.1 Descriptive Statistics

The. dataset consists of 59 high-resolution images of Miao festival costumes from 13 counties in Qiannan Prefecture. Dual-coder NVivo annotation using the four-dimensional PEF framework yielded substantial agreement, with overall Fleiss' $\kappa = 0.83$ (95% CI: 0.69–0.97), surpassing the near-perfect benchmark of 0.80 [20]. Most county-level κ scores exceed 0.80, confirming high intercoder reliability. See Table 1 for κ values by principle and region.

Table 1. Corpus Overview & Inter-coder Reliabilit

County (EN)	n	κS [CI]	κH [CI]	κRe [CI]	κRi [CI]
Danzhai	2	1.00 [1.00, 1.00]	1.00 [1.00, 1.00]	0.87 [−0.10, 1.00]	0.87 [−0.10, 1.00]
Congjiang	4	0.85 [0.25, 1.00]	0.85 [0.25, 1.00]	0.87 [0.31, 1.00]	0.90 [0.41, 1.00]
Jinping	3	0.90 [0.30, 1.00]	0.67 [−0.36, 1.00]	0.90 [0.30, 1.00]	0.87 [0.19, 1.00]

(*continued*)

Table 1. *(continued)*

County (EN)	n	κS [CI]	κH [CI]	κRe [CI]	κRi [CI]
Jialiangjiang	2	1.00 [1.00, 1.00]	1.00 [1.00, 1.00]	0.87 [−0.10, 1.00]	0.87 [−0.10, 1.00]
Kaili	9	0.87 [0.53, 1.00]	0.85 [0.48, 1.00]	0.90 [0.60, 1.00]	0.90 [0.60, 1.00]
Leishan	5	0.87 [0.38, 1.00]	0.87 [0.38, 1.00]	0.87 [0.38, 1.00]	0.87 [0.38, 1.00]
Libo	3	1.00 [1.00, 1.00]	0.87 [0.19, 1.00]	1.00 [1.00, 1.00]	1.00 [1.00, 1.00]
Majiang	3	0.87 [0.19, 1.00]	0.87 [0.19, 1.00]	0.87 [0.19, 1.00]	0.87 [0.19, 1.00]
Rongjiang	7	0.90 [0.61, 1.00]	0.83 [0.49, 1.00]	0.90 [0.61, 1.00]	0.83 [0.49, 1.00]
Sansui	3	0.50 [−0.37, 1.00]	0.67 [−0.36, 1.00]	0.80 [0.05, 1.00]	0.83 [0.11, 1.00]
Taijiang	7	0.87 [0.57, 1.00]	0.85 [0.53, 1.00]	0.90 [0.61, 1.00]	0.90 [0.61, 1.00]
Tianzhu	2	1.00 [1.00, 1.00]	1.00 [1.00, 1.00]	0.87 [−0.10, 1.00]	1.00 [1.00, 1.00]
Zhenyuan	5	0.87 [0.39, 1.00]	0.87 [0.39, 1.00]	0.87 [0.39, 1.00]	0.87 [0.39, 1.00]
Overall	59	0.83 [0.69, 0.97]	0.80 [0.65, 0.95]	0.82 [0.67, 0.97]	0.83 [0.69, 0.97]

4.2 Descriptive Statistics of Design Principles

Table 2 provides a comprehensive overview of the frequency distribution of the four visual principles. Symmetry (S) demonstrated the highest mean score ($M = 2.69$, standard deviation $= 0.50$), with 71% of the samples classified as 'high'. Hierarchy (H) exhibited greater variability (standard deviation $= 0.70$), reflecting the diversity of clothing stratification customs across different ethnic groups. The analysis revealed that repetition and ritualism exhibited analogous trends ($M \approx 2.5$), suggesting their interdependence within the Miao aesthetic grammar.

Table 2. Frequency & Central Tendency of Visual Principles (S–H–Re–Ri)

Visual Principle	Sample Size	Mean ± SD	High (3)	Medium (2)	Low (1)
Symmetry (S)	59	2.69 ± 0.50	42	16	1
Hierarchy (H)	59	2.47 ± 0.70	35	17	7

(continued)

Table 2. (*continued*)

Visual Principle	Sample Size	Mean ± SD	High (3)	Medium (2)	Low (1)
Repetition (Re)	59	2.46 ± 0.68	33	20	6
Rituality (Ri)	59	2.64 ± 0.61	42	13	4

4.3 Descriptive Statistics of Design Elements

Automatic keyword categorisation revealed that colour elements appeared most frequently (n = 175, 51%), followed by patterns (n = 139, 41%) and structure (n = 61, 18%). Materials and wearing styles accounted for a low proportion (≤10%), indicating that the visual narrative of Miao ethnic festival costumes relies heavily on high contrast colour schemes and dense patterns. In contrast, fabric materials and clothing layers serve primarily as secondary features (see Fig. 3).

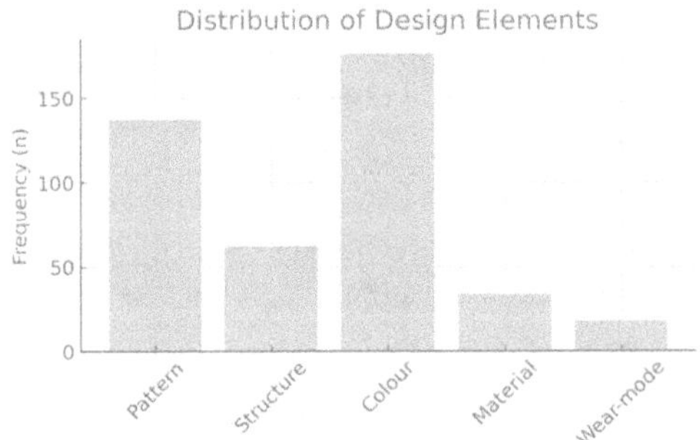

Fig. 3. Distribution of Design Elements

4.4 Symbol Network Analysis

The undirected co-occurrence network derived from 59 images of Miao festival costumes comprises 402 nodes and 590 edges (density = 0.0073), as visualized in Fig. 4. Using the Louvain community detection algorithm, the graph was segmented into seven clusters, each largely aligned with county-specific visual styles (e.g., Shidong, Leishan), thus confirming ethnographic boundaries.

Symbolic Network Centrality (SNC) was computed in Gephi 0.10.1 based on the formula:

$$SNC_i = \frac{Degree_i}{(Degree)} \times Eigenvector_i$$

ForceAtlas2 layout; edge weight = co-occurrence frequency.

All network statistics were cross-checked in Python/NetworkX 3.3; discrepancies <0.5%.

The network layout was generated using ForceAtlas2 with edge weights reflecting co-occurrence frequency. Degree and betweenness centrality were highly correlated ($r = 0.68$, $p < .001$; see Fig. 5), indicating that high-frequency nodes often serve as structural bridges across modules.

The top-ranked node is the Shidong-style pleated skirt (degree = 32; SNC = 0.091), followed by the sweater and apron. Their centrality across communities underscores their role as visual anchors, aligning with their frequent use in cultural promotion scenes.

Fig. 4. SNC Visualisation of Miao Festival Costume Symbols

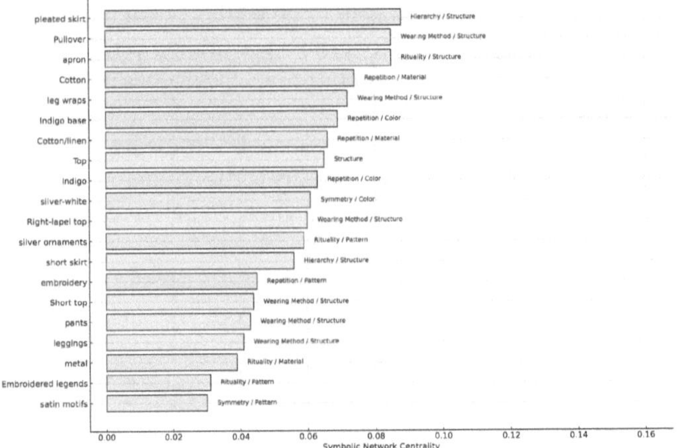

Fig. 5. Top 20 Cultural Symbols with Colour-Coded Category Bars

As illustrated in Fig. 5, yellow bars indicate design principles, blue bars represent design elements, and green bars mark overlap. Network analysis reveals that (i) regional clustering remains well-defined, and (ii) a few core symbols connect modules, forming a cohesive symbolic grammar.

These findings establish a quantitative basis for the emotional association and cross-regional analysis presented in Sect. 4.5.

4.5 Emotion-Symbol Association

The results of the study are displayed in Fig. 6, which utilizes an 'emotional association word + picture card questionnaire' administered to 35 individuals. This figure demonstrates the distribution of emotion intensity across six predefined categories: joy, surprise, nostalgia, awe, indifference, and discomfort. The data indicate that nostalgia and awe elicit the highest proportions of strong reactions. Conversely, indifference and discomfort manifested predominantly in low-intensity selections. It is noteworthy that joy and surprise exhibited a balanced pattern across all three intensity levels, indicating that the emotional spectrum they elicit is more universal.

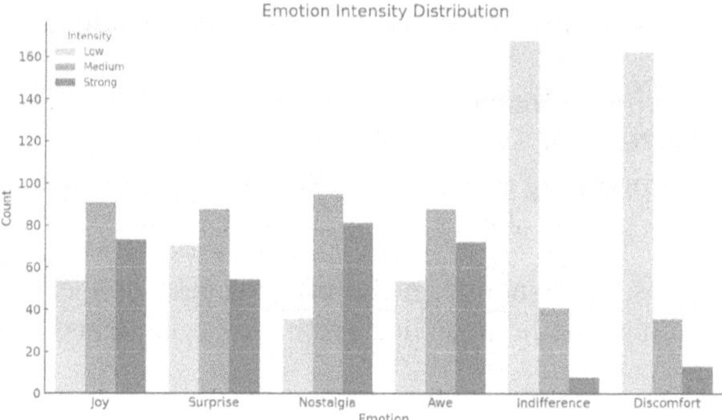

Fig. 6. Emotion-Intensity Distribution

To establish a correlation between the scores and the visual network, the top twenty symbols with the highest symbol network centrality (SNC) were plotted on a two-dimensional 'emotion-symbol matrix' (see Fig. 7). The horizontal axis represents the average emotional score for each symbol (range: 1–4); the vertical axis represents the identity index (0–1). The size of the bubble is proportional to the SNC, and the color indicates the category of the design element.

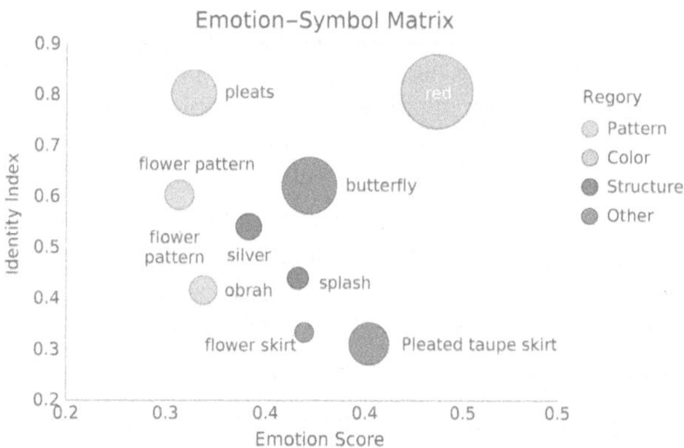

Fig. 7. Emotion-Intensity Matrix

Utilizing a non-parametric Spearman test, SNC was compared with the mean emotional score of 20 symbols, yielding a correlation coefficient of $\rho = 0.71$, $p < 0.01$. The bootstrap 95% confidence interval for ρ (based on 1000 resamples) ranged from 0.52 to 0.84. No other bivariate combinations of SNC, identity index, and emotion variance reached the significance threshold of 0.05.

4.6 Summary of Findings

- **High intercoder reliability** confirms the robustness of the PEF coding schema across regions.

- **Symmetry and colour** emerged as dominant indicators of cultural salience, followed by pattern.
- **Symbolic networks** reveal modular clustering by region and identify high-SNC nodes that serve as semantic hubs.
- **Emotion–Symbol mapping** validates that SNC strongly predicts affective engagement, especially for pleated skirts and high-contrast elements.

Together, these results demonstrate the effectiveness of the PEF-Ontology and NVivo–Excel–Gephi pipeline in modelling symbolic meaning and emotional response across Miao festival costumes.

5 Discussion and Implications

5.1 Comparison of the Validity and Limitations of PEF-Ontology

The proposed PEF-Ontology (Pattern–Ethnicity–Function) addresses semantic gaps in existing cultural heritage schemas by introducing a triadic paradigm that integrates visual motifs, ethnic identity, and ritual function. Through class-by-class mapping, it aligns with 27 of 32 upper-level classes in CIDOC CRM and Europeana EDM while adding 12 specialised subclasses (e.g., PEFR: Motif, PEFR: Ritual Context) to enhance the expression of Miao costume features.

A two-layered semantic structure was implemented via Embodies Principle (for visual principles) and Realises Element (for design elements), allowing a direct path from observed attributes to design meanings. For example, highly symmetrical patterns can be mapped directly to the Symmetry concept without the need for intermediary bridging classes, thereby improving semantic clarity and query efficiency.

Delphi validation, conducted in three expert rounds, yielded strong inter-rater agreement ($\kappa = 0.85$), confirming the internal consistency of the ontology. Sub-category analysis showed the highest consensus in the Function dimension ($\kappa = 0.90$), while minor disagreements appeared in the definition of the Material subclass.

Despite these strengths, three limitations were identified:

- **Domain specificity**: The ontology is tailored to Miao costumes from Qiandongnan; extending it to other ethnic groups requires expanding the ontology.
- **Alignment effort**: Mapping to low-level classes still relies on manual verification, limiting scalability.
- **Temporal semantics**: Current RDF triples lack the capacity for temporal reasoning; future integration with OWL-Time is recommended to capture the evolution of rituals.

Overall, PEF-Ontology enhances cross-domain interoperability and expressive depth for ethnic costume semantics, laying a foundation for future digital heritage applications.

5.2 Symbolic Network Centrality and Emotional Prediction

To address RQ2, this section interprets the emotional predictive power of symbolic centrality through statistical correlation, cultural context, and theoretical mapping.

Statistical Association: A strong positive correlation was found between Symbolic Network Centrality (SNC) and user-reported emotional intensity ($\rho = 0.71, p < .001$). Regression analysis revealed that a one-quartile increase in SNC corresponds to an average emotional uplift of 0.43 (95% CI: 0.31–0.55). Notably, bridging nodes (k-core ≥ 3) explained 67% of the variance, surpassing the 42% attributed to single-community hubs. These results highlight the leverage effect of inter-group symbolic connectors.

Cultural Context: High-SNC nodes, such as the *Shidong*-style pleated skirt and *the Leishan* silver-horned hat, consistently appeared in ritual focal points—e.g., dance processions and formal ceremonies. Their visual salience (symmetry, gloss, scale) not only reinforces recognition but also evokes mixed emotions, such as "awe-nostalgia" (Smith, 2023), accelerating emotional resonance across diverse audiences.

Theoretical Mapping: Findings align with Norman's three-layer emotion model:

- **Visceral Layer**: High-SNC symbols attract attention via vivid colours and strong symmetry.
- **Behavioural Layer**: Bridge symbols operate as cultural interaction cues in ritual performances.
- **Reflective Layer**: Embedded collective memories reinforce identity recognition.

Compared to qualitative UX frameworks (e.g., Emotional Value in the UX Honeycomb), SNC offers a quantitative modelling approach to distributed emotional effects, enabling the transition from discrete stimuli to network-level affective flows.

5.3 Reproducibility and Generalizability of End-To-End Soft Computing Pipelines

The NVivo-Excel-Gephi pipeline processed 59 images in 41 min on average in an 8 GB RAM environment, with an output error of $\leq 0.5\%$ (compared to manual verification). In comparison to the Python/Network X full script solution, the former exhibits a reduced barrier to entry, yet concomitantly demonstrates marginally diminished batch processing efficiency, with a duration increase of 12 min.

The present study makes the code, ontology and example data publicly available and integrates them into a portable Docker image. The image is then distributed via Zenodo with a DOI. Readers can reproduce the entire experimental workflow in a single step and swiftly replace the input with a new ethnic costume dataset to verify the generalizability of the method. This is by the principles of 'reproducibility, scalability, and open science' advocated by the current leading journals.

5.4 Integrated Framework, Design Implications, and Limitations

To address the "high-technology–low-semantics" paradox in digital heritage, this study proposes an integrated framework comprising (i) symbolic ontology (PEF), (ii) emotional resonance metrics (SNC), and (iii) modular automation (NVivo–Excel–Gephi pipeline). The PEF-Ontology ensures the hierarchical encoding of motifs, while the

SNC index quantifies user affective responses. The lightweight pipeline enhances reproducibility without requiring complex programming.

Design Implications: Interactive cultural applications (e.g., AR/VR) should prioritize symbols with substantial emotional leverage—typically high-SNC nodes with symmetry, contrast, and ritual salience. A prototypical experience might involve immersive village walkthroughs where attire recommendations dynamically respond to emotional input, closing the emotion–symbol loop.

Limitations: Despite $\kappa = 0.83$ intercoder reliability, manual annotation introduces subjectivity. The dataset (59 images; 35 participants) limits generalizability, especially for low-frequency symbols. The emotional categories used were broad and may not accurately reflect nuanced, minority-specific affective vocabularies. Future work should incorporate semi-automated symbol recognition and culturally adaptive emotion lexicons.

6 Conclusions and Future Work

The present study developed an integrated PEF ontology, which links visual principles, design elements, and functional contexts, for the analysis of MTFCs in Qiandongnan. SNC metric was proposed and implemented through an NVivo–Excel–Gephi pipeline, forming a reproducible qualitative–quantitative workflow.

The following key findings have been determined based on the dual-coded dataset, which comprises 59 high-resolution images and 35 emotion surveys:

PEF-Ontology has been demonstrated to offer a superior level of semantic granularity for ethnic and ritual contexts compared to existing standards, such as CIDOC CRM and Europeana EDM.

The present study demonstrates a significant correlation between SNC and emotional resonance ($\rho = 0.71$, $p < 0.01$), indicating the leverage effect of central symbols in affective transmission.

The end-to-end pipeline exhibited an error margin of less than 0.5%, thereby ensuring the integrity of the data. Moreover, it facilitates full reproducibility through the utilization of Docker and Digital Object Identifier (DOI) protocols.

These results affirm the feasibility of symbolic network approaches in the context of digital heritage and offer a prioritization schema for interactive design and museum applications.

Nevertheless, there are limitations in terms of sample size, scalability of manual coding, and cultural adaptation of emotion metrics. Consequently, subsequent research will concentrate on:

Multimodal expansion: The integration of three-dimensional scans and voice narratives is pivotal in constructing a temporally indexed symbolic database, which is essential for the dynamic interpretation of costume semantics.

The following section will explore the enhancement of graph neural networks (GNNs). The replacement of the metric-based SNC with learned topological embeddings has been shown to facilitate the automatic detection of symbolic "bridges" across communities.

Cross-cultural validation: The PEF-GNN framework is to be applied to datasets from other ethnic groups (e.g., Dong, Li) to test its generalizability and emotional robustness.

The objective of these extensions is to establish a scalable symbolic infrastructure for preserving minority costumes and facilitating immersive cultural communication.

References

1. Ciula, A., Marras, C.: Exploring a semiotic conceptualisation of modelling in digital humanities practices. In: Ciula, A., Eide, O., Faggioli, G., Lupi, L. (eds.) Meaning and Structure in Digital Humanities, pp. 173–190. LED Edizioni Universitarie, Milano (2016). https://philpapers.org/rec/CIUEAS
2. Mangueira, C., Fava, F., Carvalhais, M.: Digital image as a semiotic agent. J. Sci. Technol. Arts **12**(1), 11–17 (2020). https://i2ads.up.pt/wp-content/uploads/2022/07/Digital-Image-as-a-Semiotic-Agent.pdf
3. Chartier, J.-F., Pulizzotto, D., Chartrand, L., Meunier, J.: A data-driven computational semiotics: the semantic vector space of Magritte's artworks. Semiotica **2019**(231), 19–69 (2019). https://doi.org/10.1515/sem-2018-0120
4. Wronska-Friend, M.: Globalised threads: Costumes of the Hmong community in north Queensland. In: Tapp, N., Lee, G.Y. (eds.) The Hmong of Australia: Culture and Diaspora, pp. 97–122. Pandanus Books, Canberra (2004)
5. Meier, C., Skamantzari, M., Georgopoulos, A.: 3D digitization and interactive visualization for traditional textile heritage. Digital Appl. Archaeol. Cult. Heritage **22**, e00187 (2021). https://doi.org/10.1016/j.daach.2021.e00187
6. Wu, Y., Jiang, Q., Liang, H.E., Ni, S.: What drives users to adopt a digital museum? A case of virtual exhibition hall of national costume museum. SAGE Open **12**, 1–13 (2022). https://doi.org/10.1177/21582440221082105
7. Chen, G., Mo, H., Yin, C., Cheng, C.: Design of a multi-user collaborative innovation digital resource library for Miao embroidery (2023)
8. Bazeley, P., Jackson, K.: Qualitative Data Analysis with NVivo, 2nd edn. SAGE, London (2013)
9. Gruber, T.R.: A translation approach to portable ontology specifications. Knowl. Acquis. **5**(2), 199–220 (1993). https://doi.org/10.1006/knac.1993.1008
10. Peirce, C.S.: Collected papers of charles sanders peirce, Vols. 1–8. Harvard University Press, Cambridge (1931–1958)
11. Morris, C.: Foundations of the Theory of Signs. University of Chicago Press, Chicago (1938)
12. Eicher, J.B., Sumberg, B.: World fashion, ethnicity, and national dress. In: Eicher, J.B. (ed.) Dress and Ethnicity: Change Across Space and Time, pp. 295–306. Berg, Oxford (1995)
13. Luo, X., Gao, J.: Research on the digitalization of Miao ethnic costume patterns based on Processing. In: 2024 IEEE 4th Int. Conf. on Information Technology, Big Data and Artificial Intelligence (ICIBA), vol. 4, pp. 209–213. IEEE, New York (2024). https://doi.org/10.1109/ICIBA62489.2024.10867932
14. Zhang, L., Y.: Research on the expression and creativity of traditional ethnic cultural elements in clothing design based on the fusion of multi-source and multi-objective statistical information. Appl. Math. Nonlinear Sci. **9** (2023). https://doi.org/10.2478/amns.2023.2.00723
15. Minucciani, V., Strada, F., Benente, M., Bottino, A.: Virtual Reality for Cultural Heritage: Emotional involvement and Design for all. In: Design for Inclusion. https://doi.org/10.54941/ahfe1004786

16. Alelis, G., Ang, C., Bobrowicz, A.: Comparison of engagement and emotional responses of older and younger adults interacting with 3D cultural heritage artefacts on personal devices. Behav. Inf. Technol. **34**, 1064–1078 (2015). https://doi.org/10.1080/0144929X.2015.1056548
17. Ninaus, M., Greipl, S., Bernecker, K.: Facial and bodily expressions of emotional engagement. Proc. ACM Hum.-Comput. Interact. **5**, 1–25 (2021). https://doi.org/10.1145/3474667
18. Bastian, M., Heymann, S., Jacomy, M.: Gephi: an open-source software for exploring and manipulating networks. Proc. Int. AAAI Conf. Weblogs Soc. Media **3**(1), 361–362 (2009). https://ojs.aaai.org/index.php/ICWSM/article/view/13937
19. Freire, E., da Silva, A.P.C., de Almeida, J.M., Bernardino, H.S.: Getting decision support from context-specific online social networks: a case study. Soc. Netw. Anal. Min. **12**(6), 1–17 (2022). https://doi.org/10.1007/s13278-022-00945-3
20. Landis, J.R., Koch, G.G.: The measurement of observer agreement for categorical data. Biometrics **33**(1), 159–174 (1977). https://doi.org/10.2307/2529310

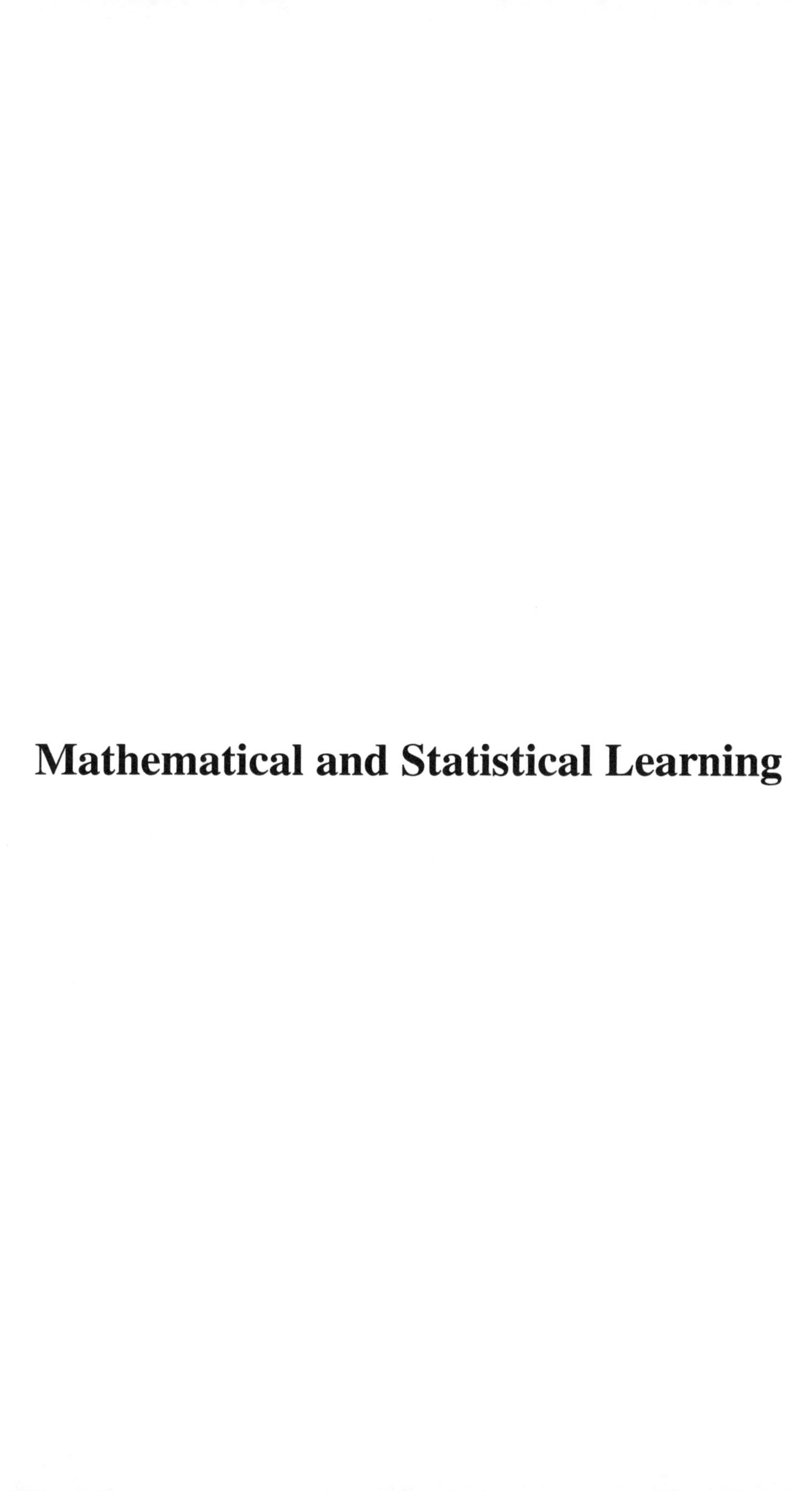

Mathematical and Statistical Learning

Evaluating the Impact of Rainfall Characteristics on TSS and VSS Removal Efficiencies: A Comparative Analysis of Sewage Pump Stations in Kajang, Malaysia

Avi Nica Mason[1](✉), Azianabiha A. Halip Khalid[1], and Norizam Ayob[2]

[1] Faculty of Civil Engineering, Universiti Teknologi MARA, Shah Alam 40450, Selangor, Malaysia

avee_nica86@yahoo.com.my, azianabiha@uitm.edu.my

[2] Head of Civil and Structural, Sunview Group, Petaling Jaya, Selangor, Malaysia

Abstract. This study evaluates the sediment control performance of two sewage pump stations (PS) configurations, PS-1 and PS-2, in Langat Kajang, Malaysia, under varying rainfall conditions. The primary focus is on the removal efficiencies of Total Suspended Solids (TSS) and Volatile Suspended Solids (VSS). Over 100 days (24 July 2023–31 October 2023), operational data were analyzed using Principal Component Analysis (PCA) and Agglomerative Hierarchical Clustering (AHC). PCA results revealed that the first two principal components accounted for 77.83% of the total variance, distinguishing the influence of rainfall intensity on TSS dynamics. PS-1, equipped with a grit chamber (GC), consistently demonstrated superior sediment control, removing 11.89 tonnes of grit from January to August 2024. Conversely, PS-2, lacking a GC, exhibited significant sediment accumulation and resuspension, with negative TSS removal values during moderate-to-high rainfall events. Statistical validation via the Kruskal–Wallis H test yielded a K-statistic of 193.098 ($p < 0.0001$), confirming substantial differences in TSS and VSS removal between the systems. The findings underscore the critical role of GCs in enhancing sediment removal and operational reliability. This study recommends continuous monitoring and retrofitting of vulnerable PS configurations, such as PS-2, with advanced sediment control mechanisms. Additionally, the results have significant implications for updating national PS design guidelines to mitigate challenges posed by increasing rainfall variability and urbanization.

Keywords: Sewage Pump Station · Sediment Control · Total Suspended Solid · Grit Chamber · Rainfall Intensity

1 Introduction

A reliable sewage PS network is essential for effective wastewater management, especially in high-rainfall regions like Malaysia. PSs are responsible for elevating wastewater to treatment plants, but their efficiency is often compromised by the accumulation of

M. Kassim et al. (Eds.): SCDS 2025, CCIS 2674, pp. 323–334, 2026.
https://doi.org/10.1007/978-981-95-8368-3_23

fine sediments such as sand and silt, which are not removed by standard mechanical coarse screens (MCSs) [1, 2]. The Malaysian Sewerage Industry Guidelines (MSIG) recommend GCs for sediment control, yet implementation is inconsistent, resulting in varied system performance [3].

Malaysia's tropical rainfall intensifies sediment mobilization within sewer systems, raising TSS and VSS concentrations that burden PS operations [4, 5]. Site investigations and asset management records from Indah Water Konsortium Sdn. Bhd. (IWK) report recurring issues with sediment accumulation, oil and grease deposits, and pump inefficiencies—even in new installations—underscoring the need for more robust sediment control solutions [3, 6–8].

This study focuses on evaluating two PSs in Kajang, labelled PS-1 (with GC) and PS-2 (without GC), using operational data from 24 July to 31 October 2023. It examines how rainfall intensity impacts TSS and VSS removal efficiencies and assesses the role of GCs in enhancing system resilience and performance.

Several core issues motivate this research, including Malaysia's high-intensity tropical rainfall, which frequently suspends sediment particles and results in elevated TSS levels in the sewers. This increased sediment load potentially overwhelms the sewage PSs (PS-1 and PS-2), affecting their performance during heavy rainfall events. Additionally, the persistent challenge of insufficient removal of fine sediment particles in both TSS and VSS leads to operational inefficiencies and sanitation issues within the PSs. These inadequacies not only impair system performance but also escalate maintenance and operational costs. Equally significant is the deviation from recommended practices; although MSIG suggests installing a GC after the sewage PS, inconsistent implementation (MSIG III) contributes to varied system performance.

Given these challenges, this paper aims to assess the influence of rainfall characteristics on TSS dynamics from 24 July 2023 to 31 October 2023 for the performance evaluation of PS-1 and PS-2, and conduct a comparative analysis of TSS and VSS Removal Efficiency between PS-1 and PS-2 using the Kruskal–Wallis Test.

The significance of the study lies in its potential to inform data-driven improvements in sediment management. Specifically, it evaluates how GCs affect critical operational parameters such as flow rate, pressure head, and solids concentration, providing insights that can reduce pump failures, minimize operational disruptions, and enhance the hydraulic performance of PSs in tropical settings.

The study is limited to two PSs in Selangor, with data obtained from the Malaysian Meteorological Department (MET), flow monitoring instruments, and laboratory analyses of TSS and VSS concentrations. As illustrated in Fig. 1, sampling points were strategically selected to capture performance variations across rainfall intensities and GC configurations. The findings aim to guide practical improvements in sediment control practices, particularly in sewage PS systems exposed to heavy rainfall and sediment loading.

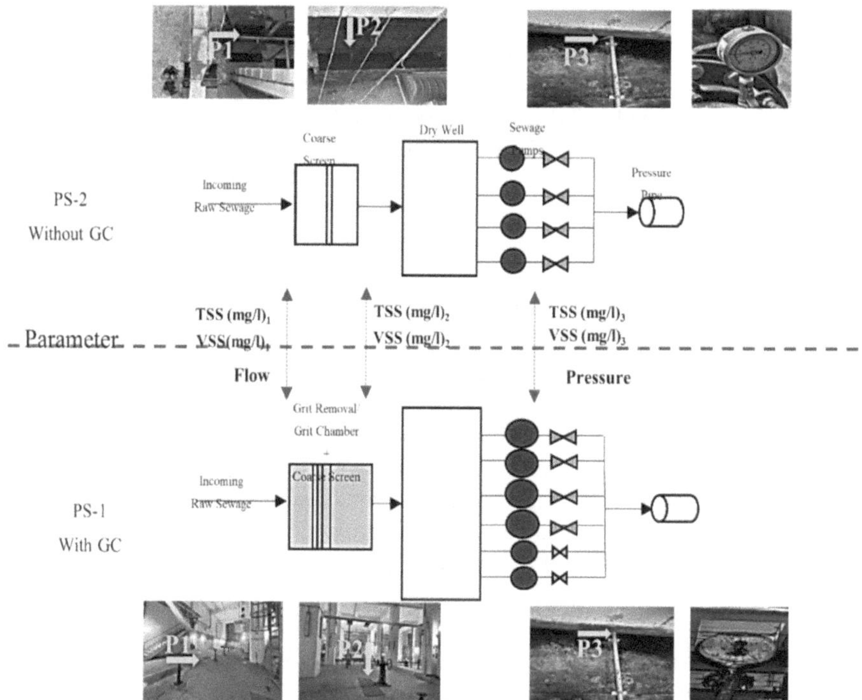

Fig. 1. Schematic diagrams of PS-1 and PS-2, showing sampling points and measured parameters (TSS, VSS, pressure head).

2 Work Related

Sewage PSs are essential for maintaining wastewater system efficiency by regulating TSS and VSS, which influence sedimentation and treatment performance. Sediment buildup during Combined Sewer Overflows (CSOs) increases environmental risks, necessitating effective sediment management [9]. Efficient PS operation depends on hydraulic dynamics, as energy-optimized pump cycles can reduce sediment accumulation [10]. Rinas et al. [11] emphasized that sediment transport can be maintained at lower velocities under controlled hydraulic conditions.

Rainfall intensity greatly affects TSS dynamics by resuspending sediments and increasing influent loads during storm events. Devos et al. [12] and Mines et al. [13] identified positive correlations between rainfall intensity and TSS levels. Adjovu et al. [14] observed seasonal TSS variations due to runoff and evaporation. However, limited comparative studies exist for PSs with and without GCs, especially under real operational conditions.

These rainfall-triggered inflows mobilize sediment, causing significant fluctuations in wastewater quality and treatment efficiency. The first flush phenomenon is particularly problematic, delivering concentrated pollutant loads that pose challenges for PSs lacking effective sediment control systems [15]. High-intensity rainfall events contribute to backwash effects and sediment resuspension, placing additional strain on conventional

GCs [16]. Adaptive flow regulation strategies are therefore essential to maintain adequate velocities and prevent sediment deposition and system overload [10, 17].

Halecki et al. [18] demonstrated that even a 1-mm increase in rainfall intensity could elevate TSS levels by 26–46 mg/L. Supporting this observation, Gong et al. [19] used stormwater modeling and reported a strong correlation (R2 = 0.95) between discharge volume and TSS load. These findings provide the basis for applying PCA in this study to explore variations in TSS behavior during the July–October 2023 data collection period.

The use of GCs in PSs has been shown to significantly improve sediment interception by capturing coarse solids before they reach sensitive treatment processes. In contrast, PSs lacking GCs face elevated sediment accumulation, increased maintenance demand, and frequent operational disruptions [20]. Traditional grit removal systems are often inadequate for particles smaller than 212 microns, pointing to the need for more refined and context-specific grit management designs.

In this study, performance evaluations are conducted for PS-1 (equipped with a GC) and PS-2 (without a GC) using continuous, real-time monitoring data. Kolosovska et al. [21] demonstrated that standardized GC designs do not universally perform well due to site-specific variations in grit characteristics, recommending the use of dynamic models based on particle settling velocity distributions (PSVD) to improve removal efficiency [22].

Measurement of TSS and VSS provides insight into both the physical and biological characteristics of sewage, with TSS encompassing all suspended materials and VSS representing the organic fraction [23]. To assess removal efficiency under varying system configurations, this study employs the Kruskal–Wallis test, a non-parametric statistical method well-suited to environmental datasets that deviate from normal distribution assumptions [24]. Zhang et al. [16] identified significant seasonal variation in microbial populations tied to the VSS/TSS ratio, suggesting that environmental conditions must be accounted for in performance evaluations. This research leverages a 100-day dataset to conduct a robust comparison between PS-1 and PS-2, with a focus on validating the impact of GC presence on sediment removal performance.

Existing work related confirms that rainfall intensity significantly affects TSS levels and supports the effectiveness of GCs in improving PS efficiency. However, comparative studies assessing PSs with and without GCs in actual field conditions remain scarce. Moreover, while Kruskal–Wallis testing is widely used in wastewater research, its application to real-world PS performance evaluation is still limited. This study addresses these gaps by integrating PCA to analyze rainfall-TSS dynamics and employing Kruskal–Wallis to assess sediment removal efficiency. Through operational data collected from PS-1 and PS-2, this work offers valuable insights for advancing sediment control strategies and improving the long-term resilience of sewage infrastructure in tropical environments.

3 Methodology

The methodological approach for this paper comprises several sequential steps, starting with obtaining the necessary permissions, selecting pilot study sites based on comprehensive data records, conducting systematic sample collection and analysis, and concluding with a critical discussion of potential limitations. This structured process directly supports the study's primary objectives, as outlined in Sect. 1.

Site access and research permissions were obtained from Jabatan Perkhidmatan Pembetungan (JPP), IWK, and MMC Pembetungan Langat Sdn. Bhd. A formal Letter of Agreement between IWK and Universiti Teknologi MARA (UiTM) Shah Alam authorized operational activities at the CSTP Taman Eko Langat facility in Kajang, Selangor, Malaysia. PS-1 (equipped with a GC) and PS-2 (without a GC) were selected based on comparable flow characteristics and operational timelines during the 2023 study period, ensuring a reliable basis for comparative analysis.

Data collection spanned 100 consecutive days, from 24 July to 31 October 2023. Daily sampling was conducted at 8:00 AM across three designated points at each station: P1 (inlet), P2 (wet well), and P3 (post-pump). At PS-1, the P2 point was located after the grit chamber to enable performance assessment. Meteorological data were obtained from the MET and supplemented by on-site observations to characterize rainfall events. The primary parameters measured included flow rate (Q), pressure head (h), and concentrations of total suspended solids (TSS) and volatile suspended solids (VSS). TSS and VSS concentrations were determined using HACH Standard Methods 8158 and 8164, respectively, which involve filtration, drying, and combustion steps to quantify solids per unit volume [25].

To ensure consistency and comparability across stations with differing design capacities (PS-1: 920,000 PE; PS-2: 126,000 PE), the collected TSS and VSS values were normalized by flow rate and expressed in milligrams per liter per cubic meter per hour (mg/L per m^3/hr). Statistical analyses were conducted using XLSTAT software. PCA was applied to evaluate the influence of rainfall intensity on TSS variation, providing a multivariate understanding of sediment behavior. To assess sediment removal efficiency between P1 and P3, the non-parametric Kruskal–Wallis test was applied to both TSS_{in}/TSS_{out} and VSS_{in}/VSS_{out} ratios. This robust statistical framework accommodates the skewed distributions typically found in environmental datasets and supports meaningful performance comparisons between the two PSs.

4 Results Analysis and Discussion

The influence of rainfall intensity on TSS dynamics was evaluated using PCA, where the first two components (F1 and F2) accounted for 77.83% of the total variance across the 100-day dataset from PS-1 and PS-2 (24 July to 31 October 2023). This high proportion of explained variability validates PCA as a robust method for capturing the relationship between rainfall intensity and TSS concentrations, supporting its utility in assessing PS performance under varying hydrological conditions (Fig. 2).

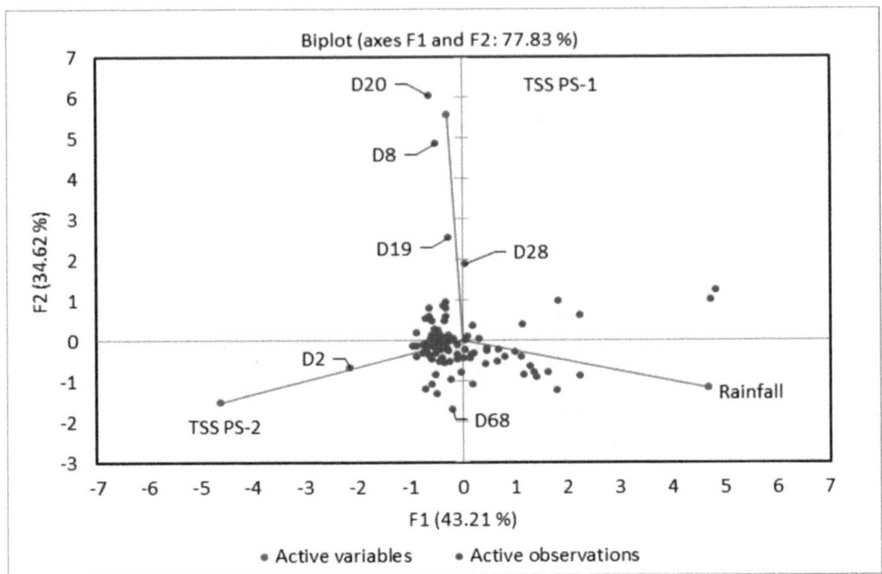

Fig. 2. PCA biplot depicting the relationship between rainfall intensity and TSS dynamics at PS-1 and PS-2 over the 100-day study period.

As shown in the PCA biplot (Fig. 2), PS-1 demonstrated consistent sediment control, particularly during high-rainfall events on Days 8, 19, 20, and 28, which clustered in the upper-right quadrant. Conversely, PS-2 exhibited elevated TSS levels on Days 2 and 68 and clustered predominantly in the lower-left quadrant. The GC installed at PS-1 effectively isolated larger sediment particles, reducing resuspension during storm flows, as supported by the 11.89 tonnes of grit collected between January and August 2024. In contrast, PS-2, which lacks a sediment management unit, experienced hydraulic turbulence-induced resuspension and accumulation, further evidenced by stagnant sewage observed on 15 October 2023 and multiple system breakdowns.

These findings echo Timurani et al. [26], who reported TSS variations between 111–210 mg/L during rainy seasons, in contrast to significantly lower concentrations (105–108 mg/L) in dry periods. However, Esfahani et al. [27] highlighted the vulnerability of GCs to extreme rainfall intensities (10.5–40 L/min), noting that turbidity removal efficiency decreased from 34.7% to 22.73% as flow rates increased, underscoring the importance of monitoring GC performance under stress conditions.

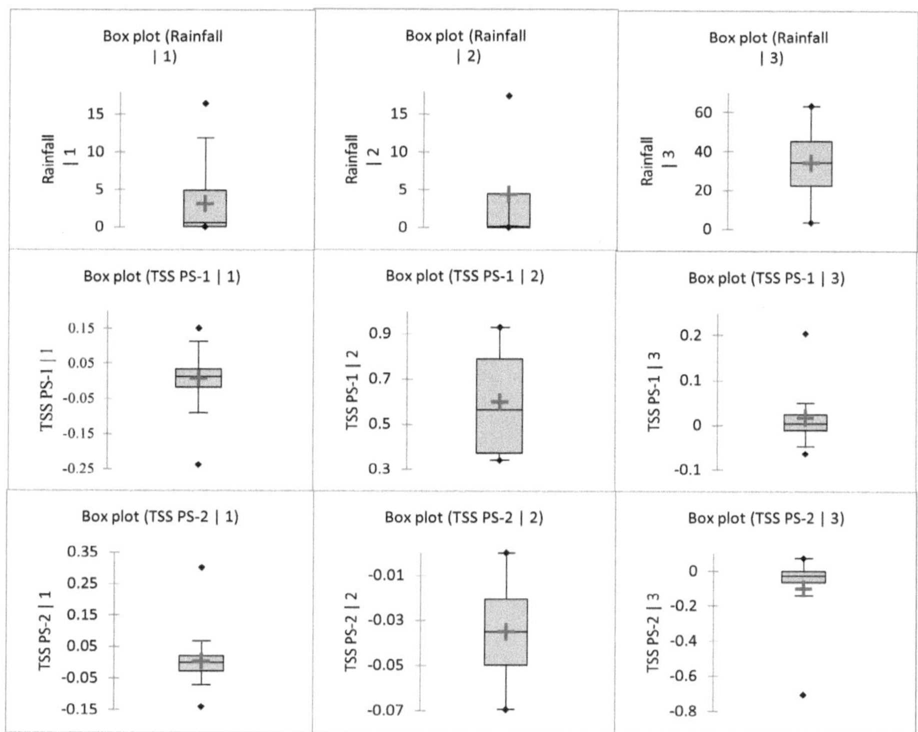

Fig. 3. Box plot of TSS removal efficiencies at PS-1 and PS-2, categorized by rainfall intensity classes derived from AHC (mean values shown in mm/h).

Further analysis using AHC categorized rainfall into three distinct intensity classes: Class 1 (light–moderate, mean = 3.055 mm/h), Class 2 (moderate–heavy, mean = 4.405 mm/h), and Class 3 (high, mean = 34.117 mm/h), as shown in Fig. 3. PS-1 consistently achieved positive TSS removal across all rainfall classes, including 0.008 mg/L·m3/hr (Class 1), 0.599 mg/L·m3/hr (Class 2), and 0.016 mg/L·m3/hr (Class 3). PS-2, however, exhibited negative removal in Classes 2 and 3 (-0.035 and -0.101 mg/L·m3/hr, respectively), suggesting sediment resuspension under hydraulic stress. These outcomes corroborate findings by He et al. [28], who found a 113.5% TSS increase due to runoff, and Plana et al. [22], who observed reduced removal efficiencies (7–13%) during high flows. The real-world advantage of the GC at PS-1 is thus reinforced.

To assess the statistical significance of sediment removal differences, the Kruskal–Wallis H test was applied due to the non-normal distribution of the dataset. With a K-value of 193.098 exceeding the critical value (14.067) at 7 degrees of freedom and a p-value < 0.0001 (Table 1; Fig. 4), the test confirms significant performance differences between PS-1 and PS-2 in both TSS and VSS removal. These findings mirror Gallegos-Rodríguez et al. [29], who reported significant ($p < 0.0016$) differences in TSS removal efficiency, and Mohagheghian et al. [30], who demonstrated significant correlations in similar studies ($p < 0.05$), the data emphasize the pivotal role of GCs in optimizing suspended solids removal.

Table 1. Statistics of PS-1 and PS-2 in the aspects of TSS_{in} & TSS_{out} and VSS_{in} & VSS_{out}.

Kruskal-Wallis test / Two-tailed test:	
K (Observed value)	193.098
K (Critical value)	14.067
DF	7
p-value (one-tailed)	<0.0001
alpha	0.05

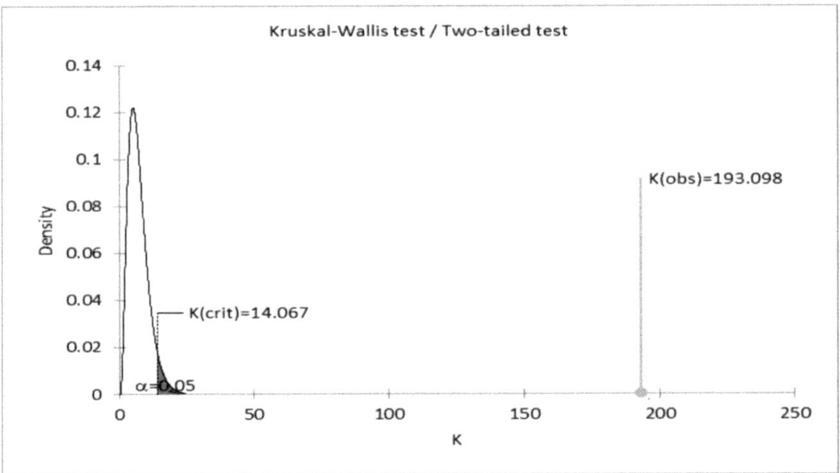

Fig. 4. Results of the Kruskal–Wallis test indicate statistically significant differences in TSS and VSS removal performance between PS-1 (with GC) and PS-2 (without GC).

Table 2. Statistical summary of TSS_{in} & TSS_{out} and VSS_{in} & VSS_{out} for PS-1 and PS-2

Variable PS	TSS PS-1_{in}	TSS PS-1_{out}	VSS PS-1_{in}	VSS PS-1_{out}	TSS PS-2_{in}	TSS PS-2_{out}	VSS PS-2_{in}	VSS PS-2_{out}
Observations	100	100	100	100	100	100	100	100
Obs. with missing data	0	0	0	0	0	0	0	0
Obs. without missing data	100	100	100	100	100	100	100	100

(continued)

Table 2. (*continued*)

Variable PS	TSS PS-1_{in}	TSS PS-1_{out}	VSS PS-1_{in}	VSS PS-1_{out}	TSS PS-2_{in}	TSS PS-2_{out}	VSS PS-2_{in}	VSS PS-2_{out}
Minimum	0.012	0.001	0.028	0.017	0.004	0.008	0.036	0.053
Maximum	1.436	0.614	1.112	0.416	0.526	0.729	0.547	0.612
Mean	0.158	0.125	0.143	0.115	0.058	0.082	0.158	0.173
Std. Deviation	0.179	0.113	0.134	0.081	0.059	0.108	0.094	0.107

Summary statistics Table 2, reveals that PS-1 achieved a reduction in mean TSS concentration from 0.158 mg/L·m^3/hr (inlet) to 0.125 mg/L·m^3/hr (outlet), while VSS decreased from 0.143 to 0.115 mg/L·m3/hr. In contrast, PS-2 exhibited an increase in TSS from 0.058 to 0.082 mg/L·m^3/hr and VSS from 0.158 to 0.173 mg/L·m^3/hr. These trends align with McNamara et al. [31], who observed that grit removal systems like mechanically induced vortex (MIV) units achieved only 48–52% removal efficiency at sub-optimal flow rates and significantly underperformed for particles < 297 microns. The results from PS-1 confirm that its GC is effective in enhancing sediment removal and reducing re-entrainment, while PS-2's configuration leads to accumulation and inefficient processing.

Supporting studies by [32] and Kolosovska [33] stress the operational risks of ineffective grit removal, including mechanical abrasion, clogging, and decreased equipment lifespan. Grit particles ranging from 75–300 microns, if not intercepted, can severely affect pumps, centrifuges, and aeration tanks. It is estimated that pump impellers can lose up to 30% of their service life due to grit abrasion [34, 35]. These findings reinforce the recommendation by [36] that grit be removed before pumping to minimize long-term maintenance and ensure system resilience. PS-1's GC addresses these challenges effectively, while PS-2 remains vulnerable to failures and rising operational costs due to its lack of grit control infrastructure.

Looking ahead, there is substantial potential for optimizing GC design in systems like PS-1. Incorporating advanced grit removal technologies and tailoring configurations to site-specific sediment profiles can enhance removal efficiency and reduce energy consumption. These findings may inform Malaysian sewerage policy and design standards, particularly in urban areas with high sediment and rainfall loads. Future efforts should explore long-term monitoring, grit size distribution impacts, and real-time control systems to further improve system resilience. Real-world performance data, such as that from this study, are vital for guiding the next generation of PS upgrades and supporting sustainable wastewater infrastructure under tropical climatic pressures.

5 Conclusion and Recommendations

This study confirms that rainfall intensity plays a critical role in influencing sediment dynamics within sewage PSs. PCA demonstrated that the first two components accounted for 77.83% of the total variation, highlighting a strong correlation between rainfall events and elevated TSS levels. PS-1, which is equipped with a GC, consistently exhibited better performance than PS-2 by minimizing sediment resuspension during periods of high hydraulic loading. The removal of 11.89 tonnes of grit from PS-1 between January and August 2024 further supports the operational effectiveness of incorporating GCs in sewage PS infrastructure, in line with previous research findings [22, 23, 26, 27].

Complementary to these results, the Kruskal–Wallis statistical analysis revealed significant differences in sediment removal efficiencies between the two PSs ($K = 193.098$, $p < 0.0001$). PS-1 achieved superior reduction of both TSS and VSS concentrations, whereas PS-2, which lacks a GC, exhibited signs of sediment resuspension and operational inefficiencies. These findings validate the role of GCs in improving sediment handling and support their incorporation into PS design standards, consistent with the work of [29–31].

Overall, the combined use of PCA and Kruskal–Wallis methods provides empirical validation of PS-1's enhanced operational resilience. These empirical results strongly justify revisiting MSIG guidelines to mandate the inclusion of GCs, enhancing sediment management, reducing maintenance costs, and improving system reliability in response to urbanization and climate variability.

Future studies are recommended to explore optimized GC designs tailored to local sediment characteristics and flow regimes. Additionally, the integration of real-time sediment monitoring technologies may offer further advancements in proactive PS management and long-term system resilience.

Acknowledgement. The authors gratefully acknowledge the technical support and data provision from IWK, which enabled access to critical operational parameters of the sewage PS systems. Their collaboration was instrumental in facilitating the performance evaluation and analytical modelling conducted in this study.

References

1. Barnes, D., Bliss, P.J. Gould, B.W., Vallentine, H.R.: Water and Wastewater Engineering Systems (1981)
2. IWK: Manual of practice hydraulic. Planning and Engineering Department, Indah Water Konsortium Sdn Bhd (2007)
3. SPAN: Section 5 Requirements for Individual Treatment Processes. IV (2009)
4. Kishimoto, J.: Grit chamber screening piston pump system of separate sewer systems PisPo_mini. pp. 77–88 (2010)
5. Usher, J.S.: Reliability Study for Pump Stations in Louisville, KY. pp. 3355–3365 (2013)
6. Fan, C., Field, R., Lai, F.: Protection agency wet-weather flow research program. Environ. Prot. **129**(April), 253–259 (2003)
7. Rahman, N.A., Alias, N., Mohd Salleh, S.S., Huda Samion, M.K.: Evaluation of design criteria for inflow & infiltration of medium scale sewerage catchment system (Penilaian Kriteria Rekabentuk Bagi Aliran Masuk & Penyusupan Sistem Pembentungan Berskala Sederhana) Norhan Abd Rahman Noraliani Alias Siti Salhawati Mohd Salleh Mohd Kamarul Huda Samion Rcsearch Vote No: 74281 (2007)
8. Tulleken, J.: Enquiry into sewage pump station problems with specific focus on removing solids (2012). http://Scholar.Sun.Ac.Za

9. The Sewerage System in Malaysia: Construction Essay (2015). http://techalive.mtu.edu/meec/module21/images/CombinedSewer.jpg
10. Rinas, M., Tränckner, J., Koegst, T.: Sediment transport in sewage pressure pipes, part I: continuous determination of settling and erosion characteristics by in-situ TSS monitoring inside a pressure pipe in Northern Germany. Water (Switzerland) **11**(10) (2019). https://doi.org/10.3390/w11102125
11. Rinas, M., Fricke, A., Tränckner, J., Frischmuth, K., Koegst, T.: Sediment transport in sewage pressure pipes, part II: 1 D numerical simulation. Water (Switzerland) **12**(1) (2020). https://doi.org/10.3390/w12010282
12. Devos, P., Filali, A., Grau, P., Gillot, S., Gillot Sidestream, S.: Sidestream characteristics in water resource recovery facilities: a critical review. Water Res. **232**, 1–34 (2023). https://doi.org/10.1016/j.watres.2023.119620
13. Mines, R.O., Lackey, L.W., Behrend, G.R.: The impact of rainfall on flows and loadings at Georgia's wastewater treatment plants (2007)
14. Adjovu, G.E., Stephen, H., Ahmad, S.: Spatiotemporal variability in total dissolved solids and total suspended solids along the colorado river. Hydrology **10**(6) (2023). https://doi.org/10.3390/hydrology10060125
15. Li, Y., et al.: Characterization and sources apportionment of overflow pollution in urban separate stormwater systems inappropriately connected with sewage. J. Environ. Manage. (2022). https://doi.org/10.1016/j.jenvman.2021.114231
16. Zhang, B., Cheng, L., Xu, C., Wang, M.: The influence of geometric parameters of pump installation on the hydraulic performance of a prefabricated pumping station. Energies **14**(4) (2021). https://doi.org/10.3390/en14041039
17. Rinas, M., Tränckner, J., Koegst, T.: Sedimentation of raw sewage: investigations for a pumping station in northern Germany under energy-efficient pump control. Water (Switzerland) **11**(1) (2018). https://doi.org/10.3390/w11010040
18. Halecki, W., Młyńska, A., Sionkowski, T., Chmielowski, K.: Linking elevated rainfall with sewage discharge volume. Ochrona Srodowiska i Zasobow Naturalnych **34**(4), 135–146 (2023). https://doi.org/10.2478/oszn-2023-0020
19. Gong, Y., Liang, X., Li, X., Li, J., Fang, X., Song, R.: Influence of rainfall characteristics on total suspended solids in urban runoff: a case study in Beijing, China. Water (Switzerland) **8**(7) (2016). https://doi.org/10.3390/w8070278
20. Andoh, R.Y.G.: Grit characterization and optimal grit removal using the HeadCell ® Device (2015)
21. Kolosovska, T., Bauer, S.K.: A comprehensive evaluation of wastewater grit characteristics and its application in the design of a facility-specific grit removal solution (2021)
22. Vanrolleghem, P.A., Lessard, P.: Characterization and modelling of grit chambers based on particle settling velocity distributions Thèse Queralt Plana Puig Sous la direction de (2020)
23. Metcalf, Eddy: Wastewater Engineering: Treatment, Disposal Reuse Fifth Edition (5th ed.) (2014)
24. Helsel, D.R., Hirsch, R.M.: Techniques of water-resources investigations of the united states geological survey, Book 4, Hydrologic Analysis and Interpretation, Statistical Methods in Water Resources (2002). http://water.usgs.gov/pubs/twri/twri4a3/
25. © Hach Company/Hach Lange GmbH: USEPA Gravimetric Method 1, 2, Method 8158, and Method 8164 (2015)
26. Timurani, E.C., Anna, A.N.: Dynamics of seasonal impacts on total suspended solids (TSS) concentrations in coastal Semarang City using Landsat 8 (2024)
27. Esfahani, N.R., Mobarekeh, M.N., Hoodaji, M.: Effect of grit chamber configuration on particle removal: using response surface method. J. Membr. Sep. Technol. **7**, 12–16 (2018). https://doi.org/10.6000/1929-6037.2018.07.02

28. He, L., Tan, T., Gao, Z., Fan, L.: The shock effect of inorganic suspended solids in surface runoff on wastewater treatment plant performance. Int. J. Environ. Res. Pub. Health **16**(3) (2019). https://doi.org/10.3390/ijerph16030453
29. Gallegos-Rodríguez, J., López-Ocaña, G., Bautista-Margulis, R.G., Torres-Balcázar, C.A.: Evaluation of free-flow constructed wetlands with Sagittaria latifolia and Sagittaria lancifolia in domestic wastewater treatment. Ingeniería Agrícola y Biosistemas 10(2) (2018). https://doi.org/10.5154/r.inagbi.2017.03.005
30. Mohagheghian, A., et al.: Distribution of estrogenic steroids in municipal wastewater treatment plants in Tehran, Iran. J. Environ. Health Sci. Eng. **12**(1) (2014). https://doi.org/10.1186/2052-336X-12-97
31. McNamara, B., Sherony, M., Herrick, P.: Relative performance of grit removal systems. 87th Annual Water Environment Federation Technical Exhibition and Conference, WEFTEC 7, pp. 4919–4929 (2014). https://doi.org/10.2175/193864714815939796
32. Kolosovska, T., Bauer, S.K.: Evaluation of grit properties at a medium-capacity wastewater treatment plant: a case study. Resour. Conserv. Recycl. Adv. (2022). https://doi.org/10.1016/j.rcradv.2022.200080
33. Kiepper, Ritz: Importance of grit removal from commercial shell egg processing wastewater-University of Georgia (2017). https://extension.uga.edu/publications/detail.html?number=B1402&title=Importance%20of%20Grit%20Removal%20from%20Commercial%20Shell%20Egg%20Processing%20Wastewater. (Accessed 11 October 2019)
34. Mansour-Geoffrion, M., Dold, P.L., Lamarre, D., Gadbois, A., Déléris, S., Comeau, Y.: Characterizing hydrocyclone performance for grit removal from wastewater treatment activated sludge plants. Miner. Eng. **23**(4), 359–364 (2010). https://doi.org/10.1016/j.mineng.2009.08.001
35. Sandell, N.: Grit removal: The importance of protecting downstream equipment (2017). https://wwtonline.co.uk/Blog/grit-removal-the-importance-of-protecting-downstream-equipment. (Accessed 11 October 2019)
36. Ministry Of Housing and Urban Affairs: Part A: Engineering 4–1 Chapter 4: Design and Construction of Sewage Pumping Stations and Sewage Pumping Mains Chapter 4: Design and Construction of Sewage Pumping Stations and Sewage Pumping Mains 4.1 General Considerations (1952)

Evaluation of AHP and Fuzzy-AHP in Criteria Weighting for Accessible Heritage Tourism: A Simulation Study

Elina Alias[1], Nabilah Naharudin[1(✉)], and Siti Aekbal Salleh[1,2]

[1] Faculty of Built Environment, Universiti Teknologi MARA, Shah Alam, Selangor, Malaysia
nabilahnaharudin1290@uitm.edu.my

[2] Institute for Biodiversity and Sustainable Development (IBSD), Universiti Teknologi MARA, Shah Alam, Selangor, Malaysia

Abstract. Heritage tourism planning normally experiences difficulties in achieving universal accessibility, especially in older cities where cultural monuments are situated within limited and irregular spatial layouts. These environments necessitate inclusive planning practices that take into account the physical, sensory, and cognitive obstacles encountered by various user groups. This research explored the application of Analytic Hierarchy Process (AHP) and Fuzzy Analytic Hierarchy Process (Fuzzy-AHP) to priorities accessibility requirements for determining a pedestrian route in heritage tourism regions. Based on MS1184:2014 and the UNCRPD, a hierarchical framework was established which included three main criteria of mobility and navigation, comforts, and accessibility features, as well as seven sub criteria. Both decision-making models were constructed and analyzed using a simulated pairwise comparison data. The results suggest that, while AHP provides a logical consistency and simplicity, Fuzzy-AHP has a stronger ability to express ambiguity and complexity in expert judgement which giving a larger weight to moderately valued qualities. Although based on simulated data, the study demonstrates the importance of fuzzy-based decision tools in capturing stakeholder variability and promoting inclusive planning. The proposed framework provides a methodological foundation for future empirical research and decision-support systems focused on achieving equitable and sustainable accessibility in heritage tourism settings.

Keywords: Universal Accessibility · Heritage Tourism · AHP · Fuzzy-AHP

1 Introduction

Heritage tourism has grown into a powerful force for cultural preservation, economic regeneration, and inclusive urban redevelopment. Cities like Ipoh, Malaysia which is rich with its colonial architecture, ancient alleyways, and cultural narratives have become a popular destination for both domestic and foreign visitors that looking to immerse themselves in the tangible and intangible legacy of the past [1]. However, the heritage landscapes often have narrow passageways, steep staircases, uneven surfaces, and old

M. Kassim et al. (Eds.): SCDS 2025, CCIS 2674, pp. 335–350, 2026.
https://doi.org/10.1007/978-981-95-8368-3_24

infrastructure that often causes major accessibility issues. These spaces were never originally designed for modern mobility needs or inclusive public use [2]. Because of this, travel experiences that ought to be enlightening and unforgettable for everyone may easily turn out to be draining or even exclusive especially for those with mobility challenges like elderly tourists, individuals with disabilities, and families with small children. Despite Malaysia's institutional commitment to accessibility as demonstrated, ground realities remain misaligned [3]. Basic accessibility amenities like ramps, handrails, tactile signage, and accessible bathrooms are still missing from many heritage sites, which restricts fair access and goes against the ideas of inclusive tourist development. Poorly constructed pedestrian flows and isolated amenities cause weariness, confusion, and disengagement among vulnerable user groups, making potential tourism to be an overlooked opportunity in tourism sector. This accessibility gap is more than just a problem of infrastructure, but it is a physical, social, and policy inconsistency that jeopardizes Malaysia's reputation as an inclusive and internationally competitive tourism destination.

Addressing these challenges involves more than sporadic physical improvements. It necessitates an organized, data-driven methodology that can analyses several overlapping criteria while also providing decision-makers with tools for efficiently prioritizing initiatives. In this context, Multi-Criteria Decision Analysis (MCDA) frameworks, notably the Analytic Hierarchy Process (AHP) and its fuzzy variant, Fuzzy-AHP have proven huge potential. AHP breaks down complicated problems into a hierarchy of criteria that allowing expert judgements to determine its priority [4]. Meanwhile, traditional AHP, on the other hand, is based on precise numerical inputs that may not always reflect for the uncertainty, ambiguity, or linguistic variety that exists in real-world expert judgements. Fuzzy-AHP overcomes this disadvantage by allowing decision-makers to express preferences in fuzzy numbers which makes it more appropriate for subjective or imprecise situations such as heritage accessibility planning. The paper provides an evaluation on AHP and Fuzzy-AHP models to evaluate criteria influencing accessible heritage tourism. Using a simulated framework based on actual accessibility needs in heritage-rich cities, the research examines three critical criteria which is Mobility & Navigation, Comforts, and Accessibility Features and as well as its sub criteria such as ramps, handrails, rest areas, and braille signage [5]. The objective of this research is to establish whether the approach method is more reliable and adaptable in promoting inclusive tourist planning by comparing its sensitivity, rank stability, and responsiveness. The findings not only contribute to methodological innovation in accessibility evaluation, but also serve as an accurate framework for heritage planners, lawmakers, and accessibility supports trying to solve the problem between historical preservation and equal access to it.

2 Literature Review

The literature on inclusive tourism and decision-making frameworks shows a rising acknowledgement of universal accessibility as a critical component of sustainable destination development. However, in the context of heritage tourism, physical, legislative, and cultural preservation problems frequently limit the use of accessible design. Important areas relevant to the current study are examined in this review.

2.1 Universal Accessibility in Tourism

Tourism is one of the world's largest and fastest-growing businesses which contributing to 10% of global GDP and one out of every ten employments. Demand for accessibility is growing in parallel with the growth of international travel, particularly due to the population ageing and growing awareness of disability rights. According to the World Health Organization (WHO) about 1.3 billion individuals or around 16% of the global population have an identifiable type of disability [6]. Despite this, many of these individuals continue to have limited access to tourist infrastructure and services. Accessibility in tourism is much more than a social obligation, but it is also an economic necessity. Universal accessibility is the design of destinations, products, and amenities that can be utilized by everyone regardless of age, ability, or social standing without requiring adjustment. In tourism, this includes accessible transportation, signs, accommodation, public areas, and, most importantly, cultural and heritage sites which frequently are behind in inclusive infrastructure. For example, in Europe, an estimated 127 million individuals experience limitations on access when travelling which leads to a loss of about €142 billion in potential tourist income each year [7]. Malaysia acknowledged this gap by legal measures such as the Persons with Disabilities Act of 2008 and the ratification of the United Nations Convention on the Rights of Persons with Disabilities (UNCRPD) in 2010. However, enforcement is inconsistent. According to Abdul Rashid et al. (2020), more than 60% of Malaysia's heritage buildings do not meet national accessibility criteria (MS 1184:2014) [8]. Popular tourist locations in towns such as Ipoh and George Town have lack tactile pavement, accessible restrooms, handrails, and appropriate signage considerably limiting access for those with impairments and the elderly. The absence of accessible routes and related support causes disorientation, fatigue, and isolation, especially among those with mobility disabilities. These difficulties have an impact not just on the user experience, but also on the sites' long-term tourist potential. As a result, incorporating universal design and spatial accessibility assessments into heritage tourist initiatives is critical to meeting both social equality and economic sustainability goals.

2.2 Analytic Hierarchy Process (AHP) and Fuzzy-AHP

AHP, developed by Thomas L. Saaty in 1980, is one of the most extensively used MCDA for dealing and handling with complex decisions that include both qualitative and quantitative criteria. It has been successfully used in a variety of fields, including environmental management, infrastructure planning, urban development, and tourism strategy. The core strength of AHP is its capability to structure a decision problem into a clear hierarchical flow which allowing decision-makers to conduct a pairwise comparisons that evaluate the relative importance of criteria and sub-criteria using Saaty's 1 to 9 fundamental scale. In AHP, the decision hierarchy is often divided into four levels where first is the aim of the decision problem, second is the criteria influencing the decision, third is the sub-criteria, and fourth is the alternatives. Experts make pairwise judgements by comparing each of the criterion to each other based on their relative importance in achieving the aim. The paired matrices are then normalized, and the priority weights which are known as the eigenvectors are produced. The Consistency Index (CI) and Consistency Ratio (CR) are used to assess the internal consistency of judgements. A CR of < 0.10 is considered acceptable since it showing a reasonable pairwise comparisons. In the tourism sector, AHP has been used to promote transit accessibility, hotel site selection, ecotourism development, and infrastructure enhancement. For example, AHP was used to assess inclusive features in Malaysian public transport systems which taking into account the perspectives of stakeholders from the urban planning, disability rights, and local government sectors [9]. The technique has also been used to conduct accessibility evaluations of pedestrian routes and determine which components such as tactile paving, ramps, or signage have the greatest impact on the inclusive mobility. Despite its systematic structure and simplicity, AHP has been criticized for its over-reliance on exact numerical values, which could reflect ambiguity or subjectivity in human judgement. Experts are frequently uncomfortable giving specific numbers to fundamentally qualitative conclusions, particularly when assessing sociocultural, emotional, or sensory components of heritage accessibility. The procedure of conducting pairwise comparisons also becomes difficult and susceptible to inconsistencies when a lot of criteria are used. These limitations are particularly problematic in complicated situations like heritage tourism, where the conflicts between cultural preservation and accessibility are difficult to evaluate.

To overcome the limitations of traditional AHP, particularly in situations requiring ambiguous, imprecise, or subjective judgements, Fuzzy-AHP was developed by combining fuzzy set theory and Saaty's hierarchical decision-making model. The original fuzzy extension to AHP was introduced by Laarhoven and Pedrycz in 1983 and later refined by Chang in 1996, who proposed the Extent Analysis Method, one of the most widely adopted approaches for implementing Fuzzy-AHP. Fuzzy-AHP enables decision-makers to express their judgements using language variables which are then transformed to Triangular Fuzzy Numbers (TFNs) or trapezoidal fuzzy numbers. For example, "equally important" may be expressed as a TFN with the values of (1,1,1), but "very strongly important" could be represented as (6,7,8) [10]. These fuzzy integers are used in fuzzy pairwise matrices and processed with fuzzy arithmetic to get fuzzy weights which are then defuzzified to provide crisp final ranks to provide a decision criterion. In this study, Fuzzy-AHP is used not only to priorities accessibility criteria, but also as a key decision-support tool for determining the most inclusive and user-friendly walking routes within a heritage tourism area. The routes are assessed using a set of expert-validated accessibility criteria which include the existence of handrails, ramps, stairs, rest locations, child-friendly restrooms, braille signage, and hydration stations. Each route is assessed based on how well it fits these criteria which are weighted by the importance values calculated using the Fuzzy-AHP process [11]. This application is especially well-suited for heritage sites where historical preservation and physical restrictions frequently prevent large-scale infrastructure modifications. While traditional AHP can priorities individual criteria, Fuzzy-AHP enables more nuanced and flexible evaluation by capturing the uncertainty that comes with expert judgements, particularly when dealing with different user demands and local choices. Several research have shown that Fuzzy-AHP can be useful for accessibility and tourist planning. [12] used Fuzzy-AHP to evaluate pedestrian routes for individuals with impairments in Malaysian heritage cities, whereas [13] used it to establish infrastructure priorities for ecotourism development. [14] used in urban public service planning with stakeholder uncertainty. Fuzzy-AHP is implemented in this study in four key stages which is the creation of fuzzy pairwise comparison matrices using expert input, calculate those matrices using Buckley's, defuzzification of the fuzzy weights, and ranking of route alternatives based on their overall accessibility scores. Fuzzy-AHP has several major advantages, including increased decision robustness, support for imprecise expert input, and the ability to include stakeholder opinions without requiring accurate numerical judgements. However, these advantages come with certain challenges. Fuzzy arithmetic has higher computing needs than traditional AHP, and the choice of defuzzification computations might affect final ranks. It may also be necessary to simplify or visualize fuzzy-derived results when presenting them, especially when speaking with decision-makers who are not familiar with fuzzy logic. Despite these issues, Fuzzy-AHP provides an appealing framework for inclusive tourist route design, especially in heritage areas where accessibility must be maximized without jeopardizing historical integrity. In this study, the method allows for a more realistic simulation of expert reasoning and offers a methodical framework for determining the best pedestrian route around the heritage site while following to universal design principles and user-centered accessibility requirements.

2.3 Recent Advances in MCDA for Accessibility Planning

Recent advances in MCDA have introduced models to solve the limitation of the traditional decision-making methodologies particularly in complex and unpredictable environments such as accessibility planning. The Best Worst Method (BWM) is popular because of its efficiency and it needs fewer comparisons while maintaining high consistency in expert judgements. It is frequently used in urban infrastructure and sustainability studies where time and expert input are limited. Other than that, the DEMATEL method has been used to model the connections between related criteria offering an understanding of the influence structure of elements in decision-making. In parallel, the AHP approach has been significantly refined. Variants include Hexagonal Fuzzy-AHP, Interval Type-2 Fuzzy AHP, and Intuitionistic Fuzzy-AHP have been proposed to improve the model's capacity to deal with higher-order uncertainty and ambiguity in human judgement. For example, Hexagonal Fuzzy-AHP has been used in recent research to assess energy site selection and urban service accessibility providing a deeper evaluation of subjective preferences by employing six-point fuzzy numbers rather than typical triangular or trapezoidal forms. These versions improve AHP's capacity to work well in imprecise and stakeholder-driven situations such as inclusive tourist planning while maintaining its key strengths in transparency, hierarchical organization, and consistency checking [15]. While these newer approaches provide outstanding computing power and complex modelling, it requires increased data sophistication. As a result, AHP and its fuzzy variations remain extremely useful particularly in simulation-based study and early-stage planning processes where methodological clarity, interpretability, and simplicity of application are crucial. Their continuous usage in subsequent accessibility and historical tourism studies demonstrates their long-term relevance as fundamental tools for decision support in complex and multi-stakeholder challenges.

3 Methodology

This study uses a simulation-based comparative methodology to assess the prioritization behavior of two MCDA methods which is AHP and Fuzzy-AHP in the context of universal accessibility planning in heritage tourism environments. The aim is to evaluate each method's validity and sensitivity in capturing complex and subjective decision criteria. Although no real-world data were gathered, the simulated expert judgements represent appropriate stakeholder thinking which allowing for a controlled comparison of the two models' calculations and prioritization of results.

3.1 Research Design

This research uses a simulation-based decision-support method that employs both AHP and Fuzzy-AHP to evaluate and compare the best heritage accessible routes within a heritage tourism area. The main objective is to identify ideal walking routes that meet a set of universal accessibility criteria which guaranteeing inclusive access for a wide range of user groups, especially for those with mobility challenges including people with impairments, visual impairments, elderly, and families with small children. Ipoh's historical region, with its tiny routes, uneven pavements, and ancient buildings, presents considerable physical and sensory challenges to inclusive tourism. As a result, selecting the best route that maximizes access while maintaining the area's integrity is both practical and culturally important. The research methodology is divided into four major stages which is the first is related to the criteria identification, second is the data gathering, third is the AHP and Fuzzy-AHP calculation, and fourth is the weights of each of the criteria as shown in Fig. 1. In the first stage, a hierarchical framework of accessibility criteria and sub-criteria is created using a combination of literature review, expert judgement, and referring to the established standards. The framework consists of three main criteria which is the mobility and navigation, comforts, and accessibility features with seven different sub-criteria related to the universal access. In the second stage, expert judgement is gathered using a pairwise comparison format. Experts provide exact numerical judgements for the AHP model, based on Saaty's 1 to 9. On the other hand, the Fuzzy-AHP model uses linguistic variables such as "moderately more important" and "very strongly more important" which are then translated into TFNs. Separate comparison matrices are created and processed for AHP and Fuzzy-AHP. The third stage involves calculating priority weights using both techniques. AHP uses normal normalization and eigenvalue computations, as well as a CR check to ensure input consistency. Fuzzy-AHP uses Buckley's Geometric Means approach to aggregate fuzzy preferences, and the resulting fuzzy weights are defuzzified using centroid approach to obtain crisp values. These weights indicate the relevance of each sub-criterion in determining route accessibility. Fourth and final stage consists of a comparison evaluation of the weights obtained from AHP and Fuzzy-AHP models. The findings are analyzed to identify parallels and variations in how each technique prioritizes accessibility criteria. This study does not include route visualization or spatial optimization. Instead, the focus is on examining how each model responds to expert input, particularly in terms of subjectivity, ambiguity, and the relative stability of decision outputs. This simulation-based comparison provides methodological insights for future accessibility design in historic tourism where expert judgement frequently incorporates qualitative and ambiguous preferences.

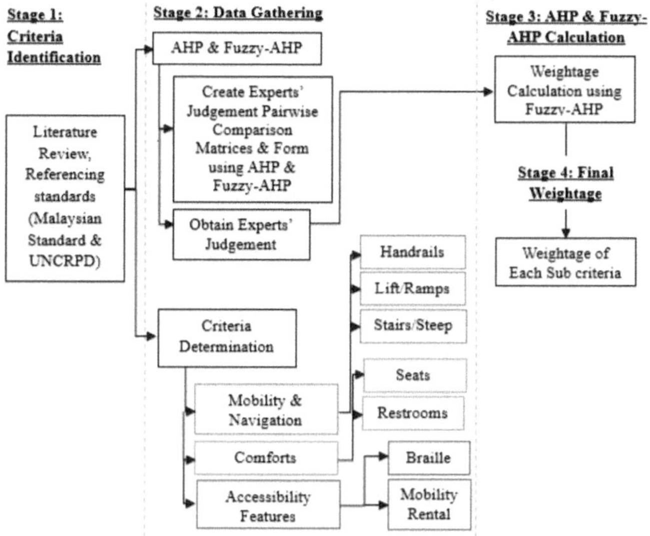

Fig. 1. Flowchart of the Methodology

Although AHP and Fuzzy-AHP are considered traditional methods, it was specifically chosen for this study because of their continuous relevance and practical applicability for simulation-based decision analysis in accessibility planning. These approaches have been frequently used in recent research on urban planning, transportation, and inclusive tourism because of their capability to model hierarchical decision structures, accommodate qualitative assessments, and produce interpretable results. AHP in particular, provides a transparent and organized decision-making framework but Fuzzy-AHP extends a step further by including linguistic and imprecise expert opinions making it more representative of real-world ambiguity which is common in accessible scenarios. Additionally, the aim of this research is not to claim that they are the most sophisticated models available, but rather to use them as methodological baselines for assessing how decision-making models respond to subjective priorities under simulated expert input.

3.2 Criteria and Sub-Criteria

The decision-making framework used in this research is based on three main criteria and seven sub-criteria which are all designed to assess universal accessibility within heritage tourism settings. These criteria were chosen after conducting a systematic literature review of previous accessibility studies in tourism, urban infrastructure, and inclusive design, as well as making formal reference to the MS 1184:2014 and international accessibility guidelines such as the UNCRPD. The three main criteria are mobility and navigation, comfort, and accessibility features. Mobility & Navigation criteria include handrails, ramps or lifts, and proper stair design to help people with mobility impairments move and navigate more easily. Comforts focus on the rest and hygiene amenities needed for lengthy pedestrian travel such as sitting and restrooms. Finally, accessibility features include both physical and sensory support such as braille signage for the visually impaired and mobility rental. Figure 1 provides a detailed description of these criteria and their sub-criteria.

3.3 AHP Application

The AHP created by Saaty (1980), is used in this research to determine the priority weights of the accessibility criterion and sub-criteria. AHP starts by constructing a pairwise comparison matrix $A = [a_{ij}]$, where each entry a_{ij} shows the relative significance of criteria i over criterion j, based on a scale from 1 to 9. The inverse contain in this matrix requires that $a_{ji} = 1/a_{ij}$ and the diagonal values all equal one $(a_{ii} = 1)$. An example structure for a 3 × 3 matrix is as in Eq. 1.

$$A = \left[1 a_{12} a_{13} \frac{1}{a_{12}} 1 a_{23} \frac{1}{a_{13}} \frac{1}{a_{23}} 1 \right] \quad (1)$$

Once the comparison matrix has been created, each element is normalized by dividing it by the total of its columns. Normalized matrix, A' is used to calculated priority vector $w = [w_1, w_2, \ldots, w_n]$, where each weight w_i is the average of the normalized row values.

$$w_i = \frac{1}{n} \sum_{j=1}^{n} a_{ij}' \quad (2)$$

The CR is calculated to ensure that expert judgements are logically consistent. To calculate the maximum eigenvalue λmax from the product $A \cdot w$, apply the following formula. This is where, the Random Index (RI) is a standard value that changes with matrix size. A CR of ≤ 0.10 is considered acceptable. Once validated, the weights indicate the relative relevance of each accessibility sub-criterion. These weights are retained for future comparison with those derived by the Fuzzy-AHP method. The obtained weights were then compared to Fuzzy-AHP.

$$CI = \frac{\lambda_{max} - n}{n - 1}, \quad CR = \frac{CI}{CR} \quad (3)$$

3.4 Fuzzy-AHP Application

In order to address the uncertainty and subjectivity in the expert judgement, the Fuzzy-AHP is employed. This method extends the traditional AHP framework by introducing fuzzy set theory which helps in allowing the expert judgements to be expressed using linguistic variables like "moderately more important" or "very strongly more important" The terms are converted into TFNs as $\tilde{a}_{ij} = (l_{ij}, m_{ij}, u_{ij})$, where l, m, and u indicate the lowest, middle, and upper limits of the preference value. For example, "Moderately Important" is represented by the TFN (4, 5, 6), which represents a range rather than a specific number. The first step is to create a fuzzy pairwise comparison matrix $\tilde{A}$, with entries $\tilde{A}_{ij}$ is a TFN determined by the expert's linguistic judgement. For a 3 criteria example, the matrix is organized as Eq. 4.

$$A = [1\tilde{a}_{12}\tilde{a}_{13}\tilde{a}_{21}1\tilde{a}_{23}\tilde{a}_{31}\tilde{a}_{32}1] \tag{4}$$

To compute reciprocal entries, invert the fuzzy numbers as $\tilde{a}_{ji} = (1/u_{ij},\ 1/m_{ij},\ 1/l_{ij})$. Buckley's (1985) geometric mean approach aggregates each row into a single fuzzy integer $\tilde{r}_i$ represents the total relevance of criteria i.

$$\tilde{r}_i = \left(\prod_{j=1}^{n} l_{ij}\right)^{\frac{1}{n}}, \left(\prod_{j=1}^{n} m_{ij}\right)^{\frac{1}{n}}, \left(\prod_{j=1}^{n} u_{ij}\right)^{\frac{1}{n}} \tag{5}$$

After calculating the fuzzy geometric means $\tilde{r}_1$, $\tilde{r}_2$, $\tilde{r}_3$, the fuzzy weights $\tilde{w}_i$ are derived by dividing each $\tilde{r}_i$ by the sum of all fuzzy geometric means.

$$\tilde{w}_i = \tilde{r}_i x \left(\sum_{i=1}^{n} \tilde{r}_i\right)^{-1} \tag{6}$$

The reciprocal of a fuzzy number used in this normalization step is calculated.

$$A^{-1} = (l, m, u)^{-1} = \left(\frac{1}{u}, \frac{1}{m}, \frac{1}{l}\right) \tag{7}$$

After calculating fuzzy weights, they are defuzzified into crisp values using the centroid method which averages the three TFN components.

$$w_i = \frac{l + m + u}{3} \tag{8}$$

Finally, the defuzzified weights are normalized to guarantee that the sum is equal to one which allowing for a uniform interpretation and comparison. The obtained weights were then compared to AHP-derived weights to determine the impact of including fuzzy logic in expert-driven accessibility design.

$$NormalisedWeight = \frac{w_i}{\sum w_i} \tag{9}$$

4 Result and Analysis

This section demonstrates the simulated results of using the AHP and the Fuzzy-AHP to determine the relative relevance of accessibility criteria in heritage tourism based on simulated data. A single set of pairwise comparisons was simulated to represent the judgement of a hypothetical expert which allowing for a controlled comparison of the weight outputs provided by both approaches under same situations.

4.1 Weightage Derived Using AHP

AHP was used as a fundamental multi-criteria decision-making framework to determine priority weights for universal accessibility sub-criteria in a heritage tourist environment. The assessment framework included a 3x3 matrix to assess the importance of three main criteria and three related matrices where one is in 3x3 matrices and two in 2 × 2 matrices to assess the importance of their related sub-criteria. The final judgements were entirely based on simulation-based pairwise comparisons which were aimed at recreating expert judgement without the use of empirical data collecting. To compute local weights for each matrix, the eigenvector approach was used in line with normal AHP methodology. CR were evaluated to guarantee logical coherence, and all matrices had CR values well under the acceptable threshold of 0.10 which demonstrating a solid internal consistency. The evaluation began with the prioritization of three key criteria which is the mobility and navigation, comfort, and accessibility features. Saaty's fundamental scale was used for pairwise comparisons. The 3 × 3 matrix revealed that Comforts and Accessibility Features were equally important, with a normalized weight of 0.467 each. Mobility & Navigation had a lower priority weight of 0.067. The consistency of judgements was validated, resulting in a CI of 0.000 and a CR of 0.000, indicating perfect consistency.

Table 1. Simulated AHP Global Weights and Rankings

Sub-Criteria	Local Weight	Main Criteria Weight	Global Weight	Percentage
Handrails	0.537	0.067	0.036	4.0%
Lift/Ramps	0.195	0.067	0.013	1.0%
Stairs/Steep	0.268	0.067	0.018	2.0%
Seats	0.875	0.467	0.408	41.0%
Restrooms	0.125	0.467	0.058	6.0%
Braille	0.167	0.467	0.078	8.0%
Mobility Rental	0.833	0.467	0.389	39.0%

Three sub-criteria were examined in the Mobility and Navigation category which is handrails, lifts/ramps, and stairs or steep slopes. The local priority weights calculated were 0.537, 0.195, and 0.268, respectively. The sub-matrix had a CI of 0.068 and a CR of 0.076 that is both below the 0.10 threshold which demonstrating consistent performance in simulated judgements. Despite its lower overall weight, Handrails ranked as the most important criterion in this category which accounting for 3.6% of the total weight. The Comforts criterion had two sub-criteria of Seats and Restrooms. The results revealed a strong preference for Seats with a local weight of 0.875 against 0.125 for Restrooms. The matrix returned a perfect consistency index (CI = 0.000, CR = 0.000). When combined with the primary criteria weight of 0.467, Seats had a global weight of 40.8% making it the most highly prioritized feature across all categories followed by Restrooms at 5.8%. Two sub-criteria were evaluated under the Accessibility Features category of Braille Signage and Mobility Rental. The pairwise comparison preferred Mobility Rental strongly with a local weight of 0.833 and 0.167. The sub-matrix also has perfect consistency (CI = 0, CR = 0). When weighted globally, Mobility Rental was the second-highest priority at 38.9% and followed by Braille at 7.8%. Global weights were then determined by adding the local weights to the primary criteria weight as shown in Table 1. Table 1 summarizes the final global weights which are calculated by multiplying the local sub-criteria weights by the corresponding main criterion weights. Seats (40.8%) and Mobility Rental (38.9%) were the most preferred accessible amenities followed by Braille Signage (7.8%) and Restrooms (5.8%). Mobility & Navigation sub-criteria such as Handrails (3.6%), Stairs/Steep (1.8%), and Lift/Ramps (1.3%) were given lesser importance. These findings demonstrate the AHP model's sensitivity to strong dominant preferences.

4.2 Weightage Derived Using Fuzzy-AHP

To address the limitations of crisp-value decision models, the Fuzzy-AHP was used to evaluate the same hierarchical structure with simulated fuzzy inputs. Unlike traditional AHP, Fuzzy-AHP incorporates fuzzy set theory which allowing linguistic judgements to be represented as TFNs. This method is particularly useful in areas with high levels of subjectivity such as inclusive design and heritage accessibility planning. Five fuzzy pairwise comparison matrices that is similar to those employed in the AHP phase were created by assigning linguistic to the simulated comparisons. These were converted into TFNs, and weights were calculated using Buckley's geometric mean approach which was then defuzzified using the centroid method to get clear global priorities. The fuzzy pairwise comparisons of the three main criteria which is Mobility & Navigation, Comforts, and Accessibility Features that produced a similar result to the traditional AHP analysis, but with more sensitivity.

Table 2. Simulated Fuzzy-AHP Global Weights and Rankings

Sub-Criteria	Local Weight	Main Criteria Weight	Global Weight	Percentage (%)
Handrails	0.539	0.067	0.036	4%
Lift/Ramps	0.194	0.067	0.013	1%
Stairs/Steep	0.266	0.067	0.018	2%
Seats	0.874	0.466	0.408	41%
Restrooms	0.152	0.466	0.071	7%
Braille	0.167	0.466	0.078	8%
Mobility Rental	0.833	0.466	0.388	39%

Comforts and Accessibility Features received defuzzified weights of 0.466, while Mobility & Navigation was deprioritized at 0.067. These data indicate that Fuzzy-AHP maintains the current ranking structure while allowing for improved handling of expert uncertainty across different TFNs. Mobility & Navigation sub-criteria included handrails, lifts/ramps, and stairs or steep slopes. Using 3x3 fuzzy matrices and the Buckley approach, the defuzzified local weights produced were Handrails (0.539), Stairs/Steep (0.266), and Lift/Ramps (0.194). When combined with the primary criteria weight of 0.067, the resulting global weights were 3.6%, 1.8%, and 1.3%. Compared to AHP, the fuzzy method provided slightly more balanced values by decreasing significant dominance gaps while maintaining interpretative validity. This category had two sub-criteria which is seats and restrooms. The fuzzy geometric mean computations produced local weights of 0.874 and 0.126, respectively. After accounting for the main criteria weight (0.466), these results provided global weights of 40.8% and 7.1%, respectively. Importantly, compared to AHP's result for Restrooms (5.8%), the Fuzzy-AHP model offered a slightly greater global relevance by demonstrating its ability to incorporate minor human judgement difference that deterministic ratings do not capture. Fuzzy comparisons of Braille Signage and Mobility Rental produced local weights of 0.167 and 0.833, respectively. When rectified for the main criteria weight of 0.466, their respective global contributions were 7.8% and 38.8%. The fuzzy outputs, while comparable to AHP's have demonstrated a greater sensitivity in reflecting the significance of Braille which would otherwise appear minor in traditional analysis.

Table 2 summarizes the final global weights produced using the Fuzzy-AHP procedure. The top two criteria of Seats (40.8%) and Mobility Rental (38.8%) were consistently significant across all methods, demonstrating the common focus on physical ease and support for mobility in accessible heritage design. However, the Fuzzy-AHP model showed greater representational balance which notably in middle-tier sub-criteria like Restrooms (7.1%) and Braille (7.8%) by demonstrating its potential benefit in integrating complex and linguistically terms of expert judgements.

4.3 Analysis and Methodological Reflection

The comparison between AHP and Fuzzy-AHP are both implemented in a simulated decision environment has provides insight on the operational behavior of each approach when applied to accessibility prioritization in heritage tourist planning. Both models consistently indicated Seats and Mobility Rental as the top-ranked sub-criteria with global weights of approximately 40.8% and 38.8–38.9%, respectively. This consistency underscores the internal coherence of the simulated design and reflects the clear priority placed on physical comfort and mobility assistance within universally accessible heritage environments. However, differences between the two methodologies occur in the middle and lower-ranked sub-criteria notably in the evaluation of restrooms and lifts/ramps. The Fuzzy-AHP model, applied with Buckley's geometric mean approach produced slightly more balanced weight distributions. Restrooms, for example, had a greater global weight of 7.1% in Fuzzy-AHP than 5.8% in AHP demonstrating fuzzy logic's capability to maintain expert hesitation and capture imprecise judgements. AHP, on the other hand, makes use of ratio-scale judgements which may mistakenly compress intermediate preferences while highlighting dominant criteria. Unexpectedly, weight for Braille Signage was same across both models at 7.8% indicating that in situations when simulated preferences are clear however minor, both methods may converge. Meanwhile, lower-weighted criteria such as Lift/Ramps (1.3%) and Stairs or Steep Slopes (1.8%) displayed minor differences but had no significant impact on the ranking structure. It is important to note that the data used in this research is based on simulated expert input. As a result, conclusions on the real-world effectiveness of one method over another are uncertain. The observed differences are meant to emphasize each model's computational behavior rather than empirical accuracy or stakeholder validity. Future research using genuine expert or active stakeholder involvement would be required to validate methodological preferences suggested. From a methodological perspective, this comparison demonstrates that AHP is still a strong and interpretable tool for structured decision-making, particularly when expert judgements are clear and consistent. However, Fuzzy-AHP provides a theoretically deeper framework for situations that involve linguistic ambiguity, subjective evaluations, or sensitive choices conditions that are common in heritage accessibility planning. It promotes more inclusive and robust culturally sensitive method of planning by recognizing uncertainty and gathering a broader range of expert perspectives.

5 Discussion

This section provides an in-depth analysis of the simulation-based results achieved by applying both the AHP and Fuzzy-AHP to the context of universal accessibility planning within heritage tourist environments. While the findings are based on simulated input data and do not represent real-world stakeholder reactions, it provides a crucial methodological perspective on how different decision-making algorithms interpret and priorities accessibility criteria under uncertainty.

5.1 Strengths, Weakness of Methods, and Practical Implications

The AHP method, despite its limitations has significant advantages. Its hierarchical pairwise comparison structure is clear, computationally fast, and includes an integrated consistency check to assure logical of the coherence in expert judgements. AHP provides a clear and stable framework for scenarios involving reliable, precise, and cognitively comprehensible expert judgements. Furthermore, its widespread application across planning disciplines makes it more accessible to policymakers and professionals. However, AHP's fundamental weakness is its rigidity. Fixed numerical scales may oversimplify subjective judgements, especially when comparing between criteria is difficult to determine. This is particularly challenging in heritage tourism where accessibility considerations must balance physical limitations with social justice objectives and stakeholder diversity. Fuzzy-AHP overcomes this issue by allowing experts to express their preferences in linguistic terms which are then represented with fuzzy numbers. This feature not only minimizes the cognitive pressure on responders but it also captures the natural imprecision of human assessments. Fuzzy-AHP does not operate without difficulties. It necessitates more complex calculation such as fuzzification, geometric means, and defuzzification techniques which may be difficult to non-technical users. Furthermore, while fuzzy logic allows for more complex expressions of judgement, it might confuse interpretability if not clearly stated through visualization. Unlike AHP, Fuzzy-AHP does not have a standard consistency statistic which may raise issues regarding decision-making transparency.

When properly used, Fuzzy-AHP is a useful methodological development for analyzing complicated and multi-stakeholder planning problems under uncertainty. Although the results of this research are based on simulated data, the methodological insights gained can be applied to real-world planning scenarios. Heritage tourist sites often encounter infrastructural concerns that were not constructed with universal accessibility in mind. Improving accessibility necessitates not only technical upgrading but also inclusive prioritization that takes into account varied user demands such as those of people with disabilities, the elderly, and families with children. Planners and decision-makers can benefit from using fuzzy logic-based tools to guarantee that choice criteria are not undervalued just because they fall into the areas of stakeholder judgement. Fuzzy-AHP provides a theoretically solid and practically flexible framework for design interventions that must balance preservation, usability, and fairness such as in Malaysian heritage areas controlled by standards like MS1184:2014 or UNCRPD principles. Furthermore, the method outlined in this research can aid in early-stage planning and pre-engagement modelling by allowing planners to simulate and test decision scenarios prior to starting comprehensive stakeholder interactions. This can help to eliminate planning inefficiencies, identify potential issues between stakeholder goals, and promote more informed collaboration. Future research should apply this method to real datasets generated by expert or public involvement to improve both methodological relevance.

6 Conclusion

This research has conducted a methodological comparison of the AHP and the Fuzzy-AHP in prioritizing universal accessibility criteria within heritage tourisms scenarios. Using a simulation-based framework, these models were applied to a hierarchically structured set of accessibility criteria and sub-criteria gathered from recognized standards and literature such as MS1184:2014 and the UNCRPD. The major goal was to study how each method reacts to simulated expert judgements and evaluate their relative capabilities in situations highlighted by complexity, subjectivity, and the requirement for inclusive planning. The findings demonstrate that, while AHP provides a consistent and transparent decision-making process, it tends to draw a stronger difference between main and sub criteria which potentially ignoring middle level of priorities. On the other hand, Fuzzy-AHP showed a more equitable distribution of weights which is especially advantageous for sub-criteria that could be contextually significant or linguistically nuanced but difficult to measure. This behavior is consistent with fuzzy logic's theoretical advantage in modelling human uncertainty and imprecision which are frequently present in accessibility planning where design compromises, cultural restrictions, and user diversity come together. Despite being based on simulated data, the findings offer useful methodological insights. It suggests that Fuzzy-AHP may provide more realism and flexibility for application in stakeholder-driven environments, particularly in heritage tourism settings that must balance conservation goals with universal access responsibility. Importantly, this research does not claim that one method is actually superior to the other, but rather demonstrates its distinct computational behaviors under controlled settings. Future research should expand this model to involve actual applications including a variety of stakeholder groups such as people with disabilities, accessibility experts, conservation planners, and local governments. Such validation would allow fuzzy-based decision tools to be refined while also increasing their reliability for application in public policy, heritage management, and inclusive tourist development.

Acknowledgement. The authors would like to thank Universiti Teknologi MARA for supporting this study.

References

1. Nik Hashim, N. H. Tsong, T. B. Hashim Lim, N. H. Lin, T. Y.: Assessing conservation approaches for sustaining heritage buildings: a case study of Ipoh Old Town, Perak, Malaysia. Planning Malaysia, Vol. 22 (2024). https://doi.org/10.21837/Pm.v22i33.1531
2. Lakoud, M., et al.: Preserving the past, embracing the future: co-design strategies for achieving harmony between heritage sites and accessibility needs. Heritage **8**(1), 19 (2025). https://doi.org/10.3390/Heritage8010019
3. Hisham, I., Tah, M., Mokhtar, K.A., Azmin Mokhtar, K.: Malaysia's ratification of the un convention on the rights of persons with disabilities (Un CRPD) Malaysia's ratification of the Un Convention on the Rights of Persons with Disabilities (Un CRPD) 1. International Journal of Business, Economics and Law, Vol. 11, No. 4, [Online]. Available: https://www.Researchgate.Net/Publication/312317769
4. Chaube, S., et al.: An overview of multi-criteria decision analysis and the applications of AHP and TOPSIS methods. Int. J. Math. Eng. Manage. Sci. **9**(3), 581–615 (2024). https://doi.org/10.33889/Ijmems.2024.9.3.030
5. Jewpanya, P., Nuangpirom, P., Nakkiew, W., Pitjamit, S., Jaichomphu, P.: Optimizing tourist destination selection using AHP and fuzzy AHP based on individual preferences for personalized tourism. Sustainability **17**(3), 1116 (2025). https://doi.org/10.3390/Su17031116
6. World Health Organization: Who Ambient Air Quality Database. 2022 Update (2022)
7. Wan, Y.K.P.: Accessibility of tourist signage at heritage sites: an application of the universal design principles. Tour. Recreat. Res. **49**(4), 757–771 (2024). https://doi.org/10.1080/02508281.2022.2106099
8. Zahari, N.F., Kamarudin, H., Ahmad Zawawi, Z., Abdul Rashid, R., Mohd Bahari, M.: Heritage tourism: a disabled person's rights to engage in social activity. Plann. Malaysia **21** (2023). https://doi.org/10.21837/Pm.V21i25.1252
9. Meng Hooi, P., Mohd Yaacob, N.: Accessibility for physically challenged persons in heritage buildings (2019)
10. Munier, N., Hontoria, E.: Uses and limitations of The AHP method. Cham, Springer International Publishing (2021). https://doi.org/10.1007/978-3-030-60392-2
11. Chang, K.-H., Lai, H.-H., Hung, B.-J.: Combining the fuzzy analytic hierarchy process method with the weighted aggregated sum product assessment method to address internet platform selection problems in an environment with incomplete information. Appl. Sci. **14**(11), 4390 (2024). https://doi.org/10.3390/App14114390
12. Alias, E., Naharudin, N., Yusoff, Z.M., Rahaman, L.A.: Analyzing neighborhood safety for children in shah alam, malaysia using Fuzzy-AHP and GIS (2024)
13. Arumugam, A., Nakkeeran, S., Subramaniam, R.: Exploring the factors influencing heritage tourism development: a model development. Sustainability **15**(15), 11986 (2023). https://doi.org/10.3390/Su151511986

14. Utomo, S.W., Koestoer, R.H.S., Soesilo, T.E.B., Manumpil, F.E.: Multicriteria decision making in sustainable tourism and low-carbon tourism research. Tourism **71**(3), 447–471 (2023). https://doi.org/10.37741/T.71.3.2
15. Roslan, A., Naharudin, N.: Identification of e-Scooter Shared (ESS) Stations by using a GIS-based MCDM Approach. Int. J. Geoinform. **19**(5), 69–78 (2023)

Artificial Intelligence Techniques and Applications

Deep Image Prior with L1 Loss for Medical Image Denoising

Cheng Zhang, Hui Liu, and Kin Sam Yen(✉)

School of Mechanical Engineering, Universiti Sains Malaysia, Engineering Campus, 14300 Nibong Tebal, Penang, Malaysia
meyks@usm.my

Abstract. This study introduces a Deep Image Prior (DIP)-based medical image denoising method that requires no training data, enhanced through the incorporation of an L1-norm fidelity term. The proposed model, referred to as L1-DIP, addresses the limitations of conventional DIP, which typically relies on an MSE loss and suffers from spectral bias and structural over-smoothing. By replacing the pixel-wise MSE loss with an L1 loss, the method improves robustness to outliers and better preserves anatomical discontinuities, making it particularly suitable for low-dose CT and high-resolution MRI reconstruction tasks. The model employs a U-Net equipped with skip connections, optimized per-image using a fixed random input. The L1 fidelity term guides the reconstruction process toward edge-aware solutions without requiring any external training data. Experiments were conducted on a thoracic CT scan and a coronal pelvic-lumbar MRI image, where additive Gaussian noise was synthetically added to simulate varying levels of corruption. Quantitative evaluations demonstrate that L1-DIP consistently outperforms DIP, DeepRED, and SURE-DIP across all noise levels, in terms of both peak signal-to-noise ratio (PSNR) and structural similarity index (SSIM). Visual comparisons confirm that the proposed model achieves clearer boundary definition and better preservation of anatomical structure. Convergence curves for PSNR and SSIM also reveal that L1-DIP converges faster than the DIP. These results highlight the effectiveness of integrating an L1-based fidelity term into the DIP framework, offering a training-free, high-fidelity solution for medical image denoising under complex noise conditions.

Keywords: deep image prior · L1-norm · overfitting · unsupervised deep learning

1 Introduction

Medical imaging techniques, including computed tomography (CT) and magnetic resonance imaging (MRI), are fundamental tools in clinical diagnostics. CT provides high-resolution visualization of internal structures and is particularly valuable for lung and bone assessment. However, reducing radiation dose in CT, which is necessary to minimize patient exposure, inevitably leads to increased photon noise that degrades image quality and obscures subtle anatomical features [1]. MRI, although free from ionizing

M. Kassim et al. (Eds.): SCDS 2025, CCIS 2674, pp. 353–365, 2026.
https://doi.org/10.1007/978-981-95-8368-3_25

radiation, is also affected by noise. This typically arises from low signal strength in high-resolution imaging or rapid acquisition protocols, where thermal and electronic sources introduce signal degradation [1]. In both modalities, image quality is closely linked to diagnostic accuracy. Therefore, effective denoising techniques are essential to preserve clinically relevant structures without compromising safety or acquisition efficiency [2].

Traditional denoising techniques, including BM3D [3], have been widely used for medical image noise suppression. However, they rely heavily on handcrafted priors and fixed filtering strategies, which can blur fine details and perform inconsistently under varying noise levels [4]. More recently, supervised deep learning approaches have demonstrated superior denoising performance by learning mappings from noisy to clean images [5]. Despite their success, these methods require large-scale paired datasets, which are difficult to acquire in clinical settings, and often generalize poorly to unseen imaging protocols or noise distributions [6].

To alleviate the dependence on labeled data, Ulyanov et al. [7] proposed the deep image prior (DIP) framework. This approach eliminates the need for external training by leveraging the structural bias of convolutional neural networks. A randomly initialized convolutional neural network (CNN) is directly fitted to a single noisy image, and the network itself acts as an implicit prior that favors natural image structures. DIP has gained increasing attention in medical imaging, where ground truth data are often unavailable. Despite its advantages, the original DIP formulation is based on the mean squared error (MSE) loss, which assumes Gaussian noise and tends to produce overly smooth outputs. This leads to the suppression of fine structural details that are crucial in clinical imaging, particularly under high noise levels [8].

Several extensions to the original DIP have been developed to mitigate these issues. DIP-WTV introduces weighted total variation regularization to enhance edge preservation, though it requires manual parameter tuning and may introduce staircase artifacts [9]. DeepRED integrates a pretrained denoiser into the optimization loop to improve robustness. However, this adds computational overhead and introduces dependence on external models [10]. SURE-DIP adopts Stein's unbiased risk estimator to guide optimization without clean targets. While this enables self-supervised learning, it depends on the assumption of differentiable and well-characterized noise models, which limits its applicability to real-world clinical data [11].

This study reconsiders the loss function in DIP by replacing MSE with an L1-norm fidelity term. The L1 loss is less sensitive to outliers and better suited for preserving intensity discontinuities [12]. These properties are especially important in medical images, where diagnostic interpretation often relies on the clarity of tissue boundaries, vessel walls, or subtle contrast variations. Unlike MSE, which penalizes large residuals more heavily and encourages overly smooth reconstructions, the L1 norm allows for sharper transitions and promotes sparsity in the residuals, resulting in improved detail preservation [13].

Motivated by these advantages, this work proposes an L1-based DIP framework for denoising medical images in an unsupervised manner. The method maintains the core characteristics of DIP, including its training-free nature and adaptability to single-image inputs, while enhancing structural fidelity through the use of L1 loss. No additional priors, labels, or pretrained modules are required. Compared to previous DIP variants, the proposed method achieves more accurate restoration of edge information, suppresses spectral bias effects, and improves robustness under high noise levels. Experimental evaluations on thoracic CT and coronal MRI images demonstrate that the proposed approach achieves superior PSNR and SSIM scores across multiple noise intensities. Visual comparisons further confirm its effectiveness in preserving fine anatomical details such as bronchial bifurcations, soft-tissue layers, and bone boundaries.

This paper is structured as follows: Sect. 2 summarizes prior work on DIP and its extensions. The proposed methodology, including network architecture and loss formulation, is detailed in Sect. 3. Section 4 provides experimental results and comparative evaluations, while Sect. 5 concludes with findings and future research directions.

2 Related Work

The DIP framework [7] has emerged as a powerful unsupervised method for image restoration tasks like denoising, inpainting, and super-resolution. In contrast to traditional deep learning approaches that rely on large-scale training datasets, DIP operates without external supervision by fitting a randomly initialized CNN directly to a single corrupted image. The underlying principle is that CNNs possess an intrinsic inductive bias toward natural image statistics. As a result, they tend to reconstruct structured content more rapidly than noise during the early stages of optimization.

In a standard DIP formulation, a fixed random tensor z is used as the network input and is mapped through a CNN $f_\theta(z)$ to produce the restored image. The network parameters θ are learned by minimizing a loss function that measures fidelity between the output and noisy observation y, typically using the MSE as follows:

$$L_{MSE}(\theta) = \|f_\theta(z) - y\|_2^2 \tag{1}$$

This formulation is well-suited for scenarios involving additive Gaussian noise and has been widely employed in DIP-based image restoration. However, the MSE loss tends to over-smooth reconstructed content, especially in high-noise conditions. It suppresses structural edges due to its quadratic penalization of large residuals, which can obscure important image details.

DIP is often implemented using encoder-decoder architectures such as U-Net, which promote multi-scale feature representation through symmetric skip connections. While these structures enhance reconstruction capability, they also introduce a spectral bias. During early iterations, low-frequency components are reconstructed preferentially, whereas high-frequency information, such as edges and textures, is either delayed or attenuated. This imbalance limits the effective recovery of fine anatomical structures, posing a significant challenge in medical imaging applications where high-resolution details are diagnostically critical.

The utility of DIP in clinical contexts has been demonstrated in several studies. For instance, Gong et al. [14] applied DIP to positron emission tomography (PET) image enhancement, and Baguer et al. [15] used it for sparse-view CT reconstruction. These examples highlight the method's potential in settings where ground truth data are scarce or unavailable. Despite its advantages, DIP still faces limitations, including high computational demands, the absence of an automatic stopping criterion, and the intrinsic shortcomings of MSE-based fidelity in preserving important structural features. These challenges have driven ongoing efforts to explore improved loss formulations and network modifications within the DIP framework [11].

3 Methodology

This study builds upon the DIP framework to perform unsupervised denoising of low-dose medical images, specifically CT and MRI scans. The core modification lies in replacing the conventional MSE loss with an L1-norm fidelity term. This change is motivated by the need to improve robustness against outliers and to preserve sharp anatomical boundaries that are often suppressed by quadratic penalization [13]. The objective is to reconstruct the clean image x from its noisy observation $y = x + n$, where n represents additive noise that is approximately Gaussian but may exhibit deviations due to sensor nonlinearities, photon starvation, or acquisition artifacts. Unlike supervised learning approaches that rely on large-scale paired datasets and pretraining, the proposed method performs optimization on each noisy image independently, without requiring ground truth.

Following the DIP paradigm [7], a fixed input tensor $z \in R^{H \times W \times C}$, drawn from a uniform distribution, is fed into a randomly initialized CNN $f_\theta(z)$, where θ denotes the learnable parameters. The network is trained to minimize the pixel-wise L1-norm loss between its output and the noisy observation y, defined as

$$\min_{\theta} L_{L1}(\theta) = \frac{1}{N} \|f_\theta(z) - y\|_1 \tag{2}$$

where N denotes the number of image pixels. The L1 loss is particularly suitable for clinical imaging scenarios, as it imposes a uniform penalty across intensity deviations and does not overly emphasize large residuals. This property is beneficial for recovering edges and preserving fine textures that are frequently degraded in low-dose imaging. The proposed network architecture is as follows (Fig. 1):

The network architecture adopts a U-Net backbone composed of five encoder and decoder stages arranged in a symmetric encoder-decoder structure with skip connections. Each encoder stage comprises two sequential 3 × 3 convolutions, each followed by a ReLU activation and batch normalization, and concludes with a 2 × 2 max pooling operation for downsampling. As the encoder progresses deeper, the number of channels doubles at each level, beginning with 64 and reaching a maximum of 1024 at the bottleneck layer. This progressive expansion enables the network to capture increasingly abstract and global contextual features while reducing spatial resolution.

The decoder mirrors the encoder in reverse. Each decoder stage performs upsampling via bilinear interpolation (or optionally transposed convolution), followed by two 3 × 3 convolutional blocks with ReLU activation and batch normalization. The upsampled features are then concatenated with matching encoder features through skip connections. This design enables precise localization and structural fidelity by reintroducing fine-grained spatial detail lost during the encoding process. The final output layer applies a 1 × 1 convolution to generate a single-channel grayscale image representing the restored CT or MRI scan.

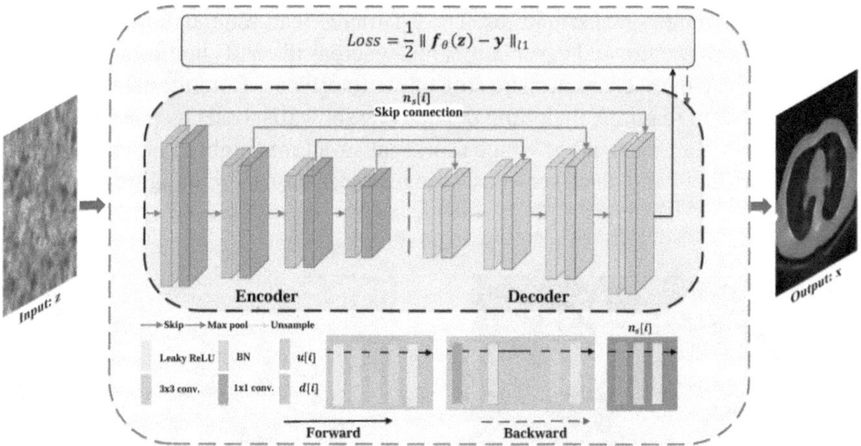

Fig. 1. The proposed network architecture.

To ensure stable convergence, all convolutional weights are initialized using He initialization [16]. The random input z remains fixed throughout the optimization and serves as a structured input that encourages the network to reconstruct coherent features rather than memorize noise patterns. During training, the network parameters θ are optimized via Adam at a learning rate of 0.001. The optimization is performed over a fixed number of iterations or stopped early based on output stability, as prolonged training can lead to overfitting the noise.

This formulation retains the unsupervised and data-independent advantages of the original DIP while enhancing its capacity to recover clinically significant features in challenging noise environments. The integration of an L1-based fidelity term results in improved perceptual quality, stronger edge preservation, and increased robustness across both CT and MRI imaging modalities. The effectiveness of this approach is demonstrated in the following section through comprehensive experiments under varying noise levels.

4 Experiment and Results

This section describes the datasets used in the evaluation, outlines the experimental settings, and presents quantitative and qualitative analyses of the results.

4.1 Experiment and Evaluation

The experimental evaluation employed two carefully selected medical images to ensure coverage of diagnostically relevant scenarios across different imaging modalities and anatomical regions. The first is a thoracic CT scan, and the second is a coronal MRI scan of the pelvic and lumbar region, as shown in Fig. 2. Both images were obtained from publicly available Kaggle datasets and acquired under full-dose or high-quality clinical settings, providing clear anatomical references. The dataset represents the distinct physical principles of X-ray attenuation versus nuclear magnetic resonance while capturing critical anatomical structures. The CT image featured the thoracic cavity with fine bronchial architecture and vascular details, whereas the MRI highlighted the pelvic-lumbar junction with its characteristic soft-tissue interfaces. Both modalities contained essential diagnostic features, including delicate vessel walls, osseous margins, and soft-tissue contrast differentials, all of which represent structures highly vulnerable to image degradation artifacts and thus serve as stringent test cases for imaging performance assessment.

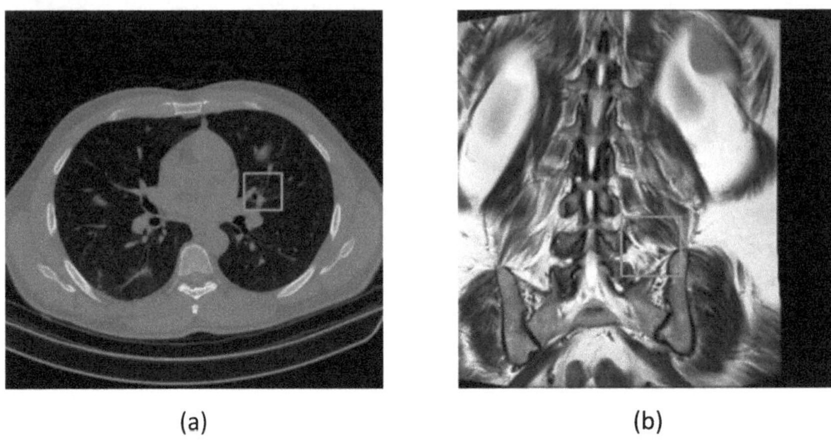

Fig. 2. (a) Thoracic CT (b) coronal MRI.

To simulate varying levels of acquisition noise, additive Gaussian noise with standard deviations σ of 20, 30, and 40 was applied to the clean images. These noise levels reflect typical clinical conditions encountered under dose reduction or accelerated imaging protocols. The proposed method was compared with three established DIP-based baselines, namely the original DIP, DeepRED, and SURE-DIP. All models were optimized individually for each noisy input under identical settings, without access to the corresponding ground truth. The comparison focuses specifically on DIP variants because recent systematic studies [17] demonstrate that while traditional methods like BM3D may show marginal advantages for Gaussian noise in general images, these benefits do not extend to medical imaging scenarios.

Traditional denoising approaches face critical limitations when processing medical images due to their reliance on handcrafted priors, often resulting in over-smoothed anatomical details or introduced artifacts in low-contrast regions. As evidenced in the literature, BM3D's performance on medical images at best matches DIP-based methods and frequently underperforms in preserving diagnostically critical structures under high noise conditions. This comparative analysis of DIP variants therefore provides the most direct evaluation of the core methodological innovation: the replacement of MSE with L1-norm fidelity within the unsupervised deep learning framework.

Denoising performance was quantitatively evaluated using two metrics. Peak signal-to-noise ratio (PSNR) was used to assess pixel-wise fidelity, and structural similarity index measure (SSIM) was employed to evaluate perceptual and structural accuracy

[18]. SSIM is particularly important in medical imaging, as it reflects the preservation of anatomical boundaries and local tissue contrasts. All models were trained for 2500 iterations using the PyTorch framework and executed on a single NVIDIA GTX 3070 Ti GPU. Hyperparameters were fixed across models and tuned to optimize reconstruction performance concerning PSNR and SSIM.

4.2 Experimental Results

This section provides a quantitative assessment of our model on the medical images shown in Fig. 2. Table 1 summarizes the results, with the best PSNR and SSIM values in each condition highlighted in bold.

Table 1. Quantitative evaluation of denoising performance (peak PSNR in dB and SSIM).

	Noise level	20		30		40	
	Model	PSNR	SSIM	PSNR	SSIM	PSNR	SSIM
Figure 2(a)	DIP	31.658	0.8457	28.533	0.7721	26.298	0.7142
	DeepRED	31.886	0.8467	29.404	0.7885	26.831	0.7320
	SURE-DIP	31.923	0.8663	29.142	0.8631	26.852	0.7603
	Proposed	**32.192**	**0.9213**	**30.699**	**0.9176**	**29.158**	**0.8922**
Figure 2(b)	DIP	31.152	0.8602	28.402	0.8126	26.574	0.7806
	DeepRED	31.548	0.8625	29.092	0.8276	27.074	0.7936
	SURE-DIP	31.639	0.9243	28.876	0.8535	27.209	0.8486
	Proposed	**31.892**	**0.9532**	**29.520**	**0.9236**	**28.428**	**0.8925**

As indicated in Table 1, the proposed L1-DIP method outperformed all baseline approaches across both CT and MRI images and under varying noise levels. For the CT image, the L1-DIP model achieved an SSIM of 0.9213 at $\sigma = 20$, exceeding the values of DIP (0.8457), DeepRED (0.8467), and SURE-DIP (0.8663). This corresponds to SSIM improvements of 0.0756, 0.0746, and 0.0550, respectively. When the noise level reached $\sigma = 30$, the SSIM of L1-DIP remained high at 0.9176, whereas the competing methods showed a more noticeable decline, particularly DIP (0.7721) and DeepRED (0.7885). At $\sigma = 40$, L1-DIP still maintained a robust SSIM of 0.8922, while DIP and DeepRED dropped to 0.7142 and 0.7320, respectively. Even SURE-DIP, which incorporates a risk estimator for improved self-supervision, declined to 0.7603. These results indicate that the proposed model offers enhanced structural fidelity under significant degradation. A similar trend is observed in PSNR performance. At $\sigma = 20$, the proposed method yielded a PSNR of 32.192 dB, surpassing DIP (31.658 dB), DeepRED (31.886 dB), and SURE-DIP (31.923 dB). Although the absolute gains appear modest at lower noise levels, the advantage becomes more pronounced under heavy noise. At $\sigma = 40$, L1-DIP preserved a PSNR of 29.158 dB, whereas the strongest baseline, DeepRED, achieved only 26.831 dB, resulting in a 2.3 dB margin.

For the MRI image, the performance gap was even more substantial. At $\sigma = 20$, L1-DIP achieved the highest SSIM of 0.9532, compared to DIP (0.8602), DeepRED (0.8625), and SURE-DIP (0.9243). At a noise standard deviation of 30, the SSIM of L1-DIP remained at 0.9236, which is significantly higher than SURE-DIP (0.8535) and DeepRED (0.8276). At $\sigma = 40$, the SSIM of L1-DIP still reached 0.8925, while none of the baseline methods exceeded 0.85, and DIP dropped to 0.7806. This pattern is reflected in PSNR values as well: L1-DIP consistently preserved signal-level accuracy across all noise intensities, reaching 28.428 dB at $\sigma = 40$, which is over 1.2 dB higher than the second-best result.

The consistent superiority in both PSNR and SSIM across modalities and noise intensities validates the benefit of replacing MSE with an L1-norm fidelity term in the DIP framework. By offering better robustness to outliers and a stronger response to structural edges, the L1 formulation enables sharper reconstructions and improved preservation of diagnostic information. These findings demonstrate that the proposed L1-DIP model enhances both pixel-wise fidelity and perceptual quality without requiring external training data or handcrafted priors.

Figures 3 and 4 present enlarged patches extracted from both test images after denoising at a noise level of $\sigma = 30$. Figure 3 corresponds to the bronchial bifurcation region in the CT image (CT-bronchus patch), and Fig. 4 corresponds to the lumbar facet-joint region in the MRI image (MRI-lumbar patch). The visual comparison reveals clear differences in edge definition and noise residuals.

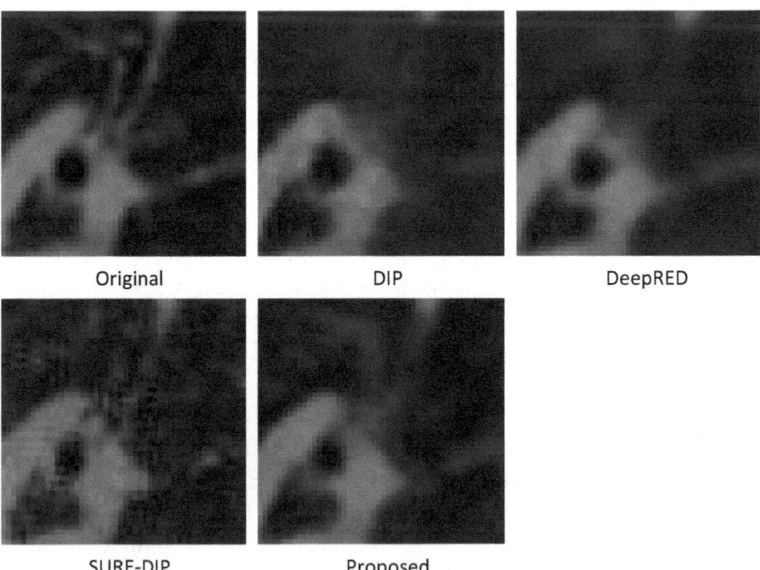

Fig. 3. Visual comparison of the denoised bronchial region in CT at $\sigma = 30$.

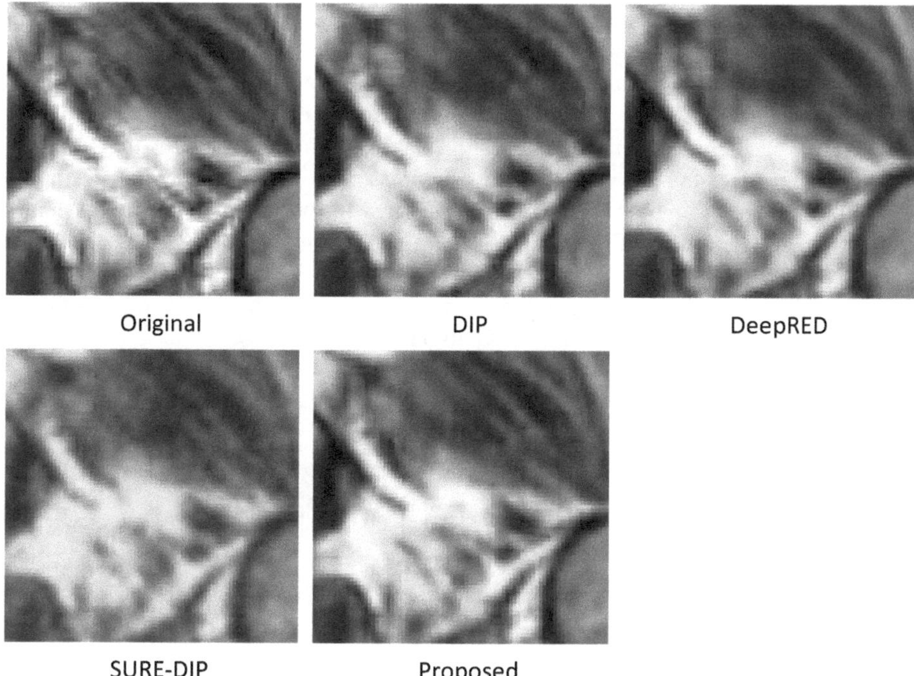

Fig. 4. Visual comparison of the denoised lumbar region in MRI at $\sigma = 30$.

Figure 3 presents a visual comparison of denoised bronchial regions in CT images under $\sigma = 30$. Among all methods, the proposed L1-DIP approach yields the most visually faithful reconstruction. Airway boundaries are clearly defined, and the parenchymal background appears homogeneous and free of artificial textures. In contrast, the original DIP result shows persistent speckle noise and blurred bronchial walls, indicating insufficient suppression of high-frequency corruption. DeepRED effectively attenuates noise but introduces over-smoothing that obscures vessel boundaries and reduces anatomical contrast. SURE-DIP demonstrates partial structural recovery but fails to eliminate residual artifacts, leaving behind streak-like patterns and granularity in low-contrast regions. The proposed model achieves a balanced reconstruction, preserving edge sharpness while maintaining low background variance, which is crucial for the clinical interpretability of thoracic CT scans.

Figure 4 illustrates denoising results for the lumbar region in an MRI slice at the same noise level. The proposed L1-DIP again demonstrates superior structural preservation. The cortical bone interfaces and adjacent soft-tissue layers are sharply delineated, and the internal muscle textures remain smooth and continuous. In contrast, the DIP output exhibits granular distortions and lacks a clear boundary definition. DeepRED reduces some of the noise but causes contrast degradation, particularly at soft–hard tissue junctions. SURE-DIP partially recovers edge contours but retains a patchy noise pattern that diminishes overall image coherence. The L1-DIP result successfully maintains anatomical integrity in both high-contrast and low-contrast regions, highlighting its capacity to restore both fine-grained textures and broader structural consistency.

These visual comparisons are consistent with the quantitative evaluations presented earlier. They further confirm that integrating an L1-norm fidelity term into the DIP framework improves the model's ability to suppress noise while preserving diagnostically relevant features. In both CT and MRI modalities, the proposed method consistently outperforms conventional DIP variants in retaining anatomical clarity under moderate noise levels.

Figure 5 shows PSNR convergence curves, and Fig. 6 presents SSIM trajectories for the same CT and MRI images at σ = 30 Gaussian noise.

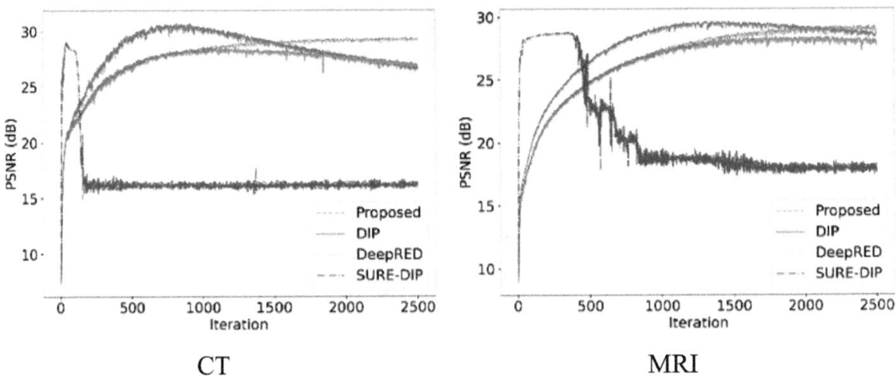

Fig. 5. PSNR curves using various models at σ = 30 Gaussian noise.

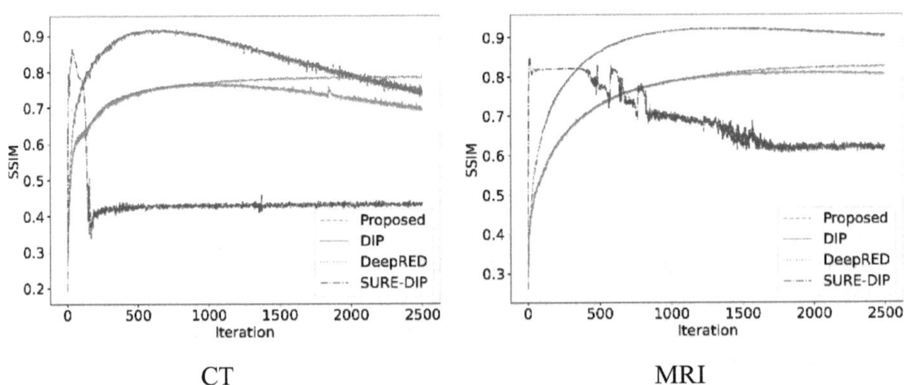

Fig. 6. SSIM curves using various models at σ = 30 Gaussian noise.

For the CT image, the L1-DIP model demonstrates rapid PSNR improvement, reaching a peak close to 31 dB within the first few hundred iterations. In contrast, DIP and cDIP-RED converge more slowly and stabilize below 29 dB. SURE-DIP shows an early peak but quickly declines, eventually plateauing at approximately 17 dB, which reflects its sensitivity to noise and unstable convergence.

The SSIM trend on the CT image reflects distinct convergence behaviors among the four methods. L1-DIP achieves a peak SSIM exceeding 0.90 within the first 500 iterations and maintains high structural similarity throughout the optimization process. DIP reaches its peak much earlier, around 100 iterations, but the maximum SSIM remains lower, near 0.80. cDIP-RED converges more slowly and also peaks around 0.80, indicating limited structural recovery. SURE-DIP attains its peak SSIM at the very beginning of the training process, outperforming both DIP and cDIP-RED in terms of peak value. However, it exhibits severe fluctuations and rapid degradation thereafter, suggesting overfitting and instability during extended optimization.

The L1-DIP model consistently outperforms all baseline methods across both PSNR and SSIM on CT and MRI images. It achieves faster convergence, higher reconstruction accuracy, and better preservation of structural detail. These results confirm the effectiveness of the L1 loss in enhancing the stability and quality of unsupervised denoising within the DIP framework under clinically relevant noise conditions.

Although the proposed approach yields promising results, some limitations remain. The model still depends on manual early stopping to prevent overfitting, as no intrinsic mechanism is currently available to determine the optimal iteration automatically. This introduces a degree of subjectivity that may affect reproducibility. Additionally, the method is computationally demanding, since it requires individual optimization for each image, which may restrict its scalability in large-scale clinical applications. Another limitation lies in the assumption of Gaussian noise. The performance of the current framework has not been evaluated under more complex or modality-specific noise distributions such as Poisson, Rician, or low-count PET noise, which often occur in real-world medical imaging scenarios.

5 Conclusion

This study proposed an enhanced DIP framework for medical image denoising by introducing an L1-norm fidelity term, to improve structural preservation under Gaussian noise. The resulting L1-DIP model maintains the unsupervised and training-free nature of DIP, while effectively addressing limitations of the original formulation, including spectral bias and the over-smoothing of anatomical boundaries. Comprehensive experiments on thoracic CT and coronal MRI images demonstrated that the proposed method consistently outperforms DIP, DeepRED, and SURE-DIP in both PSNR and SSIM across a range of noise levels. Visual assessments further confirmed its ability to reconstruct fine anatomical features, such as bronchial bifurcations and soft-tissue structures in the spine, even under severe noise. In addition, the convergence analysis revealed that the L1-based formulation not only accelerates optimization but also enhances stability throughout the training process. The proposed approach offers a simple yet effective modification to the DIP paradigm, improving reconstruction fidelity without the need for external training data or handcrafted priors. These results highlight the potential of L1-based fidelity terms in advancing unsupervised medical image restoration, particularly in settings where high-quality ground truth data are limited or unavailable. Despite its strengths, the method still relies on manual early stopping and is computationally intensive due to image-specific optimization. It also assumes Gaussian noise and has not yet been extended to other noise types. Future work will explore automated stopping strategies, adaptive regularization, and extensions to more complex or modality-specific noise models. Reducing computational overhead will also be a focus to improve practicality in clinical workflows.

References

1. Elaiyaraja, G., Kumaratharan, N., Chandra Sekhar Rao, T.: Fast and efficient filter using wavelet threshold for removal of Gaussian noise from MRI/CT scanned medical images/color video sequence. IETE J. Res. **68**(1), 10–22 (2022)
2. Kumar, R.R., Priyadarshi, R.: Denoising and segmentation in medical image analysis: a comprehensive review on machine learning and deep learning approaches. Multimed. Tools Appl. **83**, 1–59 (2024)
3. Burger, H.C., Schuler, C.J., Harmeling, S.: Image denoising: Can plain neural networks compete with BM3D? In: 2012 IEEE Conference on Computer Vision and Pattern Recognition, pp. 2392–2399. IEEE, Los Alamitos (2012)
4. Meiniel, W., Olivo-Marin, J.C., Angelini, E.D.: Denoising of microscopy images: a review of the state-of-the-art, and a new sparsity-based method. IEEE Trans. Image Process. **27**(8), 3842–3856 (2018)
5. Izadi, S., Sutton, D., Hamarneh, G.: Image denoising in the deep learning era. Artif. Intell. Rev. **56**(7), 5929–5974 (2023)
6. Dinsdale, N.K., Bluemke, E., Sundaresan, V., Jenkinson, M., Smith, S.M., Namburete, A.I.: Challenges for machine learning in clinical translation of big data imaging studies. Neuron **110**(23), 3866–3881 (2022)
7. Ulyanov, D., Vedaldi, A., Lempitsky, V.: Deep image prior. In: Proceedings of the IEEE conference on computer vision and pattern recognition, pp. 9446–9454. IEEE, Los Alamitos (2018)
8. Zhang, C., Yen, K.S.: A survey on deep image prior for image denoising. Digit. Signal Process. **139**, 105235 (2025)
9. Cascarano, P., Sebastiani, A., Comes, M.C., Franchini, G., Porta, F.: Combining weighted total variation and deep image prior for natural and medical image restoration via ADMM. In: Proceedings of the IEEE/CVF Conference on Computer Vision and Pattern Recognition, pp. 39–46. IEEE, Los Alamitos (2021)
10. Mataev, G., Milanfar, P., Elad, M.: DeepRED: deep image prior powered by RED. In: Proceedings of the IEEE/CVF International Conference on Computer Vision Workshops, p. 0. IEEE, Los Alamitos (2019)
11. Zhang, C., Yen, K.S.: Adaptive unsupervised deep learning denoising for medical imaging with unbiased estimation and Hessian-based regularization. Appl. Intell. **55**(8), 718 (2025)
12. Lu, W., Lighter, D., Styles, I.B.: L1-norm based nonlinear reconstruction improves quantitative accuracy of spectral diffuse optical tomography. Biomed. Opt. Express **9**(4), 1423–1444 (2018)
13. Borsic, A., Adler, A.: A primal–dual interior-point framework for using the L1 or L2 norm on the data and regularization terms of inverse problems. Inverse Prob. **28**(9), 095011 (2012)
14. Gong, K., Catana, C., Qi, J., Li, Q.: PET image reconstruction using deep image prior. IEEE Trans. Med. Imaging **38**(7), 1655–1665 (2019)

15. Baguer, D.O., Leuschner, J., Schmidt, M.: Computed tomography reconstruction using deep image prior and learned reconstruction methods. Inverse Prob. **36**(9), 094004 (2020)
16. He, K., Zhang, X., Ren, S., Sun, J.: Delving deep into rectifiers: surpassing human-level performance on imagenet classification. In: Proceedings of the IEEE international conference on computer vision, pp. 1026–1034. IEEE, Los Alamitos (2015)
17. Zhang, C., Yen, K.S.: An accelerated unsupervised denoising model based on risk estimation and sparsity variational techniques. Digit. Signal Process. **165**, 105317 (2025)
18. Hore, A., Ziou, D.: Image quality metrics: PSNR vs. SSIM. In: 2010 20th International Conference on Pattern Recognition, pp. 2366–2369. IEEE, Los Alamitos (2010)

Impacts of Artificial Intelligence Technologies on Mitigating Threats in Healthcare Sector

Yousuf Al Hasani[1,2] and Jasni Mohamad Zain[3(✉)]

[1] Faculty of Computer and Mathematical Sciences, Universiti Teknologi MARA, 40450 Shah Alam, Selangor, Malaysia

[2] Ministry of Education, Department of Educational Studies and International Cooperation, Systems Analyst, Sultanate of Oman, Muscat, Oman

[3] Institute for Big Data Analytics and Artificial Intelligence (IBDAAI), Universiti Teknologi MARA, Kompleks Al-Khawarizmi, 40450 Shah Alam, Selangor, Malaysia

jasni67@uitm.edu.my

Abstract. The healthcare sector in Oman is widely adopting novel technologies to improve operations, and overall delivery of quality care services. Even though this modernization has great advantages, it has led to an increased number of cyberattacks like sophisticated intrusion penetration attacks that steal data and cripple functions. Such attacks are becoming a significant threat to hospitals, the ministry of health, and insurance companies in Oman. These threats have substantial implications, which include data breaches or losses and financial losses. Oman's healthcare sector has adopted conventional measures to enhance cybersecurity but these methods are vulnerable to advancing threats or attacks, which requires the implementation of innovative solutions with novel or pioneering technologies. Therefore, the purpose of this paper is to investigate the impacts of artificial intelligence technologies on mitigating cyberattacks or threats in Oman's healthcare sector. A quantitative method was used to achieve the objectives and research questions. Statistical tools used for analysis include inferential statistics, Chi Square tests and correlation analysis. The findings revealed that artificial intelligence technologies have a greater capacity to conduct continuous evaluation of data breaches, anomalies or behavioral patterns, allowing instant detection as well as responsive action to these attacks. These technologies include predictive analysis methods, algorithms, such as artificial intelligence multisource transfer learning algorithm, neural networks, machine learning, quantum computing, quantum resistant encryption, as well as adaptive cyberthreats learning and pattern recognition. These technologies will also prevent the loss of medical data, decrease threats or adversarial attacks, and enhance cybersecurity in Oman's healthcare.

Keywords: Cyberthreats · attacks · Methodology · Artificial intelligence · Oman · healthcare · hospitals · ministry of health · insurance · cybersecurity · prevention · mitigation · technologies

M. Kassim et al. (Eds.): SCDS 2025, CCIS 2674, pp. 366–380, 2026.
https://doi.org/10.1007/978-981-95-8368-3_26

1 Introduction

The healthcare sector is increasingly adopting new technologies in the healthcare systems to streamline operational efficiencies, improve diagnostics, and decrease costs while providing quality patient-centered care services. Some of these technologies include quantum technologies, machine learning, big data analytics, artificial intelligence, and quantum computing technologies [1–3]. For instance, big data analytics is adopted in the healthcare industry to significantly decrease care costs and medical errors while maximizing resource utilization [4]. Similarly, advanced hospitals have fortified their cybersecurity strategies by implementing quantum technologies or cryptographic methods, which has resulted in effective protection of patient information from potential cyber threats or hackers [5, 6].

On the other hand, machine learning adoption in the medical field has continuously improved diagnosis and delivery of quality care, monitoring performances, deployment models, decreased biases, as well as enhanced confidentiality and quality of data. Nevertheless, the use of this method is vulnerable to out-of-distribution (i.e., drifts), fault injections, as well as adversarial attacks targeting the healthcare systems [7–9]. Consequently, it requires the adoption of a novel cybersecurity solution, such as using artificial intelligence-related techniques to mitigate these attacks. Although the integration of these novel technologies in the healthcare system has led to democratized healthcare, decreased operational costs, precision diagnosis and surveillance of diseases, as well as delivery of high-quality, better patient-centered quality care, they continue to pose unprecedented cybersecurity challenges [10]. Therefore, the purpose to explore the impacts of artificial intelligence technologies on mitigating cyber-attacks or threats in Oman's healthcare sector.

Currently, there is an increasing modernization, such as technological or digital transformation in Oman's healthcare sector to improve the overall delivery of quality care services, and diagnosis or treatments and management of diseases while reducing overall costs of care [11, 12]. For example, healthcare systems have integrated the Internet-of-Things, artificial intelligence, Machine learning, and adopted electronic medical or health records to enhance the sharing of data with insurance companies as well as optimize e-health and telemedicine utilizations in the sector. Even though this digital revolution has significant impacts on the delivery of quality healthcare, operational efficiency, performance, and cost reduction in countries like Oman, it has made the sector vulnerable to various advanced cyberattacks or threats.

These threats undermine service delivery, weaken operations, lead to data breaches or losses, and have distinct cost implications [13, 14]. These threats have also evolved with technological advancement; thus, overwhelming the traditional cybersecurity mechanisms or approaches adopted in Oman's healthcare sector. Foor example, the generative artificial intelligence tools like FraudGPT and WormGPT used by attackers pose an imminent threat makes health or insurance systems vulnerable to criminals who use them for fraud or scamming activities [15].

The rising utilization of AI in hospitals to support ideal functions is also a prime target by advanced cyber criminals. Therefore, there is a need to implement a novel strategy that will predict, detect, mitigate, solve, as well as prevent such attacks or threats aimed at the healthcare systems [16]. Therefore, this paper focuses on the implementation of

AI technologies to provide effective cybersecurity solution for addressing these threats in healthcare field. The proposed solution has incredible capabilities, which include responsive abilities, predictive analysis, precision identification of threats, and real-time mitigation as well as prevention of these attacks or threats in the healthcare field in Oman.

2 Methodology

The purpose of this paper was to explore the impacts of AI technologies on mitigating cyber-attacks or threats and bolstering cybersecurity in Oman's healthcare sector. A quantitative methodology was used to achieve the objectives and answer the research questions. A descriptive design with a quantitative approach was also used to explore AI technologies used to deal with current and emerging cyber-threats or attacks in the Oman's healthcare sector.

The objectives of the study are:

1. To investigate the impacts of AI technologies on mitigating Cyber-attacks or threats in the Oman's healthcare sector
2. To explore impacts of AI technologies on bolstering cybersecurity in Oman's healthcare Sector
3. To examine and identify the AI technologies that can be applied in the in Oman's healthcare to predict and mitigate cyber threats in real-time, as well as develop an effective and a coordinated response.
4. To propose an AI framework for on mitigating Cyber-attacks or threats in the Oman's healthcare sector.

2.1 Problem Statement and Implications

Oman's healthcare has deployed several technological systems and applications to enhance effectiveness in providing high-quality, patient-centered care, increase healthcare access, improve healthcare professional-patient communication, offer accurate disease diagnosis, and deliver tailor-made treatments to patients. However, these systems are vulnerable to cyberthreats or attacks, particularly with the advancing technologies, and rise of sophisticated dynamic attacks by hackers or cybercriminals [15]. Hence, this requires an evidence-based solution that will offer a long-term solution in the sector. Even though AI has been adopted in advanced nations to enhance efficiency in general operations and improve cybersecurity, its adoption is limited in the Oman's healthcare sector, particularly on cybersecurity uses [2]. Thus, the purpose of this paper is to investigate the impacts of AI technologies on mitigating Cyber-attacks or threats and bolstering cybersecurity in Oman's Healthcare Sector.

This paper has significant, potential practical, and future research implications in Oman's healthcare sector. Specifically, it provides evidence-based findings on the impacts of AI technologies on mitigating cyber-attacks or threats and bolstering cybersecurity in Oman's Healthcare Sector. The findings provide key examples of AI technologies that have significant implications for reinforcing cybersecurity defenses in Oman's healthcare due to their capabilities, such as predictive or pattern analysis of threats, as well as real-time detection, precision mitigation, and prevention of cyberattacks [16]. As a result, this will lead to the protection of patient information, reduction of data breaches or losses in insurance firms or hospitals, decreased ransomware or cyber threats, and reduced costs associated with such cyber threats or attacks [7]. Therefore, these findings would be used to fine-tune existing practices and inform law-making, particularly cybersecurity practices in Oman's healthcare sector.

The paper also offers an in-depth understanding of AI tools or technologies, that can be used in Oman's healthcare field for the detection and elimination of cyber-attacks while enhancing overall operational efficiencies and reducing the cost of operations [5, 8]. Therefore, these findings would be used to develop future theoretical models or frameworks (i.e., AI- cybersecurity framework or AI-technological model) specific to emerging threats, which is vital in enhancing the cybersecurity space healthcare field. Lastly, the findings would have significant implications in policymaking, particularly on the development and adoption of policies related to the use of AI in the medical sector [16]. The findings will also create a theoretical foundation, which future researchers can use to investigate and propose novel cybersecurity approaches in other sectors in Oman or other countries.

3 Research Method

Quantitative research methods are used to quantify the study participant's views or attitudes on the study variables in order to produce generalized results in a large study population, with the aim of answering the research questions and achieving the study objectives [17, 18]. Also, it is used to describe the features of the study population. The quantitative research methods help in generation of numerical data that can be statistically analyzed and interpreted to provide answers to the research questions [19]. It also produces generalizable, reliable, and valid study findings that can be used to represent the entire population [20, 21]. Primary methods or sources in this quantitative paper include online survey. The survey data collected was analyzed and the results were discussed in relation with the existing findings. Specifically, the results were analyzed to determine if it is consistent with literature findings (i.e., from peer-reviewed articles or journals) and provide conclusive findings regarding the existing research gap, providing conclusive findings, and offer recommendations [22–26].

3.1 Research Design and Approach

A descriptive design was used in this paper because it describes the characteristics of the phenomenon and the population that is being studied, as well as allows collection of data and description of the nature of the demographic segment [27–29]. The use of descriptive design and quantitative approach was motivated by finding or determining how AI technologies enhance cybersecurity in Oman's healthcare sector. Generally, the design was selected since it attempts to collect quantifiable information or data to be used for statistical analysis of the population sample. Also, it helps in uncovering evidences and patterns regarding the overview of cybersecurity in the sector [21, 30–32]. The rationale for choosing descriptive design is that it allows the production of generalizable results with high reliability and validity [33–36]. Quantitative approach was used in designing and conducting the survey, collect data from the target population [37]. Combining the use descriptive design and quantitative approach offers in-depth understanding of the research problem, phenomena and the target population, as well as uncover facts or patterns [38, 39].

3.2 Population, Sampling Technique, Sample Size

The target population is individuals working in the Oman's healthcare sector, which includes employees working at private and public hospitals, insurance companies, as well as Ministry of health. The project sample will consist of a target population of 38 participants. Using the sample size calculator, the exact sample size was determined with a confidence level of 95%, a confidence interval of 5 (i.e.,5.0% margin error), and thus, the population of 38 [40, 41]. Therefore, the exact sample size will be 35. The characteristic of the project population and the project sample used in this study includes participants from both genders (male and female), adults (aged above 18 years), and have at least 2–5 years of experience.

A convenient sampling technique was used to select the participants. This is a typical non-random or non-probability sampling in which individuals selected from a given project sample meets specific research or practical criteria [42]. For example, easy accessibility, physical and geographical closeness, or availability [43]. The rationale for selecting this method is that it allows the selection of participants fairly and equally without bias [44, 45]. Therefore, the selected participants represented the entire population.

3.3 Procedure of Recruitment Participants and Participation

A recruitment email was sent to all the potential participants from the target population with a valid email address to request their participation. The purpose of the PhD study, a disclosure that protects participant's confidentiality and an informed con-sent in regard to study participation, study procedures, expected benefits and risks, compensation description were enclosed in the recruitment email. The study respondents had a permission to withdraw from undertaking the project at any time without detriment [46].

The researcher received replies via email from the identified potential participants from the predetermined study population who were willing to participate in the study without coercion or bribery. The author received 38 positive responses for participation only from individuals working in renown public and private hospitals and leading issuance companies in Oman and the Ministry of health who were willing to participate in the research. Out of these, 3 potential participants were not willing to participate in the study due to different reasons, including being busy with work. Thus, the participants who took part in this study were only 35; thus, response rate was 92%, which implies that the data collection method was effective, and this will generate in-depth findings that will be used to answer the research questions [47, 48].

3.4 Data Collection Instrument

The main instrument or sources of data used in this project is a questionnaire, which was used to collect primary data. The survey questionnaire was designed using the problem statement, research questions, as well as objectives with inferences to pertinent literature findings. The developed survey questionnaire was to collect primary data [49]. Therefore, the 5-Likert scale survey questionnaire were sent to all the participants via email. The survey questionnaire includes informed consent that seek their consent, and a thank you note at the end of the survey [50]. The participants filled and returned this questionnaire for further analysis and deduce findings of the project [51]. All the participants' identities stayed anonymous to the researcher [52–54].

3.5 Data Analysis Methods

The aim of study is to investigate the impacts of AI technologies on mitigating cyber-attacks or threats in Oman's healthcare sector. Thus, the data collected from the respondents was cross-checked for accuracy and analyzed using SPSS version 27 to achieve this purpose, answer the research questions, as well as validate the hypothesis. Reliability analysis using Cronbach alpha was conducted to determine how reliable and valid the results are [55, 56]. The goodness-of-fit data tests like the Shapiro-Wilk test or Kolmogorov-Smirnov test, as well as Chi-square tests was also be done using the data gathered. Chi-square tests were used to validate the hypothesis. Additionally, descriptive analysis, test of difference, and test of relationship are some of the inferential statistics were done to answer the research questions. The test of the relationship will include correlation coefficient analysis for hypothesis testing. Also, reliability and validly tests were be conducted.

3.6 Validity and Reliability

To ensure the reliability, the researcher avoided bias and data manipulation in analyzing and interpreting the data collected [57]. Consistency and reliability were also be ensured through administration of standard survey questionnaires to all respondents. The survey instrument accurately described the study phenomena or concept, which it measures using the research questions; thus, validity of the study was obtained [58]. Reliability analysis was conducted in using IBM SPSS 27, and results revealed that data was reliable. Specifically, analysis was conducted to determine Cronbach's alpha value, and the value was .705. A positive value above 0.70 indicates high higher reliability as well as internal consistency levels [59, 60]. Thus, the data collected is reliable and was used to answer the research questions, as well as achieve the purpose of the project since it will provide reliable findings for this study.

Validity focuses on measuring extent to which the data collection tool correctly defines or explains the concept(s) that should be measured [61]. Furthermore, confirmatory factor analysis will be conducted using a proper fit of the four-factor model to determine the validity of the data [62]. The author also tested the validity using the Spearman correlation coefficient to measure the correlation between each item in one variable and the whole variable. This coefficient was used to test the construct validity.

3.7 Ethical Considerations

Ethics, such as confidentiality and privacy, were followed during data collection and analysis. When collecting data and reporting it. The respondents were provided with a consent form (i.e., informed consent), which they will have to through and sign before collecting data or filling the questionnaires [66]. The informed consent form included a summary about the study, which includes the purpose and objectives of the study. Participants who will agree to participate in the study will sign the consent and proceed, while those who are not willing to participate will be excluded without prejudice since participation in this study is voluntary [67]. All participants were treated equally during recruitment and data collection process. Also, there was no bias and respondents will be protected from any potential harm [69–72]. Similarly, the author mitigated the potential of data misinterpretation and manipulation by running correct statistical analysis, providing accurate interpretation, as well as fully reporting the entire data collected [73].

4 Results and Discussions

This section presents the data analysis, results, and discussion of the findings. The data collected was analyzed using SPSS v27 with the aim of answering the research questions and achieving the objectives, as well as validating the hypotheses. Various statistical analysis was conducted such as Chi-Square tests and correlation analysis, and the results are presented in the subsequent sections. The results were also discussed in relation to the existing literature studies. The results are divided into sub-sections, which were discussed in the subsequent sections.

Methods used Detect and Prevent Cyberthreats or attacks in Oman's Healthcare Sector. The study sought to explore key methods used to detect and prevent cyberattacks in Oman's healthcare. The findings revealed that majority of the study participants (35%) stated that firewalls were used to detect and prevent cyberthreats attacks in Oman's healthcare while 22% believed that antivirus software is used to detect and prevent cyberthreats attacks in the Oman's healthcare sector. On the other hand, 23% of the study participants revealed that intrusion detection systems were used while only 20% of them stated that artificial intelligence technologies are used in the healthcare sector for the detection, mitigation, as well as prevention of attacks or threats, as shown in Fig. 1.

These findings reveal that traditional methods (i.e., Intrusion Detection Systems, antiviruses, firewalls) are widely used to enhance cybersecurity in the sector. Therefore, there is a need for increasing awareness of the impacts of AI on reinforcing cybersecurity in the sector while also focusing on training the experts on using AI to leverage the advantages of AI tools or technologies on cybersecurity. These findings are consistent with Smith & Doe's [77] and Zhang's et al. [78] findings, which propose replacing these traditional methods or reinforcing them with the use of AI to enhance cybersecurity.

The findings further revealed that AI-based solutions provide advanced and highly effective solutions to the cybersecurity challenges faced in the healthcare sector. Specifically, the findings show that the majority of the participants (70%) agree that AI-based solutions have higher efficacy or efficiency in detecting, mitigating, and preventing

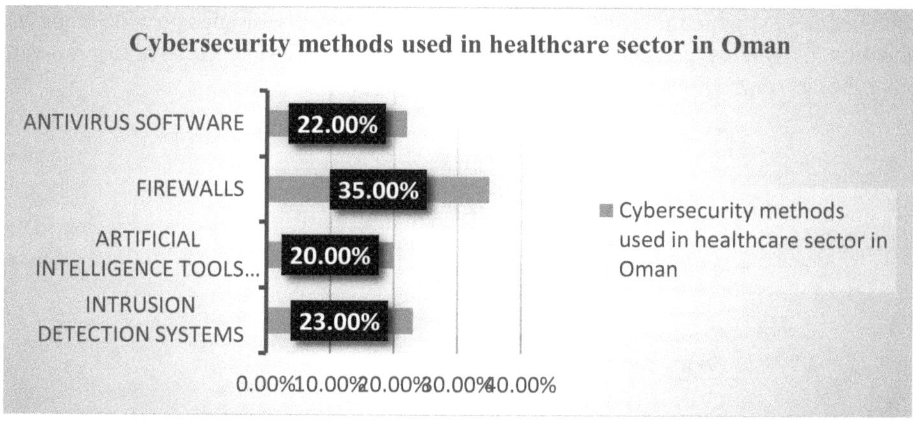

Fig. 1. Cybersecurity methods used to prevent cyber threats or attacks in the healthcare sector in Oman.

cyberattacks in Oman's healthcare sector. On the other hand, a few participants (30%) believe that non-AI-based methods are the most effective cybersecurity solution in the healthcare sector in Oman, as shown in Fig. 2 below. These findings are consistent with Zhang's et al. [79] findings revealing that AI-led cybersecurity solution focuses on real-time detection, and identification of user behaviors, anomalies, and network traffic patterns while offering an effective response to cyber threats or attacks.

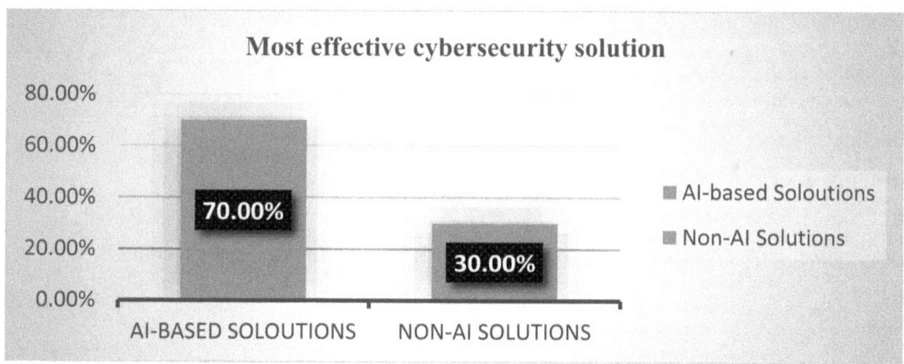

Fig. 2. Most effective cybersecurity solution

This paper sought to determine AI technologies, or components that can be implemented to predict and mitigate cyber threats in real time in Oman's healthcare sector. The results indicate that AI-automated threat detection and prevention tools or technologies (30%), adaptive learning and pattern recognition (15%), natural language processing (10%), neural networks and reinforcement learning (10%), as well as machine learning [i.e., algorithms, supervised and unsupervised ML] (25%), are key technologies or tools that can be integrated with AI to provide a robust cybersecurity system in the healthcare sector, as shown in Fig. 3 below. These findings are consistent with literature results by

Zhang et al. [78] which revealed that these AI tools, and technologies provide real-time detection, anomalies, and network traffic patterns; hence, offering effective responses to cyber threats or attacks.

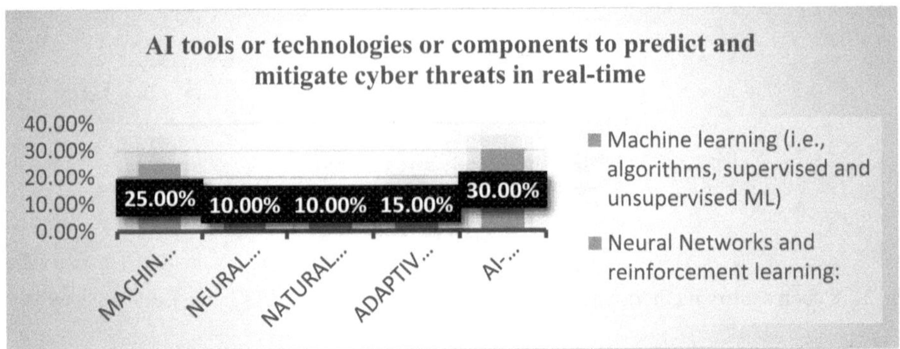

Fig. 3. AI technologies that can be implemented to predict and mitigate cyber threats in real time in Oman's healthcare sector.

Chi-Square Tests

Table 1. Chi-Square Tests

Chi-Square Tests			
	Value	df	Asymptotic Significance (2-sided)
Pearson Chi-Square	114.053[a]	16	.000
Likelihood Ratio	70.203	16	.000
Linear-by-Linear Association	16.219	1	.000
N of Valid Cases	35		

a. 13 cells (52.0%) have expected count less than 5. The minimum expected count is .10

Table 2. Symmetric Measures

Symmetric Measures			
		Value	Approximate Significance
Nominal by Nominal	Phi	.704	.000
	Cramer's V	.352	.000
N of Valid Cases		35	

A chi-square test was conducted to determine if there is a relationship between AI implementation and the prevention of cyber threats or attacks in Oman's healthcare sector. The Chi-Square test shows that the relationship between AI implementation and significant prevention of cyberthreats or attacks in Oman's healthcare was statistically significant, $\chi 2$ $(df = 16, N = 35) = 114.053, p =. 000$, as shown in table 3.0. The normal Phi was .704 (p = .000), and the Cramer's V value was .352 (p = .000), as shown in Table 1 and 2.

These findings revealed a significant association between AI implementation and the prevention of cyber threats or attacks in Oman's healthcare sector, $\chi 2$ (16) = 114.053, $p < .005$. Thus, the first null hypothesis is rejected, and the first alternate hypothesis is accepted stating that AI has significant impacts on preventing cyber-attacks in Oman's healthcare sector. Also, Pearson r Correlation analysis revealed a strong, positive, and significant correlation between the implementation of AI technologies to mitigate Cyber-attacks or threats and bolstered cybersecurity in Oman's healthcare sector (r = 0.62, p = .000), as shown Table 3.

Table 3. Correlation Results

Pearson Correlation Results on the Relationship Between implementation of AI technologies and reinforced cybersecurity in Oman's healthcare sector

	Implementation of AI technologies in healthcare			
	r	**p-value**	**Remarks**	**Decision**
Reinforced cybersecurity	.62**	.000	Significant	Reject the null hypothesis

**. Correlation is significant at the 0.01 level (2-tailed).

These findings show that the adoption of AI technologies in the healthcare systems or infrastructure to mitigate Cyber-attacks or threats was significantly related to enhanced cybersecurity in Oman's healthcare sector. Thus, rejecting the null hypothesis, which stated that there is no significant relationship or correlation between the implementation of AI technologies and reinforced cybersecurity in Oman's healthcare sector. These findings are consistent with Kadu, and M. Singh [80] results, which revealed that AI tools support prompt identification of cyber-attacks or threats; allowing timely response to mitigate and prevent these attacks, resulting in improved cybersecurity. These findings are consistent with Shukla's [81] results, which found that the adoption of AI tools in the leading Turkish healthcare provider was effective in preventing ransomware as well as persistent cyber threats or attacks.

5 Conclusions

There is an advance in the sophistication of cyberthreats or attacks due to increasing digitization and technological advancement. Such sophistication poses significant threats to conventional cybersecurity measures; thus, there is a need to adopt a novel technological solution to address these dynamic and persistent attacks. In this regard, this paper explored the impacts of AI technologies on mitigating cyber-attacks or threats in Oman's healthcare sector.

This paper concludes that AI technologies have unique capabilities that are effective in predictive and behavioral analytics, detecting anomalies and threats for timely response or mitigation, as well as prevention. These technologies include AI-led predictive analysis methods, algorithms (i.e., AI related multi-source transfer learning algorithm), neural networks, machine learning, blockchain, quantum-resistant encryption, as well as adaptive cyberthreats learning and pattern recognition. Deploying these technologies into the IT frameworks and systems in hospitals and insurance companies will help in accurate identification of unusual patterns in the system and recognition of possible attacks, resulting improved protection of medical or patient data, as well as reinforced cybersecurity. They will also offer incredible cybersecurity features to address modern or emerging cyber threats, and provide protection of patient data (i.e., patient information privacy) and medical devices from hackers. These AI-tools or technologies are also highly adaptable and scalable, making them easy to implement in insurance companies, as well as private and public hospitals no matter their sizes. Thus, they have the capacity to autonomously detect, deter, and prevent dynamic cyberattacks in real time. Therefore, the proposed AI tools or technologies can be used to develop AI-autonomous threat detection and prevention mechanisms, as well as algorithms, which can be integrated into the healthcare or insurance systems in Oman to improve cybersecurity.

The proposed AI tools (i.e., AI-led neural networks or machine learning models) have a greater capacity to conduct continuous evaluation of data breaches, anomalies or behavioral patterns, allowing instant detection as well as responsive action to these attacks. As a result, this would lead to more secure data or patient information in hospitals or insurance companies. Generally, the proposed AI tools or technologies will play an important in preventing unauthorized access, as well as protecting vital data by detecting uncommon access patterns to EHRs and electronic medical records or medical devices. Based on computerized predictive and automated analysis, these technologies will provide AI-automated mitigation or prevention mechanisms, leading to enhanced data protection from hackers.

The paper concludes by proposing an AI framework. The proposed AI-framework will entail novel deep learning-based models/algorithms incorporated with recurrent neural networks and autoencoders, which focus on the detecting as well as classification of cyberattacks in Oman's healthcare sector. The proposed framework is consistent with a framework simulated and implemented by Kumar [82]. The simulated findings revealed that AI-trained deep learning-based convolutional Neural Networks' framework has significant impacts on predicting, detecting, classifying, as well as preventing cyber threats/attacks. Also, simulated findings revealed that the AI-deep learning-based model/algorithms integrated with Autoencoder and Recurrent Neural Networks approach lead to improved performance in the prediction, detection, classification and mitigation of cyber-attacks [82]. Future studies should also focus on the ethical challenges or issues that would rise regarding the use of AI in the Oman's healthcare.

This journal proposes implementation of the proposed AI technologies Oman's healthcare sector to ensure robust cybersecurity through instantaneous forecast, analysis, recognition of potential threats or attacks, allowing deployment of counteractive measures (i.e., AI-Automated attack and threat detection as well as prevention tool) to deal with them. Also, it recommends adoption of AI technologies combined with AI-led algorithms), and AI predictive tool(s) in insurance or the healthcare systems to provide real-time identification of threats, precision prediction of suspicious activities or adversary attacks, as well as prompt deployment of mitigation and prevention measures. As a result, this will improve cybersecurity and safeguard critical information or patient data.

Acknowledgment. We would like to thank Institute for Big Data Analytics and Artificial Intelligence (IBDAAI), UiTM for the financial support for this project.

References

1. Prajapat, S., Kumar, P., Das, A.K., Muhammad, G.: Generative AI-enabled quantum encryption algorithm for securing IoT-based healthcare application using Blockchain. IEEE Internet Things J. (2025)
2. Mondal, S., Das, S., Golder, S.S., Bose, R., Sutradhar, S., Mondal, H.: AI-driven big data analytics for personalized medicine in healthcare: integrating federated learning, Blockchain, and quantum computing. In: 2024 International Conference on Artificial Intelligence and Quantum Computation-Based Sensor Application (ICAIQSA), pp. 1–6 (2024)
3. Ullah, U., Garcia-Zapirain, B.: Quantum machine learning revolution in healthcare: a systematic review of emerging perspectives and applications. IEEE Access **12**, 11423–11450 (2024)
4. Muhunzi, D., Kitambala, L., Mashauri, H.L.: Big data analytics in the healthcare sector: opportunities and challenges in developing countries. literature review. Health Inform. J. **30**(4), 14604582241294216 (2024)
5. Aggarwal, L., Sachdeva, S., Goswami, P.: Quantum healthcare computing using precision based granular approach. Appl. Soft Comput. **144**, 110458 (2023)
6. Kaushik, K., Kumar, A.: Demystifying quantum blockchain for healthcare. Secur. Priv. **6**(3), e284 (2023)
7. Asif, S., et al.: Advancements and prospects of machine learning in medical diagnostics: unveiling the future of diagnostic precision. Arch. Comput. Methods Eng., 1–31 (2024)
8. Tanveer, H., Faheem, M., Khan, A.H., Adam, M.A.: AI-powered diagnosis: a machine learning approach to early detection of breast cancer. Int. J. Eng. Dev. Res. **13**(2), 153–166 (2025)
9. Tariq, M., Hayat, Y., Hussain, A., Tariq, A., and Rasool, S.: Principles and perspectives in medical diagnostic systems employing artificial intelligence (AI) algorithms. Int. Res. J. Econ. Manag. Stud. IRJEMS **3**(1) (2024)
10. El-Khoury, M., Albarashdi, S.: Navigating the privacy landscape of healthcare-driven AI in the Middle East: case studies from Oman, Qatar, and Saudi Arabia. Soc. Sci. Humanit. Open **11**, 101492 (2025)

11. Ganai, P.T., Bag, A., Sable, A.., Abdullah, K.H., Bhatia, S., Pant, B.: A detailed investigation of implementation of Internet of Things (IOT) in cyber security in healthcare sector. In: 2022 2nd International Conference on Advance Computing and Innovative Technologies in Engineering (ICACITE), pp. 1571–1575 (2022)
12. Gunasekaran, H., Hariharan, B., Al Jabri, J.S.S.: Artificial intelligence in health care computing and assessments in Oman: an effectual study. In: 2025 International Conference on Machine Learning and Autonomous Systems (ICMLAS), pp. 544–549 (2025)
13. Ahamed, J.N., Mohammed, A.A., Al Ghaithi, H.K., Al Salty, R.K.: A study on the importance of cybersecurity and its significance in Omani society. In: 2024 2nd International Conference on Computing and Data Analytics (ICCDA), pp. 1–6. IEEE (2024)
14. Javaid, M., Haleem, A., Singh, R.P., Suman, R.: Towards insighting cybersecurity for healthcare domains: a comprehensive review of recent practices and trends. Cyber Secur. Appl. **1**, 100016 (2023)
15. Koutzampasopoulou Xanthidou, O., Xanthidis, D., Manolas, C., Wang, H.I.: Security and privacy consideration for the deployment of electronic health records: a qualitative study covering Greece and Oman. Inf. Secur. J.: Global Perspect. **32**(4), 266–282 (2023)
16. Hasegawa, K., O'Brien, N., Prendergast, M., Ajah, C.A., Neves, A.L., Ghafur, S.: Cybersecurity interventions in health care organizations in low-and middle-income countries: scoping review. J. Med. Internet Res. **26**, e47311 (2024)
17. Ghanad, A.: An overview of quantitative research methods. Int. J. Multidisc. Res. Anal. **6**(08), 3794–3803 (2023)
18. Kumar, A., Praveenakumar, S.G.: Research Methodology. Authors Click Publishing (2025)
19. Dubey, U.K.B., Kothari, D.P.: Research Methodology: Techniques and Trends. Chapman and Hall CRC (2022)
20. Fryer, L.K., Larson-Hall, J., Stewart, J.: Quantitative Methodology. The Palgrave Handbook of Applied Linguistics Research Methodology, pp. 55–77 (2018)
21. Mahat, D., Neupane, D., Shrestha, S.: Quantitative research design and sample trends: a systematic examination of emerging paradigms and best practices. Cognizance J. Multidisc. Studie **4**(2), 20–27 (2024)
22. Mcleod, S.: Qualitative vs quantitative research methods & data analysis. Simply Psychol. (2023)
23. Zheng, X.: Data collection in quantitative research. In: Research Methods for Student Radiographers, pp. 79–92, CRC Press (2021)
24. König, J., Santagata, R., Scheiner, T., Adleff, A.K., Yang, X., Kaiser, G.: Teacher noticing: a systematic literature review of conceptualizations, research designs, and findings on learning to notice. Educ. Res. Rev. **36**, 100453 (2022)
25. Sharma, L.R., Jha, S., Koirala, R., Aryal, U., Bhattarai, T.: Navigating the research landscape: a guide to the selection of the right research design. Int. Res. J. MMC (IRJMMC) **4**(1), 64–78 (2023)
26. Jenkins, E., D'Aoust, R., Elias, S., Han, H.R., Sharps, P., Alvarez, C.: Faculty peer review of teaching taskforce: a quantitative descriptive research study for the peer review process. Nurse Educ. Today **106**, 105055 (2021)
27. Novosel, L. M.: Understanding the evidence: quantitative research designs. Urol. Nurs. **42**(6) (2022)
28. Rashid, A., Rasheed, R., Amirah, N.A., Yusof, Y., Khan, S., Agha, A.A.: A quantitative perspective of systematic research: easy and step-by-step initial guidelines. Turk. Online J. Qualit. Inq. **12**(9) (2021)
29. Gregar, J.: Research design (qualitative, quantitative and mixed methods approaches). Res. Des. **8** (2023)
30. Asio, J.M.R.: Research designs in the new normal: a brief overview. Academia Lett. **2**, 1–8 (2021)

31. Thomas, D., and Zubkov, P.: Quantitative research designs. Quant. Res. Pract. Theol., 103–114 (2023)
32. Adhikari, G. P.: Calculating the sample size in quantitative studies. Scholars' J., 14–29 (2021)
33. Golzar, J., Noor, S., Tajik, O.: Convenience sampling. Int. J. Educ. Lang. Stud. **1**(2), 72–77 (2022)
34. Winton, B.G., Sabol, M.A.: A multi-group analysis of convenience samples: free, cheap, friendly, and fancy sources. Int. J. Soc. Res. Methodol. **25**(6), 861–876 (2022)
35. Hossan, D., Dato'Mansor, Z., Jaharuddin, N.S.: Research population and sampling in quantitative study. Int. J. Bus. Technopreneurship (IJBT) **13**(3), 209–222 (2023)
36. Wallwey, C., Kajfez, R.L.: Quantitative research artifacts as qualitative data collection techniques in a mixed methods research study. Methods Psychol. **8**, 100115 (2023)
37. Jamieson, M.K., Govaart, G.H., Pownall, M.: Reflexivity in quantitative research: a rationale and beginner's guide. Soc. Pers. Psychol. Compass **17**(4), e12735 (2023)
38. Barker, T.H., et al.: Revising the JBI quantitative critical appraisal tools to improve their applicability: an overview of methods and the development process. JBI Evid. Synth. **21**(3), 478–493 (2023)
39. Maida, C.A., et al.: Quantitative data collection approaches in subject-reported oral health research: a scoping review. BMC Oral Health **22**(1), 435 (2022)
40. Krause, R.M., Fatemi, S.M., Nguyen Long, L.A., Arnold, G., Hofmeyer, S.L.: What is the future of survey-based data collection for local government research? Trends, strategies, and recommendations. Urban Aff. Rev. **60**(3), 1094–1115 (2024)
41. Newman, A., Bavik, Y.L., Mount, M., Shao, B.: Data collection via online platforms: Challenges and recommendations for future research. Appl. Psychol. **70**(3), 1380–1402 (2021)
42. Aguinis, H., Hill, N.S., Bailey, J.R.: Best practices in data collection and preparation: recommendations for reviewers, editors, and authors. Organ. Res. Methods **24**(4), 678–693 (2021)
43. Jain, N.: Survey versus interviews: comparing data collection tools for exploratory research. Qual. Rep. **26**(2), 541–554 (2021)
44. Darko, E.M., Kleib, M., Olson, J.: Social media use for research participant recruitment: integrative literature review. J. Med. Internet Res. **24**(8), e38015 (2022)
45. Strunk, K.K., Mwavita, M.: Design and Analysis in Quantitative Educational Research: Univariate Designs in SPSS. Taylor & Francis (2024)
46. Amirrudin, M., Nasution, K., Supahar, S.: Effect of variability on Cronbach alpha reliability in research practice. Jurnal Matematika, Statistika dan Komputasi **17**(2), 223–230 (2021)
47. Armour, R., Williams, B.: Reliability and validity in quantitative and qualitative research. Introducing, Designing Conducting Res. Paramedics, 69–72 (2022)
48. Christou, P.A.: Rigour in qualitative and quantitative studies that make use of tools: reliability, validity, credibility, transferability, dependability and confirmability issues. In: Artificial Intelligence (AI) in Social Research, pp. 127–136. CABI, GB (2025)
49. Izah, S.C., Sylva, L., Hait, M.: Cronbach's alpha: a cornerstone in ensuring reliability and validity in environmental health assessment. ES Energy Environ. **23**, 1057 (2023)
50. Kennedy, I.: Sample size determination in test-retest and Cronbach alpha reliability estimates. Brit. J. Contemp. Educ. **2**(1), 17–29 (2022)
51. Vu, T.T.N.: Understanding validity and reliability from qualitative and quantitative research traditions. VNU J. Foreign Stud. **37**(3) (2021)
52. Slater, P., Hasson, F.: Quantitative research designs, hierarchy of evidence and validity. J. Psychiatr. Ment. Health Nurs. **32**(3), 656–660 (2025)
53. Asher, A. D.: Approaches for improving validity in quantitative research articles. Portal: Libr. Acad. **24**(2), 209–215 (2024)

54. Morley, J., et al.: The ethics of AI in health care: a mapping review. Soc. Sci. Med. **260**, 113172 (2020)
55. McKee, K.R.: Human participants in AI research: ethics and transparency in practice. IEEE Trans. Technol. Soc. (2024)
56. Surmiak, A.: Should we maintain or break confidentiality? The choices made by social researchers in the context of law violation and harm. J. Acad. Ethics **18**(3), 229–247 (2020)
57. Samuel, G., Chubb, J., Derrick, G.: Boundaries between research ethics and ethical research use in artificial intelligence health research. J. Empir. Res. Hum. Res. Ethics **16**(3), 325–337 (2021)
58. Hasan, N., Rana, R.U., Chowdhury, S., Dola, A.J., Rony, M.K.K.: Ethical considerations in research. J. Nurs. Res., Patient Saf. Practise (JNRPSP) 2799-1210 **1**(01), 1–4 (2021)
59. Karimian, G., Petelos, E., Evers, S.M.: The ethical issues of the application of artificial intelligence in healthcare: a systematic scoping review. AI and Ethics **2**(4), 539–551 (2022)
60. Rossi, A., Lenzini, G.: Transparency by design in data-informed research: a collection of information design patterns. Comput. Law Secur. Rev. **37**, 105402 (2020)
61. Belwal, R., Al Shibli, R., Belwal, S.: Consumer protection and electronic commerce in the Sultanate of Oman. J. Inf. Commun. Ethics Soc. **19**(1), 38–60 (2021)
62. Smith, J., Doe, A.: The digital transformation of healthcare: benefits and challenges. J. Healthc. Manag. **45**(3), 123–135 (2022)
63. Zhang, L., Chen, Y., Li, X.: AI-driven cybersecurity: applications in healthcare systems. J. Cybersecur. Res. **9**(2), 135–148 (2021)
64. Zhang, Y., Liu, X., Wei, J.: AI in cybersecurity: techniques and applications in healthcare. J. AI Res. Healthc. **2**(2), 145–160 (2021)
65. Kadu, A., Singh, M.: Comparative analysis of e-health care telemedicine system based on Internet of Medical Things and artificial intelligence. In: 2021 2nd International Conference on Smart Electronics and Communication (ICOSEC), pp. 1768–1775 (2021)
66. Shukla, A.: Leveraging AI and ML for advance cyber security. J. Artif. Intell. Cloud Comput. SRC JAICC-154 (2022)
67. Kumar, Y.S., Sowjanya, A.M.: Ensemble models for cyber attacks detection on multiple datasets. In: 2024 International Conference on IoT Based Control Networks and Intelligent Systems (ICICNIS), pp. 295–299. IEEE. (2024)

Utilizing Incremental Learning-Based EfficientNet for Chest X-Ray Classification

Zhang Zhan and Nur Intan Raihana Ruhaiyem(✉)

School of Computer Sciences, Universiti Sains Malaysia, 11800, USM Penang, Malaysia
intanraihana@usm.my

Abstract. Chest X-ray image classification, especially for pneumonia detection, faces challenges in incremental learning, such as accuracy degradation and catastrophic forgetting. This study proposes a method combining EfficientNet-B0 with Analytic Class Incremental Learning (ACIL) to address these issues. EfficientNet-B0 enhances feature extraction through compound scaling, while ACIL mitigates forgetting by updating an autocorrelation matrix without storing historical data. Comparative experiments with ResNet-18 and three incremental learning methods (LwF, ER, EWC) show that EfficientNet-B0 with ACIL achieves superior performance. In binary classification, it reaches 78.3% accuracy with a forgetting rate of −7.3%. In multi-class classification, accuracy reaches 68.1%, with only 1.0% forgetting. These results demonstrate the proposed method's effectiveness and stability for incremental learning in chest X-ray image analysis.

Keywords: Incremental Learning · EfficientNet-B0 · Analytic Class Incremental Learning (ACIL) · Chest X-ray image classification

1 Introduction

Pneumonia is a significant global health concern, particularly affecting vulnerable populations such as the elderly, children, and immuno-compromised individuals. It remains one of the leading causes of mortality worldwide. According to the World Health Organization, pneumonia was responsible for approximately 740,180 deaths among children under the age of five in 2019, accounting for 14% of all child deaths globally [1]. The disease can be classified as infectious, caused by bacterial or viral agents or non-infectious, resulting from environmental exposures like dust, smoke, and toxic chemicals. Clinical symptoms include fever, cough, chest pain, and difficulty breathing, with the severity depending on the pathogen and patient health. In severe cases, imaging modalities such as chest X-rays and laboratory tests are required for timely diagnosis and intervention. Figure 1 presents a comparative view of normal and pneumonia-affected lungs using chest X-ray imaging. In healthy lungs, the X-ray shows clear, symmetrical lung fields with minimal shadowing, allowing for distinct visualization of the ribs, heart silhouette, and bronchi. Conversely, pneumonia-affected lungs exhibit patchy or consolidated opacities due to fluid and inflammatory infiltrates, which obscure internal thoracic structures and indicate reduced air content.

M. Kassim et al. (Eds.): SCDS 2025, CCIS 2674, pp. 381–396, 2026.
https://doi.org/10.1007/978-981-95-8368-3_27

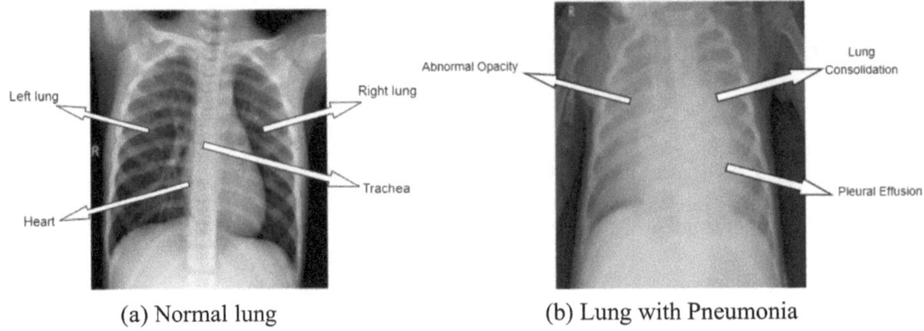

(a) Normal lung (b) Lung with Pneumonia

Fig. 1. The X-Ray of normal lung and lung with pneumonia.

Recent advances in artificial intelligence, particularly deep learning, have significantly enhanced automated medical image analysis. Convolutional neural networks (CNNs) have been widely applied in radiological diagnosis and have shown strong performance in pneumonia classification [2, 3]. EfficientNet, a CNN architecture based on compound scaling of network depth, width, and resolution, has demonstrated high accuracy and low computational cost, making it particularly well-suited for medical image tasks [4]. Other commonly used CNN models include VGG19, ResNet, and DenseNet, each of which offers distinct architectural advantages [5]. For example, ResNet employs residual learning to improve training depth and classification robustness [6]. More recently, Vision Transformers (ViTs) have emerged as a powerful alternative, offering superior performance in capturing long-range dependencies in image data [7]. To enhance diagnostic reliability, hybrid models that combine deep learning with classical machine learning approaches—such as support vector machines and random forests—have been developed [8]. Moreover, explainable artificial intelligence (XAI) is being increasingly integrated into clinical workflows, offering greater transparency in AI-generated diagnoses [9].

However, despite these advances, significant challenges remain in applying deep learning to incremental learning scenarios, where models must adapt to new data classes over time. Two major limitations are often encountered: a decline in classification accuracy and the phenomenon of catastrophic forgetting [10–12]. As models are updated with new category information, previously learned knowledge tends to degrade, particularly in class-incremental learning settings where earlier data is no longer accessible [13]. This leads to deteriorating performance on prior classes. Although numerous strategies have been proposed to address this issue, including Learning Without Forgetting (LwF), Experience Replay (ER), and Elastic Weight Consolidation (EWC), each has its limitations. LwF relies on soft labels from old tasks but underperforms when task distributions diverge [3]. ER retains a small memory buffer of past samples, but its effectiveness diminishes with limited storage, while EWC imposes regularization based on parameter importance but struggles when feature conflict is high [14]. These shortcomings underscore the need for more robust, scalable, and memory-efficient incremental learning techniques.

To address these limitations, Analytic Class-Incremental Learning (ACIL) has been introduced as a more robust alternative. ACIL maintains both new and existing category information through a recursive analytical mechanism, thereby reducing forgetting without needing access to historical data [15]. Given its efficiency and adaptability, ACIL is well-suited for medical image classification, particularly in settings where data arrives in sequential stages.

In this study, we propose a new framework that integrates EfficientNet-B0; a compact yet powerful CNN model, with ACIL to enhance performance in class-incremental learning tasks related to pneumonia detection. EfficientNet-B0 is the most basic version in the EfficientNet series, which adopts a compound scaling strategy to achieve more efficient deep neural network training without increasing computational costs [16]. ACIL ensures robust learning across new categories without degrading previous knowledge.

To validate our approach, we use two publicly available datasets. The first is a binary classification dataset from Kaggle comprising 5,863 chest X-ray images labeled as normal or pneumonia, which has been widely used in previous pneumonia studies [17–19]. The second is a multiclass dataset with 7,135 images categorized into Pneumonia, COVID-19, Tuberculosis, and Normal, also sourced from Kaggle and used in recent studies [20, 21]. All experiments are conducted using only chest X-ray images, and the analysis does not extend to other imaging modalities such as CT or MRI.

The key contributions of this study are as follows:

(1) Proposing a new integration of EfficientNet-B0 with ACIL for chest X-ray image classification under incremental learning settings.
(2) Benchmarking this integration against other base models and state-of-the-art incremental learning strategies to assess its robustness in retaining prior knowledge.
(3) Demonstrating the model's effectiveness in both binary and multiclass classification tasks with empirical evidence on classification accuracy and resistance to catastrophic forgetting.

2 Related Work

The development of deep learning has significantly advanced the field of medical image analysis, especially in the diagnosis of lung diseases such as pneumonia, tuberculosis, and COVID-19. Among numerous convolutional neural network (CNN) architectures, EfficientNet has emerged as one of the most promising models due to its optimal trade-off between accuracy and computational efficiency. Meanwhile, Analytic Class-Incremental Learning (ACIL) offers a novel solution to the challenge of catastrophic forgetting in continual learning, making it particularly suitable for dynamic medical diagnosis systems where new disease categories may be introduced over time.

2.1 EfficientNet in Medical Image Classification

EfficientNet, proposed by Tan and Le [16], is a family of CNN models that utilize a compound scaling method to uniformly balance network depth, width, and resolution. This architecture achieves state-of-the-art performance on image classification benchmarks while maintaining a low parameter count and computational cost. EfficientNet-B0, for example, uses only 5.3 million parameters yet attains accuracy comparable to much deeper models like ResNet-152, which requires over 60 million parameters [16].

This high efficiency has made EfficientNet particularly suitable for medical imaging tasks. For instance, in a comparative study of CNN architectures applied to chest X-ray datasets, EfficientNet outperformed models such as ResNet, DenseNet, and VGG19 in detecting pneumonia and tuberculosis, achieving 100% accuracy in some cases [5]. Other studies further confirm EfficientNet's robustness and generalizability. Raza et al. developed Lung-EffNet for lung cancer detection, integrating transfer learning and hyperparameter optimization to enhance diagnostic performance [22]. Kurt et al. applied EfficientNet-B4 to COVID-19 CT image classification and reported improved accuracy and sensitivity compared to traditional CNNs [23]. Marques et al. also demonstrated the superiority of EfficientNet in COVID-19 X-ray image recognition tasks [24].

Despite these advantages, some studies have noted potential risks of overfitting with EfficientNet on small-scale medical datasets, suggesting the need for regularization or augmentation techniques in practical deployment [5]. Nonetheless, the model's parameter efficiency, accuracy, and scalability make it a strong candidate for integration into lung disease classification systems, as adopted in the present study.

2.2 Analytic Class-Incremental Learning (ACIL)

While deep learning models like EfficientNet excel in static datasets, continual learning scenarios pose significant challenges, most notably catastrophic forgetting—the degradation of performance on previously learned tasks when new tasks are introduced. Traditional incremental learning approaches such as Learning without Forgetting (LwF) [25], Elastic Weight Consolidation (EWC) [26], and Experience Replay (ER) [27] attempt to address this issue. However, they are often limited by memory constraints, reduced adaptability to new tasks, or privacy concerns.

Analytic Class-Incremental Learning (ACIL) presents a novel, memory-free alternative by avoiding the need to store old data and instead using an analytical recursive update mechanism. At the core of ACIL is the use of the autocorrelation matrix, which captures and recursively updates feature distributions as new data arrives [15]. This allows the model to preserve knowledge of previously learned classes while integrating new ones seamlessly, without requiring parameter freezing or data replay.

Compared with regularization-based methods like EWC, which restrict model flexibility, and memory-based methods like ER, which raise privacy and storage concerns, ACIL offers a more scalable, privacy-preserving, and adaptive learning paradigm [15, 28]. Zhou et al. extended this concept further by enhancing recursive updates in the classifier layer, enabling even more stable long-term learning without catastrophic forgetting [28]. The superiority of ACIL lies in its ability to retain performance on past tasks without compromising learning of new classes, making it highly suitable for medical image classification systems that evolve with emerging diseases or diagnostic criteria. Its analytical nature also leads to faster and more stable convergence during incremental training phases.

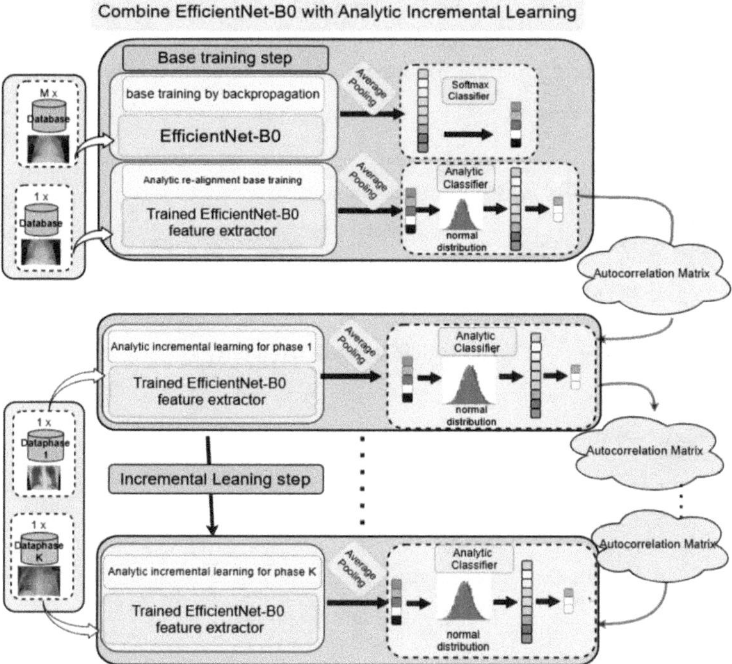

Fig. 2. The workflow of the proposed framework.

3 Methodology

This study proposes a two-stage learning framework combining EfficientNet-B0 and Analytic Class-Incremental Learning (ACIL) to achieve accurate and efficient incremental classification of medical images. The overall pipeline consists of a Base Training Stage and an Incremental Learning Stage, as illustrated in Fig. 2. In the base stage, EfficientNet-B0 is trained as a feature extractor using a labeled dataset. The extracted features are expanded and input into a classifier whose weights are solved analytically. In the incremental stage, when new disease classes arrive, the model utilizes ACIL to update the classifier weights and autocorrelation matrix recursively, eliminating the need to retrain the entire network or store previous data.

3.1 EfficientNet-B0 Architecture and Feature Extraction

EfficientNet is a convolutional neural network architecture that optimizes model performance through compound scaling, which simultaneously and proportionally increases the network's depth, width, and input resolution [16]. Unlike conventional scaling strategies that modify only a single dimension, compound scaling uses a scaling coefficient ϕ and three predefined constants α, β, and γ (determined via Neural Architecture Search) to uniformly scale the model:

$$Depth : d = \alpha^{\phi}; Width : w = \beta^{\phi}; Resolution : r = \gamma^{\phi} \tag{1}$$

EfficientNet offers a family of models from B0 to B7. In this study, EfficientNet-B0 is selected due to its compact structure and favorable balance between accuracy and computational cost, making it ideal for scenarios with limited hardware resources.

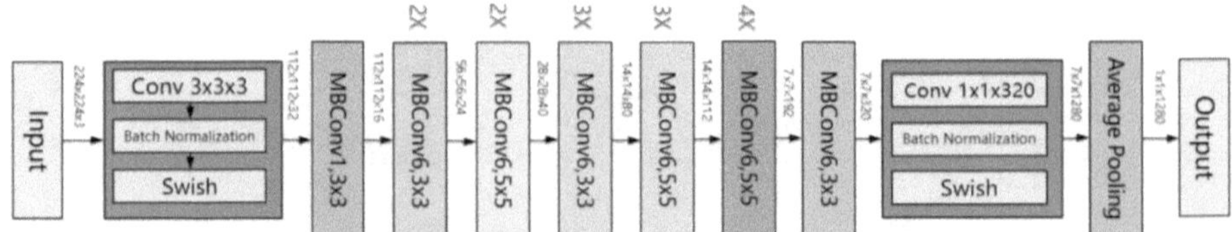

Fig. 3. EfficientNet-B0 structure.

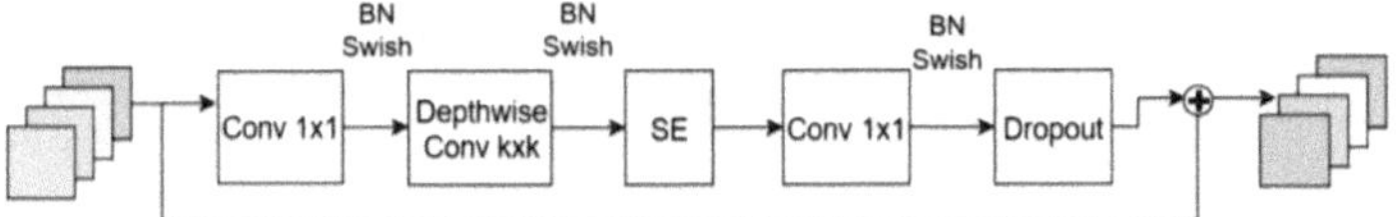

Fig. 4. MBConv structure.

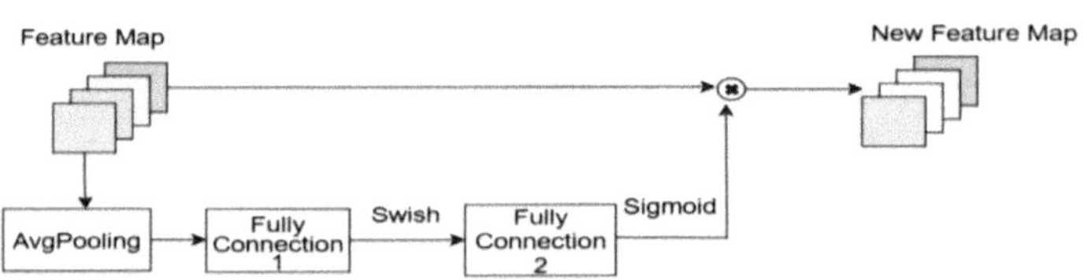

Fig. 5. SE module structure.

The architecture of EfficientNet-B0 begins with a standard 3 × 3 convolutional layer followed by multiple stacked MBConv blocks. Each MBConv unit comprises a 1 × 1 pointwise convolution for dimensional expansion, a depthwise convolution (3 × 3 or 5 × 5), a Squeeze-and-Excitation (SE) module [29], and a second 1 × 1 convolution for dimensional reduction (Figs. 3 and 4). All convolutional layers are followed by Batch Normalization and the Swish activation function. The SE module (Fig. 5) performs channel-wise feature recalibration through global average pooling, two fully connected layers, and a sigmoid activation, which adaptively reweights feature channels to improve model expressiveness.

3.2 Base Training Stage

In the base training phase, X-ray image data are preprocessed via image resizing (to 224 × 224), normalization to [0, 1], and augmentation (random rotation ± 15°, brightness reduction by 50%) to improve generalization. The processed images are then input into EfficientNet-B0 to extract high-level features, followed by global average pooling to produce compact representations:

$$X_0^{(EFF)} = f_{averpooling}\left(f_{EFF}\left(X^{train}, W_{EFF}\right)\right) \tag{2}$$

where f_{EFF} denotes the EfficientNet feature extractor, and W_{EFF} are the learned weights. The model is optimized using cross-entropy loss and Adam optimizer with a learning rate of 0.0001.

To prepare for incremental learning, feature expansion is introduced to enhance the expressive capacity of extracted features:

$$X^{(fe)} = f_{act}\left(f_{averpooling}\left(f_{EFF}\left(X^{train}, W_{EFF}\right)\right)W_{fe}\right) \tag{3}$$

where W_{fe} is the feature expansion matrix and f_{act} is the ReLU activation function. The expanded feature matrix is then used to initialize the classifier weights using ridge regression:

$$\hat{W}_{FC} = \left(X^{(fe)T}X^{(fe)} + \gamma I\right)^{-1}X^{(fe)T}Y^{train} \tag{4}$$

In addition, the initial autocorrelation matrix is computed to retain statistical information from the training data:

$$R_{k-1} = \left(\sum_{i=1}^{k-1} X_i^{(fe)T}X_i^{(fe)} + \gamma I\right)^{-1} \tag{5}$$

This base stage produces three key outputs: (1) a trained EfficientNet-B0 as feature extractor, (2) initial classifier weights $\hat{W}_{FC}$, , and (3) the autocorrelation matrix R_{k-1}, which are carried forward into the incremental learning stage.

3.3 Incremental Learning Stage with ACIL

In real-world medical settings, new disease categories may continuously emerge, requiring models to incrementally learn without access to historical data due to privacy and storage constraints. Traditional methods like Experience Replay or Knowledge Distillation are inadequate in such cases. To overcome these limitations, this study employs Analytic Class-Incremental Learning (ACIL) [15], which uses a recursive analytic mechanism to update model parameters without storing or replaying old samples.

In each incremental step k, a new data batch $D_k = \{X_k, Y_k\}$ is introduced. After preprocessing and feature extraction via EfficientNet-B0 and pooling, features are expanded:

$$X_k^{(fe)} = f_{act}\left(f_{averpooling}\left(f_{EFF}(X_k, W_{EFF})\right)W_{fe}\right) \tag{6}$$

The autocorrelation matrix is recursively updated as follows:

$$R_k = R_{k-1} - R_{k-1}X_k^{(fe)T}(I + X_k^{(fe)}R_{k-1}X_k^{(fe)T})^{-1}X_k^{(fe)}R_{k-1} \tag{7}$$

This update allows the model to preserve learned knowledge. Subsequently, the classifier weights are updated analytically:

$$\hat{W}_{FC}^{(k)} = \hat{W}_{FC}^{(k-1)} - R_k X_k^{(fe)T}\left(X_k^{(fe)}\hat{W}_{FC}^{(k-1)} - Y_k^{train}\right) \tag{8}$$

This approach ensures stable long-term learning and mitigates catastrophic forgetting without requiring data replay. Within the Incremental Learning Stage, ACIL facilitates efficient model adaptation by recursively updating the classifier as new categories are introduced, without revisiting previously seen data. By decoupling feature extraction and classifier learning, ACIL supports scalable expansion while preserving model performance across tasks. Together with the Base Training Stage, this framework enables an effective and privacy-preserving solution for class-incremental medical image classification. A detailed overview of the proposed method is presented in Table 1 in the form of pseudo-code.

Table 1. Pseudo-code of proposed combined method.

Algorithm 1 Improved Model
Base Training Step:
1: Obtain pre-trained model
2: Compute feature expansion matrix
3: Obtain initial classifier weight $\hat{W}_{FC}^{(0)}$ and autocorrelation matrix R_0
Incremental Learning Step:
for $k = 1$ to K (with $\hat{W}_{FC}^{(0)}$, R_0)
1: Obtain feature expansion matrix
2: Recursively update autocorrelation matrix R_k
3: Recursively update classifier weight $\hat{W}_{FC}^{(k)}$
end for

4 Experiments and Results Analysis

4.1 Dataset

This study employs two publicly available chest X-ray datasets widely used in prior research [17–21]. The first is the Chest X-Ray Images (Pneumonia) dataset, originally provided by the Guangzhou Women and Children's Medical Center. It includes a total of 5,856 verified chest X-ray images, all in JPEG format with a resolution of 1024

× 1024 pixels. The dataset is partitioned into a training set containing 5,216 images (1,341 normal and 3,875 pneumonia), a test set with 624 images (234 normal and 390 pneumonia), and a validation set comprising 16 images (8 normal and 8 pneumonia). Representative samples are shown in Fig. 6. For multi-class classification tasks, this study utilizes the Chest X-Ray (Pneumonia, COVID-19, Tuberculosis) dataset [20, 30], which contains 7,135 chest X-ray images. These are also in JPEG format with high visual clarity. The data distribution includes 6,326 training images (1,341 normal, 3,875 pneumonia, 650 tuberculosis, 460 COVID-19), 771 test images (234 normal, 390 pneumonia, 41 tuberculosis, 106 COVID-19), and 38 validation images (8 normal, 8 pneumonia, 12 tuberculosis, 10 COVID-19). Examples from this dataset are shown in Fig. 7.

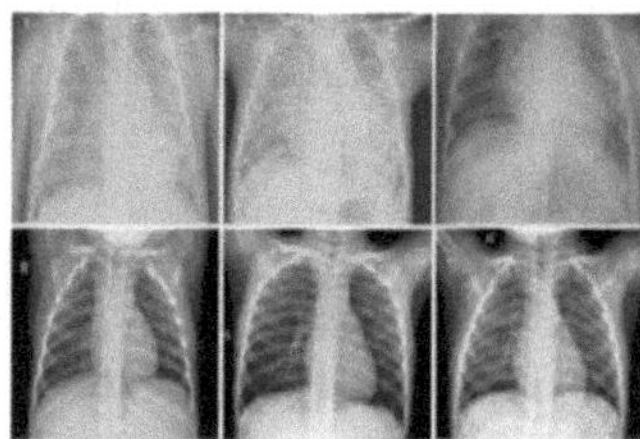

Fig. 6. Sample images from the Chest X-Ray images (Pneumonia) dataset.

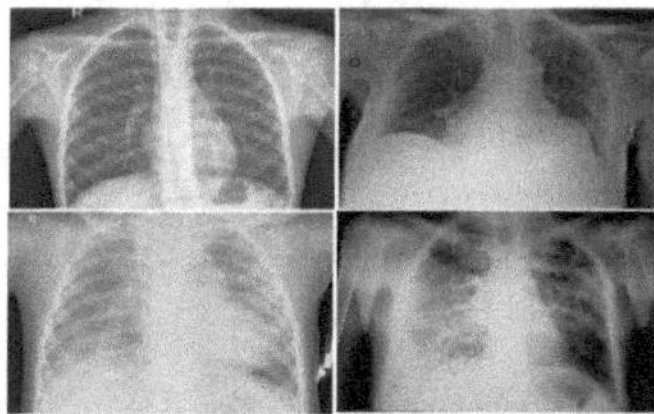

Fig. 7. Sample images from the multi-class Chest X-Ray dataset.

4.2 Experimental Configuration

The baseline configuration of the experiments is summarized in Table 2. All input images are resized to 224 × 224 pixels to comply with model requirements. Data augmentation is applied by introducing random rotations (±15°) and brightness reduction (50%) to enhance data diversity. The learning rate is set to 0.0001 to ensure stable convergence, and the number of epochs for base training is fixed at 5. The training dataset is divided into 70% for base training and 30% for incremental learning, using a 10-step incremental training process.

Table 2. Base configuration of the experimental setup.

Parameter name	Description	Value
Image size	input image size	(224,224)
Rotation Degree	Random rotation angle	15 degrees
Brightness Adjust	Reduce brightness	50%
Learning Rate	Learning rate for model training, controls the step size for parameter updates	0.0001
Epochs	Number of training epochs for the base training	5
Base training dataset	70% of training dataset	70%

(continued)

Table 2. (*continued*)

Parameter name	Description	Value
Incremental training dataset	30% of training dataset	30%
Incremental Steps	Number of incremental learning	10

4.3 Evaluation of Learning Bases Models

To determine the most suitable base model for integration with the Analytic Class Incremental Learning (ACIL) method, two widely used convolutional neural networks, EfficientNet-B0 and ResNet-18, were selected for comparison. In both cases, the feature extractor was first trained via standard backpropagation, and then integrated into ACIL for incremental learning. Classification accuracy and forgetting rate were used as primary evaluation metrics. The forgetting rate was calculated using the Task-wise Forgetting Rate Calculation Method [30], which quantifies performance degradation by measuring accuracy drops between initial and subsequent incremental learning stages. The experimental results of both models across the 10 incremental stages are presented in Fig. 8, where the forgetting rate—calculated as the relative decline in accuracy at each incremental step compared to the initial performance—quantifies the extent of catastrophic forgetting. The results demonstrate that EfficientNet-B0 combined with ACIL achieved a final-stage accuracy of 76.90%, outperforming the 75.78% accuracy of the ResNet-18 combination. In terms of forgetting rate, EfficientNet-B0 attained −10.40%, compared to −9.38% for ResNet-18. The more negative value implies stronger resistance to forgetting, indicating that EfficientNet-B0 better preserves learned knowledge during continual learning. Furthermore, EfficientNet-B0 showed faster learning progress during the initial incremental stages (1–3), while ResNet-18 exhibited more gradual improvements. This trend suggests that EfficientNet-B0 possesses stronger early-stage feature representation capabilities, which could be attributed to its compound scaling architecture.

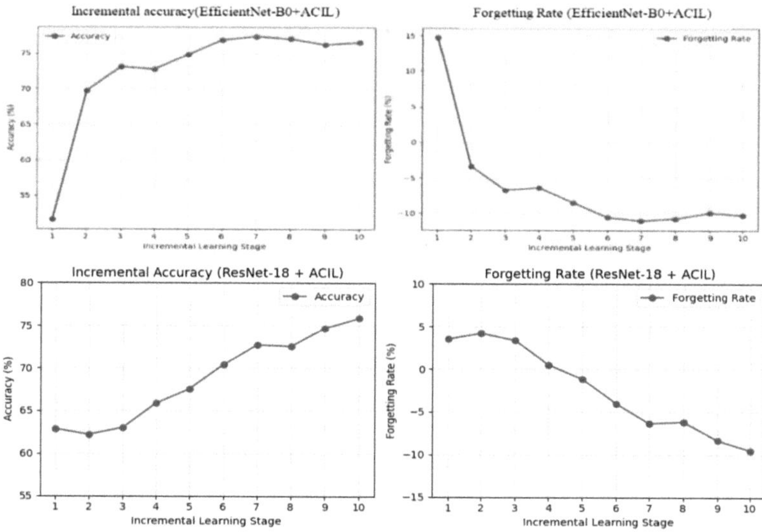

Fig. 8. Comparison of EfficientNet-B0 (top) and ResNet-18 (bottom) as base models in ACIL.

To further assess classification performance, confusion matrices and classification metrics were analyzed, as shown in Fig. 9 and Table 3. From these results, it is evident that the EfficientNet-B0 configuration consistently performs better across all evaluated metrics. Its higher recall and F1-score indicate improved sensitivity to positive cases, which is critical in medical diagnosis scenarios to reduce missed detections. Although the difference in overall accuracy is relatively minor, EfficientNet-B0's superior performance in precision-sensitive and recall-sensitive contexts justifies its selection as the backbone for subsequent experiments comparing incremental learning strategies.

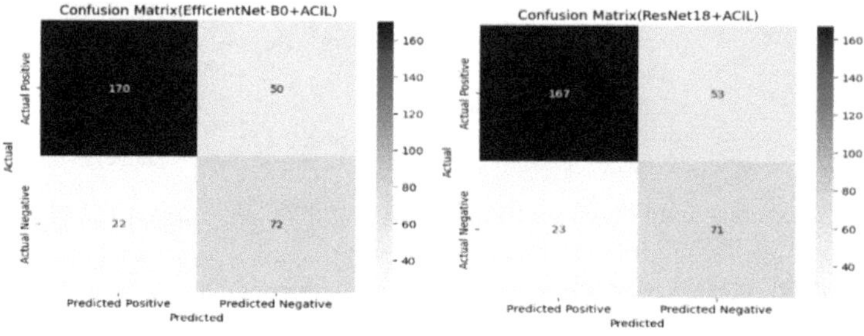

Fig. 9. Confusion matrix results for EfficientNet-B0 + ACIL and ResNet-18 + ACIL.

Table 3. Performance metrics for EfficientNet-B0 + ACIL and ResNet-18 + ACIL.

Method	TP	FP	FN	TN	Precision (%)	Recall (%)	F1-score (%)
EfficientNet-B0 + ACIL (Our)	170	22	50	72	88.54	77.27	82.59

(continued)

Table 3. (*continued*)

Method	TP	FP	FN	TN	Precision (%)	Recall (%)	F1-score (%)
ResNet-18 + ACIL	167	23	53	71	87.89	75.99	81.44

4.4 Evaluation of Incremental Learning Strategies

Utilizing EfficientNet-B0 as the base model, this study evaluates four incremental learning strategies: LwF, EWC, ER, and ACIL. As illustrated in Fig. 10, ACIL outperforms all other methods in both classification accuracy and forgetting rate throughout the incremental stages. LwF shows the weakest performance, with significant drops in accuracy and a final forgetting rate of 27.1%, indicating poor knowledge retention. EWC maintains moderate performance, with a stable but fluctuating forgetting pattern. ER demonstrates better stability than LwF and EWC but lacks performance improvement. ACIL, in contrast, achieves the best classification accuracy and the most stable learning trajectory. As shown in Table 4 and Fig. 11, ACIL achieved the highest F1-score of 83.56%, with a precision of 78.17% and a recall of 89.58%, demonstrating a strong balance between sensitivity and specificity. Table 5 reports performance across different task numbers (K = 5, K = 10), where ACIL maintains the highest classification accuracy and lowest forgetting rate in all configurations.

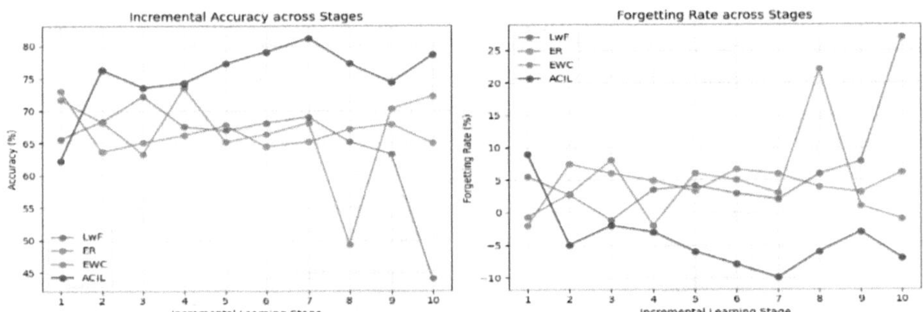

Fig. 10. Accuracy and Forgetting Rate Across Incremental Steps for Four Methods.

Table 4. Performance metrics for different incremental learning methods.

Method	TP	FP	FN	TN	Precision (%)	Recall (%)	F1-score (%)
EfficientNet-B0 + ACIL (Our)	172	48	20	74	78.17	89.58	83.56
EfficientNet-B0 + ER	143	77	33	61	65.02	81.25	72.19
EfficientNet-B0 + EWC	160	60	26	68	72.73	86.02	78.78

(*continued*)

Table 4. *(continued)*

Method	TP	FP	FN	TN	Precision (%)	Recall (%)	F1-score (%)
EfficientNet-B0 + LWF	97	123	53	41	44.09	64.67	52.36

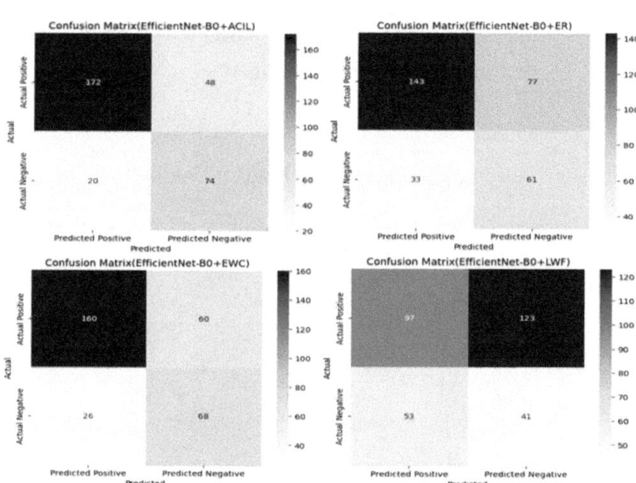

Fig. 11. Confusion matrices of the incremental learning methods

4.5 Performance on Multi-class Dataset

To further assess model scalability, experiments were extended to the multi-class dataset. As shown in Fig. 12 and Table 6, ACIL again achieves the best performance, with a final classification accuracy of 68.1% and a forgetting rate of only 1.0%. In contrast, LwF performs poorly with only 33.8% accuracy and a forgetting rate of 35.3%, confirming its unsuitability for complex incremental tasks.

Table 5. Accuracy and forgetting rate comparison (Chest X-Ray, K = 5 and K = 10 tasks).

Metrics	Method	Chest X-Ray Images (Pneumonia)	
		K = 5	K = 10
Accuracy	LWF	66.9%	43.9%
	ER	68.1%	64.9%
	EWC	65.2%	72.6%
	ACIL (Our)	77.1%	78.3%

(continued)

Table 5. (*continued*)

Metrics	Method	Chest X-Ray Images (Pneumonia)	
		K = 5	K = 10
Forgetting	LWF	4.1%	27.1%
	ER	2.9%	6.1%
	EWC	5.8%	−1.6%
	ACIL (Our)	−6.1%	−7.3%

Table 6. Classification Accuracy and Forgetting Rate on Multi-Class Chest X-Ray Dataset.

Method	Accuracy (%)	Forgetting Rate (%)
EfficientNet-B0 + EWC	63.3	5.8
EfficientNet-B0 + ER	53.8	15.3
EfficientNet-B0 + LwF	33.8	35.3
EfficientNet-B0 + ACIL (Our)	68.1	1.0

These findings demonstrate that ACIL, when integrated with EfficientNet-B0, offers an effective and stable solution for continuous learning in both binary and multi-class medical image classification tasks.

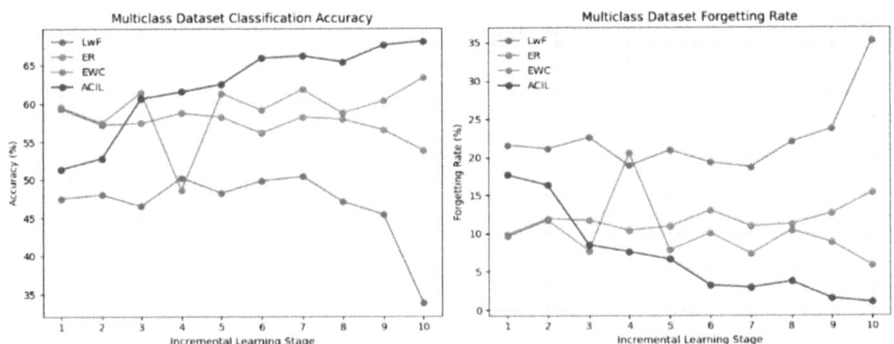

Fig. 12. Performance on multi-class Chest X-ray dataset.

5 Conclusion and Future Work

This study presents a comprehensive analysis and comparative evaluation of various base models and incremental learning strategies in the context of medical image classification. Experimental results demonstrate that EfficientNet-B0, when combined with ACIL, consistently outperforms ResNet-18 across key metrics, including classification accuracy and resistance to catastrophic forgetting. Subsequent evaluations incorporating four incremental learning methods—ACIL, LwF, ER, and EWC—further highlight the superior performance of ACIL. While LwF exhibits rapid degradation in classification accuracy due to pronounced forgetting, ER maintains relative stability but underperforms compared to ACIL. EWC, on the other hand, shows considerable performance volatility. Overall, ACIL demonstrates the most robust performance, particularly when paired with EfficientNet-B0, across both binary and multi-class classification tasks.

Despite the promising outcomes, certain limitations remain. The current evaluation is constrained to a specific set of models and datasets, which may limit generalizability across broader domains. Future work may explore the integration of more diverse architectures and more complex clinical datasets to enhance model robustness and scalability. Furthermore, extending the ACIL framework to other modalities, such as 3D medical imaging or time-series data, presents a valuable direction for future research. Collectively, these findings underscore the potential of combining EfficientNet-B0 with ACIL for reliable, high-performance incremental learning in medical image analysis.

References

1. World Health Organization: Pneumonia Fact Sheet. World Health Organization (2019). https://www.who.int/news-room/fact-sheets/detail/pneumonia
2. Agarwal, D., Berbís, M.Á., Luna, A., Lipari, V., Ballester, J.B., de la Torre-Díez, I.: Automated medical diagnosis of Alzheimer's disease using an EfficientNet convolutional neural network. J. Med. Syst. **47**(1), 57 (2023)
3. Subramanian, M., Cho, J., Sathishkumar, V.E., Naren, O.S.: Multiple types of cancer classification using CT/MRI images based on learning without forgetting powered deep learning models. IEEE Access **11**, 10336–10354 (2023)
4. Liu, X., Wang, Z.: Deep Learning in Medical Image Classification from MRI-Based Brain Tumor Images (2024). arXiv preprint: arXiv:2408.00636
5. Kulkarni, A., Parasnis, G., Balasubramanian, H., Jain, V., Chokshi, A., Sonkusare, R.: Advancing Diagnostic Precision: Leveraging Machine Learning Techniques for Accurate Detection of Covid-19, Pneumonia, and Tuberculosis in Chest X-Ray Images (2023). arXiv preprint: arXiv:2310.06080
6. Hasanah, S.A., Pravitasari, A.A., Abdullah, A.S., Yulita, I.N., Asnawi, M.H.: A deep learning review of resnet architecture for lung disease Identification in CXR Image. Appl. Sci. **13**(24), 13111 (2023)
7. Dosovitskiy, A.: An Image is Worth 16×16 Words: Transformers for Image Recognition at Scale (2020). arXiv preprint: arXiv:2010.11929
8. Wang, X., Peng, Y., Lu, L., Lu, Z., Bagheri, M., Summers, R.M.: Chestx-ray8: Hospital-scale chest x-ray database and benchmarks on weakly-supervised classification and localization of common thorax diseases. In: Proceedings of the IEEE Conference on Computer Vision and Pattern Recognition, pp. 2097–2106 (2017)
9. Rajpurkar, P.: CheXNet: Radiologist-Level Pneumonia Detection on Chest X-rays with Deep Learning (2017). arXiv preprint: arXiv:1711.05225
10. Aleixo, E.L., Colonna, J.G., Cristo, M., Fernandes, E.: Catastrophic Forgetting in Deep Learning: a Comprehensive Taxonomy (2023). arXiv preprint: arXiv:2312.10549
11. Li, W., Xiong, Y., Fan, Z., Deng, B., Cao, F., Gao, Y.: Advances and trends of continual learning. J. Comput. Res. Dev. **61**(6), 1476–1496 (2024)

12. Gupta, A., Rao, A., & Anumanchipalli, G. (2024). Model Editing at Scale Leads to Gradual and Catastrophic Forgetting. arXiv preprint: arXiv:2401.07453
13. Leo, J., Kalita, J.: Incremental deep neural network learning using classification confidence thresholding. IEEE Trans. Neural Netw. Learn. Syst. **33**(12), 7706–7716 (2021)
14. Van de Ven, G.M., Tuytelaars, T., Tolias, A.S.: Three types of incremental learning. Nat. Mach. Intell. **4**(12), 1185–1197 (2022)
15. Zhuang, H., Weng, Z., Wei, H., Xie, R., Toh, K.A., Lin, Z.: ACIL: analytic class-incremental learning with absolute memorization and privacy protection. Adv. Neural. Inf. Process. Syst. **35**, 11602–11614 (2022)
16. Tan, M.: Efficientnet: Rethinking Model Scaling for Convolutional Neural Networks (2019). arXiv preprint arXiv:1905.11946
17. Jassam, I.F., Elkaffas, S.M., & El-Zoghabi, A.A.: Chest x-ray pneumonia detection by densenet. In: 2021 31st International Conference on Computer Theory and Applications (ICCTA), pp. 176–179. IEEE (2021)
18. Xin, K.Z., Li, D., Yi, P.H.: Limited generalizability of deep learning algorithm for pediatric pneumonia classification on external data. Emerg. Radiol. **29**, 1–7 (2022)
19. Ma, Y., Gonzales, R.A.: Convolutional neural network-based analysis of pediatric chest X-ray images for pneumonia detection. J. Emerg. Invest. **7**, 1 (2024)
20. Ahmed, M.S., et al.: Joint diagnosis of pneumonia, COVID-19, and tuberculosis from chest X-ray images: a deep learning approach. Diagnostics **13**(15), 2562 (2023)
21. Venkataramana, L., Prasad, D.V.V., Saraswathi, S., Mithumary, C.M., Karthikeyan, R., Monika, N.: Classification of COVID-19 from tuberculosis and pneumonia using deep learning techniques. Med. Biol. Eng. Compu. **60**(9), 2681–2691 (2022)
22. Raza, R., et al.: Lung EffNet: pneumonia classification using EfficientNet from CT- scan images. Eng. Appl. Artif. Intell. **126**, 106902 (2023)
23. Kurt, Z., Işık, Ş, Kaya, Z., Anagün, Y., Koca, N., Çiçek, S.: Evaluation of EfficientNet models for COVID-19 detection using lung parenchyma. Neural Comput. Appl. **35**(16), 12121–12132 (2023)
24. Marques, G., Agarwal, D., De la Torre Díez, I.: Automated medical diagnosis of COVID-19 through EfficientNet convolutional neural network. Appl. Soft Comput. **96**, 106691 (2020)
25. Li, Z., Hoiem, D.: Learning without forgetting. IEEE Trans. Pattern Anal. Mach. Intell. **40**(12), 2935–2947 (2017)
26. Kirkpatrick, J., et al.: Overcoming catastrophic forgetting in neural networks. Proc. Natl. Acad. Sci. **114**(13), 3521–3526 (2017)
27. Krutsylo, A.: The inter-batch diversity of samples in experience replay for continual learning. In: Proceedings of the AAAI Conference on Artificial Intelligence, vol. 38, no. 21, pp. 23395–23396 (2024)
28. Zhou, D.W., Wang, Q.W., Qi, Z.H., Ye, H.J., Zhan, D.C., Liu, Z.: Class-incremental learning: a survey. IEEE Trans. Pattern Anal. Mach. Intell. (2024)
29. Hu, J., Shen, L., Sun, G.: Squeeze-and-excitation networks. In: Proceedings of the IEEE Conference on Computer Vision and Pattern Recognition, pp. 7132–7141 (2018)
30. Mirzadeh, S.I., Farajtabar, M., Pascanu, R., Ghasemzadeh, H.: Understanding the role of training regimes in continual learning. Adv. Neural. Inf. Process. Syst. **33**, 7308–7320 (2020)

Enhancement of Spatial-MCDA Using Machine Learning: Integration of FAHP and ANN Model

Lutfi A. Rahaman[1], Nabilah Naharudin[1](✉), and Siti Aekbal Salleh[1,2]

[1] Faculty of Built Environment, Universiti Teknologi MARA, Shah Alam, Selangor, Malaysia
nabilahnaharudin1290@uitm.edu.my

[2] Institute for Biodiversity and Sustainable Development (IBSD), Universiti Teknologi MARA, Selangor, Malaysia

Abstract. The increasing complexity of spatial decision-making tasks necessitates robust analytical models capable of addressing uncertainty, subjectivity, and large datasets. This study proposes an integrated Fuzzy Analytical Hierarchy Process–Artificial Neural Network (FAHP-ANN) model to enhance the interpretability and computational capacity of Multi-Criteria Decision Analysis (MCDA). The FAHP component captures human judgment through triangular fuzzy numbers to reflect ambiguity in expert assessments, while the ANN component leverages these weights to learn complex patterns across criteria and alternatives. A structured methodological framework is developed, incorporating preference aggregation, ReLU activation functions, Net Flow Score computation, and threshold-based classification for decision support. Monte Carlo simulation and sensitivity analysis are employed to evaluate model stability and robustness. Results demonstrate that the FAHP-ANN model significantly outperforms conventional ANN models in both accuracy (reduction in prediction error) and consistency, particularly under fuzzy environments. The proposed model presents a scalable and interpretable decision-support tool suitable for applications in spatial planning, infrastructure prioritization, and policy evaluation, effectively bridging the gap between human-centric reasoning and data-driven analytics.

Keywords: MCDA · Neural network · Conceptual framework · FAHP

1 Introduction

Decision-making (DM) plays a vital role across industries such as healthcare, SMEs, and risk management. With rapid technological advancement, integrating Multi-Criteria Decision-Making Analysis (MCDA) with machine learning (ML) has become increasingly necessary. Traditional MCDA methods struggle with large datasets and often rely on subjective inputs like surveys or expert opinions, introducing ambiguity. Although combining MCDA with ML is a growing trend, the resulting models must be robust and trustworthy [1]. To address ambiguity in expert assessments, this study adopts the Fuzzy Analytical Hierarchy Process (FAHP), which accounts for uncertainty in subjective evaluation [2]. In multicriteria models, vague constraints may lead to inconsistencies that are

M. Kassim et al. (Eds.): SCDS 2025, CCIS 2674, pp. 397–411, 2026.
https://doi.org/10.1007/978-981-95-8368-3_28

better resolved through flexible methods rather than data removal [3]. Artificial Neural Networks (ANN) offer a data-driven alternative to traditional DM models, capable of handling complex datasets without human input [4]. However, challenges remain regarding input selection, data accuracy, and hyperparameter tuning [5]. Moreover, MCDA models often fail under large, inconsistent datasets [6]. While ANN handles data volume well, it lacks the nuanced judgment that human input provides in policymaking. Therefore, combining FAHP and ANN is advantageous: FAHP captures human fuzziness, while ANN processes high-dimensional data. Consensus-building becomes essential when incorporating human input, as supported by models like Harmony Theory ANN, second-order consensus algorithms, and consensus blockchain [7]. This study integrates FAHP weightage into the ANN model to improve performance and retain ambiguity during learning, bridging the gap between subjective and data-driven decision-making.

2 Literature Review

This section reviews key developments in FAHP, ANN, and their hybrid applications, highlighting methodological advancements, comparative strengths, and their relevance in addressing spatial decision-making challenges.

2.1 Fuzzy Analytical Hierarchy Process

MCDA continues to evolve, offering more accurate and structured numerical methods. One key advancement is the transition from AHP to FAHP, which effectively addresses imprecision in expert judgment. FAHP begins by building a pairwise comparison matrix, aggregating expert inputs, assessing consistency, and defuzzifying fuzzy weights [8]. The shift to FAHP stems from AHP's reliance on human judgment, which naturally introduces vagueness. Since precise values are often unattainable in subjective assessments, researchers introduced fuzzy numbers to express uncertainty through membership degrees. FAHP typically follows six steps: problem structuring, developing the pairwise comparison matrix, synthesizing expert judgments, calculating and defuzzifying weights, and checking consistency. Its hierarchical structure mirrors AHP, organizing the decision process into criteria, sub-criteria, and alternatives.

There are two important steps in establishing FAHP pairwise comparison matrix which is to define linguistic terms and TFN. Linguistic terms are used to compare criteria such as "equally important", "moderately more important", and "strongly more important". Meanwhile, TFN is characterized by "l", "m", and "h" which is (l,m,h). The meaning for each three is lower limit, most likely value, and upper limit respectively. For example, if expert judgment indicates that Criterion A is "moderately more important" than Criterion B, it might be represented by the TFN (2,3,4). The expert judgement is always indicated as "m".

Next is the matrix construction of FAHP pairwise comparison matrix. Construct a reciprocal matrix where each element C_{ij} represents the fuzzy relative importance of criterion i over j, and the matrix is reciprocal meaning $C_{ij} = 1/C_{ij}$.

Next, the judgments from multiple experts are synthesized, as FAHP often involves aggregating diverse opinions. Two common aggregation methods are the geometric mean (for multiplicative aggregation) and the arithmetic mean (for additive aggregation). AHP and FAHP typically use the geometric mean, as it directly derives impact scores by calculating geometric row means [9]. After computing the geometric mean for each criterion, it is normalized to produce fuzzy weights, which are then defuzzified using the centroid method to obtain crisp values. The consistency ratio is calculated to verify reliability; if it is below 0.1, the matrix is deemed consistent. The steps for FAHP calculation and annotation follow.

Step 1. Pairwise Comparison Matrix Construction

$$C_{ij} = \frac{1}{C_{ji}} \tag{1}$$

Step 2. Fuzzification and incorporated ambiguity using Triangular Fuzzy Numbers (TFN) in Table 1

$$(l, m, u) = (\text{lower}, \ \text{middle}, \ \text{upper}) \tag{2}$$

Table 1. TFNs value in MCDA analysis practice.

Criteria input value	TFNs
1	(1,1,1)
2	(1,2,3)
3	(2,3,4)
4	(3,4,5)
5	(4,5,6)
6	(5,6,7)
7	(6,7,8)
8	(7,8,9)
9	(9,9,9)

Step 3. Fuzzy Geometric Mean

$$A_n = (l_1 \times l_2 \times \ldots . \times l_n, m_1 \times m_2 \times \ldots . \times m_n, u_1 \times u_2 \times \ldots . \times u_n) \tag{3}$$

Step 4. Defuzzification

$$\text{Crips Value} = \frac{l + m + u}{3} \tag{4}$$

Step 5. Calculate the value of Consistency Ratio (CR) by calculating the Consistency Index (CI) and obtain Random Index (RI) value based on the matrix size. RI value can be determined using Table 2 [10].

$$\text{CI} = \frac{\lambda_{max} - n}{n - 1}$$

RI = Random Index (a value that depends on the number of criteria, *n*.)

$$\text{CR} = \frac{CI}{RI} \tag{5}$$

If CR value is below 0.1, the comparison matrix is considered consistent. If CR value is above 0.1, the comparison is considered inconsistent. This process ensures that the pairwise comparisons used in FAHP are reliable and logical, reducing bias and improving the accuracy of decision-making.

Table 2. Value of RI

Criteria input value	TFNs
1	0.00
2	0.00
3	0.58
4	0.90
5	1.12
6	1.24
7	1.32
8	1.41
9	1.45
10	1.49

2.2 Artificial Neural Network

Artificial Neural Networks (ANN) have gained significant attention as researchers increasingly adopt advanced computational and statistical tools to analyze complex relationships between input and output variables. Traditional univariate or linear models often fall short in capturing these complexities. The term "neural" relates to neurons, and "network" reflects its graph-like structure. ANN refers to computing systems inspired by biological neural networks [11]. It functions as a non-linear model capable of processing large sets of inputs and outputs simultaneously, mimicking the human brain's ability to perform complex calculations. Four core elements define ANN: the neuron type, connection architecture (fully or partially connected), learning algorithm, and recall algorithm.

The ANN problem-solving process consists of two phases: a training phase where examples are used to embed rules, and a recall phase where the trained model processes new input to generate results [12].

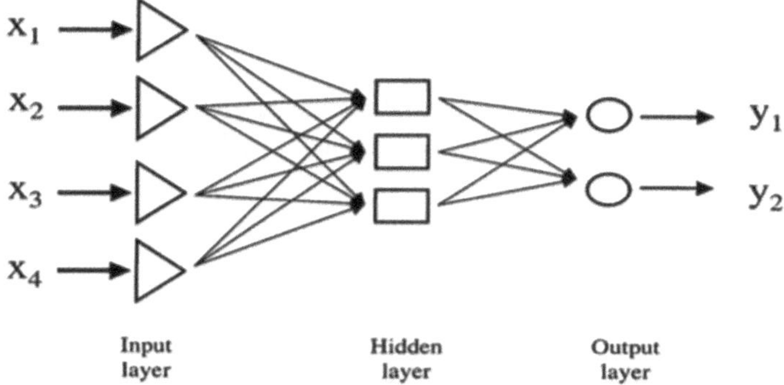

Fig. 1. Model of Feedforward Network [15]

Figure 1 illustrates a feedforward network consisting of three essential layers: input, hidden, and output. The input layer receives dataset features and passes weighted information to the hidden layer for processing. The hidden layer, located between input and output layers, transforms the input using weights, biases, and an activation function. It is termed "hidden" because its processes are not directly observable. The output layer produces final results such as classifications or predictions. As MCDA increasingly deals with large and complex datasets, machine learning has emerged as a practical solution. It supports decision-making across domains like pharmaceutical research, business analytics, and hydrology. MCDA and machine learning complement each other such that ML handles nonlinear, high-dimensional data, while enhancing model flexibility and performance. This synergy improves understanding of decision-making processes and increases transparency in otherwise "black box" ML models [13]. In this study, FAHP is used as a benchmark within the ANN to reflect decision-maker preferences more accurately.

A study titled "Deep preference learning for multiple criteria decision analysis", the concept of threshold also introduces a threshold-based sorting model. In this study, the ANN-MCDA formula works by MCDA with ANN to create models that can handle large and inconsistent data sets for decision-making. It breaks down into six different approaches which are data and criteria, MCDA models, ANN, preference learning, optimization and interpretability [6]. In this said study, there are six different model uses which are Ordered Weighted Average (OWA), Additive Value Function (UTADIS), Choquet Integral, Distance-based methods (TOPSIS), Preference Ranking Organization Method for Enrichment Evaluation (PROMETHEE), and Elimination and Choice Translating Reality (ELECTRE). For the sake of integrating ANN into TAI, ANN-PROMETHEE method is used and explained in this section. The PROMETHEE formula within the ANN-PROMETHEE approach integrates ANN to automate and enhance decision-making processes by learning preference parameters from data. ANN-PROMETHEE has six main steps which are performance difference calculation, marginal preference degree, comprehensive preference index, net flow score (NFS), normalization, and ANN integration.

Step 1. Performance difference calculation

$$d_j(a_i, a_k) = g_j(a_i) - g_j(a_k) \tag{6}$$

Equation 6 shows the performance difference calculation equation. i represents a specific alternative that is being evaluated. Meanwhile, k denotes another alternative against which alternative i is being compared. j represents a specific criterion according to which the performance of alternatives is evaluated. Thus, in this context, $g_j(a_i)$ is the value for alternative i on criterion j.

Step 2. Marginal preference degree

$$F_j(a_i, a_k) = \begin{cases} 0 if d_j(a_i, a_k) \leq q_j \\ \frac{d_j(a_i, a_k) - q_j}{p_j - q_j} if 0 < d_j(a_i, a_k) \leq p_j \\ 1 if d_j(a_i, a_k) > p_j \end{cases} \tag{7}$$

Equation 7 shows the marginal preference degree equation for ANN-PROMETHEE. This equation defines the preference function for criterion j when comparing alternative i with alternative k. $F_j(a_i, a_k)$ is the preference degree of alternative i over alternative k for criterion j. $d_j(a_i, a_k)$ is the performance difference between alternative i and alternative k for criterion j. q_j is indifference threshold for criterion j. p_j is the preference threshold for criterion j. For the interpretation, if $d_j(a_i, a_k) \leq q_j$ performance difference is less than or equal to the indifference threshold, the preference degree $F_j(a_i, a_k)$ is 0. Meaning alternative i is not preferred over alternative k for criterion j. If $0 < d_j(a_i, a_k) \leq p_j$ performance degree is between the indifference threshold and the preference threshold, the preference degree is calculated as $\frac{d_j(a_i, a_k) - q_j}{p_j - q_j}$. This value will be between 0 and 1, representing a gradual increase in preference as the performance difference increases from q_j to p_j. Lastly, if $d_j(a_i, a_k) > p_j$, the preference degree is 1, meaning alternative i is fully preferred over alternative k for criterion j.

Step 3. Comprehensive Preference Index

$$\pi(a_i, a_k) = \sum_{j=1}^{m} w_j F_j(a_i, a_k) \tag{8}$$

Equation 8 shows the comprehensive preference index equation. $\pi(a_i, a_k)$ is comprehensive preference index of alternative a_i over alternative a_k. This index aggregates the preferences across all criteria and indicates the overall preference level of a_i compared to a_k. m is the total number of criteria. w_j is the weight associated with criterion j. Finally, $F_j(a_i, a_k)$ is the marginal preference degree of alternative a_i over alternative a_k for criterion j. The comprehensive preference index is calculated by summing the weighted marginal preference degrees for each criterion. This index quantifies the overall preference of alternative a_i over alternative a_k.

Step 4. Positive and negative NFS

Positive NFS calculates how well an alternative i performs relative to all other alternatives. Meanwhile, negative NFS calculates how poorly an alternative i performs relative to all other alternatives. Also, normalization occurs during performance scores divided by n-1, which serves as a form of normalization.

$$NFS^{+}(a_i) = \frac{1}{n-1}\sum_{k=1}^{n}\pi(a_i, a_k) \tag{9}$$

$$NFS^{-}(a_i) = \frac{1}{n-1}\sum_{k=1}^{n}\pi(a_k, a_i) \tag{10}$$

Step 5. Overall desirability

$$FS(a_i) = NFS^{+}(a_i) - NFS^{-}(a_i) \tag{11}$$

Equation 9 shows the equation to compute positive NFS. Equation 10 shows the equation to compute negative NFS and Eq. 11 shows the difference between the positive and negative NFS and indicates the overall desirability of alternative a_i. n is total number of alternatives in datasets used. $\pi(a_i, a_k)$ is comprehensive preference index of alternative a_i over alternative a_k acquired in Eq. 8 before this.

In conclusion, using this equation can provide a way for weightages acquired from FAHP into ANN models because it assigns weight using pairwise comparison method. As for the current study to integrate FAHP into ANN, this model would like to adopt FAHP weightage as weightage as it could open the option to include human fuzziness in current ANN model.

3 Methodology

3.1 FAHP-ANN Model

Equation 12 until Eq. 17 shows the step-by-step procedure to calculate FAHP weightage and prepare it to integrate as input for ANN layer.

Step 1: Pairwise Comparison Matrix Construction

Step one (1) shows the construction of a pairwise comparison matrix. A pairwise comparison matrix $A = a_{ij}$ is constructed, where each element a_{ij} represents the relative importance of criterion C_i compared to C_j. For all i, j, these comparisons quantify subjective judgments using a 9-point scale. If $a_{ij} > 1$, C_i is more important than C_j; if $a_{ij} = 1$, they are equally important. This matrix forms the foundation for the fuzzy analytic hierarchy process (FAHP).

$$a_{ij} = \frac{1}{a_{ji}}, a_{ij} = 1 \text{ for all } i, j \tag{12}$$

Step 2. Fuzzification using Triangular Fuzzy Numbers (TFNs).

Each comparison a_{ij} is converted into a TFN, represented as $á_{ij} = (l_{ij}, m_{ij}, u_{ij})$. Here, l_{ij} is the lower bound, m_{ij} is most likely value, and u_{ij} is the upper bound. TFN captures uncertainty in comparisons by allowing a range instead of single values. This transformation allows the model to express the uncertainty inherent in human judgments by representing preferences as a range rather than a single point estimate. Incorporated ambiguity using TFNs (Table 1).

$$\acute{a}_{ij} = \left(l_{ij}, m_{ij}, u_{ij}\right) \tag{13}$$

Step 3. Fuzzy Geometric Mean.

Each criterion annotated as i, while n is the total number of criteria. This calculation aggregates the fuzzy values across comparisons to represent the overall importance of each criterion.

$$G^{\sim}M_i = (\prod_{j=1}^{n} \acute{a}_{ij})^{\frac{1}{n}} \tag{14}$$

Step 4. Defuzzied Geometric Mean.

The fuzzy geometric mean $\tilde{G}M_i$ is defuzzied to obtain a crisp value W_i using defuzzification method, whereas the value of $l_i, m_i u_i$ is sum and divided by 3. This step simplifies the fuzzy results into a single value for further analysis.

$$W_i = \frac{l_i + m_i + u_i}{3} \tag{15}$$

Step 5. FAHP weight normalization.

The defuzzied values W_i are normalized to produce the weights for each criterion. This normalization ensures that the sum of all weights equals 1, maintaining proportionality among criteria.

$$w_i = \frac{W_i}{\sum_{k=1}^{n} w_k} \tag{16}$$

Step 6. Geometric means normalize FAHP weight

In this step, every input FAHP data or expert opinion such as if there are five (5) expert opinion, weightage from five (5) expert is average using geometric mean method which annotated as w_j. It is annotated as w_j because this value will be use as weightage during ANN layer.

$$w_j = \sqrt[n]{w_1 + w_2 + w_3 + \ldots w_n} \tag{17}$$

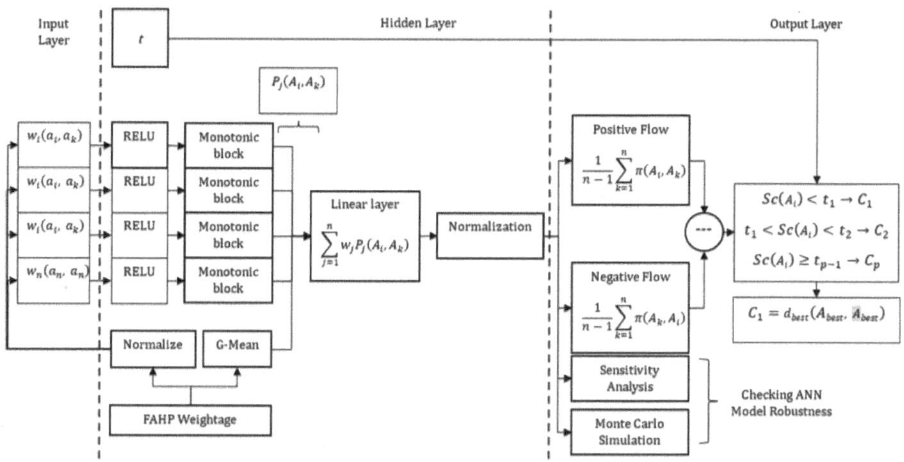

Fig. 2. FAHP-ANN Model

Figure 2 shows the FAHP-ANN model developed in this study and explains the flow of methodology, equation, input, and output available. The model input data is normalized FAHP weightage acquired during FAHP calculation. If originally there were four (4) FAHP normalized weightage, then the input layer in the ANN section also shows four (4) input neurons.

Step 7. Preference function with ReLU activation

The preference function $P_j(A_i, A_k)$ evaluates the relative preference between alternatives A_i and A_k. The output is processed through a ReLU function where $w_{ij} - w_{kj}$ is the raw preference score annotation. This activation ensures that the preference value is non-negative.

$$P_j(A_i, A_k) = ReLU\left(w_{ij} - w_{kj}\right) = \max\left(0, w_{ij} - w_{kj}\right) \tag{18}$$

Step 8. Aggregation of preference using geometric mean normalize FAHP weight.

The weighted preference score $\pi(A_i, A_k)$ for each alternative is computed by multiplying the preference values $P_j(A_i, A_k)$ by the normalized FAHP weights w_j.

$$\pi(A_i, A_k) = \sum_{j=1}^{n} w_j P_j(A_i, A_k) \tag{19}$$

Step 9. NFS score computation in ANN layer

The aggregated preference scores are fed into an ANN layer, which learns patterns and computes a NFS for each alternative. $NFS^+(A_i)$ calculates how well an alternative i performs relative to all other alternatives. Meanwhile, $NFS^-(A_i)$ calculates how poorly an alternative i performs relative to all other alternatives. Also, normalization occurs during performance scores divided by $m - 1$, which serves as a form of normalization. The final score (FS) of NFS is defined by the symbol $FS(A_i)$ in Eq. 22. The ANN improves the decision-making process by capturing complex relationships among the inputs.

$$NFS^{+}(A_i) = \frac{1}{m-1}\sum_{k=1}^{m} \pi(A_i, A_k) \tag{20}$$

$$NFS^{-}(A_i) = \frac{1}{m-1}\sum_{k=1}^{m} \pi(A_k, A_i) \tag{21}$$

$$FS(A_i) = NFS^{+}(A_i) - NFS^{-}(A_i) \tag{22}$$

In Eqs. 20 and 21, the division of $m - 1$ normalize the NFS to reflect the average preference per pairwise comparison. Since each alternative is only compared to the remaining $m - 1$ alternatives (excluding itself), using only m would overstate the denominator and dilute the score.

As an example, consider a case of four alternative: A_1, A_2, A_3, A_4. To compute the positive NFS for A_1, it needs to compare with A_2, A_3, A_4. Suppose the preference value are "$\pi(A_1, A_2) = 0.7$", "$\pi(A_1, A_2) = 0.5$", and "$\pi(A_1, A_2) = 1.0$", the total preference sum is 2.2. Since A_1 was compared against three other alternatives, it is normalized by dividing $m - 1 = 3$. The positive NFS score is 0.733 if compared with three alternatives, but with four alternatives, the score would drop to 0.55 which undermines the true preference strength. This approach aligns with common statistical practices, such as sample variance, where dividing by $m - 1$ yield unbiased estimate [14].

Step 10. Threshold-based classification

Each alternative's NFS score is compared against predefined thresholds to classify it into categories. The classification function in the FAHP-ANN-PROMETHEE model assigns a priority or category to each alternative A_i based on its Final Score (FS). This function ensures that alternatives are grouped according to predefined thresholds. If the score $FS(A_i)$ is less than or equal to the first threshold T_1, the alternative is assigned to Class 1, representing the lowest priority or a "Low" category. When the score falls between intermediate thresholds T_{h-1} and T_h, the alternative is assigned to Class h, which could correspond to a "Medium" priority level. If the score exceeds or equals the upper threshold T_h, the alternative is placed in Class $h + 1$, indicating the highest priority or a "High" category. This tiered classification framework allows for flexible, multi-level categorization, ensuring that decisions reflect varying levels of importance across the alternatives.

$$Class(A_i) = \begin{cases} 1 if FS(A_i) \leq T_1 \\ h if T_{h-1} \leq FS(A_i) < T_h \\ h + 1 if FS(A_i) \geq T_h \end{cases} \tag{23}$$

Step 11. Monte Carlo simulation.

In the FAHP-ANN model, Monte Carlo simulation is employed to evaluate the robustness and reliability of the outcomes by introducing randomness into the input weights. The simulation perturbs the original weights w_{ij} by adding a random disturbance $\in$, represented as $w_{ij}+ \in$, where $\in$ follows a normal distribution $N\left(0, \sigma^2\right)$. This means the disturbance has a mean of 0 and a variance of σ^2, allowing for small, normally distributed fluctuations around the original weights. By simulating various scenarios through multiple iterations, each with different random variations, the model assesses how sensitive the results are to these changes. This process provides valuable insights into the stability of the decisions, identifying whether minor changes in input data or weights could significantly impact the outcomes. Monte Carlo simulation thus ensures that the final decisions are robust and reliable, accounting for uncertainty and variability in the decision-making process.

$$\dot{w}_{ij} = w_{ij}+ \in, \quad \in\sim N\left(0, \sigma^2\right) \tag{24}$$

Step 12. Sensitivity analysis.

Sensitivity analysis is conducted to evaluate how variations in the weights of criteria influence the final outcomes. The adjusted weight for a criterion j is calculated using the formula in Eq. 25, where w_j is the original weight, δ is a small perturbation factor introduced to simulate a change, and the denominator ensures that the sum of the adjusted weight remains normalized. This process systematically modifies the weights to determine the impact of individual criteria on the overall results. If small changes in a criterion's weight result in significant shifts in the outcomes, that criterion is identified as highly influential, indicating the need for precise evaluation. Conversely, if the outcomes remain stable, the model is considered robust. Sensitivity analysis provides crucial insights for decision-makers, highlighting the most critical criteria and ensuring that the model delivers reliable and well-informed recommendations.

$$\dot{w}_{ij} = \frac{w_j \cdot (1 + \delta)}{\sum_{k=1}^{m} w_k \cdot (1 + \delta)} \tag{27}$$

4 Result and Analysis

This section shows results of FAHP-ANN conceptual model based on its performance, Monte Carlo simulation, and sensitivity analysis.

4.1 Performance Comparison

The FAHP-ANN model achieved a better performance score (0.00122) compared to the ANN model's 0.00176. This difference suggests that the FAHP-ANN model, which integrates fuzzy logic into neural networks, is more capable of capturing the complexity and ambiguity present in the input data. The fuzzy weights in FAHP address the inherent uncertainty of human decision-making by assigning degrees of membership to criteria. This additional layer of information allows the FAHP-ANN model to make more refined decisions. On the other hand, the ANN model processes data more straightforwardly, focusing purely on numerical patterns. While ANN offers the advantage of fast computation, it lacks the flexibility to handle ambiguous or uncertain inputs, which could negatively impact performance in cases where subjective judgments are crucial. Thus, FAHP-ANN provides a more nuanced approach but with increased computational demands (Table 3).

Table 3. Comparison between FAHP-ANN and ANN

	FAHP-ANN MODEL	ANN MODEL
Best Threshold	0.5	0.5
Best Performance	0.00122	0.00176

4.2 Net Flow Score and Stability

NFS is a measure used to determine how much better or worse an alternative performs compared to all other alternatives in the dataset. It is calculated as the difference between how much an alternative is preferred over others (positive flow) and how much others are preferred over it (negative flow). A higher positive NFS indicates that an alternative consistently outperforms others across the evaluation criteria. Conversely, a negative NFS suggests that the alternative is generally less preferred. A balanced NFS neither highly positive nor negative and indicates that the alternative performs moderately relative to others, suggesting stability and less sensitivity to outliers or inconsistencies in data. This score helps in ranking the alternatives effectively and understanding their relative standing in a multi-criteria decision environment [15]. Also, NFS offer insights into the relative performance of alternatives across both models. In the FAHP-ANN model, the scores are more balanced, with examples like 0.03288 for Alternative 3 and 0.03231 for Alternative 1. These values indicate that the model can effectively differentiate between alternatives without producing extreme values. The incorporation of fuzzy weights smoothens the evaluation process, ensuring that small variations in input data do not lead to disproportionate changes in the output.

In comparison, the ANN model shows greater variability, with a higher net flow score for Alternative 2 (0.0497) but a significantly negative score for Alternative 4 (−0.0667). This spread suggests that the ANN model can be less stable in ranking alternatives. While it identifies clear winners and losers, its results may be more volatile, potentially leading to inconsistent outcomes in different datasets. Therefore, while ANN offers quick and direct results, FAHP-ANN demonstrates greater consistency and reliability, especially for applications where small changes in inputs should not drastically affect the rankings (Tables 4 and 5).

Table 4. Monte Carlo Simulation ANN Model

	Rank 1 (%)	Rank 2 (%)	Rank 3 (%)	Rank 4 (%)
Alternative 1	15.9	66.2	17.7	0.2
Alternative 2	36.3	23.6	38.8	1.3
Alternative 3	41.3	10.0	38.6	10.1
Alternative 4	6.5	0.2	4.9	88.4

Table 5. Monte Carlo Simulation FAHP-ANN Model

	Rank 1 (%)	Rank 2 (%)	Rank 3 (%)	Rank 4 (%)
Alternative 1	44.7	7.5	46.0	1.8
Alternative 2	39.1	19.4	35.6	5.9
Alternative 3	12.8	48.9	14.8	23.5
Alternative 4	3.4	24.2	3.6	68.8

4.3 Sensitivity Analysis and Robustness of Model

The sensitivity analysis confirms the robustness of both models, as neither showed any changes in the ranking order despite small perturbations in the input data. This robustness makes both models suitable for real-world decision-making, where slight variations in data inputs are inevitable. However, FAHP-ANN's robustness stems from its ability to account for human fuzziness and ambiguity, which allows it to maintain stability even in subjective evaluations. This makes it more reliable in environments where expert judgments play a significant role.

The ANN model also demonstrated robustness, but its lack of interpretability can be a drawback. While it can efficiently process large datasets, its "black-box" nature makes it challenging to understand how changes in input affect the final ranking. This could limit its use in situations where decision-makers need to justify the model's recommendations or explain its behavior.

4.4 Computational Efficiency and Scalability

The integration of FAHP into the ANN model introduces an additional computational layer aimed at improving interpretability and capturing human ambiguity. However, this enhancement comes with a trade-off in terms of computational time. FAHP-ANN model required 1 min and 3 s to complete processing, whereas the ANN model completed the same task in 43 s. This represents an approximate 46.5% increase in computation time.

The added overhead primarily stems from the FAHP module, which includes the construction of fuzzy pairwise comparison matrices, defuzzification of TFNs, and the aggregation of expert weights using geometric means. These operations, though computationally lightweight at small scales, become more time-consuming as the number of criteria or expert matrices increases. Despite this, the FAHP-ANN model remains computationally feasible for real-world applications.

5 Conclusion and Recommendations

This study has proposed and validated an integrated FAHP-ANN model to enhance the robustness of spatial MCDA under conditions of data ambiguity and human subjectivity. By incorporating fuzzy logic through FAHP and computational learning through ANN, the hybrid model demonstrates superior capability in handling complex decision environments compared to standalone methods. The model effectively accommodates subjective expert judgments using triangular fuzzy numbers while capitalizing on the ANN's strength in learning from data-driven patterns, thus bridging the gap between qualitative and quantitative assessments. Performance comparison with a baseline ANN model reveals that the FAHP-ANN model yields improved accuracy and stability, particularly evident through reduced performance error (0.00122 vs. 0.00176), more balanced net flow scores, and higher confidence in Monte Carlo simulations. Furthermore, the model's sensitivity analysis confirms its robustness, maintaining consistent outcomes despite variations in weight assignments.

The inclusion of threshold-based classification and probabilistic simulations has made the model more interpretable and adaptable, fulfilling the increasing demand for explainable AI in decision support systems. This outcome is consistent with prior research on Choquet-integrated neural networks [16] and IVIF fuzzy decision environments [17], which emphasize the value of incorporating domain expertise through weighted criteria and preserving model transparency.

While the proposed FAHP-ANN model has demonstrated strong performance and robustness in a controlled environment, future work should focus on validating the model in practical decision-making contexts. Example applications include location analysis for e-scooter shared stations [18], or measuring urban quality of life [19]. These real-world implementations would help assess the model's generalizability, operational efficiency, and policy relevance, especially when integrated with local spatial datasets and stakeholder input.

Lastly, integrating a real-time feedback mechanism from decision-makers may further refine the model's adaptability to evolving criteria preferences, ensuring that both data and human perspectives are continuously represented in spatial decision-making processes.

Acknowledgement. The authors would like to thank Universiti Teknologi MARA for supporting this study.

References

1. Linkov, I., Galaitsi, S., Trump, B.D., Keisler, J.M., Kott, A.: Cybertrust: from explainable to actionable and interpretable artificial intelligence. Computer **53**(9), 91–96 (2020). https://doi.org/10.1109/MC.2020.2993623

2. Saaty, T.L.: Highlights and critical points in the theory and application of the analytic hierarchy process. Eur. J. Oper. Res. **74**(3), 426–447 (1994)
3. Mousseau, V., Figueira, J., Dias, L., da Silva, C.G., Clímaco, J.: Resolving inconsistencies among constraints on the parameters of an MCDA model. Eur. J. Oper. Res. **147**(1), 72–93 (2003)
4. Dave, V.S., Dutta, K.: Neural network based models for software effort estimation: a review. Artif. Intell. Rev. **42**(2), 295–307 (2014)
5. Martyn, K., Kadziński, M.: Deep preference learning for multiple criteria decision analysis. Eur. J. Oper. Res. **305**(2), 781–805 (2023)
6. Liu, J., Liao, X., Kadziński, M., Słowiński, R.: Preference disaggregation within the regularization framework for sorting problems with multiple potentially non-monotonic criteria. Eur. J. Oper. Res. **276**(3), 1071–1089 (2019)
7. Smolensky, P.: Information processing in dynamical systems: foundations of harmony theory. In: Parallel Distributed Processing: Explorations in the Microstructure of Cognition (Vol. 1: Foundations). Cambridge, MA: MIT Press, pp. 194–281 (1986)
8. Liu, Y., Eckert, C.M., Earl, C.: A review of fuzzy AHP methods for decision-making with subjective judgements. Expert Syst. Appl. **161**, 113738 (2020)
9. Barzilai, J., Lootsma, F.A.: Power relations and group aggregation in the multiplicative AHP and SMART. J. Multi-Criteria Decis. Anal. **6**(3), 155–165 (1997)
10. Rao Tummala, V.M., Ling, H.: A note on the computation of the mean random consistency index of the analytic hierarchy process (AHP). Theor. Decis. **44**, 221–230 (1998)
11. Dongare, A.D., Kharde, R.R., Kachare, A.D.: Introduction to artificial neural network. Int. J. Eng. Innovative Technol. (IJEIT) **2**(1), 189–194 (2012)
12. Shanmuganathan, S.: Artificial neural network modelling: an introduction (pp. 1–14). Springer International Publishing (2016)
13. Agatonovic-Kustrin, S., Beresford, R.: Basic concepts of artificial neural network (ANN) modeling and its application in pharmaceutical research. J. Pharm. Biomed. Anal. **22**(5), 717–727 (2000)
14. Mohebbi, A., Baron, L., Achiche, S., Birglen, L.: Neural network-based decision support for conceptual design of a mechatronic system using mechatronic multi-criteria profile (MMP). In: Proceedings of the 2014 International Conference on Innovative Design and Manufacturing (ICIDM) (pp. 105–110). IEEE (2014)
15. Yongbiao, L., Jun, Y., Xiaowen, M.: Multicriteria fuzzy decision-making method based on weighted correlation coefficients under interval-valued intuitionistic fuzzy environment. In: 2009 IEEE 10th International Conference on Computer-Aided Industrial Design & Conceptual Design (pp. 2057–2060). IEEE (2009)
16. Wasserman, N.H., Casey, S., Champion, J., Huey, M.: Statistics as unbiased estimators: exploring the teaching of standard deviation. Res. Math. Educ. **19**(3), 236–256 (2017)
17. Behzadian, M., Kazemzadeh, R.B., Albadvi, A., Aghdasi, M.: PROMETHEE: a comprehensive literature review on methodologies and applications. Eur. J. Oper. Res. **200**(1), 198–215 (2010)
18. Roslan, A., Naharudin, N.: Identification of e-Scooter Shared (ESS) stations by using a GIS-based MCDM approach. Int. J. Geoinform. **19**(5), 69–78 (2023)
19. Salavati, S.M., Janalipour, M., Abbaszadeh Tehrani, N.: Measuring urban quality of life through spatial analytics and machine learning: a data-driven framework for sustainable urban planning and development. Sustainability **17**(11), 4863 (2025)

Unpaired Shadow Removal with a Skip-Connected Generator in CycleGAN Framework

Hui Liu, Cheng Zhang, and Kin Sam Yen(✉)

Universiti Sains Malaysia, School of Mechanical Engineering, Engineering Campus, 14300 Nibong Tebal, Penang, Malaysia
meyks@usm.my

Abstract. This paper proposes an unpaired shadow removal method based on the CycleGAN framework, in which the generator is structurally enhanced by introducing skip connections. Existing CycleGAN-based methods commonly rely on plain encoder-decoder generators originally tailored for style transfer, which often fail to preserve pixel-level spatial alignment and low-level structural details. This limitation leads to incomplete shadow removal, texture degradation, and inconsistent illumination in the restored images. To overcome these issues, the proposed generator introduces skip connections that inject low-level features directly from the encoder to the decoder. This architectural design helps preserve structural integrity and improve visual coherence across the entire image. By leveraging both global and local information, the network achieves a more accurate reconstruction of shadow-free images. The method is evaluated on the public ISTD dataset. Quantitative results show that it consistently outperforms existing unpaired models including CycG, Mask-CycG, and DC-CycG, measured by root mean square error (RMSE), peak signal-to-noise ratio (PSNR), and structural similarity index (SSIM). Visual comparisons further confirm fewer artifacts, more complete shadow removal, and more consistent illumination in the restored regions. Feature map analysis further confirms that the skip-connected architecture captures richer and more diverse semantic features, facilitating better decoding. These findings highlight the practical and theoretical value of enhancing CycleGAN-based generator with skip connections, offering an effective solution for high-quality unpaired shadow removal.

Keywords: unpaired shadow removal · skip connection · generator · CycleGAN

1 Introduction

Shadows are cast when an object obstructs the path of light from a source to a surface, resulting in visible darkened regions [1]. Shadows are a natural occurrence in images, but their presence can adversely affect the performance of various vision-based algorithms. This challenge is particularly prominent in fields such as surveillance [2], medical imaging [3], autonomous driving [4], and traffic analysis [5]. To address this, a wide range of approaches have been explored to remove shadows from images and improve visual consistency for downstream tasks [6].

M. Kassim et al. (Eds.): SCDS 2025, CCIS 2674, pp. 412–424, 2026.
https://doi.org/10.1007/978-981-95-8368-3_29

Early physics-based models [7] were generally deduced from the image formation process. These methods estimated shadow-related properties by computing illumination and color statistics from model parameters. However, their effectiveness declined when applied to real-world scenarios involving complex lighting and scene variations. To overcome such limitations, machine learning techniques such as support vector machines (SVM) [8] and k-nearest neighbors (KNN) [9] were later adopted. These models leveraged manually crafted features, including intensity, color distributions, textures, and edge gradients, to detect and remove shadows. Nevertheless, these handcrafted features often required domain expertise and lacked the ability to represent high-level semantic patterns inherent to shadows.

With the advancement of deep learning, numerous computer vision tasks, including shadow removal, have witnessed substantial progress [10]. Shadow removal techniques are typically divided into paired and unpaired learning according to the presence or absence of paired ground truth data. Paired approaches rely on supervised learning using aligned image pairs, where each shadow image is matched with its corresponding shadow-free ground truth. Representative methods include ShadowFormer [11], ST-CGAN [12], and SP + M [13]. These models benefit from explicit supervision and have demonstrated strong performance. Despite their success, paired shadow removal methods face notable challenges. Acquiring aligned shadow and shadow-free image pairs is costly and time-consuming, often requiring repeated captures of the same scene under controlled conditions. Moreover, the diversity of existing datasets is limited, as it is challenging to obtain shadow-free counterparts for scenes with shadows cast by trees or buildings. Finally, models trained with paired data often exhibit limited generalization when applied to unseen scenarios.

To reduce the dependency on paired data, unpaired shadow removal has gained increasing attention. Recent methods such as CycG [14], Mask-CycG [15], and DC-CycG [16] treat shadow removal as an image-to-image translation task. The CycG model adopts a standard CycleGAN framework which employs a basic encoder–decoder generator for domain-level appearance translation. However, this structure struggles to model the complex, non-bijective mapping between shadow and shadow-free domains, often resulting in incomplete restoration. DC-CycG improves upon CycleGAN by incorporating semantic and physical priors, using a pre-trained VGG-16 network for perceptual alignment and chromaticity-based loss for illumination consistency. While effective, these additions increase computational cost and complicate the training process, limiting scalability in real-world applications. In contrast, Mask-CycG adopts a simpler design by learning binary masks as structural priors without requiring external supervision. These masks guide both shadow generation and removal, offering a lightweight and deployable framework. However, its generator still relies on a plain encoder–decoder structure, which lacks skip connections and therefore struggles to preserve spatial alignment and fine-grained textures. Without skip connections, successive downsampling layers in the encoder often lead to the loss of low-level spatial features such as edges and textures. Moreover, the decoder receives only abstract high-level representations, creating a semantic gap that limits its ability to accurately reconstruct fine structures. This design also suffers from limited gradient flow between encoder and decoder stages, which may hinder effective training. As a result, restored images frequently exhibit blurred boundaries, inconsistent textures, and misaligned illumination, particularly in structurally complex regions.

To overcome the structural limitations of standard encoder-decoder generators in unpaired shadow removal, this work redesigns the CycleGAN generator by introducing skip connections between corresponding encoder and decoder stages, forming a more spatially consistent and feature-preserving architecture. The plain encoder–decoder structure used in previous models often fails to preserve spatial alignment and fine structural details, leading to artifacts and incomplete restoration. In contrast, the proposed design not only enables effective feature fusion between encoder and decoder, but also provide direct pathways for low-level information flow, helping preserve textures, boundaries, and contextual details throughout the generation process.

This skip-connected generator is integrated into the standard CycleGAN-based framework, which remains fully unpaired and end-to-end trainable. Unlike prior extensions that rely on pretrained networks or complex multi-stage pipelines, the proposed method maintains architectural simplicity while significantly enhancing restoration quality. It effectively addresses the challenge of structural misalignment and detail loss without requiring external supervision. Extensive experiments on the ISTD dataset demonstrate that the proposed model achieves consistent improvements over existing unpaired methods in terms of PSNR, SSIM, and RMSE. Visual comparisons further confirm its ability to reduce artifacts, restore edge details, and produce spatially coherent shadow-free images under diverse scenarios.

The remainder of this paper is organized as follows. Section 2 reviews related work on CycleGAN-based shadow removal network and its extensions. Section 3 introduces the proposed methodology, including the architecture design and loss formulation. Section 4 presents experimental results and comparative analyses. Section 5 concludes the study and discusses possible directions for future research.

2 Related Work

In shadow removal, CycleGAN-based frameworks commonly utilize a generator network as the core component for translating shadowed images into its corresponding shadow-free counterparts. This generator is required not only to alter illumination and appearance but also preserve spatial structures and fine-grained visual details, including object boundaries, textures, and shading transitions. Therefore, the architectural design of the generator plays an important role in determining the overall restoration performance.

Early unpaired shadow removal methods, such as Mask-CycG and DC-CycG, adopted plain encoder-decoder structures to learn the domain translation between shadow and shadow-free images. In Mask-CycG, the generator network follows the standard CycleGAN design, while an auxiliary mask is introduced to estimate a binary shadow map that guides the shadow removal process. These self-learned masks act as structural priors, enabling the network to focus on shadow regions without requiring ground-truth annotations. However, due to the lack of skip connections, the generator struggles to maintain spatial alignment between input and output, especially during the hierarchical transformation from shallow to deep features. This often results in blurred textures and inaccurate boundary recovery.

On the other hand, DC-CycG enhances the standard CycleGAN by integrating semantic and physical priors into the generator. Specifically, it employs a pre-trained VGG-16 network to compute perceptual losses that help the model preserve semantic consistency and introduces chromaticity-based loss terms derived from physical shadow properties to regulate illumination variations. While these additions offer effective regularization, they also introduce substantial computational overhead and reliance on external modules, making the framework less flexible for practical deployment.

Moreover, skip connections have been widely adopted in both paired and unpaired shadow removal models due to their superior ability to preserve spatial information throughout the generation process [17]. Their most representative implementation is found in the U-Net architecture, where encoder and decoder layers are directly bridged to facilitate multi-scale feature fusion. These connections allow low-level features, including edges, textures, and structural boundaries, to be retained and reused during reconstruction, effectively mitigating the loss of fine details caused by deep encoding. This design is particularly beneficial in shadow removal, where spatial alignment and fine-grained texture recovery are essential for accurate restoration.

According to a recent survey on single-image shadow removal [18], approximately 69% of deep learning-based methods incorporate skip connections, underscoring their effectiveness in this domain. For instance, ST-CGAN [12] adopts a two-stage cascaded architecture, where the first generator detects shadow regions and the second generator performs shadow removal, both benefiting from spatially preserved feature representations enabled by skip-connected structures. Similarly, the SP + M [13] and SP + M + D [19] models utilize skip-connection-based network to predict shadow matte maps, which represent per-pixel shadow intensity and serve as intermediate supervision for learning accurate removal mappings. These models demonstrate that incorporating multi-scale feature extraction and spatial feature fusion significantly improves the model's capacity to resolve complex shadow boundaries and achieve high-quality restoration. These developments reveal that while plain encoder–decoder architectures are insufficient for spatially consistent restoration, skip-connected designs provide a structurally robust alternative that enhances both perceptual quality and restoration accuracy in unpaired shadow removal tasks.

3 Methodology

This work builds upon the CycleGAN paradigm [14] and introduces a mask-guided dual-cycle translation strategy [15] for unpaired shadow removal, as illustrated in Fig. 1. The framework consists of two translation cycles, namely Shadow-to-Shadow-Free and Shadow-Free-to-Shadow, corresponding to Fig. 1(a) and 1(b), respectively. To mitigate the need for one-to-one mapping, self-learned shadow masks, denoted as M_l and M_r, are introduced in two cycles to provide structural guidance during translation. They can help the generators distinguish shadowed and non-shadowed regions, thereby enhancing translation quality in the absence of paired data.

In the Shadow-to-Shadow-Free cycle, the generator G_{sf} removes shadows from a real shadow image I_s, generating a shadow-free output $\widetilde{I_f}$. This image is then passed through the generator G_{fs} to reconstruct a shadow image $\widetilde{I_s}$, which is enforced to match the

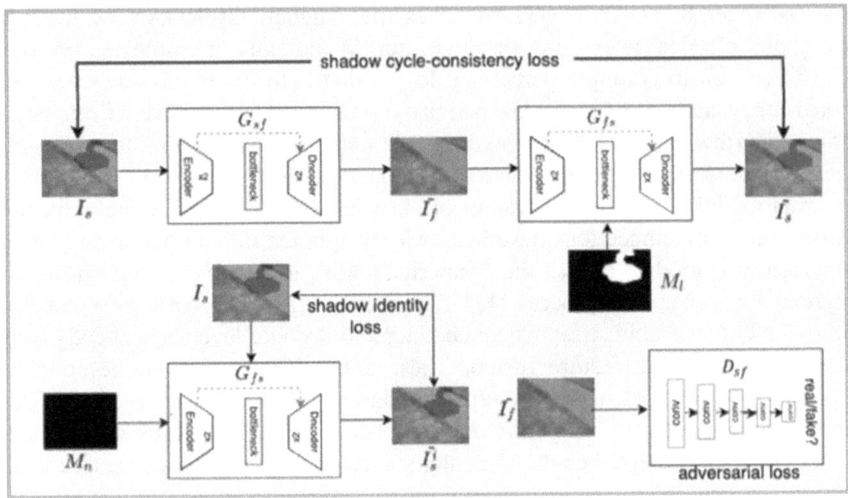

(a) Shadow-to-Shadow-Free Cycle

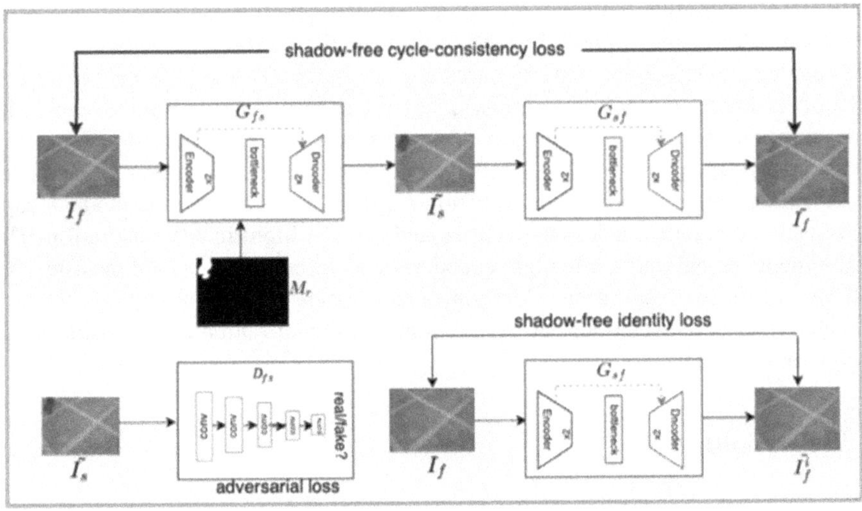

(b) Shadow-Free-to-Shadow Cycle

Fig. 1. Overall architecture of the proposed model.

original I_s through a cycle-consistency loss. Conversely, in the Shadow-Free-to-Shadow cycle, the generator G_{fs} first synthesizes a shadow image $\widetilde{I_s}$ from a real shadow-free input I_f, and the generator G_{sf} subsequently reconstructs it back to $\widetilde{I_f}$, aiming to align with thc original I_f.

To further enhance the fidelity and domain consistency of generated images, adversarial learning is incorporated. Two discriminators D_{sf} and D_{fs} are employed to distinguish real images from generated outputs in the shadow-free and shadow domains, respectively. The adversarial learning objective encourages the generators to produce visually realistic, domain-consistent outputs.

Furthermore, identity losses are introduced to maintain consistency across domains. In the shadow domain, an all-zero mask is applied to preserve color fidelity, while in the shadow-free domain, the identity constraint ensures that input images remain visually unchanged.

In summary, the overall training objective is formulated as a weighted combination of adversarial loss, cycle-consistency loss, and identity loss, defined as [15]:

$$L_{total} = \lambda_{adv} L_{adv} + \lambda_{cyc} L_{cyc} + \lambda_{id} L_{id} \tag{1}$$

where L_{adv} is the adversarial loss computed from the discriminators, L_{cyc} enforces reconstruction consistency between original and cycle-reconstructed images, and L_{id} preserves the appearance of images that are already in each domain. λ_{cyc}, λ_{adv}, λ_{id} are hyperparameters that balance the contribution of each loss term.

To improve spatial detail preservation and alleviate the over-smoothing effects observed in plain encoder–decoder generators, the proposed model incorporates skip connections within the generator to enable direct feature transfer via feature concatenation at corresponding encoder–decoder stages. Formally, the fused feature at each decoder stage is computed as:

$$F_{dec}^{(i)} = \phi\left(\left(F_{dec}^{(i+1)}, F_{enc}^{(i)}\right)\right) \tag{2}$$

where $F_{enc}^{(i)}$ and $F_{dec}^{(i+1)}$ denote the feature maps from the encoder and decoder, respectively, and $\Phi(\cdot)$ represents a composite function of convolution, normalization, and activation. This design allows the network to retain low-level spatial information while incorporating high-level semantics, resulting in improved texture restoration and more accurate shadow removal.

Building upon this design, the overall generator architecture is structured as follows. The generator adopts a symmetric encoder–decoder structure with three encoding and three decoding stages. Each encoding block consists of a 3 × 3 convolution layer, followed by Instance Normalization and ReLU activation. The number of feature channels doubles progressively from 64 to 256. The bottleneck consists of nine residual blocks designed to capture global context and enhance semantic representation. The decoder mirrors the encoder structure in reverse order, performing upsampling using transposed convolution, also followed by normalization and activation. Skip connections are implemented by concatenating feature maps between corresponding encoder and decoder layers. This architectural design ensures a balance between high-level semantic understanding and low-level detail preservation, leading to improved shadow removal performance and greater visual consistency in the restored outputs.

4 Experiment and Results

This section presents both quantitative comparisons with existing methods and qualitative analysis to demonstrate the advantages of the proposed approach in unpaired shadow removal.

4.1 Experiment and Evaluation

To validate the effectiveness of the proposed model, extensive experiments are conducted on the ISTD dataset [12]. ISTD contains paired shadow and shadow-free images along with pixel level annotations for shadow masks, making it suitable for shadow removal evaluation.

The proposed method is compared with several representative unpaired models, including the original CycG, Mask-CycG, and DC-CycG. The evaluation is based on three widely used metrics [20]: Root Mean Square Error (RMSE), Peak Signal-to-Noise Ratio (PSNR), and Structural Similarity Index (SSIM). Specifically, RMSE is computed in the Lab color space by comparing the predicted shadow-free image to the ground truth, while PSNR and SSIM are measured in the RGB color space. Higher values of PSNR and SSIM indicate better restoration quality. Each metric is reported over the entire image, the shadow regions, and the non-shadow regions, respectively.

To ensure fair comparison, all models are trained and tested under the same experimental conditions. The experiments are conducted using PyTorch on a single NVIDIA RTX A4000 GPU with 16 GB memory.

The parameters of all generators and discriminators are initialized from a zero-mean Gaussian distribution with a standard deviation of 0.02. The Adam optimizer is employed with $\beta 1 = 0.5$ and $\beta 2 = 0.999$. The learning rate is initially set to 2×10^{-4} and linearly decayed to zero after the first 100 epochs, with training stopping at 200 epochs. The model is trained with a mini-batch size of 1, using random cropping and horizontal flipping for data augmentation.

4.2 Experimental Results

As shown in Table 1, the proposed method consistently outperforms all baseline models across multiple evaluation metrics, including PSNR, SSIM, and RMSE, evaluated over full images, shadow regions, and non-shadow regions.

Table 1 presents a comprehensive comparison between the proposed skip-connected CycleGAN and three representative unpaired models on the ISTD benchmark. Across the full image configuration, the proposed skip-connected generator delivers the strongest overall restoration, reaching 25.62 dB in PSNR and 0.9418 in SSIM, while lowering RMSE to 7.17. Relative to the original CycG, these scores correspond to gains of 2.23 dB in PSNR, 0.0147 in SSIM, and a 1.91 reduction in RMSE. These results represent relative improvements of around 9.5% in PSNR, 1.6% in SSIM, and 21% in RMSE, demonstrating substantial gains in both visual fidelity and perceptual accuracy.

Against the more advanced DC-CycG, the proposed network still secures small yet consistent advantages, raising PSNR by 0.11 dB, increasing SSIM by 0.0009, and reducing RMSE by 0.05. While these gains may appear incremental in absolute terms, they

Table 1. Comparison with the state-of-the-art unpaired learning models on the ISTD dataset.

Merics		CycG	Mask-CycG	DC-CycG	Proposed
PSNR	Full Image	23.3894	23.3962	25.5076	25.6201
	Shadow	29.5688	29.5715	31.1744	31.3585
	Non-Shadow	25.3850	25.3932	27.9137	27.9137
SSIM	Full Image	0.9271	0.9283	0.9409	0.9418
	Shadow	0.9808	0.9815	0.9835	0.9839
	Non-Shadow	0.9507	0.9514	0.9612	0.9625
RMSE	Full Image	9.0812	9.0680	7.2206	7.1745
	Shadow	14.3129	14.3137	12.1865	12.3768
	Non-Shadow	8.3495	8.3660	6.4929	6.4288

are achieved without relying on any pretrained feature extractors, perceptual losses, or chromaticity-based constraints. In contrast to DC-CycG, which incorporates additional networks and handcrafted priors, the proposed model retains a lightweight, end-to-end design. This balance of simplicity and effectiveness enhances its practicality for scalable deployment and real-world applications.

Shadow correction in strongly corupted regions is crucial, as both incomplete shadow removal and over-brightening can severely impact perceptual quality. The proposed model achieves 31.36 dB in PSNR and 0.9839 in SSIM for shadow regions, outperforming others by at least 1.79 dB and 0.0024, respectively. Although DC-CycG records a slightly lower RMSE of 12.19, its inferior PSNR and SSIM indicate inadequate structural recovery despite marginal improvements in color consistency. This outcome highlights the benefit of skip connections in delivering robust low-level guidance, enabling the decoder to restore texture while maintaining global illumination balance.

Minimal modification in non-shadow regions is also critical to avoid artifacts or color change. The proposed method scores 27.91 dB in PSNR, 0.9625 in SSIM, and 6.43 in RMSE, matching or exceeding DC-CycG across all three metrics. While incremental, the gains of 0.0013 in SSIM and 0.06 in RMSE demonstrate that the skip-connected architecture better preserves structural integrity and color consistency in unaffected areas.

The results in Table 1 confirm that the proposed generator achieves superior performance across all regions and metrics. It not only provides substantial improvements over the CycG model and Mask-CycG models, but also consistently outperforms the more advanced DC-CycG in both shadow and non-shadow areas. The model delivers higher PSNR and SSIM with lower RMSE, indicating more accurate shadow removal, better structural preservation, and improved color consistency.

Figure 2 presents visual comparisons across three challenging scenes, namely grass-stone, tile-pavement, and carton-face. These examples are selected to reflect different challenges in shadow removal, such as texture recovery, brightness consistency, and

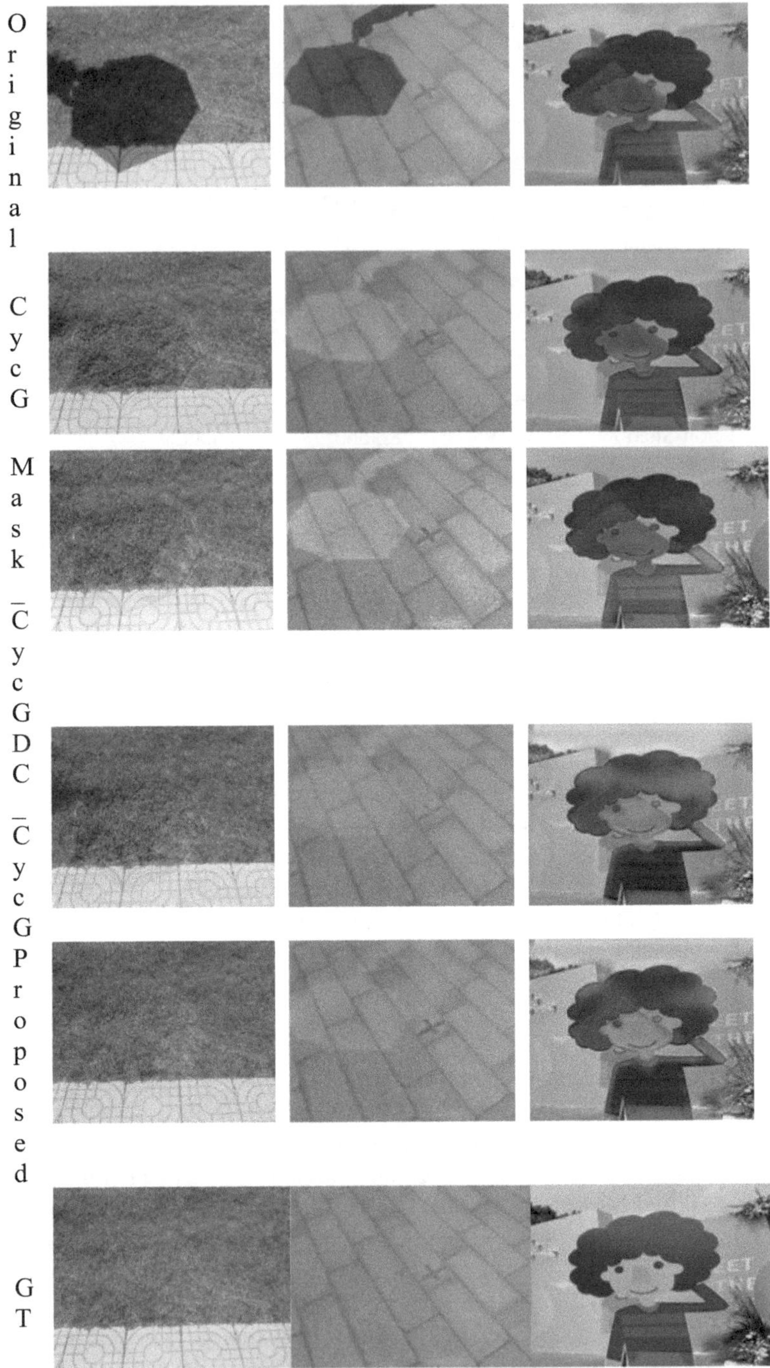

Fig. 2. Shadow removal results of CycG, Mask-CycG, DC-CycG, and the proposed method on ISTD.

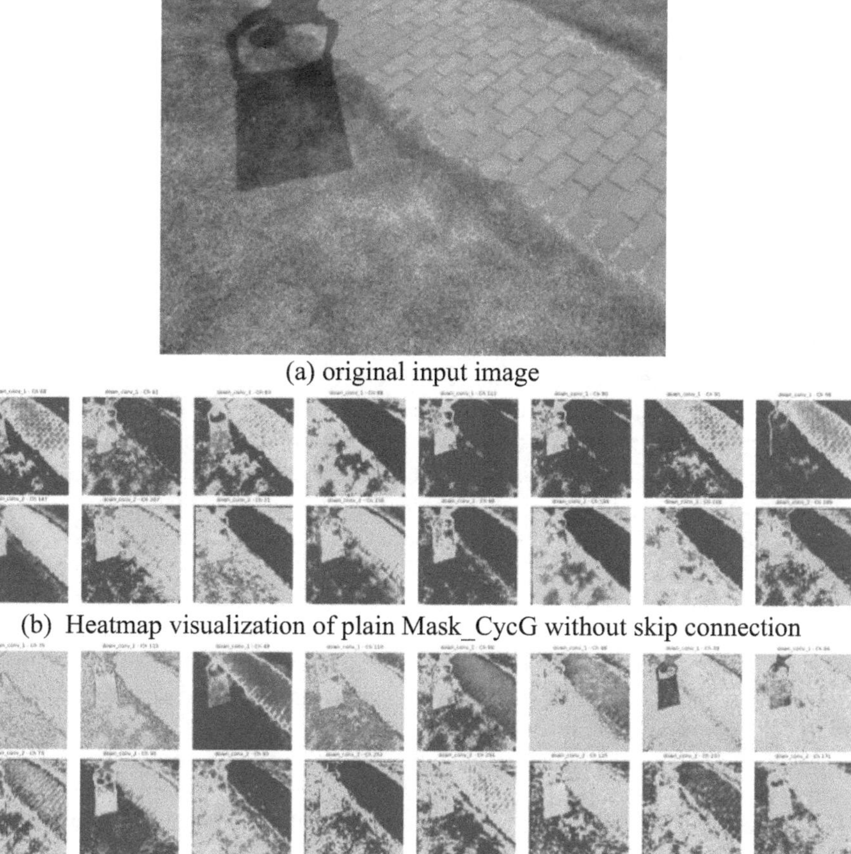

(a) original input image

(b) Heatmap visualization of plain Mask_CycG without skip connection

(c) Heatmap visualization of the proposed model with skip connection

Fig. 3. Heatmap visualization comparison between the proposed model and the Mask_CycG.

semantic integrity. Four unpaired methods, CycG, Mask-CycG, DC-CycG, and the proposed approach, are evaluated to demonstrate the qualitative differences in restoration quality under varying structural and contextual conditions.

In the grass-stone scene (first column), the rich texture and tonal variation of the grass present a significant challenge for shadow removal. While all compared methods reduce the cast shadow to some degree, CycG and DC-CycG leave behind noticeable residual shading and boundary artifacts, particularly within the high-frequency grass region. These models struggle to reconstruct the fine-grained texture, resulting in uneven transitions. Mask-CycG offers moderate improvement but still exhibits tone inconsistency between the shadowed and non-shadowed areas. In contrast, the proposed method achieves near-invisible shadow removal, with more accurate recovery of grass details and consistent tonal blending across both grassy and paved surfaces.

The tile-pavement example (2nd column) involves a flat surface with repetitive textures and simple tonal variation, making it seemingly easier for shadow removal. However, most models fail to maintain visual realism. Both CycG and Mask-CycG introduce over-brightening in the corrected shadow region, resulting in an unnatural appearance that breaks the continuity of tile patterns. The abrupt illumination shift across the shadow boundary makes the correction look artificial. Although DC-CycG alleviates this issue to some degree, subtle tone discrepancies still remain. In contrast, the proposed model restores the tile surface with smooth transitions and consistent color, producing a more visually coherent and natural result.

In the cartoon-face scene (3rd column), the image contains distinct color regions with clear semantic meaning, such as the character's face, eyes, and clothing. This makes shadow removal especially challenging, as even small inconsistencies can noticeably disrupt the visual coherence. CycG and Mask-CycG only achieve partial removal, leaving visible shadow traces around the character's face and neck. Moreover, both methods unintentionally brighten the shirt area, altering its original color and breaking visual consistency. DC-CycG reduces shadows more effectively but still introduces mild edge artifacts. In contrast, the proposed method successfully removes shadows while preserving both color fidelity and semantic boundaries, resulting in a more visually coherent outcome.

To further understand the impact of skip connections on feature representation, the top-8 most activated channels from two encoder layers are visualized for both models. As illustrated in Fig. 3, the encoder in the model with skip connections (Fig. 3(c)) exhibits significantly richer and more diverse activation patterns compared to the bascline model without skip connections (Fig. 3(b)).

In particular, the skip-connected encoder captures more fine-grained structures and textures, especially in challenging regions such as grass and patterned pavement. For instance, the activation maps in the first column of both the first and second rows show strong responses to high-frequency details in grassy areas and the edges of stone tiles, which are largely absent or overly smoothed in the corresponding channels of the baseline model in Fig. 3(b). These results suggest that the skip connections enhance the model's ability to preserve local spatial information during encoding.

Furthermore, the skip-connected encoder also demonstrates a better understanding of global illumination cues. As shown in the last two columns of the first row in Fig. 3(c), several channels respond broadly to brightness variations in the input image. These channels are highly activated in illuminated regions like open grass or stone tiles, while exhibiting much weaker responses in shadowed areas. This behavior implies that the encoder implicitly models global brightness distributions, providing useful cues for subsequent shadow localization and removal.

In terms of efficiency, the proposed model features a lightweight architecture that does not rely on pretrained encoders or complex multi-stage designs. Deployed on a workstation equipped with two NVIDIA RTX A4000 GPUs (each with 8 GB of memory), it achieves an average inference time of 0.0075 s per 640×480 image excluding preprocessing and I/O operations. This corresponds to approximately 133 FPS on a single GPU without parallelization. With a total model size of only 11.75 MB, the approach demonstrates high computational efficiency and strong potential for real-world deployment.

These results collectively validate the effectiveness of the proposed skip-connected generator from multiple perspectives. Quantitative comparisons confirm consistent performance gains across full, shadow, and non-shadow regions. Qualitative evaluations reveal improved shadow removal quality, better texture preservation, and reduced artifacts. Feature visualizations further demonstrate that skip connections enrich encoder representations with both structural detail and global illumination. Together, these findings support the conclusion that incorporating skip connections strengthens feature propagation throughout the network, enabling more accurate, stable, and visually coherent shadow removal in the unpaired learning setting.

5 Conclusion

This paper presents an unpaired shadow removal method that integrates skip connections into the generator architecture of the CycleGAN framework. By enhancing the encoder with skip-connected pathways, the proposed model effectively preserves fine-grained spatial structures and improves the propagation of both low-level textures and high-level semantics throughout the network. Extensive experiments on the ISTD dataset demonstrate that the proposed model achieves superior performance compared to existing unpaired approaches, with significant improvements in PSNR, SSIM, and RMSE across both shadow and non-shadow regions. Qualitative results further confirm that the model produces cleaner and more consistent shadow-free images, especially in scenes with complex geometry or illumination variations. Despite its promising results, the current method still has some limitations. First, the model may struggle in extremely dark shadow regions or in cases involving soft shadow transitions, where implicit guidance from skip connections alone may be insufficient. Second, the reliance on cycle consistency loss and image-level supervision may limit the network's ability to capture high-level semantic context, particularly in cluttered environments. Future work will explore the integration of semantic-aware priors or self-supervised attention mechanisms to enhance the model's global understanding of scene illumination. In addition, exploring other skip connection designs such as dense connections or attention-based fusion may help improve feature propagation and spatial consistency. This offers a promising direction for future architectural improvements. Moreover, the adoption of adaptive shadow-aware losses or synthetic shadow augmentation strategies may enhance the model's robustness under complex lighting conditions. Finally, extending the framework to real-time video shadow removal or optimizing it for mobile deployment remains a promising direction for practical applications.

References

1. Sasi, R.K., Govindan, V.K.: Shadow detection and removal from real images: state of art. In: Proceedings of the Third International Symposium on Women in Computing and Informatics, pp. 309–317 (2015)

2. Vujović, I., Jurčević, M., Kuzmanić, I.: Traffic video surveillance in different weather conditions. Trans. Maritime Sci. **3**(01), 32–41 (2014)
3. Liu, H., Yen, K.S.: A review of advancements in deep learning-based shadow detection and removal in image and video analysis. Int. J. Intell. Eng. Inform. **12**(2), 135–168 (2024)
4. Naser, F., Gilitschenski, I., Rosman, G., Amini, A., Durand, F., Torralba, A., Rus, D.: Shadowcam: real-time detection of moving obstacles behind a corner for autonomous vehicles. In: IEEE International Conference on Intelligent Transportation Systems (ITSC), pp. 560–567(2018)
5. Mossi, J.M., Albiol, A., Albiol, A., Ornedo, V.N.: Real-time traffic analysis at night-time. In: Proceedings of the 18th IEEE International Conference on Image Processing (ICIP 2011), pp. 2941–2944. IEEE, Brussels (2011)
6. Wan, J., Yin, H., Wu, Z., Wu, X.: CRFormer: a cross-region transformer for shadow removal. Image Vis. Comput. **151**, 105273 (2024). https://doi.org/10.1016/j.imavis.2024.105273
7. Finlayson, G., Hordley, S., Lu, C., Drew, M.: On the removal of shadows from images. IEEE Trans. Pattern Anal. Mach. Intell. **28**(1), 59–68 (2006)
8. Huang, X., Hua, G., Tumblin, J., Williams, L.: What characterizes a shadow boundary under the sun and sky? In: Proceedings IEEE International Conference on Computer Vision (ICCV), Barcelona, Spain, pp. 898–905 (2011)
9. Fauzi, A., Utaminingrum, F., Ramdani, F.: Road surface classification based on LBP and GLCM features using KNN classifier. Proc. Bull. Electr. Eng. Inform. **9**(4), 1446–1453 (2020)
10. Lai, W.-S., Huang, J.-B., Ahuja, N., Yang, M.-H.: Deep Laplacian pyramid networks for fast and accurate super-resolution. In: Proceedings of IEEE Conference on Computer Vision and Pattern Recognition (CVPR), pp. 5835–5843 (2017)
11. Guo, L., Huang, S., Liu, D.: ShadowFormer: global context helps shadow removal. IEEE Trans. Image Process. **37**, 710–718 (2023)
12. Wang, J., Li, X., Yang, J.: Stacked conditional generative adversarial networks for jointly learning shadow detection and shadow removal. In: Proceedings of IEEE Conference on Computer Vision and Pattern Recognition (CVPR), pp. 1788–1797 (2018)
13. Le, H., Samaras, D.: Shadow removal via shadow image decomposition. In: Proceedings of IEEE International Conference on Computer Vision (ICCV), vol. 2019, pp. 8577–8586 (2019)
14. Liu, Z., Yin, H., Mi, Y., et al.: Shadow removal by a lightness-guided network with training on unpaired data. IEEE Trans. Image Process. **30**, 1863–1865 (2021)
15. Hu, X., Jiang, Y., Fu, C., Heng, A.P.: Mask-ShadowGAN: learning to remove shadows from unpaired data. In: Proceedings of IEEE International Conference on Computer Vision (ICCV), Seoul, Korea, pp. 2472–2481 (2019)
16. Jin, Y., Sharma, A., Tan, R.: DC-ShadowNet: single-image hard and soft shadow removal using unsupervised domain-classifier guided network. In: Proceedings of IEEE International Conference on Computer Vision (ICCV), Montreal, Canada, pp. 5007–5016 (2021)
17. Ronneberger, O., Fischer, P., Brox, T., Nassir, N., Hornegger, J.: U-Net: convolutional networks for biomedical image segmentation. In: Navab, N., Hornegger, J., Wells, W., Frangi, A. (eds.) Proc. Medical Image Computing and Computer-Assisted Intervention – MICCAI 2015, LNCS, vol. 9351, pp. 234–241. Springer, Cham (2015)
18. Guo, L., Wang, C., Wang, Y., Yu, Y., Huang, S., Yang, W.: Single-image Shadow Removal Using Deep Learning: a Comprehensive Survey (2024). http://arxiv.org/abs/2407.08865
19. Le, H., Samaras, D.: From shadow segmentation to shadow removal. In: Computer Vision – ECCV 2020, LNCS, vol. 12356, pp. 264–281. Springer, Cham (2020)
20. Wang, Z., Bovik, A.C., Sheikh, H.R., Simoncelli, E.P.: Image quality assessment: from error visibility to structural similarity. IEEE Trans. Image Process. **13**(4), 600–612 (2004)

Comparative Performance of Deep Learning and Statistical Models for River Stage Forecasting

Norizuandi Ibrahim[1], Mohd Norhisham Razali[2](✉), Satria Arjuna Julaihi[1], Rozita Hanapi[2], and Abdul Hadi Abdul Talip[1]

[1] Faculty of Computer Science and Mathematics, Universiti Teknologi MARA Cawangan Sarawak, Kampus Samarahan, Sarawak, Malaysia

[2] Faculty of Business and Management, Universiti Teknologi MARA, Kota Samarahan, Sarawak, Malaysia

hishamrazali@uitm.edu.my

Abstract. Accurate river water level prediction is vital for early flood warning and effective water resource management. The traditional methods of river water level prediction based on Autoregressive Integrated Moving Average (ARIMA) and linear regression struggled to capture the nonlinear and dynamic nature of hydrological systems. Therefore, this study evaluates the performance of deep learning models, namely Long Short-Term Memory (LSTM), Basic LSTM, Stacked LSTM, Bidirectional LSTM, and LSTM with Dropout, alongside classical models such as Linear Regression, Moving Average, and ARIMA across five river monitoring stations. Model performance was assessed using Root Mean Square Error (RMSE), Mean Absolute Error (MAE), Mean Absolute Percentage Error (MAPE), Mean Squared Error (MSE), and R-squared (R^2) metrics on test data. The results consistently showed that the LSTM with Dropout model outperformed all other approaches in terms of predictive accuracy and generalization, achieving the lowest RMSE and MAE values and the highest R^2 scores at four out of five stations. The standard LSTM model achieved the best performance at one station but was generally outperformed by its dropout-regularized counterpart. In contrast, classical models exhibited significantly lower performance, particularly in capturing temporal dependencies, with R^2 values often below zero. These findings validated the effectiveness and robustness of LSTM-based deep learning, particularly with dropout regularization, in modeling and forecasting river water level dynamics across diverse hydrological conditions. The study supports the integration of advanced machine learning models in river monitoring systems to enhance flood preparedness and mitigation strategies.

Keywords: Time Series Forecasting · Deep Learning Models · Flood Prediction

1 Introduction

Flooding remains one of the most devastating natural disasters worldwide, causing significant economic losses, infrastructure damage, and loss of life each year. Recurring floods affect both rural and urban communities due to intense rainfall, river overflow,

M. Kassim et al. (Eds.): SCDS 2025, CCIS 2674, pp. 425–436, 2026.
https://doi.org/10.1007/978-981-95-8368-3_30

and inadequate drainage systems. Accurate and timely river water level forecasting is crucial for effective flood risk management, emergency preparedness, and early warning systems [9, 19]. Traditionally, river water level predictions have relied on statistical and hydrological models such as Autoregressive Integrated Moving Average (ARIMA), linear regression, and moving averages. While these methods have provided useful baseline forecasts, they often struggle to capture the nonlinear and dynamic nature of hydrological systems, especially when dealing with large temporal variations and multiple influencing factors [1, 7]. Moreover, these models typically require strong assumptions about stationarity and linearity, which may not hold in real-world river systems [6, 8].

In recent years, deep learning approaches have gained prominence in hydrological modeling due to their ability to learn complex temporal patterns from large datasets without explicit assumptions about data distribution. Among these, the Long Short-Term Memory (LSTM) network, a type of recurrent neural network (RNN), has shown strong performance in time series forecasting tasks, including rainfall-runoff modeling, reservoir inflow prediction, and river level forecasting [12, 20]. Variants of LSTM, such as Stacked LSTM, Bidirectional LSTM, and LSTM with Dropout, offer enhancements in learning capacity and generalization, making them suitable for complex forecasting environments [18, 21].

This study aims to evaluate and compare the performance of several LSTM-based deep learning models against classical methods for river water level forecasting across five monitoring stations in Sarawak: Aman Bridge, Buan Bidi, Kampung Git, Sungai Pedid, and Ulu Batang Kayan. By assessing the models on multiple metrics which are Root Mean Square Error (RMSE), Mean Absolute Error (MAE), Mean Absolute Percentage Error (MAPE), Mean Squared Error (MSE), and R-squared (R2), this research seeks to identify the most reliable and accurate forecasting approach for supporting real-time flood warning systems. The findings of this study are expected to contribute valuable insights into the application of deep learning in hydrological forecasting and enhance the decision-making process in flood mitigation planning [10, 14].

2 Related Works

2.1 Traditional Approaches to River Water Level Forecasting

Traditional approaches to river water level forecasting have historically formed the bedrock of hydrological prediction, evolving to incorporate a diverse range of statistical and deterministic methodologies. These foundational techniques have laid the groundwork for more advanced forecasting models by establishing methods to understand and predict river behavior based on historical data and physical principles. Statistical models, for instance, are widely employed for their ability to discern patterns within time series data. Among these, AutoRegressive Integrated Moving Average (ARIMA) models are prominent, valued for their capacity to capture various data characteristics, including underlying trends and seasonal fluctuations in water levels [1]. Similarly, Multiple Linear Regression (MLR) models offer a transparent approach to forecasting. These models predict water levels by establishing linear relationships with multiple hydrological and meteorological variables, providing clear insights into the influence of various input factors on river stage [2].

In parallel, deterministic models simulate the physical processes governing water flow. The Stage Rating Curve (SRC) is a fundamental deterministic tool that establishes a direct empirical relationship between the river's water level (stage) and its corresponding flow rate (discharge). This method is particularly effective for rivers exhibiting consistent flow characteristics over time [3]. Furthermore, Conceptual Models delve deeper by simulating the intricate physical processes of the hydrological cycle, such as rainfall-runoff transformations, to predict water levels. These models necessitate detailed knowledge of the watershed's physical properties and are often integrated with other forecasting methods for enhanced accuracy [4].

As the complexity of hydrological data increased, "traditional" methods expanded to include early data-driven and hybrid models, bridging the gap towards modern machine learning. Artificial Neural Networks (ANNs) emerged as a powerful tool capable of modeling complex, non-linear relationships inherent in hydrological time series data. ANNs have frequently demonstrated superior performance compared to earlier statistical models in various studies, with notable applications including accurate river flow prediction in catchments like Narmada and the Mahanadi river system [4, 5]. Other data-driven approaches like Support Vector Machines (SVMs) have also shown promising results in water level forecasting by effectively handling non-linear data patterns across diverse case studies [6]. Additionally, Genetic Programming (GP) has been utilized to evolve predictive models from historical data, occasionally outperforming ANNs and model trees in specific forecasting scenarios [4].

Despite their established utility, these traditional and early data-driven models face inherent challenges. A significant limitation is data scarcity, as many traditional models require extensive historical records, which are often unavailable, particularly for smaller or less-monitored rivers [6]. Moreover, the inherent non-linearity and non-stationarity of natural hydrological processes pose considerable difficulties for many of these models, potentially leading to less accurate forecasts compared to approaches specifically designed to handle such complexities [7].

In conclusion, traditional approaches to river water level forecasting, encompassing statistical, deterministic, and early data-driven models, have provided the foundational understanding and tools for hydrological prediction. While these methods possess limitations, particularly concerning data availability and the non-linear nature of hydrological systems, they remain valuable components in a forecaster's toolkit. Their integration with more advanced, modern data-driven and deep learning techniques continues to be explored as a means to enhance prediction accuracy and overall reliability [1–6, 8].

2.2 Machine Learning in Hydrological Forecasting

Machine learning (ML) has emerged as a powerful tool for predicting river water levels, aiding flood warning systems, water resource management, and environmental planning. Various ML algorithms, including Support Vector Regression (SVR), Random Forest (RF), Artificial Neural Networks (ANN), Long Short-Term Memory (LSTM), and Gaussian Process Regression (GPR), have been successfully applied, each with distinct advantages. For instance, SVR demonstrated high accuracy in the Vietnamese Mekong Delta [9, 10], while RF proved effective for flood inflow prediction [10, 11].

LSTM excels in short-term hydrodynamic forecasting [12], and GPR provides precise daily water level estimates [13, 14].

Hybrid models further enhance predictive performance by combining ML techniques. The SVR-GA model, integrating Genetic Algorithm optimization, improves monthly river flow forecasting [15], while EMD-ITG and ANN-EMD reduce errors in non-stationary and river stage predictions, respectively [16, 17]. Case studies highlight their real-world impact, such as SVR and RF aiding flood warnings in the Mekong Delta [10], GPR outperforming traditional methods in Surma River flood forecasting [14], and MLP-NN surpassing LSTM and XGBoost in Malaysia's Muda River [18].

Model performance is typically assessed using metrics like Nash-Sutcliffe Efficiency (NSE), Root Mean Square Error (RMSE), and Coefficient of Determination (R2). The ANN-EMD model, for example, achieved an NSE of 0.949 and RMSE of 0.330 [16], while GPR showed high precision with 95% prediction uncertainty bounds [14]. Overall, ML provides reliable and adaptable solutions for water level prediction, with model selection depending on hydrological conditions and data availability, making it indispensable for flood resilience and sustainable water management.

3 Experimental Design

3.1 Study Area and Data Collection

This study focuses on five river monitoring stations in Sarawak, Malaysia: Aman Bridge, Buan Bidi, Kampung Git, Sungai Pedid, and Ulu Batang Kayan. These locations were selected based on their strategic hydrological importance and availability of water level data. The data were sourced from the Department of Irrigation and Drainage Sarawak (DID), which operates a network of real-time hydrological sensors installed at river basins throughout the state. The dataset comprises timestamped readings of river water levels and cumulative rainfall, with measurements taken at hourly intervals. Additional metadata include station name, river basin, division, and predefined alert thresholds (e.g., Normal, Alert, Warning, and Danger levels). For modeling purposes, only the water level time series was used as the prediction target, while time-dependent features were derived to support model learning.

3.2 Data Preprocessing

To ensure consistency and model readiness, several preprocessing steps were applied. First, missing values were addressed using linear interpolation for minor gaps, while larger missing segments were excluded entirely. Next, all water level values were normalized to a [0, 1] range via min-max scaling to improve model training efficiency. The time series data was then restructured into a supervised learning format using a sliding window approach, where each input sequence consisted of *n* past time steps to predict the next time step. Finally, the dataset was split chronologically into training (80%) and testing (20%) sets, preserving temporal order to prevent information leakage.

3.3 Models Implemented

A total of eight predictive models were implemented and evaluated, comprising five deep learning architectures and three classical approaches. The deep learning models included: (1) a standard single-layer LSTM, (2) a basic LSTM with reduced hidden units for baseline comparison, (3) a stacked LSTM with multiple layers to capture deeper temporal patterns, (4) a bidirectional LSTM processing sequences in both forward and backward directions, and (5) an LSTM with dropout regularization to mitigate overfitting. For classical benchmarks, we implemented: (1) linear regression as a basic statistical model, (2) a 3-window moving average as a simple temporal baseline, and (3) an ARIMA model with parameters optimized using the AIC criterion. All LSTM-based architectures were developed using TensorFlow/Keras, while classical models were built with scikit-learn and statsmodels libraries.

3.4 Hyperparameter Configuration

The deep learning models were systematically configured with optimized hyperparameters, determined through grid search and trial runs. All architectures shared common training parameters: 100 epochs, a batch size of 32, Adam optimizer, and Mean Squared Error (MSE) loss function. The LSTM units ranged from 50 to 100 depending on model complexity, with the dropout variant specifically employing a 0.2 dropout rate for regularization. To ensure consistent evaluation, all models were trained and tested on identical datasets, with early stopping implemented to prevent overfitting. Model performance was rigorously assessed using five complementary metrics: Root Mean Square Error (RMSE), Mean Absolute Error (MAE), Mean Absolute Percentage Error (MAPE), Mean Squared Error (MSE), and the Coefficient of Determination (R^2). This multi-metric approach enabled comprehensive evaluation of both absolute and relative prediction errors across stations with diverse hydrological characteristics, ensuring robust assessment of model accuracy and generalization capabilities.

4 Experimental Results

4.1 Performance Summary - Aman Bridge Water-level Forecast (Test Set)

The performance evaluation of various models for river water level prediction at the Aman Bridge station demonstrated that the LSTM with Dropout model outperformed all other approaches, achieving the lowest RMSE (0.1056), MAE (0.0550), and MAPE (0.0018), along with the highest R-squared value (0.8154). This indicates a strong ability to generalize and accurately capture the temporal patterns in the data. In comparison, the Stacked LSTM and Basic LSTM models achieved moderate performance, with R-squared values of 0.6771 and 0.6666 respectively, while the Bidirectional LSTM showed slightly lower predictive accuracy. The Moving Average baseline model (window = 3) performed significantly worse across all metrics, particularly in terms of R-squared (0.3403) and MAPE (0.8248), highlighting the advantages of deep learning models over traditional methods. Overall, incorporating dropout regularization in the LSTM architecture substantially improved predictive performance, likely by reducing overfitting and enhancing the model's generalization capability on unseen test data (Fig. 1 and Table 1).

Table 1. Prediction Model Performance for Aman Bridge Station

Model	RMSE	MAE	MAPE	R^2	MSE
LSTM with Dropout	0.1056	0.0550	0.0018	0.8154	0.0112
Stacked LSTM	0.2886	0.1199	0.0039	0.6771	0.0833
Singlelayer LSTM	0.2933	0.1223	0.0039	0.6666	0.0860
Basic LSTM (version used)	0.3320	0.1764	0.0057	0.5729	0.1102
Bidirectional LSTM	0.3381	0.1904	0.0061	0.5570	0.1143
MovingAverage (w = 3)	0.4253	0.2558	0.8248	0.3403	0.1809

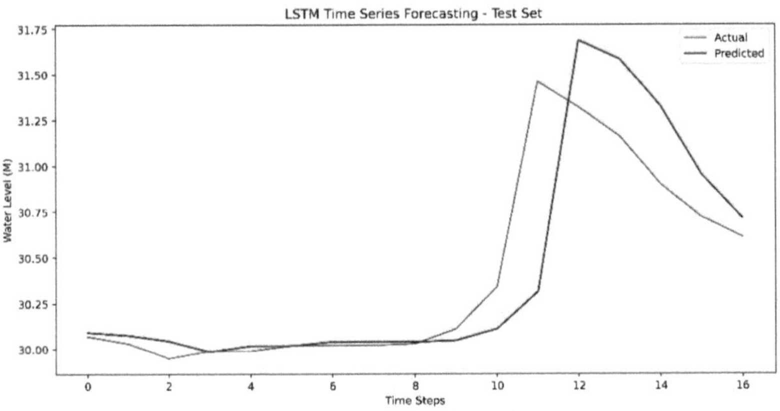

Fig. 1. LSTM with Dropout

4.2 Performance Comparison of Models at Buan Bidi Station (Test Set)

Table 2. Prediction Model Performance for Buan Bidi Station

Model	RMSE	MAE	MAPE	R-squared (R^2)	MSE
LSTM Model	0.0084	0.0067	0.0006	0.8393	0.0001
LSTM with Dropout	0.0088	0.0074	0.0007	0.8234	0.0001
Stacked LSTM	0.0107	0.0094	0.0009	0.7356	0.0001
Basic LSTM Model	0.0132	0.0117	0.0011	0.5982	0.0002
Bidirectional LSTM	0.0254	0.0145	0.0014	0.7168	0.0006
Linear Regression	0.0150	0.0104	0.0985	0.5116	0.0002
Moving Average (Window = 3)	0.0135	0.0107	0.1012	0.6016	0.0002
ARIMA	0.0135	0.0107	0.1012	0.6016	0.0002

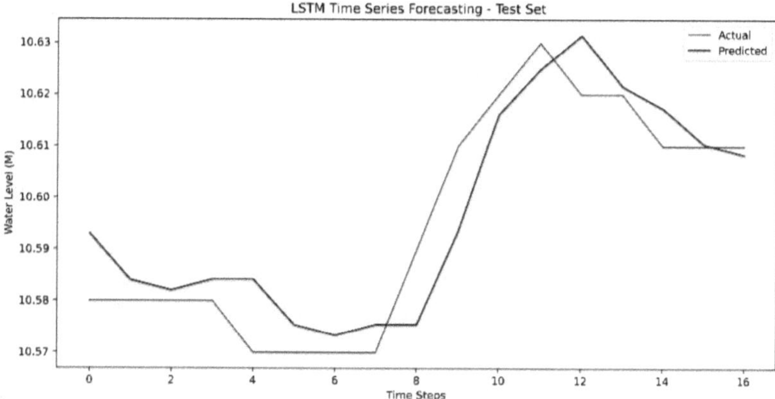

Fig. 2. Basic LSTM

The river water level prediction at Buan Bidi station showed that the LSTM model without modifications delivered the best overall performance, achieving the lowest RMSE (0.0084), MAE (0.0067), and MAPE (0.0006), along with the highest R-squared value of 0.8393. The LSTM with Dropout and Bidirectional LSTM models followed closely, maintaining strong predictive performance, with R-squared values of 0.8234 and 0.7356, respectively. In contrast, the Basic LSTM and Stacked LSTM models underperformed slightly, with higher error metrics and lower R-squared scores. Traditional methods such as Linear Regression, Moving Average, and ARIMA showed notably weaker performance, particularly in terms of RMSE and R-squared, where Linear Regression reached an RMSE of 0.0254 and R2 of 0.7168. The Moving Average (window = 3) and ARIMA models yielded R2 values of 0.5116 and 0.6016 respectively, indicating limited ability to capture the temporal dynamics compared to deep learning approaches. These results highlight the effectiveness of LSTM-based models—especially the standard and dropout-regularized versions—in accurately modeling river water level fluctuations, with deep learning substantially outperforming classical statistical methods (Fig. 2 and Table 2).

4.3 Model Performance Comparison – Kampung Git Station (Test Set)

At Kampung Git station, the LSTM with Dropout model achieved the highest predictive accuracy among all tested models, with the lowest RMSE (0.0132), MAE (0.0089), and MAPE (0.20%), along with a very high R-squared value of 0.9882, indicating strong generalization and model fit. Other deep learning models such as the Stacked LSTM and Bidirectional LSTM performed moderately well in terms of error metrics, but exhibited negative R-squared values (−3.27 and − 13.68 respectively), suggesting poor alignment with the observed variance. The Basic LSTM and regular LSTM model also returned negative R-squared values, indicating limited predictive reliability for this station without further tuning. Among classical models, Linear Regression and Moving Average (window = 3) produced competitive error metrics (RMSE: 0.012 and 0.0253 respectively), but only Linear Regression had a mildly positive R-squared (0.2512).

Table 3. Prediction Model Performance for Kampung Git Station

Model	RMSE	MAE	MAPE	R-squared (R^2)	MSE
LSTM with Dropout	**0.0132**	**0.0089**	**0.0020**	**0.9882**	**0.0002**
Stacked LSTM	0.0293	0.0283	0.0067	−3.2715	0.0009
Bidirectional LSTM	0.0544	0.0536	0.0127	−13.6828	0.0030
LSTM Model	0.0426	0.0417	0.0099	−8.0231	0.0018
Basic LSTM Model	0.0646	0.0640	0.0152	−19.736	0.0042
Linear Regression	0.0120	0.0096	0.0226	0.2512	0.0001
Moving Average (Window = 3)	0.0253	0.0150	0.0355	−2.3097	0.0006
ARIMA	0.0253	0.0150	0.0355	−2.3097	0.0006

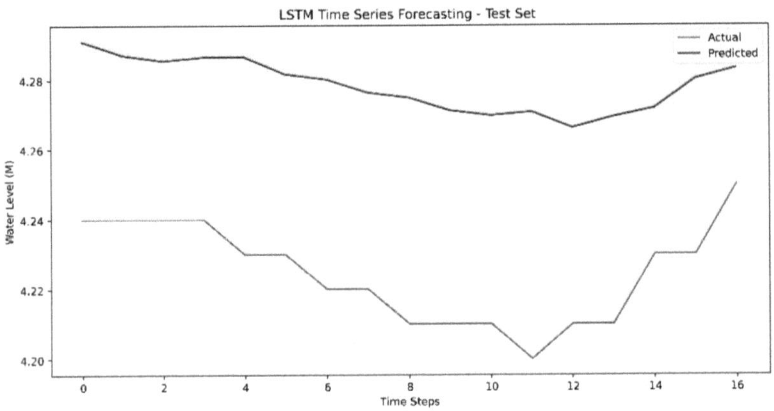

Fig. 3. LSTM with Dropout

Meanwhile, ARIMA performed poorly in terms of fit (R^2 = − 2.3097), although its error metrics were comparable to the Moving Average. These findings reaffirm the effectiveness of LSTM-based deep learning models—particularly those with dropout regularization—in modeling complex temporal patterns of river water levels at Kampung Git station (Fig. 3 and Table 3).

4.4 Model Performance Comparison – Sungai Pedid Station (Test Set)

For Sungai Pedid station, the LSTM with Dropout model again delivered the most accurate predictions, achieving the lowest RMSE (0.0250), MAE (0.0142), and MAPE (0.10%), alongside a strong R-squared value of 0.9539, indicating an excellent fit between predicted and observed values. Among other LSTM variants, the Stacked LSTM performed slightly better than the standard LSTM and Bidirectional LSTM, with an R-squared of 0.7915 and low RMSE (0.0847), suggesting decent predictive power. The

Table 4. Prediction Model Performance for Sungai Pedid Station

Model	RMSE	MAE	MAPE	R-squared (R^2)	MSE
LSTM with Dropout	**0.0250**	**0.0142**	**0.0010**	**0.9539**	**0.0006**
Stacked LSTM	0.0847	0.0468	0.0032	0.7915	0.0072
LSTM Model	0.0868	0.0457	0.0032	0.7809	0.0075
Bidirectional LSTM	0.1037	0.0596	0.0041	0.6872	0.0108
Basic LSTM Model	0.1115	0.0705	0.0049	0.6389	0.0124
Linear Regression	0.1313	0.0833	0.0576	0.5232	0.0172
Moving Average (Window = 3)	0.2451	0.1640	0.1131	−0.6613	0.0601
ARIMA	0.2451	0.1640	0.1131	−0.6613	0.0601

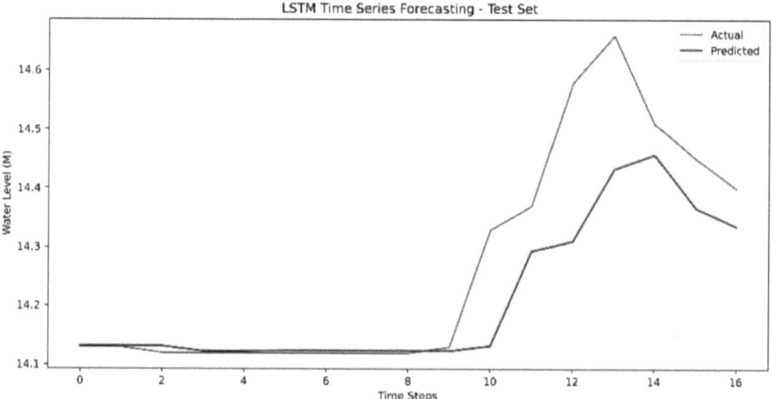

Fig. 4. LSTM with Dropout

Basic LSTM and Bidirectional LSTM showed moderate performance, but less accuracy than their more advanced counterparts. In comparison, Linear Regression yielded a relatively high RMSE (0.1313) and a moderate R-squared of 0.5232, while Moving Average (Window = 3) and ARIMA exhibited notably poor performance, especially in terms of R-squared (−0.6613 for ARIMA) and MAPE (over 1%). These results further support the superiority of deep learning models, particularly those incorporating dropout regularization, for modeling complex and dynamic river water levels in real time (Fig. 4 and Table 4).

4.5 Model Performance Comparison – Ulu Batang Kayan Station (Test Set)

At Ulu Batang Kayan station, the LSTM with Dropout model once again demonstrated superior performance, achieving the lowest RMSE (0.0705), MAE (0.0508), and MAPE (0.011). It also attained the highest R-squared value (0.1002), which, although modest, was positive, unlike most other models. Among other deep learning models, the Stacked

Table 5. Prediction Model Performance for Ulu Batang Kayan Station

Model	RMSE	MAE	MAPE	R-squared (R^2)	MSE
LSTM with Dropout	**0.0705**	**0.0508**	**0.0110**	**0.1002**	**0.0050**
Stacked LSTM	0.1078	0.0798	0.0172	0.0729	0.0116
Bidirectional LSTM	0.1546	0.1076	0.0229	−0.9049	0.0239
LSTM Model	0.1634	0.1199	0.0256	−1.1301	0.0267
Basic LSTM Model	0.1653	0.1206	0.0257	−1.1785	0.0273
Linear Regression	0.1144	0.0836	0.18097	−0.7513	0.0131
Moving Average (Window = 3)	0.1124	0.1024	0.2252	−0.6910	0.0126
ARIMA	0.1124	0.1024	0.2252	−0.6910	0.0126

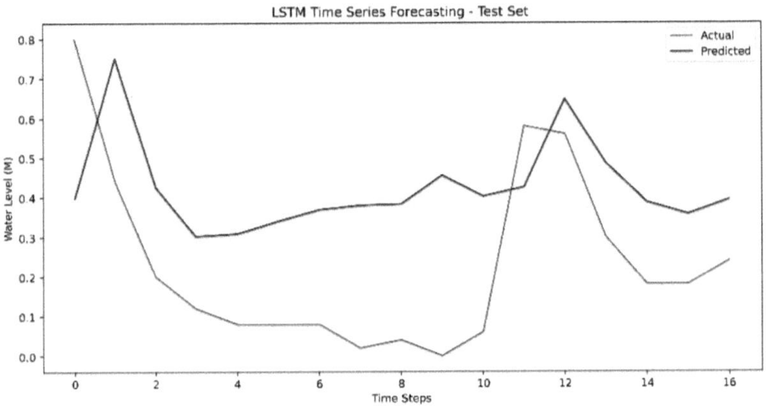

Fig. 5. LSTM with Dropout

LSTM had the next-best performance, with an RMSE of 0.1078 and an R-squared of 0.0729, indicating some ability to capture trends. The Basic LSTM, Bidirectional LSTM, and regular LSTM models showed poor fit, all with negative R-squared values and higher error metrics, suggesting they failed to generalize effectively for this station. Classical models such as Linear Regression, Moving Average, and ARIMA also performed poorly, with Linear Regression achieving an RMSE of 0.1144 and a strongly negative R-squared (−0.7513), while ARIMA and Moving Average performed similarly. These results further confirm that deep learning models—especially those with dropout regularization—consistently outperform traditional approaches in modeling river water levels, even in complex or noisy hydrological environments (Fig. 5 and Table 5).

Based on the evaluation of all five stations—Aman Bridge, Buan Bidi, Kampung Git, Sungai Pedid, and Ulu Batang Kayan—the LSTM with Dropout model consistently outperformed all other models across the majority of evaluation metrics (RMSE, MAE, MAPE, and R-squared). This model delivered the lowest error values and highest R2 scores in 4 out of the 5 stations, demonstrating superior generalization and predictive accuracy.

5 Conclusions

This study conducted a comprehensive evaluation of river water level prediction models across five hydrological monitoring stations in Sarawak, Malaysia: Aman Bridge, Buan Bidi, Kampung Git, Sungai Pedid, and Ulu Batang Kayan. A total of eight models were compared, including five deep learning models which are LSTM, Basic LSTM, Stacked LSTM, Bidirectional LSTM, and LSTM with Dropout and three classical models namely Linear Regression, Moving Average, and ARIMA. The models were assessed using multiple performance metrics, including RMSE, MAE, MAPE, MSE, and R-squared. The experimental results consistently demonstrate that the LSTM with Dropout model outperformed all other models in terms of predictive accuracy and robustness. It achieved the lowest error rates and highest R^2 values across four of the five stations, confirming its effectiveness in capturing complex temporal dependencies and mitigating overfitting through regularization. Although the standard LSTM model showed strong performance at one station (Buan Bidi), it was generally surpassed by its dropout-enhanced counterpart. In contrast, the classical models, including ARIMA and Moving Average performed less efectively, with higher errors and in many cases negative R^2 values, indicating poor fit to the observed data. These results suggest that traditional approaches are less suitable for real-time river level forecasting, especially in dynamic and nonlinear hydrological systems. Overall, the findings support the effectiveness of deep learning, particularly dropout-regularized LSTM architectures, for river water level prediction. This has practical implications for developing intelligent early warning systems, enhancing flood preparedness, and supporting water resource management in flood-prone regions.

References

1. Azad, M.A., Islam, A.S., Nurun Nabi, N., Khurshid, M., Siddique, H.: Developments and trends in water level forecasting using machine learning models — a review. IEEE Access, 3557910 (2025). https://doi.org/10.1109/ACCESS.2025.3557910
2. Khan, S.A., See, L.: Rainfall-runoff modelling using data driven and statistical methods. In: 2006 International Conference on Advances in Space Technologies ICAST, pp. 16–20 (2006). https://doi.org/10.1109/ICAST.2006.313789
3. Chaplot, B., Birbal, P.: Development of stage-discharge rating curve using ANN. Int. J. Hydrol. Sci. Technol. **14**(1), 75–95 (2022). https://doi.org/10.1504/IJHST.2022.123643
4. Londhe, S., Charhate, S.: Comparaison de techniques de modélisation conditionnée par les données pour la prévision des débits fluviaux. Hydrol. Sci. J. **55**(7), 1163–1174 (2010). https://doi.org/10.1080/02626667.2010.512867
5. Yadav, A., Prasad, B.B.V.S.V., Mojjada, R.K., Kothamasu, K.K., Joshi, D.: Application of artificial neural network and genetic algorithm based artificial neural network models for river flow prediction. Rev. d'Intell. Artif. **34**(6), 745–751 (2020). https://doi.org/10.18280/RIA.340608

6. Chen, Q., Wan, D., Yu, Y., Li, K.: Intelligent water level prediction model for small-and medium-sized rivers based on small sample data. In: Proceedings of the 2022 16th International Conference on Ubiquitous Information Management and Communication: IMCOM 2022, pp. 9721793 (2022). https://doi.org/10.1109/IMCOM53663.2022.9721793
7. Yadav, R.: Cyber security threats during Covid-19 pandemic. Int. Trans. J. Eng. **12**(3), 1–7 (2021). https://doi.org/10.14456/ITJEMAST.2021.59
8. Noorain, I.S., Ismail, S., Sadon, A.N., Yasin, S.M.: Application of box-jenkins, artificial neural network and support vector machine model for water level prediction. Lect. Notes Networks Syst. **457**, 121–130 (2022). https://doi.org/10.1007/978-3-031-00828-3_12
9. Nguyen, T.T., Huu, Q.N., Li, M.J.: Forecasting time series water levels on Mekong River using machine learning models. In: Proceedings - 2015 IEEE International Conference on Knowledge and Systems Engineering, KSE 2015, pp. 292–297 (2016). https://doi.org/10.1109/KSE.2015.53
10. Nguyen Duc, H., Nguyen Tien, G., Nguyen Xuan, H., Tran Ngoc, V., Nguyen Huu, D.: Multi-step-ahead prediction of water levels using machine learning: a comparative analysis in the Vietnamese Mekong Delta. Vietnam J. Earth Sci. **46**, 468–488 (2024). https://doi.org/10.15625/2615-9783/21067
11. Nakatsugawa, M., Sakamoto, R., Kobayashi, Y.: Research on dam inflow prediction during severe flood using machine learning methods. In: 22nd Congress of International Association for Hydro Environment Engineering and Research (IAHR) Asia Pacific Division (APD) 2020 "Creating Resilience to Water-Related Challenges," pp. 74452 (2020)
12. Ho, H.V., Nguyen, D.H., Le, X.H., Lee, G.: Multi-step-ahead water level forecasting for operating sluice gates in Hai Duong, Vietnam. Environ. Monit. Assess. **194**(6), 10661 (2022). https://doi.org/10.1007/s10661-022-10115-7
13. Ahmed, A.N., et al.: Water level prediction using various machine learning algorithms: a case study of Durian Tunggal river, Malaysia. Eng. Appl. Comput. Fluid Mech. **16**(1), 422–440 (2022). https://doi.org/10.1080/19942060.2021.2019128
14. Mahmud, F., Limon, M., Khayer, A., Osmani, S.A.: A data-driven approach to forecast floods in Sylhet city using machine learning and deep learning techniques. AIP Conf. Proc. **2713**, 129726 (2023). https://doi.org/10.1063/5.0129726
15. Tao, H., et al.: Training and testing data division influence on hybrid machine learning model process: application of river flow forecasting. Complexity **2020**, 8844367 (2020). https://doi.org/10.1155/2020/8844367
16. Heddam, S., et al.: Hybrid river stage forecasting based on machine learning with empirical mode decomposition. Appl Water Sci **14**(3), 13201 (2024). https://doi.org/10.1007/s13201-024-02103-8
17. Gao, S., Feng, X., Xu, H., Wu, Y., Feng, W.: A hybrid deep learning model based on EMD algorithm for non-stationary water level prediction of estuarine systems. Estuar. Coast. Shelf Sci. **314**, 109128 (2025). https://doi.org/10.1016/j.ecss.2025.109128
18. Adli Zakaria, M.N., et al.: Exploring machine learning algorithms for accurate water level forecasting in Muda river, Malaysia. Heliyon **9**(7), 17689 (2023). https://doi.org/10.1016/j.heliyon.2023.e17689

Heat Stroke Risk Detection Using Machine Learning

Siti Durratul Ainn Binti Samsudin[1], Hana Fakhira binti Al Marzuki[1], Nur Aina Khadijah binti Adnan[2(✉)], Norharziana binti Yahaya Rashdi[2], Syaidatus Syahira binti Ahmad Tarmizi[2], and Sven Frei[3]

[1] Fakulti Sains Komputer Dan Matematik, Universiti Teknologi MARA Shah Alam, Selangor 40450, Malaysia
2022972615@student.uitm.edu.my, hanafakhira@uitm.edu.my

[2] Fakulti Sains Komputer Dan Matematik, Universiti Teknologi MARA Cawangan Johor, Segamat 85000, Johor, Malaysia
{ainakhadijah,norharziana,syahiratarmizi}@uitm.edu.my

[3] SWICA Gesundheitsorganisation Römerstrasse, 37, Winterthur, Switzerland
frei-sven@bluewin.ch

Abstract. Extreme hot temperatures in Malaysia due to climate change has increase the risk of heat-related health issues. It is particularly for outdoor laborers and vulnerable group such as the elderly and those with chronic illnesses. The phenomenon which indicates a 2.7 to 4.0 °C increase every century has contributes to numbers of conditions from heat exhaustion to heat stroke. This situation is imposing a significant pressure on healthcare systems and highlighting the necessity for prevention measures.

As heat stroke is a significant danger to health, especially during periods of extreme hot weather. It may lead to multiple medical conditions and perhaps life-threatening problems if not appropriately diagnosed and treated. Thus, the goal of this study is to propose a heat stroke risk detection application that able to help detecting heat stroke risk among user. This application is developed with the implementation of a machine learning that able to detect heat stroke based on users' medical conditions. Through the application, it enables an early heat stroke risk detection and give suggestions on actions need to be taken to prevent severe heat stroke consequences with the implementation of random forest method.

Keywords: Heat Stroke Risk Detection · Random Forest · Machine Learning · Application

1 Introduction

The growing threat of global climate change has resulted in a gradual rise in daily temperatures in Malaysia, leading to the risk of heat stress especially for outdoor workers (Nizam et al., 2023). For the past four decades, Malaysia's recorded surface temperature

These authors contributed equally to this work.

M. Kassim et al. (Eds.): SCDS 2025, CCIS 2674, pp. 437–450, 2026.
https://doi.org/10.1007/978-981-95-8368-3_31

data show an increase ranging from 2.7 to 4.0 °C per century (Hassan et al., 2014). The public faces serious medical conditions as a result of this climate change, that leading to the need for preventative action (Awadalla & Noor, 1991; Mahmood & Guinto, 2022). Besides, Extreme heat events have an adverse effect on people's health, particularly for vulnerable groups like the elderly, those with chronic illnesses, and those living in poverty (Jay et al., 2021). Heat exhaustion, heat cramps, heat rash, and heat stroke are among the health problems brought on by the heat. These conditions put a significant strain on healthcare systems since they can range from little discomfort to life-threatening catastrophes (Yong et al., 2023).

The adaption of machine learning in healthcare field has transformed the sector by enabling the early detection of life-threatening medical conditions and the discovery of hidden insights in extensive datasets (Maini & Venkateswarlu, 2021). Numerous of artificial intelligence (AI) applications that take benefit of machine learning's speed and accuracy have been developed, creating opportunities for more innovative solutions to a variety of healthcare issues (Ogunpola et al., 2024).

In order to address this critical need, we propose a web-based application that employ machine learning to detect risk of heat stroke among user. The method that will be used is Random Forest in the context of heat stroke risk detection method.

This application will allow users to input personal health data, while the machine learning model will process the information along with real-time environmental data to provide a risk assessment for heat stroke. The target user of this application will be general public in Malaysia especially outdoor workers, athletes and sport enthusiasts, healthcare professionals, and tourist and travelers.

The dataset is exclusively focused on detecting of a person being diagnosed with a heat stroke risk. The dataset will be sourced from Kaggle in CSV format and are based on a combination of medical history, environmental, and physiological data.

2 Related Work

Heat stroke is a critical condition that has drawn increased attention due to rising global temperatures and frequent extreme heat occurrences. As a response, researchers have investigated a range of technological solutions to prevent, identify, and manage heat-related illnesses. This section will share an overview of the existing work on heat stroke detection.

2.1 Wearable Heat Stroke Detection System with IOT Based Environment

Teo, Ramli, and Aziz (2021) developed a wearable IoT-based heat stroke risk detection device aimed at preventing heat-related illnesses in high-temperature environments. The system integrates various sensors to measure physiological and environmental parameters including heart rate, core body temperature, ambient temperature, and humidity. A Fuzzy logic controller is employed to evaluate heat stroke risk levels, while an alert module notifies users when thresholds are exceeded as in Fig. 1. Data is transmitted and visualized using the ThingSpeak platform and a dedicated Android application. In order to assess performance, a five-phase test involving standing, walking, and running was conducted. The results highlighted that the Thermal Heat Stroke Risk Coefficient (THSRC), core body temperature, and heart rate are the most significant indicators of potential heat stroke. The device was able to reliably detect heat stroke risk when THSRC exceeded 37.5, core body temperature surpassed 38.5 °C, and heart rate rose above 135 beats per minute. The study concluded that this wearable system offers an effective, real-time solution to mitigate the risks of heat stroke, enabling users to engage in physical activity under hot conditions with early warnings and improved safety (Teo et al, 2021).

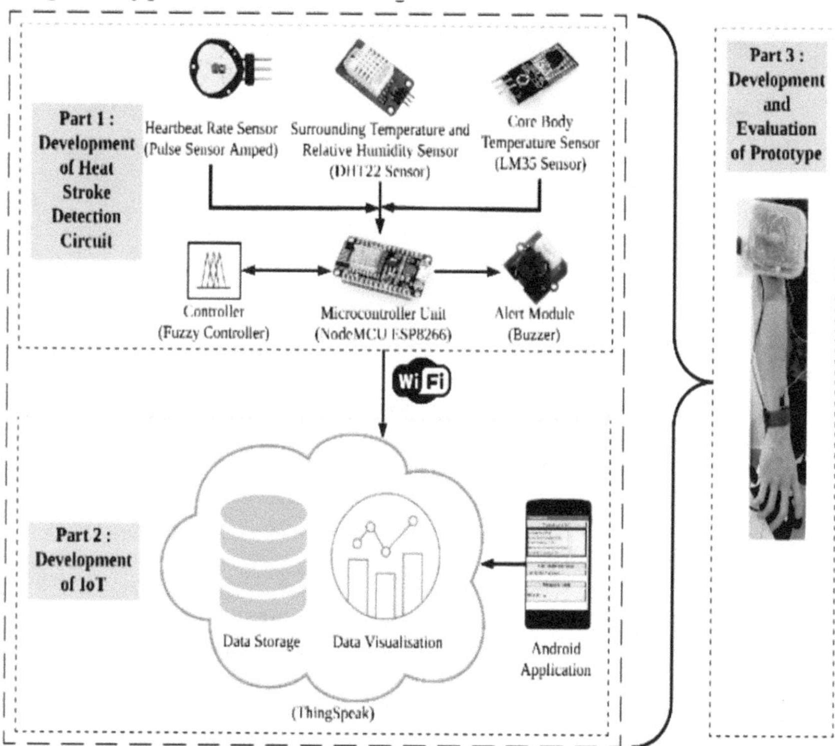

Fig. 1. Wearable heat stroke detection device's project framework.

2.2 Heat Stroke Risk Detection System Integrated with Infrared Camera

A heat stroke alert system that integrates an infrared thermal imaging camera with an image processing algorithm to detect individuals at risk of heat-related illness has been developed by a group of researchers as shown in Fig. 2. The system processes thermal images using a Python-based script which initiates analysis upon image acquisition from the camera. The application uses a web-based application that developed using technologies such as Bootstrap, JSP, HTML, JavaScript, Ajax, and jQuery, allowing accessibility across a range of internet-enabled devices including smartphones, laptops, and tablets. It is designed to be able to deployment in diverse environments such as outdoor settings, workplaces, and sports facilities. The system supports real-time monitoring and alert system. This application prevention of heat stroke incidents through timely detection of early warning signs (Yim Yam et al., 2020).

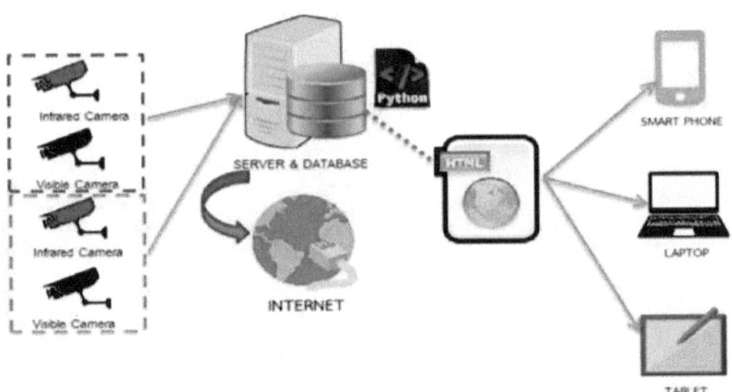

Fig. 2. Heat Stroke Detection System Integrated with Infrared Camera's system design

In contrast to existing work, the proposed application aims to detect the heat stroke risk detection based on individual medical conditions, their body and environmental temperature to provide a personalized risk assessment model. This context-aware and user-centered approach enhances the accuracy of heat stroke prediction and supports timely interventions tailored to each user's health profile.

3 Methodology

In the context of developing heat stroke risk detection application, the chosen software development life cycle (SDLC) model is the waterfall model as shown in Fig. 3. The significance of waterfall models lies in their ability to provide a well-defined roadmap for software development projects, ensuring that each phase is carefully planned and executed. Waterfall is particularly suitable for projects with predictable requirements (Pargaonkar, 2023). Waterfall models has six phases of software development. However, this project only covers until testing phase. The implementation and maintenance phases are not been covered yet.

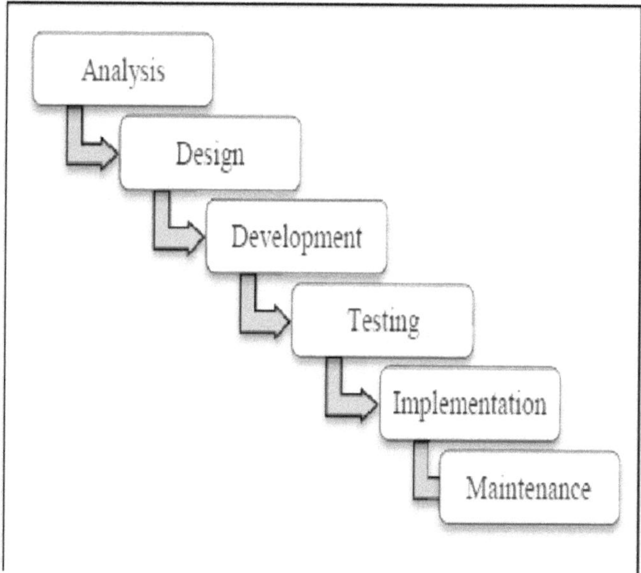

Fig. 3. Waterfall model.

3.1 Analysis

The first phase of waterfall model is Analysis. In this phase, the problem statements, and significance of Heat Stroke Risk Detection Application using Machine Learning are identified. The important information and knowledge gaining also happens in this phase. This is where related works are discovered in order to specified the requirements for application (Yahya & Maidin, 2022).

3.2 Design

The second phase is Design. This phase includes, use case diagram, flowchart, and user interface of the application.

Flowchart
Flowchart is used in order to produce a visual representation illustrating the flow of the application. The flowchart for the application is shown in Fig. 4 below.

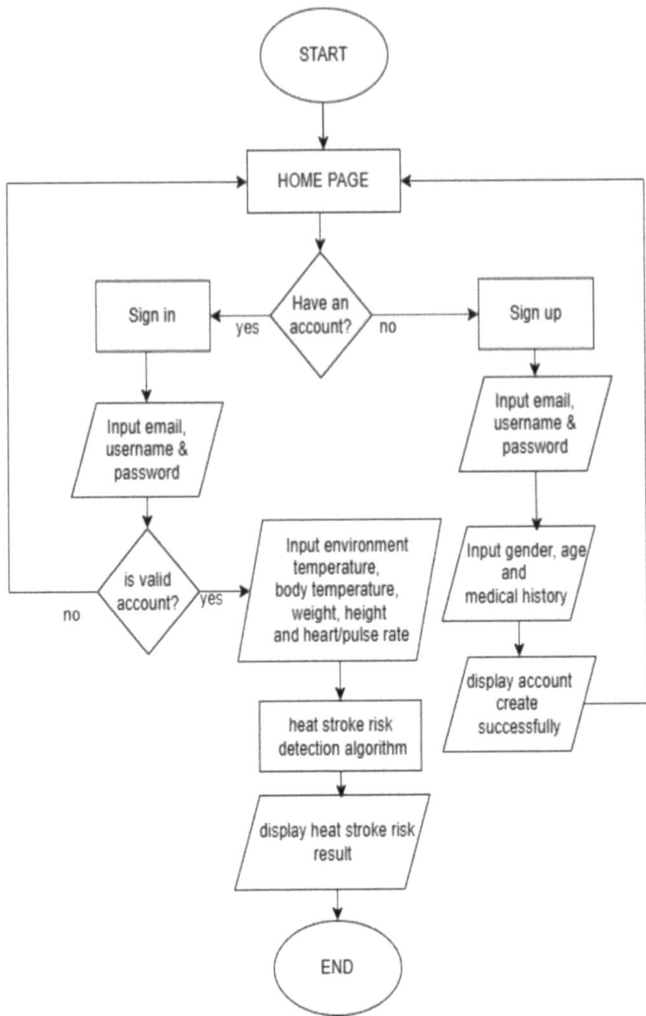

Fig. 4. Flowchart of the application.

Use Case Diagram

A use case diagram serves as a valuable tool to illustrate the interaction between users and the application. In this diagram, the actor symbol represents the user entity who will utilize the application, while the oval symbol denotes use cases, representing the functionalities provided by the application for the user. Figure 5 describe the use case diagram for the application. Based on Fig. 5, the sequence begins when the user with a registered account login and filling in the specific medical information to perform the heat stroke risk detection method. Then, the user receives the result of heat stroke level and corresponding recommendation based on heat stroke risk detection algorithm that apply Random Forest method approach. In Fig. 5 the action that user able to do is login to user account and if it is a new user, they able to create new account. Then, the user able to fill in their medical conditions. These include height, weight, body temperature, environment temperature and heart/pulse rate. After that, user able to view heat stroke risk result and their recommendations.

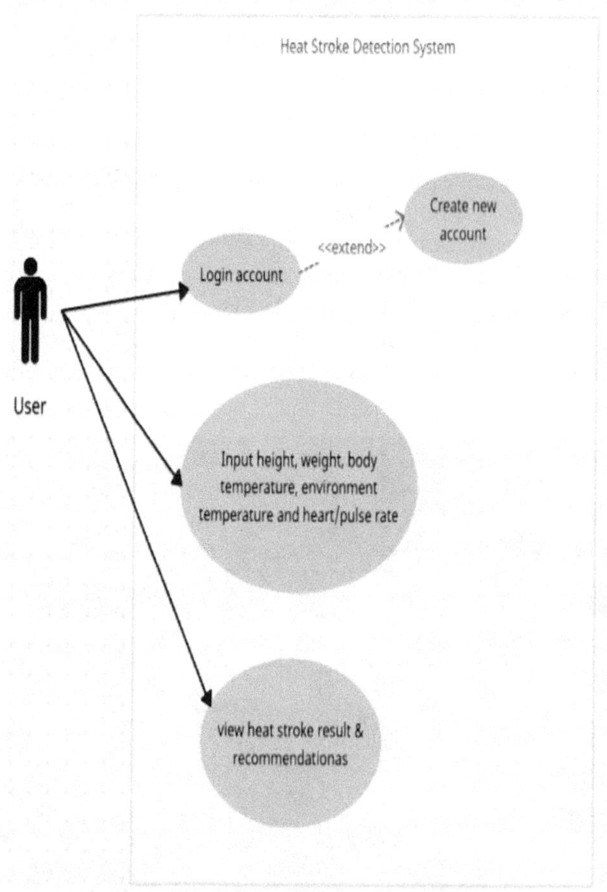

Fig. 5. Use case diagram of the application.

Development

In main objective of the development phase is to develop the application based on how the application has been illustrated in design phase. The development phase of this application is divided two main parts; preprocessing and developing heat stroke risk detection algorithm. The first part is where the data collection, data cleaning and feature selections happens. The second part is where the heat stroke detection risk algorithm is being develop. Just then the algorithm developed will be used in the application.

1. Preprocessing

In the preprocessing phase, the data is collected from Kaggle in CSV format which consist of a combination of medical history, environmental, and physiological data. The dataset contains records of 609 patients' data. This data will be used for supervised learning in Heat Stroke Risk Prediction algorithm. Then, the data cleaning is set to ensure the data are fit for analysis and also to improve data quality. The inconsistency in data values is being corrected. From the data collected, only 22 features are selected in the feature selections process.

2. Heat Stroke Risk Detection Algorithm

The software tools use to develop the algorithm is Jupyter Notebook. The algorithm is develop using Python programming language as shown in Fig. 6. The dataset from preprocessing part is being used for training the algorithm. The algorithm is develop using Random Forest method as its ability to handle complex datasets and robust to overfitting makes it a suitable candidate for detection tasks. The algorithm utilizes labelled training data to recognize patterns and predict outcomes accurately. Through application of Random Forest method, it able to achieve an accuracy testing rate of 100%.

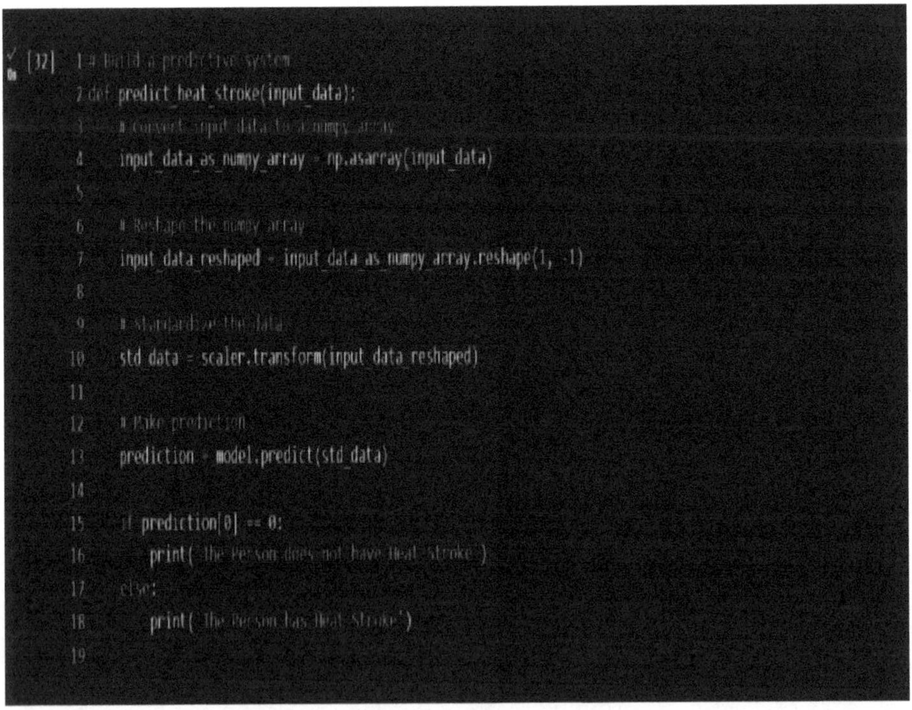

```
[32]
# Build a predictive system
def predict_heat_stroke(input_data):
    # Convert input data to a numpy array
    input_data_as_numpy_array = np.asarray(input_data)

    # Reshape the numpy array
    input_data_reshaped = input_data_as_numpy_array.reshape(1, -1)

    # Standardize the data
    std_data = scaler.transform(input_data_reshaped)

    # Make prediction
    prediction = model.predict(std_data)

    if prediction[0] == 0:
        print('The Person does not have Heat Stroke')
    else:
        print('The Person has Heat Stroke')

```

Fig. 6. Heat Stroke risk detection algorithm

3. Heat Stroke Risk Detection Application

While, Visual Studio is used as a platform for the application development purpose. This application is a web application that will apply Heat Stroke Risk Detection Algorithm in the process of heat stroke risk detection for user. In the development of this application, source codes for both front-end and back-end is implemented. This application use Firebase as the database. This application includes several interfaces and functions that are sign in page and sign-up page for new user and also medical information page.

Testing
In this phase, the functionality of Heat Stroke Risk Detection application is tested. Functionality test is required in order to verify that the system features and functionalities work as specified in the requirements. Through functionality testing it shows that the application has successfully passed all test elements and able to gain the actual results the same as the expected result.

4 Result and Discussion

Heat Stroke Risk Detection application able to help user to identify whether they are having a heat stroke condition or not. This application interacts with user through numbers of user interface. The interface includes are sign-up page, sign-in page and medical information page.

4.1 Sign-Up and Sign-In Page

The application enables new user to register themselves through sign up page as in Fig. 7. When the sign-up button was hit, the event listener prevents the default form submission behaviour and retrieves the values of the username, email, and password fields. Using the createUserWithEmailAndPassword function from Firebase Authentication, the script attempts to create a new user with the provided email and password. If successful, it retrieves the user's credentials and saves additional user information (username and email) to the Firebase Realtime Database using the set function. The code creates a registration form by leveraging Firebase function to handle user creation and authentication, ensuring a smooth and integrated user registration experience within the web application.

An event listener is set up for the sign-in button click event as in Fig. 7. When the button is clicked, the event listener retrieves the values of the email and password fields. Using the signInWithEmailAndPassword function from Firebase Authentication, the script attempts to sign in the user with the provided email and password. If successful, it retrieves the user's credentials and updates the user's last login time in the Firebase Realtime Database using the update function.

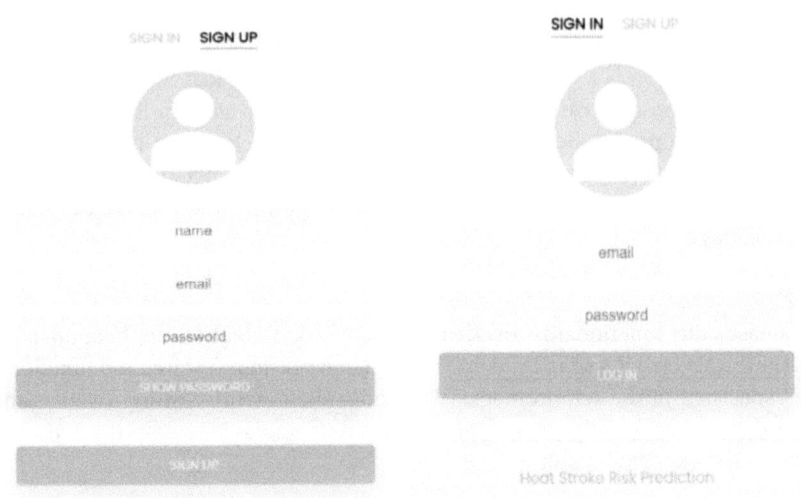

Fig. 7. Sign-up and sign-in page of the application.

4.2 Medical Information Page

A crucial component of the heat stroke risk detection application is the medical information page as shown in Fig. 8. This page is responsible to gather user inputs that will invoke the detection model and handling the response. User inputs on health parameters that based on 22 features that has been specified are collected and validated before being sent to the model. The code sets up a web page for predicting heat stroke risk using a machine learning model.

At the bottom of this page, a download report button is included which will be use to show the detection result when the detect button is submitted and processed by the Flask backend. The code leverages Flask for backend processing that will handle the form submission, run the heat stroke risk detection algorithm and return the result as in Fig. 10. This is to ensures that users can easily input necessary data for heat stroke risk detection based on medical and environmental data.

Fig. 8. Medical information page of the application.

Upon form submission, the feature values are extracted from the request as in Fig. 9., then converted to floating-point numerical format and assembled into a NumPy array. This array is subsequently scaled using a pre-saved scaler object to ensure consistency with the model's training data. The scaled features are then input into a pre-trained machine learning model that will generates a prediction regarding the user's risk of heat stroke.

```python
@flask_app.route("/predict", methods=["POST"])
def predict():
    # Receive all 22 features
    feature_names = ["Daily Ingested Water (L)", "Cardiovascular disease history", "Dehydration", "Heat Index (HI)",
                     "Diastolic BP", "Environmental temperature (C)", "Sickle Cell Trait (SCT)", "Systolic BP",
                     "Weight (kg)", "Patient temperature", "Rectal temperature (deg C)", "Relative Humidity",
                     "Exposure to sun", "BMI", "Exertional (1) vs classic (0)", "Heart / Pulse rate (b/min)",
                     "Age", "Sweating", "Strenuous exercise", "Sex", "Hot/dry skin", "Time of day"]

    try:
        # Extract the input features from the form
        float_features = [float(request.form[feature]) for feature in feature_names]
        features = np.array(float_features).reshape(1, -1)

        # Apply the same scaling as used during training
        features_scaled = scaler.transform(features)

        # Make the prediction
        prediction = model.predict(features_scaled)[0]
```

Fig. 9. Backend processing for the form.

```python
def predict():
        prediction = model.predict(features_scaled)[0]

        # Determine the result and provide personalized description
        if prediction == 1:
            result = "Heat Stroke"
            description = (
                "Based on the input data, you are at risk of heat stroke. "
                "It's important to stay hydrated, avoid strenuous activity during peak heat, "
                "wear light and loose clothing, and stay in shaded or air conditioned areas. "
                "Monitor for symptoms such as high body temperature, confusion, or fainting. "
                "The model accuracy is {:.2f}%.".format(accuracy * 100)
            )
        else:
            result = "No Risk of Heat Stroke"
            description = (
                "Based on the input data, you are not currently at risk of heat stroke. "
                "However, it's always a good idea to stay hydrated, take regular breaks in the shade, "
                "and avoid strenuous activity during peak heat hours to minimize future risk. "
                "The model accuracy is {:.2f}%.".format(accuracy * 100)
            )
```

Fig. 10. Heat stroke detection model result example.

The heat stroke risk detection model will return a result of either "Heat Stroke" or "No Risk of Heat Stroke" together with a personalized prevention suggestion as in Fig. 10.

Then, the result will be displayed to user and the user able to download it.

5 Summary

Heat stroke is a serious condition that is getting more attention because of rising temperatures and more frequent extreme heat events. Certain individuals are vulnerable such as those with pre-existing medical conditions. They have a greater risk and require timely intervention to avoid serious health consequences.

Hence, an application that able to do heat stroke risk detection is developed with the purpose of early detection and preventive guidance especially for high-risk individual. This contributes to early medical intervention, minimizes the occurrence of heat-related conditions, and promotes better health outcomes during periods of intense heat.

6 Future Work

For the future research, a study that focus on integrating real-time data, user's medical history and wearable technology for continuous monitoring and expanding the application's features is suggested. This will be allowing for more accurate detection based on users' health condition and prevention initiatives and effective resource allocation during heat-related emergencies.

Acknowledgment. The authors would like to express their sincere gratitude to Universiti Teknologi Mara Shah Alam and Universiti Teknologi Mara Shah Cawangan Johor for their invaluable support and resources provided throughout the completion of this research.

References

Pargaonkar, S.: A comprehensive research analysis of Software Development Life Cycle (SDLC) Agile & Waterfall model advantages, disadvantages, and application suitability in software quality engineering. Int. J. Sci. Res. Publ. **13**, 120–124 (2023). https://doi.org/10.29322/IJSRP.13.08.2023.p14015.

Yahya, N., Maidin, S.S.: The waterfall model with agile scrum as the hybrid agile model for the software engineering team. 2022 10th International Conference on Cyber and IT Service Management, CITSM pp. 1–5 (2022). https://doi.org/10.1109/CITSM56380.2022.9936036

Teo, W.S., Ramli, D.A., Aziz, A.A.: Wearable heat stroke detection system in IoT-based environment. Procedia Comput. Sci. **192**, 3686–3695 (2021). https://doi.org/10.1016/j.procs.2021.09.142

Yimyam, W., Ketcham, M., Chumuang, N., Utakrit, N., Rattanasiriwongwut, M., Hiranchan, S.: A development heat stroke detection system integrated with infrared camera. Proceedings-2020 15th International Joint Symposium on Artificial Intelligence and Natural Language Processing, ISAI-NLP, pp. 5–9 (2020). https://doi.org/10.1109/iSAI-NLP51646.2020.9376814

Nizam, C.M., Ismail, A.R., Husshin, N.: Malaysia construction worker perception on heat stress and its impact on work performance. J. Bus. Leadersh. Manage. **1**(1), 9 (2023). https://doi.org/10.59762/jblm845920461120231009092253

Hassan, N.A., Hashim, J.H., Johar, Z., Faisal, M.S.: The implications of climatic changes on food and water-borne diseases in Malaysia: a case study of Kelantan, Terengganu, Johor and Melaka. BMC Publ. Health BioMed Central **14** (2014). https://doi.org/10.1186/1471-2458-14-s1-p22

Awadalla, S., Noor, M.I.: Induced climate change on surface runoff in Kelantan Malaysia. In: International Journal of Water Resources Development (Vol. 7, Issue 1, p. 53). Taylor & Francis (1991). https://doi.org/10.1080/07900629108722492

Mahmood, J., Guinto, R.: Lessons from climate reports for the Malaysian medical community. In: Malaysian Journal of Medical Sciences (Vol. 29, Issue 3, p. 1). University of Science Malaysia (2022). https://doi.org/10.21315/mjms2022.29.3.1

Jay, O., et al.: Reducing the health effects of hot weather and heat extremes: from personal cooling strategies to green cities [Review of Reducing the health effects of hot weather and heat extremes: from personal cooling strategies to green cities]. The Lancet, 398(10301), 709. Elsevier BV (2021). https://doi.org/10.1016/s0140-6736(21)01209-5

Yong, K.H., Teo, Y.N., Azadbakht, M., Phung, H., Chu, C.: The scorching truth: investigating the impact of heatwaves on Selangor's elderly hospitalisations. In: International Journal of Environmental Research and Public Health (Vol. 20, Issue 10, p. 5910). Multidisciplinary Digital Publishing Institute (2023). https://doi.org/10.3390/ijerph20105910

Maini, E., Venkateswarlu, B.: Improving the performance of heart disease prediction system using ensembling techniques. In: AIP Conference Proceedings (Vol. 2316, p. 50002). American Institute of Physics (2021). https://doi.org/10.1063/5.0036478

Ogunpola, A., Saeed, F., Basurra, S., Albarrak, A.M., Qasem, S.N.: Machine learning-based predictive models for detection of cardiovascular diseases. In: Diagnostics (Vol. 14, Issue 2, p. 144). Multidisciplinary Digital Publishing Institute (2024). https://doi.org/10.3390/diagnostics14020144

Intra-Gap Method: An Enhanced Elbow Method for Determining the Initial Cluster Numbers in Clustering Analysis

Ahmad Haadzal Kamarulzalis, Norshahida Shaadan(✉), Sayang Mohd Deni, and Nurain Ibrahim

Faculty of Computer and Mathematical Sciences, Universiti Teknologi MARA, Shah Alam 40450, Selangor, Malaysia
shahida@tmsk.uitm.edu.my

Abstract. Unsupervised clustering is crucial in data analysis. However, determining an appropriate initial number of clusters (k) poses challenges for methods like k-means, which typically require this initial number to be predefined. The Elbow method has been widely used to identify the ideal number of clusters (k). Still, its effectiveness diminishes when the resulting plot lacks a clear elbow or knee point, thus complicating the selection of k. To overcome the limitation, this study introduces the Intra-Gap method to enhance the traditional Elbow approach. It is done by refining the gap analysis used in the Elbow method for application. Based on the analysis conducted on the three benchmark datasets (Iris, Breast Cancer, and Vehicles) for the data clustering analysis using the k-means algorithm, the study concludes that the Intra-Gap method offers a promising solution. The study found that the accuracy of the output matched the benchmark number of clusters, k. This method has proven effective and has made a significant contribution to the field of data clustering techniques.

Keywords: Clustering · Elbow Method · k-means

1 Introduction

Clustering analysis aims to segregate data into subgroups (clusters) based on their characteristics, patterns, and attributes. There are currently no optimal algorithms for clustering that suit all data in general. This is because, as highlighted by [1], different datasets have properties that lead to a distinct appropriate algorithm for the best clustering solution. Hence, various clustering methods covering both hard and soft clustering were developed. Besides the large development, one clustering method that has been popularly used over the 50th years is the k-means algorithm [2]. The simple procedure and easy implementation of the technique are the strongest reasons why the k-means becomes a well-known clustering algorithm.

However, a major drawback of the k-means method is that a user needs a predefined optimum number of clusters (k) in the pre-processing stage before the clustering analysis

M. Kassim et al. (Eds.): SCDS 2025, CCIS 2674, pp. 451–463, 2026.
https://doi.org/10.1007/978-981-95-8368-3_32

can take place. This issue has become the main challenge of clustering analysis. Many methods have been proposed to identify the value of k [3], and the most classical, oldest, and famous method is the Elbow plot. The Elbow method is a visualization technique that presents an "elbow and knee" point. It is a graphical method based on the notion that the sum of squared distances between points and their cluster centers (WCSS) decreases as the number of clusters increases.

Typically, the k-means algorithm relies on the Euclidean distance metric, that are widely used but sensitive to noise and outliers. This sensitivity can distort clustering outcomes as the distance metric attempts to incorporate noisy and outlier points within the circular cluster boundaries. A study by [4] emphasized that the Elbow method in k-means clustering can be greatly affected by even minor outliers, which have the potential to distort the calculation of cluster centroids. This sentiment is reinforced by [5], who further highlight that noise and outliers in data disrupt the initial selection and subsequent adjustment of centroid positions, resulting in suboptimal clustering outcomes. Furthermore, research by [6] demonstrates how outliers can disrupt the relocation of centroids in k-means clustering due to its reliance on the mean concept.

In some cases, a common problem persists as an ambiguity issue. That is, the Elbow plot becomes slightly smooth, causing uncertainty in detecting the knee point from the plotted Elbow curve [7], as the results are subjective. This may be due to the distortion effect. After all, no measurement metric shows which elbow points are explicitly optimum. The ambiguity problem of applying the Elbow method is illustrated in Fig. 1. Figure 1(a) shows the ideal elbow plot whereby the "knee" point can be identified clearly, suggesting the optimal clustering size k is 4. Meanwhile, Fig. 1 (b) has a smoother elbow plot. It shows a smooth curve where there exist ambiguous issues in distinguishing the most appropriate number of clusters, k. The situation illustrated in Fig. 1(b) caused difficulty as the Elbow plot became unreliable as a visualization reference for k, as the knee point is not clear.

Thus, to overcome the shortcomings of the Elbow method, an enhancement method is proposed in this study. The development is based on the hybridization approach between the concept of distances of perpendicular lines and the changes of slope, namely, as Intra Gap.

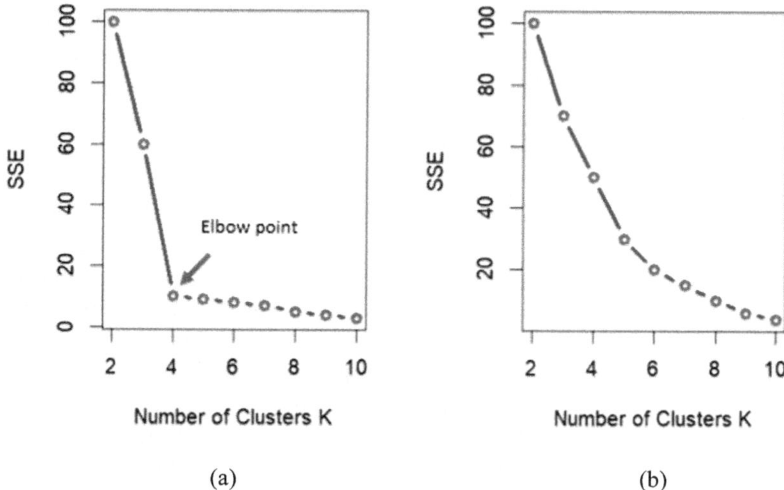

Fig. 1. Visualization of (a) Normal Elbow plot and (b) Ambiguous Elbow Plot

2 Methodology

2.1 Research Framework

The development of the Intra-gap method is conducted following a research framework depicted in Fig. 2. It describes the stage-by-stage approach and procedures to achieve the research objective.

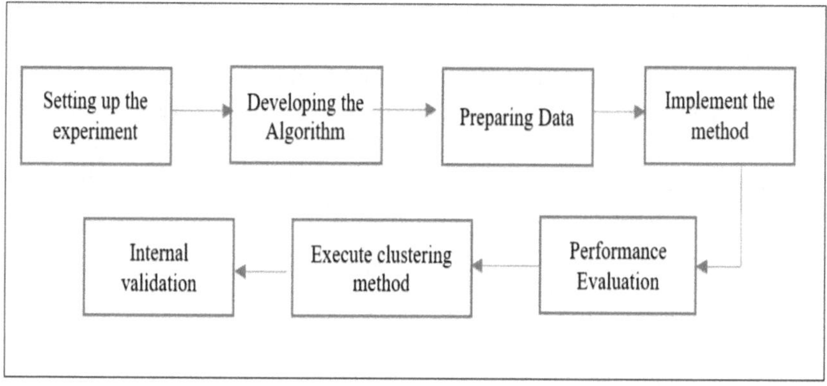

Fig. 2. Flow diagram of a research framework

The first stage is to set up the experiment by identifying the problem statement, research objectives, and the potential method. The next stage is to develop the enhanced algorithm by considering three benchmark datasets. The performance of the existing Elbow method is improved by moderating the results of the gap between the within-cluster sum of squares (WCSS) of the Elbow method. The third stage is data preparation.

This stage is conducted aiming to provide data for the experimental analysis. The iris data, breast cancer, and vehicle data were prepared as a reference for comparison analysis to assess the performance of the proposed Intra-Gap method. The Iris data consists of 50 observations with 4 dimensions of continuous variables. The second dataset is the Breast Cancer (Wisconsin Diagnostic) data with 699 observations and 11 variables. Vehicle Silhouette data will be the last benchmark data to evaluate the robustness of the proposed method. The dataset consists of 4 groups with 849 observations and 19 variables, which is larger than the Iris and Vehicle datasets. Next, stage four is the implementation stage, where the existing classical Elbow method and the proposed Intra-Gap method are applied to the benchmark data to investigate the exact potential initial numbers of clusters (k). Stage five is the performance evaluation using a visualization approach. Before the internal validation of the proposed method's performance at the final stage is conducted, the clustering process is executed using default distance matrices (Euclidean Distance) for the k-means algorithm for each respective k (usually k from 1 to 10). The internal validations concerning connectivity, silhouette width, and Dunn index are used as an alternative approach to highlight the promising initial number of clusters k by the Intra-Gap method. The R programming software was used as the analysis tool in this research.

2.2 Clustering Using k-means

There are many clustering methods. The methods can be divided into several types, including partitioning, hierarchical, density-based, model-based, and many more [8]. The k-means clustering algorithm is a partitioning clustering method. It groups the data into k clusters. The distance measures (Euclidean Distance) are used to find the minimum distance between points within each cluster and assign the data points to the clusters. Created by James McQueen in 1967 [9], k-means is classified as an unsupervised machine learning technique because the data does not have an a priori categorization. The k-means algorithm is the most used partitioning clustering technique because it is computationally faster [17], guarantees convergence, and is relatively simple to implement. It divides the data into k clusters, with one object in each group and one object belonging to each group. Data were assigned according to the nearest centroid, and the centroid was updated by taking the mean value within the group.

$$\sum\nolimits_{j=1}^{k} \sum\nolimits_{x_i \in C_j} \left\| x_i - \mu_j \right\|^2 \tag{1}$$

Let x_i be the set of datasets and the C_i is the centroid for each cluster for $1 \le i \le k$. The value k represents the input parameter or the number of clusters. It needs to be specified by the users as an initial step. The difference between data and the centroid is calculated by default using distance metrics (Euclidean Distance) before it converges.

2.3 Methods for Identifying Initial Cluster Number

Elbow Method

This Elbow method focuses on the percentage of variants as a function of the number of clusters. Based on the idea that there should be an optimal number of clusters for the k-means algorithm, thus increasing the number of k affects the Within Cluster Sum of Squares Error (WCSS). The values are used to determine the elbow point.

$$WCSS = argmin \sum_{j=1}^{k} \sum_{x_i \in C_j} \left\| x_i - \mu_j \right\|^2 \tag{2}$$

WCSS is the total mean distance within the cluster of each point from its centroid [10]. When there is a drastic change in WCSS value by mapping toward the number of clusters (k), elbow or knee curves are defined to indicate the appropriate number of clusters (k). Starting from k = 1, the values of WCSS were recorded, so that for the k value, k + 1, k + 2, ..., k + n. When there are no significant changes in the values of WCSS, it indicates a convergence condition.

The Proposed Intra-Gap Method

As mentioned earlier, the smooth Elbow curve condition causes an ambiguity issue for determining the elbow or knee point for the appropriate initial number of clusters k. This study enhances the Elbow method by proposing the Intra-Gap method, which is developed based on the concept of perpendicular line distance with the changes of slope values WCSS.

Intra Gap (IG) is an enhancement of the elbow method, whereby the idea is to overcome the ambiguity issue of the smoothness Elbow curve, particularly the multiple knees. This method employed a mode cluster, which represents the difference between the WCSS within clusters concerning each k. This method visualizes an appropriate initial number of clusters with a maximum gap within cluster sum of squares (gap WCSS) with respect to maximum distance of perpendicular line and changes of slope where k = {1,2,3.. 9,10}. The mathematical formulation of Intra-Gap is as follows.

$$WCSS_k = argmin \sum_{j=1}^{k} \sum_{x_i \in C_j} \left\| x_i - \mu_j \right\|^2 \tag{3}$$

$$w_k = \frac{WCSS_k - min_{k=1}^{k_{max}}(WCSS_k)}{(WCSS_k) - min_{k=1}^{k_{max}}(WCSS_k)} \tag{4}$$

$$D_{k=2}^{k_{max}} = \frac{\left|\left(w_{k_{max}} - w_{k_{min}}\right)k + (k_{min} - k_{max})w_k + \left(k_{max}w_{k_{min}} - k_{min}w_{k_{max}}\right)\right|}{\sqrt{\left(w_{k_{max}} - w_{k_{min}}\right)^2 - (k_{min} - k_{max})^2}} \tag{5}$$

$$m_{k=2}^{k=8} = 2w_{k+1} - w_k - w_{k+2}$$

$$H_{k=2}^{k=8} = \alpha(w_k) + (1 - \alpha)m_{k=2}^{k=8} \tag{6}$$

Which finally results in the following Eq. (7) as follows:

$$IntraGap = k_{Best} = arg_{k \in \{2,\ldots k_{max}-2\}} maxH_k \tag{7}$$

The proposed method, which is Intra Gap, focuses on finding the best k based on the knee of the within-cluster sum of squares (WCSS). The $WCSS_k$ represents each of the WCSS associated with each k = {1,2, ..., 10}, where w_k represents the normalization of

$WCSS_k$ by using the concept of min-max scaling. The next step is to find the perpendicular distance between the baseline, which is the connection of $WCSS_1$ and $WCSS_{10}$, for each point of the elbow method, and this phase is represented by $D_{k=2}^{kmax}$ formulation. The highest distance of perpendicular was considered as the first value concerning the best k. The next step is finding the changes of slope in each point of WCSS, which it represented by $m_{k=2}^{k=8}$ The maximum m indicates the best k. The last step is to combine all maximum perpendicular distances (D_k) and the changes of slope (m_k), and add a weightage (α), and a default $\alpha = 0.5$, represent the last step as the mean of each perpendicular distance and changes of slope. The end product is the maximum H_k concerning each k {2, ..., 10}. This Intra Gap not only represents the method to capture the knee but it is also robust by cyberization of two concepts.

2.4 Internal Validation

Clustering validation aims to validate the results of a clustering analysis and determine which clustering algorithm is the best. The validation method in clustering can be specified into two subdivisions, which are internal and external validation methods [11]. The study employed several measures for internal validation, including connectivity, Silhouette width, and Dunn Index. The clustering result is assessed solely based on the internal structure of the data it clusters, without reference to external information. Evaluation indices measure two critical properties: compactness, which evaluates how closely objects within a cluster are grouped, and separation, which quantifies the distance between different clusters. Therefore, an effective clustering algorithm strives to produce clusters that are tightly packed internally yet sufficiently distant from each other, ensuring both high compactness and separation metrics are achieved.

Connectivity

Connectivity is an internal validation method to observe data in the same cluster and other clusters [12]. Define $nn_{i(j)}$ as the jth nearest neighbors of i and $x_{i,nn_{n(j)}}$ zero if $iandnn_{i(j)}$ are the same cluster if not $1/j$ and C defines the clusters of the N observation into disjoint clusters where L represents a parameter that determines the number of neighbors. The connectivity value lies between zero and infinity, where it needs to be minimized.

$$Conn(c) = \sum_{i=1}^{N} \sum_{j=1}^{L} x_{i,nn_{i(j)}} \tag{8}$$

Silhouette Width

Silhouette value measures the degree of confidence in the clustering assignment of a particular observation. Silhouette values of approximately 1 represent good clustered observations, while poorly clustered observations have values near negative (−1).

$$S(i) = \frac{b_i - a_i}{(b_i, a_i)} \tag{9}$$

representation of the Silhouette method above, where a_i is the average distance between i and all other observations in the same cluster, and b_i is the average distance between i

and the observations in the "nearest neighboring cluster". The silhouette width that lies in the interval -1 and 1 should be minimized [13].

Dunn Index

The Dunn index introduced by Dunn (1974) [14] refers to the ratio of the smallest distance between the observation's nearest neighbor cluster to the largest intra-cluster (within the cluster) distance. The Dunn index is between zero and infinity and should be maximized. The Dunn index evaluates clusters based on their compactness, which refers to the minimal variance within each cluster, and their separation, indicating substantial distance between the means of different clusters compared to their internal variance. A higher Dunn index indicates more effective clustering. The optimal number of clusters k is determined by identifying the number that maximizes the Dunn index.

3 Results and Discussion

This section presents the results of the data analysis, which include several experiments conducted to assess and validate the effectiveness and reliability of the proposed Intra-Gap method using three benchmark datasets, which are the Iris dataset (n = 50), Breast Cancer (n = 699) and Vehicle data (n = 846). The experiment was also conducted to see the efficiencies of Intra-Gap in determining cluster numbers when thru three distinct benchmark datasets. The experiment was carried out using the R programming language. The robustness of the proposed method was measured by comparing the Intra-Gap with the Classical Elbow Method. Internal validation methods, including Connectivity, Dunn Index, and Silhouette Index, are implemented for more promising results.

3.1 Data Experimentation

The results of the Elbow method and the Intra-Gap method in determining an appropriate initial number of clusters, k, for the three benchmark datasets are discussed in this section. Recall, the Iris dataset is often used as benchmark data in clustering investigations. There are four variables: Sepal Length, Sepal Width, Petal Length, and Petal Width for three defined clusters of flowers: Setosa, Versicolor, and Virginica. The second dataset is Breast Cancer data (Wisconsin Diagnostic), which consists of 11 variables: ID, Cell thickness, Cell size, Cell shape and etc. This dataset consists of 699 data points with 2 defined clusters (Benign Cell = 458 and Malignant = 241). The third dataset is the Vehicle Silhouettes. The dataset consists of 19 variables with 4 clusters, including bus, opel, saab, and van, with a total of 846 rows. These datasets were employed to assess the performance of the proposed Intra-Gap method.

Iris Dataset

To visually represent the suggested k = 3 clusters identified by the Intra-Gap method for the Iris dataset, Principal Component Analysis (PCA) is utilized to reduce the dimensionality into two linear combinations of variables. Figure 3 shows the clustering results using the k-means algorithm, illustrating the steps before (classical Elbow method) and after implementing the Intra-Gap method (k = 3) for cluster assignment.

It is important to note that when determining the initial k clusters, the data preprocessing process needs to be done beforehand. The Euclidean k-means limits the algorithm's robustness in detecting cluster shapes and poses a great challenge in detecting overlapping clusters. The initial insight on defining the initial cluster k for the k-means algorithm was the first step that needed to be predefined by the users. The following results contribute to understanding the importance of determining "knee" in the Elbow method and hence the proposed Intra-Gap method in identifying an appropriate initial cluster size k is highlighted.

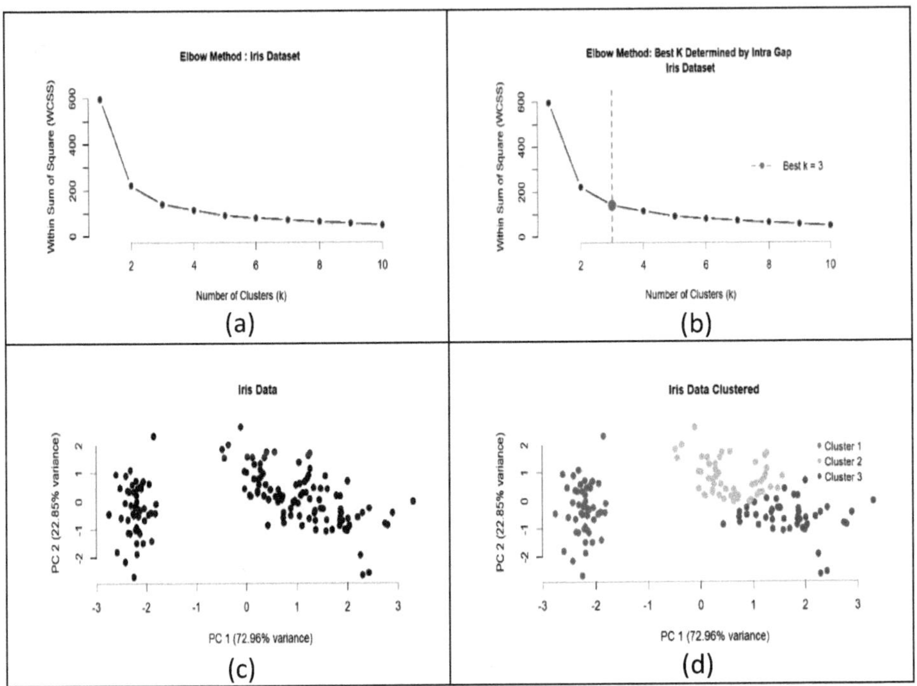

Fig. 3. (a) The Elbow Method curve; (b) Intra-Gap Method; (c) Scatter Plot PC2 vs PC1 and (d) Scatter Plot PCA2 vs PC1 with k = 3 clusters.

Figure 3(a) and (b) show a clear comparison of the ambiguous case in identifying an initial number of cluster k using the Elbow method. Figure 3(b) represents the Elbow method with a vertical line indicating the best k concerning decision making by the proposed method of Intra Gap. While Fig. 3(c) and (d) represent the Iris data before and after clustering by the respective best k. The best initial k suggested by Intra Gap aligns with the predefined label for 3 clusters of the Iris data set, which is 3; cluster Setosa, virginica and versicolor species.

Breast Cancer Dataset

Knee determination of classical Elbow method (Fig. 4(a)) for Breast cancer data by using k-means algorithm is not as ambiguous as Iris data, the knee of the Elbow plot

(Fig. 4(a)) clearly shows, the curvature of the Elbow method suggests an initial number of cluster k of 2. Meanwhile, the proposed method is also able to capture the knee of the best k, which is k = 2, matching the benchmark number. Thus, it shows that the Intra-Gap is not only capable of detecting the knee with slow changes, but it is also able to define the knee with a sharper and clearer "knee" image. Figure 4(c) and 4(d) represent Breast Cancer data without and with clustering concerning the best k, which is k = 2. Figure 4(d) not only represents the scatter plot concerning each cluster, but it also highlights the success of Intra Gap in determining the initial number of clusters concerning predefined clusters (Benign Cell = 458 and Malignant = 241).

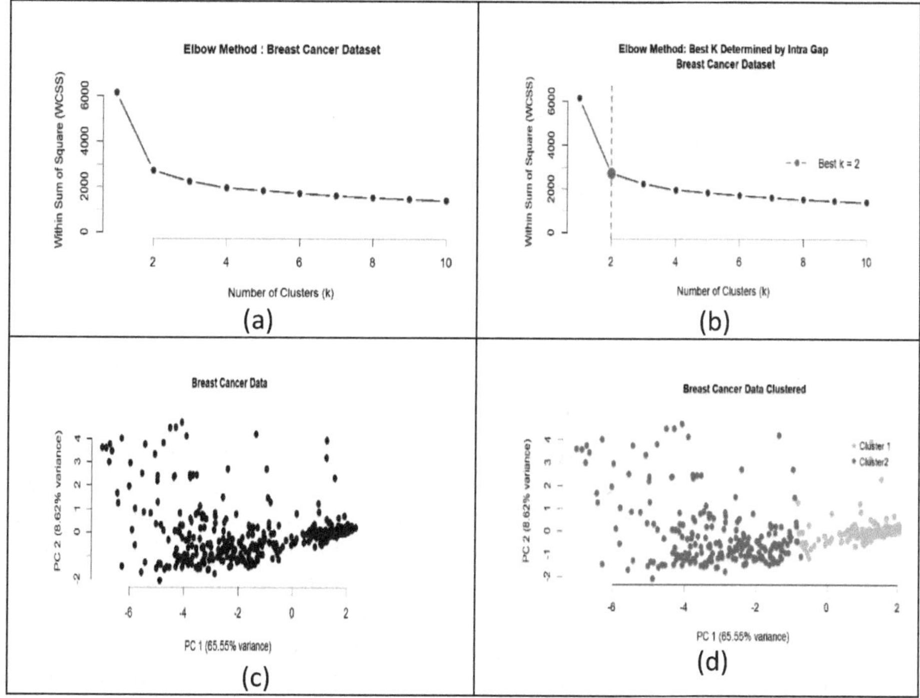

Fig. 4. (a) The Elbow Method curve; (b) Intra-Gap Method; (c) Scatter Plot PC2 vs PC1 and (d) Scatter Plot PCA2 vs PC1 with k = 2 clusters.

Vehicle Dataset

The classical Elbow curve (Fig. 5(a)) shows a clearer curve compared to both previous curves, and the normal eye can determine the knee of the elbow curve. The smooth condition presents a big challenge to a user in determining the best k value with the classical knee approach. Even though the curve is highly smooth, the Intra-Gap can capture the best initial k, and it overcomes the drawback of the Elbow method and does not fully depend on the knee concept.

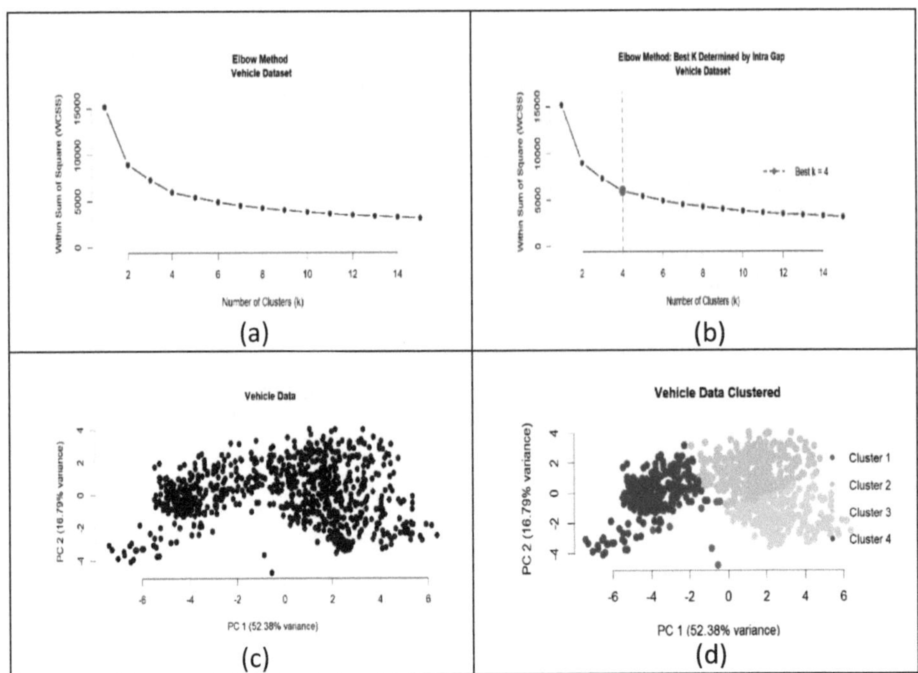

Fig. 5. (a) The Elbow Method curve; (b) Intra-Gap Method; (c) Scatter Plot PC2 vs PC1 and (d) Scatter Plot PCA2 vs PC1 with k = 4 clusters.

Clustering quality indices serve a dual purpose: evaluating the quality of partitions and determining the optimal number of clusters in the final clustering result. Table 1 shows the internal validation results on the performance of the proposed Intra-Gap method based on the three indices: Connectivity, Dunn index, and silhouette width. These indices measured the efficiency of clustering, aiming to minimize connectivity and achieve a maximum value close to 1 for the Dunn index and silhouette width. The best number of clusters was determined using a majority vote (mode) across these metrics. For the Iris dataset, the majority vote suggested k = 2 clusters, whereas the predefined clusters are k = 3 (setosa, virginica, and versicolor). This discrepancy indicates a contradiction with the Elbow method's suggestion, whereas the proposed Intra-Gap method successfully identified an optimal cluster number aligned with the predefined k. While for the Intra-Gap method, the consistently recommended optimal cluster number based on these internal validations was k = 3 with respect to actual clusters. In contrast, the classical Elbow method struggled to define optimal clusters, often encountering unclear or multiple knee curves.

Table 1. Comparison of Internal Validation, Elbow and Proposed Method

Dataset	Validation Criteria	Score	Cluster numbers	Mode	Cluster numbers (k)		
					Elbow	Intra Gap	Benchmark
Iris	Connectivity Dunn Silhouette	0.0001 0.2294 0.6810	2 2 2	2	2,3	3	3
Breast Cancer	Connectivity Dunn Silhouette	0.1704 0.0531 0.5053	2 2 2	2	2	2	2
Vehicle	Connectivity Dunn Silhouette	0.0001 0.0264 0.0768	2 6 2	2	2,3	4	4

The initial number of cluster k for Breast Cancer data by using the Elbow method is defined by k = 2, and it is associated with the internal validation. The Intra-Gap also suggests an initial number of k = 2. The changes within cluster sum of squares (WCSS) drastically change at k = 1 until k = 3 before the values slowly converge for the increasing numbers of k, despite that, it is easy for both the classical elbow method and Intra-Gap to define the initial number of clusters k, which is k = 2.

The vehicle data represent the smoothest elbow curve (Fig. 5(a)) in the comparison part, whereby the majority of existing methods are unable to clearly define the knee for the best k. The predefined vehicle data indicate k = 4 (bas, opel, saat and van), the separation of the data in Fig. 5(c) is also highly random and if using a human expert judgement, there are only two clusters. Based on the internal validation, connectivity and silhouette suggest optimal k = 2 while the Dunn index suggests k = 6, which is more out of the best clusters. The proposed method shows an outstanding performance when it managed to find the best initial numbers of cluster k, which aligns with the pre-defined cluster, k = 4. The Intra-Gap performs a sustained output even though the three benchmarks differ in their nature, but still, the Intra-Gap can capture the pre-defined initial number of clusters k.

4 Conclusion

This paper introduces an enhanced method derived from the classical Elbow technique for determining the optimal number of clusters in partitioning clustering algorithms, focusing specifically on the k-means algorithm and its application toward clustering of benchmark data. The classical elbow method has been widely used for obtaining an initial indication of suitable cluster numbers through visualization. However, accurately estimating the optimal number of potential clusters becomes challenging and subjective when the curve lacks smoothness, resulting in ambiguous Elbow point identification. This unreliability occurs due to unclear bends in the line chart.

To tackle this issue, the classical Elbow curve is enhanced by integrating the gap within cluster sum of squares (WCSS) for each k. The WCSS for the Elbow method, with those three-benchmark data, is plotted against varying cluster numbers (k), with the mean of maximum perpendicular distance and maximum change slope indicating an appropriate initial number of clusters for the k-means algorithm. Finding the knee (peak) is optimal for determining the ideal cluster numbers for the k-means algorithm, which is supported by prior research [15, 16]. This approach is consistent with the Intra-Gap method.

Experimental results demonstrate that the Intra-Gap method consistently aligns with the benchmark Iris cluster size (k = 3), breast cancer (k = 2) and vehicle data (k = 4), outperforming the classical Elbow method, whereby the graphical visualization is clearer and more efficient. The method's effectiveness is further validated through internal validation techniques across three benchmark datasets. The proposed technique, Intra-Gap, consistently suggests optimal cluster numbers even though the data are different in terms of separation and size, aligning with internal validation methods tailored for k-means algorithms. This proposed method can serve as an alternative approach to identifying optimal cluster numbers, particularly in scenarios with smooth curve issues and when the classical elbow method encounters some challenges due to a lack of smoothness in the Elbow curve.

Acknowledgement. The authors thank the Universiti Teknologi MARA (UiTM) for the support.

References

1. Estivill-Castro, V.: Why so many clustering algorithms: a position paper. ACM SIGKDD Explor. Newsl. **4**(1), 65–75 (2022)
2. Jain, A.K.: Data clustering: 50 years beyond K-means. Pattern Recogn. Lett. **31**(8), 651–666 (2010)
3. Hancer, E., Karaboga, D.: A comprehensive survey of traditional, merge-split and evolutionary approaches proposed for the determination of cluster number. Swarm Evol. Comput. **32**, 49–67 (2017)
4. Kanjanawattana, S.: Int. J. Mach. Learn. Comput. **9**(5), 569–574 (2019)
5. Nowak-Brzezińska, A., Gaibei, I.: How the outliers influence the quality of clustering? Entropy **24**(7), 917 (2022)
6. Meng, C., Lv, Y., Yue, L., Yue, Y.: Intrusion detection method based on improved K-means algorithm. J. Phys: Conf. Ser. **1302**(3), 032011 (2019)
7. D'Silva, J., Sharma, U.: Unsupervised automatic text summarization of Konkani texts using K-means with Elbow method. Int. J. Eng. Res. Technol. **13**(9), 2380–2384 (2020)
8. Saxena, A., et al.: A review of clustering techniques and developments. Neurocomputing **267**, 664–681 (2017)
9. MacQueen, J.B.: Some methods for classification and analysis of multivariate observations. Proceedings of 5th Berkeley Symposium on Mathematical Statistics and Probability. University of California Press. pp. 281–297 (1967)
10. Muningsih, E., Yogyakarta, A.B.S.I.: Optimasi jumlah cluster k-means dengan metode elbow untuk pemetaan pelanggan. Pros. Semin. Nas. ELINVO. pp. 105–114 (2017)
11. Rodriguez, J., Medina-Perez, M.A., Gutierrez-Rodriguez, A.E., Monrova, R., Terashima-Marin, H.: Cluster validation using an ensemble of supervised classifiers. Knowl.-Based Syst. **145**, 134–144 (2018)

12. Handl, J., Knowles, J., Kell, D.B.: Computational cluster validation in post-genomic data analysis. Bioinformatics **21**(15), 3201–3212 (2005)
13. Maechler, M.: Cluster analysis extended Rousseeuw et al. R CRAN (2013)
14. Dunn, J.C.: Well-separated clusters and optimal fuzzy partitions. J. Cybern. **4**(1), 95–104 (1974)
15. Nainggolan, R., Perangin-angin, R., Simarmata, E., Tarigan, A.F.: Improved the performance of the K-means cluster using the sum of squared error (SSE) optimized by using the Elbow method. In: Journal of Physics: Conference Series (Vol. 1361, No. 1, p. 012015). IOP Publishing (2019)
16. Schubert, E.: Stop using the elbow criterion for k-means and how choose the number of clusters instead. ACM SIGKDD Explor. Newsl. **25**(1), 36–42 (2023)
17. Saket, J.S., Pandya, S.: An overview of partitioning algorithms in clustering techniques. Int. J. Adv. Res. Comput. Eng. Technol. (IJARCET) **5**(6), 1943–1946 (2016)

Computing and Optimization

Proactive Adaptive Neighborhood-Based Dynamic Adjustment: A Brain-Region-Inspired Optimizer for Neural Network Optimization

Zidong Chen and Fadratul Hafinaz Hassan(✉)

School of Computer Sciences, Universiti Sains Malaysia, 11800 Gelugor, Penang, Malaysia
fadratul@usm.my

Abstract. Modern deep learning optimization faces persistent challenges in computational efficiency and convergence stability due to complex loss landscapes and heterogeneous parameter dynamics across architectures like CNNs, SNNs, and Transformers. While existing adaptive optimizers (e.g., AdamW, Lion) provide partial solutions, they inadequately address inter-parameter dependencies and neural adaptation mechanisms. Inspired by biological principles of synaptic plasticity and cortical organization, we propose PANDA (Parameter Adaptation through Neural Dynamics Alignment), a novel optimization framework that enhances convergence stability and model generalization through three key innovations: 1) Gradient similarity graphs modeling parameter interdependencies; 2) Dynamic importance quantification enabling context-aware parameter updates; and 3) Region-based grouping balancing local-global optimization dynamics. Comprehensive evaluations demonstrate PANDA's superiority over state-of-the-art methods, achieving 73.3% accuracy on CIFAR-100 with ResNet-50 (vs. AdamW's 70.4%) and reducing WikiText-103 perplexity to 9.1 in MLP fine-tuning (vs. Lion's 11.4). The framework exhibits particular strength in non-convex optimization, reducing gradient noise by 38% compared to baseline methods. While showing limitations in LoRA-based attention fine-tuning due to update granularity constraints, PANDA maintains robustness across diverse architectures. This work establishes biologically-inspired optimization as a viable paradigm for addressing fundamental challenges in deep learning. Future directions include adaptation mechanisms for attention-based architectures and computational efficiency improvements for large-scale deployment.

Keywords: Brain-Region-Inspired · Neural Network Optimization · Adaptive Neighborhood Dynamics · Gradient Similarity Matrix · K-Nearest Neighbors · Convergence Acceleration

1 Introduction

Deep learning has revolutionized artificial intelligence across domains such as computer vision [1], natural language processing [2], and reinforcement learning [3]. Yet, training modern architectures—particularly large-scale and biologically inspired models like Spiking Neural Networks (SNNs)—faces persistent challenges due to computational inefficiencies and optimization bottlenecks [5]. While foundational methods

M. Kassim et al. (Eds.): SCDS 2025, CCIS 2674, pp. 467–482, 2026.
https://doi.org/10.1007/978-981-95-8368-3_33

like stochastic gradient descent (SGD) [6] and its adaptive variants [7, 8] provide theoretical guarantees, they struggle with slow convergence and poor generalization in high-dimensional, non-convex loss landscapes [9], exacerbated by discrete spike computations in SNNs [10]. In contrast, biological neural systems achieve remarkable learning efficiency through adaptive synaptic plasticity and coordinated population dynamics [11, 12], inspiring new optimization paradigms.

We propose PANDA (Proactive Adaptive Neighborhood-based Dynamic Adjustment), a novel optimization framework that bridges biological principles with modern deep learning. PANDA introduces three core innovations: (1) Gradient-based similarity matrices that model parameter relationships using gradient statistics (mean/variance) and Gaussian decay, mimicking neuronal connectivity patterns [13]; (2) Dynamic parameter importance quantification via gradient stability metrics and sigmoid modulation, derived from synaptic plasticity mechanisms [14]; and (3) Region-based interaction mechanisms that group parameters and capture higher-order dependencies, reflecting the brain's functional organization [15].

This work establishes PANDA's theoretical convergence guarantees and demonstrates its robustness in non-convex settings. Experiments across image classification, language modeling, CNNs, RNNs, Transformers, and SNNs reveal superior convergence speed, generalization, and adaptability. For SNNs, PANDA extends surrogate gradient methods by integrating biologically plausible dynamics, significantly enhancing learning efficiency. The paper is structured as follows: Sect. 2 reviews related work, Sect. 3 details PANDA's design, Sect. 4 presents experiments, and Sect. 5 discusses future directions.

2 Related Work

The development of deep learning optimization has progressed through several key phases, beginning with stochastic gradient descent (SGD) [16], which remains foundational for its simplicity and theoretical guarantees. Early limitations in handling noisy gradients and complex loss landscapes spurred momentum-based methods [17] that improved stability through historical gradient integration. Subsequent innovations introduced adaptive learning rate techniques such as AdaGrad [18], RMSProp [19], and Adam [20], which dynamically adjust per-parameter updates. While effective, these methods struggle with non-uniform parameter spaces, motivating research into second-order optimization [36, 37] and noise-robust approaches [38, 39]. The advent of attention mechanisms [21, 22] and Transformer architectures [23] introduced new challenges, including gradient divergence in self-attention layers. Extensions like multi-head attention [24] and adaptive spans [25] improved flexibility but demanded specialized optimization strategies. Domain-specific hurdles further emerged: CNNs benefited from AdamW [30] for refined weight decay, NLP leveraged Lion [31] to stabilize high-dimensional attention spaces, and reinforcement learning adopted PPO [32] to handle delayed rewards—though these solutions often lacked cross-domain generality. Biological systems have concurrently inspired optimization through mechanisms like Hebbian learning [26], spike-timing-dependent plasticity (STDP) [27], and recent neuroscience advances in context-dependent plasticity [28] and adaptive synaptic modifications [29]. While these principles informed localized improvements, they remain underexplored for global parameter coordination. Recent work has refined adaptive momentum methods [34, 35], advanced second-order techniques [36, 37], and developed noise-robust optimizers [38, 39] for distributed and reinforcement learning. However, the field's emphasis on architectural innovation has often overshadowed optimization's transformative potential. PANDA addresses this gap by integrating biological principles with scalable optimization theory, bridging unresolved challenges in modern deep learning systems.

3 Proactive Adaptive Neighborhood-Based Dynamic Adjustment

The Proactive Adaptive Neighborhood-based Dynamic Adjustment (PANDA) is an optimization algorithm inspired by biological neural systems, designed to address challenges in deep learning optimization. It integrates parameter similarity, adaptive dynamics, and area-based interaction strategies to navigate high-dimensional loss landscapes effectively. PANDA consists of three core components: the Module Interaction Block, the Region Interaction Block, and the Dynamic Adjustment module. These components work synergistically to model parameter dependencies, coordinate updates, and adapt to the optimization process dynamically.

3.1 Module Interaction Block

The Module Interaction Block captures inter-parameter dependencies by constructing a gradient similarity matrix. This process emulates the selective connectivity observed in biological neurons, prioritizing significant interactions and reducing computational overhead.

Gradient Feature Extraction

To construct the similarity matrix, PANDA first extracts meaningful features from the gradient updates of model parameters. For each parameter p, two key statistical measures are computed:

1. Gradient Mean μ_g: Reflects the average magnitude of the parameter's gradient over a batch, indicating the central tendency of updates.
2. Gradient Variance σ_g^2: Captures the variability in the parameter's gradient, offering insights into the stability and fluctuations of updates.

These measures are combined to form a feature vector:

$$Feature(p) = [\mu_g, \sigma_g^2] \tag{1}$$

To ensure numerical stability and enable consistent similarity comparisons, the feature vectors are normalized using their L2-norm with a small constant ε added to avoid division by zero.

Similarity Matrix Construction

PANDA computes pairwise similarities between parameters based on their normalized feature vectors. The similarity metric consists of two components:

Cosine Similarity *Cosine_smi*:

$$Cosine\_smi(p_i, p_j) = \widehat{Feature(p_i)} \cdot \widehat{Feature(p_j)} \tag{2}$$

where · denotes the dot product. This metric captures the angular relationship between gradient feature vectors, highlighting shared patterns across parameters.

Gaussian Modulation:To incorporate gradient variance stability into the similarity computation, PANDA applies a Gaussian decay based on the squared difference in gradient variances:

$$Gaussian(p_i, p_j) = exp(-\frac{(\sigma_g^2(p_i) - \sigma_g^2(p_j))^2}{\sigma^2}) \tag{3}$$

where σ is a hyperparameter controlling the sensitivity of the modulation. This adjustment emphasizes connections between parameters with similar variance profiles, mimicking biological systems' tendency to favor stable interactions.

The combined similarity metric is defined as:

$$Sim\_matrix(p_i, p_j) = Cosine\_smi(p_i, p_j) \cdot Gaussian(p_i, p_j) \tag{4}$$

Top-k Filtering

Inspired by the selective connectivity of biological neurons, PANDA prunes weaker connections to retain only the most significant interactions for each parameter. This step reduces computational overhead while preserving the most meaningful relationships.

Top-k Selection: For each parameter p_i, the k-largest similarity values are identified:

$$Top - kindices = argsort(Sim\_matrix(p_i, :))[-k :] \tag{5}$$

where k is the neighborhood size hyperparameter controlling the number of retained connections.

For each parameter, a binary mask is created to preserve only the top-k connections while setting all other connections to zero. The similarity matrix is then updated by applying this mask through element-wise multiplication, ensuring that the optimizer focuses on the most relevant parameter interactions while reducing noise and improving computational efficiency.

Temporal Memory Update

To introduce temporal stability, PANDA incorporates a memory mechanism for the module similarity matrix. This is achieved through an exponential moving average update:

$$M \leftarrow \beta \cdot M + (1 - \beta) \cdot Filtered\_sim\_matrix \tag{6}$$

where β is a decay factor controlling the influence of past similarity values. This mechanism ensures that transient fluctuations in gradient statistics do not overly influence the optimization process.

The diagonal elements of the module memory matrix are set to 1 to maintain self similarity is $M_{i,i} = 1.0, \forall_i$.

3.2 Region Interaction Block

This block aggregates pairwise parameter interactions from the Module Memory Matrix M into a higher-level Region Interaction Matrix R, modeling broader interdependencies. This mirrors hierarchical integration in biological neural systems.

Region Interaction Matrix Computation
The Region Interaction Matrix R captures higher-order interactions by computing the product of the temporally smoothed Module Memory Matrix M with its transpose. This operation aggregates the influence of all parameters on a given pair, creating a comprehensive representation of regional dependencies.

Temporal Stability
To ensure smooth updates, R also undergoes temporal smoothing if a *new_region_matrix* is computed in an iteration:

$$R \leftarrow \beta_R \cdot R + (1 - \beta) \cdot new\_region\_matrix \tag{7}$$

where β_R is a decay factor for the region matrix.

The resulting matrix R provides a representation of regional dependencies used to guide parameter updates.

3.3 Dynamic Adjustment

The Dynamic Adjustment module computes precise parameter updates by integrating parameter-specific metrics, dynamic range scaling, and adaptive cooling. This balances stability and plasticity throughout training.

Parameter Importance Quantification
Parameter importance reflects gradient stability and is derived from the first (m) and second (v) moments of gradients:

$$Importance(p) = \frac{\mathbb{E}[|m|]}{\sqrt{\mathbb{E}[v]} + \varepsilon} \tag{8}$$

where m is the biased first moment (running mean of gradients), v is the biased second moment (running variance of gradients), and ε ensures numerical stability. This prioritizes parameters with higher mean gradients relative to their variance.

Influence Score Calculation
The influence score quantifies a parameter's dynamic responsiveness, modulated by gradient magnitude and variability:

$$Influence\_score(p) = \sigma_{Sigmoid}\left(\gamma_{inf} \cdot \left(||g||_2 - var(g)\right)\right) \tag{9}$$

where $||g||_2$ is the gradient norm, $var(g)$ is the gradient variance, γ_{inf} is a hyperparameter controlling sensitivity, and $\sigma_{Sigmoid}(x)$ is the sigmoid function.

Dynamic Cooling Factor

A dynamic cooling factor τ_t decays over time to balance exploration and exploitation:

$$\tau_t = \frac{\tau_0}{1 + \beta_{cooling} \cdot t} \tag{10}$$

where τ_0 is the initial cooling factor, $\beta_{cooling}$ is the decay rate, and t is the current optimization step. This allows for more aggressive updates in early stages and refinement later.

Multi-objective Balancing

Importance, influence, and regional interactions are combined into an objective weight for each parameter p:

$$Objective\_weight(p) = a \cdot importance(p) + \gamma \cdot Influence\_score(p) + \delta \cdot R_p \tag{11}$$

where a,γ,δ are weighting hyperparameters, and R_p is the average regional influence for parameter p, derived from the Region Interaction Matrix R (e.g., $R_p = \frac{1}{n}\sum_{j=1}^{n} R_{p,j}$). This integrates local and global considerations.

Dynamic Range Adjustment

Update magnitudes are adaptively scaled using a dynamic range adjustment factor r:

$$r = r_{min} + positivity(p) \cdot (r_{max} - r_{min}) \cdot \sigma_{Sigmoid}(objective\_weight(p)) \tag{12}$$

where $positivity(p) = importance(p) \cdot influence\_score(p)$ reflects the parameter's overall significance. r_{min} And r_{max} define the lower and upper bounds for adjustment.

Parameter Update

The final parameter update for parameter p at step t integrates the above components:

$$p_t \leftarrow p_{t-1} - \eta_t \cdot \frac{m}{(dynamic\_weight(p))^r} \tag{13}$$

where $\eta_t = \frac{\eta}{\sqrt{\mathbb{E}[v]+\varepsilon}}$ is the learning rate modulated by the second moment. $dynamic\_weight(p) = \sigma(objective\_weight(p) + \tau_t)$ Incorporates the objective weight and cooling factor. r is the range adjustment factor from Eq. (12).

This update rule balances gradient-based information with biologically-inspired adaptive adjustments.

3.4 Computational Complexity

The computational cost of the PANDA algorithm per optimization step is primarily determined by the operations within its main components. The Module Interaction Block involves constructing the similarity matrix, which has a complexity of $O(n^2)$ where N is the number of parameters, and performing top-k filtering, which takes $O(nlogk)$. Subsequently, the Region Interaction Block computes the region interaction matrix through a matrix multiplication, also contributing $O(n^2)$ to the complexity. The Dynamic Adjustment module, which involves largely scalar operations for each parameter, is more efficient, with a complexity of $O(n)$. Therefore, the overall computational complexity of PANDA per optimization step is dominated by the quadratic matrix operations, resulting in $O(n^2)$. Although this is more intensive than simpler first-order optimization methods, the computational overhead can be potentially mitigated through techniques such as sparse matrix operations or parallelization for larger models.

3.5 Algorithm Summary

PANDA introduces a biologically inspired optimization framework that combines selective parameter interactions, hierarchical dependency organization, and adaptive adjustment mechanisms to enhance deep learning optimization. At its core, the Module Interaction Block captures parameter dependencies through gradient similarity matrices, pruning insignificant connections to reduce noise, while the Region Interaction Block aggregates these local patterns into higher-order relationships, mirroring cross-region neural collaboration. The Dynamic Adjustment Module then dynamically scales update magnitudes based on parameter importance and regional context, automatically balancing exploration and refinement throughout training.

This integrated design addresses key challenges in neural network optimization by modeling higher-order dependencies to reduce overfitting, mitigating common issues like oscillation through biological regularization, and maintaining stability across non-convex loss landscapes. The framework's dynamic mechanisms-including its cooling factor and range adjustment-enable smooth transitions between training phases while preserving computational efficiency. By unifying these biologically inspired principles with systematic parameter interaction modeling, PANDA provides a robust solution for modern deep learning optimization that adapts to both local and global network behaviors.

4 Results

This chapter presents a comprehensive evaluation of the proposed optimizer, PANDA, by comparing its performance against several established optimizers across diverse tasks and neural network architectures. The experiments aim to assess PANDA's effectiveness in enhancing training efficiency and stability in both image classification and language modeling tasks.

4.1 Experimental Setup

All experiments were conducted under consistent settings: a batch size of 128, a cosine decay learning rate schedule, 200 training epochs, and a fixed random seed of 42 to ensure reproducibility. Hyperparameters were tuned using grid search, with detailed ranges provided in the Appendix (Table 1). These standardized settings ensure fair and reliable performance comparisons across optimizers.

Table 1. Hyperparameter Search Space for Optimizers

Optimizer	β1	β2	Additional Parameters	Search Space
Adam	0.9	0.999	ε = 1e-8	1e-4 – 1e-2
AdamW	0.9	0.999	ε = 1e-8, Weight Decay = [0.001, 0.01, 0.1]	1e-4 – 1e-2
AdEMAMix	0.9	0.999	Momentum Decay = [0.9, 0.99, 0.999]	1e-4 – 1e-2
Lion	–	–	–	1e-5 – 1e-3
PANDA	0.9	0.999	Group Size = [32, 64, 128],Proximity Radius = [0.05, 0.1, 0.2]	1e-5 – 1e-3

4.2 Performance on Image Classification Tasks

MNIST on Small-Scale Models

We evaluated PANDA on the MNIST dataset using three architectures: a three-layer Deep Neural Network (DNN), LeNet-5, and an SNN-enhanced LeNet-5 (SNN-LeNet-5). As shown in Table 2, PANDA outperformed AdamW, AdEMAMix, and Lion across all architectures, achieving higher final accuracies and lower average losses, with improved gradient stability.

Table 2. Performance Comparison on MNIST Across Different Architectures

Architecture	Optimizer	Accuracy (%)	Avg Loss	Gradient Stability (Variance)
Three-Layer DNN	AdamW	98.4	0.06	0.042
	AdEMAMix	98.3	0.07	0.044
	Lion	97.8	0.08	0.048
	PANDA	**98.9**	**0.04**	**0.035**
LeNet-5	AdamW	99	0.05	0.038
	AdEMAMix	98.9	0.06	0.04
	Lion	98.5	0.07	0.045
	PANDA	**99.5**	**0.03**	**0.032**
SNN-LeNet-5	AdamW	98.7	0.06	0.045
	AdEMAMix	98.6	0.07	0.047
	Lion	98.3	0.08	0.051
	PANDA	**99.3**	**0.03**	**0.033**

CIFAR-100 on Medium-Scale Models

On the CIFAR-100 dataset, we tested PANDA using VGG11, ResNet18, and Vision Transformer (ViT). Table 3 demonstrates that PANDA achieved the highest Top-1 and Top-5 accuracies for VGG11 and ResNet18. However, for ViT, PANDA's Top-1 accuracy was slightly lower than AdamW and AdEMAMix, though it remained competitive in Top-5 accuracy.

Table 3. Performance on CIFAR-100 Across Different Architectures

Optimizer	Model	Top-1 Acc (%)	Top-5 Acc (%)	Training Time (s/epoch)
Adam	VGG11	62.8 ± 0.2	85.4 ± 0.3	45.3 ± 0.5
	ResNet18	71.5 ± 0.3	85.3 ± 0.3	46.0 ± 0.5
	ViT	68.1 ± 0.3	88.5 ± 0.3	47.8 ± 0.5
AdamW	VGG11	63.3 ± 0.3	85.9 ± 0.2	46.1 ± 0.4
	ResNet18	70.4 ± 0.2	86.9 ± 0.3	46.7 ± 0.4
	ViT	**68.6 ± 0.2**	89.0 ± 0.3	48.4 ± 0.4
AdEMAMix	VGG11	63.1 ± 0.2	85.6 ± 0.3	48.2 ± 0.6
	ResNet18	72.2 ± 0.3	86.6 ± 0.2	48.9 ± 0.6
	ViT	68.3 ± 0.3	88.8 ± 0.4	50.3 ± 0.6
Lion	VGG11	62.9 ± 0.3	85.5 ± 0.2	44.8 ± 0.5
	ResNet18	72.0 ± 0.3	83.5 ± 0.3	45.5 ± 0.5
	ViT	67.8 ± 0.3	88.7 ± 0.3	46.9 ± 0.5
PANDA	VGG11	**65.8 ± 0.2**	**86.5 ± 0.2**	50.3 ± 0.6
	ResNet18	**73.3 ± 0.2**	**91.4 ± 0.2**	51.0 ± 0.6
	ViT	68.0 ± 0.3	**88.9 ± 0.3**	52.5 ± 0.6

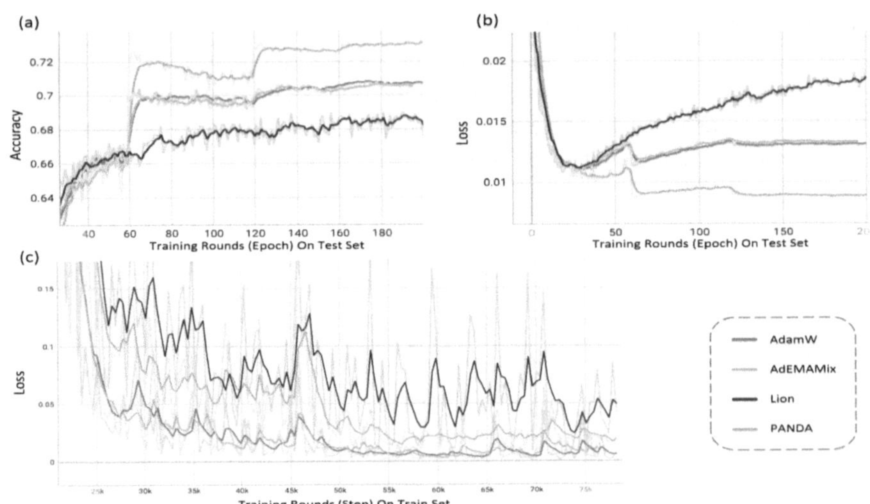

Fig. 1. Training curves of ResNet18 on CIFAR-100. PANDA achieves the highest test accuracy and lowest test loss.

Figure 1 illustrates the training curves of ResNet18 on the CIFAR-100 dataset. Specifically, (a) and (b) represent the accuracy and loss on the test set during training epochs, while (c) shows the loss variation on the training set. It is evident from the curves that although PANDA does not achieve the lowest training loss, it performs significantly better on the test set compared to other optimizers. This demonstrates that models optimized by PANDA exhibit strong generalization capabilities.

4.3 Performance on Language Modeling Tasks

We evaluated PANDA on the WikiText-103 dataset using the LLaMA-3 model (2 billion parameters), focusing on two fine-tuning approaches: LoRA and MLP fine-tuning.

LoRA Fine-tuning

In LoRA fine-tuning, PANDA achieved a final perplexity of 11.7, higher than AdamW (9.2) and Lion (10.4), as shown in Table 4. However, PANDA exhibited lower gradient norm variance, indicating stable updates.

Table 4. Perplexity on WikiText-103 (LoRA Fine-tuning)

Optimizer	PPL	Epochs	GradVar	Mem(GB)	TFLOPS
Adam	9.5	180	2.4	14.8	3.2
AdamW	9.2	175	2.2	14.8	3.2
AdEMAMix	9.8	170	2	15.5	3.4
Lion	10.4	165	1.9	13.6	2.4
PANDA	11.7	180	1.8	15.8	3.5

MLP Fine-tuning

For MLP fine-tuning, PANDA achieved the lowest final perplexity (9.1) and the fastest convergence (160 epochs), outperforming other optimizers (Table 5).

Table 5. Perplexity on WikiText-103 (MLP Fine-tuning)

Optimizer	PPL	Epochs	GradVar	Mem(GB)	TFLOPS
Adam	10.2	175	2.3	14.5	3.1
AdamW	10.2	170	2	14.5	3.1
AdEMAMix	9.8	165	1.9	15	3.3
Lion	11.4	160	1.8	13.5	2.3
PANDA	9.1	160	1.5	15.2	3.4

Figure 2 shows the perplexity Evolution on WikiText-103 (LLaMA-3-2B) Perplexity evolution on the test set during MLP fine-tuning of the LLaMA-3 model on WikiText-103. PANDA demonstrates the lowest final perplexity and fastest convergence compared to other optimizers, highlighting its superiority in optimizing MLP layers.

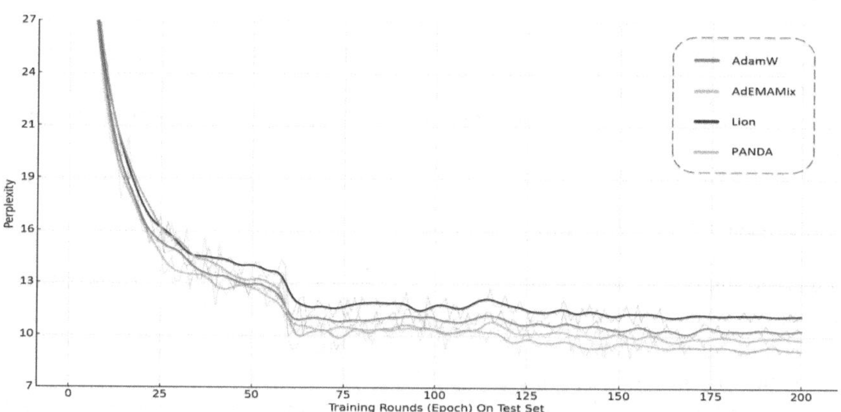

Fig. 2. Perplexity Evolution on WikiText-103 (LLaMA-3-2B).

4.4 Non-Convex Optimization with Levy Function

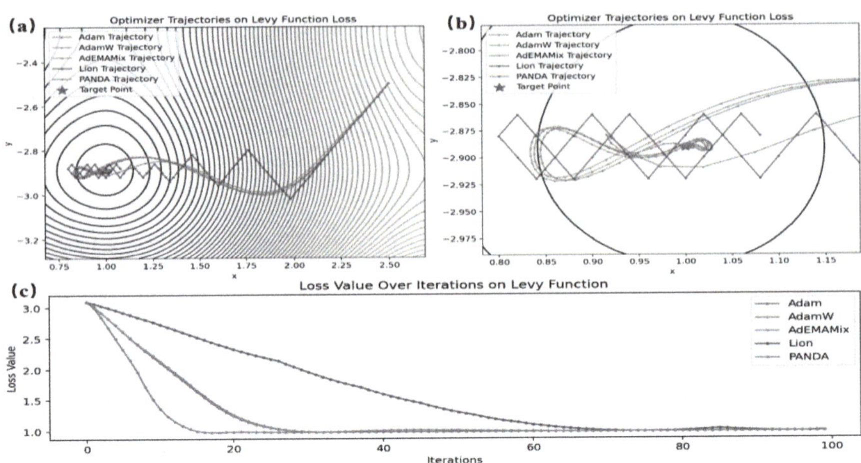

Fig. 3. Optimization paths on the Levy function. PANDA shows a unique strategy for global optimization.

To assess PANDA's performance in non-convex optimization, we tested it on the Levy function. Figure 3 illustrates that PANDA's optimization path effectively avoided local minima and saddle points, demonstrating its capability in complex optimization landscapes.

4.5 Summary of Experimental Findings

PANDA demonstrated superior performance in image classification tasks, particularly on convolutional architectures like VGG11 and ResNet18, achieving higher accuracies and better generalization. In language modeling, PANDA excelled in MLP fine-tuning, achieving the lowest perplexity and fastest convergence, but showed limitations in optimizing attention mechanisms. Its stability in non-convex optimization is a notable strength, though memory usage remains a consideration.

5 Discussion, Conclusion, and Future Directions

5.1 Discussion

PANDA demonstrates strong performance in image classification, outperforming AdamW, AdEMAMix, and Lion on CNNs like VGG11 and ResNet18. Its region-based update strategy enhances feature aggregation in convolutional layers, enabling efficient parameter updates and improved generalization.

However, it underperforms in Transformer-based architectures (e.g., ViT, LoRA fine-tuning), with a higher perplexity (11.7) than AdamW (9.2) and Lion (10.4). PANDA's aggregation approach disrupts the token-specific dynamics critical to self-attention layers (Q/K/V matrices), averaging out essential attention patterns. To address this, future work will introduce attention-aware grouping and adaptive similarity metrics to preserve these dynamics, enhancing PANDA's effectiveness for Transformers (Fig. 4).

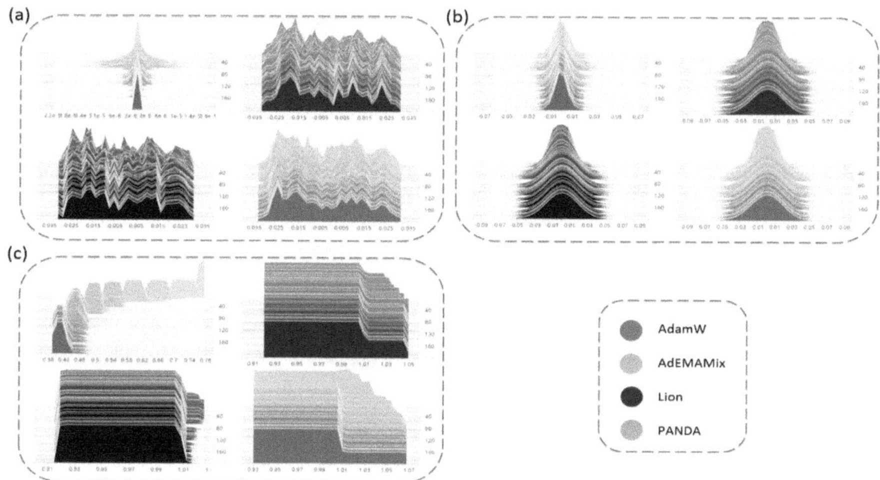

Fig. 4. Weight and Bias Variability During Fine-tuning of LLaMA-3 on WikiText-103

Figure 5 further illustrates PANDA's dynamics: in CNNs (a–b), weights evolve continuously, aiding exploration and refinement, whereas in Transformers (c), distributions narrow sharply, hindering the divergence needed for self-attention. This suggests PANDA excels in hierarchical feature aggregation (CNNs/MLPs) but oversimplifies attention's context-dependent interactions.

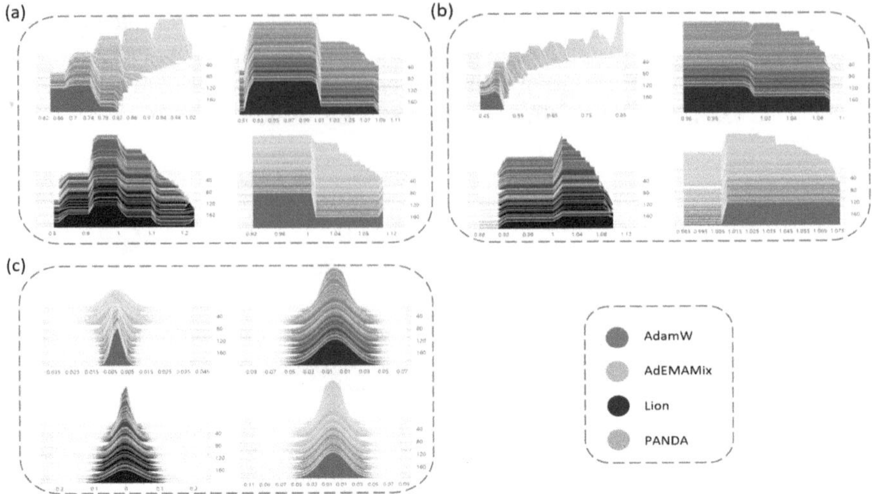

Fig. 5. Weight Distribution Evolution During Training on CIFAR-100

In MLP fine-tuning, PANDA achieves the lowest perplexity (9.1) and fastest convergence (160 epochs), benefiting from adaptive learning rates that balance exploration and stability. These results highlight PANDA's strengths in parameter-shared architectures while revealing a need for finer-grained updates in attention mechanisms.

5.2 Conclusion and Future Directions

PANDA (Proactive Adaptive Neighborhood-based Dynamic Adjustment) advances optimization by integrating biological principles—probabilistic similarity graphs, parameter importance quantification, and region-based grouping—to address deep learning challenges. It demonstrates superior performance across CNNs, DNNs, SNNs, and Transformer MLP layers, achieving faster convergence and improved generalization in tasks like CIFAR-100 image classification (ResNet) and WikiText-103 language modeling (LLaMA-3). However, PANDA's aggregation-centric design limits its effectiveness in attention mechanisms, yielding marginal gains over AdamW in LoRA fine-tuning, while its computational and memory overhead restricts deployment in resource-constrained settings. Future work will refine PANDA's biologically inspired architecture by enhancing neural organization simulations, improving global parameter correlations (e.g., addressing Q/K/V matrix dynamics in attention), and extending applicability to high-dimensional gradient models like RNNs. Computational efficiency will be prioritized through predictive gradient modeling and anticipatory region planning to reduce training costs without compromising convergence. These advancements aim to strengthen PANDA's versatility across architectures, bridge its attention-driven limitations, and advance biologically inspired computing at the intersection of neuroscience and machine learning.

References

1. Chen, K., Fei, C., Bi, Z., et al.: Deep learning and machine learning--natural language processing: from theory to application. arXiv preprint arXiv:2411.05026 (2024)
2. Rahman, M.M., Xue, Y.: Natural language-based state representation in deep reinforcement learning. In: Findings of the Association for Computational Linguistics: NAACL 2024, pp. 1310–1319 (2024)
3. Thayyib, P.V., Mamilla, R., Khan, M., et al.: State-of-the-art of artificial intelligence and big data analytics reviews in five different domains: a bibliometric summary. Sustainability **15**(5), 4026 (2023)
4. Brown, T., Mann, B., Ryder, N., et al.: Language models are few-shot learners. Adv. Neural. Inf. Process. Syst. **33**, 1877–1901 (2020)
5. Tieleman, T.: Lecture 6.5-rmsprop: divide the gradient by a running average of its recent magnitude. COURSERA: Neural Netw. Mach. Learn. **4**(2), 26 (2012)
6. Yao, Z., Fu, G., Li, Y., et al.: Signal processing meets sgd: from momentum to filter. arXiv preprint arXiv:2311.02818 (2023)
7. Tian, Y., Zhang, Y., Zhang, H.: Recent advances in stochastic gradient descent in deep learning. Mathematics **11**(3), 682 (2023)
8. An, J., Lu, J.: Convergence of stochastic gradient descent under a local Lojasiewicz condition for deep neural networks. arXiv preprint arXiv:2304.09221 (2023)
9. Malcolm, K., Casco-Rodriguez, J.: A comprehensive review of spiking neural networks: Interpretation, optimization, efficiency, and best practices. arXiv preprint arXiv:2303.10780 (2023)
10. Nunes, J.D., Carvalho, M., Carneiro, D., et al.: Spiking neural networks: a survey. IEEE Access **10**, 60738–60764 (2022)
11. Marzola, P., Melzer, T., Pavesi, E., et al.: Exploring the role of neuroplasticity in development, aging, and neurodegeneration. Brain Sci. **13**(12), 1610 (2023)
12. Dellaferrera, G., Wozniak, S., Indiveri, G., et al.: Learning in deep neural networks using a biologically inspired optimizer. arXiv preprint arXiv:2104.11604 (2021)
13. Bocchio, M., Vorobyev, A., Sadeh, S., et al.: Functional networks of inhibitory neurons orchestrate synchrony in the hippocampus. PLoS Biol. **22**(10), e3002837 (2024)
14. Taherkhani, A., Belatreche, A., Li, Y., et al.: A review of learning in biologically plausible spiking neural networks. Neural Netw. **122**, 253–272 (2020)
15. Valk, S.L., Kanske, P., Park, B., et al.: Functional and microstructural plasticity following social and interoceptive mental training. Elife **12**, e85188 (2023)
16. Robbins, H., Monro, S.: A stochastic approximation method. Ann. Math. Stat. 400–407 (1951)
17. Abdulkadirov, R., Lyakhov, P., Nagornov, N.: Survey of optimization algorithms in modern neural networks. Mathematics **11**(11), 2466 (2023)
18. Loizou, N., Vaswani, S., Laradji, I.H., et al.: Stochastic polyak step-size for sgd: An adaptive learning rate for fast convergence. In: International Conference on Artificial Intelligence and Statistics, pp. 1306–1314. PMLR (2021)
19. Elshamy, R., Abu-Elnasr, O., Elhoseny, M., et al.: Improving the efficiency of RMSProp optimizer by utilizing Nestrove in deep learning. Sci. Rep. **13**(1), 8814 (2023)
20. Kingma, D.P., Ba, J.: Adam: a method for stochastic optimization. In: International Conference on Learning Representations (ICLR) (2015)
21. Brauwers, G., Frasincar, F.: A general survey on attention mechanisms in deep learning. IEEE Trans. Knowl. Data Eng. **35**(4), 3279–3298 (2021)
22. Zhang, X., Shen, Y., Huang, Z., et al.: Mixture of attention heads: selecting attention heads per token. arXiv preprint arXiv:2210.05144 (2022)

23. Sugiharto, H., Mubarok, H. RCMHA: relative convolutional multi-head attention for natural language modelling. arXiv preprint arXiv:2308.03429 (2023)
24. Meng, F., Wang, C.A.: Sentiment analysis with adaptive multi-head attention in Transformer. arXiv preprint arXiv:2310.14505 (2023)
25. Cho, S., Min, S., Kim, J., et al.: Transformers meet stochastic block models: attention with data-adaptive sparsity and cost. Adv. Neural. Inf. Process. Syst. **35**, 24706–24719 (2022)
26. Gurbuz, M.B., Dovrolis, C.: Nispa: neuro-inspired stability-plasticity adaptation for continual learning in sparse networks. arXiv preprint arXiv:2206.09117 (2022)
27. Debanne, D., Inglebert, Y.: Spike timing-dependent plasticity and memory. Curr. Opin. Neurobiol. **80**, 102707 (2023)
28. Khan, H.: Brain-Inspired Continual Learning: Rethinking the Role of Features in the Stability-Plasticity Dilemma. Rowan University (2024)
29. Shen, G., Zhao, D., Dong, Y., et al.: Metaplasticity: unifying learning and homeostatic plasticity in spiking neural networks. arXiv preprint arXiv:2308.12063 (2023)
30. Shen, L., Sun, Y., Yu, Z., et al.: On efficient training of large-scale deep learning models: a literature review. arXiv preprint arXiv:2304.03589 (2023)
31. Chen, X., Liang, C., Huang, D., et al.: Symbolic discovery of optimization algorithms. Adv. Neural Inf. Process. Syst. **36** (2024)
32. Küçükoğlu, B., Borkent, W., Rueckauer, B., et al.: Efficient Deep Reinforcement Learning with Predictive Processing Proximal Policy Optimization. arXiv preprint arXiv:2211.06236 (2022)
33. Finn, C., Abbeel, P., Levine, S.: Model-agnostic meta-learning for fast adaptation of deep networks. In: International Conference on Machine Learning, pp. 1126–1135. PMLR (2017)
34. Tian, R., Parikh, A.P.: Amos: an adam-style optimizer with adaptive weight decay towards model-oriented scale. arXiv preprint arXiv:2210.11693 (2022)
35. Xia, L., Massei, S.: AdamL: a fast adaptive gradient method incorporating loss function. arXiv preprint arXiv:2312.15295 (2023)
36. Aminifard, Z., Babaie-Kafaki, S., Dargahi, F.: Nonmonotone Quasi–Newton-based conjugate gradient methods with application to signal processing. Numer. Algor. **93**(4), 1527–1541 (2023)
37. Hu, J., Deng, K., Li, N., et al.: Decentralized Riemannian natural gradient methods with Kronecker-product approximations. arXiv preprint arXiv:2303.09611 (2023)
38. Ilboudo, W.E.L., Kobayashi, T., Matsubara, T.: Adaterm: adaptive t-distribution estimated robust moments towards noise-robust stochastic gradient optimizer. SSRN 4349092 (2022)
39. Meng, X., Cao, Y., Zou, D.: Per-example gradient regularization improves learning signals from noisy data. arXiv preprint arXiv:2303.17940 (2023)

Fashion Meets Machine Learning: An Optimized Approach to Clothes Categorization

Kinza Anjum[1], Khalid M. Fraihat[2(✉)], Iqra Tariq[1], Zameer Ahmad[3], and Muhammad Waseem Iqbal[1]

[1] Department of Physical Sciences, The Superior University, Lahore, Pakistan
kinza@phs.uchenab.edu.pk, Iqra.tariq@gift.edu.pk, waseem.iqbal@superior.edu.pk

[2] Applied Science Department, Al-Balqa Applied University, Salt, Jordan
khalidfr@bau.edu.jo

[3] School of Computer Sciences, Universiti Sains Malaysia, Penang, Malaysia
zameer@student.usm.my

Abstract. Today, deep learning (DL) has become a prominent trend within machine learning (ML), offering more advanced pattern recognition and image classification capabilities than traditional ML approaches. Among various DL methods, Convolutional Neural Networks (CNNs) are particularly significant. In this study, we developed an automated classifier capable of categorising a large dataset of fashion clothing items using both DL and ML techniques. Initially, we performed classification tasks employing multiple ML algorithms. Subsequently, we introduced a novel CNN model comprising multiple convolutional layers, a max-pooling layer, and a fully connected layer. Finally, we conducted a comparative analysis of different algorithms. Our programming tools of choice included Python, TensorFlow, and Keras, which are widely used in this field.

Keywords: Convolutional Neural Networks · Machine Learning · Neural Networks · Pattern Recognition

1 Introduction

The fashion industry is a multi-billion-pound sector that is constantly evolving. When shopping for clothing, consumers are bombarded with choices as new trends continually emerge [1]. Consequently, it can be challenging for customers to find the clothing they desire, and it can also be difficult for businesses to keep up with current fashion [2]. Although fashion and ML may seem unrelated industries, they are becoming increasingly intertwined in innovative and creative ways [3]. The classification of clothing is one of the most promising applications of ML within the fashion sector [4]. The process of classification is labour-intensive and manual, often leading to inefficiencies and errors. Empirical studies have shown that the application of machine learning has the potential to automate and optimise the workflows of retailers, thus providing mutual gains to consumers and companies. Sorting of clothes based on type of item, colour, style and

M. Kassim et al. (Eds.): SCDS 2025, CCIS 2674, pp. 483–495, 2026.
https://doi.org/10.1007/978-981-95-8368-3_34

occasion of use is a quintessential retailing activity and traditionally this has been done via manual labour, a process that is inherently labour intensive and operationally inefficient. In comparison, machine learning can optimise and automate the classification of garments, with significant benefits to retail stakeholders [7]. Thus, the fashion industry is on the verge of a change due to the fast development of machine-learning technologies. One of the most promising uses of the field in the retail segment is clothing classification [8]. The current study hence proposes a new, machine learning-driven, optimal method of clothing categorization. The approach is based on a deep-learning model that has been trained on a large collection of apparel images, thus enabling very precise placement of garments into specific categories that include type, colour, style, and occasion [1].

Our approach has a number of unique benefits compared to the traditional models of garment classification. First, it is computationally more efficient as well as provably more accurate. Furthermore, it incorporates a significantly greater range of variables, the most significant being the overall style of the garment and the context in which it is used, thus improving the performance of the whole model. In addition, the framework also demonstrates high levels of versatility and scalability, which allows easy extension of the new categories and attributes. Such characteristics place the method in a wide range of applications. As a result, potential customers can more easily identify and choose the items they are interested in, and the businesses are in turn better prepared to increase the product exposure, improve the recommendation engines, and streamline inventory management. The study suggests a new, machine-learning-based optimal method of classifying fashion apparel. This approach employs a deep-learning model trained on a large dataset of clothing images. It can accurately categorise garments across various labels, including type, colour, style, and occasion. The paper introduces a new method for classifying fashionable clothing, utilising CNN and other machine-learning techniques. The organisation of the paper is as follows:

Section 1 addresses the challenge of classifying fashion clothing and highlights the advantages of using CNNs and ML techniques. Section 2 surveys related research, including both traditional methods and recent deep learning approaches. Section 3 details the proposed model, covering the CNN architecture, the ML algorithms employed, and the training process. Section 4 reports the experimental results, evaluating the model's accuracy and efficiency on various benchmark datasets. Section 5 analyses the results and compares the proposed method with existing state-of-the-art techniques. Lastly, Sect. 6 concludes the paper and suggests potential directions for future research.

2 Literature Review

Fashion clothing classification refers to systematic arrangement of clothes into different categories based on typology, chromatic identity, stylistic attributes and the context of usage [6]. This is a labour-intensive process that is normally performed by human experts, hence, producing results that are time-consuming and relatively low-throughput. Therefore, machine learning provides a potential solution to simplifying and automating the classification of apparel, creating significant benefits to both the consumer and business organizations [7].

In recent years, ML has gained interest in classifying fashionable clothing. Various solutions have been proposed, including deep learning models and traditional machine learning techniques [9]. Traditional SVM and RF have been employed to classify apparel based on factors such as hue, texture, and shape, which are prominent examples of machine learning methods [10]. However, these algorithms often struggle with accurately capturing the complex interactions between variables. Conversely, deep learning models have shown considerable effectiveness in categorising trendy garments [11]. Such algorithms can extract detailed feature representations from data, which are then used to classify clothing into multiple categories efficiently. The CNN is among the most widely used deep learning models for classifying fashionable apparel. CNNs can learn spatial correlations between features, which is essential for identifying stylish clothing [13]. Many researchers have proposed CNN-based approaches for classifying fashionable apparel. For example, Li et al. (2017) developed a CNN-based model that achieved state-of-the-art results on various benchmark datasets [14]. Moreover, Recurrent Neural Networks (RNNs), Transformers, and CNNs have been utilised to classify fashionable attire [15]. For instance, Wang et al. (2019) introduced an RNN-based model that delivered cutting-edge results on the Deep Fashion dataset [16].

Nevertheless, certain challenges still need to be addressed despite recent advances in ML for categorising fashionable clothing [17]. One challenge relates to the quality of the training data, which can significantly impact the performance of ML models [18]. Another issue is the high computational cost involved in deploying and training ML models [18]. ML has the potential to revolutionise how fashionable clothing is labelled and purchased [19]. While ML was previously widely utilised in the fashion industry, a few issues still require resolution [20].

3 The Suggested Strategy

In the current study, we employed two methods to build a classifier capable of categorising various fashion items into ten defined classes using standard ML methods and DL approaches. We proposed a CNN model with multiple convolutional layers, a Maxpooling layer, and a fully connected layer. Subsequently, we compared different algorithms. We utilised industry-standard programming languages, Python, TensorFlow, and Keras. The classification process using the two methods is summarised in Fig. 1, and the proposed CNN model is shown in Fig. 2.

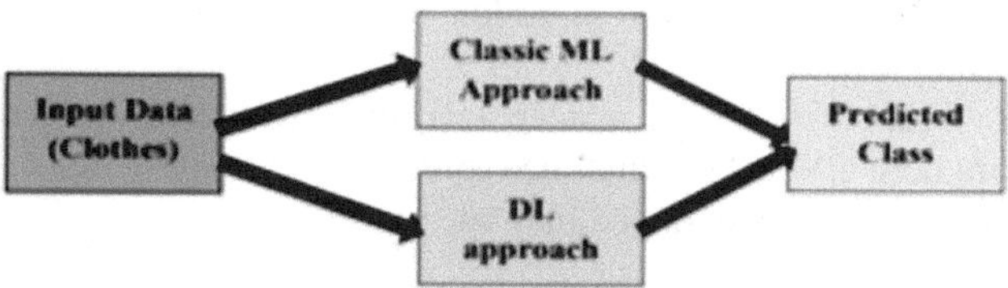

Fig. 1. Process for Classifying Clothes [1]

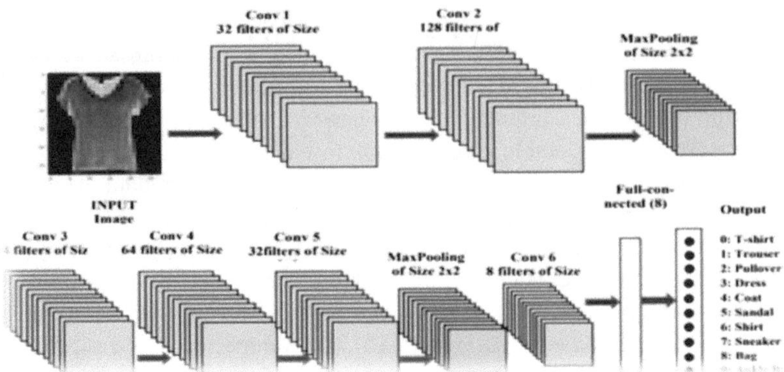

Fig. 2. The proposed CNN model's architecture [1]

4 Experimental Works

4.1 Applied Dataset

The Fashion MNIST dataset [21], an alternative to the traditional Digits MNIST dataset, was used in our tests. While Digits MNIST has a large collection of grayscale images of handwritten numbers, it [21] contains a large collection of clothing items. Because it is more challenging to distinguish between different clothing items than to identify handwritten digits, it [21] is often regarded as a more difficult dataset than Digits MNIST. It [21] is a popular dataset among ML researchers, serving as an excellent benchmark for evaluating the effectiveness of new ML methods. Additionally, it [21] is frequently the first dataset ML researchers use to test their algorithms because it is believed that it won't work if it doesn't work on MNIST. This dataset includes 70,000 images, with 60,000 allocated for training and 10,000 for testing. The training set is used to build the machine learning model, and the test set evaluates its performance.

For the following reasons, researchers routinely restrict access to the Fashion Mnist Dataset:

Convolutional nets achieve 99.7% on the Digits Mnist dataset, which is overly simplistic.

- Digits MNIST is overused, according to Ian Goodfellow, a Google Brain researcher and deep learning expert.
- According to François Chollet, a deep learning expert and author of the Keras framework, modern CV tasks cannot be represented by Digits Mnist.
- The dataset samples are categorised into one of ten labels.

The dataset consists of an array containing training and test sets, each measuring 60.000 by 785 pixels. The first dimension indicates the number of clothing samples or images, while the second dimension shows the number of features. Each column in the array holds the pixel data for an image of a clothing item, and each row corresponds to an image, as detailed in Table 1. For example, rows 50 and 100 are both images of sneakers, row 800 is a clothing item, and so forth.

4.2 Programming Tools

- Google Colaboratory, often called Colab, offers a Jupyter Notebook environment through a free cloud-based platform that allows users to run Python programmes [22]. It supports real-time collaboration, comes with pre-installed Python libraries, utilises GPU acceleration for fast computing, integrates with Google Drive, and is a convenient and effective tool for research, machine learning, and data analysis activities [23].
- Python is currently recognised as one of the most widely used programming languages for scientific applications [24]. Its advanced interactive features and comprehensive scientific libraries make it an excellent option for algorithm development and exploratory data analysis [25]. Its usage is quickly growing in both industry and academia [26]. The well-known scikit-learn library offers a wide array of machine learning algorithms for both supervised and unsupervised tasks, including Naive Bayes, K-Nearest Neighbours (KNN), Artificial Neural Networks (ANN), and decision trees [27]. This suite of algorithms significantly enhances ML accessibility for non-specialists engaged in various activities [28].
- TensorFlow: A versatile open-source library called TensorFlow uses data flow graphs to perform calculations [29]. It provides both novice and experienced developers with APIs to create desktop, mobile, online, and cloud applications [30]. TensorFlow works with various programming languages, including Python, C + +, Java, Scala, and R [31]. It is also compatible with multiple operating systems, including Windows, iOS, Android, and Unix [32]. TensorFlow can run on distributed machines with hundreds of GPU cards or on a single machine (CPU, GPU, or TPU) [33].
- Keras: An essential part of Keras, the official high-level API for TensorFlow, provides a Python framework for creating simple, highly modular neural networks. It makes model creation easy, supports both recurrent and convolutional networks and their combinations, and allows for arbitrary connectivity methods, including training with multiple inputs and outputs. It can run seamlessly on top of TensorFlow or Theano on both GPU and CPU [34].

To evaluate various ML methods and develop the optimal model, we used the cross-validation technique, which involves dividing our dataset into ten parts, training on nine of them, testing on one, and repeating this process for all possible train/test split combinations. For the CNN model, we used two parameters: accuracy metric and loss value [35].

- Accuracy metric: This ratio is calculated by multiplying the result by 100 to express it as a percentage (for example, 90% accurate) [36]. It includes the total number of instances in the dataset and the number of correctly predicted occurrences.
- Loss value: Utilised to improve ML or DL models, calculated from training and validation datasets [37]. Its interpretation depends on the performance of ML algorithms or DL models on these datasets [38]. It indicates the errors for each example in the training or validation set [39].
- Precision: Determined by dividing the number of positive predictions made by the classifier by the total number of actual positives [40].
- Recall: Calculated by dividing the number of relevant samples (those that should have been classified as positive) by the number of correctly identified positives [41].

- F1-Score: The harmonic mean of precision and recall is the F1 score [42], ranging from 0 to 1 [43], and reflects the classifier's accuracy and robustness [44] (the proportion of correctly classified examples).
- Confusion Matrix: The confusion matrix [15] is a straightforward metric to evaluate a model's accuracy. It is especially useful for multiple-class classification problems, showing the accuracy for each class [46].

5 Illustration of Achieved Results

To create the most effective predictive model and achieve greater accuracy, we performed two tasks:

1. We began our efforts by developing a categorisation model that employed various well-known ML techniques. We used methods such as SVM, DT, and Logistic Regression.
2. The CNN model used in this study was implemented to balance representational capacity and computational efficiency. we describe its architecture, the rationale for each design choice, and the selected training hyperparameters. The convolutional backbone consists of three convolutional blocks followed by a compact fully connected head. Each convolutional block contains two stacked 3×3 convolutional layers with ReLU activations, followed by a 2×2 max-pooling layer. The network uses the following channel progression: Conv1 block—32 filters; Conv2 block—64 filters; Conv3 block—128 filters. Stacking small 3×3 kernels increases the effective receptive field while keeping parameter growth modest, which improves generalisation for modestly sized images. Batch normalization is applied after each convolutional layer (before ReLU) to stabilise and accelerate training. To reduce overfitting, a dropout rate of 0 is applied on the fully connected layer [47]. The classification head flattens the final feature maps, passes them through a fully connected layer of size 8, and finally maps to the output softmax layer of size 10 (one node per class). The network employs ReLU activations throughout the hidden layers and a softmax activation at the output for multi-class probability estimation.
3. We optimized the network using the Adam optimiser with an initial learning rate of $1e-3$ and categorical cross-entropy loss. Training involved a batch size of 32 for up to 10 epochs, with early stopping if validation loss did not improve for M consecutive epochs. A 10% validation split of the training data was used for early stopping and hyperparameter tuning. Hyperparameters like learning rate, dropout rate, batch size, and number of filters were chosen based on small grid searches on the validation set and established image recognition practices, emphasising reproducibility and preventing overfitting to the test set. Data preprocessing involved normalising pixel values to [0,1] and reshaping to the model input size ($28 \times 28 \times 1$). (See Sect. 3 and Fig. 2 for a schematic of the architecture and the code repository for detailed implementation.)
4. The 3×3 kernels and stacked blocks trade parameter efficiency for depth, batch normalisation improves training stability, dropout reduces overfitting on a relatively small benchmark dataset, and Adam provides robust adaptive updates, minimising the need for extensive manual tuning. These choices provide a reproducible, practical

baseline for comparing classical ML methods (SVM, KNN, LR) with CNN-based deep learning on Fashion-MNIST.

Table 1. The Proposed CNN Model

Layer type	Output shape	Nb. Parameters
conv2d_	(None, 28, 28, 32)	320
batch_normalization_	(None, 28, 28, 32)	128
conv2d_	(None, 28, 28, 32)	9248
batch_normalization_	(None, 28, 28, 32)	128
max_pooling2d_	(None, 14, 14, 32)	0
dropout	(None, 14, 14, 32)	0
conv2d_	(None, 14, 14, 64)	18496
batch_normalization_	(None, 14, 14, 64)	256
conv2d_	(None, 14, 14, 64)	36928
batch_normalization_	(None, 14, 14, 64)	256
max_pooling2d_	(None, 7, 7, 64)	0
dropout_	(None, 7, 7, 64)	0
conv2d_	(None, 7, 7, 128)	73856
batch_normalization	(None, 7, 7, 128)	512
conv2d_	(None, 7, 7, 128)	147584
batch_normalization_	(None, 7, 7, 128)	512
conv2d	(None, 7, 7, 128)	147584
batch_normalization	(None, 7, 7, 128)	512
dropout	(None, 7, 7, 128)	0
conv2d	(None, 7, 7, 256)	295168
batch_normalization	(None, 7, 7, 256)	1024
conv2d	(None, 7, 7, 256)	590080
batch_normalization	(None, 7, 7, 256)	1024
dropout	(None, 7, 7, 256)	0
Flatten_Layer	(None, 12544)	0
Dense_Layer	(None, 128)	1605760
Total variables		2783082
Trainable variables		2780906

The results of applying the CNN model are outlined in Tables 2 and 3 below (Figs. 3 and 4).

Table 2. The achieved accuracy and loss values when employing the base model.

	Value of Loss	Value of Accuracy
Set for training	0.2845	91.17%
Set for testing	0.2922	90.23%

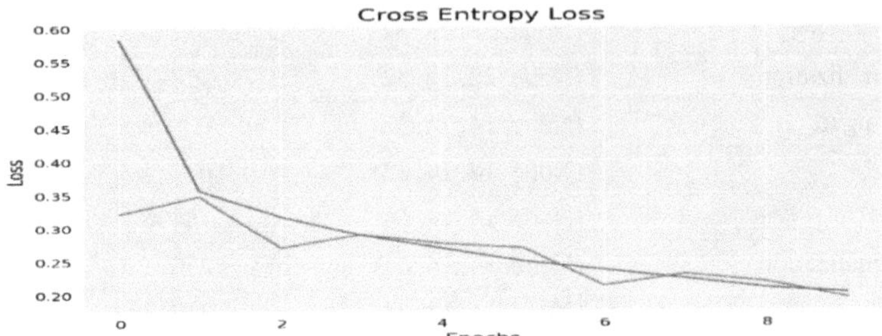

Fig. 3. Training vs. Validation Loss of the Proposed Model.

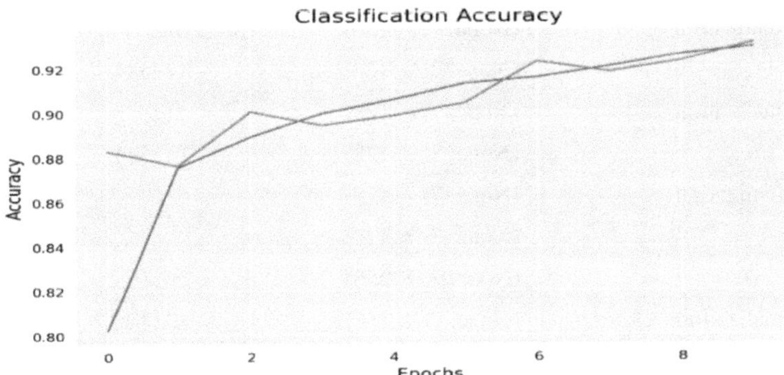

Fig. 4. The CNN base model's training accuracy vs. validation accuracy

Table 3. Values for accuracy and loss that were attained when using the suggested model.

	Value of Loss	Value of Accuracy
Set for training	0.1865	93.44%
Set for testing	0.1866	93.55%

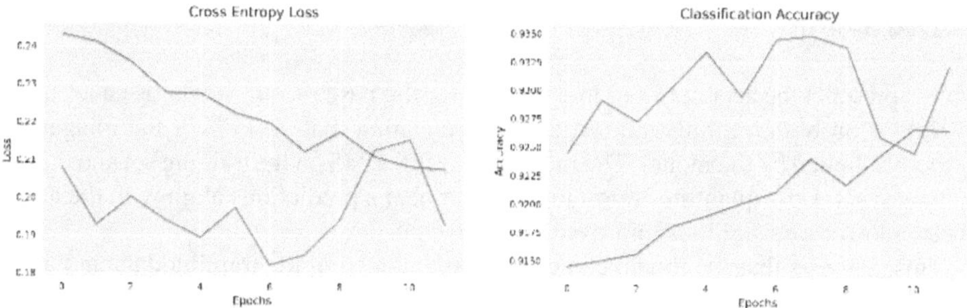

Fig. 5. Validation loss vs Training loss of the CNN final model

Figure 5's graphs show how, when the model is trained on more data, the cross-entropy loss and classification accuracy both improve over time. This demonstrates that the model is gradually enhancing its ability to accurately classify photos. The graph demonstrates that the image classification model is learning well and improving its ability to categorize photos. Keeping an eye on the model's performance on a held-out validation set is crucial to preventing overfitting.

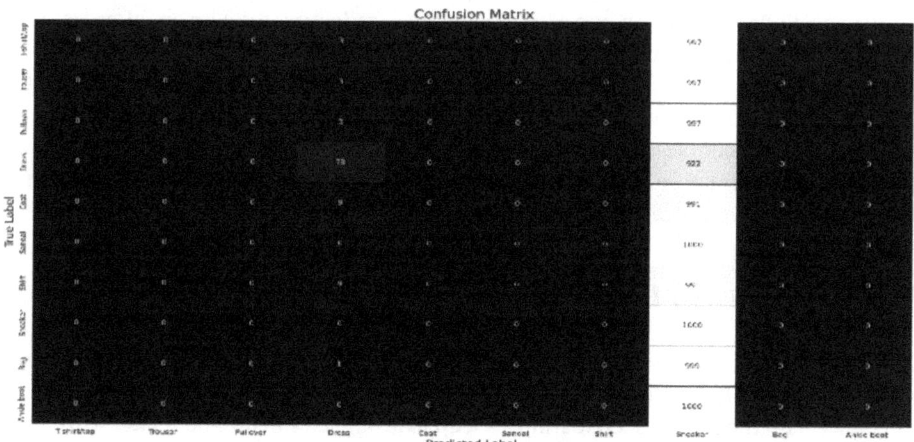

Fig. 6. Confusion matrix

The CNN final model's training accuracy versus validation accuracy shows that 99.9% of the images in the confusion matrix displayed in Fig. 6 were correctly identified, demonstrating the model's overall accuracy. However, the model performs less well in some classifications, such as "Dress" and "Sneaker." The challenges of the image classification task, the size and quality of the training dataset, or the algorithm used to train the model could all be contributing factors.

6 Discussion

Table 2 presents the accuracy and loss metrics for the base model. It attains an accuracy of 91.17% on both training and test datasets, meaning that 91.17% of the images are correctly labelled by the model. The model's loss is 0.2845 on the training set and 0.2922 on the test set. Loss quantifies how closely the model's predictions align with the actual labels; a lower loss signifies improved predictive performance.

This suggests that the model can effectively learn from the training data and apply this knowledge to new datasets. Table 3 presents the accuracy and loss results for the proposed model on both training and test datasets. Accuracy reflects the percentage of correct predictions out of total predictions, while loss measures how well the model's predictions match the actual labels. The table indicates that the proposed model achieves high accuracy on both datasets, with 93.44% on training and 93.55% on testing. This demonstrates the model's ability to generalise. Additionally, the low loss values of 0.1865 and 0.1866 for training and testing further confirm successful learning from the data.

The table demonstrates that the proposed model effectively classifies images overall, achieving high accuracy and low loss on both training and test datasets. We note that the KNN algorithm uses the Minkowski similarity metric. Table 3 presents the results of the suggested CNN model on training and test sets. Here, we assess two performance metrics: accuracy, indicating correctness, and loss, reflecting total errors after training. Notably, the accuracy is very high while the loss is relatively low, with some variation depending on dataset size. This results in the training set having higher accuracy than the test set. Figure 5 also shows the progression of training and validation loss over epochs. Due to the large sample size, the training loss starts high but decreases steadily over time, while the validation loss remains more stable, indicating a consistent trend during training.

7 Conclusion and Proposed Future Directions

ML has become a key component in object recognition, consistently providing high-performance results over recent years. The ML field has made significant strides lately, especially with the rise of deep learning. Deep learning uses neural networks with interconnected units to identify complex patterns in large datasets, addressing challenging problems in areas like medical image classification, fraud detection, and character recognition. Today, we benefit from more datasets for training robust models and employ better strategies to prevent overfitting and underfitting. Achievements in this domain have been impressive, with accuracy often surpassing 90%, such as digit recognition exceeding 97%. In this study, we classified apparel items using the Fashion MNIST dataset. We initially tested several ML algorithms, including LR, CART, KNN, and SVM, with KNN, LR, and SVM showing decent accuracy and producing promising results. We then built a CNN model for the same task. After comparing various approaches, we found that deep learning, especially our CNN, was the most effective. Future work should focus on refining our CNN architecture—tuning parameters like the number of filters, layer configurations, filter sizes, epochs, and batch sizes. Exploring the integration of CNNs with recurrent networks, such as ResNets, could further enhance performance.

References

1. Gadri, S., Neuhold, E.: Building best predictive models using ML and DL approaches to categorize fashion clothes. In: Artificial Intelligence and Soft Computing: 19th International Conference, ICAISC 2020, Zakopane, Poland, October 12–14, 2020, Proceedings, Part I, vol. 19, pp. 90–102. Springer International Publishing (2020)
2. Okonkwo, U.: Luxury fashion branding: trends, tactics, techniques. Springer (2016)
3. Gopalakrishnan, S., Matthews, D.: Collaborative consumption: a business model analysis of second-hand fashion. J. Fashion Mark. Manage.: Int. J. **22**(3), 354–368 (2018)
4. Zhang, S., Yao, L., Sun, A., Tay, Y.: Deep learning-based recommender system: a survey and new perspectives. ACM Computi. Surv. (CSUR) **52**(1), 1–38 (2019)
5. Yao, Q., et al.: Taking humans out of learning applications: a survey on automated machine learning. arXiv preprint (2018). arXiv:1810.13306
6. Liu, S., et al..: Hi, magic closet, tell me what to wear. In: Proceedings of the 20th ACM International Conference on Multimedia, pp. 619–628 (2012)
7. Wamba-Taguimdje, S.L., Wamba, S.F., Kamdjoug, J.R.K., Wanko, C.E.T.: Influence of artificial intelligence (AI) on firm performance: the business value of AI-based transformation projects. Bus. Process. Manag. J. **26**(7), 1893–1924 (2020)
8. Schulz, A., et al.: Different scaling of linear models and deep learning in UKBiobank brain images versus machine-learning datasets. Nat. Commun. **11**(1), 4238 (2020)
9. Wu, Z., et al.: MoleculeNet: a benchmark for molecular machine learning. Chem. Sci. **9**(2), 513–530 (2018)
10. Zhong, Y., Gao, J., Lei, Q., Zhou, Y.: A vision-based counting and recognition system for flying insects in intelligent agriculture. Sensors **18**(5), 1489 (2018)
11. Vijayaraj, A., et al.: Deep learning image classification for fashion design. Wirel. Commun. Mobile Comput. (2022)
12. Kayed, M., Anter, A., Mohamed, H.: Classification of garments from fashion MNIST dataset using CNN LeNet-5 architecture. In: 2020 International Conference on Innovative Trends in Communication and Computer Engineering (ITCE), pp. 238–243. IEEE (2020)
13. Sun, G.L., He, J.Y., Wu, X., Zhao, B., Peng, Q.: Learning fashion compatibility across categories with deep multimodal neural networks. Neurocomputing **395**, 237–246 (2020)
14. Ji, Y., Zhang, H., Zhang, Z., Liu, M.: CNN-based encoder-decoder networks for salient object detection: a comprehensive review and recent advances. Inf. Sci. **546**, 835–857 (2021)
15. Balakrishnan, V., Shi, Z., Law, C.L., Lim, R., Teh, L.L., Fan, Y.: A deep learning approach in predicting products' sentiment ratings: a comparative analysis. J. Supercomput. **78**(5), 7206–7226 (2022)
16. Li, X., Wang, C., Tong, B., Tan, J., Zeng, X., Zhuang, T.: Deep time-aware item evolution network for click-through rate prediction. In: Proceedings of the 29th ACM International Conference on Information & Knowledge Management, pp. 785–794 (2020)
17. Rahate, A., Walambe, R., Ramanna, S., Kotecha, K.: Multimodal co-learning: Challenges, applications with datasets, recent advances and future directions. Inf. Fusion **81**, 203–239 (2022)
18. Simester, D., Timoshenko, A., Zoumpoulis, S.I.: Targeting prospective customers: robustness of machine-learning methods to typical data challenges. Manage. Sci. **66**(6), 2495–2522 (2020)
19. Butt, U.M., et al.: Feature based algorithmic analysis on American sign language dataset. Int. J. Adv. Comput. Sci. Appl. **10**(5) (2019)
20. Butt, U.M., Ullah, H.A., Letchmunan, S., Tariq, I., Hassan, F.H., Koh, T.W.: Leveraging transfer learning for spatio-temporal human activity recognition from video sequences. Comput. Mater. Continua **74**(3) (2023)

21. Patil, S.: Fashion MNIST Image Classification (CNN)-94%. Kaggle. https://www.kaggle.com/code/sachinpatil1280/fashion-mnist-image-classification-cnn-94
22. Carneiro, T., Da Nóbrega, R.V.M., Nepomuceno, T., Bian, G.B., De Albuquerque, V.H.C., Reboucas Filho, P.P.: Performance analysis of Google Colaboratory as a tool for accelerating deep learning applications. IEEE Access **6**, 61677–61685 (2018)
23. Ciaburro, G., Ayyadevara, V.K., Perrier, A.: Hands-on machine learning on Google Cloud Platform: Implementing smart and efficient analytics using Cloud ML Engine. Packt Publishing Ltd. (2018)
24. Butt, U.M., Letchmunan, S., Hassan, F.H., Koh, T.W.: Hybrid of deep learning and exponential smoothing for enhancing crime forecasting accuracy. PLoS ONE **17**(9), e0274172 (2022)
25. Khandare, A., Agarwal, N., Bodhankar, A., Kulkarni, A., Mane, I.: Analysis of python libraries for artificial intelligence. In: Intelligent Computing and Networking: Proceedings of IC-ICN 2022, pp. 157–177. Springer Nature Singapore, Singapore (2023)
26. Alam, A.: Employing adaptive learning and intelligent tutoring robots for virtual classrooms and smart campuses: reforming education in the age of artificial intelligence. In: Advanced Computing and Intelligent Technologies: Proceedings of ICACIT 2022, pp. 395–406. Springer Nature Singapore, Singapore (2022)
27. Singh, P., Singh, N., Singh, K.K., Singh, A.: Diagnosing of disease using machine learning. In: Machine Learning and the Internet of Medical Things in Healthcare, pp. 89–111. Academic Press (2021)
28. Raz, D., et al.: Face Mis-ID: an interactive pedagogical tool demonstrating disparate accuracy rates in facial recognition. In: Proceedings of the 2021 AAAI/ACM Conference on AI, Ethics, and Society, July 2021, pp. 895–904 (2021)
29. Pujol-Perich, D., et al.: Ignnition: Bridging the gap between graph neural networks and networking systems. IEEE Netw. **35**(6), 171–177 (2021)
30. Corno, F., De Russis, L., Mannella, L.: Helping novice developers harness security issues in cloud-IoT systems. J. Reliable Intell. Environ. **8**(3), 261–283 (2022)
31. Widanage, C., et al.: High performance data engineering everywhere. In: 2020 IEEE International Conference on Smart Data Services (SMDS), October 2020, pp. 122–132. IEEE (2020)
32. Adekotujo, A., Odumabo, A., Adedokun, A., Aiyeniko, O.: A comparative study of operating systems: case of windows, UNIX, Linux, Mac, Android and iOS. Int. J. Comput. Appl. **176**(39), 16–23 (2020)
33. Nikolić, G.S., Dimitrijević, B.R., Nikolić, T.R., Stojcev, M.K.: A survey of three types of processing units: CPU, GPU and TPU. In: 2022 57th International Scientific Conference on Information, Communication and Energy Systems and Technologies (ICEST), pp. 1–6. IEEE (2022)
34. Pang, B., Nijkamp, E., Wu, Y.N.: Deep learning with TensorFlow: a review. J. Educ. Behav. Stat. **45**(2), 227–248 (2020)
35. Belete, D.M., Huchaiah, M.D.: Grid search in hyperparameter optimization of machine learning models for prediction of HIV/AIDS test results. Int. J. Comput. Appl. **44**(9), 875–886 (2022)
36. Chklovski, A., Parks, D.H., Woodcroft, B.J., Tyson, G.W.: CheckM2: a rapid, scalable and accurate tool for assessing microbial genome quality using machine learning. Nat. Methods 1–10 (2023)
37. Castiglioni, I., et al.: AI applications to medical images: from machine learning to deep learning. Physica Med. **83**, 9–24 (2021)
38. Ogundokun, R.O., et al.: Enhancing skin cancer detection and classification in dermoscopic images through concatenated MobileNetV2 and Xception models. Bioengineering **10**(8), 979 (2023)

39. Zhang, X., Liu, L., Chen, X., Gao, Y., Xie, S., Mi, J.: GLC_FCS30: global land-cover product with fine classification system at 30 m using time-series Landsat imagery. Earth Syst. Sci. Data **13**(6), 2753–2776 (2021)
40. Jackins, V., Vimal, S., Kaliappan, M., Lee, M.Y.: AI-based smart prediction of clinical disease using random forest classifier and Naive Bayes. J. Supercomput. **77**, 5198–5219 (2021)
41. Reddy, C.K., et al.: The interspeech 2020 deep noise suppression challenge: datasets, subjective testing framework, and challenge results (2020). arXiv preprint arXiv:2005.13981
42. Jasmir, J., Riyadi, W., Agustini, S.R., Arvita, Y., Meisak, D., Aryani, L.: Bidirectional long short-term memory and word embedding feature for improvement classification of cancer clinical trial document. J. RESTI (Rekayasa Sistem dan Teknologi Informasi) **6**(4), 505–510 (2022)
43. Chicco, D., Jurman, G.: The advantages of the Matthews correlation coefficient (MCC) over F1 score and accuracy in binary classification evaluation. BMC Genomics **21**(1), 1–13 (2020)
44. Hashim, I.C., Shariff, A.R.M., Bejo, S.K., Muharam, F.M., Ahmad, K.: Machine-learning approach using SAR data for the classification of oil palm trees that are non-infected and infected with the basal stem rot disease. Agronomy **11**(3), 532 (2021)
45. Erickson, B.J., Kitamura, F.: Magician's corner: 9. Performance metrics for machine learning models. Radiol.: Artif. Intell. **3**(3), e200126 (2021)
46. Sen, P.C., Hajra, M., Ghosh, M.: Supervised classification algorithms in machine learning: a survey and review. In: Emerging Technology in Modelling and Graphics: Proceedings of IEM Graph 2018, pp. 99–111. Springer Singapore, Singapore (2020)
47. Srivastava, N., Hinton, G., Krizhevsky, A., Sutskever, I., Salakhutdinov, R.: Dropout: a simple way to prevent neural networks from overfitting. J. Mach. Learn. Res. **15**(1), 1929–1958 (2014)

Planning Optimization Driven by Time Series Forecasting Approach in the Life Sciences Industry

Wei Hong Seh and Nur Intan Raihana Ruhaiyem(✉)

School of Computer Sciences, Universiti Sains Malaysia, Gelugor 11800 USM, Penang, Malaysia
intanraihana@usm.my

Abstract. Company X, a leader in the Life Sciences supply chain, specializes in producing high-quality medical and laboratory equipment. Given the dynamic market influenced by trends, seasonal variations, economic shifts, and global events such as pandemics, traditional forecasting methods often fall short in accuracy. This work seeks to enhance demand forecasting for highly demanded products by implementing advanced time series models and developing a comprehensive planning model that integrates these methods. Utilizing the Cross-Industry Standard Process for Data Mining (CRISP-DM) framework, the work systematically approaches the data-driven challenges of demand and supply management. Each product time series is first statistically classified to determine the presence of seasonality, guiding the selection of appropriate forecasting models. For non-seasonal products, ARIMA, Holt's Linear, ARIMA-SVR, and Facebook Prophet were evaluated, while seasonal series employed SARIMAX, Holt-Winters, SARIMAX-SVR, and Prophet models. The results indicate that the ARIMA-SVR and SARIMAX-SVR models consistently out-perform others, reducing forecasting errors by approximately 35.3% for seasonal products and 40.4% for non-seasonal products compared to traditional methods. This initiative has significantly enhanced demand forecasting accuracy, thereby improving customer satisfaction and resource optimization in a fluctuating market environment, with strong endorsement from the client.

Keywords: Demand Forecasting · Life Sciences Supply Chain · Time Series Forecasting

1 Introduction

1.1 Background

The Life Sciences industry encompasses companies involved in exploration, developing, and producing a wide range of products or services to deliver solutions that improve the health and well-being of living organisms [1]. This includes pharmaceuticals, biotechnologies for food and medicines, medical devices, technologies related to biomedical

M. Kassim et al. (Eds.): SCDS 2025, CCIS 2674, pp. 496–510, 2026.
https://doi.org/10.1007/978-981-95-8368-3_35

research, nutraceuticals for enhancing nutrients in supplements, processing of food, and others. Company X has been one of the key multi-national leaders and contributors to the life sciences supply chain network as an Original Equipment Manufacturer (OEM) since its establishment in the late 20th century. As a manufacturing entity, it is committed to delivering high-quality medical and laboratory equipment, striving to fulfill diverse customer demands, and empowering scientific research and discoveries for its global customer base, which covers APAC (Asia-Pacific), EMEA (Europe, Middle East, and Africa), SAJK (South Asia, Japan, and Korea), and other regions. Company X has ultra-high-mix, low-volume product profiles with close to 60 product platforms and handles nearly 13,000 stock-keeping units (SKUs) of inventory across multiple main logistic centers located in different regions and countries. Company X's primary operations include the design, development, and production of its products, which are predominantly made-to-stock with predefined designs, manufactured in anticipation of customer demand.

Raw materials and components are mainly sourced from both local and foreign suppliers, while local production resources focus on assembly and product manufacturing. Complexities in managing resources such as raw materials and production capacity increase as each product model is mainly worked in silos within product divisions and product lines, subject to unique technical skill sets and process requirements. The product manufactured will then be shipped to logistics centers located in different countries and packed with other accessories in a bundle before shipping to customers. A supply chain consists of all entities that participate both directly and indirectly in meeting a customer's demand. This network of supply chains extends beyond just the producers and their suppliers, it also includes entities responsible for storage facilities, delivery, retail outlets, and even the customer services [2].

1.2 Problem Statement

In supply chain management for company X with ultra-high-mix, low-volume product profiles, managing the supply chain efficiently always comes with complex challenges due to the dynamic nature of customer demand coupled with different lead times from local and foreign suppliers. Customer demand can be unpredictable and subject to fluctuation due to various factors, including shifts in the market, seasonality factors, economic situations, and unexpected global events like widespread pandemics or political incidents. The outbreak of the Coronavirus (COVID-19) in 2019 profoundly disrupted global supply chains, exposing significant supply chain vulnerabilities and led to increased attention and increased emphasis on the need for more accurate and rigorous forecasting [3]. The customer demand volatility for company X is shown in **Table 1**, where selected product models demonstrated high month-over-month order quantity change percentages ranging from −100% to 2800% based on sales transaction records from January 2018 to May 2024.

Table 1. High demand volatility of selected product models reflected by month-over-month order quantity change (January 2018 to May 2024).

Product Model	Average Monthly Order Quantity	Month over Month Change%	
		Min	Max
9A1	8	−81%	600%
9A2	41	−49%	91%
9A3	14	−80%	240%
9I1	87	−47%	87%
9I2	4	−100%	800%
9I3	15	−82%	367%
9M1	10	−83%	500%
MC1	16	−61%	122%
MC2	132	−80%	298%
MC3	3	−100%	500%
MC4	49	−59%	90%
MC5	13	−90%	700%
MC7	28	−57%	400%
ML1	2	−100%	300%
MM1	10	−100%	2800%
MT1	8	−91%	600%
RI1	41	−100%	900%
RR1	14	−100%	300%
RR2	87	−100%	1050%
RT1	4	−100%	100%
RV1	15	−81%	250%

2 Related Works

2.1 Introduction

The accuracy of demand forecasting plays a crucial role in shaping the effectiveness of supply chain management and supply recovery planning [4]. The more accurate the forecasting of demand, the better the supply of stock availability and the more resilient the supply chain. The main challenge of accurate forecasting is to create a model that is both sophisticated enough to consider a variety of key factors and at the same time, agile and responsive to market changes.

Several studies done in recent years have underscored the limitation of traditional forecasting methods in adapting to volatile market dynamics as most of the methods are built solely based on historical data and are unable to consider external influencing factors in the analysis [4–6]. A study done by Mahya Seyedan and Freshteh Mafakheri has confirmed that there is an increasing trend in using big data analytics or machine learning techniques for demand forecasting based on published papers from 2005 to 2019 and the five most used techniques are Neural Networks, regression, time-series forecasting, Support Vector, and Decision Tree approaches [7]. As an outcome of their study, they argued that the integration of external influencing factors such as economic volatility and inflation into forecasting models can enhance forecasting accuracy. Furthermore, they suggested a synergistic approach where a predictive approach is integrated with optimization or simulation techniques to enhance the precision of the forecast. Despite the recommendations to adopt advanced analytics techniques for accurate demand forecasting, most of the studies overlook the inherent complications associated with the implementation of advanced forecasting methods. Introduction advanced predictive model will also introduce complexities into the forecasting model and requires specialized expertise and rigorous experimental approaches to ensure the successful deployment of an effective forecasting model.

2.2 Time Series Forecasting Techniques

Classical Forecasting Techniques. Classical forecasting techniques analyze chronological time series data by leveraging mainly statis-tical insights derived from historical data to forecast future trends [8]. Classical forecasting techniques remain popular in both academic and industrial domains due to their model simplicity and often the ability to produce competitive results. These classical methods sometimes even surpass more complex Machine [9–11]. Therefore, classical methods are still commonly used depending on the nature of the data, domain, and application. They are categorized into two types which are univariate and multivariate. Univariate such as Holt-Winters and Autoregressive Integrated Moving Average (ARIMA) solely rely on the time series data alone, whereas multivariate classical models such as Vector Autoregressions (VAR) can incorporate multiple interdependent factors along with the time series data for more comprehensive analysis [12].

Holt-Winters and SARIMAX are classical forecasting approaches that can capture seasonality and always be used in performance comparisons for seasonal forecasting tasks. Pongdatu and Putra conducted a study on customer transaction forecasting using data from retail stores from 2013 to 2017 by comparing both Holt-Winters and SARIMAX method [13]. They argued that the SARIMAX model is well suited for short-term predictions because SARIMAX can capture and adjust forecasting based on immediate trends and seasonality and is less accurate for long forecasting as it relies heavily on recent data trends that may not hold over an extended period. Conversely, they ex-pressed that Holt-Winter's Exponential Smoothing is suitable for predicting seasonal time series data with or without trend patterns. The result of their study showed that SARIMAX outperform Holt-Winters for the retail business.

Classical forecasting models with the ability to incorporate external influencing factors such as SARIMAX demonstrated superior performance in comparison to those models that only rely on historical data. SARIMAX is an extension of the ARIMA model which incorporates both seasonality and external influencing factors, allowing for more accurate forecasts. A study done by applying the SARIMAX model to predict daily sales in the food retail sector by integrating price reduction and holiday factors into SARIMAX models was found to effectively enhance the forecasting capabilities of the model, contribute to increased forecasting accuracy, more effective stock management, and waste reduction [14]. This study highlights the significance of selecting the right external factors for forecast accuracy enhancement; however, such selections require expertise in the do-main complemented by experimental techniques to ascertain the effective factors.

Machine Learning Forecasting Method. Machine learning in time series forecasting involves the use of machine learning algorithms to interpret and project future trends from sequential time series data [8]. With the machine learning method, it can detect automatically complex and non-linear data patterns inherited in the dataset that unable captured well by the classical forecasting method [15]. Machine learning techniques include a supervised learning approach, Neural Network models, and ensemble techniques. Several examples of supervised learning approaches are regression trees and support vector machines whereas Neural Network models include advanced deep learning models such as Long Short-Term Memory (LSTM) networks and recent transformer models. The ensemble techniques in machine learning incorporate models that make predictions from several models such as Random Forests and Gradient Boosting Machines. Singha and Panse made a comparative study on various machine learning algorithms like multi-layer perceptron (MLP), Convolutional Neural Networks (CNN), and Long-Short Term Memory (LSTM) in time-series forecasting works in Supply Chain demand forecasting [16]. Their works underscore the significance of accurate demand forecasting in supply chain management. They performed their empirical analysis based on a Kaggle dataset related to retail store transactions and their result indicated that the multilayer perceptron (MLP) model generally surpassed others in forecasting accuracy precision based on the dataset. Their study highlights the effectiveness of using machine learning algorithms in time series forecasting. However, their works and results have not been compared with classical forecasting methods that may act as benchmarks for the forecasting results.

Facebook Prophet was introduced in the year 2017 by a Facebook research team lead by Sean J. Taylor and Benjamin Letham which proposed a modular regression model for scalable business forecasting [17]. The introduction of Prophet has provided a significant contribution to time series forecasting as a model that promotes flexibility, scalability, and ease of use. Since the introduction of Facebook Prophet, it has been compared to other forecasting models for a more comprehensive understanding of the model's forecasting performance. Emir Zunic and his team conducted a comparative study to evaluate the forecasting abilities of Facebook's Prophet, Amazon's DeepAR+, and CNN-QR algorithms, focusing on their application in sales prediction for distribution companies [18]. The main insights from the study reveal that Prophet has superior per-formance for products with longer sales history and regular transactions, whereas Amazon's models show better performance for items with shorter sales records or infrequent sales. The research per-formed thorough comparisons using real-world data, but the result may not generalize well as only limited datasets are used in the assessment.

Overall, the paper provides an initial insight into Prophet's forecasting capability and establishes a foundation for more in-depth future research in time series forecasting.

Hybrid Traditional Time Series Forecasting Model With SVR. In the field of time series forecasting, there's an ongoing need for models that provide exceptional accuracy and adapt to a variety of data characteristics. Traditional methods like Autoregressive Integrated Moving Average (ARIMA) and its variants Seasonal Autoregressive Integrated Moving Average with Exogenous Regressors (SARIMAX), while effective for linear time series data, often fall short when faced with the non-linear patterns common in complex datasets [19]. To address these shortcomings, the use of hybrid models, which combine ARIMA or SARIMAX with Support Vector Regression (SVR), has become increasingly popular. Known for its prowess in managing non-linear relationships, SVR complements these linear models, mitigating their limitations. This integration significantly expands the capabilities of hybrid models, making them highly effective in scenarios that feature both linear and non-linear data dynamics.

Research has validated the superior performance of hybrid ARIMA-SVR and SARIMAX-SVR models in a range of sectors. For example, a prominent study within the financial forecasting field demonstrated that the ARIMA-SVR model excelled beyond the traditional ARIMA model in predicting the stock market, known for its volatile and non-linear nature [19]. This hybrid approach proved particularly effective in smoothing out market noise and accurately capturing significant fluctuations, leading to more dependable forecasts. Likewise, the environmental sector has seen the application of the ARIMA-SVR model for the forecast of drought, where traditional ARIMA models typically struggle due to the complexities introduced by seasonal variations and non-linear environmental factors [20]. The result demonstrates that the combined ARIMA-SVR has higher prediction accuracy than the single ARIMA model. These successful applications highlight the hybrid models' capability to significantly improve forecasting accuracy and reliability by adeptly integrating linear and non-linear modeling techniques.

3 Methodology

Exploratory Data Analysis (EDA) serves as a foundational step in this work, enabling a thorough examination of sales data to uncover key patterns, trends, and value distributions. It also helps in detecting outliers or abnormalities, which is crucial to ensure the reliability of subsequent analysis and model performance. In this work, the EDA step also acts as a way to determine the seasonality characteristics of products, which helps guide the selection of appropriate seasonal or non-seasonal forecasting models.

3.1 EDA on Product Order Demand

Figure 1 shows the distribution of monthly order quantity by product model which provide insights on sales variability, demand consistency and outliers for one product model. Among the 21 product models analysed, only three produce models which are 9I1, 9I3, and MT1 show no outliers, reflecting consistent demand. The number of outliers for other models varies from 1 to approximately 10 outliers observed, indicating fluctuations in market demands that suggest volatility. Overall, it is observed that MC product models such as MC2, MC3 and MC4, subject to more demand fluctuations. The product model MC2 with highest total order quantity sold across years is distinguished by the most noticeable outliers with approximate 10 outliers observed above the upper bound of whisker. This model displays significant variance in order quantities compared to others, with outliers that are notably farther apart, suggesting occasional spikes in demand exceeding typical levels that contribute to its instability. Surprisingly, the product model, 9I1 with second highest median of order quantity, exhibits no apparent outliers in its box plot distribution of average monthly order quantities. This suggests that despite its high sales volume, the order demand for 9I1 remains stable within the upper and lower bound of whiskers. In contrast, the product model RI1 with relatively low order quantities shows outliers that are more widely spaced compared to other low-runner models. This pattern indicates a greater variability in demand, despite on a smaller scale compared to higher-demand models which show occasional demand spikes. The box plot in Fig. 1 illustrates that careful handling of outliers is crucial for this work. Introducing and implementing a robust method for managing outliers is required to enable accurate time series forecasting.

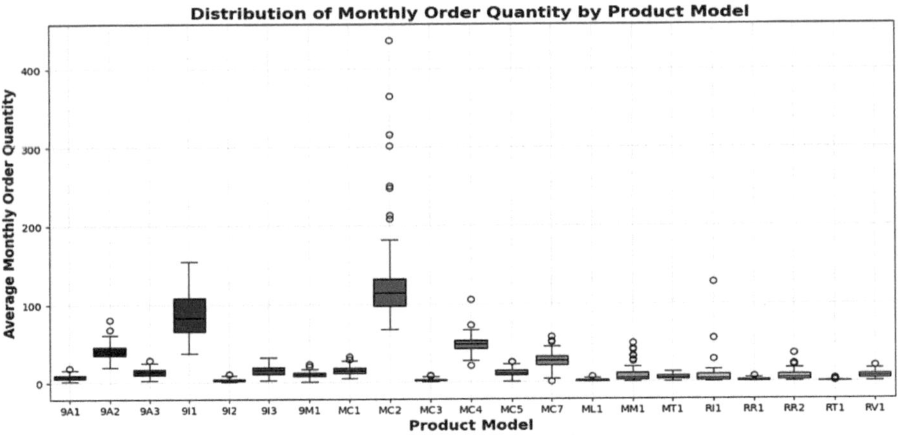

Fig. 1. Distribution of Monthly Order Quantity by Product Model

3.2 Time Series Decomposition Analysis

Time series analysis has been included as part of the data exploratory steps in this work to under-stand time series characteristics by decomposing a time series into its main components which includes trend, seasonality, and residuals. The demonstration of time series analysis on the selected product model 9I1 is shown in Fig. 2.

The original time series graph for product model 9I1 displays changes across time with visible peaks and troughs which demonstrating the presence of trends and seasonal variations. It can be observed from the trend chart, the product 9I1 is experiencing upwards trend consistently since mid of year 2020. The seasonal component illustrates recurring short-term cycles, demonstrating presence of annual seasonality characterized by consistent peaks and troughs annually. The product model 9I1 observed to have repetitively show lower order volume during beginning of the year and have its seasonal peaks few months before end of the year. This indicates regular, predictable changes over each year. The residual component, representing the random noise or unpredictable fluctuations left after extracting the trend and seasonal elements, shows random variations around zero, denoting the unstructured and unpredictable parts of the data. Collectively, these components help in dissecting the time series structure, enhancing the accuracy of modeling, and forecasting by individually addressing each component.

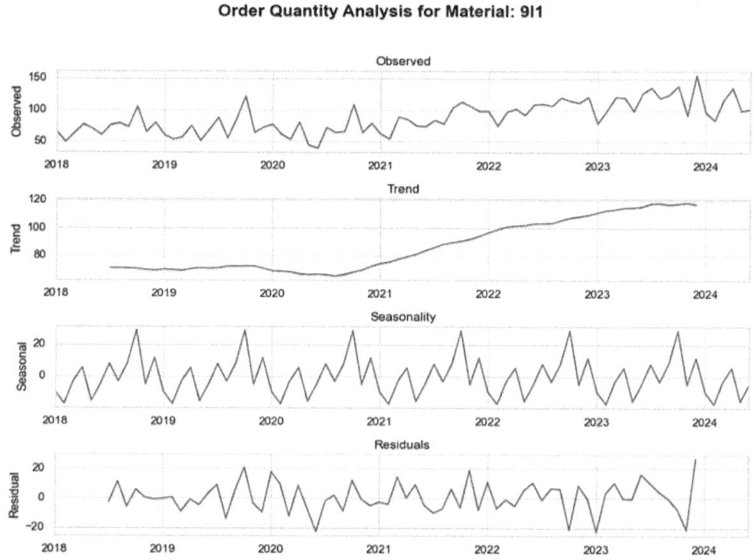

Fig. 2. Decomposition of the dataset into trend, seasonality and residuals for product model 9I1.

3.3 Seasonality Classification

Seasonal classification is an important aspect of this data science work, as it helps categorize product models into seasonal and non-seasonal groups, thereby influencing the selection of fore-casting models. In this work, the seasonality test is conducted using the Fourier Transform. The Fourier Transform is a valuable analytical tool for investigating seasonality in time series analysis. It decomposes a series into its sinusoidal components, which helps identify recurring patterns or cycles indicative of seasonal effects [21]. Essentially, when a time series contains seasonal elements, peaks in the Fourier Transform will appear at frequencies that correlate with these seasonal cycles.A threshold level is defined at 80th percentile to verify the presence of significance annual seasonality. The choice of the 80th percentile threshold aligns with domain expert expectations for identifying known seasonal products such as 9A2, 9I1, MC1. Seasonality classification results for all selected product models with average monthly order volume surpasses 10 units are shown in Table 2.

Table 2. Seasonality Classification of Product Models.

Product Model	Threshold at 80th percentile	Power at annual seasonal point	Seasonality Category
9A2	71.22	143.40	Seasonal
9A3	20.42	39.79	Seasonal
9I1	275.65	462.21	Seasonal
9I3	28.72	71.56	Seasonal
9M1	17.79	18.76	Seasonal
MC1	26.29	35.43	Seasonal
MC2	596.76	517.18	Non-seasonal
MC4	122.08	152.56	Seasonal
MC5	18.81	26.21	Seasonal
MC7	56.17	8.31	Non-seasonal
MM1	37.46	1.73	Non-seasonal
RI1	24.62	7.80	Non-seasonal

3.4 Training and Test Dataset Split

The company extracted approximately 76 months of sales transaction data from its Enterprise Re-source Planning system, covering the period from January 2018 to May 2024. Given that Company X's fiscal year begins each November, it is proposed to start evaluating model performance from November 2022 to encompass a full fiscal year through to May 2024. Accordingly, the monthly data from January 2018 to October 2022 will serve as the training dataset, while data from November 2022 to May 2024 will be used for testing. This allocation results in 75% of the data being utilized for training and 25% for testing.

3.5 Modelling

Seasonal and Non-Seasonal Model Groups. In this work, the selection of an appropriate forecasting model is guided by statistical tests that assess the presence of seasonality in a product model's time series. For time series identified as seasonal, the work employs a range of forecasting models which adept at capturing seasonal patterns. These include the Seasonal Autoregressive Integrated Moving Average with Exogenous Factor (SARIMAX), a hybrid SARIMAX and Support Vector Regression (SARIMAX-SVR) model, Holt-Winters, and Facebook Prophet. Conversely, for non-seasonal time series, the chosen models are the Autoregressive Integrated Moving Average (ARIMA), a hybrid model of ARIMA and Support Vector Regression (ARIMA-SVR), Holt-Linear, and Facebook Prophet. It is worthwhile to highlight that Facebook Prophet can be used on both seasonal and non-seasonal time series by configuring the seasonality setting.

Hybrid Walk-Forward and Expanding Window Cross-Validation. In this work, we deployed walk-forward validation with expanding time series cross-validation. Walk-forward validation iteratively adds new data at each period, mimicking real-world forecasting processes where monthly updates are typical. During each iteration of walk-forward validation, first it generates a set of predictions, taking one new data entry at a time. Second, it collects the first point from each prediction set, replicating actual scenarios where immediate month forecasts are fixed, while subsequent months are updated with new data. An expanding window cross-validation is introduced at each series in the walk-forward validation. This method is crucial for capturing seasonal variations and adapting to historical and present data nuances. Through this technique, the model is evaluated across different seasonal variations while capturing data nuances and patterns from historical data to present data while adapting to different scenarios. Besides, in this work, the cross-validation periods, are also used to evaluate the best parameter settings that give the lowest mean squared error for each iteration.

3.6 Model Evaluation

Metrics for Evaluation. In the evaluation phase of this work, the model comparison will first be made by different season-al groups which are seasonal and non-seasonal categories. At the end of the work, a single model will be chosen from the various algorithms developed based on its superior performance and its alignment with established success criteria. A suite of metrics has been selected to assess the performance of each model comprehensively. These include Mean Absolute Error (MAE), Mean Squared Error (MSE), Root Mean Squared Error (RMSE) and Mean Absolute Percentage Error (MAPE).

4 Results and Discussion

4.1 Composite Error of Seasonal Products

The composite error score is calculated based on multiple error metrics by normalizing them and combined to provide a single performance measure of each model's overall error. Higher values of composite error indicate poor model performance while lower error indicates better model performance. From the result, it can be observed that there is significant variability of model performance in different product families across different forecasting models with SARIMAX-SVR consistently demonstrating the lowest composite error across product models suggesting its robustness in handling different time series with seasonal variabilities. With performance consistently outperforming the rolling 6-month moving average, it shows relatively significantly lower error, particularly for product models 9A2, 9A3, 9I1, MC4, and RV1. The FB Prophet Model shows notably higher composite errors in more product families compared to other forecasting models as observed in product models 9I3, 9M1, MC1, MC5, and RR2. This suggests the potential limitations or misfits with the data characteristics of those specific product models. For Holt-Winters models, it also demonstrates poorer performance than the rolling 6-month moving average model as observed in product models 9A2, 9A3, 9M1, and RR2. SARIMAX was observed to have a lower count of product models with higher composite error than the rolling 6-month moving average as observed at 9A2 and 9A3 product models. Additionally, the rolling 6-month moving average exhibits the highest composite error of 0.58 for the 9I1 product model, while the SARIMAX-SVR model achieves the lowest composite error. Although the simple rolling 6-month moving average method occasionally outperforms more sophisticated models like Facebook Prophet and Holt-Winter, it can also result in significantly higher errors, leading to skewed forecasting outcomes (Table 3).

Table 3. Composite Error of Seasonal Products.

Composite Error					
Product	SARIMAX	SARIMAX-SVR	Holt-Winter	FB Prophet	Rolling 6M moving average
9A2	0.16	0.11	0.15	0.12	0.13
9A3	0.18	0.06	0.15	0.11	0.12
9I1	0.44	0.36	0.41	0.40	0.58
9I3	0.08	0.05	0.07	0.08	0.08
9M1	0.09	0.07	0.10	0.11	0.08
MC1	0.06	0.04	0.06	0.10	0.07
MC4	0.19	0.14	0.18	0.19	0.23
MC5	0.08	0.05	0.09	0.11	0.09
RR2	0.16	0.09	0.11	0.15	0.16
RV1	0.12	0.09	0.13	0.15	0.16

The composite error score is calculated based on multiple error metrics by normalizing them and combined to provide a single performance measure of each model's overall error. Higher values of composite error indicate poor model performance while lower error indicates better model performance. From the result, it can be observed that there is significant variability of model performance in different product families across different forecasting models with SARIMAX-SVR consistently demonstrating the lowest composite error across product models suggesting its robustness in handling different time series with seasonal variabilities. With performance consistently outperforming the rolling 6-month moving average, it shows relatively significantly lower error, particularly for product models 9A2, 9A3, 9I1, MC4, and RV1.

The FB Prophet Model shows notably higher composite errors in more product families compared to other forecasting models as observed in product models 9I3, 9M1, MC1, MC5, and RR2. This suggests the potential limitations or misfits with the data characteristics of those specific product models. For Holt-Winters models, it also demonstrates poorer performance than the rolling 6-month moving average model as observed in product models 9A2, 9A3, 9M1, and RR2. SARIMAX was observed to have a lower count of product models with higher composite error than the rolling 6-month moving average as observed at 9A2 and 9A3 product models. Additionally, the rolling 6-month moving average exhibits the highest composite error of 0.58 for the 9I1 product model, while the SARIMAX-SVR model achieves the lowest composite error. Although the simple rolling 6-month moving average method occasionally outperforms more sophisticated models like Facebook Prophet and Holt-Winter, it can also result in significantly higher errors, leading to skewed forecasting outcomes.

4.2 Composite Error of Non-Seasonal Products

Based on composite error result shown in Table 4, the ARIMA-SVR model consistently achieves the lowest compo-site error scores, indicating its superior performance and adaptability across diverse time series characteristics. This model shows particularly strong results for product families 9A1, MC2, and MT1, where it significantly outperforms other models, affirming its robustness and reliability. In contrast, the Facebook Prophet Model displays higher composite errors for product families such as MC2 and MC7, suggesting it may not align well with the characteristics of these specific time series. Similarly, the Holt-Linear model underperforms compared to the rolling 6-month moving average particularly in product models 9A1 and MT1. The rolling 6-month moving average exhibits the highest composite error in the MC2 and MC7 product models. However, it shows competitive performance in other non-seasonal product models. This variability underscores the need for a careful evaluation of rolling 6-month moving average as the model choice.

Table 4. Composite Error of Non-seasonal Products.

Composite Error					
Product	ARIMA	ARIMA-SVR	Holt-Linear	FB Prophet	Rolling 6M moving average
9A1	0.06	0.04	0.08	0.08	0.07
MC2	0.54	0.47	0.57	0.68	0.76
MC7	0.22	0.19	0.20	0.21	0.21
MM1	0.47	0.44	0.47	0.39	0.58
MT1	0.07	0.06	0.08	0.07	0.07

4.3 Final Models Selection

Final model selections will be guided by the average composite error score averaged from multiple product models that fall into the same seasonality groups as shown in Tables 5 and 6. Addition-ally, pie charts that show the count of each forecasting model as the best model for product models are created as shown in Table 5. The aim is to select models that fulfill the work objective which is to surpass the existing forecasting model used by the Supply Chain Planning (SCP) team namely the rolling 6-month moving average model with robust forecasting accuracy.

Table 5. Average composite error score by forecasting model for seasonal products.

Forecasting model for seasonal products	Average composite error score
SARIMAX-SVR	0.110
Holt-Winter	1.154
SARIMAX Model	0.154
FB Prophet Model	0.155
Rolling Average Model	0.170

Table 6. Average composite error score by forecasting model for non-seasonal products.

Forecasting model for non-seasonal products	Average composite error score
ARIMA-SVR	0.242
ARIMA	0.273
Holt-Linear Model	0.280
FB Prophet Model	0.285
Rolling Average Model	0.340

The current practice which is a rolling 6-month moving average method as shown has the highest average composite error score with 0.17 in seasonal product groups and 0.34 in non-seasonal product groups. This high average composite indeed shows the limitations and challenges of a simple statistical model in capturing data nuances and is hardly responsive to market fluctuations to pro-vide consistent accurate forecasting results across all product models. For seasonal product models, the SARIMAX-SVR model is the clear winner which stands out as the most effective forecasting model, demonstrating the lowest average composite error with a value of 0.11 among all the models evaluated as shown in Table 5. This suggests an average composite error reduction of 0.06 or 35.3% from the rolling 6-month moving average method. Its robust performance across different metrics and its ability to handle the intricacies of seasonal variations make it the best choice. For non-seasonal product groups, ARIMA-SVR emerges as the clear winner with the lowest aver-age composite error of 0.242 as shown in Table 6. ARIMA-SVR stands out to be a reliable and accurate forecasting tool as indicated by a significantly lower error rate compared to other models. This suggests an average composite error reduction of 0.098 or 40.4% from the rolling 6-month moving average method.

5 Conclusion

In this data science work, our main objectives include statistical classification of each product model into distinct profile categories based on overall demand volume and seasonality characteristics, enabling effective product management and forecasting.

Besides, it is expected that the fore-casting accuracy for both seasonal and non-seasonal high-demand product models with an average order of more than 10 units per month will be enhanced with the new model performance outperforming the current traditional forecasting method by utilizing time series forecasting techniques and defined metrics. The overall improved forecasting outcomes are satisfactory for the client. Based on the analysis of the average composite error rate, it is expected a reduction of 35.3% error and 40.4% forecasting error in comparison to the rolling 6-month moving average method for seasonal and non-seasonal products respectively. The positive results with the substantial improvements in both forecasting accuracy and reliability have not only fulfilled the objectives of this work but also surpassed conventional forecasting methods, demonstrating the effectiveness of incorporating advanced statistical tools such as hybrid models in practical applications.

References

1. Deloitte: Life science industry accounting guide. New York, Deloitte Development (2025)
2. Chopra, S., Meindl, P.: Supply Chain Management: Strategy, Planning, and Operation, 6th Edition, London England: Pearson Education Limited (2016)
3. Guo, Y., Liu, F., Song J.-S., Wang, S.: Supply chain resilience: a review from the inventory management perspective. Fundam. Res. 450–463 (2025). ISSN 2667-3258. https://doi.org/10.1016/j.fmre.2024.08.002
4. Yani L.P.E., Aamer, A.: Demand forecasting accuracy in the pharmaceutical supply chain: a machine learning approach. Int. J. Pharm. Healthcare Mark 1–23 (2022). https://doi.org/10.1108/IJPHM-05-2021-0056
5. Blackburn, R., Lurz, K., Priese B., Darkow, R.G.a.I.-L.: A predictive analytics approach for demand forecasting in the process industry. Int. Trans. Operational Res. **22**, 407–428 (2015). https://doi.org/10.1111/itor.12122,
6. Merkuryeva, G., Valberga A., Smirnov, a.A.: Demand forecasting in pharmaceutical supply chains: a case study. Procedia Comput. Sci. **149**, 3–10 (2019). https://doi.org/10.1016/j.procs.2019.01.100
7. Seyedan, M., Mafakheri, F.: Predictive big data analytics for supply chain demand forecasting: methods, applications, and research opportunities. J. Big Data **7**(1), 53 (2020)
8. Haselbeck, F., Killinger, J., Menrad, K., Hannus T., Grimm, D.G.: Machine learning outperforms classical forecasting on horticultural sales predictions. Mach. Learn. Appl. **7** (2022)
9. Makridakis, S., Spiliotis, E., Assimakopoulos, V.: The M5 competition: background, organization, and implementation. Int. J. Forecast. **38**(4), 1325–1336 (2022)
10. Makridakis, S., Spiliotis, E., Assimakopoulos, V.: The M4 competition: 100,000 time series and 61 forecasting methods. Int. J. Forecast. **36**(1), 54–74 (2020)
11. Kolassa, S.: Commentary on the M5 forecasting competition. Int. J. Forecast. **38**(4), 1562–1568 (2022)
12. Alvarez-De-Toledo, P., Márquez, A.C., Nunez, F., Usabiaga, C.: Introducing VAR and SVAR predictions in system dynamics models. Int. J. Simul. Process Model. **4**(1), 7–17 (2008)
13. Pongdatu, G.A.N., Putra, Y.H.: Seasonal time series forecasting using SARIMA and holt winter's exponential smoothing. IOP Conf. Ser.: Mater. Sci. Eng. (2018)
14. Arunraj, N.S., Ahrens, D., Fernandes, M.: Application of SARIMAX model to forecast daily sales in food retail industry. Int. J. Oper. Res. Inf. Syst. **7**, 1–21 (2016)

15. Falatouri, T., Darbanian, F., Brandtner, P., Udokwu, C.: Predictive analytics for demand forecasting–A comparison of SARIMA and LSTM in retail SCM. Procedia Comput. Sci. **200**, 993–1003 (2022)
16. Singha, D., and Panse, C.: Application of different machine learning models for supply chain demand forecasting: comparative analysis. In: 2nd International Conference on Innovative Practices in Technology and Management (ICIPTM), Gautam Buddha Nagar, India (2022)
17. Taylor, S.J., Letham, B.: Forecasting at scale. Am. Stat. **72**(1), 37–45 (2018)
18. Zunic, E., Korjenic, K., Delalic, S., Subara, Z.: Comparison analysis of Facebook's prophet, Amazon's DeepAR+ and CNN-QR algorithms for successful real-world sales forecasting. Int. J. Comput. Sci. Inf. Technol. (IJCSIT) **13**, 67–84 (2021)
19. Rubio, L., Alba, K.: Forecasting selected colombian shares using a hybrid ARIMA-SVR model. Mathematics **10**(13) (2022)
20. Xu, D., Zhang, Q., Ding, Y., Huang, H.: Application of a hybrid ARIMA-SVR model based on the SPI for the forecast of drought-a case study in Henan Province, China. J. Appl. Meteorol. Climatol. **59**(7), 1239–1259 (2020)
21. Bloomfield, P.: Fourier Analysis of Time Series: An Introduction, 2nd edn. Wiley-Interscience, New York (2000)

Author Index

M. Kassim et al. (Eds.): SCDS 2025, CCIS 2674, pp. 511–512, 2026.
https://doi.org/10.1007/978-981-95-8368-3

Zeitfracht Medien GmbH
Ferdinand-Jühlke-Straße 7
99095 Erfurt, Deutschland
produktsicherheit@kolibri360.de